D1387991

Allez France!

Richard Binns

Chiltern House

For
Anne
for a million loving reasons

A special thank you to P&O European Ferries for their help in providing some complimentary ferry crossings on our numerous research trips.

Published in October 1994 by Richard & Anne Binns – trading as Chiltern House Publishers, Honeywood House, Avon Dassett, Leamington Spa, Warwickshire CV33 0AH

ISBN 0-9516930-3-4

The contents of the guide are believed correct at the time of printing. Nevertheless Chiltern House Publishers cannot accept responsibility for errors or omissions, or for changes in details given. The prices indicated in the guide were supplied to us during the summer of 1994.

Maps drawn by the author
Typeset in Concorde (text) and Gill (maps) by Art Photoset Limited, 64 London End, Beaconsfield, Bucks HP9 2JD
Printed by Butler & Tanner Limited, The Selwood Printing Works, Caxton Road, Frome, Somerset BA11 1NF

MAPAHOLICS' FRANCE

France remains the "First Lady of Europe". She is as beguiling as ever, a country both deeply rural and highly civilised. An added plus is that the tourist "industry" is run by individuals for individuals. And, joy of joys, *Marianne* still clutches to her breasts endless delights – hidden corners where Nature's priceless legacies and majestic man-made creations are ignored by all but a few enterprising visitors.

How can you prise out of *La Belle France* your share of her cornucopia of pleasures? One golden rule applies as much as ever: maps are the essential key if you are to open the door to France's seductive charms. Good large-scale maps repay their outlay a thousand times over.

A second golden rule goes like this: "The more you run the risk of getting lost the more certain you are of seeing the real France." In *Mapaholics' France* I've chosen an idiosyncratic way of persuading you to emulate my freewheeling philosophy of exploration. I've selected 44 map sheet pages from the spiral-bound *Michelin Motoring Atlas France* – the finest investment you can make. (For easier use I detach map sheets from the spiral binding, as needed, and bulldog clip them to a piece of cardboard. I never use hardboard.) Each map sheet forms the basis of a chapter, in which I detail as many as possible of the widely differing natural and man-made treats on the ground. Though much of the material I have unearthed is not listed in Michelin's green guides I do not claim to have done anything more than scratch the surface of each area.

If you want to enjoy France's varied topography then you must have a go at "navigating". By that I mean you must use as many of the Michelin maps' "yellow" and "white" lanes as you can manage. There's a foolproof system which helps you enormously: all but a few French minor roads have an identifying number which is shown on both maps and signposts. Dyed-in-the-wool readers, doing a "Binns", will already be familiar with the term "mapaholic". Join the club – the guidelines are simple: immerse yourself in maps; get lost often; laugh over your wrong turns; and always remember a third golden rule – the best parts of any country are found, more often than not, at the end of roads that go nowhere.

Some important advice: make use of France's tourist offices. Your *Maison de la France* (MDLF) will provide you with lists of the departmental and regional (22) tourist offices; all of them are useful sources of information. Hundreds of *Office de Tourisme* and *Syndicat d'Initiative* addresses in France (and their phone numbers) are listed under village and town names in the Michelin red guide.

Hotels and restaurants: use the 1,000 or so recommendations made in my *Franc-wise France* and *French Leave Encore* guides. The map sheets in the spiral-bound Michelin atlas also highlight all towns and villages with hotels and restaurants (underlined in red) in the Michelin red guide.

Notes on Maps, Text and Contents page opposite

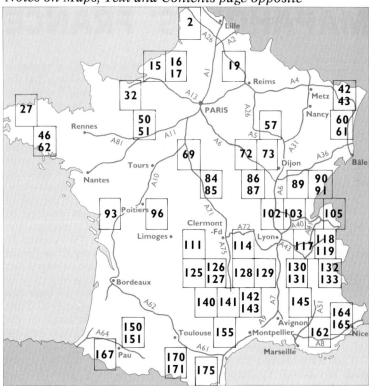

1) The map above and the first column on the opposite page: the figures shown are the page numbers in the spiral-bound *Michelin Motoring Atlas France*. If two numbers are printed together these refer to adjoining pages in the same atlas. (The 44 maps which follow also provide details of alternative Michelin 1/200 000 map products on which the terrain described is shown: see the box at the top of each map.)

2) Many places of interest – towns, villages, rivers and other sights – referred to in each area text (in **bold** print) are shown on the corresponding map in black/grey print   •**Fontgombault**

A letter and number (A1, C3, etc.), following any place name, refers to the grid square on the corresponding page in the spiral-bound atlas. (The grid squares are also shown on the maps in *Mapaholics' France* – to help those of you using other Michelin map products.)

3) Map scales 1/600 000: 1 cm is 6 km; 1 inch is just under 10 miles.

4) Map tints: under 200m/660ft ☐ 200m/660ft to 1000m/3300ft ☐
1000m/3300ft to 3000m/9900ft ☐ over 3000m/9900ft ■

Contents

5

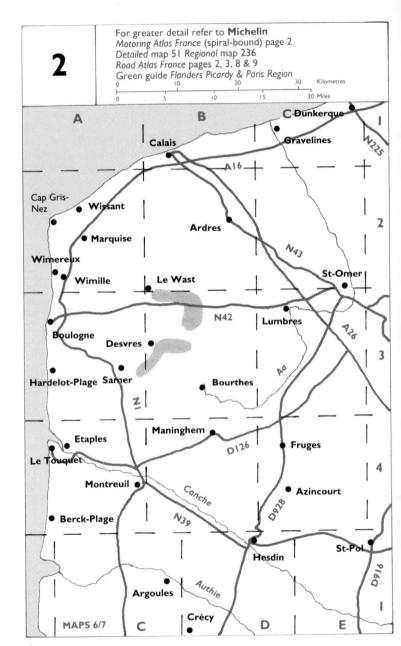

2

For greater detail refer to **Michelin**
Motoring Atlas France (spiral-bound) page 2
Detailed map 51 *Regional* map 236
Road Atlas France pages 2, 3, 8 & 9
Green guide *Flanders Picardy & Paris Region*

Kilometres
0   10   20   30
0   5   10   15   20 Miles

A   **B**   **C** Dunkerque

Calais   Gravelines

N225

A16

Cap Gris-Nez   Wissant   Ardres   N43   2

Marquise   St-Omer

Wimereux   Le Wast

Wimille   N42   Lumbres   A26

Boulogne   Desvres   3

Aa

Hardelot-Plage   Samer   Bourthes

N   3

Etaples   Maninghem   D126   Fruges   4

Le Touquet   Montreuil   Canche   Azincourt

D928

Berck-Plage   N39   St-Pol

Hesdin   D916

Argoules   Authie

MAPS 6/7   **C**   Crécy   **D**   **E**   1

6

I shall begin the first of the 44 chapters in *Mapaholics' France* with a classic example – and explanation – of what I mean by a "freewheeling philosophy of exploration": look beyond the obvious; get used to using Michelin's yellow and white lanes; laugh over your wrong slots; see France as few tourists do; and, above all, enjoy yourselves.

Study both the map on the left and the Michelin spiral-bound atlas map sheet 2. Most Brits, heading south and east, or returning home, rush across the Pas-de-Calais. (The French are just as bad: witness the Parisians on the new D126 (B4) which connects exit 4 on the A26 and **Le Touquet**.) As a consequence most tourists miss out: you and I know better – so let me help you seek out the not-so-obvious.

Start at **Fruges** (C4). Hereabouts a handful of enterprising farmers, producers and craftsmen deserve your support. First the Ferme Auberge du Sire de Créquy (tel 21 90 60 24), route de Créquy, 62310 Fruges. (Exact location: north of D130 by the word "Préhédré" on the map.) What a thriving affair: buy their farm-produced cheeses, butter and other products; but, better still, relish their terrific menus (lunch or dinner but you must book ahead). Their own produce features strongly, of course; especially *flamiche au fromage* and their home-made cheeses. Menu prices are modest. On Sundays the place is buzzing, packed to the rafters with an exclusively French clientele.

South-east of Fruges is Verchin and to the south of the hamlet is the Ferme Bocquet; buy breads, tarts and *brioches cuits au feu de bois* by Patricia and Jacqueline (21 04 43 66). Purchase dried flowers at the home of Marie-Christine and Chantal Carrez – at Crépy, south-east of Verchin (21 04 65 43). Relatives of the Sire de Créquy owners make *brebis* (ewe's milk) cheeses at their farm alongside the road immediately to the south of the D130, just above the word "Coupelle", south-west of Fruges. Buy wines from Les Caves du Vieux Chai at Fressin, south of Créquy and in the Planquette Valley (21 90 61 43).

All the neighbouring terrain is unassuming, unspoilt and unseen – with extensive views from high ground and, as a contrast, pastoral valleys. The Créquoise Valley is especially eye-catching at Royon (B4): here the D130 crosses the stream; trees provide shade on the "green" alongside the water; there's an *auberge*, handsome small château and minute waterfall to the south-west. Enjoy the river aspect from the bridge at Loison-sur-Créquoise – and then pay a call on the enterprise Delobel, on the D130 south of the village, where you can try, and buy, *perlé de groseille* or *framboise* (slightly sparkling *apéritifs*). Embry (B4) is a scenic treat from the hillside to the south.

Now to Maninghem where, just north of the church, you can purchase *foie gras*, *rillettes*, duck *cassoulet* and *pâtés* at the whitewashed farm of Christine and Hubert Dellerie (21 90 52 77). Spare a minute for the single Commonwealth War Grave of Captain G.W.W. Morris, who was killed on 22 May 1940. I wonder how the captain came to be buried at Maninghem? After the harvest, dive down to Clenleu (south-west of

7

Maninghem) and admire the *tressage de blé* (corn dollies) made at the farm of Hervé Vielliard (21 90 50 25); then tuck into pancakes and cider across the road. Be sure to leave by the steep 14% climb.

I have long loved the Course Valley which flows south from near **Desvres** (B3) to **Montreuil** (A4). Today there are many swish new villas at the southern end of the valley but the famous old *auberge* at Inxent still captivates. The Course is at its most appealing where the borders of Inxent and Beussent (B4) rub together. Just north of the latter one unusual producer makes highly reputed *chocolat frais*; you can try and buy (21 86 17 62). Rest awhile at Doudeauville (B3): what could be more refreshing than sitting on the bank by the stream, shaded by trees, with a drink in your hand (buy the latter at the Café des Sports)? Nearby **Samer** (A3) is renowned for strawberries.

As I said in the introduction, I can only scratch the surface in each chapter. Do your own exploration in the *pays* between the Course and **Bourthes** (B3) and Maninghem to the east: churches, old manors, footpaths, vales, streams and houses with a Spanish influence at Hucqueliers (B4) are just some of the surprises awaiting you.

Before leaving the countryside around Fruges detour to Agincourt (**Azincourt** on the map: C4). Here, on 25 October 1415, Henry V won his great battle. With the help of a new information centre and noticeboards you can see why the French *chevaliers* were massacred by Henry's deadly archers – trapped as the former were between the woods of Azincourt and Tramecourt. Further south (7:D2) is the battlefield of **Crécy**, where 69 years earlier, on 26 August 1346, Edward III won his famous victory, the start of the Hundred Years War. From a viewing tower you can survey the same scene that Edward witnessed and where, for the first and not the last time, the French learned the bitter lesson of the stunning use made of the longbow by the English and Welsh archers. On that same day cannonballs were also used for the first time.

Other valleys appeal too. North of Crécy is the **Authie** where, on either side of the river, you pass through communities and scenery a world away from the hectic N1. I have a soft spot for **Argoules** (6:C2) and its small *auberge* lost under a lime tree umbrella. The nearby Cistercian Abbey of Valloires and its renowned gardens present an impressive mixture of landscape and architecture; there's a vast collection of thousands of roses and shrubs.

The **Aa** Valley, from the source near Bourthes (B3) to **Lumbres** (C3), is seen by few. You have to work hard to get the best of the river views: wherever possible use side roads that bridge the stream. The mill at Renty (C3) is easily seen from the D129; one surprise, the wheel still turns. The owners of the handsome château, with a black-hatted tower, at the junction of the D191/D225, just north of St-Martin, have gone to some trouble to hide their property. Park and peek.

What of lesser-known treats? On map 6 (B2) is the huge Marquenterre Bird Sanctuary. There are many hides where you can watch migrating species; details from the Domain du Marquenterre at 80120 St-Quentin-en-Tourmont (22 25 03 06). Between the **Canche** and Authie valleys, at Buire-le-Sec (6:C1), is the Maison de l'Art et de l'Artisant, where several dozen artists show their varied work. Desvres (B3) is famous for its delicately decorated pottery (*faïence*); visit both the Maison de la Faïence and the workshop/exhibition of one of the manufacturers, Les Artistes Faïenciers (39 rue Rodolphe Minguet).

Tasting treats abound too. In **Boulogne** (A3) Philippe Olivier's treasure-trove *fromagerie* must not be missed: 43-45 rue Thiers. Hidden in the maze of Le Touquet's streets (A4) is Serge Pérard's exhilarating fish restaurant at 64 rue de Metz (see Michelin red guide): his *soupe de poissons* is fabulous. At Neufchâtel-Hardelot, between Boulogne and Le Touquet, pay a call on the *boulangerie-pâtisserie* of André Trupin, 20 rue du Chemin (on the D119E west of the village) and marvel at his old wood and traditional ovens: taste his handiwork too. At **Berck-Plage** (A4) see how *berlingots* (humbugs) are made in the traditional way; try them and buy them at Le Succés Berckois, 56 rue Carnot.

In the hills east of Boulogne, Le Boulonnais, are quiet villages and lanes – part of the Parc Naturel Régional Nord Pas-de-Calais: Réty (A2) and **Le Wast** (B2) are just two. The park is split into two parts: a semicircle to the east of Boulogne; and a circle of terrain around **St-Omer** (C2). For information on events and places to see, call on the Maison du Parc, "Manoir du Huisbos", at 62142 Le Wast; and the Maison du Parc, "Le Grand Vannage", at 62510 Arques (south of St-Omer). North of Boulogne is the Côte d'Opale, renowned for sandy beaches, dunes, cliffs and the glorious views from **Cap Gris-Nez**. Explore Le Boulonnais and the Côte d'Opale by bike. Many firms hire them, including Cyclo Plein Air at **Wissant** and Cycles Marius at **Wimille**.

There are many varied museums in the Boulogne area: the Maison du Marbre et de la Géologie at Rinxent (A2, east of **Marquise**) – note the many marble and stone quarries; the creepy V3 base at the Forteresse de Mimoyecques (north-east of Marquise); the Atlantic Wall Museum at Audinghen (north-west of Marquise); the Musée 39-45 at Ambleteuse (west of Marquise). Don't miss Boulogne's superb Nausicaa, the world's largest sea centre: there's an aquarium for the public and research facilities for marine professionals. Visit tropical lagoons with rainbow-coloured fish and see conger eels in a rusting wreck.

Many other Pas-de-Calais museums appeal: the impressive fine arts museum at the gracious Hôtel Sandelin in St-Omer; the Musée Municipal at Berck-Plage – specialising in ethnology and archaeology; the fine arts Musée du Château at Boulogne; the fine arts, scientific and technical culture of the Musée des Beaux Arts et de la Dentelle at **Calais**; the fine arts Musée du Touquet at Le Touquet; the regional archaeology exhibits at the Musée Quentovic in **Etaples** (A4); the modern and contemporary art displays at the Musée du Dessin et de l'Estampe Originale at **Gravelines** (C1); and, finally, the contemporary art at the

9

Musée d'Art Contemporain at **Dunkerque** (and the Jardin de Sculptures which surrounds the ultra-modern building).

Not surprisingly the Pas-de-Calais has many links with wars fought over the centuries. Between Calais and St-Omer is one of man's more hideous creations: a monstrosity of reinforced concrete called the Blockhaus d'Eperlecques (C2). The blockhouse was planned to be a firing pad for V2 rockets aimed at London. Three centuries ago the legendary and crafty military architect, Vauban, was associated with most of the formidable fortresses built throughout France: seek out the red-brick ramparts at Montreuil (A4); the well conserved fortress at Gravelines; Fort Nieulay, west of Calais (B1); the Fort d'Ambleteuse (north of Boulogne); and the St-Omer fortifications.

Other more pleasing examples of man's architectural skills abound. The entertaining Grisendal Water Mill near Wimille (A2), built in 1811, where Monsieur Roy, the miller, still passionately perpetuates the craft handed down from generation to generation. (The mill is alongside the Wimereux, to the east of Wimille.) Montreuil (A4), once a Roman port, is now a small hilltop town more than 10 km inland. Enter through the northern medieval town gates. Wander through cobbled streets and walk the Vauban ramparts circuit (three km). Both Victor Hugo, in his epic *Les Misérables*, and Laurence Stern, in *A Sentimental Journey*, wrote about the town. **Hesdin** (7:D1), like Montreuil, is a film-makers' delight (many of the original *Maigret* TV episodes were shot there).

Some readers will be interested in festivals, *son et lumière* shows and other events held in the area. (If you want information on festivals, spectacles and similar events throughout France contact your MDLF.) Here's a handful held in the Pas-de-Calais (phone numbers in brackets): "Music and Ramparts" at Boulogne (first three weeks in June: 21 31 68 38); the Medieval Festival at the Château d'Hardelot (A3) (July/August: 21 83 71 22); the Hardelot Festival of classical music (July/mid August: 21 83 02 65); the International Kite Meeting at Berck (early April: 21 09 50 00); and the Flobart (traditional fishing boat) Festival at Wissant (A2) (end August: 21 85 15 62).

Just as our children have enjoyed the long, sandy beaches of the area in past years so will yours too. The best known are the beaches at **Hardelot-Plage**, stretching over 17 km and bordered by pine woods; the beach at Le Touquet, backed by the elegant promenade and resort; the smaller version at **Wimereux** (don't miss the dunes to the north, at de la Slack); and the sands and dunes at Berck-Plage and Fort-Mahon Plage (6:B2). An added attraction here is the Aquaclub Côte Picarde – fun and recreation with water slides and bubbling pools.

Poking noses and fingers into markets could well be an irresistible idea for many of you. Here is a list of some of the smaller markets held in the area: St-Omer (Saturday morning); Desvres (Tuesday morning); Etaples (A4) (Tuesday and Friday morning); Montreuil (Saturday morning); Samer (A3) (Monday morning); Wimereux (Tuesday and Friday morning).

Finally, I'll finish by reminding you of some of the more illustrious tourist attractions in the bigger towns and resorts.

Le Touquet. A sophisticated seaside resort with wide and long sandy beaches. Designer boutiques on the main street and casinos cater for the posher Porsche-owning Parisians. The Aqualud indoor watersports centre on the sea front keeps children happy for hours. The covered market, too, is a lively affair: Thursday and Saturday mornings (and Monday mornings, too, from mid June to mid September).

Calais. Don't bypass Rodin's bronze sculpture, The Burghers of Calais, in front of the town hall; the work commemorates the surrender of six townsmen in 1347 to King Edward III. The lighthouse, near the Gare Maritime, offers exceptional views across the Channel to the English coast on clear days. The Musée des Beaux Arts, already mentioned and in the heart of the town, contains exhibits of Flemish lace and linen. To the south is the vast Channel Tunnel terminal; note, too, the line of the new TGV track. Bridges on the roads south of **Ardres** (B2) provide many a chance to see the bullet trains on the move.

Boulogne. After Nausicaa, already referred to, spend time in the Ville Haute, the 13th-century hilltop town, with the Basilica of Notre-Dame and ramparts; the oldest church, St-Nicolas, in *place* Dalton; and the museum, in the castle, noted for Egyptian treasures. Don't forget the *fromagerie* treasures, over 200 varieties, at Philippe Olivier's cheese shop at 43-45 rue Thiers. The display is a roll-call of French cheeses. Northern varieties have pride of place but you will also encounter many unknown regional versions rarely seen elsewhere: *Le Bergues* (near Dunkerque); *Le St-Winoc* (made at an abbey); *Le Belval* (near Hesdin and **St-Pol**); *Le Crayeux de Roncq*; and *Le Vieux Boulogne*.

St-Omer. The ancient wool town's charm has survived extensive war damage. There are pretty, old canalside houses, handsome main square, impressive Basilica of Notre Dame and the exceptional museum in the Hôtel de Sandelin (displays of fine and decorative arts, especially clay pipes and ceramics). Tour the *marais* (marshes) and waterways (explore by punt) north and east of the town. At nearby Arques (to the immediate south) the astonishing Ascenseur des Fontinettes has been preserved: the hydraulic lift was built in 1887 to replace a series of locks and raised canal barges a distance of 40 feet.

And last, but not least, may I put in a special word for one of my favourite small towns, Bergues, just off the edge of the map (7:D1). A peaceful place, with walled fortifications, belfry (a copy of the original destroyed in 1944), first-rate Musée Municipal (in the Mont-de-Piété) and a network of canals fringed by Flemish-styled houses. North of the ramparts is the star-shaped Couronne d'Hondschoote, a defensive complex of moats and walls designed by Vauban, the military architect, which now provides a delightful walk along a canal and lakes. I wonder what the wily genius would make of the fort's new use? Peace, not war, is an appropriate end to this Pas-de-Calais chapter.

11

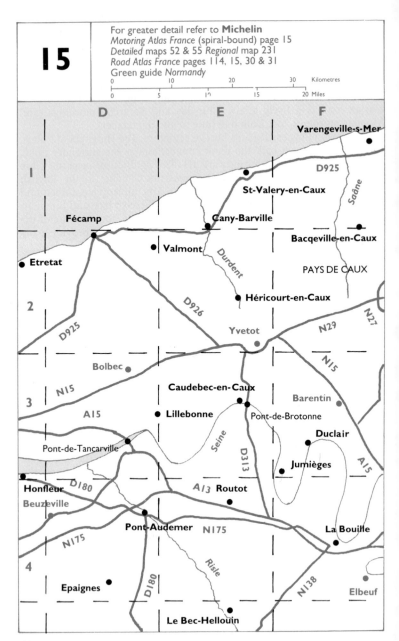

15

For greater detail refer to **Michelin**
Motoring Atlas France (spiral-bound) page 15
Detailed maps 52 & 55 *Regional* map 231
Road Atlas France pages 114, 15, 30 & 31
Green guide *Normandy*

0   10   20   30   Kilometres

0   5   10   15   20   Miles

D   E   F

Varengeville-s-Mer

D925   *Saâne*

St-Valery-en-Caux

I

Fécamp   **Cany-Barville**

Bacqeville-en-Caux

Etretat   **Valmont**   *Durdent*

PAYS DE CAUX

D926   **Héricourt-en-Caux**

2   N29   N27

D925   **Yvetot**   N15

Bolbec

3   N15

A15   **Caudebec-en-Caux**   **Barentin**

Lillebonne   Pont-de-Brotonne

Seine   **Duclair**

Pont-de-Tancarville   D313   A15

Jumièges

Honfleur   D180   A13 **Routot**

Beuzeville

La Bouille

Pont-Audemer   N175

4   N175

Risle   D180   N138   Elbeuf

Epaignes

Le Bec-Hellouin

12

The map on the left is a cartographic image of contrasting countryside. The plateau area north of the **Seine** is called the **Pays de Caux**.

The coast is renowned for the high chalk cliffs (*falaises*) which dominate the shoreline. In the hinterland tiny picturesque chalk streams are very much my own cup of tea though I cannot say I like the extensive hedge-less prairies which cover much of the Caux plateau. The Seine estuary and valley are uglier than ever; industrial complexes and urban sprawl have crept into every available corner. Thankfully, there are numerous man-made treasures to compensate and, on the left bank of the Seine, the Parc Régional de Brotonne is a welcome and refreshing green lung. I'll start with my personal scenic favourites: the valleys of the River **Durdent** (E1/E2) and the River **Saâne** (F1/F2).

The Durdent is pretty as a picture. One big plus is that roads are in constant touch with the stream. Start with a scenic splash at a gorgeous spot. Locate **Cany-Barville** (E1), head south on the D131 for a mile or so and turn left towards the church marked on the map. At the point the lane crosses the stream (a ford) you'll find the church and a small hotel, the Manoir de Barville. Park, and take a stroll; even if you don't use the hotel's facilities no-one is likely to bite your head off.

A few hundred yards upstream is the 17th-century Château de Cany. Moated and full of handsome furniture, the severe-looking château, redeemed by the pastoral river setting, managed to survive the Revolution. Continue south and do some detailed navigation, nosing out in the process some striking examples of *colombiers cauchois*, the dovecotes of Caux. Built of stone and red bricks, and with tiled cone-shaped roofs, each one is a treat; don't miss them.

The first, at Grainville-la-Teinturière (E2), is easily spotted, near the church. The second is harder to find. Do not use the signposted route from the church alongside the D131 at Oherville. Instead, drive up the one-car-wide lane half a mile to the north, between two banks cut out of the hillside covered with a dense beech wood. At the top, among the trees to the left, you'll spot the fortified Manoir d'Auffay and, nearer the entrance from the road, the exceedingly handsome dovecote, built in a mosaic of brick patterns. This is also the site of a new Musée des Colombiers Cauchois (open weekends in May and June and every day from July to mid September). Now back to the river.

The third dovecote is also hard to locate. Head north on the D149 from **Héricourt-en-Caux** (E2). At the top of the hill, after the bend, turn right towards Anvéville; the *colombier* is part of a farm which is on the right in half a mile or so. You are allowed to enter.

You will love the Durdent Valley, the unspoilt villages and the mix of meadows, trees and gentle stream. There are several water mills between Grainville and Héricourt and, at the latter, a riverside *auberge*. Autretot (E2), south of Héricourt, is a four-star *village fleuri*. One enterprising business is S.A. Sotrosa at Ouainville (E1), west of Cany-Barville. Here you can buy *oeufs de truite* – used to such good effect at the Manoir de

Barville – smoked fish, varying *confits*, *soupe de poisson* and other goodies, including *cidre*, *calvados* and *pommeau* (apple juice and *calvados*). Finally, there's an Ecomusée de Moulin St-Martin at Cany-Barville which explains local crafts during the last century (open p.m. at weekends from June to September).

The Saâne (F1/F2), together with its tiny tributary, the Vienne (the Michelin maps do not identify, by name, the marked stream which flows north from **Bacqeville-en-Caux**: F1/F2), are not as seductive as the Durdent. But do seek them out. The many villages are prosperous places. All have differently-styled churches. The D2 road is never really in contact with the Saâne and the only way to best appreciate the water vistas is to constantly cross, by car or foot, the numerous bridges which cross the river. Make an effort to find the stern looking, multi-towered Château d'Imbleville (F2), the ancient stone house with half-timbered balcony at Auzouville-sur-Saâne and, to the east, the handsome Manoir d'Herbouville at St-Ouen-le-Mauger (F2).

The smaller ports and resorts on the Caux coastline leave me cold. Over the decades I have visited them out of season, in winter, spring and autumn; perhaps on a hot summer's day I would see them at their best. However, there are several sites worth a detour.

Start in the woods surrounding **Varengeville-sur-Mer** (F1). The Renaissance Manoir d'Ango is a pleasing Italian-styled diversion; note the fine dovecote. To the north of the D75, on the D27 leading to the sea, is the renowned, somewhat too much I think, Parc Floral des Moutiers: a Lutyens house and the Gertrude Jekyll inspired gardens attract thousands of visitors. The wooded grounds and the many hidden corners please the eye, especially the fabulous rhododendrons which we were so lucky to see at the end of May. Drive the narrow one-way lanes near Vasterival (F1), lined with cottages and houses galore, some simple, some swish. Enjoy the vistas from the viewpoints.

Continue west. Admire the vast église at Bourg-Dun (F1); the thatched cottages and one of the smallest rivers in France at Veules-les-Roses (F1: both villages have a first-class restaurant); and the colourful harbour at **St-Valery-en-Caux** (E1). Visit the over-the-top Palais Bénédictine at **Fécamp** (D2): a mixture of ornate Gothic and Renaissance buildings; an art museum housing paintings, sculptures and ivory; and a history of the Bénédictine story, explaining how the spirit is distilled and a fascinating demonstration of the 27 spices and plants which are used to make the heady liqueur. Before leaving the port don't forget the impressively-proportioned interior of La Trinité Church.

The best route to **Etretat** (C2) is along the minor roads, not the D940. Leave the car whenever you can and walk the GR21 footpath, which runs along the top of the cliffs; this advice also applies to both sides of Etretat, the only way to marvel at the Falaise d'Amont, the Falaise d'Aval and the famous natural arches to the west of the resort.

Inland from Fécamp two châteaux deserve your attention. **Valmont**

(D2) is particularly creditworthy as a considerable effort has been made to lay on all sorts of attractions. The 15th-century castle has a medieval, 11th-century keep, a 16th-century Renaissance wing and a large leisure park. The Château de Bailleul (D2), south-west of Valmont, is a 16th-century square building, noted for its kitchen and a bedroom where Mary Queen of Scots stayed after she fled from Scotland in 1561; just as noteworthy are the gardens and trees in the park.

Man has certainly left his mark on the banks of the Seine. I've grumbled already about the bleak features: what of the more positive benefits? Two *ponts*, the **Tancarville** suspension bridge (D3) and the harp-like, cable-stayed **Brotonne** (E3), are massive. An even larger one, the Pont de Normandie, is being built east of **Honfleur** (14:C3); at 856 m between the two towers, this will be the world's longest cable-stayed bridge (Brotonne is 320 m). **Caudebec-en-Caux** (E3) and **Duclair** (F3) are pleasant but busy spots; cross the Seine by car ferry from the latter. Do that, too, at **La Bouille** (F4), squeezed onto the river's left bank; walk the narrow streets and promenade.

Four renowned abbeys are located on map sheet 15: the austere, three-sided Cistercian Abbaye de Valasse (D3), north of **Lillebonne** (see the ruins of the latter's grass-banked Roman theatre); the Abbaye de St-Wandrille (E3), east of Caudebec, a Bénédictine glory and the home of Europe's oldest dining room (*le réfectoire*); the mighty abbey ruins at **Jumièges** (F3), still a stunning reminder of the many once great Norman abbeys; and, the last of the quartet, the Bénédictine Abbaye St-Georges at St-Martin-de-Boscherville (F3), east of Jumièges.

South of the river is the green lung I referred to earlier: the two sections of the Parc Régional de Brotonne, one the great beech and oak forest (E3), the other the Marais Vernier (D3). Call at the Maison du Parc at Notre-Dame-de-Bliquetuit (E3), south of the bridge, for details of several points of interest: the new Maison du Lin (flax) at **Routot** (E4); the Musée du Sabotier and Le Four à Pain (a rural bakery) at La Haye-de-Routot, north of Routot; the Maison des Métiers at Bourneville (E4); the Musée de la Marine at Caudebec (E3); and the Maison de la Pomme and La Forge at St-Opportune-la-Mare (D4/E4).

Now three favourites. **Pont-Audemer** (D4) is full of half-timbered houses between the two arms of the **Risle** (connected by tiny canals, the town is tagged la Venise Normande); market day is Monday. Honfleur, an atmospheric port where the *vieux bassin* is a magnet for painters. The abbey at **Le Bec-Hellouin** (33:F1) has a lovely setting: walk through the shady grounds and don't be intimidated by St-Nicholas' Tower; study the plaque before making the 200-step climb.

Finally, some man-made delights as you head for the Pays d'Auge (map 32): the *église* at St-Germain-Village (D4); the 1,000-year-old yew tree and the church at St-Symphorien (D4); the church and half-timbered houses at **Epaignes** (D4); and the delectable church at Le-Bois-Hellain (D4). Relish, too, the many half-timbered *maisons Normandes*.

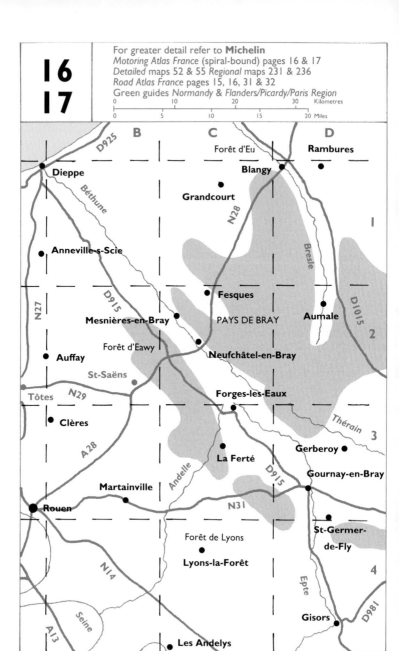

16
17

For greater detail refer to **Michelin**
Motoring Atlas France (spiral-bound) pages 16 & 17
Detailed maps 52 & 55 *Regional* maps 231 & 236
Road Atlas France pages 15, 16, 31 & 32
Green guides *Normandy & Flanders/Picardy/Paris Region*

0   10   20   30   Kilometres

0   5   10   15   20 Miles

B   **C**   **D**

Forêt d'Eu

Rambures

Blangy

Dieppe

D925

Béthune

Grandcourt

N28

Anneville-s-Scie

Bresle

I

Fesques

D915

N27

Mesnières-en-Bray

PAYS DE BRAY

Aumale

D1015

2

Forêt d'Eawy

Neufchâtel-en-Bray

Auffay

St-Saëns

Tôtes   N29

Forges-les-Eaux

Thérain

3

Clères

A28

Gerberoy ●

Andelle

La Ferté

D915

Gournay-en-Bray

Martainville

N31

Rouen

**St-Germer-
de-Fly**

Forêt de Lyons

Lyons-la-Forêt

N14

Epte

4

Seine

D981

A13

Gisors

Les Andelys

16

Most of the northern half of the countryside covered by the map on the left is known as the **Pays de Bray**. In sharp contrast to the open plateau of Caux (map 15), Bray is a land of broad river valleys, undulating hills, beech forests and emerald pastures. Increasingly hedges have been ripped out and some of the upland stretches now resemble prairies. To the south is the **Seine** Valley and the vast beech **Forêt de Lyons**. Streams and rivers abound, flowing both north and south. No wonder the area was nicknamed "The Paris Larder" in the last century.

Where do you start your exploration of this unassuming farming landscape? I suggest at one of the more off-the-beaten-track spots, a quiet corner where you will be reminded, in an unassuming, contemplative way, of the tragic loss of life in the Normandy countryside 50 years ago. Head for the Commonwealth War Cemetery to the north-east of **Grandcourt** (C1), one of the most unusual in Normandy. At Grandcourt there are only 58 graves, ten more than the smallest of the Commission's Normandy cemeteries, at Jerusalem (see map 32). Study the register and the exceptionally interesting table and map which, together, explain how the 58 souls came to be buried at Grandcourt. You will not regret the minimal effort needed to seek out the inspiring spot.

Between the cemetery and the **Bresle** Valley, to the north-east, is the refreshing **Forêt d'Eu**. I have seen all the Bray forests in the spring when the beech glades are carpeted with bluebells. In autumn the same glades become crunchy copper carpets when the trees above shed their dying leafy cloaks. Explore the Forêt d'Eu and the varied flora and fauna. Seek out the viewpoint at the Poteau de Ste-Catherine, east of Grandcourt cemetery; walk the last few hundred yards.

The Vallée de Bresle is famous for glassware. The *verreries* range from huge factories at Hodeng-au-Bosc and Senarpont (D1), both south-east of **Blangy**, to smaller ones at Vieux-Rouen-s-Bresle (D1) and Blangy. The latter are renowned for their colourful perfume bottles, vases and lampshades. For factory visits call at the tourist offices in Blangy (tel 35 93 52 48) or **Aumale** (D2: 35 93 41 68).

One man-made structure is a rewarding detour: the château at **Rambures** (D1). There is no prissiness about this virile château: surrounded by trees is a small castle with broad, thick-walled towers built of red brick and topped with cone-shaped roofs. Built in the 15th century, the castle played an important part in the Hundred Years War (March to October, a.m. and p.m.; closed Wednesdays; 22 25 10 93).

Now west to the heart of Bray, to **Neufchâtel-en-Bray** (C2). Bray is cheese country: *Bondon, Bondard, Carré, Petit Suisse*; there are many names and shapes but the version which is associated with the area more than any other is *Coeur de Bray*, a fruity-tasting, heart-shaped cream cheese. There's a Route du Fromage de Neufchâtel; get a map from the Office de Tourisme, 6 place Notre-Dame, 76270 Neufchâtel-en-Bray (you can also taste the cheese here during the summer). You can buy the cheese at the Ferme des Fontaines, on the D135 south-east of Neufchâtel and 200 yards before the left turn to Nesle-Hodeng (C2).

The hills on both sides of Neufchâtel are reputed for their wild flowers. The same tourist office (35 93 22 96) has laid out several walks and produced a map to identify where the routes go. In the nearby Eaulne Valley there's a small nature reserve, alongside the stream, at **Fesques** (C1/C2). Varying flora and fauna can be seen; details from the same tourist office or the *mairie* at Fesques (35 94 36 04). Of the man-made sites in the **Béthune** Valley the best known is the large Château de Mesnières (C2). A mixture of fortress and château, the Renaissance structure is a glorious building. Take my tip and approach **Mesnières-en-Bray** (C2) from Fresles (B2), much the best way to admire the imposing 15th-century château (open p.m. only at weekends from Easter to All Saints' Day). Bures-en-Bray (B2) is another attractive spot; again, much the best way of enjoying the view of the manor house and church is on the descent from the south-west.

The **Forêt d'Eawy** (B2) should be crossed and re-crossed; there's many a forest glade to catch the eye. So too will "apple" country to the west; cider is the tipple hereabouts. The Varenne Valley is a sparkling scenic tonic. Be sure to include these two roads on your route: the climb from St-Germain-d'Etables to Le Bois-Robert (B1); and the climb on the D476 from Muchedent to Le Catelier (B2). If you want to buy cider then seek out the Cidrerie du Duché de Longueville at **Anneville-sur-Scie** (A1) or the Cidreries Mignard at **Auffay** (A2). The Scie Valley is lined with villages and churches and, at Heugleville-sur-Scie (A2), just north of Auffay, spare time for the commune's enterprising arboretum walk (June to mid October: details from the *mairie*).

On your way north to **Dieppe** detour to the Château de Miromesnil (A1). The handsome château has two utterly different façades: red brick and twin towers, capped with cone-shaped roofs, at the rear (not pepperpots M. Michelin); ornate richness at the front. As appealing as the man-made building is, Anne and I were as interested in the park and walled kitchen garden, an extrovert mix of flowers and vegetables.

Dieppe (A1/B1) is my favourite Channel port. Crammed with character there's much to waylay you: the bustling port, the wide promenade, the cathedral-sized Eglise St-Jacques, the narrow lanes surrounding the church and the castle-museum above the town. Sadly, the events of 19 August 1942 weigh heavily on the memory: the Operation Jubilee raids by the Canadians at Puys, to the east, and Pourville-sur-Mer, to the west, caused tragic loss of life. Do visit the Museum of 19 August 1942, on the D75 towards Pourville, which details the story of that horrendous day. One point of interest: the site of the present-day open-air swimming pool and tennis courts was once the home of Dieppe's casino, demolished by the Germans after the 1942 raid.

Leave the coast and head inland to **Forges-les-Eaux** (C2/C3). This small spa is as unassuming as the rest of Bray: a combination of woods, lake, park and varied leisure activities give the resort a healthy vitality.

The casino will attract some; for others the Musée de la Résistance et de la Déportation will be much more interesting (p.m. March to September). Very much to our liking is the tiny hilltop hamlet of **La Ferté** (C3), south of the spa: the church and its yew trees, the *mairie*, the mix of old and new houses around a small green and the majestic small half-timbered Maison Henri IV combine to reveal the hidden face of Normandy, one rarely seen by the majority of tourists. The nearby *ancienne abbatiale* at Sigy-en-Bray (C3) is another treat bypassed by travellers relying solely on small-scale maps.

Before heading south to **Lyons-la-Forêt** (C4) seek out three man-made attractions to the east. First **Gerberoy** (D3), a tiny, precious jewel of a village on an elevated site. Second, **St-Germer-de-Fly** (D3), south of **Gournay-en-Bray**, where a gigantic 12th-century *église* dwarfs the village below its high walls and tower. Third, to **Gisors** (D4) and an imposing castle; ruins now but the commanding position confirms just why the original structure was built by William the Conqueror's son at the end of the 11th century.

The Forêt de Lyons is best approached from Beauvoir-en-Lyons (C3); be certain to walk to the viewpoint marked on the map. Lyons-la-Forêt is a startling contrast to tiny La Ferté, mentioned earlier. The largish village, elegantly groomed and sophisticated, has many superb half-timbered houses. We've spent time in the past criss-crossing the forest's numerous roads. One mysterious spot is on the steep lane which climbs north-west from the Abbaye de Mortemer, south of Lyons: 300 yards from the abbey there's a monument to 11 Frenchmen killed on the 23/24/25 August 1944. What is the story behind the memorial?

There's a ring of numerous sites to the east, south and west of Lyons-la-Forêt. The Château de Fleury, to the north-east, has a rose garden, handsome panelling, a display of dolls and an old kitchen. The ruins of the Abbaye de Mortemer lie in a delightful wooded valley site; a museum explains the Cistercian monastic life. The Château de Vascoeuil (C3), in the **Andelle** Valley, is more a stone castle housing an art exhibition; the gardens, river, stepped cascade and cottages win hands down (the Musée Michelet houses the historian's memorabilia). The nearby Château de **Martainville**, due west, is an intriguing Musée des Traditions et Arts Normands. At **Les Andelys** (34:C1), the ruins of the once commanding fortress, built by Richard the Lionheart, dominate both the town and River Seine. Finally, the Château de **Clères** (A3/B3), north of Rouen, is the site of a fine zoo in a natural setting and the home of a super motor museum (open every day).

Finally, **Rouen** (A3/A4). Our last visit was a traffic nightmare. Try to visit on a Sunday – the best time to absorb the many treasures: the fabulous Notre-Dame Cathedral, several churches, the old quarter with flamboyant half-timbered houses, museums galore and the exquisite rue du Gros-Horloge. Write to the Office de Tourisme for information: 25 place de la Cathédrale, 76008 Rouen Cedex (35 71 41 77).

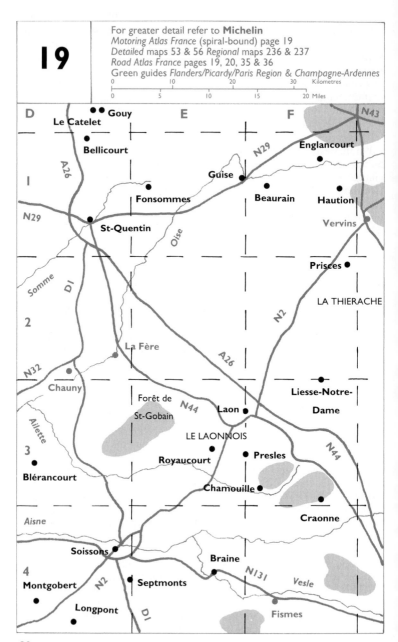

19

For greater detail refer to **Michelin**
Motoring Atlas France (spiral-bound) page 19
Detailed maps 53 & 56 *Regional maps* 236 & 237
Road Atlas France pages 19, 20, 35 & 36
Green guides *Flanders/Picardy/Paris Region & Champagne-Ardennes*

0   10   20   30   Kilometres

0   5   10   15   20 Miles

D   **E**   **F**   N43

● ● **Gouy**
Le Catelet

Bellicourt   N29   **Englancourt**

A26

1   **Guise** ●

Fonsommes ●   **Beaurain** ●   **Haution** ●

N29   **Vervins** ●

St-Quentin ●   Oise

Prisces ●

Somme   D1   **LA THIERACHE**

2   N2

La Fère ●   A26

N32   Chauny ●   **Liesse-Notre-**

Chauny   Forêt de   N44   **Laon** ●   **Dame** ●

Aillette   St-Gobain   **LE LAONNOIS**

3   **Royaucourt** ●   ● **Presles**   N44

● **Blérancourt**   **Chamouille** ●

Aisne   ● **Craonne**

Soissons ●

4   **Braine** ●   N131   Vesle

Montgobert   N2   ● **Septmonts**

● ● **Longpont**   D1   **Fismes** ●

20

Is there a name more synonymous with slaughter than the word "Somme"? No matter how many times I visit, or cross, northern France, I am always reminded of the inconceivable slaughter which took place 80 years ago in the killing fields of both Flanders and Picardy. We must never forget and we should all give a little time, every year, to quietly remembering the supreme sacrifice made by so many of our forefathers.

Most of map sheet 19 is part of Picardy. The Source de la Somme (E1) is north-east of **Fonsommes**. The ancient spring has been turned into an "attraction" (1993) with an explanatory map and board, gardens and toilets. The 245 km-long **Somme** flows west, past so much consecrated ground. Now seek out some of the nearby cemeteries and memorials.

The Prospect Hill Cemetery is between **Gouy** and Beaurevoir, east of the N44 (8:C4). The cemetery is the last resting place of 451 UK, 77 Australian and 10 South African soldiers who fell in the October 1918 advance, just weeks before the end of the war. Read the notes in the register and study the explanatory plate behind the shelter. Quite different, and set out in 14 acres of tree-lined grounds, is the American Cemetery at Bony (8:C4), south-west of **Le Catelet**. 1837 soldiers are buried here; their names, and those of 333 missing in action, are commemorated in the chapel alongside the cemetery.

Give time, too, to the nearby impressive Bellicourt American Memorial on the west side of the N44 (8:C4). Look at the monument's western façade where a large map explains the attack, at the end of September 1918, which pierced the Hindenburg Line, the ultra-strong German defensive position, just west of the canal tunnel below you.

Canal tunnel? You can trace the 6,200 yard-long Canal de St-Quentin tunnel, built by Napoléon between 1802 and 1810, on the map. Just south of **Bellicourt** (D1), stop on the west side of the N44, at the Vermandois Tourist Office, and walk down the zig-zags to the tunnel's southern entrance. Note the blue water, electric lights and the canal details at the entrance. Call, too, at the first-class tourist office.

Let's change tack and head east from the monotonous, hedge-less *pays*, where maize and sugar beet predominate, to **Guise** (E1). In the terrain to the east the **Oise** Valley is an eye-opening treat: wooded, hilly and with pastures where cows munch contentedly. Note that Michelin use few green markings alongside the roads (to signify pretty routes); yet, further downstream from Origny-Ste-Benoite (E1), the D13 is edged all the way. Michelin are wrong: the Oise thereabouts is no great shakes and Origny has a hideous cement works dominating the town.

East of Guise is **La Thiérache**, a pastoral area famed for fortified churches built of brick and stone and with varying towers. Just as interesting are the villages where houses, cottages, gardens and barns catch the eye. Start at **Beaurain** (F1) where clever use is made of agricultural machinery to win a two-star *village fleuri* rating. The 16th-century church is to the north-west; note the small cone-topped turrets. At Gomont, further east on the D31, smile at the tiles on the red-brick façade of the house at the D26 junction.

Englancourt (F1) is high above the right bank of the Oise. The church has four towers with sharpened pencil hats. Admire, too, the attractive red-brick farms and cottages. Now south to the Brune Valley, stopping first at the Ferme de la Fontaine Orion, where Claire Halleux produces *Maroilles* cheese – soft, slightly salty and gold – and the regional classic, *tarte aux maroilles*. Her farm is on the D464 at **Haution** (F1) and is open p.m. only except Sun and *fête* days.

In the pleasant Brune Valley make a start at **Prisces** (F2). Here the church's red-brick tower has the look of a formidable castle keep; note, too, the wattle and daub cottages. At Burelles (20:B2), the *église* is all red brick; see the wash house opposite. Further east the church at Hary is the first, on my route, to have a cone-topped tower.

South-west now to one of France's greatest glories, **Laon** (E3/F3), calling on the way at the pilgrimage site of **Liesse-Notre-Dame** (F2) where the white-stoned *église* has some striking stained glass windows. Laon, once the capital of France, sits majestically on a solitary hill. The stunning Gothic cathedral, one of the oldest and finest in France, is both the centrepiece and a proud landmark, seen from miles away. The western towers; the glorious façade below them; the pulse-racing purity of the nave; the stained glass windows; I defy anyone not to be moved by this medieval wonder. To access the high old town use either the rack railway from the SNCF station or drive up the *lacets* on the hill's south side. Enjoy the town gates, the old houses and streets, the ramparts and cliff-top promenades.

To the west of Laon is the **Forêt de St-Gobain** (E3) – a self-contained beech forest, gently undulating with hidden valleys, *étangs*, smallholdings, ruined priories and abbeys, swooping owls, beech tunnels and villages where houses are built of either white stone or small red bricks. In late autumn the forest is a sensual sight. Seek out the 14th-century priory of Le Tortoir, a collection of white stone buildings with a fortified look and a solitary tower; access is possible. The 15th-century Bénédictine abbey at St-Nicholas, further south, has an idyllic setting with *étangs*, woods and, among the trees, a tantalising glimpse of distant towers; the building is not accessible.

The vast abbey at Prémontré, rebuilt in the 18th century, is now a psychiatric hospital; parts of the classical buildings can be visited. The *étangs* to the east are much to my liking. South of Prémontré, at Brancourt-en-Laonnois, is a 1920s *église* noted for a pierced tower. Finally, at Coucy-le-Château Auffrique (D3), outside the forest, little remains of what was once a massive 13th-century fortress; but the ruined walls, towers, gate and views make a worthwhile detour.

To the west and south of Laon is the appealing wooded and hilly *pays* of **Le Laonnois**. Nose out some of the man-made attractions. Mons (E3), south-west of Laon, has a 13th/14th century *église*; drive up to the end of the tarmac road at Les Creuttes for a fine view of Laon to the east.

Climb, too, to the modern church at Montbavin. The 13th/14th-century *église* at **Royaucourt** is a mini cathedral: drive the one-way system and relish the lofty exterior, flying buttresses and several towers with tops like knights' lances. The restored Romanesque church at **Urcel** (E3) is a handsome, balanced structure with ingenious use made of arches in the porch and tower (east of the N2).

North-east to the Romanesque church at Nouvion-le-Vineux, an admirable building in an appealing site above the village; note the 1841 wooden *lavoir*, with running water, to the east. **Presles** (F3) is a smart *village fleuri*. The Romanesque church has a cemetery where three RAF crew are buried (they died on 17 May 1940). Vorges has a 13th-century *église* with an open bell-tower and large rose window in an agreeable *place*. The church at Bruyères-et-Montbérault has a massive bell-tower; look out for the good-looking *mairie* and paved *place.*

Now climb the wooded ridge to the south of the previous four villages and make for the Parc Nautique de l'Ailette, south-east of **Chamouille** (F3): here the River **Ailette** has been turned into an inviting lake with excellent use made of trees and woods. Savour the walks, picnic areas, sailing, *pédalos*, super children's playground and wild life. To the east is the ruined and accessible Cistercian Abbaye de Vauclair; note the garden of medicinal plants and the *étang* across the road.

Next, to another tragic reminder of the futile fighting in the 1914-18 war. The sacred Chemin des Dames (E3/F3) runs east to west, along the crest of hills between the Ailette and **Aisne** valleys. Just north of **Craonne** (F3), on the south side of the D895, is a *table d'orientation* which explains how the hideous fighting between the French and Germans lasted almost throughout World War One in the valley below. Visit, too, the Caverne du Dragon (closed Tues) to the west, a *musée* explaining the futile four-year engagement. Wrap up as you get cold underground.

What else? On the small scale there's a 13th-century *église*, in a colourful garden setting, at **Braine** (E4); the flamboyant Gothic keep at **Septmonts** (D4); the château and Musée de Bois at **Montgobert** (D4), approached by an avenue of handsome trees (open p.m. weekends) – admire, too, the village's smart stone houses; the ruined Cistercian abbey at **Longpont** (D4) where the village has a beguiling cobbled terrace, flowers, stone buildings, the vine-covered Hôtel de l'Abbaye, and stone gate under an old half-timbered house with cone-hatted towers; and, at **Blérancourt** (D3), there's a Franco-American *musée* evoking the historical links between the two nations.

On a larger scale admire the vast interior of the Gothic cathedral at **Soissons** (D4) – and the dagger-like spires of the ruined 14th-century Abbaye de St-Jean des Vignes where the west front is still intact; and, finally, the Gothic basilica at **St-Quentin** (D1), with double transept, stained glass windows and 75-stop organ. (Spare time, too, for the nearby flamboyant Gothic Hôtel de Ville and the Marais d'Isle de St-Quentin – a nature reserve north-east of the station.)

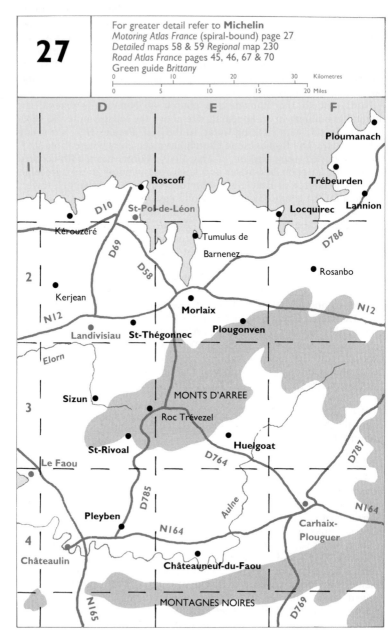

27

For greater detail refer to **Michelin**
Motoring Atlas France (spiral-bound) page 27
Detailed maps 58 & 59 *Regional* map 230
Road Atlas France pages 45, 46, 67 & 70
Green guide *Brittany*

| 0 | | 10 | | 20 | | 30 | Kilometres |

| 0 | 5 | 10 | 15 | 20 Miles |

D   **E**   **F**

1

Ploumanach

Trébeurden

Roscoff

St-Pol-de-Léon

Locquirec   Lannion

D10

Kérouzéré

Tumulus de
Barnenez

D786

D69

D58

Rosanbo

2

Kerjean

Morlaix

N12

N12

Landivisiau   **St-Thégonnec**

Plougonven

Elorn

Sizun

MONTS D'ARREE

3

Roc Trévezel

St-Rivoal

Huelgoat

D787

Le Faou

D764

D785

Aulne

N164

Pleyben

**Carhaix-
Plouguer**

N164

4

Châteaulin

Châteauneuf-du-Faou

D769

N165

MONTAGNES NOIRES

24

"Brittany has a thousand and one faces." At first you smile and dismiss the claim as typical of any made by tourist boards the world over. Yet there's a ring of truth to the bold claim. This north-west corner of France is a land of patriotic people, proud to be Bretons, who guard their language with great fervour; and where the landscape, both natural and man-made, is always changing and always pleasing.

In the two Brittany chapters I shall lead you to many facets of the emerald called Bretagne. Inland Brittany is known as Argoat, "the land of the woods". The coast is Armor, "the land of the sea". Map sheet 27 gives you a taste of the Argoat and the northern Armor coast.

I'll start at the very heart of map sheet 27, in the **Monts d'Arrée** and the Parc Régional d'Armorique (D3/E3). To get your first sight and taste of the Argoat do one, or both, of two things: use leg power to make the short ascent of the **Roc Trévezel** (D3); or sit comfortably in your car and drive to the top of the Montagne St-Michel, further south, where you have a brief lung-testing hike to the chapel and observation table. In both cases your reward is a 360-degree panorama.

What do you see? To the east the terrain appears to be a shallow but massive crater, almost treeless and with a man-made reservoir at the centre (let's forget the nuclear power station); the western rim is a spine of rocky vertebrae. To the west, north and far east is refreshing wooded country. Now head east for some of the best, to **Huelgoat** (E3), beyond the crater ringed by a circle of *routes nationales*.

Huelgoat is a delight. The village sits contentedly at the eastern end of a small lake; beyond the granite houses is a most enticing forest. Oak, beech, pine and spruce blanket the hills and hide outcrops of granite and sandstone and a series of streams and springs. This is a walkers' paradise. Several woodland walks start at the eastern end of the lake, where there's a gurgling cascade; all have fanciful names. Further east, off the D769A, other walks entice (use the car parks): one is a safe and level path, alongside a narrow canal, built to connect the lake with old silver-bearing lead mines. Access to the mines can be made by car; use the track further east off the D769A.

Now back to the arc of countryside on the western side of the crater with its high landmark, the communications mast at the D764 and D785 crossroads (E3). As you criss-cross the Argoat, and use as many of the minor lanes as possible, you realise Brittany is a mammoth yellow eiderdown of broom and gorse where, in late spring, the landscape is illuminated by thousands of rhododendron and azalea spotlights. One man-made aspect will also stand out: the region is well endowed with newly-built roads. If only Devon and Cornwall were so lucky.

Brittany is full of reminders of prehistoric times, among them *menhirs*, standing stones, *dolmens*, cairns and passage graves. Of the latter none is more intriguing than Mougau-Bian (D3), near Roc Trévezel: a corridor 14 metres long with a roof of five granite blocks.

The Armorique Regional Nature Park is run as well as any in France.

The enterprise shows in various ways. Let me lead you to a handful of the dozen and more first-class museums and *maisons* managed with so much care. Start at the Maison de la Rivière de l'Eau et de la Pêche at the Moulin de Vergraon, north-west of **Sizun** (D3), between the D764 and the River **Elorn**. The fascinating displays dramatically and graphically tell the story of Brittany's water and the wildlife associated with the region's rivers, streams and lakes. Do ask for the excellent notes, in English, which help you to understand all the exhibits (every day June to September; otherwise p.m. on Sunday and Wednesday).

To the east, on the D764, are the Moulins de Kerouat (D3). The Argoat must have had thousands of working water mills in centuries past. Here, a collection of 15 buildings, in 15 acres, is the epitome of what a good *ecomusée* should be: houses, mills, bread ovens, washing pool, small waterfall and lake combine to illustrate precisely what the life of rural millers must have been like in times past. A new *accueil centre* is being built and will have opened by the summer of 1994.

South through the lanes for a few minutes to the fish farming museum at the foot of the Barrage du Drennec (D3), east of Sizun and upstream on the Elorn: here there's a wide ranging exhibition of aquaculture throughout the world and the chance to observe salmonoids at various stages of their development. Continue south to **St-Rivoal** (D3), to the Maison Cornec, to see how a country family lived in the 18th century. Then climb through pretty wooded terrain to the Domaine de Menez-Meur (F3), a *parc animalier* where a range of different wild and farm animals are kept in open enclosures surrounded by woods.

One must: the quite exceptional Maison des Artisans (F3), alongside the D785 and just south of the Montagne St-Michel, where the brilliantly designed and crafted work of over 100 artisans is displayed; even if you cannot buy do still go (closed Tuesday and Wednesday).

Another facet of Brittany's heritage, religious architecture, is the great number of ornate *enclos paroissiaux* (parish enclosures). Built from the 15th to the 17th centuries, the finest examples consist of a church with granite calvaries containing most intricate sculptures of the Passion and crucifixion, triumphal arch and charnel house (ossuary). Seek out the most glittering: **St-Thégonnec** and Lampaul-Guimiliau (both D2); Guimiliau and Le Martyre (both D3); **Plougonven** (E2), south-east of **Morlaix**; and, further south, **Pleyben** (D4).

Before leaving the Argoat for the northern Armor coast let me highlight some scenic treats on the south edge of map sheet 27. You'll notice the word Noires in F4; turn to sheet 45 to discover the full name of **Montagnes Noires**. In reality these are no more than a long line of rounded hills noted for super woods and numerous viewpoints. The best of the latter are from near Laz (45:E1) and the Roc de Toullaëron (E4). As you drive the steep, narrow lanes take in the tiny Notre-Dame du Crann chapel, enjoy the views across the River **Aulne** towards the Monts d'Arrée, and visit the château and park at the Domaine de Trévarez (E4), south of **Châteauneuf-du-Faou**: there's nothing to see in the dark red brick and granite château, but the park, in late spring, when we had the good fortune to walk through the 200-acre grounds, is a wonderland of rhododendrons and azaleas. There's something to see at all seasons (all day July and August; p.m. April, May, June, September, except Tuesday; p.m. weekends October to March).

Why not approach the northern coastline by an alternative road to the main D785 to Morlaix (E2). Instead use the D769 from Huelgoat: the wooded valley, with so few houses, is a classic example of the dividends which accrue when you have the right large-scale maps to hand.

I'll describe the coastline in two parts: first east of Morlaix, then west. The eastern section has two parts: Corniche Armorique (west of **Lannion**: F1) and Corniche Bretonne (north of Lannion).

The Morlaix-**Ploumanach** (F1) coastline is dotted with what seems like thousands of spick-and-span cottages, most of which are whitewashed; some are exceptionally well designed. Broom and gorse are everywhere. There are many fine sandy beaches; those south of **Locquirec** (F1) are the colour of Cornish cream. The Corniche Bretonne is also known as the Pink Granite Coast where huge rose-red and almost purple-hued rocks have been worn by wind and tide into all sorts of weird shapes.

The terrain around **Trébeurden** (F1) is full of interesting sites: the headland at Ploumanach, a geological and botanical treat; the Ile Milliau, a mini version of the mainland (tel 96 23 68 28); the unspoilt cliffs at Trédrez (F1), west of Lannion; the Aquarium Marin at Trégastel (F1); and the Station Ornithologique and Nature Reserve on the Ile Grande (F1). There's more – a quartet round Pleumeur-Bodou, east of Trébeurden: the protected woodland of Le Bois de Lann Ar Waremm; the brilliantly laid out Musée des Télécommunication; the Planetarium; and Le Village de Meem Le Gaulois, a Gallic village built by youngsters to profit schools in Togo. The last three are grouped together.

Something different: admire the superb work by artist Bernard Louédin at his Atelier Louédin, on the west side of the D65 south of Trébeurden. Visit two man-made sites. North of Morlaix is a remarkable dry-stone cairn, the **Tumulus de Barnenez** (E2), an ancient burial site. South-west of Lannion is the sombre yet elegant Château de **Rosanbo** (F2) with handsome rooms and a small pepperpot tower.

The coast north-west of Morlaix has fewer attractions. The submersible road to Ile Callot (E1) fascinated us, as did the Jardin Exotique at **Roscoff** (D1), off the D58 to the ferry. This is a five-acre rocky outcrop garden, newly-created, covered with exotic plants. Seek out two châteaux: **Kérouzéré** (D1) is a small building, perfectly proportioned and with capped turrets at each corner. **Kerjean** (D2) is at the end of a long tree-lined avenue. This structure, part fortress, part mansion, is certainly not perfectly balanced; but the owners work hard and hold all sorts of exhibitions, events and evening spectacles (every day July and August; for rest of year – tel 98 69 93 69).

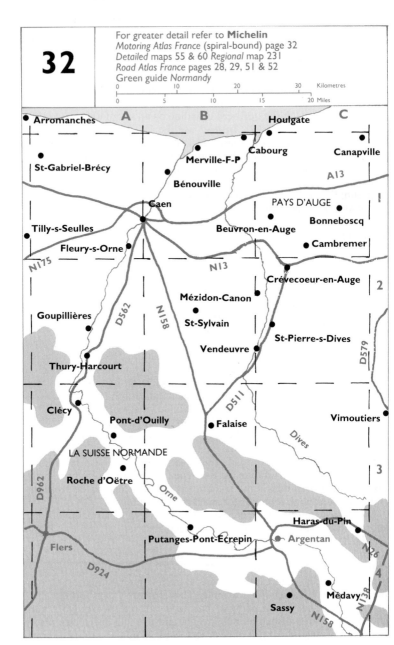

32

For greater detail refer to **Michelin**
Motoring Atlas France (spiral-bound) page 32
Detailed maps 55 & 60 *Regional* map 231
Road Atlas France pages 28, 29, 51 & 52
Green guide *Normandy*

0   10   20   30   Kilometres
0   5   10   15   20 Miles

A   **B**   **C**

Arromanches

Houlgate

Cabourg

Canapville

St-Gabriel-Brécy

Merville-F-P

A13

Bénouville

PAYS D'AUGE

Caen

I

Tilly-s-Seulles

Beuvron-en-Auge

Bonneboscq

Fleury-s-Orne

Cambremer

N175

N13

Crèvecoeur-en-Auge

2

Mézidon-Canon

Goupillières

D562

N158

St-Sylvain

St-Pierre-s-Dives

D579

Vendeuvre

Thury-Harcourt

D511

Clécy

Pont-d'Ouilly

Falaise

Vimoutiers

LA SUISSE NORMANDE

Dives

3

Roche d'Oëtre

Orne

D962

Haras-du-Pin

N26

Putanges-Pont-Écrepin

Argentan

Flers

D924

A

Médavy

N138

Sassy

N158

For me Normandy, Britain's "partner-in-history", is an extension of our island home. The map on the left will take you to a land of wooded hills, easy-going rivers, beech forests and handsome towns and villages, many of which were rebuilt after the devastation of 1944.

I have divided the chapter into three parts. First I'll provide you with some ideas on the best countryside to explore; the landscape, both man-made and natural, is well coiffured with hardly a hair out of place. Then I'll give you details of four producers and suppliers from whom you can buy some of Normandy's renowned "5C" culinary delights: cream, cheese, cider, *calvados* and *charcuterie*. Finally, I'll devote some space to numerous man-made sights and museums, many of which span the vast swathe of history during this turbulent millennium.

I'll start part one in the **Pays d'Auge** (C1/C2), a land of dazzling brown and white timbered cottages. In spring the Pays d'Auge is an enchanting, intoxicating sight. Intoxicating? Literally, as the apple orchards are laden down with blossom, destined to become that fiery amber-hued brandy, *calvados*, or, alternatively, sparkling cider with an almost russet glow. In April the hedgerows are lined with primroses; later, wild flowers replace their sunny faces (that's true of all Normandy). In May fields are awash with wild yellow irises.

Seek out **Beuvron-en-Auge** (C1), east of **Caen**, an unbelievably evocative Normandy village; no wonder the community "protects" the superb half-timbered houses. Then head north-east on the D146; be sure to make the short walk to the *chapelle* at Clermont-en-Auge for the extensive panorama to the west. Continue on to Rumesnil, follow the Dorette upstream to La Roque-Baignard (C1), south-east to La Boissière (C2), west to **Cambremer** and finish on the D101, with views to the south, towards **Crèvecoeur-en-Auge** (C2).

Next, south-west to **La Suisse Normande**, in reality the middle section of the **Orne** Valley, where wooded hills and river aspects please the eye. Start at **Thury Harcourt** (A2). Walk the Boucle du Hom where a loop of the Orne does an almost 360-degree clockwise turn. At St-Rémy, north of **Clécy** (A3), follow the signposted Route des Crêtes to the Pain de Sucre viewpoint – Normandy personified.

A riverside café, south of the bridge between Clécy and Le Vey and on the Orne's left bank, is the ideal spot for a cooler. Just south of a weir, the terrace also proves to be a good "hide" for watching dragon flies skimming the surface, birds going about their hectic business and fishermen working the fall in the river. See the Orne at **Pont-d'Ouilly** (A3), continue south on the D167, cross the river and then climb to the **Roche d'Oëtre**. Here the viewpoint, reached through the heady aroma of a pine wood, overlooks the River Rouvre, hardly visible in high summer, so dense are the forests far below you.

Drive the lanes on both banks to **Putanges-Pont-Ecrepin** (B4), enjoy the river scenes there, and continue south-east, taking in the views north-east of Ménil-Jean. At Ménil-Glaise (B4), most easily reached by the lane 400 yards north-east of the cemetery at Batilly, man and Nature combine to shape the most seductive of river aspects.

North of Thury-Harcourt, and not part of La Suisse Normande, the Orne has a more unassuming face. Start from **Goupillières** (A2), head north on the D171 and D212, use the lane which runs alongside the river south of Pont-du-Coudray and continue north, on both banks, to **Fleury-sur-Orne** (A1). The latter is on a hill; seek out the riverside site of the Ile Enchantée restaurant. Here the Orne is enchanting, a pretty contrast to the wretched urban sprawl surrounding Caen. (At Pont-du-Coudray detour east to the *poterie* at La Ruelle, south of Clinchamps-sur-Orne (A2). The potter, Gérard Quinchez, produces stunning work; he was taught his craft by Owen Watson – *FLE* p197/198.)

Visit the newly-created 750-acre nature reserves in the Orne estuary. These are north of Sallenelles (B1): call at the Maison de la Nature et de l'Estuaire in the village for details of walks, viewpoints and the different birds to be seen. There is nothing wretched about the superb seaside resorts that line the shore to the north-east of Sallenelles: **Cabourg**, **Houlgate**, Villers-sur-Mer, Deauville and Trouville are smart, sophisticated and have marvellous leisure facilities.

Now for part two. First, pay a call on Pierre Huet at "La Brière des Fontaines", on the D101 south-west of Cabremer (C1): here you'll find the highest quality *calvados*, cider and *pommeau* (an amber *apéritif*, a blend of apple juice and *calvados*) in a variety of different-sized bottles. Second, to the Domaine de St-Loup, two km south of Crevècoeur (C2) and to the east of the D16; here you can buy the finest Camembert cheese. Third, to the hard-to-find Ferme Le Boquet, where you can purchase farm-made *Pavé d'Auge* and *Pont-l'Evèque* cheeses (leave them to mature): find Vieux-Pont, north-east of **St-Pierre-sur-Dives** (C2), locate the cross between the village and Boquet, and 400 to 500 yards to the south, on the D154, you'll spot the farm with white gates on the left. Finally, if you want to savour some of the tasty treats made from every part of a pig (other than the squeak), then call at the Baratte *charcuterie* at **St-Sylvain** (B2), south-east of Caen.

Part three and some man-made sights. I've divided the map into two sections, right and left, and listed them from north to south.

Canapville (C1), north-east of Pont-l'Evêque: the picturesque stone and half-timbered Manoir des Evêques (p.m. mid June to Aug, except Tues; rest of year p.m. Fri and weekends). Pont-l'Evêque (33: D1): the motor museum at the Château de Betteville, south of the A13 (tel 31 65 05 02); and the Musée du Calvados et des Métiers Anciens which explains the skills of local craftsmen in past times (open every day).

Bonnebosq (C1), east of Beuvron: a gorgeous 16th/17th century Auge manor house (31 65 11 07). Crèvecoeur-en-Auge (C2): a collection of half-timbered buildings on a small site with art and science exhibitions (July and Aug every day; p.m. April to Sept; p.m. rest of year). **Mézidon-Canon** (C2): an 18th-century mansion and park of woodland, wild flower meadows, water features and walled gardens (July to Sept: p.m. except Tues. April to June: p.m. weekends).

St-Germain-de-Livet (33:D2), south of Lisieux: small château of differently-shaded stone and brick; towers, moat and timbers (p.m. April to September; rest of year tel 31 31 00 03). St-Pierre-dur-Dives (C2): the vast covered market (not a nail or screw in sight) and the Gothic abbey church; and the Musée des Techniques Fromagères in the abbey grounds which explains the process of cheese making (31 20 97 90).

South-east of St-Pierre is **Vendeuvre** (C2): visit the 18th-century château, a sober building; more fun is the museum of miniature furniture (p.m. June to mid September). Lisores, north of **Vimoutiers** (33:D3): Fernand Léger Museum; outdoor and indoor exhibits of his ceramics, mosaics and, especially striking, seven stained glass windows; isolated, attractive site (April to October; not Wednesday).

Crouttes, west of Vimoutiers (C3): St-Michel Priory, a collection of eight buildings, one a tithe barn (p.m. mid June to mid Sept). Vimoutiers: the Musée du Camembert, a reconstruction of a traditional farm *fromagerie* (May to Oct: every day except Monday p.m.). **Haras-du-Pin** (C4): National Stud with handsome buildings and attractive grounds (a.m. and p.m. every day mid April to Sept; p.m. rest of year except Tuesdays; 33 39 92 01). Château de **Médavy**, south-west of Haras (C4): interesting moats (every day mid July to mid Sept). Château de **Sassy** (C4), west of Médavy: formal gardens and terraces (weekends April to Nov; every day July and Aug).

Arromanches (13:F3): the Musée du Débarquement tells the story of the 1944 Mulberry Harbour. Courseulles, to the east: La Musée de la Mer, a super aquarium (31 37 92 58). **St-Gabriel-Brécy** (A1): château, church and exquisite French formal garden (closed Wed). **Merville-Franceville-Plage** (B2): the prodigious fortifications of a German coastal battery. **Bénouville** (B1), north-east of Caen: the Pegasus Bridge Museum (Apl to Oct) and the Café Gondrée, the first building to be liberated in 1944. **Tilly-sur-Seulles** (31:F1): a village taken and re-taken 23 times in June 1944; a museum tells the story of those devastating days. (Don't miss the poignant Jerusalem Cemetery where 48 souls are buried: alongside the D61 at Chouain, north-west of Tilly.)

Caen (A1/B1): abbeys, churches, castle and museums (including the "Memorial", a modern structure alongside the bypass, which explains the history of the period from 1929 to today, how the Second World War came about, the years of occupation and the Battle of Normandy).

Thury-Harcourt (A2): château ruins, burned by the Germans in 1944, and 170 acres of picturesque grounds and gardens (p.m. May to September). Clécy (A3): the Musée Hardy; the work (mainly of La Suisse Normande) and memorabilia of the artist André Hardy (31 69 79 95). **Falaise** (B3), fittingly the final entry and two sites which span 900 years of history: the castle where William the Conqueror was born in 1027; and the Musée Août 1944 which explains the fierce battle for the town.

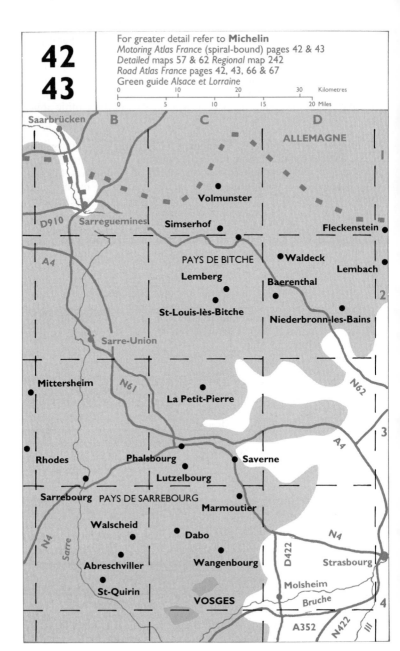

42
43

For greater detail refer to **Michelin**
Motoring Atlas France (spiral-bound) pages 42 & 43
Detailed maps 57 & 62 *Regional* map 242
Road Atlas France pages 42, 43, 66 & 67
Green guide *Alsace et Lorraine*

| 0 | 10 | 20 | 30 | Kilometres |

| 0 | 5 | 10 | 15 | 20 Miles |

Saarbrücken

B   C   D

ALLEMAGNE

I

Volmunster

D910

Sarreguemines   Simserhof   Fleckenstein

A4   PAYS DE BITCHE   Waldeck

Lemberg   Baerenthal   Lembach

2

St-Louis-lès-Bitche   Niederbronn-les-Bains

Sarre-Union

N62

Mittersheim   N61   La Petit-Pierre

A4   3

Rhodes   Phalsbourg   Saverne

Lutzelbourg

Sarrebourg   PAYS DE SARREBOURG

Marmoutier

N4

Walscheid   Dabo   N4

Sarre   D422   Strasbourg

Abreschviller   Wangenbourg   Molsheim

St-Quirin   VOSGES   Bruche   4

A352   N422

32

Most tourists ignore this north-eastern corner of France. I plead guilty too; until my detailed exploration last year my only knowledge of the terrain was the **A4** *autoroute* and the wooded **Vosges** hills to the south. I implore you: don't use the A4 as a bypass; get the maps out.

First, I'll describe the wooded hills and valleys of the Parc Régional des Vosges du Nord, the area between the A4 and the German border. Make your first port of call the town of **Bitche** (C2), at the heart of a boat-shaped area tagged the **Pays de Bitche**. Hereabouts the houses and villages have a typical neat and tidy German look and are painted in pastel shades only rarely seen elsewhere in France.

Looming over the town is a monster of a fort, originally designed by that military architect superman, Vauban. First built in the 1680s, the fort's high, impregnable walls are a masterpiece of military engineering. High-tech aids, in the shape of headsets providing an English commentary, help you to understand the place. See two museums: one in the old chapel where the scale model of the fort, made 200 years ago, is a fascinating exhibit; the second *musée* is in the old bakery and evokes life in the local *pays* in times past. (Throughout the Vosges, here and to the south on map sheet 61, you will see scores of castles and forts, some built centuries ago, others this century.)

Now savour Nature's handiwork. Head south-east to Schweizerlaendel (D2). Explore the lanes around the ruined tower of the Château du **Waldeck**: the landscape is Swiss-like but with many outcrops of red sandstone which look just as impressive as any of man's efforts. Much more impressive ruins, where walls merge with the sandstone rocks, are at the high viewpoint of the Château de Falkenstein (D2); the only snag is the 45-minute hike from the D87A. The most renowned of the ruined castles is the Château de **Fleckenstein** (E1/E2): easily accessible, this once remarkable fortress combined man-made walls and halls with passages and a watch-tower carved out of the sandstone rocks.

The Etang de Hanau, between Waldeck and Falkenstein, is a tranquil, triangular pool, surrounded by trees and with a beach and two small hotels. The valley from **Baerenthal** (D2) to **Lemberg** (C2) is delicious: sandstone walls, some so weathered that see-through holes have appeared; mixed woods; pools; smallholdings, including a deer farm; and a *plage* and nature reserve at the Ramstein *étang* (E2) all appeal.

Several villages south of Bitche are renowned for their glassware. **St-Louis-lès-Bitche** (C2) is especially famous. Hidden in a valley, the ugly little place compensates with the production, since the 16th century, of flamboyant glass creations (shop/exhibition open a.m. and p.m. on weekdays; Sun p.m. only). A little further south, in another valley, is Meisenthal: here there's an exceptional *musée*, La Maison du Verre et du Cristal, which explains all the intricate workings involved in the making of fine crystal (Easter to Oct; p.m. only). Two km away, at Soucht, is La Musée du Sabotier: this museum evokes the skills of the dozens of clogmakers who worked in the village before the last war and explains the old art of clog making (July/Aug; p.m. every day. May/June and Sept/Oct; p.m. weekends only).

What else is there to see in the Pays de Bitche? To the west, at **Simserhof** (C1), high above the D35, is the subterranean artillery fort built in the 30s as part of the Maginot Line (tours 9.00 and 14.00 – mid Mar to mid Dec, except Mon). A little further north, near the church at Schorbach, is an ossuary dating back to Roman times – housed behind a row of 11 arches and columns. Continuing north there's a restored water mill, the Moulin d'Eschviller, north of **Volmunster** (C1), where the power of the River Schwalb is used to grind corn (p.m. every day July/Aug; p.m. weekends Easter to June and Sept). South-east of Meisenthal, mentioned earlier, seek out the *menhir*, four metres high, near the D12 (Pierre des 12 Apôtres – 12 apostles); enjoy, too, as you leave the *pays*, the beech woods on the descent to Wimmenau (C2).

Head south-west to **La Petite-Pierre** (C3), passing through grand beech woods. The "new" town is flower-filled; in the old town, on a rocky spur high above the surrounding valleys, much use is made of sandstone. At the very end of the spur are the ruined walls of an ancient castle; the more modern, high-walled adjacent château houses the HQ of the Regional Park. Other sites in the park merit attention. Especially refreshing is the spa of **Niederbronn-les-Bains** (D2), a mixture of old and new. See, too, the nearby village of Oberbronn where some houses have the "trade" sculptures of their owners carved on the lintels above the doors. Windstein, to the north, has two ruined castles; also admire the *rocher*, a vertical sandstone needle. Finally, spare time for yet another vast underground Maginot Line fort – the Ouvrage du Four à Chaux, just south of **Lembach** (E2): built in the 30s the monumental subterranean town (folly?) was used in anger for just two weeks in 1940 (tours 10.00 to 16.00 every day May to Sept).

Now enjoy yourself in the much higher Vosges mountains to the south of the A4. I'll divide what follows into two: first the country to the east of the north-south crest of peaks; then the terrain to the west.

Start at **Saverne** (C3). As you make the steep descent on the N4 park on the left and then cross the road to the Jardin Botanique where, among the trees, are over 2,000 varied plants. In the town is a small rose garden, the Roseraie, beside the N4 and near the railway, where over 1,000 varieties are planted in soil which is changed every three years. Parts of the old town are eye-catching (especially the richly decorated 17th-century Maison Katz) but I can't say that about the vast slab of a façade, built in neo-classical style, on the Château des Rohans. Much more pleasing are the ruins of the Haut-Barr castle built among three huge sandstone outcrops high above the town; enjoy, too, the tiny chapel with a Romanesque nave. Two other churches worth seeing are at St-Jean, north of Saverne – with three naves, sculptures and Romanesque paintings; and the massive sandstone *église* at **Marmoutier** (C4), south of Saverne, with three lofty Romanesque towers.

In the past we've enjoyed driving the high roads of La Suisse d'Alsace – the wooded slopes and valleys around **Wangenbourg** (C4) and connecting with Niederhaslach, further south. Ruined castles, forests, waterfalls (it's well worth the climb to see the Cascade du Nideck) and churches (don't miss the *église* at Niederhaslach) combine to please.

What of the terrain to the west? The **Pays de Sarrebourg** has many treats in its valleys and hills. First the two main towns. Phalsbourg (C3) was yet another Vauban fortified creation: see the large *place* and the two massive town gates with their helmet-like tops and walls with ornate stone carvings. **Sarrebourg** (B3) has one exceptional treasure: the Chapelle des Cordeliers with a mammoth Marc Chagall stained glass window which almost fills one end of the *église*.

My preference is for out-of-town pleasures. Start at **Lutzelbourg** (C3) with its site alongside the Canal de la Marne au Rhin. Much the most interesting engineering wonder on this vital canal link is the unique 45 metre-high boat and barge lift built in 1969 to replace 17 locks (Plan incliné on the map, south-west of Lutzelbourg). There's a *musée* in a barge; long and short boat trips using the lift; a motorised train tour; or a simple guided tour. (Every day from Mar to Oct.)

Another highly enjoyable "engineering" treat is the Chemin de Fer Forestier d'**Abreschviller** (B4), a five km-long 70 cm-gauge railway up the wooded valley to Grand Soldat. Originally a logging railway, the humble little line is a real delight. Steamers at weekends, otherwise diesels; round trip 80 mins. (Apl to Sept. Timetable: G. Baillet, Hôtel des Cigognes, 57560 Abreschviller; tel 87 03 79 12.)

Don't bypass the St-Léon chapel at **Dabo** (C3), on a high sandstone cone accessed by the corkscrew D45A. Nearby you'll see many signs advertising glass and crystal producers. Of the smaller workshops none come better than the home, literally, of Bruno Lehrer at the D45/D98 junction below Haselbourg (C4). Of the bigger factories the Cristallerie de Vallérystal (B4) has a large showroom and you can also see glass and crystalware being made (a.m. and p.m. every weekday; p.m. Sat/Sun).

More surprises come in the shape of the area's many church organs. Of the six which we saw these two were notable: the large church at **Walscheid** (B4), richly decorated and with a highly colourful mural on the nave ceiling – the organ is a big one too; and **St-Quirin** (B4), where the large *église* has high salt and pepper-pot matching towers, fine stained glass and wood sculptures around the organ.

Anything else? To the west of Sarrebourg is a line of *étangs*, hidden by trees, linked by the Canal des Houillères de la Sarre (from the Marne to the Saarbrucken coalfields) and part of the Lorraine Regional Park. All sorts of watersport facilities are available near **Mittersheim** (A3); on the Etang du Stock, further south; and on the Etang de Gondrexange (A4). Visit, too, the Parc Animalier de Ste-Croix, north of **Rhodes** (A3), where scores of breeds roam freely in 175 acres of woodland and *étangs* (every day Easter to Oct; closed Mon Apl/May/Sept/Oct).

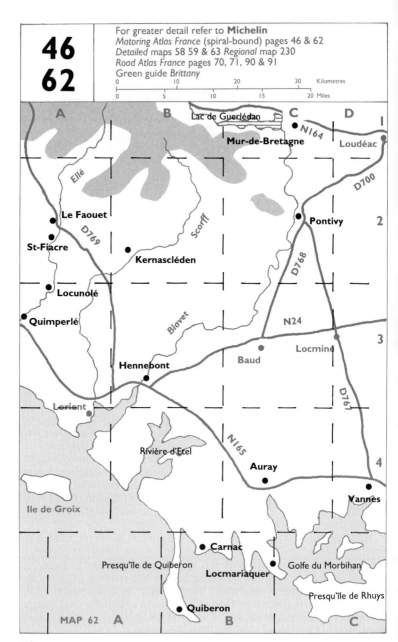

46
62

For greater detail refer to **Michelin**
Motoring Atlas France (spiral-bound) pages 46 & 62
Detailed maps 58 59 & 63 *Regional* map 230
Road Atlas France pages 70, 71, 90 & 91
Green guide *Brittany*

Kilometres
0   10   20   30
0   5   10   15   20 Miles

A   B   Lac de Guerlédan   C   D   I

N164

Mur-de-Bretagne   Loudéac

Ellé   D700

Le Faouet   Pontivy   2

Scorff

St-Fiacre

D769   Kernascléden   D768

Locunolé   N24

Blavet   Locmine   3

Quimperlé   Baud

Hennebont   D767

Lorient

N165

Rivière d'Etel   Auray   4

Vannes

Ile de Groix

Carnac

Presqu'île de Quiberon   Locmariaquer   Golfe du Morbihan

Presqu'île de Rhuys

Quiberon

MAP 62   A   B   C

36

This chapter will add even further weight to the regional board's claim that "Brittany is a land of 1,001 faces."

I shall start with the **Golfe du Morbihan** (62:C2) which, in Breton, means "Little Sea" – an inland lagoon, dotted with scores of islands. The protected gulf has an almost sub-tropical climate; the islands and coastline are ideal for birdwatchers; and the calm waters are perfect for sailing enthusiasts, especially beginners.

Fate treated us kindly last year when we revelled in the captivating beauty of the "Little Sea". On two glorious days in May the sun shone from an azure sky and the landscape sparkled. Our most magical highlight was the day we spent on the Ile aux Moines (62:C2).

The ferry from Port Blanc takes just five minutes to make the crossing to the island. Within 100 yards of the landing stage you have the chance to hire a bike. Do just that. The island is not quite flat, but almost so. What an island: peace and quiet, narrow lanes and alleys, palm trees, camellias, wisteria, fig trees, lilac, old roses (climbers are particularly vigorous) and flowers of every kind. We had laser-sharp views of wooded inlets, whitewashed cottages and myriad small craft moving to and fro on the calm blue waters. There's only a single entry to the gulf and that, in turn, is protected by the headland of the **Presqu'île de Quiberon** (62:B3). Magical is the word.

A second short ferry crossing from Larmor-Baden, just west of the Ile aux Moines, took us to the tiny Ile Gavrinis, famed for an exceptional tumulus (burial mound). The intricate patterns of carved lines on the supports of the cairn are fascinating. We voted Gavrinis the most intriguing of the megaliths we've seen in Brittany; perhaps the reason is the site and the mystical remoteness of the cairn.

Now explore a kite-shaped piece of *pays* with **Quimperlé** (46:A3) at one end and **Kernascléden** (B2) at the other.

Start at the Manoir de Kernault, a *domaine* owned by the Finistère *département*. From Mellac (A3), north of Quimperlé, head west, cross the railway and keep going right. The 15th to 19th century *manoir* is in a 50-acre park: differing exhibitions are laid on (p.m.); there are walks in the grounds; *goûter Breton* tastings are held on Sundays; and horses feature in some of the summer's events (tel 98 71 90 60).

Head east, to an unassuming quartet of churches, just four among thousands of Brittany's rich heritage of religious architecture. First, the tiny church in Tréméven (A4), north of Quimperlé: miniature in every respect, including the spire; and the bells are easily seen. (Just south of the village is Loc-Yvi: 100 metres from the *chapelle* is La Fontaine de Sant Diboan, a regular feature of Brittany's churches.) Next the Renaissance-styled church at Arzano (A3), east of Quimperlé: there's an Italianate look about the octagonal-topped tower with an accurate clock. The église at Guilligomarc'h, north of Arzano, is as tiny as the version at Tréméven: the porch is shaded by a solitary yew tree and note the stone carvings. **Locunolé**, to the west, has both an *église* and *chapelle*, sitting side by side; note the bell towers.

Immediately north of Locunolé are the Roches du Diable. The rocks are high above an especially alluring wooded valley. Use the road to drive to the top of the hill; park and then scramble up, through the oaks, to the rocks. Far below you is the River **Ellé** which, in May, made quite a roar. Other walks in the woods require more time.

Two churches near **Le Faouet** (A2) are more spectacular than the earlier quartet – for different reasons. First, the triple-spired 15th-century chapel at **St-Fiacre**, south of Le Faouet: the lace-like wood carvings of the rood-screen are marvellous. Note the old bread oven on the village green; and, more than welcome, the new modern toilets. (A caveat: the church is only open from 10-12 and 14-18 hours.) The chapel at Ste-Barbe, north of Le Faouet, can be reached in two ways: the energetic can park on the D132, where the road crosses the Ellé, walk *par la fontaine* and then climb the steep cliff; others, like us, can approach by the access road off the D769. The flamboyant chapel is hidden when you park the car; the small structure clings to a ledge at the top of a cliff, 100 m above the wooded Ellé Valley. Note the bell tower: will you be able to resist pulling the rope?

Finish your exploration of the "kite" with a visit to Kernascléden (B2). The 15th-century church is a stunner, for us the best in Brittany. The overall balance of the building, statuary, rose carvings and frescoes are a celebration of medieval man's superb skills. Nature, too, lays on an exuberant show: the D110, heading south from a point just west of the church, passes through an unspoilt wooded valley. For five km the road runs alongside the River **Scorff**; for us a blissful drive.

I'll give you another example of terrain rarely seen by tourists. Start at **Mur-de-Bretagne** (C1). (Bibendum says: "one of the liveliest towns in the interior of Brittany". Is that his idea of a joke?) To the west is the 1,000-acre man-made **Lac de Guerlédan** and, south of the lake, is the Forêt de Quénécan *massif*. Mixed woods, with some beautiful beech trees, views to the east and west, and leisure facilities on both banks of the lake combine to please. We liked the hamlet at Les Forges-des-Salles where, until 100 years ago, iron ore was smelted in several furnaces. We also loved the River **Blavet** vista at Bon Repos to the north. The Gorges de Daoulas (C1) is a wooded valley where the torrent has many stepped falls. Beneath the high barrage at the eastern end of the lake, at St-Aignan, there's a small Musée de l'Electricité which tells the story of the dam's construction.

Head south to **Pontivy** (C2). Here *la vieille ville* appeals, as does the 15th-century fortress with two cone-topped towers. (Why do Michelin call them "pepperpots"?) At Stival, on the D764 to the north, the Chapelle St-Mériadec has fine stained glass windows and 16th-century paintings. St-Tréphine, just west of Pontivy, is an unassuming stone-built hamlet with a *chapelle*, two *manoirs*, houses and old bread ovens. Don't use the D768 to the coast; instead enjoy the Blavet Valley, with villages, churches and river views.

Brittany's **N165** *Voie Express* cuts across the southern half of the map. Like all similar roads, the highway has attracted a ribbon of industrial and commercial sites – none of which has any scenic merit. However, there's much to see within a few minutes drive of the motorway.

Leave the N165 at the **Auray** east exit (62:B2): ignore the town and head instead for St-Goustan, on the opposite bank, a maze of alleys and old houses and once the busiest port in Brittany. The quayside is where Benjamin Franklin landed in 1776 to seek help from France. The traffic in **Vannes** (62:C2) can be hell: persevere and nose out the old town, the Cathedral of St-Pierre and, nearby, the ramparts, gardens, and ancient half-timbered wash-houses alongside a stream. The Aquarium de Vannes, in a huge purpose-built building, is reckoned to be unique in France; the site is on the road to Conleau. The old town in Quimperlé (46:A3), at the confluence of the Isole and Ellé, is a mix of old houses, narrow lanes, unusually-shaped church, brick-patterned covered market and much else besides – including swooping swallows.

The **Rivière d'Etel** (46:B4) is a land-locked bay with many inlets. St-Cado is the best treat: reached by a causeway the cottages and houses on the tiny island are pretty sights. There are also nature reserves, megaliths galore, churches and fountains. Typical of the last two are the 16th-century chapel at Locador, south of **Hennebont** (B4), hidden behind houses; further south, at St-Efflam, is *la fontaine*.

Beyond the Etel is an amazing world of megaliths: thousands of *menhirs* (standing stones) in serried ranks; *dolmens* (burial places of standing stones and stone caps); *allées couvertes* (covered stone passageways) and, here and there, a tumulus (an earth covered cairn, or burial monument, where stones form underground passageways). Visit the Prehistoric Museum in **Carnac** (62:B2) and also the new ArcheOscope (on the D196): the latter, in a semi-subterranean building, makes use of screens, film, slides, lasers, mirrors and lighting to lay on a dramatic spectacle to explain the theories behind the megaliths.

We were taken with the Dolmen de Crucuno, north-west of Carnac: nine pillars support a capstone of 40 tonnes (two other broken stones give no help). Also impressive was the massive St-Michel Tumulus, east of Carnac; here a guide leads you through a maze of tunnels buried beneath a site 390 ft long, 189 ft wide and 37 ft high. The Table des Marchands, a *dolmen* at **Locmariaquer** (62:B2), also captured our interest.

What remains to be seen? All I have space to tell you about is the **Quiberon** peninsular (62:B3). We saw the Côte Sauvage (D186) on a wild, wet and windy day; ferocious Atlantic breakers crashed against the rocks, throwing spray across the road. Another *presqu'île* is south of the Golfe du Morbihan, the **Presqu'île de Rhuys** (62:C3): don't miss Port Navalo; the point north of Arzon; the ruined Château de Suscinio with moat and towers, a Welsh castle look-alike; and the views, both east and west, from the Pointe de Penvins (62:C3).

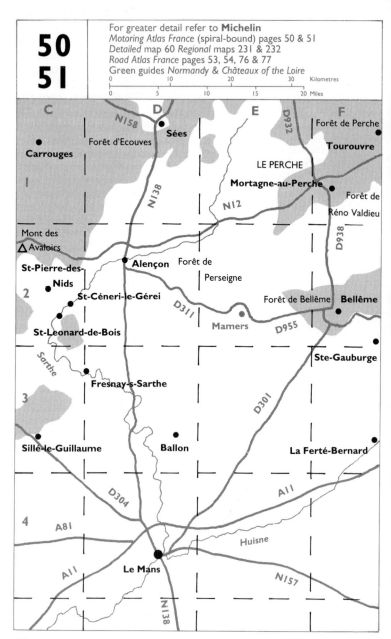

50
51

For greater detail refer to **Michelin**
Motoring Atlas France (spiral-bound) pages 50 & 51
Detailed map 60 *Regional maps* 231 & 232
Road Atlas France pages 53, 54, 76 & 77
Green guides *Normandy* & *Châteaux of the Loire*

Kilometres
0   10   20   30
0   5   10   15   20 Miles

C   D   E   F

N158   Forêt de Perche

Sées

Forêt d'Ecouves   D932   Tourouvre

Carrouges   LE PERCHE

N138   Mortagne-au-Perche   Forêt de
Réno Valdieu

N12   D938

Mont des
△ Avaloirs

Alençon   Forêt de
Perseigne

St-Pierre-des-
Nids   2   Forêt de Bellême   Bellême

St-Céneri-le-Gérei   D311

Mamers   D955

St-Léonard-de-Bois

Sarthe   Ste-Gauburge

Fresnay-s-Sarthe   D301

3

Sillé-le-Guillaume   Ballon   La Ferté-Bernard

D304

4   A81   Huisne

A11   N157

Le Mans   N138

40

This is the fourth chapter devoted to Normandy (as Michelin define the region) though, to be absolutely correct, the bottom half of the map on the left is part of the *département* of Sarthe in the Pays de la Loire region. Whatever the name, most tourists rush through the area.

I'll divide the chapter into four: first, the top right-hand quarter, the mysteriously-tagged **Le Perche**; second, the arc of forests and man-made attractions to the north and east of **Alençon** (D2); third, the endearing hills to the south-west of Alençon; and, last, the exhilarating man-made thrills in and around **Le Mans** (D4).

Le Perche was the name of an ancient province founded in 1114, only to be dissolved in 1790 when French *départements* were first formed. Half of Le Perche is on map sheet 51; the rest is on 52. Le Perche is a land of rolling hills, massive forests and fortified manor houses.

Start at **Mortagne-au-Perche** (F1). High on a hill the town is proud to be called the "Black Pudding World Capital". Equally odd-ball, and a Mortagne curiosity, are 27 sun dials; only half a dozen are easily spotted. Explore the town's medieval heart, clustered around the 16th-century Eglise Notre-Dame; the gardens with fine views on the western edge; the Maison des Comtes du Perche, the site of the Musée Alain which has the memorabilia of the French philosopher born in Mortagne; and the bulky Porte St-Denis with two floors above the fortified gate (the home of the Musée Percheron). Both the latter are near the *église*. Market day, a showpiece affair, is on Saturday morning.

In the 17th century Le Perche was the cradle of emigration to Canada. There's even a museum devoted to the historical importance of those first French settlers at **Tourouvre** (F1), north-east of Mortagne (every day June to Sept, except Monday). The village church has two stained glass windows devoted to the first Quebec settlers. Another fascinating museum, which we thoroughly enjoyed, is at **Ste-Gauburge** (F2), south-east of Bellême (p.m. May to October): based in two buildings, one custom built, the other a church, the *musée* explains the old crafts and skills of Le Perche inhabitants.

Among the stone-built manor houses three remain vivid memories: the Manoir de Courboyer (F2), like a vision of Scotland and to the east of **Bellême**; the high-pitched roofs and cone-topped towers of the Manoir de la Vove (F2), north-east of Bellême; and the handsome small Manoir de l'Angenardière (F2), sandwiched between two strong towers (near the Ste-Gauburge museum). The Château des Feugerets (F2), alongside the D7 south of Bellême, is more a castle with towers and moat.

Broadleaved forests play a part in the appeal of Le Perche. The **Forêt de Réno Valdieu** has some l00-ft-high oaks with names Aberdeen, Oxford and Forestry Commission; they're marked as *vieux arbres*, east of Mortagne (F1). The **Forêt du Perche** (F1), north-east of Mortagne, is a classic example of how important regeneration is in the management of ancient hardwood forests: here several *étangs* (pools) and the Abbaye de la Trappe, a working monastery, are bonuses. The **Forêt de Bellême**, north of the town, is a cool haven; we recall the extensive views from the pretty village of La Perrière, at the western end of the forest (use the cemetery path at the church).

A last detour will require some navigational effort. I'm sending you to the Ferme du Perrier, the isolated home of Liliane and Gérard Gosselin, lost on the edge of the Forêt de Réno Valdieu, and surrounded by gorgeous rhododendrons. Here you can buy *foies gras* (both duck and goose), *confits*, *magrets* and *rillettes*. Or, better still, you can tuck into appetite-quenching, home-cooked fare in the shape of traditional farm meals (120, 135 and 235 francs in 1993). For the latter you must book ahead, two days in advance (tel 33 83 86 80). How do you find the farm? Leave La Chapelle-Montligeon (F1/F2), south-east of Mortagne, to the south (on the east side of the basilica); at the D213 T junction turn left and, in a few hundred yards, left again to Courthenou and beyond, following signs for the Ferme du Perrier.

The second of the four segments is an arc on the east and northern sides of Alençon (D2). The town is, to say the least, a busy place. We had a hectic Thursday morning there on a hot summer's day: first walking the extensive open-air market which takes over much of the town centre; we enjoyed the Eglise Notre-Dame, a flamboyant Gothic extravaganza; and, more than anything else, we were hooked on the Musée des Beaux-Arts et de la Dentelle. Alençon is famed for lace-making; the museum houses fascinating displays of superb lace (open every day except Monday). We were glad to escape the heat and head east to the refrigerator coolness of the **Forêt de Perseigne**, an undulating forest with fine trees, viewpoints and the mysterious Vallée d'Enfer.

More recently we have explored the **Forêt d'Ecouves** (D1), to the north of Alençon. This is a giant-sized forest of mixed trees with extensive numbers of beech. Ecouves is another excellent example of how well the French manage their forests. La Croix de Médavy is a spot where a small tank is the monument to the French who died between the 10 and 23 August 1944; a display board and map explains the battle for Alençon in August of that year. The Rochers du Vignage is an outcrop of granite hidden among the trees to the west of the D26; here the road lies alongside a tiny stream and is an ideal picnic spot. Further west, La Croix Madame rewards all those who make the short walk from the crossroads with an exhilarating southern panorama.

Several man-made treats are to the north of Alençon. The Château de **Carrouges** (C1) is a favourite (north-west of Alençon): the stone and brick structure has many eye-pleasing patterns and hues, a moat and a lived-in feel – yet still manages to give the impression of being a strong fortress. Just north of the château, on the D16, is the Maison du Parc (of the Parc Régional Normandie-Maine), housed in an old farm with the unusual living exhibit of over 100 different apple and pear trees in an adjoining orchard (weekdays only). **Sées** (D1) is the site of a massive twin-spired Gothic cathedral; the stained glass windows are a special joy. Château d'O (D1), north-west of Sées, is an exuberant ornate mix of Gothic and Renaissance with stunning stonework and moat.

The third segment is my favourite on map sheets 50/51. Start at the viewpoint on the **Mont des Avaloirs** (C2), west of Alençon. Some years ago the tower providing the 360-degree panorama was overtaken by events: the surrounding trees outgrew the platform. By the time this book goes to press a modern structure will have been built; the top of the new tower will be above the tree tops. Explore **St-Pierre-des-Nids** (C2): at the heart of the village is a cracking fruit and veg shop; an almost as good *boulangerie/pâtisserie*; and the lively, English-speaking Jean Etienne, the chef/patron at the Hôtel Dauphin.

Now south, to the Alpes Mancelles. Alps they most certainly are not; deserted they most assuredly are. **St-Ceneri-le-Gérei** (C2) is a gem of unspoilt charm, bustling with character; a combination of centuries-old houses, Romanesque church high above the Sarthe, bridge across the river and weir humming away upstream. **St-Léonard-de-Bois**, to the south, is less appealing but you'll grasp why the hills have the label "Alpes"; the wooded cliff above the river has a Swiss look.

Finally, the last segment – Le Mans and the terrain around the city, all of which was once inextricably linked with the Plantagenets. When I first visited **La Ferté-Bernard** (F3) I didn't realise this "Little Venice of the West" was built on marshes; most buildings are on piles. The Notre-Dame-des-Marais (well-named) is a flamboyant Gothic masterpiece. At **Ballon** (D3) the Jardins du Donjon (see map) are a medieval rarity (p.m. mid July to Aug, except Wed). **Fresnay-sur-Sarthe** (C3/D3) has an attractive setting above a Sarthe meander; walk the narrow streets with old houses. **Sillé-le-Guillaume** (C3) has a castle, forest and *étang* used for numerous watersports

I plead guilty, along with many others, to having always associated the name Le Mans with the 24-hour sports car race. Not now. Le Vieux Mans is breathtaking. First spare time for St-Julian's Cathedral with an inspiring interior, especially the "crown of light" windows above the chancel. Then step into the old streets to the south-west for the surprise of your life: 1,700-year-old Roman stone and brick mosaics, murals and patterns abound; and, in addition, there are medieval half-timbered houses, cobbled alleyways and stone towers. To the east of Le Mans is the Abbaye de l'Epau, founded in 1229 by Queen Berengaria, widow of Richard the Lionheart. Altogether more restful, the abbey and 32-acre park, alongside the River **Huisne**, is a relaxing spot.

I'll finish by reminding you of the 24-hour circuit south of Le Mans (D4 and 67:D1). There's always something going on at the shorter Bugatti Circuit. The Musée Automobile de la Sarthe, inside the circuit, is the main draw: owned by the *département* the museum, and over 100 cars, tell the story of the automobile and the events which make the words Le Mans synonymous with motor racing (every day June to September; closed Tuesday October to May and in January weekends only).

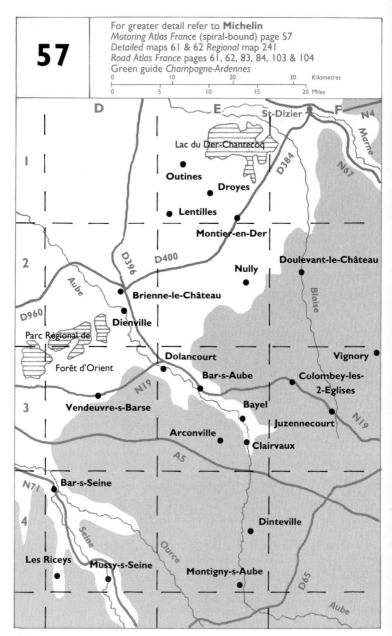

57

For greater detail refer to **Michelin**
Motoring Atlas France (spiral-bound) page 57
Detailed maps 61 & 62 *Regional* map 241
Road Atlas France pages 61, 62, 83, 84, 103 & 104
Green guide *Champagne-Ardennes*

| 0 | 10 | 20 | 30 | Kilometres |

| 0 | 5 | 10 | 15 | 20 Miles |

D **E** St-Dizier **F** N4

Marne

Lac du Der-Chantecoq D384 N67

1

Outines

Droyes

Lentilles

Montier-en-Der

2 D396 D400

Nully **Doulevant-le-Château**

Brienne-le-Château Blaise

Aube

D960

Dienville

Parc Régional de

Forêt d'Orient

Dolancourt **Vignory**

Bar-s-Aube **Colombey-les-2-Eglises**

N19

3

Bayel

Vendeuvre-s-Barse **Juzennecourt** N19

Arconville

Clairvaux

A5

N71

Bar-s-Seine

4

Dinteville

Seine

 Source

Les Riceys

Mussy-s-Seine **Montigny-s-Aube** D65

Aube

44

The roadside sign, with a drawing of two rabbits, was simple enough: "*Ralentir. Passage de lapins.*" I can think of nothing which emphasises so amusingly – and emphatically – my claim that the terrain on map sheet 57 is as good an example as any of *la France profonde*.

I have divided the map into five. I'll start in the bottom right-hand quarter – the *pays* to the east of **Bar-sur-Aube** (E3) and the **Aube** Valley (E3/E4). Then I'll deal with the bottom left-hand quarter which includes a bottle-shaped mass of Champagne country – from **Les Riceys** (D4) to Bar-sur-Aube. In parts three and four I'll describe two lakeland areas (man-made *lacs* built, during the last 30 years, to control the flow of the **Seine**, Aube and **Marne**): the terrain in the Parc **Régional de Forêt d'Orient** (D2/D3); and the **Lac du Der-Chantecoq** (E1). I'll finish with some ecclesiastical surprises.

Start part one in the Aube Valley. **Montigny-sur-Aube** (E4) has a half-moated Renaissance château with a diamond-shaped chapel/tower alongside the moat. At the rear there's a black-hatted tower which pre-dates what remains of the present 16th-century structure. Another 16th-century château, refurbished in the 18th/19th centuries, is at **Dinteville** (E3): the kitchen, tower and park are worth seeing.

North now to **Clairvaux** (E3). In map sheet chapters 72 and 73 I refer to St-Bernard and his immense influence in the 12th century. In 1098 the Cistercian order was founded at Cîteaux (88:B2) – a breakaway group which felt that the Bénédictine order, based at Cluny (102:B2), had moved too far from the principles of poverty, prayer, simplicity and self-sufficiency. Bernard entered Cîteaux in 1112; three years later he founded Clairvaux. His influence and charisma was such that when he preached he drew thousands of listeners. Both Fontenay (73:D2) and Pontigny (72:B1) were among Clairvaux's first daughters.

There's little to see now of what was, once, the linchpin of the Cistercian order. Most of the site is a prison but every Sat p.m., from May to Oct, you can visit what remains of the great abbey.

Nearby **Bayel** (E3) is renowned for its crystal. You can see the stages involved in making the glassware at the Cristalleries Royales de Champagne; there's a shop with displays of dazzling modern work – from goblets and glasses to decanters and vases. Another shop, just off the D396, also has fine displays of work created by smaller producers (*artisans cristalliers*). (Both are open every day; p.m. only Sun.)

Colombey-les-deux-Eglises (F3) is synonymous with Charles de Gaulle. High on a hill and dominating the horizon is the huge granite Cross of Lorraine, a memorial to the general who maintained a home in the village for nearly 40 years. You can visit the house, La Boisserie, every day except Tues. De Gaulle's grave is in the village cemetery. Further east, at **Vignory** (58:A2), approached by a delectable wooded descent, is the pre-Romanesque and Romanesque Eglise St-Etienne; the interior is magnificent with beams, arches, pillars and sculptures.

Now drive the quiet lanes in the **Blaise** Valley, from **Juzennecourt**

(F3) to **Doulevant-le-Château** (F2). Relish the pastoral landscape and, whenever possible, cross the village bridges to see the best of the river. There's a covered market at Cirey-sur-Blaise (F2) and the château is famed for its links with Voltaire who lived there from 1734 to 1749 (p.m. mid June to mid Sept; also a.m. Aug).

Start part two at **Mussy-sur-Seine** (D4). As you approach Les Riceys (D4) on the D17 the map indicates nothing but woodland; but, in reality, trees share the extensive hilly vistas with thousands of vines. Les Riceys, part of the Aube Champagne area, is renowned for its *rosé* sparklers (*Rosé des Riceys*), non-sparkling wines (*Coteaux Champenois*) and fruity-tasting cow's milk cheese.

The Aube Champagne-producing area extends north-east to Bar-sur-Aube and beyond. I can particularly recommend the wares of Bernard Gaucher at **Arconville** (E3) – he also makes a Pinot Noir *rouge*.

There are four man-made sites worthy of note in the bottom left-hand quarter of map sheet 57. North of Les Riceys and Ricey-Bas is the Musée des Vieux Tacots – 70 models and makes of car from 1902 to 1960 (p.m. Sun or tel Christian Fournier at 25 29 31 53). Seek out the medieval half-timbered *maisons* in **Bar-sur-Seine** (D4); there's a particularly fine 16th-century house west of the church, in the road parallel to the N71. **Vendeuvre-sur-Barse** (D3) has a dour-looking château – well-known for its *son et lumière spectacle historique* (Fri and Sat July/Aug: details 25 41 44 76). Finally, there's Nigoland, beside the N19 at **Dolancourt** (E3): a mini-miniature Euro Disney which provides children with hours of fun and, unlike its Val de Marne counterpart, has survived happily for years (Easter to Sept).

Part three and the Parc Régional de Forêt d'Orient (D2/D3). Call first at the Maison du Parc, north-west of Vendeuvre-sur-Barse, and collect leaflets describing the nature park's amenities. The Lac d'Orient (Lac Seine) and the forest to the east are the main attractions. Several leaflets map out, in detail, marked walks in the woods and alongside both the lake and the newly-built Lac du Temple. Others explain the sights in the nearby villages; there are watersport facilities; flora and fauna; a *plage* and much else besides. One interesting site is the newly-created *ecomusée*, an old mill beside the River Aube and the D11B south-west of **Brienne-le-Château** (D2).

Two man-made sites worth a detour are: the Musée Napoléon in the old Ecole Militaire at Brienne (the great man studied there); and **Dienville** (D2), south of Brienne, where the 16th-century *église* and covered stonebuilt market will appeal. There's also a new marina and watersport facilities at the nearby Port Dienville on Lac Amance.

Part four and the Lac du Der-Chantecoq (E1), a 12,000-acre man-made lake with 50 miles of shoreline. Call first at the Maison du Lac, just east of Giffaumont-Champaubert, on the south shore. Facilities around the lake include motor-boat rides, sailing, a motorised train and beaches (note the following caveat). Seasonal variations in the water level expose huge tracts of mudflats – especially in the autumn and winter. No wonder the lake is a magnet for over 100 species of migrating and resident birds: waders, geese, ducks and others in the autumn; followed by swans, cranes and others in winter; and terns, grebe and herons in spring. Don't miss the *musée-village* at Ste-Marie-du-Lac on the north shore where there's a series of half-timbered buildings – a school, church, barns, café, *pigeonnier* and others (Mar to Nov). The newly-built Maison de l'Oiseau et du Poisson evokes the lake's bird and fish life in a graphic way (Port de Chantecoq).

Finally, part five and the ecclesiastical surprises. The arc of terrain to the west and south of the Lac du Der-Chantecoq is called Der, part of "wet" Champagne – a Normandy-like *bocage* of fields, oak woods, marshy ground and villages with half-timbered buildings and white-washed walls of clay and earth. Last year we visited 12 villages and their 16th-century half-timbered *églises*. I'll describe, briefly, the four we reckoned to be the best of the dozen.

Start at Châtillon-sur-Broué (E1), south of the lake. The 17th-century structure is stunning; inside, photographs show the before and after condition, following recent rebuilding. **Outines**, further west, is the largest of the half-timbered churches: an ornate altar and rose and other fine windows catch the eye – as do some cottages opposite the entrance. South to Bailly-le-Franc, with its lance steeple and simple, down-to-earth interior. Now south-west, to **Lentilles**: a richly-endowed oak interior, a steeple with wooden scales and 16th-century stained glass windows are the highlights.

(All four, and eight others at Drosnay, Arrembécourt, Chassericourt, Joncreuil, Chavagnes, Villeret, Puellemontier and Droyes are floodlit at weekends and every evening from May to September.)

I've not finished with the ecclesiastical surprises. You can also enjoy some glorious stained glass windows (of the Troyes School) – most of them created as "explosions of colour" in the early 16th century. **Droyes** and Puellemontier (E1) are half-timbered *églises* with brilliant windows. Ceffonds, just south of **Montier-en-Der** (E1), has a 16th-century church with Romanesque tower and outstanding stained glass. **Nully** (E2), further south, has a 15th/16th-century *église* with a warm, proud, lived-in interior; the paintings, roof and several windows are a joyful sight. Nearby Trémilly also has remarkable windows.

The last ecclesiastical wonder is neither half-timbered nor are its Max Ingrand windows especially enthralling. But on no account miss the *église* at Montier-en-Der (E1). Terribly damaged in 1940, the church was rebuilt in primitive style and there are still traces of the past: the vast Romanesque nave is a grand sight but the most thrilling pleasure is the Gothic choir with an arc of multi-level "cloisters", each with numerous arches. See, too, the adjoining National Stud, housed in what was a former monastery. (Every Thurs at 15.00, from Sept to mid Nov, a colourful horse show is laid on in both the yard and town.)

47

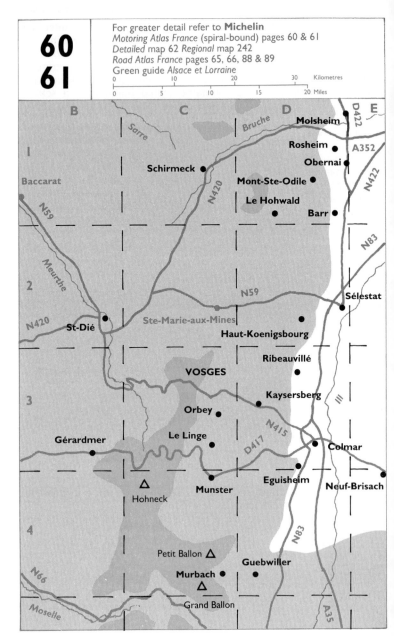

For greater detail refer to **Michelin**
Motoring Atlas France (spiral-bound) pages 60 & 61
Detailed map 62 *Regional* map 242
Road Atlas France pages 65, 66, 88 & 89
Green guide *Alsace et Lorraine*

Kilometres

0   10   20   30

0   5   10   15   20 Miles

B   C   D   E

Molsheim

Rosheim •   A352

Schirmeck •   Obernai •

Baccarat   Mont-Ste-Odile •

Le Hohwald •

Barr •

N420

Meurthe

N59

Ste-Marie-aux-Mines

St-Dié •

Haut-Koenigsbourg

Ribeauvillé •

VOSGES

Kaysersberg •

Orbey •

Gérardmer •

Le Linge •

Colmar

Munster •

Eguisheim •

Hohneck

Neuf-Brisach

Petit Ballon △   Guebwiller •

Murbach •

Grand Ballon

Moselle

N66

Sélestat

N83

N422

D422

N415

D417

Sarre

Bruche

48

There's a surfeit of riches within the terrain to the left – all part of Alsace. This is a *pays* where you can enjoy yourself in each of the four seasons. There's an abundance of man-made creations and Nature's handiwork: scores of *villages fleuris*; a dark curtain of mountains, the wooded **Vosges**; beneath them, to the east, the flat Rhine plain and Ried (marshland); and, as bonuses, some of France's most drinkable wines and a larder full of appetite-busting regional dishes.

I shall find the job of fitting everything into 138 lines of text impossible. To make more sense of my task I've split the map into three parts: imagine a line drawn from **Sélestat** (D2) to **St-Dié** (B2); and another from **Colmar** (D3) following the **D417** west to **Gérardmer** (B3). I'll start in the southernmost section.

Before we head west to the high Vosges *ballons* let's see what the Ried has to offer. **Neuf-Brisach** (E4): what a pity we can't all be eagles and admire the town from one-mile high. The perfect octagonal outline, with its complex exterior star-defence system, was one of Vauban's most masterful creations; within the octagon is a grid of criss-crossing streets and, at the very centre, a large *place*. To the north-east there's something different: the Chemin du Fer du Rhin. Take a steam train north to Baltzenheim, enjoy a boat trip on the Rhine, and then return by the same puffer (weekends from Whit Sun to 2nd Sun in Sept: details Office de Tourisme, 68000 Colmar; tel 89 20 68 92).

Another significant attraction on the Rhine plain is the Ecomusée d'Alsace at Ungersheim (D4), east of **Guebwiller**. Here, scores of houses in a village layout take you back in time and explain the old traditions and skills of the region (open every day, except Jan/Feb).

Colmar is a seductive charmer. Many of the old town's streets have been pedestrianised: relish the multi-hued, half-timbered, 16th-century houses (the Maison Pfister is said to be the world's most beautiful); the area nicknamed La Petite Venise; and the Musée d'Unterlinden with its majestic Issenheim reredos. Nearby **Eguisheim** is another smasher: walk the narrow streets, circle after circle of them, their half-timbered houses groaning with flower-laden displays.

Seek out two churches in this southern segment: the Romanesque St-Léger *église* in Guebwiller (D4) with triple naves and a magnificent western façade under two towers; and the superb Romanesque half church at **Murbach** (C4) where only the twin towers, transept and choir remain – a vision of both austerity and elegance at the same time. Michelin rate the Guebwiller Valley very highly: why? The houses have less of the wine-village glitz, which is no bad thing; the beech woods are fine, especially on the D430 run to Westhalten (D4); and the climb to Le Markstein (C4), past the minute Lac de la Lauch, is exhilarating.

At Le Markstein you join the Route des Crêtes, a spectacular mountain-top run, which snakes north from Cernay (77:E1) to the Col du Bonhomme (C3). Detour south to the highest of the Vosges peaks, the **Grand Ballon** (1424 m), with a *table d'orientation* and a monument

49

to the Chasseurs Alpins (mountain troops); the views are memorable.

Another way of accessing the Route des Crêtes is by driving up the **Munster** Valley (C4). Locals claim this the best in the Vosges. Munster cheese is certainly top-notch; so are the lanes which wind up to the **Petit Ballon** summit (1267 m); and arguably the handful of small lakes to the north of the valley, bordered by woods, are tranquil, soothing sights – especially the Fischboedlé and Schiessrothried *lacs* west of Muhlbach (C4). Whatever route you take aim for **Hohneck** (C4: 1362 m), the best of all the mountain summits; minimal effort is required for you to absorb the far-reaching views.

West of Hohneck is some of our favourite Vosges terrain. In the spring we've thrilled at the sight of wild daffodils in the pastures high above Gérardmer (B3); in June we've admired the carpets of wild flowers at altitude; we've driven the forest roads (RF) between Xonrupt-Longemer (B3) and Gérardmer with their hidden views; in high summer we've cooled ourselves by the unspoilt lakes of Longemer and Retournemer (C3), east of Gérardmer, and the larger, much busier Lac de Gérardmer; we've picked bilberries and blackberries in August and September; and, in late autumn, we've adored the varied hues of dying leaves on broadleaved trees. One must: don't bypass the Jardin Botanique de la Schlucht, north of Hohneck – an Alpine flora wonderland in early summer.

Now for the middle segment. Complete the rest of the Route des Crêtes run north. Then drive the lanes, through dense woods, to four lakes: Blanc, Noir, Forlet and Vert (C3: north to south). Admire the stunning views south from Hohrodberg (C3) and then give time to nearby **Le Linge** – a football pitch-sized hilltop where, in 1915, 17,000 Chasseurs Alpins (note the nearby cemetery on the map) and German soldiers lost their lives in futile fighting. The opposing trenches, often just yards apart, have been left as they were, rusty barbed wire and all. A small museum tells the story of the massacre: some of the finds unearthed from the site are chilling; others are both morbid and poignant human effects. To the east, Les Trois Epis (D3) is a cool haven of peace – high above the Rhine plain and a world away from Le Linge.

Of the Vosges valleys my vote goes to the Vallée de la Weiss – from above **Orbey** (C3) and east to the plain. Enjoy Orbey, Lapoutroie and the four-star *village fleuri* of **Kaysersberg** (D3). There's much to see. But for the four weekends prior to Christmas the place both buzzes and sparkles. The buzz comes from the Christmas market stalls where hand-made, quality products are on sale. The sparkle comes free every evening during the four weeks. Every window, balcony and tower is garlanded with traditional festive decorations and lights.

Give your attention now to man-made attractions. To a trio of villages to the south: Ammerschwihr, Niedermorschwihr and Turckheim (all C3) – each one associated with wine and the latter two with picturesque ancient treasures. Head north to Riquewihr (D3) – an unbelievably delectable village where the medieval heart is weighed down with richly decorated 15th/17th-century stone and half-timbered houses. Nearby **Ribeauvillé** is also a treasure chest of old houses with ornate façades, complemented by flowers seemingly everywhere.

A trio of differing pleasures. The Parc des Cigognes, on the D1 east of Ribeauvillé, is a stork-breeding reserve (a.m. and p.m every day Apl to Oct). To the south-east, west of the **N83**, is the Parc Naturel de Schoppenwihr – an English garden (a.m. and p.m. every day July/Aug). On the D416 western exit from Ribeauvillé is the Beauvillé textile factory. Save your francs before you call: the range of products and designs is fabulous – from teacloths to tablecloths, from curtains to clothes, from scarves to serviettes. You'll not leave empty-handed.

Finish the middle section at Sélestat (D2) with its medieval heart, old houses, Romanesque and Gothic churches, and the unique Humanist Library (detour north-east, too, to the extravagantly decorated Baroque Eglise d'Ebersmunster); and the perched, perfect conception of a castle at **Haut-Koenigsbourg** – restored in 1900 by Kaiser Bill.

Finally, the northernmost section. Last year we spent some time in the hills around the Donon peak (C1) and in the Bruche Valley, south and north-east of **Schirmeck** (C1). Fine, as they go; but I suggest you leave that terrain until you've explored everything to the east.

Start in **Le Hohwald**, the wooded peaks and valleys circling the village of the same name (D1). To get a flavour of the delectable *pays*, drive a clockwise loop from the village, via the Champ du Feu (D1/D2); views of woods and pastures – all quintessential Vosges. Then aim north-east for **Mont-Ste-Odile** (D1): the site, on yet another sandstone table, has for thousands of years been both fortress and place of pilgrimage. The large present-day convent was rebuilt 300 years ago. Admire the views, see the various chapels (especially the mosaic roof of the Chapelle des Larmes), and wonder most at the 10 km-long Mur Païen (Pagan Wall) that loops around the hill on which the convent is perched.

Which way now? To the south there's **Barr** (D1), guarded by two perched ruined castles, and renowned for its Musée Folio Marco; enjoy the house, the various designs of furniture and exhibits evoking local life.

To the north of Mont-Ste-Odile are three further attractions. First, the ancient heart of **Obernai** (D1) where you'll find the famed Place du Marché, narrow lanes radiating off, half-timbered and stone houses, high belfry, richly-decorated town hall and the elegant 16th-century stone Puits (well) aux Six-Seaux. Then north to **Rosheim**, where the pride and joy is the Romanesque church of Sts-Pierre-et-Paul – which, for balance and supreme clarity of construction, is unbeaten in Alsace. Finally, head for **Molsheim** (D1) and the town centre: admire the stylish Renaissance Le Metzig building and, a few strides away, visit the Musée de la Chartreuse/Fondation Bugatti – the latter with exhibits, including cars, which evoke the story of the town where the classic vehicles were made earlier this century (a.m. and p.m. weekdays; p.m. weekends; mid June to mid Sept; closed Tues).

51

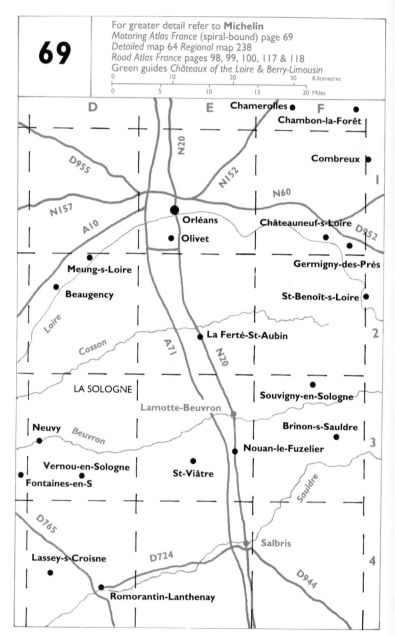

For greater detail refer to **Michelin**
Motoring Atlas France (spiral-bound) page 69
Detailed map 64 Regional map 238
Road Atlas France pages 98, 99, 100, 117 & 118
Green guides *Châteaux of the Loire & Berry-Limousin*

| 0 | | 10 | | 20 | | 30 | Kilometres |

| 0 | 5 | | 10 | | 15 | 20 Miles |

D   E   **Chamerolles**

Chambon-la-Forêt

D955   N20   **Combreux**

N152

N157   N60   I

A10   **Orléans**   **Châteauneuf-s-Loire**   D952

Olivet

Meung-s-Loire   **Germigny-des-Prés**

Beaugency   **St-Benoît-s-Loire**

Loire   2

Cosson   A71   **La Ferté-St-Aubin**

N20

LA SOLOGNE   **Souvigny-en-Sologne**

Lamotte-Beuvron

Neuvy   Beuvron   **Brinon-s-Sauldre**

Vernou-en-Sologne   **Nouan-le-Fuzelier**   3

Fontaines-en-S   **St-Viâtre**

Sauldre

D765

Salbris

Lassey-s-Croisne   D724   D944   4

Romorantin-Lanthenay

In selecting the 44 map sheet chapters for *Mapaholics' France* I made a deliberate decision to turn my back on a handful of France's most celebrated tourist areas. Instead I have concentrated on those parts of France bypassed by the majority of tourists.

One of the "honeypot" areas I have ignored lies to the south-west of map sheet 69, the central section of the **Loire** Valley. There you will find superb examples of man's architectural and artistic skills. In selecting map sheet 69 I have turned instead to my favourite part of the Loire: **La Sologne** – a land of silver birches, oaks, beech, chestnuts and pine, *étangs* (pools), streams, sandy soil, heather and broom. The area is a wildlife paradise, renowned for fish, wildfowl, game, asparagus, fungi, strawberries, *pâtés* and *tarte Tatin*.

Map sheet 69 is literally a sea of green. I've driven through the extensive forests in early spring, when the first Chartreuse tints refresh the clear air; a month or two later wild flowers tease the senses; and in the misty months of October and November I've seen the armies of trees aglow with their autumn-tinted cloaks.

Let me try to persuade you to seek out the lanes which criss-cross La Sologne. I'll start with a trio of short drives, each one of which will give you a taste of the terrain I described above. First, locate **St-Viâtre** (E3), to the west of the **A71**. Seek out the Maison des Etangs, a small half-timbered house on the south side of the village; here there's an *écomusée* which explains the hows and whys of the Sologne *étangs* and the area's flora and fauna (every day mid June to mid October; weekends rest of the year). If time allows see the church and its main treasure: *le polyptique*, four 16th-century paintings on wood panels. Then follow this route, stopping as often as you can to make short detours, on foot, to absorb the restful terrain.

Drive south from St-Viâtre, on the D49, to Marcilly-en-Gault. Leave Marcilly to the north-west, on the D121. Within one km or so turn right at Le Carroin and head north on the V6. The woodland and *étang* landscape is superb. At the cross-roads detour east to a romantic visual delight, the Château Favelle (E3), a classically balanced small building of red brick and stone. Finish the diamond-shaped run by driving north to La Ferté-Beauharnais and then back to St-Viâtre. Walks are ten a penny. But if you are keen to join accompanied *balades nature* (starting from a trio of nearby villages) then contact Sologne Nature Environnement, 1 av. de Toulouse, 41600 **Nouan-le-Fuzelier** (tel 54 88 79 74).

A second typical Sologne drive. Start at **Fontaines-en-Sologne** (68:C3 and 69:D3). Have a look at the half-timbered houses, west and south of the church, and the *église* itself, a part 12th/part 17th-century fortified structure (key from Madame Porcher whose house is 50 yards south of the *boulangerie* on the east side of the D119 just before the bend). Detour briefly on the D120 towards Courmemin, to the Ferme de Jaugeny; here you can buy *fumé d'agneau* and *plats cuisinés conservés*. From Fontaines head towards Bauzy (D3), being sure to take the loop that is marked in green shortly after La Ravinière. The loop winds past *étangs*, through mixed woods and alongside fields of asparagus and strawberries. Irises and wildlife abound and there's many a picnic spot. Finally, just north-west of Bauzy, have a look at the château at Veillenne, an eye-pleasing structure built with the small red bricks which suit the unassuming Sologne so perfectly.

South-east now for drive three. But first stop at **Vernou-en-Sologne** (D3), typical of many communities which make the most of an *étang*; witness the pool at the village's northern entrance. On the south-east side of the *commune* is La Borde where the vista is perhaps the finest in La Sologne. Man and Nature combine to create perfection: relish the water, trees, elegant château and inquisitive swallows.

Start drive three from the **Romorantin-Lanthenay** (D4) bypass. Head west on the D59. Soon the Etang de Batarde appears on your right. Note the sluice gate alongside the road; this enables the large pool to be emptied and cleaned periodically, an essential requirement for all *étangs*. The Etang de Paris is covered with water lilies in summer, unless the sluice gate has been used to empty the pool; in the year following the "cleaning-up" blooms do not appear.

At **Lassay-sur-Croisne** (D4) admire the *église* with a slender spire. Get the key from Monsieur Martin at his house beside the phone kiosk; once inside enjoy the rose window and the 16th-century fresco. Continue on to one of the subjects in the fresco: the Château du Moulin. Access is by a woodland lane (mind the sleeping policemen). The site of the red brick and stone château, with cone-hatted towers and moat, is idyllic (open every day March to mid Nov: 54 83 83 51). Finish at La Straize, north-west of the château; here the Musée de la Straize (follow signs for Locature de la Straize), north of Gy-en-Sologne (D4), is a tiny, old cottage which illustrates the way of life of a 16th-century Solognote farm (weekends and public holidays only).

What of other man-made attractions in La Sologne? Romorantin-Lanthenay (D4) is the capital. Stand on the bridge across the River Sauldre; admire the happy mix of Nature and man's handiwork; walk the narrow streets upstream on the right bank past old Solognote houses (the tiny Musée d'Archeologie is a treat); and visit both the Musée de Sologne and the Musée Municipal de la Course Automobile. To the east of the town, at Villeherviers (D4), is the newly-opened Aliotis – a high-tech series of varying-sized aquariums (closed Sun & Mon from Sept to Apl).

Don't miss **Souvigny-en-Sologne** or **Brinon-sur-Sauldre** (both F3). Souvigny is a pretty village: admire the old stone and half-timbered houses, village green, trees and *église* with an original feature called a *caquetoire*, a timbered porch on the south and west sides. Brinon's church, too, has its own *caquetoire*. Visit the 17th-century château, alongside the **Cosson**, at **La Ferté-St-Aubin**. The splendid moat (the river is one side of the water defences) and a *parc animalier* share the honours with the château.

Before I round off my all-too-brief words on La Sologne let me remind you that the area was a *maquis* (Resistance) stronghold during the last war. One book is a must: the wonderfully poignant *Jacqueline: Pioneer Heroine of the Resistance* by Stella King (for the Arms and Armour Press hardback try a library if shops are sold out; hopefully Transworld will soon be publishing a paperback version). The book tells the story of Yvonne Rudellat, known as Jacqueline, the first British woman SOE agent sent into German-occupied France – to the secretive Sologne.

Read the book and then, on the ground, relate geography to history. Stella captures the spirit and bravery of the people and the very essence of the landscape. Visit the Château de Nanteuil (now an hotel and in *FLE*) at Huisseau-sur-Cosson (68:C3). Visit **Neuvy** (69:D3) and read about the "incident" there (seek out the isolated church and the Resistance monument and graves in the cemetery). Moune Gardnor-Beard, part of the "Jacqueline" story, was Owen Watson's wife (the talented potter's life is detailed in *FLE*). Recently Owen gave me a warning to pass on to readers tempted to swim in an *étang*: beware leeches, as both he and Moune once found to their painful cost.

Continuing the theme of off-the-beaten track France I'll identify some of the pleasures in the Forêt d'Orléans, north-east of Orléans (E1). First, head for the Château-Promenade des Parfums at **Chamerolles**, beside the D109 (54:A4). The small 16th-century stone and brick-patterned structure, and the gardens at the rear, have been extensively restored by the owners, the Loiret Regional Council. The moated Renaissance building and formal gardens (restored to their original layout) are a delight; the château houses a museum which explains the use of perfume through the ages. **Chambon-la-Forêt**, to the east, is a two-star *village fleuri*; the area near the church is pretty. Nibelle, to the south, claims three stars for its summer flower show.

The Etang de la Vallée (69:F1) has all sorts of leisure facilities. The best picnic spots are to the east, alongside the Canal d'Orléans. On no account miss **Combreux** (70:A1) and the fairytale château to the north; constructed of small red bricks, and with super stone work and black cone-topped towers, the building dazzles.

What else? Don't miss the small church at **Germigny-des-Prés** (F1); the tiny mosaic roof is a jewel. Don't bypass the Romanesque abbey at **St-Benoît-sur-Loire** (F2) and its breathtaking belfry porch. Make two essential detours: to the Parc Floral at **Orléans** La Source (E1) where, from April to October, there's always a colourful show of flowers; and to **Olivet**, to the west, where you should walk the wooded right bank of the Loiret (or take the *bateau mouche*, *La Sologne*, from the mooring behind the Rest. Madagascar).

I've no space to tell you about the châteaux, *églises* and museums at **Beaugency**, **Meung-sur-Loire** (both D2) and **Châteauneuf-sur-Loire** (F1); and the cathedral and museums at Orléans. Shed no tears if you bypass them; I know where I would head for first.

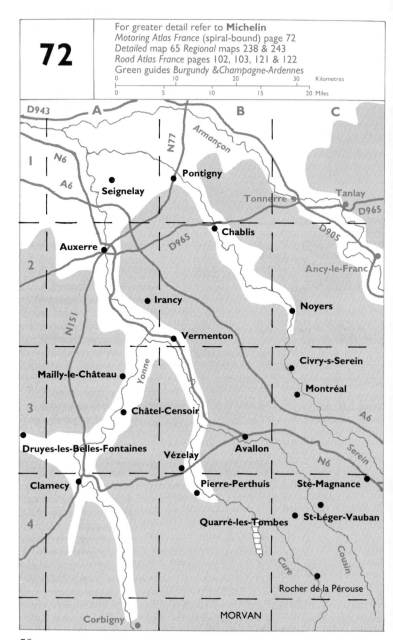

72

For greater detail refer to **Michelin**
Motoring Atlas France (spiral-bound) page 72
Detailed map 65 *Regional* maps 238 & 243
Road Atlas France pages 102, 103, 121 & 122
Green guides *Burgundy &Champagne-Ardennes*

| 0 | 10 | 20 | 30 | Kilometres |

| 0 | 5 | 10 | 15 | 20 Miles |

D943

A

B

C

1

N6

A6

N77

Armançon

● Pontigny

● **Seignelay**

Tonnerre

Tanlay

D965

Auxerre ●

● **Chablis**

D965

D905

2

N151

Ancy-le-Franc

● **Irancy**

● **Noyers**

● **Vermenton**

Mailly-le-Château ●

Yonne

● **Civry-s-Serein**

● **Montréal**

3

● **Châtel-Censoir**

A6

Serein

●
Druyes-les-Belles-Fontaines

● **Vézelay**

Avallon ●

N6

Clamecy ●

● **Pierre-Perthuis**

Ste-Magnance

●

4

Quarré-les-Tombes

● **St-Léger-Vauban**

Cure

Cousin

● Rocher de la Pérouse

Corbigny ●

MORVAN

56

MICHELIN MAP PAGE 72

Don't make the same mistake which Anne and I made for so many years. In our rush across France, first on the **N6** and, later on the **A6**, we were quite oblivious to the myriad Burgundian pleasures on each side of the busy highways which slice across map sheets 72 and 73. Yes, we visited the great historical sites: **Auxerre** (A2), **Vézelay** and **Avallon** (both B3) and to the south-east, Dijon (74:B4) and Beaune (88:A2). But we ignored all the lesser-known attractions. For much of this chapter, and the next, I'll concentrate primarily on the latter.

On the bottom of map sheet 72 you can trace, with some difficulty, the northern border of the Parc Naturel Régional du Morvan (the green dotted line). In the chapter for map sheets 86/87 I describe the **Morvan** and the best of the park's countryside. Here, I'll finish off the job by looking at what remains of the park on map sheet 72.

Let's assume you follow my advice in 86/87 and make the climb to the top of the **Rocher de la Pérouse** (C4) with its quintessential Morvan panorama. Here wooded hills surround you and, far below your feet, you may catch sight of canoeists taking on the challenge of the white water in the River **Cure**. The hills rise slowly but surely to their highest point, 901 m, some 25 miles further south.

From the rocks follow this route to get a real taste of just what makes the Morvan special. Continue up the one-way forest road to the D10, turn right and head for St-Agnan (C4); but, just before Les Amans, aim north for Trinquelin. Driving in these lanes is akin to time travel with your *Tardis* – taking you back to rural, rustic Burgundy as she used to be. At Les Brizards you'll pass an *auberge* on your left where you can tuck into hearty, anything but prissy, Morvan fare. At **St-Léger-Vauban** (C4) keep turning right and then south, through conifer and beech woods, and under a memorable beech tunnel, to the Bénédictine Abbaye de la Pierre-qui-Vire – founded just over 100 years ago at the site of a granite *dolmen* (a legend claims that the "stone that turns" can be moved by one hand). There's an exhibition on monastic life but what makes the trip worthwhile is the chance to buy the small, organically-produced, herb-flavoured cows' milk cheese made by the monks.

Which way now? Head north through the lanes to **Ste-Magnance** (C4) and its Gothic church with flamboyant vaulting on the apse and the Romanesque tomb of Ste-Magnance. Or re-trace your steps to St-Léger. The elevated village was the birthplace of the military architect, Vauban (a genius I've referred to often in this book). There's a Maison Vauban, in the handsome *mairie* beside the church, which tells his life story – and note the statue on the D55 (the *musée* is open a.m. and p.m. June to Sept; weekends only May and Oct). **Quarré-les-Tombes** (C4), also on an elevated site, has an unusual "attraction"; outside the church walls are 100 or so 7th/8th-century limestone sarcophagi.

Continue west and then north along the western banks of the lake formed by the Barrage du Crescent (B4) to Chastellux-sur-Cure (B4). I reckon the château, on its perched site, is one of the most handsome in

Burgundy. Now north and then west on the D20 with its first eye-catching vista of Vézelay's hill-top basilica. Dive down the D353 to the wooded valley and the old bridge over the Cure at **Pierre-Perthuis**; wind through St-Père with its proud Gothic *église*; and then climb to the majestic ecclesiastical marvel high above you, at Vézelay.

For Anne and me the Romanesque Basilica of Ste-Madeleine is one of the most inspiring places in France – for 900 years a pilgrimage site second to none. Whether you admire the tympanum sculpture of the main doorway, or the glorious rounded arches and capitals of the interior, or the views from the tree-shaded terrace, you'll most certainly be filled with an overpowering sense of history past. This is where, in 1146, St-Bernard, the Abbot of Clairvaux (57:E3), preached the second Crusade; and where the arch-enemies, Richard the Lionheart and Philippe-Auguste, undertook jointly the Third Crusade in 1190.

Vézelay marks the top-most edge of the regional park. I'll describe what remains on map 72 in three parts: the rest of the Cure Valley (B2/B3) – upstream stretches have already been mentioned – and its tributary, the **Cousin** (B3); the **Yonne** Valley (A1 to A4); and the **Serein** Valley (C3 to A1). I shall refer to the short stretch of the **Armançon** (B1/C2) in the next chapter where I can make more sense of the many sights along its entire length.

The Cousin packs a scenic punch below the town of Avallon (B3). Explore the latter, on a granite table, first: the Romanesque church of St-Lazare with its exuberant carvings on the two main doorways; the extensive ramparts; and the views over the Cousin from the south gate. Descend and follow the Cousin downstream through a small wooded valley, which is as pretty as a picture. Spare time for the Romanesque *église* at Pontaubert (B3) and the mammoth 16th-century fresco in the church at nearby Vault-de-Lugny. Continue on to the Cure.

Further downstream on the latter, head for the Grottes d'Arcy (B3) – 500 metres of underground caves carved out millions of years ago by the river. They are full of stalagmites and stalactites and, at the end of the caves, the floor surface looks as if a tiny part of the moon's surface has been brought back to earth (open every day Mar to Nov). A hop-step-and-jump to the north is the 16th-century Manoir du Chastenay; tucked away the manor house may well be, but do take a peek and admire the exterior Renaissance features. Two Romanesque churches are also worth a look: Sacy (B2), to the north-east, has a striking octagonal tower; and **Vermenton** (B2) has a fine stone spire and western doorway, though the statues on the latter are in poor condition.

Now to the west and the Yonne. Study the map and you'll soon grasp that for much of the valley's length the Canal du Nivernais keeps the river company (in times past the Yonne was used to float timber downstream from the Morvan). The canal is much loved by holidaymakers who hire craft at Auxerre (A2) and then chug south to **Clamecy** (A4) and beyond. Explore Clamecy: the church with its flamboyant-style west front and tower; and the old houses in the nearby streets. **Châtel-Censoir** (A3) has a church with a 12th-century triple apse (note the capitals); further downstream, Ste-Pallaye (A2), too, has a Romanesque *eglise*. But please don't bypass **Mailly-le-Château** (A3). See the fortified church at the heart of the village; the neighbouring 400-year-old lime tree; and then drink in the tonic of a view from the terrace around the corner – below you the tree-lined arms of the Yonne, the canal, wooded hills and the lower half of Mailly.

At Bailly (A2) explore the vast underground caves, once quarried to provide stone for buildings and now used to store millions of bottles of wine. Above the caves are St-Bris-le-Vineux and **Irancy** (both A2), renowned for their largely-ignored wines: whites from the former; reds and *rosés* from the latter. Admire the views too.

Before heading for Auxerre I'll tell you about two spots just west of the Yonne. We fell in love last year with **Druyes-les-Belles-Fontaines** (71:F3). The source of the short-lived River Druyes is some springs at the foot of a low cliff, the latter ringed by a small park. There's also a tiny lake and a buzzing weir – all-in-all a soothing scene. High above the village are the ruins of a once formidable 12th-century castle (p.m. every day July/Aug).

Auxerre is an always busy town – but be patient, endure the traffic, park under the shady trees alongside the Yonne and then make the short walk to its two most famed treasures: the massive and impressive Gothic cathedral (the crypt is Romanesque); and, just to the north, the pre-Romanesque crypt at the Abbey Church of St-Germain.

Finally, the serene Serein Valley. Start at **Montréal** (C3). Turn off the D957 and pass under three combined arches into a medieval village with stone houses, paved lanes and views over the Serein; don't miss the church with its 26 elaborately carved oak stalls. Note the fortified farm beside the D11; and make the detour to hidden **Civry-sur-Serein** – humble but proud and with a smashing church porch.

Noyers (C2) is a must. I know of few places which deserve a *cité médiévale* label so much. *Maisons* of stone and timber; *portes*, arches and tiny *places*; walk the maze of alleys which pass under both houses and gates. Walk, too, the promenade to the east, between the Serein and the ancient ramparts and towers. **Chablis** (B2), shining with good wealth, has become a cult wine word; enjoy the new park beside the Serein and the excellent Sat a.m. market. The *église* at Ligny-le-Châtel (B1) is a mixture of styles: Romanesque nave, transept and tower; and huge Renaissance choir (smile, too, at the exterior gargoyles).

Continue to the Cistercian abbey at **Pontigny** (B1), built during the transition period between Romanesque and Gothic. The nave is vast, enhanced by numerous tall windows; and admire the huge *chevet*, plus flying buttresses, from the lane to the south. Finish at **Seignelay** (A1) on a Saturday morning – when you can enjoy both the *marché* and the 17th-century covered market hall with its timbered roof.

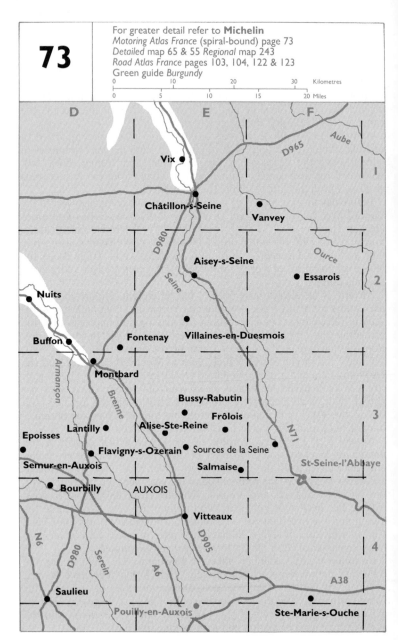

For greater detail refer to **Michelin**
Motoring Atlas France (spiral-bound) page 73
Detailed map 65 & 55 *Regional* map 243
Road Atlas France pages 103, 104, 122 & 123
Green guide *Burgundy*

0	10	20	30	Kilometres
0	5	10	15	20 Miles

D

E

F

Aube

D965

Vix

Châtillon-s-Seine

Vanvey

D980

Aisey-s-Seine

Ource

Seine

Essarois

2

Nuits

Fontenay

Villaines-en-Duesmois

Buffon

Armançon

Montbard

Brenne

Bussy-Rabutin

Frôlois

Epoisses

Lantilly

Alise-Ste-Reine

3

N71

Flavigny-s-Ozerain

Sources de la Seine

St-Seine-l'Abbaye

Semur-en-Auxois

Salmaise

Bourbilly

AUXOIS

Vitteaux

N6

D980

Serein

A6

D905

4

A38

Saulieu

Pouilly-en-Auxois

Ste-Marie-s-Ouche

A quick glance at map sheets 72 and 73 will confirm that much of the landscape is tree covered. On 73 I would guess that 90 per cent of the terrain is wood-washed on the northern half of the map; when you drive the lanes on the ground you'll not argue with that statistic. The second principal geographical feature is a series of river valleys: the **Seine** rises on the eastern edge (F3); on the western side the **Armançon** threads a path north; and, between them, many minor streams and rivers wind their way north-west to join the Armançon. I've divided what follows into the three parts described in the previous sentence.

I'll start with the last of the three parts – the rivers and hills of **Auxois**. Study the map and trace these rivers: the Lavau (F3) and Vau (E3); Oze (E3/F4); Ozerain (E3/E4) and **Brenne** (E3/E4). To the east is the Langres plateau. But between the four valleys are lines of hills where big-dipper lanes rise and dive between the rivers. There are many scenic treats: some famous, others quite unknown.

Begin your Auxois exploration of map sheet 73 (the southernmost part is on the northern edge of map 87) at **Ste-Marie-sur-Ouche** (F4); here a Roman bridge will capture your attention. At nearby Pont-de-Pany you can watch holidaymakers work a lock on the Canal de Bourgogne.

North-west to **Vitteaux** (E4): at the heart of the town look out for some old half-timbered houses and a 13th-century covered market. Drive east, on the D26, to Villy-en-Auxois (E4): here a simple *maquis* memorial honours 11 dead and explains how, when and where they came to die. **Salmaise** (E3) sits high above the Oze: note the wash-house with fountain, the long and narrow restored covered market, the tree-lined *place* and the château's high walls; all-in-all a pleasing spot. Detour, briefly, towards Blessey and the Swiss-like Lavau Valley.

Frôlois (E3) has two halves: La Montagne and Le Vallon. The restored 18th-century château has a commanding site above the valley (p.m. July/Aug). After heavy rain nose out an amazing surprise. From Darcey (E3) follow signs for La Douix and, 300 metres after the cemetery, the Grotte Douix; a short, steep descent, through the trees, leads you to a roaring rush of water from a cave – a Jura-like resurgent stream (*douix* is the local name for this type of spring).

Flavigny-sur-Ozerain (E3) next, high above the river. The medieval fortified town is an architectural marvel. See the machicolated 15th-century Porte du Bourg, the evocative Rue de l'Eglise, the old stone houses and the pre-Romanesque remains at the ancient Abbey of St-Pierre where, incidentally, the village's famed aniseed sweets are made. On to **Alise-Ste-Reine** (E3) where Julius Caesar finally defeated the Gauls, led by Vercingétorix, in 52BC. The Battle of Alésia, where his legions were outnumbered by five to one, was Caesar's greatest and most audacious victory. On Mont Auxois visit the excavations of the Gallo-Roman town of Alésia and, in the village, the *musée* housing the finds. Also high above the village is a giant statue of Vercingétorix, looking north; there's also a covered *table d'orientation* nearby. Finish with a loop to the north, to **Bussy-Rabutin**, where you have to work hard to catch a glimpse of the handsome, moated and superbly balanced 16th/17th-century château with four round, black-coned towers. Drive up the lane, as far as you can, to the south. (Apl to Sept: every day. Oct to Mar: every day but not Tues/Wed.)

Detour west to **Lantilly** (D3) where the 18th-century château, with 100 windows, has a commanding hill-top site (every day July to mid Oct; not Tues). Immediately west of the village, on the D103, is a memorial to *maquisards* who were killed on the spot on 25 May 1944. The monument's words pull no punches: *"Ici les barbares Hitleriens ont martyrisé et massacré 23 jeunes maquisards du groupe Henri Bourgogne."*

Montbard (D3), to the north, has little to offer – other than the cleverly-designed Buffon Park. **Fontenay** (D2), to the east, offers a treasure chest of riches. In an idyllic wooded setting, the restored Cistercian abbey was founded in 1118 by two of St-Bernard's uncles. Fontenay was the second daughter of St-Bernard's Clairvaux (57:E3) and there is no finer place in Burgundy for you to grasp just why the region, the mother of all the arts, and the Cistercians – led by the saint who was thought then to be Christianity's spiritual leader – had such a vital and important influence throughout Europe. Detour, too, upstream, to a delectable scene of woods and meanders.

Part two and the Armançon Valley. Approach the valley from the south, via **Saulieu** (D4) and the **Serein** Valley (see map sheet 72). At Saulieu the renowned attraction is the Romanesque Basilica of St-Andoche, famed for its carved capitals covering a wide spectrum of subjects. Continue north and ensure you seek out the isolated château at **Bourbilly** (D4), south-east of **Epoisses** (C3/D3). The restored structure, originally built in the 14th century, with seductive, sleek towers at each corner, almost rivals Bussy for eye-appeal: set in the wooded Serein Valley the detour is well worthwhile (every day July/Aug; closed Mon). Epoisses is renowned for both its cheese and château, a mixture of buildings flanked by 12th-century towers.

Now to **Semur-en-Auxois** (D3), as eye-catching and impregnable as ever. The Armançon loops in a circle below the town's massive 14th-century round towers and walls. Both the latter, together with the river, narrow alleys, lovely views and the much-altered 13th-century Eglise Notre-Dame make Semur hard to resist. Admire, too, the views from the riverside lanes below the town walls and from the Pont Joly.

North to the Forges de Buffon (**Buffon**: D2) where the Taylor-Whiteheads have done such sterling work in restoring the once model factory (with furnace, forge and roller-mills), built in 1768, and powered by the Armançon (July/Aug: p.m. every day; a.m. Wed/Thurs/Fri. June and Sept: p.m. every day except Tues). Detour to Cry (D2) where the river, canal and wooded hillside combine well. **Nuits** has a 16th-century château, a small building hidden behind a curtain of trees (every day).

To the north-west are two world-famous Renaissance châteaux. Ancy-le-Franc (72:C2) is a priceless 16th-century treasure; the austere, square-cut exterior is outshone by the rich elegance of the interior's 25 apartments (every day Apl to Oct). Tanlay (72: C1) is a sumptuous, 16th-century moated structure – though the white stone is looking a bit dirty these days (every day Apl to mid Nov but not Tues). Finish at Tonnerre (72:C1). You'll not fail to see the large, striking-looking Eglise St-Pierre; visit the church and the immense 12th-century Hôtel-Dieu (or Ancien Hôpital) but what pleases me, just as much, is the Fosse Dionne where a spring feeds a basin of deep blue-green colouring, ringed by a picturesque 18th-century wash-house.

Part three and the Seine Valley. Start at the **Sources de la Seine** (F3). Approach from the north-west, through a beech tunnel, to a wooded park and its several springs (the Goddess Sequana reclines gracefully in a grotto over the largest source). A board explains the importance of the springs in ancient times. Head north: first, along the D103C from St-Germain-Source-Seine to Chanceaux; then to Jours-lès-Baigneux (E2/E3) with a small Renaissance manor house and a pepper-pot tower tagged La Tour Joyeuse; and then, north-west, to **Villaines-en-Duesmois** (E2), where all that remains of a medieval castle are four ruined towers (p.m. every day except Tues).

The **N71** from St-Marc-sur-Seine (E2) is a pretty run; nearing Brémuret-Vaurois look right through the trees for the multi-towered château across the river. **Aisey-sur-Seine** (E2), from the N71, presents a beguiling scene of river, pastures, woods and village. Now a must. Drive east along the Brevon Valley (E2/F2): a winding and unspoilt river, pools, cascades, woods, villages and, at Rochefort, a handsome château in a classic setting – all combine to refresh the senses.

At **Essarois** (F2) take the lane which heads north-west from the church. Just above the village stop and walk 20 metres to a monument to five *maquisards "massacrés par les Barbares"* on 11 June 1944. Soon you pass the 12th-century abbey at Val-des-Choues, in an isolated woodland site (open all year). Stop at the Etangs des Marots (F1/F2). The pools and woods make an ideal picnic site: we were amused by the ducks and water fowl but we were not so lucky as an Oxford reader who saw two beavers swim past. On to **Châtillon-sur-Seine** (E1), either through the forest or via the *lavoir* at **Vanvey** (F1).

At Châtillon seek out first the Musée Archéologique (in the Maison Philandrier). This houses many Gallo-Roman finds made in the locality. The most stunning is the Vix treasure – a collection of jewellery, goblets and a massive ornately-decorated bronze vase dating from the 5th century BC and excavated on Mont Lassois at **Vix** (E1) in 1953. Then proceed 400 metres to the north-east, to a remarkable resurgent spring, the source of the 100-metre-long Douix, surely France's shortest river. The small stepped cascade, pool and park is a visual tonic. Finish at the Romanesque St-Vorles *église*, with its Lombardian arcades, perched high on a terrace between the *musée* and source.

63

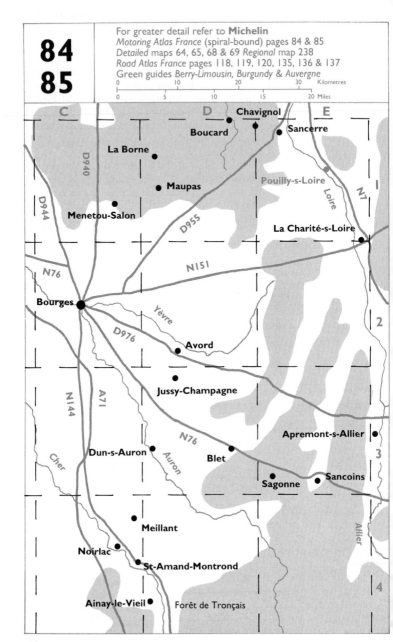

84 85

For greater detail refer to **Michelin**
Motoring Atlas France (spiral-bound) pages 84 & 85
Detailed maps 64, 65, 68 & 69 *Regional* map 238
Road Atlas France pages 118, 119, 120, 135, 136 & 137
Green guides *Berry-Limousin, Burgundy & Auvergne*

0   10   20   30   Kilometres
0   5   10   15   20 Miles

C   D   Chavignol   E

Boucard   ● Sancerre

La Borne ●

D940   Pouilly-s-Loire   N7   1

Maupas ●   Loire

Menetou-Salon ●   La Charité-s-Loire ●

D944   D955

N151

N76

Bourges ●   Yèvre   2

D976   Avord ●

Jussy-Champagne ●

N144   A71   Apremont-s-Allier ●

N76   3

Dun-s-Auron ●   Auron   Blet ●   Sancoins

Cher   Sagonne ●   ●

Meillant ●   Allier

Noirlac ●

St-Amand-Montrond ●   4

Ainay-le-Vieil ●   Forêt de Tronçais

64

Please do not make the mistake I did for three decades and ignore the numerous sights which pepper map sheets 84 and 85. Nature takes second place here – in the geographical centre of France; man-made structures, scores of them, win almost all the honours. With one or two exceptions the landscape is flat and dull. Almost all the *pays* covered by the map to the left is in the *département* of Cher, itself part of the Berry region. The country to the east of the River **Loire** is in Burgundy and the bottom edge of map 85 is known as Bourbonnais.

I'll start the chapter by taking Nature's side and describing three inviting corners where she makes a truly commendable contribution. I'll follow that with two tours: one highlighting man-made ecclesiastical treasures; the second identifying a string of sumptuous châteaux. I'll finish in medieval **Bourges** (C2), the capital of Berry.

The **Forêt de Tronçais** (D4/E4 and 99:D1/E1), on the northern edges of Bourbonnais and one of France's finest forests, is a rich tapestry of proud and handsome oaks. Careful regeneration and management since the last war, and continuing thinning out in the decades to come, will ensure that in future centuries some majestic specimens will be growing in the forest. Walks abound and, in the autumn, locals have a whale of a time picking *cèpes*, *girolles* and other fungi. Make great use of the excellent notice boards which you'll find at numerous points throughout the forest; Tronçais (D4) is just one example.

Seek out three *étangs*: walk the promenade circling the Etang de St-Bonnet (D4); the same goes for the Etang de Saloup (99:E1); and walk the Futaie Colbert on the north-east corner of the Etang de Morat, the pool north of Tronçais. Many individual oaks, or groups of trees, are marked on the map: nose out those north of St-Bonnet-Tronçais (D4) and the ones near the D978A, east of the D953 (D4).

Nature's second significant contribution is at **Apremont-sur-Allier** (F3) – where she gets more than a little help from man. Apremont is unbelievably picturesque with an unspoilt riverside setting where a wide grass walkway is shaded by willows. Beside the grass bank there's a line of brown-shuttered, ivy-covered stone houses, each one different from the others. Nothing is too precious and the overall scene is easy on the eye. Throughout the village there's a profusion of flowers, particularly lapis lazuli. Sitting peacefully above the houses is an elegant château, owned by the same family since 1722. Below the château walls is the 10-acre Parc Floral d'Apremont: lakes, a Chinese-style bridge, an arboretum, the famed long pergola walk, and the "white garden", inspired by Vita Sackville-West's Sissinghurst, combine magnificently (open every day, except Tues a.m., Easter to mid Sept).

Nature's third contribution is north of the D955 from Bourges to **Sancerre** (E1). What a refreshing change the hilly, wooded landscape, the Pays de Sancerrois, makes from the monotonous countryside to the south. Sancerre snoozes smugly on a high dome, casting a satisfied eye over the vineyards which have brought the area so much fame since the

Sauvignon white wine became so chic when first "discovered" 30 years ago. You'll have plenty of chances to buy whites and reds (made from Pinot Noir grapes – try the wine chilled) and the *rosés* from Bué (D1/E1). Another tip: do buy the goat's milk cheeses from **Chavignol** (E1) and Crézancy-en-Sancerre (D1). Other Sauvignon whites, as good and cheaper, come from the **Menetou-Salon** (C1) vineyards.

Seek out **La Borne** (D1), the potters' village, on an elevated site at the western end of Le Sancerrois. Bornoise pottery dates back as far as the 12th century. During the 19th century the potters prospered but, after the 1914-18 War, with an increasing demand for galvanised iron, the industry withered away. Today some four dozen or so potters have workshops in the village and surrounding countryside. Their varied and individualistic *grès* pottery, using local clays, is often stunning in appearance. On the D22 eastern exit from La Borne there's both a *musée*, housed in a church (open every day Easter to Oct; weekends rest of the year) and a nearby exhibition centre (open weekends only).

Now the first of two tours. This is an ecclesiastical route, starting and finishing at two memorable sites. Commence with a bang at the Abbaye de **Noirlac** (C4), the only Cistercian monastery to have survived relatively intact. Approach from the north-west, on the D35 alongside the River **Cher**. The 12th-century abbey is a graceful structure and the initial sight of Saracen chimneys is an intriguing one. The interior's cloisters and arches are eye-catching – austere and simple but a perfect reflection of Cistercian architecture. An annual music festival is held from mid July to mid Aug (contact Assoc. des Amis de l'Abbé de Noirlac, 5 rue de Séraucourt, 18000 Bourges; tel 48 67 00 18).

Continue by seeking out some of Berry's numerous Romanesque churches. We saw the following *églises*, many of which are illuminated every evening during the summer. (I've used the word "illuminated" to identify them.) Start at La Celle (C4), north of Noirlac: the Eglise St-Blaise has surprisingly large flying buttresses, some fine capitals and an elegant chevet. The Eglise St-Amand is at the heart of **St-Amand-Montrond** (C4): admire the choir, nave, capitals and 15th-century chapels. The Eglise St-Etienne at **Dun-sur-Auron** (D3) is a large multi-coloured stone building with handsome chevet, chapels and has an attractive *place* on the southern side. We were not so struck with the town's ancient ramparts. There's a bustling Sat morning market and a Musée du Canal de Berry (open May to Sept).

Next **Blet**, on the N76 (D3). Don't be put off by the church's hideous tower and spire. The 12th-century interior is remarkable, especially the capitals and columns with frescoes. Nearby Charly (illuminated) also has a banal exterior; savour instead the pillars, topped with capitals, the side chapels and the rather too enthusiastically decorated choir. Vereaux (E3: illuminated) is a modest structure; the highlight is the west door and façade. **Jussy-Champagne** (D3: illuminated) is renowned for an extravagant three-level façade which contrasts dramatically with the simplicity of the church. **Avord** (D2: illuminated) is also worth a detour just to admire the three-part façade.

Finish the tour with a flourish at the glorious Eglise Notre-Dame in **La Charité-sur-Loire** (E1). One of Burgundy's best Romanesque treasures, the vast structure is noted for its chevet, domed transept, handsome choir and radiating chapels, and Max Ingrand stained glass windows. Once, after Cluny, this was the largest church in France, capable of housing a congregation of 5,000 worshippers.

The châteaux tour also starts in the south, at **Ainay-le-Vieil** (C4/D4), south of St-Amand-Montrond. Access the *village fleuri* from the east and look out for the fisherman and the lady with a parasol. The octagonal walls of the small moated château have been tagged Le petit Carcassonne; notable, too, is the rose garden (open every day Feb to Nov except Tues in Feb/Mar/Nov). **Meillant** (C4) is a Renaissance stunner – the exterior a mix of flamboyant Gothic and medieval and the interior elegantly furnished (every day except Tues from mid Nov to Jan).

The moated Château de **Sagonne** (E3), west of **Sancoins**, is a small circular fortress. Relish the 14th-century site, moat, keep and furnished rooms (every day July to Sept). Jussy-Champagne (D3) is a more modern structure from the 17th century – a happy mix of brick and stone, pastoral landscape, river and splendid furnishings (every day Apl to mid Nov). The ornate and grandiose Château de Menetou-Salon (C1) was rebuilt in the 19th century and is particularly renowned for a collection of carriages and cars (every day Apl to Oct). The nearby 15th-century Château de **Maupas** (D1) is to the east; the many-floored building has furnished rooms and a staircase decorated with 887 earthenware plates (p.m. every day from Palm Sunday to Sept).

To finish tour two, detour north to map sheet 70. First, to the moated and multi-towered 14th-century fortress at **Boucard** (C4), west of Sancerre, with an austere exterior which is softened by the pools and water meadows of the Sauldre Valley (open every day). Next, the 15th-century Château de la Verrerie with many Scottish links. If you were asked to draw your perception of a château this is the image you would put on paper: water, trees, parkland and man's subtle efforts with differently-styled towers, walls and stone combine to create Renaissance perfection (every day Mar to Nov).

Finally, despite the heavy traffic, head for the medieval centre of Bourges and the superb Gothic Cathédrale St-Etienne: be bowled over, as we have been, by the gigantic nave; the stained glass; the flying buttresses; the ornate chevet; the west front; and the restored organ. Rest awhile in the adjacent Jardins de l'Archevêche; then head north, past half-timbered houses to the Jardin des Prés-Fichaux. Visit the flamboyant Palais Jacques-Coeur; and the many museums, especially the Musée Estève, an art gallery *par excellence*, and the Musée du Berry in the 16th-century Hôtel Cujas. (Details of all the above from Office du Tourisme, 21 rue Victor Hugo, 18000 Bourges; tel 48 24 75 33.)

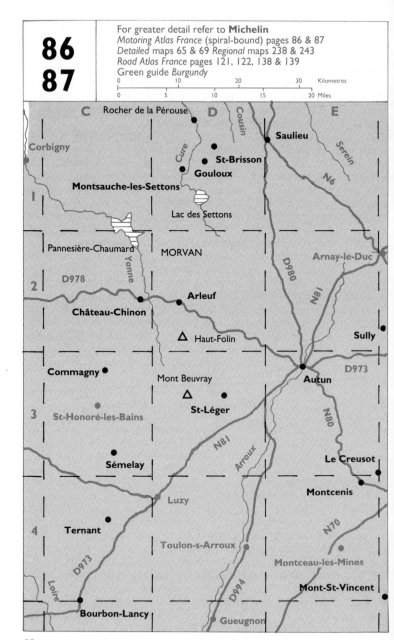

86
87

For greater detail refer to **Michelin**
Motoring Atlas France (spiral-bound) pages 86 & 87
Detailed maps 65 & 69 *Regional* maps 238 & 243
Road Atlas France pages 121, 122, 138 & 139
Green guide *Burgundy*

Kilometres
0   10   20   30
0   5   10   15   20 Miles

C   Rocher de la Pérouse   D   Cousin   E

Corbigny   Cure   Saulieu

St-Brisson   Serein

Gouloux   N6

Montsauche-les-Settons

1   Lac des Settons

Pannesière-Chaumard   MORVAN   Arnay-le-Duc

Yonne   D980

2   D978   N81

Arleuf

Château-Chinon

△ Haut-Folin   Sully

Commagny   Mont Beuvray   D973

△   Autun

3   St-Honoré-les-Bains   St-Léger   N80

N81

Arroux   Le Creusot

Sémelay

Montcenis

Luzy

4   N70

Ternant   Toulon-s-Arroux

Montceau-les-Mines

D973   D994

Loire   Mont-St-Vincent

Bourbon-Lancy   Gueugnon

The opening paragraph for map sheet chapter 72 is even more valid for 86/87: few tourists venture to these Burgundian corners. I'll deal first with one of my favourite "mountainous" areas in France – the Parc Naturel Régional du **Morvan** (C1/C3:D1/D3). Tomorrow, next week, in a month from now, Anne and I are always willing to return to the soothing calm of the park. At their highest point the granite "hills", a more apt label, rise to 2956 ft. The park, 40 miles long by 30 miles wide, is extensively wooded, in the main with broadleaved trees, and is notable for its many rivers, lakes and sylvan valleys.

We've seen the Morvan in every season. On one of our autumn trips we entered the park in the south, at **St-Léger** (D3), and climbed out of the village, along the D3, past several placards advertising *marrons à vendre* (chestnuts for sale). We drove the anti-clockwise D274 circuit to the top of **Mont Beuvray**, 821 m. Once the Gallic oppidum of Bibracte, the fortified camp commands extensive views south and covers a large area of the Beuvray summit. At several points on the heavily wooded mountain, archaeological digs continue. (By the end of 1994 a new museum, housing treasures of the European Celtic heritage, should be open at the Col du Rebout, the start of the anti-clockwise run.)

Now head north to the **D978** (C2/D2). One option could take you past Glux-en-Glenne (D3), where the European Archaeological Centre should have moved into new buildings during 1994; through the spruce and fir trees of the Forêt de St-Prix – detour to the base of the communication tower atop **Haut-Folin** (F2), the Morvan's highest summit (901 m); and then on the D197, alongside the infant **Yonne**, and the D177 to **Arleuf**. Alternatively, you could have driven through the Forêt de la Gravelle (C2/D3), further east. The panoramas, in autumn, are glorious: from afar the tops of beech, oak, sweet chestnut and silver birch resemble giant cobblestones of differing hues.

At Arleuf (D2) use the remote D500 north of the Touron Valley: high hills, dense woods with handsome beech trees, and utter isolation will be your rewards. Aim for **Château-Chinon** (C2). Before visiting the two excellent museums, follow the signs for the *table d'orientation* high above the town (you'll have to walk the final steep 200 m). At the 609 m summit there's a hand-painted observation table, made in 1914; Morvan's wooded *monts* lie to the east and south; and, below you, the town's slate roofs are as dark as the backdrop of surrounding forests. Now follow the Promenade du Château sign, on a road which loops to the north: more views and, on the northern edge, a beech tunnel.

Below the *table* you'll pass two museums: the Musée du Septennat and the Musée du Costume. The former is an entertaining thrill – housing all the many objects which Président Mitterrand has received as gifts, from countries all over the globe, since his 1981 election. Some of the gifts are fabulous works of art, of all sorts and sizes (every day May to Sept; weekends rest of year but closed Jan/Feb). The second museum houses a fascinating 17th to 20th-century collection of French clothing and accessories (every day May to Oct; otherwise weekends).

Both the **Lac des Settons** (D1) and the lake at **Pannesière-Chaumard** (C2) are attractive and the roads around them are rewarding drives. Settons offers all sorts of watersport facilities. Pannèsiere-Chaumard is often emptied for cleaning and is usually only full during the first half of the year. Between the two man-made reservoirs is the tiny hamlet of Planchez (D2), alongside the D37. Here sniff out the most unpretentious café in France, Chez Millette, where simple, local fare is cooked and served by the owner: *jambon du Morvan*, *rosette* (pork sausage), *boudin blanc* and *crapinaude* (bacon pancake).

During the last war the Morvan was renowned for its many formidable Resistance groups operating from the protective wooded hills. One was the Maquis Bernard – the latter a pseudonym for the leader, Louis Aubin, who, before the outbreak of hostilities, had been a *gendarme*. The group operated around **Montsauche-les-Settons** (D1).

Drive south-west from Montsauche on the D977 and, at Le Boulard, follow the signs for Maquis Bernard Cimetière Franco-Anglais. In 1982, when I first "discovered" this most unusual cemetery, the track was rough and there wasn't a clue to its history. Today the lane is smooth and surviving members of the *maquis* have erected large boards along the route and at the cemetery explaining some of the events in the Morvan during 1943-44. What the signs do not tell you, and something I've only recently established, is that the bodies of the 21 *maquis* and seven RAF airmen, initially buried in the sacred ground, were moved in February 1947 to other cemeteries in France.

Nevertheless, there remains an overpowering air of pride in this secret wooded corner. During the last 12 years hundreds of readers, urged on by me, have visited the poignant spot. I know many of you have sensed a human "presence" at this most overwhelming of memorials: one visitor remarked that "souls were still alive there".

In the days after the D-Day landings there was a huge increase in Resistance activity in the Morvan. The *maquis* groups were joined by many SAS teams, parachuted into the area between 6 and 22 June 1944. German soldiers were ambushed and killed. Revenge was horrific and savage. On 25 June Montsauche was put to the torch; 131 houses were burnt to the ground. The next day Germans murdered 17 inhabitants of Dun-les-Places (D1), north of Montsauche, including the mayor and *curé*; houses were burnt, women raped. Planchez, too, was destroyed. The story of the Morvan resistance is told at the *musée* in the Maison du Parc at **St-Brisson** (D1), north-east of Montsauche; open from June to Sept, the spot is well worth visiting for its park, lake and setting.

Recently I have had the most rewarding and satisfying contact with a Beckenham reader who told me that one of the RAF crew, Sgt Richold, had been a friend of hers. Returning from a raid on Dijon, on the night of 10/11 August 1944, his Halifax had been attacked over **Saulieu** (E1) and crashed two km north of **Gouloux** (D1). She also told me that a

70

member of one of the SAS teams, a Church of Scotland padre, J. Fraser McLuskey, had "paid the last honours" to the airmen at their initial burial. In turn I was able to put her in touch with Alex Muirhead, the leader of one of the SAS teams, who gave her the scorched remains of a silk "survival" scarf found at the crash site. She cherishes the precious gift enormously because, after all, there's a one-in-seven chance that the scarf belonged to her friend.

Gouloux has two attractions: to the west, the River **Cure** drops 10 metres over the Saut de Gouloux – a worthwhile walk from the D977; and the clog-maker's shop belongs to the mayor, who once gave me some useful information about the Maquis Bernard cemetery. Be sure, too, to make the rewarding drive and not-too-steep and not-too-long climb on foot to the hand-painted tiles on the observation table at the **Rocher de la Perouse** (D1); the panorama is quintessential Morvan.

What's south of the Morvan? Start at **Mont-St-Vincent** (F4). Climb the 20-ft-high observation tower with its five separate ceramic tile panels: the views are great. Visit the 12th-century granite *église*, once a Bénédictine priory, which lost its tower over the transept in 1794. Nearby, at Gourdon, is another granite Romanesque church. Admire the perched site from the D164 to the north; and seek out the striking stone sculptures 50 metres beyond the *église*.

You can easily track the TGV railway line across the length of map sheet 87. Why not take a ride on a bullet train? Board the TGV at **Le Creusot** station – to the south-east, at Les 7 Ecluses (F4). Leave at 9.20, arrive Lyon at 10.02; leave Lyon 11.00, arrive back 11.45. Or leave 14.27, arrive Lyon 15.08; leave Lyon 16.07, back at 16.45.

Montcenis (E4) is an idiosyncratic hill-top town with handsome paved streets. The D47 run to the west is a south Shropshire-like drive with gentle hills, woods of oak, beech and chestnut, hedges, views, conkers, farms, châteaux, cattle, sheep and few cars. Detour to Uchon (E3) and another great viewpoint, the Signal d'Uchon. Further west seek out two Romanesque treasures: at **Sémelay** (C3), in peaceful, pastoral terrain, the 12th-century *église* has a long nave and barrel-vaulted apse with carved decorations; **Commagny** (C3), further north, has a 12th-century priory church above the tiny hamlet – admire the handsome apse and some fine capitals. Two other ecclesiastical marvels are the 15th-century Flemish triptychs in the small church at **Ternant** (C4), north of **Bourbon-Lancy**, a super small spa.

Now to a treasure-chest town. **Autun** (E3) was once called the "sister of Rome" by Julius Caesar. Relish the 800-year-old St-Lazare Cathedral, a glorious Romanesque work of art (the tall spire is 15th century); the theatre, Temple of Janus, gateways and town walls from its Roman past; the many medieval and Renaissance sights; and the richly-endowed Rolin Museum (closed Tues and pub hols). Finish at the 16th-century château at **Sully** (F2), to the north-east, once described as the "Fontainebleau of Burgundy" (open every day Palm Sunday to Oct).

71

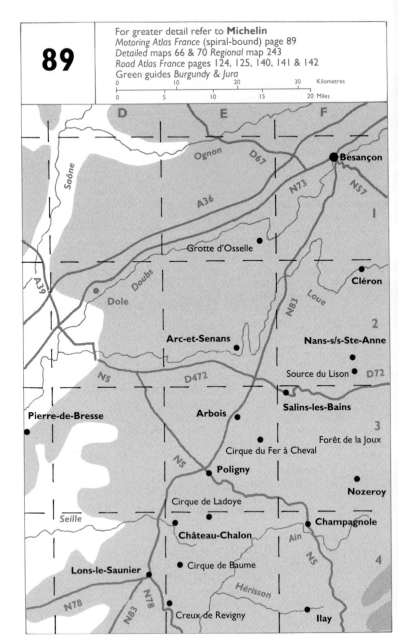

89

For greater detail refer to **Michelin**
Motoring Atlas France (spiral-bound) page 89
Detailed maps 66 & 70 *Regional* map 243
Road Atlas France pages 124, 125, 140, 141 & 142
Green guides *Burgundy & Jura*

Kilometres
0   10   20   30

Miles
0   5   10   15   20

D   E   F

Ognon

D67

Besançon

Saône

A36

N73

N57

1

Grotte d'Osselle

Cléron

A39

Doubs

Loue

Dole

N83

2

Arc-et-Senans

Nans-s/s-Ste-Anne

N5

D472

Source du Lison

D72

Pierre-de-Bresse

Arbois

Salins-les-Bains

3

Forêt de la Joux

Cirque du Fer à Cheval

N5

Poligny

Nozeroy

Cirque de Ladoye

Champagnole

Seille

Château-Chalon

Ain

N5

Lons-le-Saunier

Cirque de Baume

4

Hérisson

N78

N83

N78

Creux de Revigny

Ilay

Map sheet 89 brings us to the first of several chapters where I shall enthuse about one of my favourite areas of France – the Jura. Please don't mistake the Jura mountains as a rival for the Alps: the highest peak in the range, which runs from Bâle to the Rhône, in both France and Switzerland, is a modest 5636 ft above sea-level.

When the spirit and senses need refreshing head for the gentle Jura, a land of densely-wooded limestone hills, imposing valleys, rock faces, emerald pastures, streams, rivers and lakes. Added pluses are the Jura's quaffable wines, encore-tempting cheeses and tasty *charcuterie*. We've seen the area in all the seasons but our favourite time is October when the mellow days – if luck is with you – can be warm, dry and benevolent. Then the landscape dazzles. The primarily broadleaved forests become gigantic swathes of autumn colours, Kaffe Fassett designs of random hues and shades: bronze, saffron, old gold, ochre, russet, chilli red and copper. The bird life is amazing: buzzards, red kites, herons, peregrines, kingfishers, woodpeckers and dippers commonplace.

Two words are synonymous with the Jura: limestone and water. The Jura – a gargantuan Gruyère cheese – is riddled with limestone caves and subterranean passages. The area is renowned for resurgent streams, where water disappears underground miles away, high above the tops of the many *cirques* (amphitheatres), to reappear in caves or falls at the bottom of the steep rock faces. The *cirques* are at the end of deep wooded valleys called *reculées*. We've seen the *cirques* and *reculées* many times during the last four decades but, on our last visit, the appalling weather, for once, returned gilt-edged bonuses: the rivers, cascades and resurgent streams were at their ferocious best. I'll describe the five most important *cirques* for you – starting in the south.

View the classic **Cirque de Baume** (E4) from the belvedere at its southern end, just off the D471. Then descend to Baume-les-Messieurs, an unspoilt village in a time-warp and guarded by two massive rock walls scowling at each other above the roof tops. The 11th/15th-century abbey snoozes behind a shaded *place*. At the head of the valley a waterfall gushes out of the rock face and tumbles over mossy rocks. The **Cirque de Ladoye** (E4) is best approached from the D5 to the north; on our most recent visit the stunning wooded valley below us was an eerie sight with whisps of cloud floating among the beech trees and hovering over the emerald pastures at the bottom. The *fontaine* which emerges at the base of the rock face is a docile affair.

The **Cirque du Fer à Cheval** (E3), at the head of a wider wooded valley, is not as spectacular as the previous duo. The Grottes des Planches below the *cirque* is a superb sight after heavy rain: emerging at the foot of a black and white overhanging cliff, the volume of water can be immense and deafening near the cave's exit (the *grottes* are open every day Apl to Oct but closed Fri in Oct). At the **Source du Lison** (F2) two caves feed the river: one, the Grotte Sarrazine, is a ten-minute walk from the car park; the thundering roar of water blasting from the base is a dramatic spectacle. Further east, the Source de la Loue (90:B2) can be reached by either a long, exciting hike from the D67 or from the D443 to the south – a less strenuous walk; this stepped version is not as impressive as the others.

Two other natural features deserve a mention. The **Creux de Revigny** (E4), south-east of **Lons-le-Saunier**, is a high cliff, pock-marked with caves, where the River Vallière emerges at the base of the rock face. The Creux Billard (F2), above the Source du Lison, is a huge gouge (*creux*) in the rock face where, after heavy rain, there's a cascade 80 metres high. The D103 descent here is gorgeous: a vista of beech woods, other valleys branching off the Lison and various moulded hills. (Detour to the Pont du Diable: a narrow bridge over a ravine with a terrific view of a densely wooded gorge to the north.)

I'll continue on the theme of water. Do not fail, under any account, to seek out the **Hérisson** Valley (E4/F4). Small the valley may be, only 20 km or so, but what an incomparable punch the Hérisson packs. There's a belvedere on the D39 to the north; view the wooded scene below you but then use the D326 from Doucier (E4) and park at the end of the lane. As you walk upstream to **Ilay** (F4) you'll pass a series of cascades; the Hérisson falls 250 metres in three km. For the lazy a 400-metre walk from the car park takes you to the best of the falls, the multi-stepped Cascade de l'Eventail. Don't bypass the Hérisson.

Note that there are several lakes in the area (E4/F4). The largest is the Lac de Chalain (E4). In summer, watersports of all kinds ensure the lake is busy; but walks on the southern banks are quiet enough. Further east, the Cascade de la Billaude (F4) is a thundering spectacle after heavy rain. (Readers speak highly of the climb to the Pic de l'Aigle (F4) with extensive views from the 993 metre-high summit.)

Not surprisingly, the limestone Jura has endowed the area with many grottoes and caves – all with their own versions of stalagmites and stalactites. Among the renowned caves are: the **Grotte d'Osselle** (E1: Apl to Oct); the cathedral-sized Gouffre de Poudrey (90:A1. Mar to Oct); the Grotte de la Glacière (90:B1. Mar to Nov); and the recently-opened Grottes des Moidons, on the D469 south of the Cirque du Fer à Cheval (E3: Apl p.m. only; all day May to Sept).

The Jura is also a land of trees – broadleaved and pines. France's best pine forest is the **Forêt de la Joux**, north-east of **Champagnole** (F4). Hidden within the 6,000-acre forest is the Sapin Président, a massive pine with a circumference of four metres (a long walk from the road). Something quite different is Mont Poupet, north of **Salins-les-Bains** (F3). The views south from the D492 and the RF (forest road) to the summit are stunning – a vista of wooded hills and valleys; there's also a lovely marked walk, with explanatory boards, starting from the D492 west of its junction with the D273.

Before I finish with some man-made sights let me tell you about a captivating river: the **Loue**. Start at the source (90:B2), mentioned earlier; then track the river downstream. Spare a few minutes at three villages, of varying size, with differing perspectives of the Loue: Mouthier-Haute-Pierre, Lods and Ornans (A2). West of the latter admire the remarkable river reflection, the Miroir de Scey, just before **Cléron** (F2). The multi-towered Château de Cléron, alongside the Loue, is an appealing scene (p.m. mid July to mid Aug).

Continue on the D103 to Lizine (F2) and then the D135 north. Do not drive past the two belvederes north of Lizine: the first, the Piquette, a five-minute walk from the road, overlooks the luminous, bowling-green waters of the Loue, hundreds of feet below the viewpoint; the other, the Moulin Sapin, is high above the River Lison.

What of the man-made attractions? Lons-le-Saunier (D4) is a bustling town; of the architectural treats the arcades and Tour de l'Horloge are the most noteworthy. **Château-Chalon** (E4) sits on a rocky seat high above the River **Seille** – with a bib of famed vineyards falling sharply away to the valley floor. In October the D5 climb to the village is especially colourful, courtesy of the dying leaves in the vineyards to the north. **Nozeroy** (F3), to the east, is a medieval, perched treat: admire the formidable tower/gate, the many stone houses, the handsome *place* with a solitary chestnut tree and the 13th/15th-century church. **Poligny** (E3) is the capital of *Comté* cheese. At the heart of the town nose out Joseph Defert's super Comté Juraflore cheese shop; all the Jura varieties, including *Comté*, are available.

Arbois (E3) is renowned for its Pasteur connection (the family house is now a *musée*); the three-star *ville fleuri* is also the Jura wine capital. Salins-les-Bains (F3) is pleasant enough around the *bains*, tourist office and *musée*. Famed in times past for the production of salt by the evaporation of brine, you can visit the ancient underground workings near the tourist office. **Arc-et-Senans** (E2), to the north-west, was an 18th-century planned town, La Saline Royale (brine, piped from Salins, was evaporated there). Built by the visionary Claude Nicolas Ledoux, the site is worth a detour with its striking stone buildings, set out in a large arc, and a *musée* showing numerous scale models of the architect's work throughout France.

Another must is the Musée de la Taillanderie, south-west of **Nans-sous-Ste-Anne** (F2): an absorbing 19th-century farm workshop where all manner of tools such as scythes and axes were made, using water to provide energy; the waterwheels, ovens, hammers and bellows are fascinating (all day May to Sept; p.m. only on Sun out of season). Far to the west, at **Pierre-de-Bresse** (88:C3), is the HQ of the Ecomusée de la Bresse (see map sheet chapter 103) – housed in a stylish, eye-pleasing moated château with black pepper-pot towers and surrounded by a park (in part of which deer roam free). The museum evokes and explains the traditions and life of Bresse, the area to the south of maps 88/89. Finally, if you can cope with the traffic, finish in **Besançon** (F1) – with its fine site, old town, *citadelle* and museums.

75

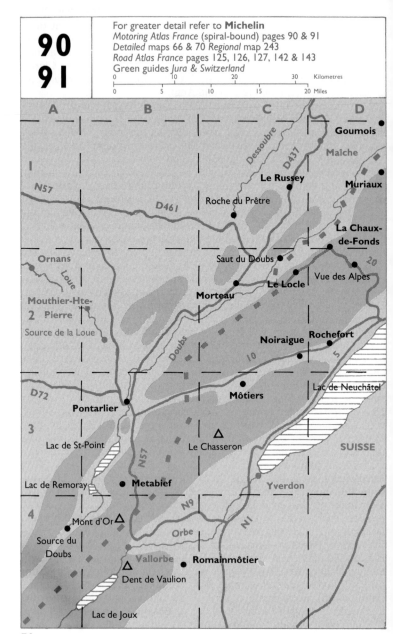

90
91

For greater detail refer to **Michelin**
Motoring Atlas France (spiral-bound) pages 90 & 91
Detailed maps 66 & 70 *Regional* map 243
Road Atlas France pages 125, 126, 127, 142 & 143
Green guides *Jura & Switzerland*

0   10   20   30   Kilometres

0   5   10   15   20 Miles

A   B   C   D

I

N57

D461

Goumois

Maîche

Le Russey

D437

Dessoubre

Roche du Prêtre

Muriaux

**La Chaux-
de-Fonds**

Ornans

Loue

Saut du Doubs

20

Le Locle

Vue des Alpes

Mouthier-Hte-
Pierre

Morteau

2

Source de la Loue

Doubs

Noiraigue

Rochefort

10

5

D72

Môtiers

Lac de Neuchâtel

Pontarlier

3

Lac de St-Point

N57

△
Le Chasseron

SUISSE

Lac de Remoray

● **Metabief**

Yverdon

N9

4

Mont d'Or △

N1

Source du
Doubs

Orbe

△ Vallorbe   **Romainmôtier**

Dent de Vaulion

Lac de Joux

This second Jura chapter includes terrain in both Switzerland and France; the border between the two countries cuts diagonally across the landscape, from the top right-hand corner to the bottom left. To enable me to describe the countless attractions more easily I have divided the chapter into three parts. I'll start in Switzerland. Then I'll cross the border and head north-east, following the **Doubs** downstream from its source (A4), looking at both sides of the French and Swiss borders. I'll finish with a brief look at one of France's most delectable small rivers, the **Dessoubre** (C1). (Another river valley, the **Loue** (A2/B2), was described in map sheet chapter 89.)

As good a place as any to start part one is the renowned **Vue des Alpes** (D2: 1283 m). With minimum effort you can enjoy the distant panorama of the Bernese Oberland peaks and the Mont Blanc *massif*. You'll be rewarded with an even better panorama if you drive south from the main road to the hotel marked on the map, park your car and make the half hour hike to the Tête de Ran (1422 m) summit. (By the end of 1994 a new six km road tunnel will be open under the high ridge.)

Now use the minor roads which head south-west to the Val de Travers (C2/C3). Above **Rochefort** (D2) relish the views of the **Lac de Neuchâtel** (D2/D3) and the flattish terrain beyond. One refreshing aspect is that the hill above Rochefort is covered with beech trees, a welcome change from the ubiquitous dark conifers. Just south-west from Rochefort dive down the minor road to the Champ du Moulin (D2). The views are scintillating: distant lake, beeches around you, mixed woods on the other side of the valley and, far below, the Gorges de l'Areuse. At the bottom you have various options: you can walk to your heart's content, upstream or down; you can cycle on the tarmac track laid down through the entire length of the Val de Travers; or you can catch a train from the Champ de Moulin station to **Noiraigue** (C2) and either walk back or return by the railway (or vice versa).

Next, leave route 10 at Noiraigue, cross the railway and climb to the Ferme Robert, a chalet café (981 m) at the heart of the Réserve du Creux du Van. Flora and fauna are protected and roe deer and *chamois* roam free in their natural habitat. Back in the valley seek out the Asphalt Rock Mines at La Presta (C2: cross the railway line). Until 1986 the mine had produced mastic asphalt for 113 years. There's a one km circuit in the old galleries and a small workshop explains the workings of the mine. At the adjacent café try the ham, wrapped in tin foil, cooked by heating asphalt to 220 degrees C. (Tours at 10.00, 14.00, 16.00 every day July/Aug; 14.00, 16.00 weekends Apl to June and Sept/Oct; 14.00, 16.00 Sun only rest of year.) **Môtiers** (C3) is the home of the Jean-Jacques Rousseau *musée* (the house where he lived from 1762 until 1765) and a covered market, the Hotel of the Six-Communes.

On our visit last year bad weather ruined the planned climbs, our first ever, to the summits of **Le Chasseron** (C3) and the **Dent de Vaulion** (B4). The former requires a long climb of over an hour to reach the top

77

with its famed views of the Alps; the latter's steep peak is reached more easily, your car taking you almost all the way. The panorama from the observation table is said to include the Jungfrau, Mont Blanc and even La Meije in the Massif des Ecrins (132:C2).

The low cloud and heavy rain didn't spoil our visit to the Romanesque abbey at **Romainmôtier** (B4): the delightful little village, with its semi-circular street, is tucked away in a hidden valley. See both the abbey and the exhibition evoking monastic life (a.m. and p.m. Apl to Oct). Another idyllic hidden valley is at Les Clées, to the immediate north: beech woods; a tower high above the hamlet; the River Orbe forcing a path through the narrow ravine; walks; and memorable, too, for our sightings of two red squirrels.

Cross into France on the D389 (A4/B4) forest road. Start part two at the **Source du Doubs**. The pouring rain paid us a rich dividend on our last visit: the resurgent source, a cave at the foot of Le Noirmont ridge, was a roaring, raving sight. Bravo to the tourist board for erecting several signs, in three languages, explaining the fabulous natural phenomenon. (Who is the diving champion?) The **Lac de Remoray** (B3) is a *réserve naturelle* where flora and fauna are protected: the Maison de La Réserve is on the east side of the D437, north of Labergement-Ste-Mairie (B3: every day p.m. only).

Shortly before the *maison*, stop at the Obertino Fonderie de Cloches (bell foundry). I guarantee anyone entering the octagonal-shaped shop will not come out empty-handed. Seek out, too, the Sancey Richard Fromagerie du Mont d'Or at **Metabief** (B3), north of the village. Arrive at 9.30 every day, except Sunday, and witness, from special galleries, the making of three Jura cheeses: *Comté*, a huge hard wheel; *Morbier*, an LP-sized record with an ash streak through the middle; and *Mont d'Or*, a creamy CD-sized *fromage* made only from Nov to Mar. Then climb the 1463 m **Mont d'Or** (B4). On one October visit, at sunset, we were fortunate enough to see the 100-mile-long range of the Swiss and French Alps at their best – glowing pink on the eastern horizon.

The **Lac de St-Point** (B3) is a long lake with numerous restful vistas. Something new is the special *sentier pédestre* (footpath) which has been laid out around the lake – with eight display boards, at various points, explaining differing aspects of the terrain covered (no bikes allowed). Further north, above a natural cleft in the Jura hills, is the imposing fortress of the Château de Joux (B3): towers, ramparts, moats and drawbridges all played a part at this strategic castle, built and rebuilt over the centuries (open Easter to October).

From **Pontarlier** (B3) to **Morteau** (C2) the Doubs is a relaxing river. Stop to have a look at the abbey at Montbenoît (B2): admire the carved choir-stalls and the pillars in the tiny cloisters. Morteau, like its Swiss counterparts, **Le Locle** (C2) and **La Chaux-de-Fonds** (D1), is a clock making centre. The Musée d'Horlogerie is housed in the 16th-century Château Pertusier with a handsome stone façade (July to Sept); Le

Locle's watch museum is at the Château des Monts (p.m. only, closed Mon); and the Musée International d'Horlogerie at La Chaux is an ambitious affair (closed Mon).

On your way to Le Locle, stop at the Col des Roches (C2), a narrow gash through the limestone ridge. Here the Moulins Souterrains are an exciting, exhilarating adventure: a series of 300-year-old underground mills which once were busy active affairs (every day May to Oct). Retrace your steps. The 90-ft-high **Saut du Doubs** (C2) – literally, where the river shoots forth a cascade of foaming water – can be reached either by a road on the French side which leaves you with a longish walk to the fall; or by boat from Villers-le-Lac (C2: France) and Les Brenets (C2: Switzerland) – from Easter to October. Both alternatives make use of the winding man-made lake to the north.

I'll finish part two with a few varying snippets. In the French Jura you'll notice the huge chimneys which dominate most farms. Visit one: La Ferme des Guinots, south-east of the crossroads at Les Cerneux-Monnots, on the D414 from Charquemont (D1) to **Le Russey** (C1); it's the first farm on the right side of the D457. Gasp at the size of the structure, called a *tué* or *tuyé*, where hundreds of hams and sausages can be smoked in the high, dark interior. Then try a slice or two (or even lunch) of *saucisse de Morteau* (also called *Jésus de Morteau*) – a tasty pork concoction; *jambon de tuyé* – smoked ham; and *brési* – wafer-thin slices of dried beef; all washed down with Jura wine.

Seek out the viewpoint, just south of **Goumois** (77:D4), where the D437A turns north-west (D1). The vista is one of the most rejuvenating in France: pure air; a pleasing panorama; distant, humming river; lush pastures; and giant duvets of trees on both sides of an immense valley. Is this not an image of eternity? Walkers and fishermen are also in heaven hereabouts; and the Doubs' white water is ideal for canoeists.

On the Swiss side visit the enterprising automobile museum at **Muriaux** (D1); open every day (p.m. only Nov to Mar). Seek out, too, the strikingly modern stained glass at the chapel, built in 1971, in Le Peuchapatte (D1), a hamlet of just 30 souls. We all know how neat and tidy the Swiss are: the changes, when you cross the border, are immediately apparent. But in the Swiss Jura even the landscape seems to be more manicured than its French counterpart.

Part three and finish with a scenic glory. Aim for a startling viewpoint, the **Roche du Prêtre** (C1). To the right is the dramatic Cirque de Consolation and, far below you, nestling under an eiderdown of tree tops, is the 17th-century Abbey of Notre Dame de Consolation. Descend to the abbey park – a wonderland of springs, grottoes, waterfalls and woodland paths. The River Dessoubre is no more than a 20-mile-long stream, flowing north to join the Doubs. As you drive the deserted roads downstream you'll pass few houses. You may smell newly-felled pine trees; you can paddle in the stream; you can taste *brési*, *saucisse or truite* at an *auberge*; here you can truly put all your senses to the test.

79

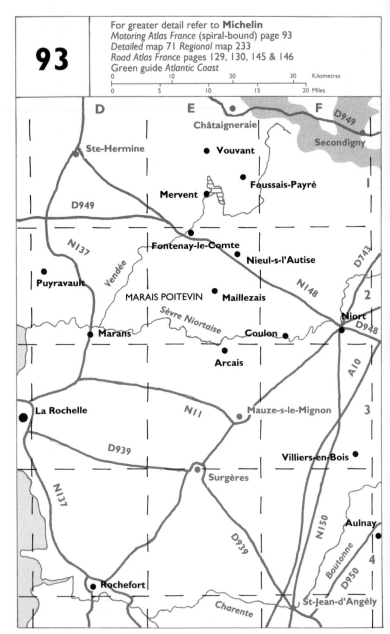

93

For greater detail refer to **Michelin**
Motoring Atlas France (spiral-bound) page 93
Detailed map 71 *Regional* map 233
Road Atlas France pages 129, 130, 145 & 146
Green guide *Atlantic Coast*

| 0 | 10 | 20 | 30 | Kilometres |

| 0 | 5 | 10 | 15 | 20 Miles |

D   E   F

D949

Châtaigneraie

Secondigny

Ste-Hermine

Vouvant

Foussais-Payré

I

D949

Mervent

N137

Fontenay-le-Comte

Nieul-s-l'Autise

Vendée

D743

Puyravault

MARAIS POITEVIN

Maillezais

N148

2

Sèvre Niortaise

Niort

Marans

Coulon

D948

Arcais

A10

La Rochelle

N11

Mauze-s-le-Mignon

3

D939

Villiers-en-Bois

Surgères

N137

N150

Aulnay

D939

Boutonne

D950

4

Rochefort

St-Jean-d'Angély

Charente

What varied countryside awaits you as you travel across the terrain covered by map sheet 93. To the north is the Vendée; to the south Charentes, part of Poitou-Charentes, a region which has so many threads of English history running through its turbulent past. Most of the landscape is unassuming – though one section is scenically both unique and curious. **La Rochelle**, just off the western edge, is the most exciting and extrovert of ports (92:C3).

I'll commence in an unusual way by bringing to your attention a site to the north of map sheet 93. As you travel south, or on your return home, seek out Le Puy-du-Fou (80:A3), south of Mortagne-sur-Sèvre. Here, every Friday and Saturday evening, from June to September, the ruined château and lake are the scene of a spectacular *spectacle*, the largest in Europe. The "stage" is 30 acres; 650 actors and 50 horsemen take part; 2,000 volunteers help out; and hundreds of fireworks are set off. Lasers, synchronised fountains, 1,500 projectors and ultra-modern sound technology all combine to put on the supreme *son et lumière show* – a *cinéscénie* epic. The show is an evocation of Vendée life, as experienced by a humble *paysan vendéen* (Vendée peasant), Jacques Maupillier. If you cannot see the show still visit the site: the permanent stands are massive, as are the car parks. There's an *écomusée* in the grounds, the Grands Parcours: this includes an 18th-century village, jugglers, jousting tournaments and falconry displays. In 1993 Le Puy-du-Fou received world-wide publicity when the annual Tour de France cycle race started from the site. (For information contact Spectacle du Puy-du-Fou, 85590 Les Epesses: tel 51 67 65 65.)

Back to map sheet 93. An unassuming landscape? As evidence of my claim consider the Pays de Mélusine. Legend says Mélusine was a siren-lady, ever frolicking through oak forests, from castle keep to country house, from *dolmen* to postern (a castle's back door). The *pays* is the area around **Vouvant** (E1). What a handsome setting the village has, perched above the River Mère: the château is a ruined castle of which the most notable part is the 12th-century Tour Mélusine (enjoy the panorama from the top of the 120-step climb); the Romanesque *église* is a splendid example of a fortified church (with a super front); and the river aspect at Le Vivier includes an old *lavoir* (wash-house).

Other Romanesque churches worth nosing out are at Cezais, north-west of Vouvant; **Foussais-Payré**, to the south-east of Vouvant, where the *église* has some fine sculptures (admire the Descent from the Cross on the façade); and St-Hilaire-des-Loges (E2), south of Foussais. There are other good reasons for visiting Foussais-Payré: enjoy a number of Renaissance stone houses (one, dating from 1552, is on the south side of the church); note, too, the wooden *halle* (covered market).

Two other man-made treats are worth seeing. First, the small moated and fortified 17th-century Château de la Citardière, hidden to the north of Les Quillères, west of Foussais-Payré. Second, the Abbey St-Vincent in **Nieul-sur-l'Autise** (E2), south of St-Hilaire-des-Loges; dating from

81

the 11th and 12th centuries, the building has a handsome façade and claims to have the only entirely arched Romanesque cloisters in western France. Your navigation efforts will be well rewarded.

The 12,500-acre Mervent-Vouvant forest (E1), to the south of Vouvant, is on hilly ground. Several roads thread their way through the woods and walks abound. The lake, a winding snake, is man-made. For the best view head for the *hôtel de ville* gardens at **Mervent**; the lake is far below you and in the middle is a postage stamp-sized island café which can only be reached by boat from the far shore.

There are some fine oak trees at the cross-roads south of the Grotte du Père Montfort. Below the cross-roads, to the east, is the 25-acre Parc de Pierre-Brune, a leisure park with 50 different fun games to suit everybody in the family, a two km-long narrow-gauge train track, tennis and mini-golf (Easter to Oct: 51 00 28 18). The map identifies two zoological gardens: the six-acre Parc Ornithologique de Pagnolle (road signs say Parc Animalier de Pagnolle) with over 250 species of exotic birds (E1: south-west of Foussais-Payré); and, just to the west, the 13-acre Parc Zoo du Gros Roc with more than 350 animals.

Now descend from the Forêt de Mervent-Vouvant, leaving the flighty Mélusine behind you, to the Renaissance town of **Fontenay-le-Comte** (E2). From afar your first glimpse of the town is the high spire of the Eglise Notre-Dame, for all the world a distant vision of England. One must before you walk the narrow streets to the east of the church: visit the Museé Vendéen (51 69 31 31) which has three floors devoted to the varied history of the town, once the capital of Bas-Poitou. Enjoy the 15th-century church, the Rue des Loges, the stone and timber-framed houses and, to the north, on the right bank of the River **Vendée**, the Fontaine des Quatre-Tias. To the west is the stylish strength of the 16th-century Château de Terre-Neuve – with famed fireplace, wood panelling, fine furniture and other oddities.

To the south of Fontenay is one of the most curious parts of France: the unique **Marais Poitevin**. Study map sheet 93: a band across the middle is an intricate maze of canals, rivers, dykes, lush marshes, meadows and wetlands. The alternative name is more apt: *la Venise verte*. The Green Venice is a realistic label for the thousand and one canals, many of which are green tunnels, and where waterways are covered in duckweed and lined with avenues of poplars, willows and pollarded ash trees. Every field is, in effect, an island. Punts are a vital means of transport: for humans, crops, animals and their feed.

Once the 37,000-acre wetlands lay beneath the waters of a shallow gulf which stretched as far as **Niort** (F2). In times past rises of ground were islands – villages such as Chaillé-les-Marais and **Puyravault** (D1) on a spiny ridge of land running west to east.

Over the decades I must have driven every lane in the Marais Poitevin. Perhaps the best way to see the wetlands by car is to drive from Thairé-le-Fagnoux (D2), east of **Marans**, along the lanes on the banks of the

Sèvre Niortaise, to La Croix-des-Mary (E2). On a weekday we had the roads to ourselves with only the company of yellow irises, herons, pike, ducks, swallows and weeping willows. Detour, briefly, to a small exhibition on the Marais fauna at Taugon, south of the river. At La Croix head north, on the D15, to **Maillezais** (E2) where the Gothic architecture of the ruins of the Abbey St-Pierre still appeals; also pleasing is the Romanesque porch of the *église* at Maillé (north of La Croix). Back to La Croix and continue upstream to **Coulon** (F2): *en route* admire the handsome tower and spire of the church at Damvix (E2); and, as you get closer to Coulon, you'll note how much smarter and busier the waterways and houses become. From the D123 you'll also glimpse, across the river, the blue-shuttered cottage which has featured on so much tourist literature.

At Coulon visit the Maison des Marais Mouillés, an evocation of local life, history and costumes, and the L'Aquarium de la Venise verte. At Coulon you can explore the Marais by means other than car. There's a green and white motorised train, *Pibalou*, which takes the strain. Or you can enjoy do-it-yourself or guided punt (*barque*) trips. Punts can also be hired at Damvix, **Arcais** (E3) or Maillezais. Alternatively, you can hire a bike at Maillezais or Damvix; take a minibus ride, *Le Grenouillou*, from Coulon; or a horse-drawn carriage at Damvix.

Let's turn our backs on the unassuming faces of the Marais Poitevin and the Pays de Mélusine and turn our attention to some of the more famed man-made sights. La Rochelle (92:C3), once a mighty Protestant stronghold and with so many important historical links, is a port of throbbing vitality: the combination of massive medieval towers, old streets, covered arcades, several museums and buzzing street life will interest and excite everyone. One absolute must: take a boat bus ride from the old harbour. And try to see the Aquarium de La Rochelle where the tunnel through the shark tank is a hair-raising experience (at the Port de Minimes, south-west of La Rochelle's old port).

Rochefort (D4) has several man-made treats. Visit the 17th-century Royal Rope Factory, a 378-metre long building beside the **Charente**. Visit the Pont du Martrou, a national monument and France's only surviving *pont transbordeur* (transporter-bridge). Today the bridge is redundant with the opening of the one km long Viaduc de Charente. Spare time, too, for the house of the novelist Pierre Loti, with a number of bizarre "exhibition rooms of marvellous elsewheres".

What else? Definitely the 12th-century Romanesque Eglise St-Pierre at **Aulnay** (94:B4); the stone carvings are superb. Further north, at **Villiers-en-Bois**, is the oak and beech Forêt de Chizé (93:F3); within the forest is the Zoorama Européen, a 62-acre zoo where you can see European animals in a natural habitat. Due north, east of Niort, is Les Ruralies (94:B2); here you can visit a museum of farm machinery, taste examples of regional produce and see local craftwork. Access to the site is from the **A10** *autoroute* or the **D948**.

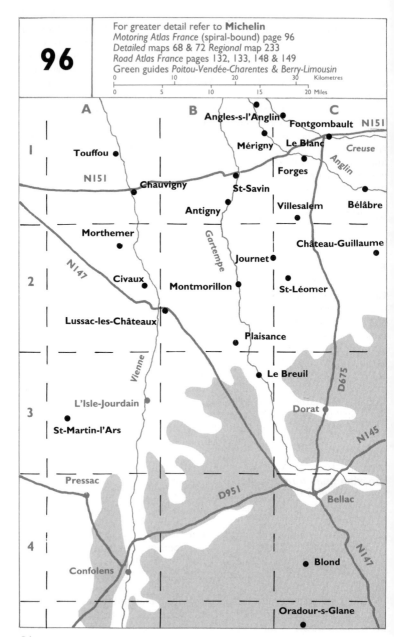

96

For greater detail refer to **Michelin**
Motoring Atlas France (spiral-bound) page 96
Detailed maps 68 & 72 *Regional* map 233
Road Atlas France pages 132, 133, 148 & 149
Green guides *Poitou-Vendée-Charentes & Berry-Limousin*

| 0 | 10 | 20 | 30 | Kilometres |
| 0 | 5 | 10 | 15 | 20 Miles |

A　　　**B**　　　**C**

I

Touffou ●

Angles-s-l'Anglin ●
Fontgombault ● N151
Mérigny ●
Le Blanc ●
Creuse

N151

Chauvigny ●
St-Savin ●
Forges ●
Anglin

Antigny ●
Villesalem ●
Bélâbre ●

Gartempe

Morthemer ●

Château-Guillaume ●

2

N147

Journet ●

Civaux ●
Montmorillon ●
St-Léomer ●

Lussac-les-Châteaux ●

Vienne

Plaisance ●

Le Breuil ●

D675

3

L'Isle-Jourdain ●

Dorat ●

St-Martin-l'Ars ●

N145

Pressac ●

D951

Bellac ●

4

N147

Blond ●

Confolens ●

Oradour-s-Glane ●

84

At first sight there seems little to entice tourists to seek out the terrain on map sheet 96. Not for the first time I shall restate the obvious: there are scores of interesting sites – if you know where to look. I emphasise the word sites because here man is the winner in his duel with Nature to attract your attention. Her contributions are of a more self-effacing nature – but both subtle and effective.

Nevertheless, to help me describe this corner of Poitou, I shall rely on Nature's more restful gifts – the river valleys which flow from south to north towards the Loire. In the top right-hand corner is the **Creuse** (C1); a few miles to the south-west is the humble **Anglin**; further west is the **Gartempe** (B1/B3); and, on the left edge of the map sheet, flowing north in an almost straight line, is the **Vienne**. I'll start with the baby of the quartet, the Anglin.

Château-Guillaume (C2) overlooks the Allemette, one of the Anglin's many tiny tributaries. Approach from the D53, to the east. The compact fortress, with high ramparts, round towers and a formidable keep, snoozes peacefully in a wooded setting. Parts of the château date back to the 11th century. Dismantled by Richelieu, the castle was restored in 1878. (Apl to Nov: p.m. every day; July/Aug a.m. also.)

Downstream, **Bélâbre** (C1) is especially eye-pleasing alongside the Anglin. Continue north-west, to **Forges**: what visual perfection awaits you as you approach from the east. The château is built of light stone and has six cone-hatted towers. The property is private; but stop and admire the structure and walk the path beside the château.

Nearby Ingrandes, with salami-sliced towers, has an attractive setting beside the Anglin. So has **Mérigny** (B1): see the river and weir from the bridge, glimpse distant views of the château at Roche-Bellusson and, if you have the time, enjoy the riverside walks. Downstream the Anglin is a charmer with rock faces adding cosmetic interest. **Angles-sur-l'Anglin** (82:B4) is a picture postcard *village fleuri*: from the bridge savour the castle ruins, medieval houses and weir.

Now east to the Creuse which, on this map sheet, is no more than 20 km long. **Le Blanc** (C1) is a busy place. To the north-east is the Brenne Regional Nature Park – an enclave of *étangs* and protected wildlife. High above Le Blanc's left bank are two museums: one, in the sombre Château Naillac, is the Musée des Oiseaux – which explains the varied bird life in the Nature Park; the other, the Maison des Amis du Blanc, evokes the life of the town and environs in times past. The drive downstream, starting under the massive viaduct, is a pretty run.

The Romanesque abbey church at **Fontgombault** (82:C4) must not be missed. Restored in the last century, the huge high-vaulted nave and stained glass are splendid; even more stirring are the Gregorian chants of the monks. Try to coincide your visit with one of the daily services: 10.00 and 18.00 (the latter is 15.30 on Thurs; and 17.00 on Sun and fête days). The monks are also dab hands as potters; see their work in an adjacent shop. You can also buy produce from the abbey farm.

Between the Anglin and Gartempe is a trio of differing man-made sites. First, the isolated Romanesque priory of **Villesalem** (C1) – constructed in the 12th century and with some delicate sculptures. The building is being restored and is open every day, except Tues. Second, the *lanterne des morts* on the green at **Journet** (C2) – one of many in the area (a few are marked on the map). *La lanterne* is a small, narrow, stone column with a hollow interior and arched windows – rising up from a base and tiny altar and topped with a minute cross. In days past an ever-lasting flame, to the memory of the dead, was placed inside the column, at the base, thus ensuring the light's glow could easily be seen.

Third, the remains of the rural Gallo-Romain Sanctuary of Masamas. Little is left now but nevertheless you will be fascinated by the site and the structure built in the first century. All the finds on the site are in the archaeological museum in the Maison Dieu at **Montmorillon** (B2). To find the sanctuary locate **St-Léomer** (C2): follow the road south past Séchaud and the site is to the left. (Also signposted from the D117, five miles from Montmorillon.)

As you criss-cross this laid-back terrain (there's nothing pretentious or chic about the scenery) you'll soon realise that maize and sunflowers seem to flood the landscape; uninteresting but colourful.

Start your Gartempe Valley exploration with a visual thump – at **St-Savin** (B1). Cross the river from the east bank. From the medieval bridge the 12th-century *église* with its tall, slim steeple and surrounding abbey buildings is a scenic feast. The interior is majestic: a high nave, classically balanced and with restful spaciousness, dominates the eye. You will have to bend your head right back to appreciate the almost child-like Romanesque paintings high above you. For some visitors the decayed frescoes are disappointing.

Seek out, too, another quite different St-Savin "attraction" – the home of two talented artists: Joanna Carrington (her professional name) and her husband, Christopher Mason. The couple's house is easy to find, at the southern end of the large square adjoining the church: 50 place de la Libération. Ring the bell and they'll show you an exhibition of their modern work in two ground floor rooms. Joanna is an inventive, imaginative artist; colour is very important for her. She and Christopher, both professionally trained, have been painting for many decades. (I found the musak, blaring out of the loudspeakers in the vast *place*, utterly out of keeping with the Romanesque treasure beside the square. Why does the mayor countenance such nonsense?)

Now upstream on the Gartempe, stopping first at **Antigny** (B1). There's a *lanterne des morts* on the green; some naive frescoes in the Romanesque church; and a *musée* which contains numerous finds from the once important Roman town which occupied the present village site two thousand years ago. Further south, Montmorillon is the home of the Romanesque Eglise Notre-Dame (Ste-Catherine's crypt has some medieval frescoes); the 12th-century Chapelle St-Laurent; and the nearby Maison Dieu with its mysterious 12th-century Octogone chapel.

Continue south. Look out for a small moated house just east of **Plaisance** (B2), alongside the D12. The stretch of river from the bridge at Chez Ragon, south to **Le Breuil**, is delicious: there's lots of white water – ideal for canoes and kayaks. If you want to see the Gartempe away from the road then park just east of the Chez Ragon bridge and walk north to the rock above the river, tagged the Portes d'Enfer. Another, shorter walk, past goats, chickens, and descending steeply through an oak wood, takes you to the Saut de la Brame, south of Le Breuil, where a river tumbles past car-sized boulders.

West to the Vienne. I'll start in the north and assume you drive upstream along its banks. First **Touffou** (A1), a most noble, inspiring and harmonious château, with towers and keep and a site beside the river (July/Aug: a.m. and p.m. but not Mon). Next **Chauvigny** where market day is Thursday. Head first for the *cité mediévale* high above the more modern town: enjoy ramparts, five ruined keeps (the restored Donjon de Gouzon has a folk and archaeological museum) and the Romanesque Eglise St-Pierre with startling grotesque capitals. Detour to another Eglise de St-Pierre, a tiny version, alongside the river south of the town; head south-west to the medieval and restored château at **Morthemer** (A2); and seek out the *cimetière mérovingien* at **Civaux** (stone coffins in the north-east corner of the cemetery north of the village centre; also visit the museum across the road).

Next, the monument to the memory of Constable John Chandos, mortally wounded at Lussac bridge on 31 December 1369. (The memorial is on the D25 just south of the N147 and west of **Lussac-les-Châteaux**.) One of England's most outstanding generals, he masterminded the victory at Poitiers on 19 September 1356. The further upstream you travel, the prettier the Vienne becomes, but tear yourself away to two magnificent man-made sites. First to the Romanesque church at Civray (95:E3) – perhaps the best in Poitou with a fabulous façade and hallucinogenic patterns painted on the interior's walls and columns. Next, to the 12th-century Abbaye de la Réau, south of **St-Martin-l'Ars** (A3); the stone and carvings are so pleasing in their simplicity.

I'll finish on a sobering note. Drive through the *village fleuri* of **Blond** with its fortified church (C4); cross the wooded Monts de Blond; relish the pastoral scene at the *étang* near Cieux; and then descend to **Oradour-sur-Glane** (109:F1). First, you'll pass through the new village. Then, to the south, you'll see the ruins of the old village which was systematically destroyed by the 22nd SS Panzer Division on 10 June 1944, as the Germans headed north to Normandy after the Allied landings. 642 human beings were massacred on that horrific June day, including 207 school children. One word greets you at the entrance to the fire-scarred ruins: REMEMBER. No word is more telling. Oradour is a silent witness to the irreducible baseness in human nature and the horrifying potential for the human race to destroy its very own.

102

For greater detail refer to **Michelin**
Motoring Atlas France (spiral-bound) page 102
Detailed maps 69, 70, 73 & 74 *Regional* maps 243 & 244
Road Atlas France pages 139, 140, 155 & 156
Green guides *Burgundy & Vallée du Rhône*

0   10   20   30   Kilometres

0   5   10   15   20 Miles

A   **B**   **C**

Seille

N6

A6

Sercy

Chapaize

Tournus

D975

Cormatin

Brancion

Taizé

Massy

Blanot

Pont-de-Vaux

Cluny

Grosne

Azé

N79

Berzé-la-Ville

Mâcon

A40

Solutré

N79

La Clayette

N6

Chauffailles

Vonnas

Fleurie

A6

Belleville

Châtillon-s-Chalaronne

Saône

LA DOMBES

Vaux-en-Beaujolais

D485

Villefranche-s-Saône

Villars-les-Dombes

N83

Oingt

Ternand

Theizé

Few other map sheets in Michelin's spiral-bound atlas hide such golden riches in their Fort Knox treasure chests of countryside. But before I signpost dozens of places for you to see I implore you to seek out a bubbly character who, in her own inimitable way, is a human treasure chest of vitality and knowledge – a remarkable lady by any measure.

You will find Yvonne Courson at **Chapaize** (B1), in the Mâconnaise hills west of **Tournus**. Park outside the *église*. Alongside the lane, on the north-west side of the church, is La Forge, a classic example of the local houses, many of which you will have already seen as you crossed the wooded hills. Fifteen steps, which lead up to a vine-covered *meurot* (the name given to the first-floor terraces), are covered with pots of pansies; Yvonne changes the varieties annually, choosing colours which link with some national or European theme. Note the silver birch growing almost out of the wall and the old forge "machinery".

Enter La Forge, full of excellent examples of work created by local artisans. But the most striking and notable is Yvonne's work. Marvel at the couple of dozen *boîtes* (boxes) hanging on the walls. Each one is an individually painted model of a Mâconnaise house: see how every one has a *meurot*, a staircase leading up to the living accommodation, and a cool, protected *cave* at the heart of the ground floor. Yvonne noses out the actual houses, paints the model and then sells the finished *boîte* to clients for use as either a salt box or post box. Our own salt box is modelled on a house in Domange, south of **Azé** (B2).

The houses in the area, not the models, were built in this way for the sole purpose of keeping the ground floor, centrally-sited *cave* at a cool and constant temperature throughout the year; remember wine has been one of the main trades hereabouts for centuries. I defy you not to purchase one of her little masterpieces. Long after you have invested in a box you will have vivid memories of Yvonne, La Forge, the *église* at Chapaize, and the area's wooded hills, every time you take a spoonful of salt from the model (La Forge, 71460 Chapaize; tel 85 50 16 88).

The striking high-towered *église Romane* at Chapaize is one of the finest in the Mâconnaise hills. The 11th-century wonder is being extensively restored. Ask Yvonne to point out Le Méditant on the bell-tower – lit at sunset between March 21 and September 23. Ask her to show you the last remaining tower of the Bénédictine monastery (for monks) and chuckle over her tale of the tunnel linking the latter with the convent for nuns a kilometre or so away. Ask her, finally, to tell you about the previous male owner of La Forge. He had never washed so hadn't bothered to install either water or electricity.

Back to the map and I'll begin the difficult task of listing the gems, both natural and man-made, which you must seek out on your travels. Tournus is the place to start (C1). The great abbey of St-Philibert, built in the 11th/12th centuries, is majestic: towers, nave, crypt, the St-Michel Chapel with its surprise view of the nave – all please enormously. The Romanesque churches in Mâconnais are built of *calcaire* (limestone), a light-coloured stone; further west and north-west the *églises* are constructed from the local *granit rose* (pink) stone (example Gourdon: A1). At St-Philibert, both have been used.

Do not desert Tournus yet. Visit the Greuze Museum (devoted to the painter) and then call at the nearby tourist office. Ask for the street map showing the location of 30 or so Renaissance houses. Many hide the most handsome of surprises. Wherever you can open the street door, enter and marvel at the courtyard at the heart of each house. For example, immediately opposite the tourist office is No 12 rue de la République (42 on the map) – a courtyard with half-timbered galleries and spiral stone staircase; at No 16 (41 on the map) is a triple gallery and spiral stone staircase. You could spend a day alone following the architectural wonders on the map's marked trail.

Into the hills again. Don't rush through Martailly-les-Brancion on the D14 (B1). Look out for Monsieur Leta, another fascinating individual, and his sculptures of stone and wood. By now you will have realised this is a land of perfumed old roses (invariably climbers and ramblers), vines, Charolais cattle (white ghosts in the twilight), woods, pastures, hills and those characteristic houses I described earlier. At **Brancion** (B1) park and walk to the medieval village. There's an austere *église Romane* masterpiece at the end of the promontory overlooking the **Grosne** Valley; a feudal castle (which you can visit); and vine-covered, ancient buildings – all a world away from the N6.

The Mâconnais area is endowed with numerous ecclesiastical riches. **Cluny** (B2) is the most important by far. Once the spiritual hub of the Christian world, the abbey, until St-Peter's was built in Rome, was the largest Christian church in Europe. Little remains of the abbey today but the site still merits your attention; apply your imagination as you tour the grounds. Cluny's influence on religious architecture and sculpture in the 12th century was enormous – as were the hundreds of Cluny's "children" (dependant abbeys and priories) which kept alive the Christian faith throughout France and Europe, not just Burgundy, in the days when Christianity almost came close to dying.

The hills are full of superb Romanesque churches. Chapaize and Brancion have already been mentioned. Nose out also the *église* at Malay (B1: hard to find as there are no signposts in the village) – a perfectly proportioned structure with a series of differently-shaped exterior levels; **Massy** (A2) – a miniature version of Chapaize with an honour guard of five lime trees below the tower; **Blanot** (B2) – again different and with an unusual top-hatted tower with a Lombardian influence; and **Berzé-la-Ville** (B2) – where, just below the village, the priory chapel of the Château des Moines hides, within its interior, glorious murals, reminiscent of Byzantine art.

Another 20th-century ecclesiastical site is at **Taizé** (B1: north of Cluny), a world-famous community founded by Brother Roger in 1940. Each year tens of thousands of young people, of all nationalities and denominations, spend time at the tented village camp. At first glance the "church" resembles a concrete bunker; but what a transformation takes place when you enter the dark interior. Peace and an overwhelming feeling of faith grips your heart. Three services of song and prayer are held every day (for details and times tel 85 50 14 14).

Now for something unusual. Locate Bissy (B1), just north-west of Chapaize. Opposite the war memorial there lies a stunning secret, lurking behind the door to what appears to be a concrete bunker. Inside is an ancient oval-shaped *lavoir* with craftily-designed roof which gives both protection to those washing and also allows rain to fall into the pool. Note the *granit rose* edgings around the pool.

There's another version, not anything like as fascinating, near Berzé-la-Ville (B2). Follow signs from the *village fleuri* which say *lavoir fleuri*. These lead you to Le Vernay to the north. Colourful both the *lavoir* and the hamlet most certainly are.

Other man-made treats are worth noting. One, the most obvious, is the TGV railway line from Paris to Lyon. Hereabouts you'll grasp, at first hand, what steep gradients the track climbs. Put aside 20 minutes or so at one of the bridges and gasp at the sight of a bullet train flashing past. At Blanot (B3) follow signs to the "Poterie" at the top of the village and admire some fine glazes (open from 2.30 p.m.).

Three châteaux deserve your attention. First, the smallest and least well known, at **Sercy** on the D981 (B1). The quartet of varyingly-topped towers appeal and so does the pool in front of the structure; to this day Anne can recall, over 10 years ago, the grunts of the frog orchestra tuning up in the water beside her. **Cormatin** (B1) is something else: truly representative of the image we all have of the word "château", with moat, gardens and extravagantly rich paintings, tapestries and furniture. Berzé-le-Châtel (B2) is a strategically-sited feudal castle, built to protect the southern approaches to Cluny.

Nature has a significant say in the wooded hills and valleys. Two renowned caves will please those who seek adventure underground: the grottoes at Blanot (B1: north of the village) – an extensive network of caves with huge examples of stalactites and stalagmites; and Azé (B2) – prehistoric caves combine with a subterranean river and museum where remarkable finds are exhibited. For those who prefer panoramas and lots of fresh air, then numerous viewpoints are identified on the map: among them Mont Romain (B1); Butte de Suin (A2); and Mont-St-Vincent (A1). The southern panorama from the hills above Berzé-la-Ville (B2) is also terrific and provides the ideal first view of Beaujolais.

Over the decades, as I've revisted many times the terrain to the west of the River **Saône,** from **Mâcon** down to Lyon, the strongest visual memories I have of the Beaujolais hills are the ones made up of upturned moulds of hills, studded with clusters of trees and filled in with vineyards and numerous increasingly prosperous villages. Flowers and roses are especially profuse. This is a land of wines and roses – literally.

Immediately behind the Beaujolais "moulds" are the higher hills of Charolais country: forested, cool, emerald terrain ignored by all but a few enterprising tourists.

Locals say there are three rivers: the Rhône, Saône and the Beaujolais. Absolutely right. There are hundreds of *vignerons* who will gladly sell you their fruity red Gamay wines. Look out, too, for rarer white and *crémant* varieties. I suggest you ask the many chefs in my various culinary guides for advice on where to buy the best wines.

One supplier is Antoine Pein at **Theizé** (115:F1). Buy his reds and cross your fingers that he has sparkling and sweet wines in stock. The terrain around Theizé sparkles in another way – known by the colourful phrase of *au pays des pierres dorées*. Buildings are constructed of the local stone – a golden-textured, warm material, much darker than Cotswold stone. Villages glow with good health – especially in the late afternoon. Enjoy Theizé, perched high at 1600 ft above sea-level and with views south to the Monts du Lyonnais and Mont d'Or, Lyon's northern guardian; nearby **Oingt** – once a strong fortress and on the first weekend in Sept the home of France's oldest mechanical organ festival; further west is **Ternand** (115:E1) – a minute, centuries-old perched hamlet; and to the north, at **Vaux-en-Beaujolais** (102:A4), soak up the charm of Gabriel Chevallier's *Clochemerle pays*.

There's much else to distract you in Beaujolais as you meander through the wine villages (**Fleurie** is my favourite: B3) – from one *dégustation* to another. Drive up to the crests above the villages. Map 102 shows many a viewpoint: the most renowned is La Terrasse, just west of Fleurie where, on clear days – rare in summer – there are vast views east, to the Jura and the Alps. Mont Brouilly, too (B4), is worth a detour; descend by the lane to the east, down to St-Lager.

Solutré (B3) is a good starting point if you enter Beaujolais from the Mâconnaise hills. You'll get your first views of the startling perpendicular cliff from the slopes above Berzé-la-Ville. Make the navigation effort to drive the lanes which encircle the historic rock face; then be certain to spare time for the first-class Musée de Solutré which explains the intriguing prehistoric finds made in the area and especially those at the foot of the high limestone outcrop.

A handful of châteaux are located in the hills: among them the château at Corcelles (B3), south-east of Fleurie – more a fortress with several towers, each with sharply-pointed roofs; Pierreclos (B2), north-west of Solutré – with Romanesque church, medieval kitchens and bakery, gardens and wine museum; nearby St-Point (to the west) – a 12th-century and neo-Gothic mix of architecture; and the park and 18th-century Adour château south of Dompierre-les-Ormes (A2). (Note, too, the 45-acre arboretum and lake at nearby Pezanin – with over 400 varieties, many from the Far East.) As a contrast there are two automobile museums: one at **Chauffailles** (101:F3); and another collection at **La Clayette** château (101:E3) – the latter building a mix of

14th century and 19th-century Gothic bordering a large lake (the site of a famed *spectacle* in July and August; for details tel 85 28 23 02).

What lies to the east of the River Saône? Called La Bresse, the contrast in landscape is remarkable. South of the **A40** *autoroute* is **La Dombes** – terrain peppered with *étangs* (pools or ponds). Around **Vonnas** (C3), a four-star *village fleuri* with trees and fountains, the land is gently undulating and wooded; further south the countryside is flatter and there are pools by the hundreds.

The latter area is a birdwatchers' paradise. Where better to start than the magnificent Parc Ornithologique at **Villars-les-Dombes** (C4); the reserve houses many hundreds of species, some on pools and others in large, open cages. There's a Maison de la Dombes (and tourist office) at the park (open Fri/Sat/Sun). Ask them for a copy, in English, of the Dombes Lakes Route (if closed, the leaflet is on display in the window). This sets out two routes around the *étangs*: I cannot recommend them enough – even if you only do them in part. For example, near Bouligneux (C4), the site of a small red-brick château with lop-sided tower, are two *étangs*: north of the village is the Etang le Château; and to the south, the especially nice Etang Forêt. At every *étang* on the two routes boards provide details of each pool.

Both north and south of the A40 are numerous *villages fleuris*. Don't miss St-Jean-sur-Reyssouze (C2), south-east of **Pont-de-Vaux**; St-Didier-d'Aussiat (C2), between St-Jean and Vonnas (C3); Vonnas itself; and another four-star winner, **Châtillon-sur-Chalaronne** (C4). Enjoy the pleasures of ancient timbered buildings (especially the 14th-century covered market), the eye-catching river through the town, the Saturday morning market, and the *triptych* (1527) in the town hall (enter and ask to see the handsome paintings).

What of the area to the north of the A40? There's a collection of over 30 superb examples of Bressane farmhouses with *cheminées sarrasines* (Saracen chimneys). Apart from the multi-varied chimneys, each built in a different style, some of the farms have other interesting features. Because so many of these farms are on map 103 I have discussed the subject in the chapter which follows. But, if time allows, navigate the lanes to spots utterly ignored by tourists: Bâgé-le-Châtel (C2), once the capital of La Bresse, with a château and *église*; nearby St-André, with a Romanesque church; Crottet (C3), south of the A40, where there's another *église*; the 13th-century Tour de l'Horloge (clocktower) at Pont-de-Veyle (C3); and, to finish, something colourfully different, the modern Château d'Epeyssoles, on the north side of the D26C between Vonnas and Mézeriat – with its own *étang* and gazebo.

I've devoted five pages to the map sheet 102 terrain and I finish knowing that I have only scratched the surface. Many a site has been missed and, worse still, I have made no mention of the bountiful larder that awaits you – especially in La Bresse: *French Leave Encore* gives you all the mouthwatering details.

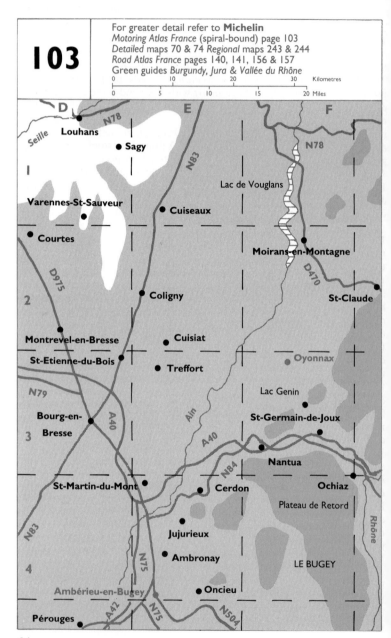

103

For greater detail refer to **Michelin**
Motoring Atlas France (spiral-bound) page 103
Detailed maps 70 & 74 *Regional* maps 243 & 244
Road Atlas France pages 140, 141, 156 & 157
Green guides *Burgundy, Jura & Vallée du Rhône*

| 0 | 10 | 20 | 30 | Kilometres |

| 0 | 5 | 10 | 15 | 20 Miles |

D **E** **F**

Seille

N78

Louhans

● **Sagy**

N83

I

Lac de Vouglans

N78

Varennes-St-Sauveur

● **Cuiseaux**

● **Courtes**

Moirans-en-Montagne

D975

D470

2

● **Coligny**

St-Claude

Montrevel-en-Bresse

● **Cuisiat**

Oyonnax

St-Etienne-du-Bois

● **Treffort**

N79

Lac Genin

Ain

Bourg-en-Bresse

A40

St-Germain-de-Joux

3

A40

N84

Nantua

St-Martin-du-Mont ●

● **Cerdon**

Ochiaz

Plateau de Retord

N83

Rhône

● **Jujurieux**

● **Ambronay**

LE BUGEY

4

N75

Ambérieu-en-Bugey

● **Oncieu**

A42

N75

N504

Pérouges ●

94

The introductory paragraph to map sheet 102 is as valid here. Map sheet 103 is a mixture of unassuming but intriguing country: the eastern half of La Bresse (the map's left side); the south-western flanks of the Jura; and the mountains of **Le Bugey** (bottom right-hand corner).

I'll begin in the relatively flat La Bresse landscape. **Louhans** (D1) makes a good starting point. See the Hôtel-Dieu with its fascinating *apothicairerie* – both of which capture the atmosphere and authenticity of a hospital a century ago (March to Sept: 10.30, 14.30. 16.00 on Mon and Wed to Sat). Admire, too, the old arcaded streets and the handsome *église* clock tower. Visit the Musée de l'Imprimerie – a real newspaper printing workshop (p.m. mid May to end Sept; not Tues). The latter is one of many satellite sites of the enterprising Ecomusée de la Bresse Bourguignonne at the Château de Pierre-de-Bresse (88:C3). The museum explains the landscape, architecture, traditions, handicraft and activities of Bresse – past and present (p.m. all year).

Two other *ecomusée* sites on 103 are: La Tuilerie (tile factory) at **Varennes-St-Sauveur** (D1: a.m. July/Aug); and Le vigneron et sa vigne (the vine-grower and his vine) at the Château des Princes d'Orange in **Cuiseaux** (E1: p.m. mid May to end Sept; not Mon).

Moulins (mills) played a vital part in the economy of La Bresse in times past. Here are three: the Moulin de Bourgchâteau (now an hotel), beside the Seille and just north of Louhans (east of Chalon road) – client or not call in to see the mill machinery; the Moulin de la Croix at Ratte (D1), north-east of Louhans; and the isolated Moulin de Cornon at Romenay (102:C1). Romenay also has two museums: de la Volaille explains the importance of the famed Bresse poultry; du Terroir evokes the agricultural past of the area (p.m. July/Aug).

There are some fine houses and buildings to seek out. The 17th-century Maison du Bailli at **Sagy** (D1); see, too, the restored Bressane farm on the south exit with its small museum of mill machinery at the rear (Sat in July/Aug). Flacey-en-Bresse (E1), east of Sagy, has an especially fine 14th-century *Bourgeoise* house and Romenay has ancient 14th-century gates and a particularly evocative half-timbered *maison*.

The most appealing buildings in La Bresse are the farms with *cheminées sarrasines* (Saracen chimneys). However enigmatic the origin of the chimneys one fact is certain: they were designed and built with local materials by Bressans. There are dozens, each with a different chimney. Here are three of the best. La Ferme de la Forêt (on map), east of **Courtes** (D2); the 17th-century farm is also a rural museum (the interior recaptures the character of the place in centuries past; p.m. mid June to mid Sept). La Ferme des Mangettes, on the west side of the N83 south of **St-Etienne-du-Bois** (D3): 16th century, half-timbered, small red bricks, chimney (p.m. July/Aug). La Ferme du Sougey, west of **Montrevel-en-Bresse** (D2: open all year). Many others are near St-Trivier (102:C2); details from the tourist office.

What else can I draw your attention to in La Bresse? One must is the

95

Eglise de Brou, beside the N75 to the south-east of **Bourg-en-Bresse** (D3). This 16th-century Gothic church is full of treasures: admire the stained glass windows, the oak choir stalls, the chapels and tombs, the cool cloisters and, in the adjoining monastery, the Ain Museum. Another priority visit must be to the hill-top citadel of **Pérouges**, south of La Bresse (116:C1). Four hundred years ago Pérouges was a thriving community with a population of 2,000; three centuries later the village had all but fallen into ruin and had no more than 50 inhabitants. Parts of Pérouges were demolished in 1909 but, thankfully, many residents (led by Anthèlme Thibault) fought to preserve and protect the village. Walk the cobbled streets, soak up the dream-like atmosphere of the tufa stone and half-timbered houses and seek out the huge lime tree at the heart of the medieval fortified village.

Let's look now at the wooded Jura hills – a series of north to south ridges and valleys – to the immediate east of the N83 (D3 to E1). Start in Cuiseaux. Park the car and walk the narrow streets, a medieval Aladdin's Cave. Enjoy arcades, fountains, old *portes* (gates), ramparts, *lavoir* (wash-house), the Château des Princes d'Orange, the *église* with its choir stalls, the 16th-century Maison de l'Echauguette, old houses with restored stone work and much else besides. (Ask at the tourist office for English notes on the signposted route.)

You'll see few tourists once you head into the hills. Here's a typical route – one of many. Leave the N83 south of **Coligny** (E2) and head for Salavre, Verjon and Pressiat (all E2). These villages, like others to the east, are still many decades back in time: roses, lilies, flowers, vines, goats, chickens, wash-houses, churches and old houses appeal. Pressiat is rated a two-star *village fleuri* – an accolade shared with others in the Ain *département* and to the immediate west: Marboz (D2), Viriat, Attignat and St-Etienne-du-Bois (all D3).

Now press on to **Cuisiat** (E2) and the fascinating Musée du Revermont (the local *pays*). Once the village primary school, the neat and tidy building is a museum on the life of the local people during the last two centuries; Anne and I found the orchard and kitchen garden just as tempting as the interior exhibits (p.m. May to Oct). **Treffort** (E3), too, is in a time warp. Though Treffort has no official *village fleuri* tag the place is nevertheless a flower-filled picture. Between the village centre and the D52 seek out the *fromagerie*: you can see the owners making *Comté* cheese, *fromage blanc*, cream and butter and, in turn, you can buy their wares and other cheeses as well.

In the past we have driven the attractive roads alongside the River **Ain**. Gorges de l'Ain says the map (E3): inevitably there are many dams, all with snaking lakes behind them, as you head upstream. The **Lac de Vouglans** (F1/F2) is much the largest, most scenic and offers a range of watersport opportunities; the various blue dots on the map indicate swimming facilities. Something new is the fascinating Musée du Jouet at **Moirans-en-Montagne** (F2), a striking structure which tells you, with the help of hundreds of exhibits, all you need to know about toys and how they are made (a.m./p.m. May to Sept but not Mon; a.m./p.m. Oct to Apl but not Mon, Sat p.m. and Sun a.m.).

St-Claude (104:A2) has long been a favourite of mine. 200 years ago the town prospered because of its reputation for making the world's finest pipe briars. St-Claude tumbles down from the hills to the floor of the Bienne and Tacon valleys. There's a fine Gothic cathedral (with stained-glass windows and glorious choir stalls) and a pipe museum. Make a special point of crossing, on foot, the Pont de Pierre (between town exits 1 and 4) and the Grand Pont (exit 3): views of the town, rivers, hills and older, smaller bridges below you. Anne and I have spent many happy hours, in every season, in the maze of lanes to the south of St-Claude: tranquil forested slopes and wild spring flowers galore beguile. Another new attraction is the Maison des Fromages at Les Moussières (104:A2), about 15 km south of St-Claude; learn how *Bleu de Gex*, *Comté*, *Morbier* and other cheeses are made.

Without fail head for **Lac Genin** (F3), the smallest of small lakes. An unspoilt emerald, the lake is protected by a circular couch of wooded cushions of beech, pine and spruce. During the week your only companions will be goldcrests hovering around your head like humming birds. Busier sites lie to the south-west: the lake at **Nantua** (F3) – try a cruise on a small paddle boat, the *Mississippi*; and both La Cuivrerie (where copper goods, of every kind, are made: open every day) and the *grottes* at **Cerdon** (E4: May to Sept). See, too, the huge Monument de la Résistance beside the N84, east of Cerdon.

The bottom right-hand corner of 103 is the northern half of Bugey. I shall tell you more about this mysterious *pays* in map sheet chapter 117. But I'll finish 103 by providing you with a few access options to Bugey. Two are from the north: either the D101 from **Ochiaz** (F3) or the D55 from **St-Germain-de-Joux** (F3). In early June the pastures around the Col de Bérentin (F3) resemble fields of snow; in reality gargantuan duvets of wild narcissi. A few weeks earlier vast swathes of yellow jonquils flood the same **Plateau de Retord** (F4).

Another access is from the west. Start at **St-Martin-du-Mont** (E4), south-east of Bourg-en-Bresse. Enjoy the views and, if you're a walker, study the plan of eight marked walks outside the *mairie*. Use the lane to Neuville-sur-Ain (E4); at the bridge over the Suran there's an enchanting vista of a weir and jade-shaded pool. **Jujurieux** (E4) claims to have 12 châteaux: make the detour if only to see two of the 12 – the Château de Valence and Château de Chenavel. Detour south to the old abbey church at **Ambronay** (F4) and then back into the hills for a dramatic climb to Boyeux-St-Jérôme. Continue south-east to Résinand. (Did you spot Le Boomerang, an Aussie restaurant, just north of the latter?) On through wooded hills to **Oncieu** (E4). This little working hamlet, shining with pride and character, is full of visual surprises; be sure to walk the circular lane.

97

105

For greater detail refer to **Michelin**
Motoring Atlas France (spiral-bound) page 105
Detailed maps 70 & 74 *Regional* maps 243 & 244
Road Atlas France pages 143, 158 & 159
Green guides *Alpes du Nord & Switzerland*

0   10   20   30   Kilometres

0   5   10   15   20 Miles

D   E   F

N1

N12

1

Lausanne

Lac Léman

Montreux

Rhône

N9

Yvoire

Evian-les-Bains

Thonon-les-Bains

N5

Bernex

2

Gorges du Pont du Diable

Avoriaz

SUISSE

3

Morzine

D902

Martigny

Col de Joux Plane

Cirque du Fer à Cheval

Barrage d'Emosson

Bonneville

Samoëns

Champex
→

A40

Cluses

Col des Montets

4

Sallanches

Arve

CHAINE DU

Chamonix

CHAINE

MONT BLANC

DES ARAVIS

St-Gervais-les-Bains

ITALIE

I'm halfway through *Mapaholics' France* and, at last, I have arrived in the terrain which I rate as one of my favourite parts of France – or, to be more specific, the area around the **Chaîne du Mont Blanc** (F4 and 119:E1). Readers of my earlier books will already know that I spent the first ten years of my life in the high Himalayas. As a result I have an insatiable love for lofty heights. No other mountain area in Europe excites me more than the varied peaks in the Mont Blanc *massif*.

If you approach Mont Blanc from the north you have two alternative routes to choose from. The less likely route is from **Martigny** (F3) in Switzerland. However impatient you may be to reach **Chamonix** (F4) make an absolutely essential detour, shortly before you reach the French border, to the **Barrage d'Emosson** (F3). The skyscraper-high dam is not far short of 7000 ft above sea-level; your reward is a spellbinding panorama of the entire Mont Blanc *chaîne*.

The second alternative approach is from Genève (104:C3) on either the **A40** or N205. At **Sallanches** (E4) turn right and climb on the D113, past numerous colourful chalets, to Cordon: once again, the panorama of the western end of the *chaîne* is breathtaking.

However impressive these two long-distance panoramas are nothing compares with the views of the mountain wall towering above you in the Chamonix Valley; these are at their best from the lanes which climb the hillside on the north-west side of the 3400 ft-high resort. Across the valley, to your right, is the mystical snow-covered dome of the 15771 ft-high Mont Blanc (119:E3), glaciers tumbling down its northern face. In front of you, and to your left, are numerous razor-sharp rock needles (*aiguilles*), set in a jagged line across the eastern horizon.

There's always enough to keep you busy in Chamonix however long you stay. The various "transport" attractions cost money. First, the cable-car climb to Aiguille du Midi, a spiky finger of rock, 12605 ft-high (done in two sections; and, if you have the time, the five-km gondola ride across the Vallée Blanche (119:E3) to Italy). Second, the less exciting cable-car climb ascent of Le Brévent (F4), one of the summits in the Aiguilles Rouges range; the panorama across the valley includes seven peaks in excess of 4000 m. Third, the gentle and relaxing rack (cog-rail) railway to the Mer de Glace at Montenvers (make the further ascent to the ice cave in the glacier, carved out anew each year). Fourth, the sedate Tramway du Mont Blanc, another rack system, which starts from Le Fayet (E4), climbs through the spa of **St-Gervais-les-Bains** (119-D1), to the 7782 ft-high terminus at Le Nid d'Aigle (119:E1). Finally, the rail line which links Chamonix to Martigny shows off many facets of the Alpine world: isolated villages, roaring streams, deep gorges, dense forests, high peaks and emerald pastures. We've done them all – and others, too.

Sporting enthusiasts have a range of options. Golf, on one of the most exhilarating courses in the Alps; tennis, swimming and ice-skating (both the latter are covered, open-all-year facilities) in a fabulous sports

99

complex; rafting and canoeing from the Base Hydroglisse, alongside the Arve and the Centre Sportif; hang-gliding from the peaks reached by cable-car; a summer *luge* on the slopes behind the Mer de Glace terminus in Chamonix; and walks and climbs galore – exercise which costs nowt. There's an excellent guide for walkers and climbers: *Mont Blanc Trails* (in English) provides details, plus a first-class map, on 162 summer walks and hikes – each one categorised according to difficulty. A favourite walk of ours starts after the *téléférique* and *télécabine* ride from Les Praz (F4) to L'Index; walk north-east to Lac Blanc and then descend to the intermediate station at La Flégère. Flora and fauna fans should seek out two sites: the Parc de Merlet, a 57-acre reserve of mountain animals west of Les Bossons (E4); and the easy path which features many varieties of Alpine flowers and plants at the **Col des Montets** (F4), part of La Reserve des Aiguilles Rouges.

Let's head north. Make your first port of call the Giffre Valley and the **Cirque du Fer à Cheval** (E3/E4). As you approach **Samöens** (E3) you'll see a handful of pyramid-shaped peaks to the north of the three-star *village fleuri*. One treat at the village is the seven-acre hillside Jardin Alpin de La Jaysinia – an extrovert mix of cascades and paths among thousands of Alpine plants from five continents (a.m. and p.m. every day). The Cirque du Fer à Cheval, in two distinct amphitheatre halves, is a rewarding dead-end road: glaciers, both snow-topped and rocky peaks (one a rhino horn shape), and a dozen waterfalls appeal. An essential detour south from Sixt is the Cascade du Rouget (E4). The waterfall, in two parts, is more a river falling over a cliff edge. The D29 runs immediately below the fall, so close you could wash your car in the spray. Walk up the natural stone staircase to hear the roar, feel the spray and to admire the rainbow.

The **Col de Joux Plane** (E3) has long been a renowned Tour de France cycle race climb. From the south you climb through broadleaved trees and pines to pastures of wild flowers and a small pool at the summit. The views are stupendous: the whole Mont Blanc range, including the Grandes Jorasses (119:E1), fills the southern horizon.

Morzine (E3) has many sporting facilities: a large swimming pool, covered all-seasons ice rink, new golf course, tennis, and walks and climbs by the score. The best of the resort is the older part to the south. Drive up the D338 hairpins: as you climb hang-gliders swoop past you going the other way. The ski-station of **Avoriaz** is a spectacular sight at the top of the Ardoisières Valley: from a distance some of the buildings appear almost as extensions of the dark rock faces. As you descend on the D338 towards Les Lindarets keep a sharp look out for the Dents du Midi to the south-east (F3).

Les Lindarets is a tiny hamlet with old chalets; count yourself lucky if you encounter a herd of goats sunning themselves on the road – as we did. The Lac de Montriond (E3), in the wooded valley below, is as green a lake as you'll ever see. Further north the **Gorges du Pont du Diable**

(D2) is a big tourist attraction (May to Sept). After you pay your money there's a steep descent to a suspended walkway past falls of rock and alongside the Dranse, part of which is subterranean. (The dam upstream has taken the sting out of the river's fast flow.)

Typical of many mountain drives in Le Chablais (D2/E2) is the D122 which winds up through La Forclaz to the Col du Grand Taillet (D2): you get terrific views south of both the Dranse Gorge and the man-made lake. Over the top the vistas change: gentler hills, cultivated fields and many more houses. **Bernex** (E2), beneath several rock peaks to the east, is another unspoilt plus. The small lake at La Beunaz (you pay for the *plage*) is so well hidden by trees you can easily pass the spot by. But you'll not miss **Lac Léman**: your first views of the gigantic arc of water are from the lanes near St-Paul-en-Chablais (D2).

As hard as I have tried over several decades I have never taken to the resorts on the French side of Lac Léman. **Evian-les-Bains** (D2) has a large slice of style: flowers are everywhere; there's a shady tree-lined lakeside promenade; and, at the heart of the spa, you'll relish a chocolate-box selection of mouthwatering buildings. The Jardin Japonais is an eye-pleasing pleasure and steamer trips on the lake (including a service to **Lausanne**) are a big bonus. **Thonon-les-Bains** (D2) has two parts: the lakeside port area has a Med feel; and a funicular takes you up to the ridge above Lac Léman where delightful gardens and views are the scenic highlights. Don't miss the picture postcard multi-towered Château de Ripaille, to the north, famed for its vineyards (a classic Savoie Chasselas grape white wine) and 47-acre arboretum. Excenevex (104:C2) has a great sandy beach.

On no account miss the stunning small medieval lakeside village of **Yvoire** (104:C2) – the epitome of a *village fleuri*. Man and Nature have succeeded too well; the honeypot hive is overrun by tourist swarms. The shops, too, are full of Far Eastern junk. All is forgotten when you enter Le Jardin des Cinq Sens at Yves and Anne-Monique d'Yvoire's château and the couple's newly-created delectable *labyrinthe* of small gardens which, in turn, appeal to each of the five senses. The property is open every day from May to Oct; try to avoid weekends.

Two final suggestions. Number one. I've written elsewhere about the **Chaîne des Aravis** (118/119). Make the scenically super *déviation* from Thorens-Glières to the Col des Glières (104:C4) – the site of the battle on March 26, 1944 between Savoie *maquisards* and a force of 5,000 Germans and French Vichy *miliciens*. At the col there are maps and a monument which explain the battle. See map sheet chapter 118/119 for details of the cemetery and museum near Thônes (C1).

Number two. Lack of space prevents me from writing about the Swiss treats on 105. But there's one gem you must unearth – the prettiest of pretty lakes. From Martigny Bourg (F4) head south and take the narrow road which climbs the Gorges du Durnand to the tiny lake and village at **Champex** – a superb mix of *lac*, forests, peaks and isolation.

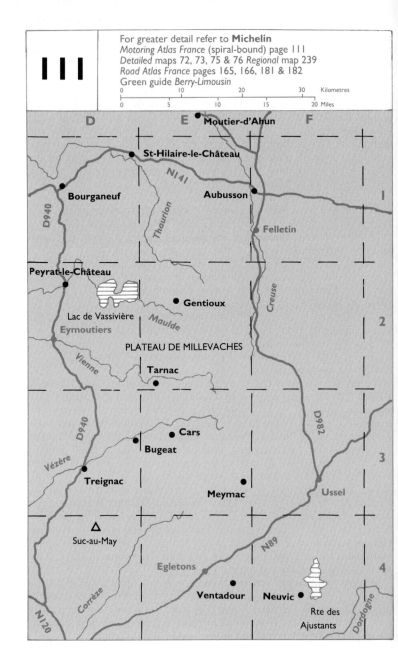

For greater detail refer to **Michelin**
Motoring Atlas France (spiral-bound) page 111
Detailed maps 72, 73, 75 & 76 *Regional* map 239
Road Atlas France pages 165, 166, 181 & 182
Green guide *Berry-Limousin*

Kilometres
Miles

D **E** Moutier-d'Ahun **F**

St-Hilaire-le-Château

N141

Bourganeuf

Aubusson

D940

Thaurion

Felletin

1

Peyrat-le-Château

Gentioux

Creuse

Lac de Vassivière

Maulde

Eymoutiers

2

PLATEAU DE MILLEVACHES

Tarnac

Vienne

D940

Cars

D982

Bugeat

Vézère

Treignac

Meymac

3

Ussel

△
Suc-au-May

N89

Egletons

4

Ventadour

Neuvic

Corrèze

Rte des
Ajustants

Dordogne

N120

102

If you travel to every corner of France for 40 years and drive a high six-figure number of miles along the nation's minor roads, as I have done, you will eventually grasp that there is no shortage of trees. I read last year that 27% of France's land mass is tree-covered – as against 7% in England. I'll not quibble over those statistics as I've seen the evidence for myself. Here, on map sheet 111, and also on 125 to the south, I reckon well over half the terrain must be tree-covered – a veritable arboretum of every variety imaginable: beech, oak, chestnut, silver birch, walnut, poplar, pine and numerous others.

Map 111 leads you to the very heart of Limousin, a region of three *départements*: Haute-Vienne, Corrèze and Creuse. The sheet includes the southern corners of the pastoral Creuse and the northern parts of the forested Corrèze. If you look hard at the centre of the map sheet you'll spot the words **Plateau de Millevaches** (E2/F2) – a large circle of country which is the very essence of unheralded Limousin.

Plateau de Millevaches: was there ever a name more likely to put off tourists? Millevaches, in this case, does not translate as a "thousand cows". The word *vaches* derives from the Celtic *batz*, meaning spring or source. The plateau, and much of the encircling terrain, is a vast granite table, topped with an absorbent covering of springs, streams, myriad trees, broom, heather, peat bogs and, here and there, long fingers and knuckles of soft, wooded hills. Many great French rivers rise on the plateau: the **Vienne** (source E3) and **Creuse** flow north to the Loire; the **Vézère** and **Corrèze** wind south to the **Dordogne**. Dozens of lesser streams feed these important tributaries.

This is a landscape of sunshine and showers and self-effacing charms. The *pays* is for dawdling, for walking, for cycling and for relishing both flora and fauna. You and Nature will be quite alone. Sophisticates, searching for the high life, must seek "chic" elsewhere.

Make a start in the bottom right-hand corner where the Dordogne cuts a deep, placid course, courtesy of man-made dams, through wooded hills. From the D982 take the D168, the **Route des Ajustants**, to the Belvédère de Gratte-Bruyère (F4). In September enjoy the heather beside the road; in October the autumn tints. At the rocky viewpoint stand and listen. No traffic, no trains and no houses; just bird calls. Similar eye-catching vistas of an impotent lake can be enjoyed from the Site de St-Nazaire (112:A4), beyond the Barrage de Marèges (F4).

Seek out the Lac de la Triouzoune, east of **Neuvic** (F4). A wooded lane encircles the lake; there's a beach and watersport facilities. The Puy de Manzagol is a 693 metre-high viewpoint with a *table d'orientation*: what a pity trees and shrubs spoil some of the views. In Neuvic nose out the Musée de la Résistance Henri Queuille, 100 m south of the *mairie*. Henri Queuille, twice prime minister of France, was born in the town and the museum occupies what was once the family home. The museum tells the story of the Haute-Corrèze *maquis* (and the wretched *déportations*); there are numerous exhibits, pictures and links with RAF

103

crews (a.m. and p.m. every day May to Sept; p.m. only every day in Oct).

West on the D991. The ruins of the Château de **Ventadour** (E4) are worth the detour – just. The 12th-century castle, once impregnable, had links with the revolutionary *troubadours* (Bernard de Ventadour, a baker's son, was one of the finest masters of the lyrical and literary art form) and the Hundred Years War. Little remains of the fortress and what does is in a dangerous condition. Use your imagination to conjure up an image of the castle, in all its glory, centuries ago.

North-west to the **Suc-au-May** (D4), in the richly wooded Massif des Monédières. Do a clockwise circuit and then climb to the observation platform atop the 2989 ft summit. The panorama is superb: surrounding you is Limousin and, to the east, the volcanic cones of Auvergne line the horizon. In August the *massif* is renowned for heather and *myrtilles* (bilberries). **Treignac** (D3), to the north, has a splendid site above the Vézère and many evocative medieval buildings.

One of the most amazing roads I have ever seen in France is the D979E from **Meymac** (E3: see the Romanesque *église* and the nearby old houses) to **Bugeat** (D3), signposted as the "Route des Hêtres". The road climbs and winds and, for 13 miles of the route, 200-year-old beech trees run more or less uninterrupted, on one side or other and often on both flanks. Napoléon's legacy of tree planting may not have benefited his armies much, but modern generations reap a rich dividend. In October the run is akin to driving past an honour guard of thousands of giant soldiers cloaked and hatted in shining gold and copper uniforms.

Six km before Bugeat detour north to the Ruines Gallo-Romaines des **Cars** (E3). There are two sites. The first, Le Sanctuaire, is the granite ruins of a temple and mausoleum. 300 yards away, down a track, is the more interesting L'Habitat du Vallon, once a residence with all sorts of 2nd-century luxury mod-cons; note the huge stone reservoir.

Many minor roads provide ideal spots for picnics – especially those with streams running alongside them. One is the Vézère beside the D164 from St-Merd-les-Oussines (E3) to Bugeat. Another is the infant **Thaurion** flowing under the D16 north of **Gentioux** (E2); here the added plus is the ruins of what was once a Roman bridge.

Tarnac (E2) is a smasher: a tiny 12/13th-century church; two oak trees – one planted in 1605 and recently pruned, the other in 1848; attractive lanes spread spider's legs in all directions; and a fine *pâtisserie* which defies economic logic in such a remote community.

The **Lac de Vassivière** (D2) is one of the better man-made lakes. Much of the charm of the 2,500-acre sheet of water comes from the series of coves and inlets, from the forests surrounding the lake, and from the sensible way the amenities and camping sites have been commercialised. For sports' enthusiasts there's much to enjoy: several beaches, riding, sailing, canoeing, *pédalos*, wind surfing and water skiing. For the less energetic there are gentle walks, motor boats, fishing and even water bus trips in craft based at the western end of the lake.

Do walk across a long concrete bridge to the wooded parkland on the Ile de Vassivière. There you'll see numerous modern sculptures, created by chiselers from around the globe, set out on both the grassy slopes and in the woods. You'll chuckle; you'll scratch your head; you'll possibly boo. Somehow though the lumps of stone graft well onto the verdant scene. One sculpture, by Andy Goldsworthy, is worth the long walk: a giant stone figure 8 with closely-planted mature trees in one of the loops, the other sloping down to the water and disappearing under the surface; the piece of work is enormously imaginative. Three years ago a new centre for contemporary art was opened on the island.

To the north of the lake is one of the most alluring enclaves of *pays*. A combination of factors gel to create a perfect rural landscape: streams, waterfalls, hidden valleys, distant views, old farms and smart houses, contented villages, birds of prey, brown hens scuttling away, milk chocolate Limousin cattle (you may even see two oxen hauling a cart full of logs – as I once did), differing-shaped churches and numerous woods with beautiful trees. Start at **Peyrat-le-Château** (D2): use the D68, D51A, St-Martin-Château (D1), D51, D13, St-Pardoux-Morterolles, D58, St-Pierre-Bellevue, D34, and finish at **St-Hilaire-le-Château** (D1). Don't miss the walk, through the trees, down to the Cascade des Jarreaux (signs say Jarrauds), north of St-Martin.

At St-Hilaire you could make the short dash west to **Bourganeuf** (D1: market day Wed a.m.), once the regional capital of the Templars and renowned for its medieval tower which was the prison for Prince Zizim, an Ottoman prince, held captive by the knights in 1483.

East to **Aubusson** (F1) and the Musée de la Tapisserie, dedicated to Jean Lurçat (1892-1966) who, from the mid 30s to his death, did so much to revitalise the ancient skills of the town's weavers. The museum houses both traditional and modern tapestries in its spacious, well-lit halls. Some modern tapestries, created from today's complete spectrum of wools, not available in the past, are stunning walls of colour. During the 80s I've been enthralled by the modern work of Lurçat, Dom Robert, Marc Saint-Saëns, Gaston Thiery and others. (Closed Tues.)

Use the D18 from Aubusson and follow the seductive left bank of the Creuse downstream. Stop at the medieval church of La Rochette (E1), with its black-spiked "hat" tower. Continue on the D18, D18A and C3 to a delectable picnic spot, on the map just below the "C" in Les Chambons (98:B4). Is there anything better for a picnic than the sound of running water, relaxing under the shade of a large tree, and watching two hoopoes at work and play? We were lucky indeed that glorious day.

Finish with a crescendo. At **Moutier-d'Ahun** (98:B4) seek out the 15th-century *église*, part Romanesque, part Gothic (open 9-12 and 14-18 hours). Within its interior is an exceptional treasure: the wooden sculptures, carved 300 years ago, of the choir stalls and altar surrounds. The oak shines as proudly as do the sculptor's skills: there are hundreds of carvings – of faces, figures, flora and fauna.

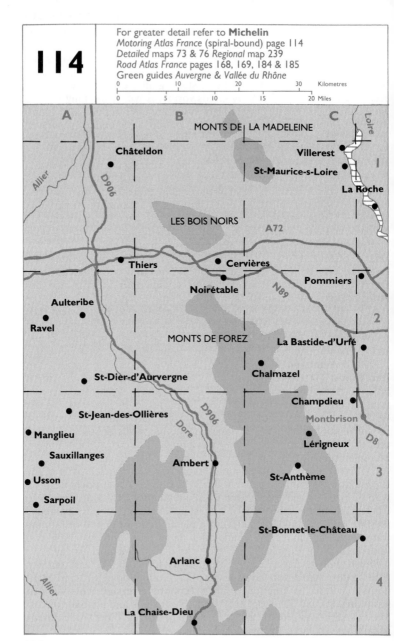

114

For greater detail refer to **Michelin**
Motoring Atlas France (spiral-bound) page 114
Detailed maps 73 & 76 *Regional* map 239
Road Atlas France pages 168, 169, 184 & 185
Green guides *Auvergne & Vallée du Rhône*

| 0 | 10 | 20 | 30 | Kilometres |

| 0 | 5 | 10 | 15 | 20 Miles |

A   B   C

Loire

MONTS DE LA MADELEINE

Châteldon

Villerest

St-Maurice-s-Loire

La Roche

Allier

D906

LES BOIS NOIRS

A72

1

Thiers

Cervières

Pommiers

Noirétable

N89

Aulteribe

MONTS DE FOREZ

La Bastide-d'Urfé

2

Ravel

St-Dier-d'Aurvergne

Chalmazel

Champdieu

St-Jean-des-Ollières

D906

Montbrison

D8

Manglieu

Dore

Lérigneux

Sauxillanges

Ambert

Usson

St-Anthème

3

Sarpoil

St-Bonnet-le-Château

Arlanc

Allier

4

La Chaise-Dieu

Can you drive for three days through some of France's most unspoilt corners without seeing more than a handful of non French-registered cars? Yes, you can: this chapter will confirm my claim. I shall also prove another aspect of my mapaholic philosophy: get off the beaten track and you'll be rewarded by a rich harvest of surprises.

Start with a view of some of the terrain you're about to explore. Drive up to **Usson** (113:E3/114:A3) and then walk to the Statue de la Vierge on top of the basalt peak: the wooded Livradois hills to the east will be your first target. Before you leave see the 15th-century *église* and the photographic museum (May-Sept).

The Livradois is endowed with many Romanesque churches. Before heading north-east detour a few km south to the 12th-century *église* at Mailhat. The small church is a mix of elegant and ornate and austere Auvergne Romanesque; note the scallop shell of St-James. North to **Sauxillanges** and **Manglieu** (both A3) and their Romanesque *églises*; the latter's abbey church is a really fine example.

Now for a more specific panoramic view of a small semi-circle of *pays* which I want to use as a classic example of the point I made in the first paragraph. Drive to the Pic de la Garde (A3), east of Manglieu. Leave the D253 and drive as far as you can; then walk the last 300 m. The 360-degree view is superb; the only blot on the landscape is the ugly quarry below you. At the summit there's another statue of the Virgin Mary and an observation platform created in 1955 by J. Roches. To the west is a long line of high volcanic cones; to the east the wooded Monts du Forez. Our target is immediately to the north.

Start at **St-Jean-des-Ollières** (A3). Leave your vehicle in front of the small but immaculate Romanesque *église* (the car park doubles up as a basketball court); ask for the key at *l'épicerie*. Relish the gorgeous window and seek out "*Je suis la roue des siècles*". Later, call at the tiny *boulangerie*. See and taste some of the breads: the large *couronne* and very tasty *seigle* (a slice or two of this rye *pain* is ideal with cheese or *charcuterie*). On to Fayet-le-Château (A2): note the beehive stone reservoir, old weighbridge and modern green bottle bank (there's always one in the remotest of spots) as you pass through. The château is to the west: the handsome tower, in such a commanding position, would make a great oversized chess piece. Now north to Mauzun and the imposing dark grey stone walled ruins of the strategically sited 12th and 13th-century castle high above the village.

As you drive the lanes among the hills note the *étangs* (pools) and the cemeteries, always 500 m or so from the *église*. South-east now to **St-Dier-d'Auvergne** (A2). Hidden behind the main street is an exquisite 12th-century fortified Romanesque church; ask for the key at the vine-covered house opposite. In the church make a point of looking at the 14 carved stone "pictures" which tell the story of the crucifixion. South of St-Dier detour off the D997 to the small, self-contained Château des Martinanches (A3) with a chapel, moat and woods (p.m. summer only;

107

out of season pop down the drive anyway).

Now I would like to recount a memorable Midsummer's Day Anne and I enjoyed some years ago in the **Monts du Forez**. We headed east from **Ambert** (B3), notable only for the stone-built, circular *mairie*. Much more interesting was the Moulin Richard-de-Bas, still producing hand-made, heavy paper and with an absorbing museum on paper making (open every day). From the *moulin* we climbed north on the D67 (chuckling at the scarecrow wearing a crash helmet), past Rimbaud and Valcivières, and then on the D106 towards the Col des Supeyres (C3: 4481 ft). Looking back the terrain resembled an upturned jelly mould of rounded hills, covered with broadleaved and evergreen trees.

We stopped near Perrier, startled by the colourful meadows straddling the road. Anne quickly identified a score or more of wild flowers: among them dog roses, orchids, marguerites, various-hued field scabious and columbine. Minutes later came another visual extravaganza: at the Col des Supeyres, above the tree line, we thrilled at the sight of pastures whitewashed with wild narcissi and speckled with blue violas, wild geranium cranes-bill, cornflowers and pink polygonum.

For botanists and ornithologists the "Hautes Chaumes", a narrow strip of terrain running north to south above the tree line, at an altitude in excess of 4200 ft, has much to offer: Alpine plants, birds of prey and solitude. Access on foot to this high upland is easy from both the Col des Supeyres and the Col du Béal (B2), further north.

The map identifies many *jasseries* in the Hautes Chaumes. These low, stone-built structures are relics of the past. Once they were used for the making and maturing of the blue-veined cow's milk cheeses called *fourmes*. Now modern methods prevail in factories at lower altitudes. The most respected Forez *fromager* is Roger Col. Don't bypass his Fromagerie de la Genette, 1.8 km south of **St-Anthème** (C3) on the left of the D996. Buy his new creation: a mini *fourme*, "*Fourmette du Livradois*" – a small one-pound cheese, perfect for picnics (Mon to Sat midday).

The *départemental* tourist office makes a song and dance of a noteworthy scenic idea, La Route des Balcons. The only snag is that neither the maps nor any signposts identify the run. On another visit last year we drove the "balcony road" which runs along the eastern flanks of the Monts du Forez. We started at **Cervières** (B1), near the north-eastern edge of the Livradois-Forez regional park and two km from exit 4 on the A72. The tiny 12th-century hamlet is in a time warp. Walk the single street and the lane behind the houses to the north; from the latter enjoy the views of the brooding **Bois Noirs** (B1) and, behind them, the **Monts de la Madeleine** (C1 and 100:D4).

I'll give you a list of road numbers and village names, in north to south order, which will allow you to trace the balcony road on map sheet 114. Cervières, D24, **Noirétable,** D53, D101 (detour to N-D l'Hermitage), Jeansagnière (C2), attractive **Chalmazel** (with dominating five-sided fortress), D101, St-Bonnet-le-Courreau, D20, D44, **Lérigneux** (C3), D44,

D496, La Bruyère, then a minor road to Chazelles-sur-Lavieu (superb views from the Fortunière crest), Gunières, D44, St-Jean-Soleymieux, D5, Marols (C3), Montarcher (C4), D14, **St-Bonnet-le-Château** (115:D4: see the old houses by the church).

What else? There's a Musée de la Dentelle at **Arlanc** (C4), a delight for lace lovers (April/May/June/mid Sept to mid Oct: p.m. July to mid Sept: a.m. and p.m.). More noteworthy Livradois Romanesque churches lie to east and west of Arlanc (which has a magnificent large version of its own): Dore-l'Eglise to the south; Beurières to the east; St-Sauveur, Doranges, Novacelles, St-Bonnet-le-Bourg and St-Germain-l'Herm to the west. For details of **La Chaise-Dieu** (see map sheet 128).

Several châteaux are further north: **Aulteribe** (A2) claims to be one of the finest furnished in France; and both **Ravel** (A2), to the west, and Montmorin (A2), to the south, are 13th-century fortress-like structures. Busy **Thiers** (A1) has an exciting hillside site; the ancient timbered houses and Musée de la Coutellerie are the highlights (the town has been making cutlery for centuries). Drive deep into the sombre pine woods of Les Bois Noirs (B1); use the D64; follow the attractive Credogne Valley (A1); and seek out **Châteldon** (A1) with a stern castle looking down on some old timbered houses.

To the east of the Madeleine and Forez hills man has left a series of mixed legacies. The first is wretched: the flooding of the Loire south of **Villerest** (C1). The winding lake is not unattractive but the sight of a marina and ugly bridge below Bully is a shock. The "new" lake view from **St-Maurice-sur-Loire** will please, as will the 12th-century *église*. But the "island" château at **La Roche** (115:D1), appearing to float on the water, comes as a real poke in the eye.

Others are kinder legacies. The history of **Pommiers** (115:D2) dates back to Roman times: enjoy the photogenic site, austere 12th-century church, chestnut-shaded *place* and 15th-century bridge. The château at **La Bastie-d'Urfé** (115:D2) is a Renaissance structure partly constructed by Italian artisans; the two-level cloister-like terraces and gardens are especially appealing (April to Oct: every day. Rest of year: p.m. but not Tues). **Champdieu** (C3) has two treats: a formidable fortified *église*; and an elegant, covered structure combining toilets, *pissoir*, waiting room, telephone, clock and fountain.

Finally, an eerie twist to paragraph one. **Sarpoil** (A3): June 9, 1993; time 22.45. Pitch black restaurant car park with only a glow worm for company. Car with yellow headlights stops. Lady's voice asks "*Je cherche pour La Chaise-Dieu*." The driver, on her own, is an English lady, of a certain age, in a French-registered car; she's quite lost and is looking for "God's chair" 60 km away. By chance I have map sheet 114 in my hand. I soon set her on her way. Our meeting must have been a million-to-one chance: an Englishman, at dead-of-night, in the middle of nowhere, giving directions to an English lady to a spot he knew well. Who was she? Did she get there safely? Did I dream our meeting?

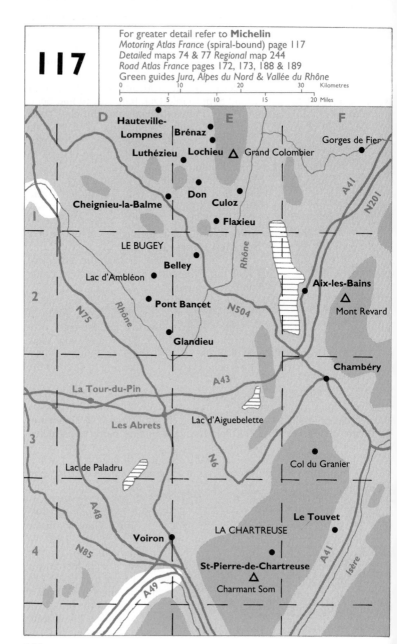

117

For greater detail refer to **Michelin**
Motoring Atlas France (spiral-bound) page 117
Detailed maps 74 & 77 *Regional* map 244
Road Atlas France pages 172, 173, 188 & 189
Green guides *Jura, Alpes du Nord & Vallée du Rhône*

0		10		20		30	Kilometres

| 0 | | 5 | | 10 | | 15 | | 20 Miles |

D

Hauteville-
Lompnes
Brénaz

E

Gorges de Fier

F

Luthézieu
Lochieu
△ Grand Colombier

Don
Culoz

Cheignieu-la-Balme

A41

N201

1

Flaxieu

LE BUGEY

Rhône

Belley

Lac d'Ambléon

Aix-les-Bains

△
Mont Revard

2

N75

Rhône

Pont Bancet

N504

Glandieu

Chambéry

A43

La Tour-du-Pin

Lac d'Aiguebelette

Les Abrets

N6

Col du Granier

3

Lac de Paladru

A48

Le Touvet

Voiron

LA CHARTREUSE

A41

Isère

4

N85

St-Pierre-de-Chartreuse
△
Charmant Som

A49

110

Mapaholic readers of my previous French books will immediately recognise that map sheet 117 allows me to enthuse about two of my favourite parts of France: **Le Bugey** and **La Chartreuse**. Three 46-1ine pages will never do justice to my passion for these two seductive corners.

"Where is Bugey?" I hear you ask. The mountains and valleys between the River Ain to the east (103:E3/E4), the A40 to the north (103:F3) and, to the south, the great "V" formed by the River **Rhône**.

Where do you start? At **Culoz** (E1) where the D120 scrambles up rocky slopes and then through woods to the **Grand Colombier** (E1: 5003 ft). On the way up detour to Fenestrez (E1), a "window" 3000 ft above Culoz. The view is stunning and the acoustics sensational: the chimes of a clock, a dog barking, or a boat chugging along the Rhône – all are many km away but seem to come from a point 20 ft below you.

The views from Grand Colombier are magnificent: Mont Blanc, the Rhône and the Lac du Bourget (E2/F2) are only part of the panorama. To the immediate west is Valromey, a wishbone-shaped valley 100 square miles in size. Visit Valromey in spring and you'll gasp at the wild flower lakes which flood the pastures between the Col de Bérentin (103:F3) and the Crêt du Nu (103:F4); see my notes in map sheet chapter 103.

But whenever you go make the most of the lanes which tumble down from the Grand Colombier and twist north to the Col de Richemont (103:F4). Walks abound and there's many an invigorating visual tonic. At the col you'll see the first of many memorials to the Bugey *maquis*. The Valromey Resistance group was one of the most courageous. Their poignant memorial is beside the D8, west of **Luthézieu** (E1): "*Nous avons combattu avec un tronçon d'epée*" (We fought with a broken sword).

To discover more about Valromey and its brave people visit the Musée Rural du Valromey at **Lochieu** (E1). The museum, once a 16th-century fortified house with unusual medieval windows, has a rare collection of local rural treasures (a.m. and p.m.: mid Apl to mid Oct).

Centuries ago every Bugey village had a *seigneur* and one of his many perks was the right to own the sole oven (*four*). Many are still used. There's an oven at **Don**, north of Artemare (E1); another at Vaux-Morets on the D131D just north of Don; and at Belmont, to the west.

Water and wine have always played an important part in Bugey. First water. Visit four sites. The 300 ft-high Charabotte *chute* (D1), southwest of **Hauteville-Lompnes** (103:F4); the nearby Gorges de l'Albarine is an exciting thrill. Next, the Source du Groin, north of Don (E1); park at Vaux-Morets and walk to the weird 30 metre-deep hole from which gushes water absorbed elsewhere in Valromey. The Cerveyrieu cascade is a 200 ft-high waterfall; access is from the D31 west of Don. The Pain Sucre is another unusual sight, a stalagmite formed by a waterfall below the D30, south-west of **Brénaz** (E1).

Wine? Visit **Flaxieu** (E1) where Camille Crussy supplies many famous restaurants; and Le Caveau Bugiste and Eugene Morin et fils at Vongnes

(E1). Savour sparklers, Chardonnay whites, various varietal reds and *rosés*. The Lac de Barterand (E2) is nearby – best seen from the north where several hilly humps provide a wooded backdrop; there's also a good *plage*. Another famed vineyard produces Manicle, the favourite tipple of Bugey's most illustrious son, Brillat-Savarin. He was born at **Belley** (E2) in 1755; read his *La Physiologie du goût – The Philosopher in the Kitchen* (Penguin p/b). (Read, too, Elizabeth Ayrton's *The Cook's Tale*; an imaginary account of a family and their Belley hotel.) The Miraillet family are restoring Manicle's reputation; their *cave* and home is near the church at **Cheignieu-la-Balme** (D1).

There's more. Nearby Contrevoz (E1) also has a *four* and on the first August weekend there's a mechanical organ fair (biennial: even years). Visit the Château d'Andert, just off the D32 to the south-east: for a 360-degree panorama; the 17th-century château; and a top-notch range of home-made *cassis* products (open every day).

Climb south-west to the **Lac d'Ambléon** (D2); the lake is an emerald gem and there's a super picnic spot; have a look, too, at the *maquis* memorial with a graphic stone carving. Something quite different is the tiny museum, Les Amis des Dinosaures, at Marchamp (D2: p.m. Sun mid Apl to mid Oct; every day summer school hols). In June the roads hereabouts pass through fields full of orchids and wild flowers. Several *vignerons* produce and sell their Bugey wines on the western flanks of the high range overlooking the Rhône: perhaps the most interesting is Les Caves de Groslée at the small medieval Château Vareppe at **Pont Bancet** (D2). Finally, the cascades at **Glandieu** (D2) are best seen from the village and not the road above.

Now to the self-contained visual joys locked within the secretive Chartreuse (E4/F4). I've driven every road in the *massif*; I've visited the mountain fastness in every season. In the spring I've relished the first hints of woodland green and the foaming rivers; in September I've been beguiled by lilac-tinted autumn crocuses and, in October, my eyes have feasted on the rich shades of dying leaves.

There are a dozen or more spots you must seek out. The northern entrance, the **Col du Granier**, is under the brooding eye of the gigantic rock slabs of Mont Granier (F3). The deserted D45 road through Corbel; views are ten a penny. The Gorges du Guiers Vif (E4/F4) thread a steep course through rock walls from the river's source at the Cirque de St-Même (don't miss the latter). The Gorges du Guiers Mort (E4) is an equally spectacular route. The forestry road from the latter to the Belvédère des Sangles is a taxing but rewarding climb. Better still is the ascent from the Col de Porte to the dead-end just below the fabulous viewpionts on the **Charmant Som** (E4).

Locate the Couvent de la Grande Chartreuse (E4) – a barracks-sized monastery hidden in a wooded fold of mountains. No wonder St-Bruno chose the isolated site over 900 years ago as the first home of the Carthusian Order. Some of Europe's first iron and steel foundries (using charcoal) were located in the Chartreuse, created and run by the Carthusians. With the advent of coke-burning smelters, 250 years ago, the mountain industry died. The monks turned to distilling what is now the world's most famous liqueur, Chartreuse. The recipe for the elixir, made from over 100 mountain plants, has been under the guardianship of the Carthusians for over 200 years: today the green and yellow liqueurs, and other varieties, are made at a distillery in **Voiron** (D4/E4: every day Easter to Oct; weekdays only rest of year). The monastery cannot be visited but La Correrie, at the southern entrance, is a museum which depicts the Carthusians' way of life in an informative way (Apl to Oct). Another, quite different, religious site is the Eglise de St-Hugues, south of **St-Pierre-de-Chartreuse** (E4). The church is a striking celebration of contemporary sacred art; the artist, Arcabas, created the paintings from 1953 to 1973 (Mar to Nov; closed Tues).

Drive the recently metalled road over the Col du Coq (F4). Enjoy the high mountain views east from the D30 and, on your descent, seek out **Le Touvet** (F4) where the château, with a man-made stepped water cascade, is a miniature Chatsworth (p.m. every day July/Aug; p.m. Sun only Easter/June and Sept/Oct). An alternative descent to the Isère is the funicular which runs between Lumbin and St-Hilaire (F4: every day June to mid Sept; weekends Apl/May and mid Sept/mid Dec).

Lack of space is proving a problem. Head east from Bugey through the Val du Fier (E1/F1) where both man and Nature have cut large slices from the rock face above the river. Further east the impressive Château Montrottier matches the **Gorges du Fier** (F1) for splendour. Visit the château, then park at the bridge over the river and descend on the protected path: first views are of woods, white rocks and water; later, beyond the café terrace, the walkways cling to the side of the rock, as the Fier slices a way through the narrowest of slits.

Visit **Aix-les-Bains** (F2), a four-star *ville fleuri* and a lakeside resort and spa (hot water springs). Across the lake is the gloriously situated Gothic-styled Abbaye de Hautecombe (E2); as peaceful as the setting is the chants of the Bénédictine monks are even more restful. Climb the zig-zag road across the Mont du Chat (E2) and descend to the tranquil and triangular **Lac d'Aiguebelette** (E3); have a swim in the warm water. Continue south-west to another of my favourite lakes, the **Lac de Paladru** (D3). Here two sites are exceptional: the underwater archaeological workings (Fouilles Archeologiques de Colletière) north-east of Charavines (D4); and the Maison de Pays du Lac de Paladru which explains the workings and the history of the villages in neolithic and medieval times (a.m. and p.m. June/Sept; p.m. Sat/Sun mid Apl/end May and Oct/Nov).

Chambéry (F3) can be a traffic nightmare. Shed no tears if you bypass the old town, the château with its Ste-Chappelle, and the Musée Savoisien. Head east towards map sheet 118 and enjoy the renowned hill climb of **Mont Revard** (F2), high above Aix: 360-degree views and, to the east, the bypassed Les Bauges. See you there over the page.

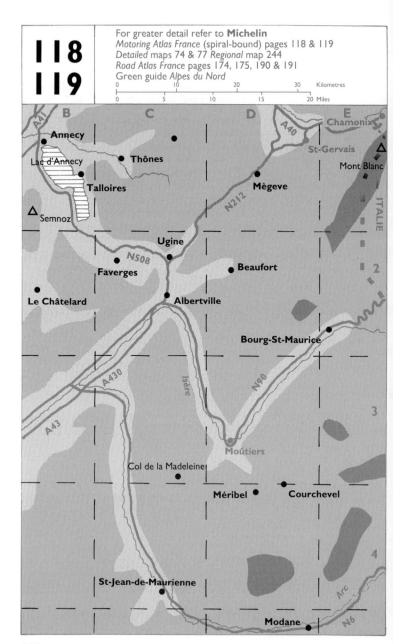

118
119

For greater detail refer to **Michelin**
Motoring Atlas France (spiral-bound) pages 118 & 119
Detailed maps 74 & 77 *Regional* map 244
Road Atlas France pages 174, 175, 190 & 191
Green guide *Alpes du Nord*

| 0 | 10 | 20 | 30 | Kilometres |
| 0 | 5 | 10 | 15 | 20 Miles |

B **C** **D** **E**

A41

Annecy

Lac d'Annecy

Thônes

Talloires

△ Semnoz

A40

Chamonix

St-Gervais

Mont Blanc

△

ITALIE

Mègeve

N212

Ugine

N508

Favergès

Beaufort

Le Châtelard

Albertville

Bourg-St-Maurice

A430

Isère

N90

A43

Moûtiers

Col de la Madeleine

Méribel

Courchevel

St-Jean-de-Maurienne

Arc

Modane

N6

By now you will have realised that I am in my element in mountain country; the Alps are where rallying mapaholics have the time of their lives. There's much to write about – so let's get motoring.

Start with a flourish. Climb to the Crêt de Châtillon on the heavily wooded **Semnoz** mountain (B1). The 5574 ft-high summit is a breathtaking viewpoint: below you is **Lac d'Annecy**; to the far south the icy peaks of the Massif des Ecrins shimmer in the sun (132:C2/C3); and, to the east, the snoozing dome of **Mont Blanc**, Europe's highest mountain (E1: see map sheet chapter 105), dominates the horizon.

In early June the marshy pastures one km south of the Crêt are dotted with lapis lazuli-tinted gentians. On the night of 15 April 1943, these same pastures, identified by bonfires, were witness to a daring wartime mission. Peter Churchill, a British SOE agent, parachuted from a Halifax and landed on the Semnoz – to be met by his future wife, the legendary Odette Sansom, and a group of local *maquis*. Within hours, disaster struck: the couple were captured at nearby St-Jorioz (B1).

Now head south to the largely ignored mountain fortress of **Les Bauges**. Call first at the local tourist office or write to Syndicat d'Initiative des Bauges, 73630 Le Châtelard (B2) for several useful leaflets (tel 79 54 84 28). One, in English, details "Strolls and summits in le Massif des Bauges"; another, far more interesting, concerns the Réserve Nationale de Faune du Massif des Bauges. This super *dépliant* explains the background to the Alpine reserve which lies between **Le Châtelard** and **Albertville**. The map in the leaflet identifies 17 marked trails, of varying lengths and difficulty, which snake into the heart of the small circle of high protected terrain.

I'll identify a handful of walks. The first is the drive up the Vallon de Bellevaux (B2), a dead-end wooded valley with roaring river and the start of several walks. Next, access the reserve from Doussard (B2); drive to and then walk in the similarly forested Combe (Valley) d'Ire, to the south. The St-Ruph Valley is reached from **Faverges** (C2); here there are more woods, a river landscape and, at Seythenex, a waterfall and subterranean promenade. From the Abbaye de Tamié, further south, two walks take you into the forests above the monastery.

Before leaving Les Bauges be sure to drive the D206 in the Aillon Valley (B2); and rise early one morning to see for yourself the relentless life led by Paul Bogey at his Fromagerie de Doucy-en-Bauges, east of Le Châtelard. Paul is the only remaining cheesemaker of the huge *Gruyère des Bauges* variety still working in the *massif*. Arrive between 8.30 and 9.00 a.m. to watch him at the critical stage of his daily production of three 40-kg "wheels" (1,500 litres of milk are needed). The much smaller 1 to 1½ kg *Tome des Bauges* is made at several farms; ask for a list at Le Châtelard SI. Finally, a tasty treat: for authentic regional specialities (*farcon, gratins* and *risolles*) visit Mme Chatelain at Chez Chatelain in La Compôte-en-Bauges, south-east of Le Châtelard (every day lunch only: telephone ahead 79 54 82 53).

Annecy (B1) is a traffic-jam most of the time. Nevertheless I, would still head for the shady parks and gardens by the *lac* (the Jardins de l'Europe, between the town hall and lake, are delectable); I would also not miss the old arcaded streets on either side of the River Thiou and the nearby château with its regional museum. A lake cruise would be a restful pleasure; for the energetic there are all sorts of watersport amenities and, as the map indicates with blue spots, there are many *plages*. Walks abound: try the lakeside promenade from St-Jorioz to Duingt (B1) or the walks around **Talloires** on the eastern bank. The latter has an exquisite setting; no trains and no busy main road are big pluses. Explore, too, the 200-acre wooded *marais* at Bout-du-Lac (B1), at the southern end of the lake.

For a different approach to Talloires why not climb the Col de La Forclaz (B1) from the south and drive along the road high above the lake? At the summit you are offered the chance to "Fly like a bird on two-seat hang glider with Instructor". Better you than me. Don't pass by the Ermitage de St-Germain: the 11th-century Bénédictine saint returned here after a pilgrimage to the Holy Land; likewise St-François de Sales came here in 1621 to see out his days. To the north of Talloires is the striking and historic Château de Menthon-St-Bernard.

Another religious site is a must: Tamié Abbey (C2). A new Centre d'Accueil has been built; an audio visual presentation explains the history of the Cistercian monastery; you can buy the tasty cheese made at the abbey; and you can purchase tapes of the chants recorded by the monks in their church. Try to find time for one of the daily services: Vespers is ideal (summer weekdays 18.15; Sun 17.00).

Faverges market is on Wednesday. A better version is the Saturday morning market at **Thônes** (C1) – an unprepossessing town with arcaded shops and an *église* with a Baroque interior. Detour three km north-west to the cemetery where many hundreds of *maquisards* are buried – Resistance fighters who died on 26 March 1944 in the hills to the north. From Thônes use the D16 to the Col de la Croix Fry and Col des Aravis (an exciting run which misses the eye-sore of **La Clusaz**); you'll note how Mont Blanc looms closer and closer. Around Thônes and Flumet C1/D1) you'll have many a chance to buy *Reblochon* cheese.

Descend to the Val d'Arly. **Megève** (D1) is a winter and summer resort and has not been spoilt like many of the high-altitude ski stations. Drive the taxing corniche road from ugly **Ugine** (C2) in a clockwise direction to the Col de l'Arpettaz and down to Héry. From Ugine take the D67 and a series of forestry roads high above the Doron Valley (D1) to the Signal de Bisanne: the panorama is astounding. An easier approach is the Col des Saisies climb from the Val d'Arly.

Now south into Le Beaufortain – centred on the village of **Beaufort** (D2), a name synonymous with a Gruyère-like cheese (but no holes). Head south to Arèches (D2) and then climb up to the Col du Pré, passing many old, traditional chalets. The Roselend lake and dam are formidable civil engineering works; the Cormet de Roselend climb is less impressive. Far more spectacular is the Col de Petit St-Bernard which zig-zags up from **Bourg-St-Maurice** (E2) in La Tarentaise; the views of the southern wall of the Chaîne du Mont Blanc are superb.

I cannot find any kind words to say about the **Isère** Valley from Albertville (C2) to Bourg-St-Maurice. Industry and winter sports dominate the economy of the Isère and Les Trois Vallées (D3/D4). In the summer months the high-altitude ski resorts are monstrosities: take **Courchevel** (D3) as one example. Man has ruined the landscape. Thankfully Nature still wins hands down – if you get away from the hundreds of hotels and ski-lifts: great forests, super views and exciting walking. One worthwhile drive is the roughish forest road from the Olympic ski jumps at Le Praz (D3) to **Méribel** (D4); the latter is nothing like as hideous as some of the other resorts.

Nor can I find much to praise in La Maurienne, the terrain straddling the **Arc** Valley from the Italian border through **Modane** (133:D1) to **St-Jean** (C4). However there are some redeeming religious treasures in both La Tarentaise and La Maurienne: the stunning Baroque interiors hidden behind the often decrepit walls of scores of churches. I'll give you details of just two where the doors are always open. Bozel (D3) is north of Courchevel. The interior of the Eglise St-François de Sales has wonderful panelling and choir stalls, a handsome pulpit with glorious carvings and a fine roof. The *église* at St-Bon-Tarentaise, on the climb to Courchevel, has a plain façade with the only colour courtesy of nine large bowls of bright flowers. The interior has intricate stained glass windows, marvellous panelling and wood carvings. For further information on other churches, their opening times and guided tours contact: Espace Baroque Maurienne, 73480 Lanslebourg-Mt-Cenis (tel 79 05 90 42); Espace Baroque Tarentaise, 73600 Moûtiers (tel 79 24 04 23). La Tarentaise and La Maurienne share another superb asset: the wondrous wilderness world of the high-altitude Parc National de la Vanoise (E3/E4). Trace the park's green dotted line border on the map and you'll soon grasp why this is a flora and fauna wonderland.

What I can rave about is the **Col de la Madeleine** (C3), the only road link between La Tarentaise and La Maurienne. As you climb the 6562 ft pass from the Isère detour to Bonneval – in a time warp and a million miles away from the ski resorts: a mix of old and new, roses and flowers, a tiny school, church, peace and quiet, walks, trees, birds and butterflies. Further south, as you ascend the unspoilt wooded valley, note the steep cobbled and stepped alleys in La Thuile.

At the summit stop and absorb the wondrous scene: Mont Blanc to the north; the Ecrins to the south. In June, on the northern side of the col, Anne and I were spellbound by myriad gentians, pansies, trollius, orchids and other wild flowers; above us skylarks sang in the clear air. On the southern slopes there were wild flowers by the million and thousands of orchids. Truly, a fantasy land sent from heaven.

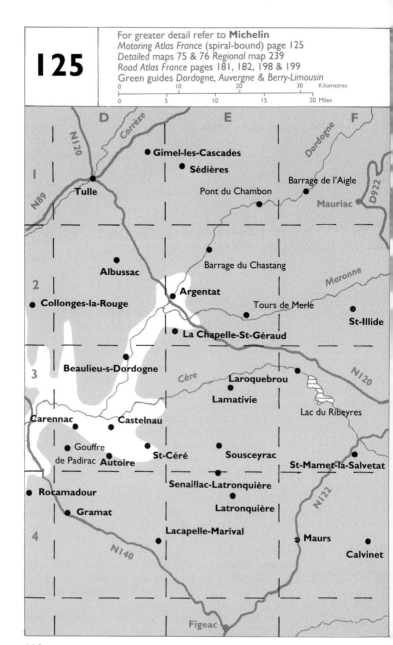

125

For greater detail refer to **Michelin**
Motoring Atlas France (spiral-bound) page 125
Detailed maps 75 & 76 *Regional* map 239
Road Atlas France pages 181, 182, 198 & 199
Green guides *Dordogne, Auvergne & Berry-Limousin*

0   10   20   30   Kilometres

0   5   10   15   20 Miles

D   E   F

Corrèze

N120

N89

Dordogne

D922

1

● **Gimel-les-Cascades**

● **Sédières**

Tulle

Pont du Chambon

Barrage de l'Aigle

Mauriac

●
Albussac

Barrage du Chastang

Maronne

2

● **Collonges-la-Rouge**

● **Argentat**

Tours de Merle

●
St-Illide

● **La Chapelle-St-Géraud**

3

● **Beaulieu-s-Dordogne**

Cère

● **Laroquebrou**

N120

● **Lamativie**

Lac du Ribeyres

Carennac

● **Castelnau**

● Gouffre
de Padirac   **Autoire**

● **St-Céré**

● **Sousceyrac**

● **St-Mamet-la-Salvetat**

● **Rocamadour**

● **Senaillac-Latronquière**

N122

● **Gramat**

● **Latronquière**

4

● **Lacapelle-Marival**

N140

● **Maurs**

● **Calvinet**

Figeac

One spot, more than any other, is the perfect entry to the captivating country on map sheet 125 – the antithesis of the two Michelin three-star honeypot sights at the end of the chapter. I suggest you start by seeking out the dead-end lane which leads to the 15th-century château at **Sédières** (E1), north-west of Clergoux. Here a natural cocktail refreshes the senses: silence; cool, still air, broken only by a cock's crow or a bird's song; mixed woods; and ferns, heather, butterflies and *étangs*. An austere small château, with Resistance links, sits contentedly in the middle of the watercolour (open every day July/Aug).

Let's stay in the *département* of Corrèze (most of the top half of the map). Later, we'll visit Cantal (the eastern edge) and we'll finish in Lot (the bottom left-hand corner). But where next in Corrèze? To **Gimel-les-Cascades** (D1), north-east of **Tulle**. Three separate waterfalls put on an extrovert show of fury and foaming sound. Walk the many steps to the bottom; but remember the steep return climb.

Corrèze remains as unspoilt as ever. Drive the myriad lanes which spread like veins through rejuvenating forests. Seek out **Albussac** (D2), south of Tulle (D1): to the east are the Cascades de Murel; to the west the observation table atop the Roche de Vic, a short hike from the D940. Detour to the 15th-century *église*, with its four-bell bell-tower, at Neuville, south of Albussac; and the church at St-Chamant, east of Albussac, with fortified tower and super stone carvings.

What of the more renowned sites? **Collonges-la-Rouge** (124:C2) is almost too good to be true with every building constructed from the local dark red sandstone. The place is so busy you have to park on the D38. Do just that and then walk the evocative streets which weave past medieval manor houses, old *maisons* and Romanesque church.

On the way to **Beaulieu-sur-Dordogne** (D3) detour to Curemonte, to the west of the town. Enjoy the ramparts, châteaux and *église* – all medieval eye-pleasers. Beaulieu has a pretty setting beside the River **Dordogne**; the Romanesque Eglise St-Pierre is the town's great magnet, especially the magnificent sculptures on the south portal. The D12 riverside run to **Argentat** (E2) is Corrèze at its most bewitching.

Argentat has a particularly eye-soothing riverside setting, one best seen from the older bridge to the east of the brand new N120 bypass. Relish the old houses with their wooden balconies and roofs of *lauzes* (local stone tiles laid on wooden slats). Until 100 years ago the upper Dordogne, untamed by gigantic modern dams, was a dangerous waterway, the vital link in getting Limousin's oak trees to the wine barrel makers in Bordeaux. Flat-bottomed barges called *gabares* did the donkey work. Each craft made only one trip downstream; at journey's end the *gabare* was scrapped. Today *gabares* are used to ferry tourists along the placid river: trips can be made from the **Barrage du Chastang** (E2) or from the **Pont du Chambon**, further upstream (E1).

The wooded hills to the east and south of Argentat are in an area called La Xaintrie – where locals claim there are over 200 calvaries. (We

119

counted 20 without trying.) Access La Xaintrie on the D33 south from Argentat: the views west, where the River **Maronne** joins the Dordogne, are gorgeous. At **La Chapelle-St-Géraud** (E2) there's a tiny *église* and the most handsome water tower we've ever seen.

The supreme treat in La Xaintrie is the wooded site of the **Tours de Merle** (E2). The best approach road is the D13 from Goulles. What a mysterious and compelling picture lies below and ahead of you: high ruined towers on a rocky outcrop with the river flowing in a double meander far beneath the remote 13th-century fortress. In July/Aug *animations médiévales*, *spectacles* and *son et lumière* shows are held (details from Mairie, 19220 St-Geniez: tel 55 28 22 31).

Leave Corrèze by heading south to the Gorges de la **Cère** and **Lamativie** (E3). The descent and ascent are more like an Alpine hillclimb. The woods are dense and you'll notice two examples of man's more modern endeavours: a rail line and power station.

What does Cantal offer? **Laroquebrou** (F3) is a valley town with a château and *église* – and humming Cère weir. If you go north be sure to use the D43 from St-Santin-Cantales to **St-Illide** (F2); the Soulane river crossing is a delight with wooded hillsides and emerald pastures on the flat-bottomed valley floor. St-Illide has a squat central-towered Romanesque *église*; the church at St-Martin-Cantalès, to the north, is a smaller building with a spire and Romanesque portal. The Gorges de la Maronne is another wooded river crossing but is not as interesting as the Cère version. Much further north is the huge **Barrage de l'Aigle** (F1), damming the Dordogne on its way south.

If you head south-east from Laroquebrou the winding arms and wooded banks of the **Lac du Ribeyres** will please; for the sports enthusiast the lake has a beach (see the diamond on the map), canoes, *pédalos* and other watersport facilities. One must is **St-Mamet-la-Salvetat** (F3). Drive to the small park on the Puy St-Laurent above the town (771 m): there's an observation table on top of the water reservoir and the views east of the Cantal mountains are fabulous. Now south to Vitrac (F4) and the D17 which follows the Rance Valley to **Maurs**.

The Rance Valley is delectable: woods, river, pastoral views and, at the lower end, 100/150 ft-high cliffs covered in heather. Use the D319 north-west from Maurs and also enjoy the densely wooded Veyre Valley. This part of Cantal (the bottom right-hand corner of 125) is tagged La Châtaigneraie. Chestnut trees are everywhere; we remember crushing thousands on a windy October day *en route* to **Calvinet** (F4).

We'll finish in the bottom left-hand corner of 125, Le Haut Quercy – part of the Lot *département*. The terrain between **Sousceyrac** (E3), **Latronquière** (E4) – both non-descript towns – and **Lacapelle-Marival** (D4) is called Le Jardin du Ségala. You may consider that pretentious: not so, as the hilly, wooded circle of *pays* is such a refreshing tonic from the dry-scrub *causse* (plateau) to the west. The views are extensive: for example, on the D48 north from Lacapelle to **St-Céré** (D3). Nose out the brand new Lac du Tolerme, west of **Senaillac-Latronquière** (E3/E4): an attractive setting, beach, children's playground and other facilities appeal.

Now head for the honeypot sites always buzzing with tourists. The Château de **Castelnau**-Bretenoux (D3) sits majestically above the Cère and Dordogne confluence; the fortress is built of ochre and caramel-shaded stone and there are numerous turrets and towers. **Carennac** (D3) has a riverside site: the combination of fortress château, 12th-century church and old houses is breathtaking. Don't miss the cloisters, Romanesque tympanum, the 16th-century life-sized carved Entombment of Christ and the views of the village from the north-west.

Medieval Loubressac (D3) has a high perch on a rocky outcrop: the dominating 15th-century château is privately-owned but savour the views, the *village fleuri*, the shaded *place*, and the stone houses with attractive balconies. Relish nearby **Autoire**, a handsome village where the houses have dark-tiled roofs; to the immediate south is a small *cirque* where a cascade and colourful rock faces add extra interest. The small 16th-century Château de Montal, west of St-Céré, is made of light, coffee-hued stone and has varying shaped towers; the most notable feature is a Renaissance stone staircase. The best of St-Céré, a town overlooked by the two sentinel towers of St-Laurent, is around the church: see the cone-topped stone towers and medieval half-timbered houses with their small red bricks and stout oak beam corbels. Visit the Jean Lurçat *musée* at St-Laurent, where you can admire varied tapestries, paintings, rugs and plates created by the celebrated artist who lived in the town from 1945 until his death in 1966.

Finally, a controversial observation. Approach **Rocamadour** (174:C4) from the south, along the D32 and past dry-stone walls and stunted oaks. Below you is the Alzou Valley with rock cliffs of pearl grey, russet, jet black, apricot and terracotta shades. Then you'll see the legendary pilgrimage town for the first time: tiers of houses with their high walls, towers and steep roofs of *lauzes* clinging to the rock faces. Visit the famed sites but, as you fight your way through the crowds and past the multitude of shops flogging junk, you'll conclude that this is commercial tourism at its most rampant. This is just as true at the **Gouffre de Padirac** (D3) – spectacular caves where you can travel hundreds of metres on a subterranean river far below the limestone *causse* (take warm clothes). You leave feeling as if you've just dropped off a fast-moving tourist production line where, at every turn, you're asked to put your hand in your pocket.

(At Rocamadour use the motorised blue and white train to ease the strain of walking the streets; there are also evening excursions to view the illuminations from the D32. In the vicinity there's a park, the Forêt des Singes, where 150 Barbary apes mingle with visitors; the Rocher des Aigles where you can watch large birds of prey flying freely; and a small zoo at the Parc de Vision (D4), south of **Gramat**.)

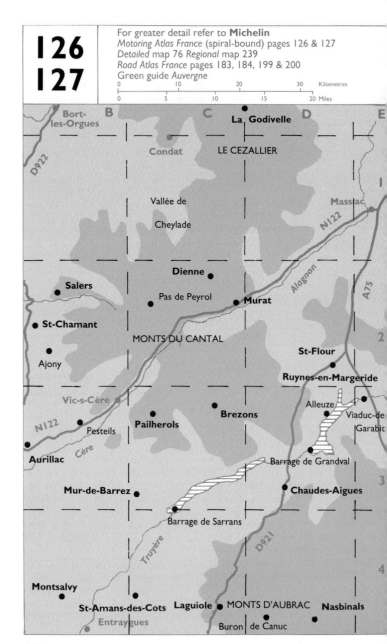

For greater detail refer to **Michelin**
Motoring Atlas France (spiral-bound) pages 126 & 127
Detailed map 76 *Regional map* 239
Road Atlas France pages 183, 184, 199 & 200
Green guide *Auvergne*

126
127

| 0 | 10 | 20 | 30 | Kilometres |
| 0 | 5 | 10 | 15 | 20 Miles |

B   **C**   **D**   **E**

Bort-
les-Orgues

D922

La Godivelle

Condat

LE CEZALLIER

Vallée de

Cheylade

Massiac

N122

1

Dienne

Salers

Pas de Peyrol   Murat

Alagnon

A75

St-Chamant

MONTS DU CANTAL

Ajony

St-Flour

2

Ruynes-en-Margeride

Vic-s-Cère

Alleuze

N122   Brezons   Viaduc-de
Garabit

Pesteils   Pailherols

Cère

Aurillac

Barrage de Grandval

Mur-de-Barrez   Chaudes-Aigues

3

Barrage de Sarrans

Truyère   D921

4

Montsalvy

St-Amans-des-Cots   Laguiole   MONTS D'AUBRAC   Nasbinals

Entraygues   Buron   de Canuc

If you value seclusion and your own company then head for Cantal-Aubrac. Not that the area will remain remote for long. The new **A75** toll-free *autoroute*, from Clermont-Ferrand (113:D2) to Aumont-Aubrac (127:E4), already pierces into the very heart of the Massif Central.

The area is one of strong visual contrasts: the volcanic cones of the **Monts du Cantal** (126:B2/C2) are separated from the desolate **Monts d'Aubrac** (south-east of **Laguiole**: C4) by one of France's most striking wooded valleys, the **Truyère** (D3 to B4).

I have visited the mountainous area many times over the decades. For this chapter I'll describe a trip Anne and I made in October a couple of years ago. I'll follow that by adding a series of notes on additional places for you to seek out, many of which we visited last year.

On our memorable October visit we entered Cantal from the south, crossing the River Lot north of Conques (140:B1). A gale-force wind was whistling away and puff-ball clouds scudded across the sky. The air was pure and clear and every view crystal sharp; some panoramas extended 50 miles and more. Near **Montsalvy** (B4) the lanes were strewn with carpets of sweet-chestnuts and the pastures were emerald dazzlers.

Our first port of call was the isolated home of Suzy and Nigel Atkins, the Poterie du Don, west of Montoursy (B4), a hamlet south-west of Montsalvy. Suzy, one of Europe's most gifted potters, produces breathtaking work: salt-glazed ceramics include both functional ware and a range of individual pieces decorated with stunning gold and metallic lustres. Some good news: the once roughish steep descent into the Auze Valley now has a tarmac surface (open every day).

We headed north to **Aurillac** (B3), a bustling modern *ville*, and then followed the signposted D35 "Route des Crêtes" north-east. After a few miles the vista to the north stopped us in our tracks: the varying patches of rapidly-changing light and shade on the Cantal peaks were reminiscent of Cumbria's fells. We took two hours to reach **Salers** (B2), following the D35 over the Col de Legal and the D135 through Le Fau. No wonder: we counted a dozen birds of prey gliding in the strong winds and we marvelled at the tiniest of tricoloured pansies glistening in the autumn air – together with campion, scabious, harebells, wild lavatera, hardy cranesbill and verbascum. And we were quite alone.

Salers is a stern, forbidding place, snoozing atop a basalt plateau bed. Explore the narrow medieval streets and the turreted basalt houses lining the Grande-Place; the fountain adds a sparkling touch. On the mountain roads you will have noticed the reddish-brown Salers cattle; their milk is used to make both *Cantal* and *Salers* cheese.

Next, we went east, to the **Pas de Peyrol** (C2: 5190 ft high). For once the mountain views came a poor second; the easy winner was the luminous beech forest clinging to the southern side of the Cirque du Falgoux (B2). At the col we detoured south, into the Vallée de Mandailles (B2). Here, too, the burnished woods were a thrilling sight. Much the most unusual of French beech forests, the Cantal versions resemble mammoth drapes and swathes of golden cloth, 2,000 to 3,000 ft long, flung down by the gods from the volcanic summits.

Continuing north-east towards **Dienne** (C2) we ran out of adjectives to describe the view ahead of us: a Capability Brown valley with long lines of chestnut, beech, maple and other trees, all wearing their autumn capes. (At other times, in April and May, we've see the same valley, and the **Vallée de Cheylade** (C1) to the north, covered with yellow jonquils and, later, peppered with white narcissi.)

From **Murat** (C2) we drove south, on the D39, to **Brezons** (C3). The high wilderness of the Prat de Bouc (C2) is a paradise for both botanists and ornithologists: locals claim that over 80 species of birds can be seen and we can vouch for the yellow gentians, lilies and other wild flowers we've encountered on our spring visits. The views north of Brezons, not mentioned in any guidebook, are show-stoppers.

The next day saw us lingering in the lanes south of **Pailherols** (C3) and beyond the Truyère, towards Laguiole (C4). Look out for several architectural treats: the open bell tower on the 13th-century *église* at Jou-sous-Monjou (C3); the château at Cropières, alongside the D59; the marvellously-sited château at Messilhac (B3), clearly visible from the D600 three km north of **Mur-de-Barrez** (C3); the bell towers at Brommat and Albinhac, east of Mur-de-Barrez; the engineering marvel of the **Barrage de Sarrans**; the terrific château at Orlhaguet (C4) with a variety of shaped towers, including one with four bells; and the *église* at Ste-Geneviève-sur-Argence (C4).

The Truyère is one of France's finest river gorges; the steep sides are wooded almost every inch of its entire length. The river is dammed at several points: the biggest of the snake-shaped lakes is to the east of the **Barrage de Grandval** (D3). The eerie, haunting ruins of the Château d'**Alleuze** (D3), atop a rocky pyramid, compares starkly with two other modern man-made marvels: the elegant and massive **Viaduc-de-Garabit** (E3) built by Eiffel to carry the railway line south; and the huge newly-completed A75 concrete bridge. A swish craft cruises on the lake from its Pont de Garabit mooring.

Now for a series of notes on other places to visit. First Laguiole (C4) and the high plateau to the east. The town has been considerably spruced up during the last decade: over 1,000 metres high, Laguiole is famed for its cattle, knives (until recently production had ceased in the town but a new factory, on the D15, is now open to the public) and cheeses (*tome*, or *tomme*, is the fresh cow's milk version, used to make *aligot*; *jeune* is a hard variety, two to four months old; and *vieux* which matures for eight to twenty months). Further east, as you climb the D15, the views south, west and north are prodigious.

Head for remote **Nasbinals** (D4). Nose out the *charcuterie* of André Souchon in the middle of the village – a porkies' palace; then, 20 metres away, the Chassang-Brunel *boulangerie* (no sign) where you should treat yourself to a slice of the crown-shaped *fougasse* bread (they insist you should not call the *pain* a *brioche*) made from flour, fresh eggs, butter, salt, sugar, yeast and orange-flower water.

In Aubrac's restaurants you are likely to be served *aligot* – a *purée* of potatoes with *Tomme de Cantal* cheese, cream, garlic and butter. But, if you want to savour *aligot* in its authentic, rustic glory then seek out one of the few remaining *burons* (there was a time when all the local cheeses were made in these remote, high-altitude stone-built structures). We had a memorable *aligot* lunch at the **Buron de Canuc** (no sign), three km north of Aubrac (141:D1) and on the west side of the D15 at the "57" km stone. Be prepared for a culture shock: this is not for the sophisticated or faint-hearted. Anne and I would return tomorrow for the superb *aligot*, with its rubbery consistency, prepared in front of our eyes. (Important: ring 65 42 29 02 the evening before, or between 8.00 and 9.00 for lunch that day – June to August.)

What else is there to see? **Chaudes-Aigues** (D3), a small spa, claims to have the hottest waters in Europe (82C). Explore the terrain to the west of Laguiole, around **St-Amans-des-Cots** and the Lac de la Selve (both C4); I've even seen an oxen-drawn cart in the lanes. The views from the Puy de Montabès (B4) are worth the detour.

Aurillac (B3), for me, is no great shakes and not worth the detour. But don't miss a handful of châteaux on the western edge of my draft map. **Anjony** (B2) is so evocative of the Auvergne: tall, narrow, stern, and, at each corner, four forbidding towers; the 16th-century frescoes are remarkable (p.m. Palm Sunday to All Saints Day); and see, too, tiny Tournemire. Conros, south of Aurillac, much less forbidding, has been in the same family's hands for over four centuries (p.m. mid July to end August). **Pesteils** (B3), north-east of Aurillac, has a Disney look and an imposing 35 metre-high 13th-century keep (a.m. and p.m. July and August; p.m. May/June/September). **St-Chamant** (B2), north of Anjony, is more a fortified manor (p.m. mid June to mid September).

St-Flour (D2) has many man-made highlights, among them the cathedral and museums, and an impressive site atop a 100 metre-high basalt table. To the south-east is something altogether more down-to-earth: the Ecomusée de la Margeride (the wooded hills in the south-east corner of 127) based at four sites around **Ruynes-en-Margeride** (E2: open mid June to mid September). At the latter there's an evocative garden by the old tower in the village. At Signalauze, to the south-west, a tiny school classroom has been kept in its 1931 state. At Loubaresse (E3), just off the N9, the Ferme de Pierre Allègre evokes a farm of a century ago (by the church with tower and three bells). At Longevialle, north of the farm and beside the Truyère, the Domaine de Longevialle chronicles the story of the men who built the Viaduc-de-Garabit.

Finally, seek out the remarkable wilderness of **Le Cézallier** (D1) – remote high plateaux, their volcanic lava pastures the home of Salers cattle and yellow gentians, and with extensive watery peat bogs. Visit **La Godivelle** (113:D4) and the nearby crater lake.

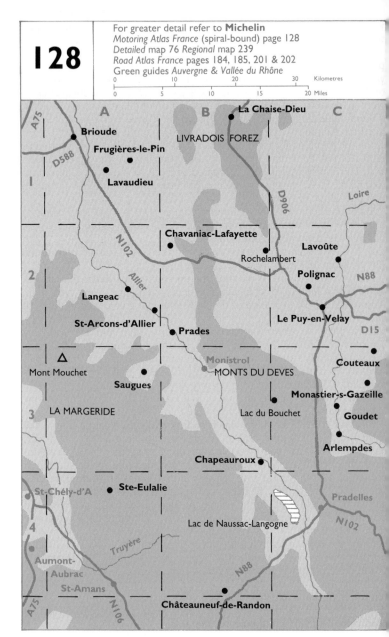

For greater detail refer to **Michelin**
Motoring Atlas France (spiral-bound) page 128
Detailed map 76 *Regional* map 239
Road Atlas France pages 184, 185, 201 & 202
Green guides *Auvergne & Vallée du Rhône*

0   10   20   30   Kilometres

0   5   10   15   20 Miles

A75

A   B   **La Chaise-Dieu**   C

Brioude

Frugières-le-Pin

LIVRADOIS FOREZ

D588

Lavaudieu

1

Loire

D906

N102

Chavaniac-Lafayette

Lavoûte

Rochelambert

Allier

Polignac

N88

2

Langeac

St-Arcons-d'Allier   **Prades**

Le Puy-en-Velay

D15

△

Mont Mouchet

Monistrol

Couteaux

MONTS DU DEVES

Sauges

Monastier-s-Gazeille

3   LA MARGERIDE

Lac du Bouchet

Goudet

Arlempdes

Chapeauroux

St-Chély-d'A   **Ste-Eulalie**

Pradelles

N102

4   Lac de Naussac-Langogne

Truyère

N88

Aumont-
Aubrac

St-Amans

A75

N106

Châteauneuf-de-Randon

Most tourists would probably decide that the terrain on map sheet 128 is not worth a detour – although those who know of unique **Le Puy-en-Velay** (C2) would disagree with such a harsh judgement. How wrong the majority would be because, for those enterprising enough to make the map-reading effort, there's many a pleasing surprise awaiting them.

I'll divide the map into three vertical slices: the Vallée de la **Loire** on the right edge; the middle tranche, Velay Volcanique, which includes the wooded hills of **Livradois Forez** (B1) and the **Monts du Devès** (B2/B3); and the western third, the Haut **Allier** Valley (A1/A2/B2/B3) and the forested **La Margeride** (A3/A4).

Let's begin at Le Puy, arguably one of the most unusual towns in France. Sharp needles of volcanic rock rise on all sides. The most needle-like has the Chapelle St-Michel d'Aiguille at the top; there's a 268-step lung-bursting climb to reach the Romanesque chapel. Another outcrop has the huge statue of Notre Dame de France on the summit. However, for me, the cathedral is the strongest magnet. The building, a mixture of Byzantine and Romanesque, has glorious 12th-century cloisters. There's one snag about Le Puy: traffic. Park in the pl. du Breuil, next door to the Office de Tourisme (43000 Le Puy-en-Velay: 71 09 38 41). Ask for their *guide pratique* which gives details of three separate walks around the town. Or, to avoid any pain, take the motorised train.

Now head for the eastern slice of country. Much the most memorable first impression of both the upper Loire Valley and the Velay, the terrain circling Le Puy, will come when you drive the high lanes on the western edge of map sheet 129, south of St-Julien-Chapteuil (D2); the latter has an especially handsome 12th-century Romanesque *église*. Use the D49 south to Laussonne. The views west and north are magnificent: a landscape of wooded, volcanic cones and mounds, the Pays des Sucs. Just west of Laussonne is **Couteaux** (128:C3) where, carved out of the red volcanic soil, are numerous old troglodyte homes. Further south, at **Le Monastier-sur-Gazeille** (C3), there are more extensive views west. This is the village where Robert Louis Stevenson started his memorable travels in 1878 with Modestine, made famous in his book *Travels with a Donkey in the Cévennes* (read the paperback).

Two exceptional sites upriver from Le Puy deserve your time. **Goudet** (C3) snoozes on the right bank of the Loire: there's a church, ruined castle and a bridge across the narrow river; paddling in the water is a hard-to-resist temptation. **Arlempdes** (C3) is on the opposite bank: here a church, ruined château, tiny *chapelle*, perched site, volcanic rocks, woods and pretty river vista combine to form a most beguiling picture. Once again, a paddle is a tonic for hot feet.

Downstream from Le Puy access to the Loire is much easier: the D103, a busy road, runs alongside the river's banks. The most striking man-made feature is the handsome stone-built Château de **Lavoûte**-Polignac (C2), atop a solid rock which rises from the very edge of the Loire's right bank. Built originally in the 13th century, and restored in

127

the 19th, the Polignac family home is open from Easter to end October. Also see the village's Romanesque church. In the autumn the valley's trees are a joy: rich shades of red, old gold, russet and copper.

At **Polignac** (C2), north-west of Le Puy, rises an impressive basalt table high above the encircling fields. On the billiard table-flat summit are the ruins of a once impregnable medieval fortress; the views are terrific. Once more seek out the Romanesque *église*.

Within the central tranche of countryside, the Velay Volcanique, is a varied mix of scenic sights. As you drive west from Le Puy you cross the Monts du Devès, a long spine of wooded summits; the views east are similar to the ones I described in the area around St-Julien-Chapteuil. At the southern end of the Chaîne du Devès (a better name), just west of the **Lac du Bouchet** (C3), the views both to east and west are equally memorable; no wonder, as the road is 4000 ft above sea-level. The circular Lac du Bouchet, once a volcanic crater, is hidden in a delectable wooded setting; walk the circuit around the lake.

Of the man-made attractions in this middle slice three are well worth nosing out. Two are in the Borne Valley, north-west of Le Puy: the medieval fortress at St-Vidal (C2) with substantial towers at each of the castle's four corners; and the 16th-century Château de la **Rochelambert** (B2). Built from dark volcanic stone the château looks more like a lived-in home; two slim towers, topped off most attractively with tiled cone-shaped roofs, add extra architectural appeal.

La Chaise-Dieu (B1) is famous for two reasons. First, the 14th-century *église*, a stern structure with thick stone walls and, in the interior, a choir of no less than 144 sculptured oak stalls; 16th-century Flanders tapestries; and a mural, created in 1460, of the *Dance Macabre*, the inspiration for Honegger's musical composition. Second, the annual music festival held during the last week of August and the first ten days in September (details: Office de Tourisme, 43160 La Chaise-Dieu). An amusing diversion is the Salle de l'Echo where Anne and I stood facing the wall at opposite corners of a large room; talking in the quietest of whispers, we could hear each other perfectly.

A drive south-west from La Chaise-Dieu leads us conveniently from the central section to the westernmost slice of *pays*. Follow the wooded Senouire Valley (B1). On the D4 near Ste-Marguerite a sign announces an "Artisanat Bois Tourné". I defy you not to buy something from Michel Estienne's showroom, full of skilfully-crafted wooden creations.

The château at **Chavaniac-Lafayette** (B2) was the birthplace of the Frenchman La Fayette, George Washington's second-in-command from 1777 to 1781. Visit the château and try to assess what motivated this French and US folk hero to marry at 16 and offer his services to Washington at the tender age of 20 (open every day Easter to end Oct).

Lavaudieu (A1), south-east of **Brioude**, is the site of a Bénédictine monastery with remarkable 12th-century cloisters, recently-uncovered frescoes and a small museum of traditional local life – all in the most rural of settings. Brioude's Basilica of St-Julien is a must: hemmed in by buildings, the church is an architectural wonder with dozens of different shades and types of patterned and layered stones. The stone and pebble floor is vast; amusingly, locals use the north and south doors to cross the nave as a shortcut between two streets.

Perhaps the best way to approach the Haut Allier – the river and the *gorges* – is the descent on the D130 to **St-Arcons d'Allier** (A2). In early summer the Allier is at its most alluring; you'll catch many a glimpse of fishermen in midstream working the river. Upstream from St-Arcons, just before the bridge at St-Julien-des-Chazes, take the unmarked road to the isolated stern-looking Chapelle Ste-Marie. (The Allier Valley has a handful of dark-stone, sombre churches. Three are downstream from **Langeac** (A2): Blassac, Aubazat and Peyrusses (all A2); Chanteuges (A2) is upstream. All have fine views.) At **Prades** (B2) there's a fearsome rock face on the Allier's right bank.

From Prades follow the road due south: stop often to enjoy the views, both east and west over the Seuge Valley; walk the short detour to the 12th-century chapel, Notre Dame d'Estours; and watch out for birds of prey hovering high above the ridge. The Ance Valley (B3) is densely wooded; upstream from the dams there's plenty of white water. Use the D33 to reach **Saugues** (A3), dominated by the massive 13th-century Tour des Anglais; another impressive tower, built on top of a huge rock, is at La Clauze, on the D335 south-west of Saugues. Continue south to the 500-acre bison park at **Ste-Eulalie**, claimed to be unique in Europe (A4: open every day; 66 31 57 01). Here you are in the remote fastness of La Margeride; you'll have the mountain lanes to yourself.

Please do not miss the drive along the Chapeauroux, a tributary of the Allier, from **Châteauneuf-de-Randon** (B4) to **Chapeauroux** (B3). The drive is an eye-teasing visual confection: in spring the fast-flowing stream is a tonic; in the autumn a 20-mile drive past a seemingly uninterrupted honour guard of colourfully-cloaked broadleaved trees. And be sure to climb to the *place* at the heart of Châteauneuf-de-Randon, a medieval treasure. If watersports are your passion, then seek out the man-made **Lac de Naussac-Langogne** (C4).

Finally, two musts. Visit the Musée de la Résistance "Joseph LHomenède" at **Frugières-le-Pin** *gare* (A1: south-east of Brioude). The museum is fascinating, filled with memorabilia of every imaginable type. Joseph was the leader of the Livradois *maquis*; his home was the adjacent Café Fayolle. Ask for access at the café. The lady who opens up the museum is Jacqueline, Joseph's daughter. Further south, on the western slopes of wooded **Mont Mouchet** (A3), in the high Margeride, is France's national monument, "*Aux Maquis de France*"; there's also an adjacent museum which explains the history of the Auvergne Resistance (see map where marked MF). Access to this place of pilgrimage is easier on the D4 from the west, alongside which there are numerous individual memorials to the brave souls who died fighting for France.

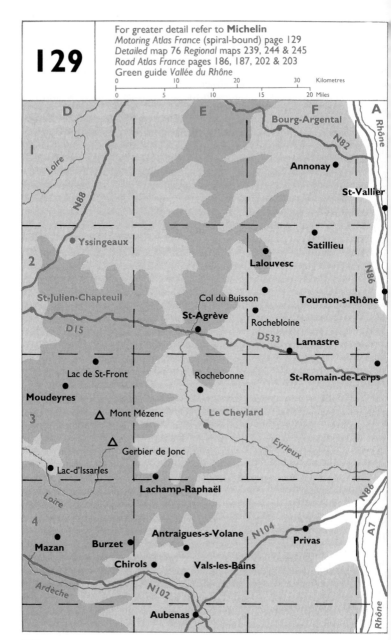

129

For greater detail refer to **Michelin**
Motoring Atlas France (spiral-bound) page 129
Detailed map 76 *Regional* maps 239, 244 & 245
Road Atlas France pages 186, 187, 202 & 203
Green guide *Vallée du Rhône*

| 0 | 10 | 20 | 30 | Kilometres |
| 0 | 5 | 10 | 15 | 20 Miles |

D E F A

Bourg-Argental

Rhône

N82

1

Loire

N88

Annonay

St-Vallier

Yssingeaux

Satillieu

N86

2

Lalouvesc

St-Julien-Chapteuil

Col du Buisson

Tournon-s-Rhône

St-Agrève

Rochebloine

D15

D533

Lamastre

Lac de St-Front

Rochebonne

St-Romain-de-Lerps

Moudeyres

△ Mont Mézenc

Le Cheylard

Eyrieux

3

△ Gerbier de Jonc

Lac-d'Issarles

N86

Loire

Lachamp-Raphaël

A7

4

Antraigues-s-Volane

N104

Privas

Mazan

Burzet

Chirols

Vals-les-Bains

Ardèche

N102

Rhône

Aubenas

The majority of tourists, speeding south on the **A7** *autoroute*, will give just a passing glance to the wooded hills on their right-hand side beyond the River **Rhône**. Some may realise that the distant summits are in the Ardèche *département*. But most drivers and their navigators, armed with small-scale maps and hell-bent on reaching the Med, will have no idea of the endless pleasures hidden in the adorable Ardèche.

Mapaholics know better. They will have the right large-scale maps and will be only too eager to cross the Rhône and head west into the Ardèche or, to give the *département* its ancient name, the Vivarais. Further west, circling Le Puy-en-Velay (128:C2), is the volcanic land of Velay. Combine map sheets 128, 129, 142 and 143 and you'll have a global cartographic view of Velay, Vivarias and most of the captivating Cévennes (see map sheet 141 for the rest of the latter).

I cannot say I find the Rhône Valley attractive; awful would be a more suitable adjective. The only redeeming features in the valley are the profuse roses, the extensive peach and cherry orchards and the vineyards – especially those of Gérard Chave, wine-maker *extraodinaire*. His *cave* is at Mauves (130:A2), south of **Tournon-sur-Rhône**; across the river, on the Hermitage hillside, is the site of his priceless vineyard. The Chave business has been handed down, from father to son, for the past 513 years, an almost unbelievable *vignerons* family history.

There are many ways you can leave the Rhône behind you and I'll start by suggesting one of the least likely of the many Ardeche *entrées*. Just north of **St-Vallier** (130: A1) is the Cance Valley. Use the narrow D270 and follow the river upstream; the valley is wooded almost every inch of the way and there are few houses. In early June, when we last saw the valley, the banks alongside the twisting road were a riot of wild flowers; Anne and I counted a couple of dozen different species, including some we had not seen before. Many rock faces were as good, if not better, than deliberately planted rock-gardens back home. Another big plus: in June the Cance is full of fast flowing water.

Continue south-west from **Annonay** (F1), past **Satillieu** (F2), and climb, through woods and past dollops of broom, to **Lalouvesc**, 1050 m above sea-level. The twin towers of the 19th-century basilica are a notable landmark, perched as they are on the edge of a high wooded cliff; enjoy the views from the east side of the church. Panoramas are the supreme feature of the D236 as you head south: the views over the Doux Valley – forested hills sharing space with sunny-side-up splashes of broom – are especially fine. At the **Col du Buisson** spare a few minutes (that's all you'll need) for the flower-filled Village Miniature, aptly named as the stone buildings are minuscule.

Shortly afterwards, when you see a track to the right marked **Rochebloine**, park and walk from the D236 up the not-too-steep bluff to the just about visible ruins of the Château de Rochebloine. The eagle's eye panorama, over the Doux Valley, is breathtaking.

Another unusual Ardèche *entrée* is one or other of the steep lanes that snake up into the hills from Châteaubourg (130:A2) or St-Péray (130:A3) to the viewpoint at **St-Romain-de-Lerps**. The views east are vast; just as intriguing are the two semi-circular observation tables, each one made of 19 ceramic tiles and hand painted by Paul Goichot from 1940-43. A third terrific access road is the steep climb north on the D266 from St-Laurent-du-Pape (130:A3) to the Château de Pierre-Gourde. Use the non-metalled track to reach the mound of stones; the view west, of line upon line of hills, is well worth the drive.

For railway buffs (including me), not one of the above suggestions bears comparison with the most exciting of the Ardèche *entreés*. You need to put aside a whole day and to leave your car in the Rhône Valley. Revel in France's best privately-owned railway line, the Chemin de Fer du Vivarais, a metre-gauge run of 33 km which climbs 250 metres from Tournon-sur-Rhône (130:A2) to **Lamastre** (F2). The railway celebrated its centenary in 1991. During the summer there's a 10.00 a.m. "steamer" from Tournon, arriving in Lamastre at midday. For a timetable write to CFTM, 8 rue d'Algérie, 69001 Lyon (tel 78 28 83 34).

There's one scenic motoring route in the Ardèche which I would not miss under any circumstances. Start at **Vals-les-Bains** (E4), a small, sleepy, old-fashioned spa. Use the D253 to **Chirols**, to the west. In the past, on a wild and windy day, I've relished the views of serried ranks of hills; the air was so clear you felt you could reach out and touch them and, far below, the River **Ardèche** sparkled. Take the D26 to **Burzet** (D4). After heavy rain the turbulent river vistas in the village will literally stop you in your tracks. The Ardèche is classic Monte-Carlo Rally country: one of the best hillclimbs is the seven km drive up the D289. The road winds and climbs 2600 ft from Burzet in that short distance – a match for anything in the Alps.

Return to Burzet and head north on the D215, up the well-named Valley of *Myrtilles* (bilberries/blueberries). Park and do the not-too-demanding 15-minute walk to the Ray-Pic cascade. Then drive, through woods, to the marshy plateau south of **Lachamp-Raphaël** (E3), to one of the most exhilarating of sights. In May Anne and I have gasped at the sheets of wild daffodils, interlaced with large yellow marsh buttercups, numerous orchids and scores of other wild flowers. A few weeks later, in June, we've been stunned anew by the same colourful pastures when pillows of intensely dark purple violas have competed with wild narcissi and myriad other wild flowers to capture our attention.

Tear yourself away and continue north-west to the lava cone of **Gerbier de Jonc** (D3); if your lungs are up to the test then make the short but very steep climb to the top. Below you is the source of the River **Loire** and, around you, an extensive panorama. But I'll lead you to an even better one, without any stiff muscle-testing exercise.

Use the D378 and D400 to the Croix de Boutières (D3), at the tail end of the sleeping dog **Mont Mézenc** (at 5751 ft the area's highest). The immediate vista to the east is remarkable for the many volcanic humps and lumps and their interconnecting wooded ridges and valleys below you; this is how a child would draw a mountain landscape. The panorama, explained by an observation table, is stunning.

In June the pastures between Les Estables and **Moudeyres** (D2) resemble snowfields; in reality wild narcissi. Hidden among them are dense pockets of purple pansies. Stop and chuckle at the entertainment provided by a meadow orchestra of skylarks and crickets. In June, on yet another visit to the seductive plateau, we've picnicked alongside the circular **Lac de St-Front** (75 acres, three km circumference and 10 m deep) with no-one else for company except a syklark and cushions of wild trollius, wild garlic, vetch, orchids and other bright flowers. We also recall a picnic on the slopes above the ruins of the Château de **Rochebonne** (E3), on the D478 south of **St-Agrève** (E2), where ruined walls appear to be part of the rocky and isolated strategic perch.

For motorists the countryside is heart-stopping stuff. For walkers the terrain is paradise. Let me commend to you a series of *pochettes*, each one of which contains superlative details of several different walks with maps and interesting notes for each suggestion. For details contact the Comité Départemental de la Randonneé, 12 boulevard P. Jourde, B.P. 198, 43005 Le Puy-en-Velay (71 05 56 50).

Now for something different. If you like the idea of walks accompanied by a pack donkey then nose out the following: Roselyne Girard at **Antraigues-sur-Volane** (E4: a village worth seeing; 75 88 24 76); or Alex and Camille Ristor at Chirols (E4: 75 94 48 39).

There's so much to tell you about and not enough space to do justice to the varied charms hidden on map sheet 129. I'll list a few in random order. The azure **Lac-d'Issarlès** (D3), nestling in the crater of an extinct volcano. The isolated ruins of the 12th-century Cistercian abbey at **Mazan** (D4). **Aubenas** (143:E1), perched high at the divide between Vivarais to the north (chestnut trees galore and cooking in butter) and the Cévennes to the south (olive trees and cooking in oil), has a castle with fine ramparts and an 11th-century tower. And for the children, the Safari park at Peaugres (F1), north-east of Annonay; 800 animals seen both from your car and on foot (open all year).

Seek out some museums. The Ecomusée du Moulinage (mill machinery) at Chirols (E4: p.m. June to Oct; not Tuesday). The Musée Vivarais César Filhol (Vivarais folk history) at Annonay (F1: p.m. every day July and Aug; p.m. Wednesday and weekends rest of year). The Musée Archéologique (150,000 years of history and an active dig) at Soyons (130:A3), south of Valence (Wednesday to Sunday May to Sept; p.m. only Wednesday, Thursday and weekends rest of year). The Château de Tournon Musée du Rhône (130:A2) brings the river's past to life (p.m. April, May, Sept and Oct; June to Aug a.m. and p.m. but not Tuesday). Two museums at **Privas** (F4): the Musée de la Terre Ardèchoise (geology and archaeology of Ardèche: p.m. Wednesday to Sunday); and the Chapelle des Recollets (Musée d'Art Religieux: p.m.).

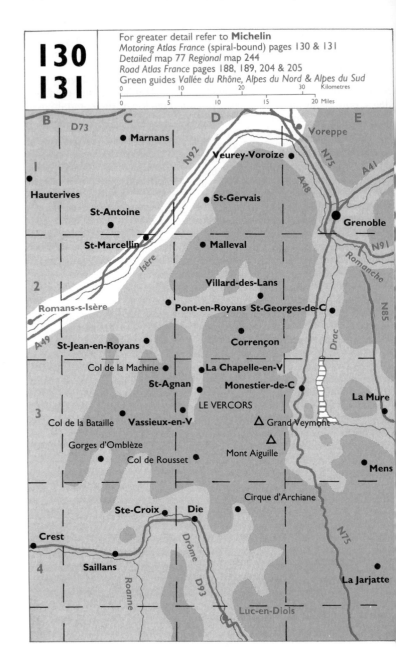

130
131

For greater detail refer to **Michelin**
Motoring Atlas France (spiral-bound) pages 130 & 131
Detailed map 77 Regional map 244
Road Atlas France pages 188, 189, 204 & 205
Green guides *Vallée du Rhône, Alpes du Nord & Alpes du Sud*

0   10   20   30   Kilometres

0   5   10   15   20 Miles

B   **C**   **D**   **E**

D73

● Marnans

N92

Voreppe

● Veurey-Voroize

A48

N75

A41

1

●
Hauterives

● St-Gervais

St-Antoine
●

Grenoble

St-Marcellin ●

Isère

● Malleval

N91

Romanche

Villard-des-Lans

2

Romans-s-Isère

● Pont-en-Royans St-Georges-de-C ●

N85

Drac

A49

● **St-Jean-en-Royans**

● Corrençon

Col de la Machine ●

● La Chapelle-en-V

St-Agnan ●

● Monestier-de-C

La Mure

LE VERCORS

3

Col de la Bataille   **Vassieux-en-V** ●

△ Grand Veymont

● **Mens**

Gorges d'Omblèze

△

●   Col de Rousset ●

Mont Aiguille

Cirque d'Archiane

Ste-Croix ●   ● **Die**
●

Drôme

N75

Crest
●

4

Saillans
●

Roanne

D93

La Jarjatte
●

Luc-en-Diois

134

The mountain terrain at the heart of map sheets 130/131 – **Le Vercors** – is a part of France I love as much as any other. The Vercors – a triangular limestone mass of mountains, 40 miles long by 25 miles wide at its base – is a natural fortress of eroded, rampart-like peaks, isolated from the French Alps by three rivers which all but encircle the *massif*: the **Isère** (C1/D1/E1), **Drac** (E2/E3) and **Drôme** (C4/D4).

Access to the Vercors is difficult: a few tortuous lanes wind up in steep zig-zags from the valleys. Within the *massif* two torrents, the Bourne and Vernaison (D2), create an even more remote inner sanctuary. This secret heart of Vercors wears a vast cloak of dense pine forests, cool in summer and a dark cover in winter. No wonder then the Vercors became a citadel of the Resistance and, later, such a legend.

Two days after the D-Day landings on 6 June 1944, the tricolour flew on numerous flag-poles in the Vercors. One of the proud flags fluttered above St-Nizier-du-Moucherotte (E1), atop the rock needles called Les Trois Pucelles and in full view of **Grenoble** far below. Inevitably the Wehrmacht were incensed and, during the weeks which followed, the Germans threw 20,000 troops into the mountains – bent on revenge because the Vercors *maquis* had long been a thorn in their sides.

The *maquisards* had counted on relief coming from the air and from the anticipated Allies' landing in Provence. The uprising came too soon, help arrived too late. Hundreds died defending the citadel and, by July, the Germans had full control of the Vercors.

As you travel the mountain roads you will see numerous monuments in memory of those who gave their lives in 1944. *Mort pour la France* say the carved words on the proud monuments: are there any finer for an epitaph? Spare time for the cemetery at St-Nizier (Les Trois Pucelles are to the south); the national cemetery at **Vassieux-en-Vercors** (D3) where there's also an evocative Resistance museum; the striking monument at **Malleval** (D2) at the top of the taxing Gorges du Nan climb; and drive the narrow D215C/D221 which wind west from **Villard-de-Lans** (D2) through dense pine forests towards Valchevrière – past numerous small memorials to *maquisards* who died as they fought valiantly, in retreat, to keep the Germans at bay. But perhaps the most poignant of all is the monument at the entrance to the Grotte de la Luire (D3), south of **La Chapelle-en-Vercors**, used by the Resistance as a hospital. The memorial's simple words carry an undemanding plea: *Thou that comest here – Bring thy soul with thee*.

The retribution and carnage reeked out by the Wehrmacht and, worse still, French collaborators, was hideous. (Most French people collaborated passively during the war. We shouldn't be too smug: what would have occurred here if Germany had over-run Britain?) Hundreds of men, women and children were murdered in cold blood. Villages were razed to the ground; new buildings in places like Vassieux and La Chapelle are a salutary reminder of the sadistic punishment meted out.

There are numerous scenic sights. Leave the **A48** at **Veurey-Voroize**

(E1), climb to La Buffe and, just before the Tunnel du Mortier, admire the view below and ahead of you. Detour south to the grassy plateau at La Molière for more extensive views east to the Chamrousse (F2). A little further north is the Gouffre Berger, the deepest and most dangerous pot-hole in France. (Much safer, and worth a visit, are the Grottes de Chorance (D2) in the Gorges de la Bourne – noted for rare pencil-thin stalactites; there's also an open-air museum.)

Another exciting access is a southerly one: starting at **Die** (D4), the **Col de Rousset** is a memorable climb of numerous hairpin bends. The best views are from the mouth of the old tunnel. The **Col de la Bataille** (C3) is the easiest entry route; views, north and south, are the highlight. The most exhilarating, frightening for some, is the engineering marvel which climbs from **St-Jean-en-Royans** (C2) up the west side of the Combe de Laval, a vast amphitheatre of rocks, to the **Col de la Machine**; the final stretch is a series of tunnels gouged out of the vertical mountain face. Another thrilling northern entry is from **St-Gervais** (D1), up the taxing D35 and then south on the Route des Ecouges (D2) with super views all the way.

Within the *massif* other man-made marvels combine with some of Nature's more violent sculptures. One is the amazing Grands Goulets (D2) where the tiny, but powerful Vernaison punches through a rocky barrier. Somehow, 150 years ago, the Jouberts (father and son) built a leech-like road alongside the torrential stream which hurtles ferociously down the narrow ravine. Equally unusual is the road that hugs the floor of the dark Gorges de la Bourne (D2) at its eastern end; steep cliffs overhang the claustrophobic bumpy tarmac ribbon. Both the above roads lead to **Pont-en-Royans**; be sure to see the colourful tall houses beside the Bourne. Something quite different is the Réserve Naturelle des Hauts Plateaux du Vercors – an exceptional high-altitude nature reserve with no roads. Information points on access to this flora and fauna paradise are at **Corrençon** (D2) and **St-Agnan** (D3).

The outer rim of the *massif* has many a natural splendour. For example, the **Gorges d'Omblèze** (C3), a dead-end with cascades and solitude as your rewards. Another, even more spectacular dead-end, is the D224 which takes you into the heart of a superb *cirque*. Here the **Cirque d'Archiane** (D4) is a stunning sight: a mammoth semi-circle stone wall rears high above the valley. Who trims the box hedges?

The best sight of all is on the descent of the Col de Menée (E4), east of the *cirque*. Ahead is the hypnotic, tilted, table-top mass of **Mont Aiguille**, one of the most startling sights in France. Or approach from the north, using roads which are renowned Monte-Carlo Rally stages – the Col de l'Arzelier (E2), St-Guillaume (E3) and Gresse-en-Vercors (D3): wooded terrain, valleys, unspoilt villages, gorges, views, streams and cols. And, at La Bâtie, the northern aspect of Mont Aiguille looms menacingly above you – a giant vertical orange and cream chisel head rising high into the sky. To the right is the grim line of **Grand Veymont**, the highest Vercors peak (almost 8000 ft).

What else is there other than the Vercors? Grenoble (E1), an almighty traffic jam, has several fine museums. But I would go elsewhere. Start to the south of Grenoble, on the Corniche du Drac road from **St-Georges-de-Commiers** (E2), past the sturdy château at La Motte-les-Bains, through Marcieu, to approach **La Mure** (E3) from the south-west. The man-made lake is turquoise and, as the road runs further south the surface below falls further and further away. At the D529/D116B junction the lake and mountain panorama is magnificent; at Les Côtes even more so. Gasp at the drop below you. The acoustics are intriguing: we heard doves cooing from a farm far below us on the other side of the Drac.

An alternative, easier-on-the-driver way of seeing the Vercors wall and lake is the Chemin de Fer de la Mure which runs from a prim station at St-Georges to La Mure. The metre-gauge line (18 tunnels and six viaducts) was opened in 1888 and was the first to use high-voltage DC current. (From one to four trains every day from mid Apl to mid Oct.) Another way of enjoying the lake is a cruise from Treffort (E3), northeast of **Monestier-de-Clermont** (June to Oct: tel 76 34 14 56).

From La Mure use the D526 and the Pont de Ponsonnas across the Drac. The bridge is an official "*Saut en Elastique*" centre. We saw several young men make bungee jumps from the bridge, leaping hundreds of feet into the gorge. What nerves of steel they have.

The circle of terrain around **Mens** (E3) is called Le Trièves – hills (one a pyramid), woods and fields with a backdrop of high rocky *têtes*. Mens is a "working" village; from afar the most pleasing aspect is the rich, earthy hues of the *lauzes* (roof tiles). Further south, beyond the Col de la Croix Haute (E4), drive up the Buëch Valley to **La Jarjatte**: a miniature Chamonix Valley with a jagged jaw of sharply-pointed peaks, wild flowers and a crystal-clear stream.

The River Drôme is at its best west of Die (D4). Savour tiny **Ste-Croix** (C4), with its vineyards (Clairette de Die sparklers) and walnut trees, and the river view from Pontaix. Do not rush past either **Saillans** (C4) or Aouste-sur-Sye (B4); relish the colourful village vistas from the left bank of the river. **Crest** (B4) has a notable architectural sight: the Tour de Crest, a formidable medieval dungeon, is reckoned to have the highest walls in France. Every Wed and Sat (15.00) the tower is used as spine-chilling abseiling wall.

Finally, some sights north of the Isère (C2). Visit **St-Marcellin**, famed for its small, mild-flavoured disks of cow's milk cheese. There's a Musée du Fromage (a.m. and p.m. except Mon a.m.). Next, the Gothic basilica at **St-Antoine**, to the north-west, has some sumptuous treasures; see, too, the Musée Départemental de Ste-Antoine l'Abbaye (both March to Nov; not Tues). On to the tiny Romanesque Eglise St-Pierre at **Marnans** (C1), north of Roybon. Then chuckle and marvel at the Palais Idéal at **Hauterives** (B1) – built of pebbles and stones a century ago by the town postman, Ferdinand Cheval.

132
133

For greater detail refer to **Michelin**
Motoring Atlas France (spiral-bound) pages 132 & 133
Detailed map 77 *Regional* map 244
Road Atlas France pages 190, 191, 206 & 207
Green guides *Alpes du Nord & Alpes du Sud*

| 0 | 10 | 20 | 30 | Kilometres |
| 0 | 5 | 10 | 15 | 20 Miles |

B   C   D   E

St-Jean-de-M

Col de la Croix de Fer

Arc   Modane   N6

1

St-Sorlin-d'Arves

Valloire

ITALIE

2   Col du
Galibier

La Grave

Les Deux-Alpes   Romanche   Col du Lautaret

Le Lauzet   Vallée de

Vénéon   la Clarée

N91

La Bérarde   MASSIF DES   N94   **Briançon**

3

Pelvoux

ECRINS   **Puy-St-Vincent**

Valgaudemer   Col d'Izoard   Guil

L'Argentière-la-B   **Arvieux**

Château-Queyras

Sommet Bucher

4   Durance   **St-Véran**

Champsaur   **Ceillac**

Guillestre

QUEYRAS

Gap   **Embrun**

138

Over the years I have had the good fortune to explore most of the terrain on the tiny map to the left of these words. Tiny indeed; but what majestic countryside is to be found on the ground: gigantic mountains and glaciers, dozens of entrancing valleys, endless dead-end roads, numerous man-made sites, cascades galore and much else besides. I wonder if I shall ever be able to say that I've seen all the mountainous *pays*; there is so much to relish in the ever-changing landscape.

In the list above I missed out, deliberately, one of Nature's most alluring legacies to the area: her incomparable display of wild flowers. In previous decades Anne and I have crossed the terrain in early spring, high summer, and the autumn. Last year we were there in late June, during a magical few days which left us utterly spellbound.

One morning we started early, leaving our overnight hotel, off the edge of the map, before 7.00 a.m. The **Romanche** Valley (B2) was nothing special: the lake behind the Barrage du Chambon was an ugly eye-sore (as is **Les Deux-Alpes**). The mighty Cascade de la Pisse was in full flow but that sight soon paled as we drove through **La Grave** (C2) and caught sight of the **Massif des Ecrins**, France's second highest mountain *chaîne*. We didn't stop: east of the village, at the end of the tunnel, we turned sharp right and snaked upwards through Les Terrasses and on towards Le Chazelet. We stopped at the Oratoire du Chazelet and climbed 300 metres to the viewing table, 1834 m high.

The time was 8.00 a.m. The sky was crystal clear, a retina-searing blue. The sun, still low, was to our left. The mountain wall above us seemed so close that you instinctively reached out to touch the glistening glaciers, shimmering snowfields and the summits of black needles. If you want to access the remote whiteness then *téléphériques* take you from La Grave to a height of 3200 m on La Meije (itself 3983 m). We were more than satisfied; in the 15 minutes we spent soaking in the wondrous panorama we had the viewing table to ourselves. Our plan to visit La Grave's 15th-century Church of Notre Dame and 17th-century Chapelle des Pénitents was put aside. The weather was superb, so we decided to make the most of our good fortune.

Half an hour later we stopped again, this time on the green pastures below the western end of the **Col du Lautaret** (C2). The "green" pastures were in fact hiding, within the lush grass, literally millions of wild flowers. We stood on one spot and, without moving our feet an inch, were able to count over 50 varieties, some of them orchids. The Lautaret is influenced by both Atlantic and Mediterranean climates and is bordered, on the southern side, by the crystalline Ecrins and, to the north, by the various sedimentary rocks of the Galibier *massif*. As a result of this climatic and geological mixture the flora, in both variety and quantity, is unique. More than 1,500 of the 4,000 plus species found in France are on these high (2000 m) Alpine slopes.

Our luck came in oversized bundles on that June day. The world-renowned Jardin Alpin on the Col du Lautaret (2058 m) had opened the previous day (25 June to 9 Sept: 10.30 to 18.30). Within the small grounds Alpine plants from all over the world prosper. The garden lies in the subalpine zone (i.e. in the upper part of the forest vegetation which reaches 2350 m in the region). The severity of the climate, particularly in winter, has long been known throughout Europe. Indeed Capt. Scott and his team spent time on the col in March 1908, preparing for their ill-fated expedition to the South Pole. There's a memorial to the explorer at the top of the garden. The site is exhilarating – with the enormous Glacier de l'Homme, on the eastern flanks of La Meije, almost appearing to be sliding out of the sky towards the *jardin*.

The **Col du Galibier** (C2) was also clear of clouds – for us the first time ever. On the ascent we became blasé about the orchids we spotted: – *nigritelle brunette*, *moucheron* and *globuleux* were just three of the varieties. At the 2646 m summit the mountain panorama was a rejuvenating tonic: to the far north the humpbacked Mont Blanc *massif*; across the road the Massif des Ecrins (with the Barre des Ecrins a striking skyscraper); and, far to the south-east, Mont Viso (F4) poked its head above the **Queyras** Regional Park. On the northern descent of the Galibier we stopped again, just below the scree where the pastures begin, to revel at the many species of gentians, pasque flowers, tiny trollious, various anemones and numerous other varieties.

Our detour to **Valloire** (C1) could almost have been an anti-climax. But we were determined not to miss the Baroque Eglise de Notre-Dame de l'Assomption, one of the few in the Alps where the doors are open all the time. Built in the middle 11th century, the modest stone exterior hides an unbelievable interior where every inch is richly decorated in one form or other: frescoes, paintings, carvings, figures, gilt, ornate nave and ceilings, a stunning rose window – and all this with the organ being played in the background. What on earth had we done to deserve such rewards on that exciting 26th day of June?

At this stage of the chapter I am feeling embarrassed. I have still got much to tell you about and, without exception, everything that follows has to be described in the same vein. Take, for example, the Vénéon Valley which runs, south of La Meije, to a dead-end barrier at **La Bérarde** (C3), bang-up against the Barre des Ecrins (4102 m). This is the ultimate three-star valley, unspoilt and laden down with scenic fruits. The road is best described as one which is akin to entering the jaws of a gigantic whale: as you ascend you lose count of the 10,000 ft-high peaks, to either side of the valley.

The River **Vénéon** is the first visual blow, both in colour and volume. There's plenty of white water: no wonder then that between the Lanchâtra lake (B2) and the river below St-Christophe (B3), you are likely to spot rafters and canoeists paddling downstream. The flora and fauna, too, is captivating: lilies, everlasting sweet peas, tiny pinks and several species of wild roses, some of which we had not seen before in the Alps; butterflies everywhere and, at the top end of the valley, we spotted two marmots and several birds of prey. The many cascades were in full spate; the descent by car and the long walk to the Cascade de la Lavey (using the two bridges which cross the Vénéon and Muande) was worth the effort. Last, but not least, the startling mountains: summits of needles, molars, pyramids, jagged saw edges, snowfields, glaciers and huge "waterfalls" of shining rock faces, thousands of feet high. What a wonderland: Nature at her supreme best.

In the top left-hand corner of my small map, to the south of **St-Jean-de-Maurienne** (C1: in the hateful **Arc** Valley), is yet another startling corner of mountain Disneyland. Follow the road up the Vallée de l'Arvan – deep gorges with, above them, vast sheets of rock, cut into slices and slabs; tar black and slate grey in the lower reaches and, higher up, lighter shades of glowing stone. All the way up the climb one is aware of three looming teeth on the southern horizon, almost a compass bearing landmark but, in reality, Les Aiguilles d'Arves.

The Baroque church at **St-Sorlin-d'Arves** (C1) keeps its doors firmly shut but do note the scores of memorials on the exterior walls, all made from tiny individual beads. As you climb the **Col de la Croix de Fer** (B1) the slopes resemble a massive rock garden of wild flowers. On the western side of the col the extensive pastures are green but, on closer inspection, they reveal myriad wild flowers.

I wonder how many of you have read *A Wild Herb Soup* (Victor Gollancz paperback) by a redoubtable French lady, Emilie Carles. The author spent most of her life (1900-1979) in the high mountains around **Briançon**, the highest *ville* in Europe (D3). The book, based on her remarkable life, is a revealing insight into the hardships suffered by the mountain people of the Briançonnais in the early decades of the 20th century.

You cannot fail to admire her ferocious courage, iron integrity, and fiery opinions. You'll agree with many of the latter; but, occasionally, you'll perhaps even despise some of her more contentious observations. One of the least contentious disagreements I have with Madame Carles is her opinion that the Vénéon Valley has been "plundered and sacked by promoters." How absurd: where on earth could she have been thinking about? Perhaps she saw Les Deux-Alpes (B2) which has a heartstopping panorama of Venosc and the river far below (from the viewpoint behind the Chalet Mounier hotel)?

I respect Madame Carles enormously because as Bernard Pivot said: "She was one hell of a woman." In the latter part of her life she discovered, as all independent free-thinkers do, that you must go for the jugular in any battle of wits with all forms of bureaucracy. Agreed?

There's not enough space here to go into the details of her book. But I'll refer to some of the more remote geographical locations which, during her teaching spells in the mountains, played such an important part in recounting the hard life that country folk endured. She taught in many tiny hamlets and villages. Locate **Le Lauzet** (C2/D2), just below the Col du Lautaret: the place is harsh even now, on a perfect summer's day. Remember what I said about Capt. Scott and severe winters? Imagine, then, her spell as a teacher here 70 years ago. Next, find La Monta (F3): in the higher reaches of the **Guil** Valley, the hamlet, today is a collection of ruined stones, destroyed by the vengeful Germans in 1945 in their typical murderous ways (you can spot the ruins just north of the church and chalet). And two more villages: Le Casset (D2), below Le Lauzet; and **Puy-St-Vincent** (D3), both of which bear little resemblance today to the locations Emilie described 70 years ago.

Much of the book recounts her upbringing and latter days in the **Vallée de la Clarée** (D2). She was born in Val-des-Près. While I would never agree with her that the valley is "the most beautiful in the world" nevertheless, I am with her all the way for the battle she fought to save *la vallée*. The heart of Val remains the same (note the sun clock, built in her time, 1920). The river and woods are the best aspects; next come the differing shaped rocks, of varying hues. Seek out, too, the many chapels at Névache (D2), marked on the map; and the wall paintings at the two churches in Plampinet with its super riverside setting. *En route* admire the great fortress at Briançon, one of Vauban's cunning military creations. He left his mark everywhere.

Let me now devote some space to the Queyras, a delectable enclave of mountains south-east of Briançon. Access this remote, wild fastness by the only open-all-the-year-road, the D902 from **Guillestre** (D4). The narrow road passes through tunnels, high above the Guil; later, the road is much easier and wider in the Combe du Queyras. But, whatever you do, don't fail to detour up the D60 to **Ceillac** (E4). The Cristillan torrent is a furious flow. In the initial climb there are no less than 18 hairpins; at one spot the river races through a tunnel and the adjacent road cuts through a small gorge. That's a unique oddity.

Ceillac is a mix of old and new and narrow lanes. The Vallon du Mélezet ends in a magnificent *cirque* but the real reason for asking you to make this *déviation* is the Cascade de la Pisse (that name again), halfway up the valley. We reckon this among our favourite waterfalls anywhere: several hundred feet high, the cascade's most unusual feature is that almost for the entire fall the water is 10 feet or so inside the rock face. Even in July the cascade is a thrilling spectacle.

Your first sight of **Château-Queyras** (E4), shortly after passing the Resistance memorial, is imposing enough. Built originally in the 14th century, the most significant strengthening of the strategic fortifications were put in place 300 years ago by that man again, Vauban. Follow the routes I now suggest and you will see the perched castle from every conceivable angle (open June to September: 9.00 to 19.00). First, the 11 km climb to the **Sommet Bucher** (E4). Every inch of the way the narrow road passes through dense woods and past wild flowers. At the top there's a 300 m walk to a *table d'orientation* (in two parts) and a refuge. The view is truly panoramic: a 360-degree circular wall of mountains. Far below is **St-Véran** (E4), Europe's highest *commune*. The only sounds are bees, the wind and bird song. The road is narrow and roughish; but the rewards are heavenly. The cherries on top of the cream are the wild flowers at the summit.

The climb from the Guil, east of Château-Queyras, to St-Véran is easy as pie. Over 6500 ft above sea-level, the village is noted for ancient timber chalets. We were also impressed by the simple church and its stained glass windows; the fine wood sculptures for sale at a couple of chalet-shops; the huge stone tiles atop many a chalet; and the interiors of two ancient houses which took you back to an *autrefois*. One caveat: there's a long climb from the car park to the village proper.

One unusual aspect of the Queyras villages is the number of wall sundials, of varying types. There are reckoned to be 15 in St-Véran alone (we could only count eight); five in Château-Queyras; four in remote Meyriès, above the latter; and four in **Arvieux** (E3).

Finally, your last long dead-end drive in the Queyras has to be the Guil Valley (F3/F4), as far as you can go by car. Park at the isolated rock, the size of a large house, and at least do the 10 minute walk to the Petit Belvédère du Mont Viso, where you win your first sight of this wondrous giant of a mountain, just across the border in Italy. Time will dictate how far you can walk up the spectacular valley, climbing ever closer to Viso. But do try to walk the 30-minute Sentier Ecologique du Pré-Michel which starts at the Petit Belvédère: the information centre at the car park explains all and a great booklet, *Sous le ciel du Viso*, provides more detail on why this superb valley is so rich in flora and fauna. (The Po is the cause of the humid micro-climate.)

Leave the Queyras by the mighty **Col d'Izoard** (E3), 2360 m high. At the summit you cross terrain which must be akin to the landscape on Mars: an orange and grey planet of needles and landslides and mammoth smooth, almost vertical, "snowfields" of stones and rock. The map tags this startling geological world as Casse Déserte.

What else is there to see? Spare time for the cathedral at **Embrun** (147:D1); the old part of the town sits contentedly on a rock table. Further north, another Vauban fortress, Mont-Dauphin (D4), also has a huge rock sideboard below the castle's walls. Leave the N94 at **L'Argentière-la-Bessée** (D3) and head north-west. Dull and boring to start, with only wall sundials of any interest in the villages but, pass through **Pelvoux** and Les Claux and, immediately after the tunnel, the run becomes exciting – through woods, dappled with shade, to Ailefroide. Then the road scrabbles up through trees to another dead-end of lofty rock faces and needles, cascades, glaciers and the highest peaks in the Ecrins *massif*. Allow time for the not-too-demanding walk north from the car park at the Pré de Madame Carle.

I have yet to visit the **Champsaur** (B4/C4) and **Valgaudemer** (B3/C3) valleys north of Gap. The former is the higher reaches of the Drac Noir and Blanc (renowned for walking); the latter is literally lined with waterfalls. As I said at the start: there's so much to explore.

140

For greater detail refer to **Michelin**
Motoring Atlas France (spiral-bound) page 140
Detailed maps 76 & 80 *Regional* maps 235 & 240
Road Atlas France pages 199, 200, 214 & 215
Green guides *Gorges du Tarn & Pyrénées-Roussillon*

| 0 | 10 | 20 | 30 | Kilometres |
| 0 | 5 | 10 | 15 | 20 Miles |

A   **B**   **C**

1

Entraygues

Flagnac

Lot

Conques

Estaing

D921

Villecomtal

Decazeville

Dourdou

Espalion

Rodelle

2

N140

Cougousse

Bozouls

D920

Montrozier

Belcastel

N88

Aveyron

La Loubière

Rodez

Lac de Pont-de-Salars

D911

3

D911

Sauveterre-de-Rouergue

Lac de Pareloup

Naucelle

Viaur

Castelpers

Pampelonne   Viaduc du Viaur

Lac de Villefranche-de-Panat

N88

4

Carmaux

Réquista

Broquiès

Brousse-le-Château

Ambialet   *Tarn*

144

I would imagine that most tourists, heading for the heart of France, would dismiss much of map sheet 140 as dull, uninteresting terrain. Once again, I shall try to prove to you the essential element of surprise, one which unfailingly rewards those who pocket their prejudices and travel instead with open minds and receptive hearts.

The landscape is dominated by river valleys. Five are especially notable: from south to north the **Tarn**, **Viaur**, **Aveyron**, **Dourdou** and **Lot**. I'll describe each valley, and the nearby countryside, in turn, giving most space to the lesser-known scenic attractions.

Start your exploration of an unknown stretch of the Tarn to the east of **Ambialet** (154:B1). The village and the aptly-named Presqui'île d'Ambialet are a scenic *tour de force* of river sculpture. As you approach Ambialet you plunge into a short 20 metre-long tunnel; beware, there's a stop sign at the tunnel exit. Turn right at the cross-roads and follow the road up to the *prieuré*; walk to the viewpoint. Now you'll see what an unusual meander lies both behind and below you. The two curves in the river to the south almost touch; at the narrowest point there's a small ornate château-style building. In fact this is an electricity generating station; water is allowed to flow through an underground channel which bridges the 15 metre-wide gap and this is the reason why the loop to the north has such a dried-up look.

To the north of Ambialet, between the old coal-mining town of **Carmaux** (A4) and **Réquista** (B4), there's a long, high ridge of hills: the villages on the D91 and D903 are really not up to much – except for the beautiful lilies you see everywhere; the views, north and south, are extensive and exceptional. I would want to get back to the Tarn. After you've seen something of the Viaur (more of that valley later) dive south again to magical **Brousse-le-Château** (C4).

What a seductive spot Brousse is, sleeping contentedly on its perch above the Tarn and alongside the Alrance. Every wall of the half-timbered and stone houses appears to be rose-covered and alongside the Alrance are many colourful vegetable and flower gardens. There's a ruined castle with towers and ramparts high above the houses; a *pont roman*; narrow alleys (*calades*) paved with giant cobblestones; an *église* with an open three-bell tower; and a weir upstream on the Tarn.

From Brousse follow the D54 to **Broquiès** (C4). Stop at La Palisse farm (marked on the map and road): there's a magnificent vista to the south of the point where the River Dourdou (not one of the five) enters the Tarn. The backdrop to the river picture is row upon row of hills to both south-east and east. The views remain excellent as you continue climbing north on the D25; the map, quite correctly, shows a particularly fine panorama at the junction with the D31, 728 metres high.

The **Lac de Villefranche-de-Panat** (C4) is a surprisingly pleasant man-made lake: the banks are wooded, there's a beach, plenty of reflections and *pédalos*. Do as we did and drive to the Tour de Peyrebrune (3000 ft above sea-level) for some fine views; there's a modern flight of stairs in the tower. We continued north-east, past Calmejane and, just west of the farm entrance to La Fraysse, we braked hard at the sight of a spectacle the like of which we had not seen anywhere else in France: a field to our right had such a dense covering of *orchis militaris* that the entire surface was washed with a dense pink colouring. No wonder the field is protected by barbed wire.

I've seen the **Lac de Pareloup** (C3) many times during the last 20 years but, in 1993, a sad sight greeted Anne and me. Disaster had struck the local hoteliers and traders: the entire lake had been emptied by EDF (the national electricity company) for "cleaning". The task of refilling the lake should start again in 1994; when full the wooded inlets are an attractive bonus, as are the beaches and watersport facilities. On the eastern shore, at Les Vernhes, there's a new marina: normally you can cruise on the lake but last year the spanking craft was high and dry. Further north, the **Lac de Pont-de-Salars** (C3) was full, looking quite smug in the June sunlight.

Back to the second river, the Viaur. I would happily give time again to the network of tributaries feeding the Viaur to the east of the **N88**, where the road crosses the wooded Gorges du Viaur (A4). Start at the grim-looking Château du Bosc (B3), associated with Toulouse-Lautrec's childhood, south-east of **Naucelle** (open April to October). After your visit descend to **Castelpers** (B4), flower-filled and alongside the Céor. Follow the stream west to its confluence with the Viaur. Detour north to the viewpoint at Puech (hill) de Rouet and then back again to the Viaur, continuing downstream. This is heavenly country: roses blooming, cattle bellowing, water murmuring and lizards scuttling.

Just before the N88 man does his bit to impress: the 100-year-old **Viaduc du Viaur** spans the gorge 120 metres above you. The single arch railway bridge, an immense necklace of steel tubing and struts, is an engineering marvel. Further downstream two spots are easily reached. Below **Pampelonne** (A4) the D78 snakes down, through woods, to the valley floor; from the tower ruins at Thuriès you'll understand why the river is throttled downstream: courtesy of an EDF dam. Pont-de-Cirou, a few km to the west, is an isolated place; one quirk is the *département* and kilometre stone bang in the middle of the old bridge.

This is very much walkers' country; note the footpath which runs along the river's left bank from Tanus, on the N88, to Pont-de-Cirou, past the remote *église* Notre-Dame de Las Planques. Naturalists among you will appreciate the absence of roads among the trees and plants. Perhaps you'll be lucky enough to catch a glimpse of otters or herons.

Between the Viaur and the Aveyron (the third of the five rivers) is a *pays* called Ségala. At its high heart is an architectural treat: the small *bastide* of **Sauveterre-de-Rouergue** (A3). The arcaded *place* is a handsome square. Also worth looking out for is the *église* at Naucelle (B3) with fine stained glass windows. Another tip: one of the best fresh cow's milk cheeses I've ever tasted in France was made at Le Taurinol farm at Taurines (B3), east of the château at Bosc.

The Aveyron, like the Viaur, has few roads alongside its banks. Certain spots are worth the detour. **Rodez** (C2) is the architectural highlight: the sandstone Cathédrale Notre-Dame is magnificent, especially the ornate high bell tower; see, too, *vieux* Rodez (south of the cathedral) with many splendid ancient houses, noted for their galleries and interior courtyards. Upstream from Rodez nose out tiny **La Loubière** with an *église* and pretty riverside aspect; that's true, too, of **Montrozier** (C2) with a sturdy looking Renaissance château. But the best site is **Belcastel** (A2/B2: west of Rodez) – a sumptuously scenic joy: a huddle of 15th-century houses, dominated by a castle high above the roof tops; cobbled *calades*; a bend in the river; and a medieval *pont* spanning the 20 metre-wide river.

Now to the fourth river, the Dourdou – the least well-known and we think perhaps the best of the five. Start at **Bozouls** (C2). From a viewpoint just yards from the D20 admire the astonishing *trou* below you: a wooded *cirque* where the river has formed a stunning loop. At the heart of the giant meander, above the river, is a Romanesque *église*, built from the local sandstone (*grès*). Continue north-west on the D20 and then drop south to **Rodelle** (C2): the deep wooded valley is the first major surprise; the village's rocky site, on a high spur, is the second. Continue downstream to the Lot. What a superb valley: by **Villecomtal** (B1) you will have noted that all buildings are made from the local *grès*, a rich ruby-hued sandstone; note, too, the shapes and shades of the *lauzes* (roof tiles) and admire the startling contrast of fallow emerald pastures and ploughed red fields.

Halfway down the Gorges du Dourdou, make the essential climb to **Conques** (B1). The 11th-century *église* is a Romanesque gem: the three spires, high nave, majestic sculptures of the peerless tympanum and the famed treasure (including the glorious gold-covered statue of Ste-Foy, enriched with precious stones) make Conques a three-star wonder.

I have never been much impressed by the Gorges du Lot, upstream from **Entraygues** (C1). The wooded river valley, downstream from Entraygues, is much more appealing (and the lanes which climb up from the Lot). I especially love the area around **Flagnac** (A1), the site of a simple but stirring annual *spectacle*: *Hier, Un Village* (details from Office de Tourisme, 12300 **Decazeville**: tel 65 43 18 36). What do win hands down in the Lot Valley are the three Es – Entraygues, **Estaing** and busy **Espalion** (C1): old bridges, ancient houses, châteaux, ruined castles and *églises* combine to please.

Finally, a highly recommended personal suggestion: painting courses at Susan and Stanley Woolston's evocative old wine makers' house in gorgeous, ideal artists' terrain (at **Cougousse** (B2), north-west of Rodez) – with personal tuition by Stanley, a supremely talented artist. (Details from Susan Woolston, Prosper Cottage, High Street, Blockley, Moreton-in-Marsh, Glos GL56 9HA: tel 0386 700219.)

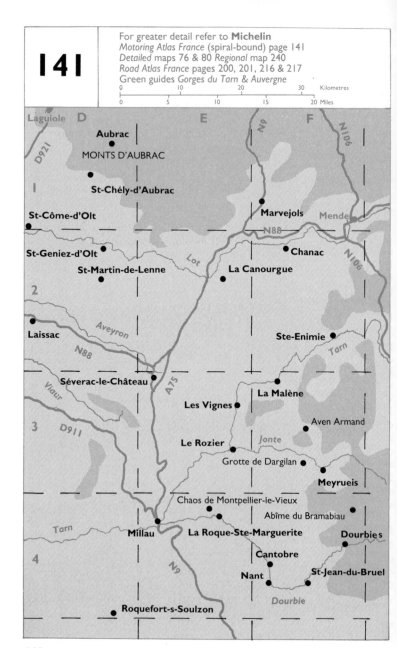

141

For greater detail refer to **Michelin**
Motoring Atlas France (spiral-bound) page 141
Detailed maps 76 & 80 *Regional map* 240
Road Atlas France pages 200, 201, 216 & 217
Green guides *Gorges du Tarn & Auvergne*

Kilometres

0   10   20   30

0   5   10   15   20   Miles

Laguiole D   E   F

Aubrac
MONTS D'AUBRAC

D921

N9

N106

St-Chély-d'Aubrac

St-Côme-d'Olt

Marvejols   Mende

N88

St-Geniez-d'Olt   Chanac

Lot

St-Martin-de-Lenne   La Canourgue

N106

Aveyron

Laissac   Ste-Enimie

N88   Tarn

Séverac-le-Château   A75   La Malène

Les Vignes

Aven Armand

Viaur   D911

Le Rozier   Jonte

Grotte de Dargilan

Meyrueis

Chaos de Montpellier-le-Vieux

Abîme du Bramabiau

Tarn   Millau   La Roque-Ste-Marguerite   Dourbies

Cantobre

N9   St-Jean-du-Bruel

Nant

Dourbie

Roquefort-s-Soulzon

In *French Leave Favourites*, published eight years ago, I started the chapter "Captivating Cévennes" with these words: "The Cévennes never fails to amaze me. For the past three decades I have been bowled over by its spectacular scenery." I then went on to describe how, a year earlier, I had been stunned anew, as I drove on the most obscure roads I could find. Well, last year, Anne was with me on my most recent exploration of map sheets 141 and 142 – and, once again, in early June, both of us were left speechless by the extrovert show Mother Nature laid on for all those lucky enough to be in the area.

For Anne, seeing the Cévennes for the first time in June, one word summed up her feelings during the course of an unforgettable morning. The word? A "wonderland". Dragging her away proved mightily difficult; she would have been quite happy to stay put. I, too, was almost prepared to forget any further "research". Let me explain why.

What thrilled both of us so much? That's simple: wild flowers and orchids in dramatic profusion, both in the numerous varieties we encountered and in the sheer numbers of each type we identified. The landscape was aflame – seemingly a sea of burning colours. I imagine I have now driven every lane in the bottom right-hand corner of 141 but the drive we made on that June morning last year was spellbinding.

We climbed north from **La Roque-Ste-Marguerite** (E4), in the **Dourbie** Valley, along the narrow lane that scrambles up the Causse Noir. Then we went east on the D29, to a point just before the ruins of a priory, the Eglise de St-Jean-de-Balmes. We turned left and drove slowly along the track. (The surface is quite safe and not unduly rough.) We kept bearing left and followed the signs showing a white arrow and two white circles on a blue background. We eventually parked at the viewpoint, a rocky outcrop, marked on the map as Corniche du Causse Noir (E3). We stopped as often as we could along the entire route. But even if you spent a day covering the 13 km run you would still not do justice to one of Nature's most breathtaking shows. One message rings out loud and clear: stop, walk and look as often as you can. There are endless opportunities to park, put your walking boots on and explore on foot; that's true everywhere on the *causses*. (The limestone "plateaux" are usually dry as water drains away quickly through numerous fissures; underground streams abound – hence the many caves.)

The route I described above crosses a tableland of exuberant wild flowers. Gigantic coverings of them, sometimes spreading across an entire pasture; words such as blankets and sheets hardly suffice. There's a richly handsome bonus in addition: orchids galore, in their thousands. Anne counted a dozen or more varieties. She was able to identify four: *céphalanthère blanche*; *orchis pyramidal*; *orchis à deux feuilles*; and *orchis à fleurs lachers*. How she wished she had had with her an authoritative book on orchids, to make identification easier. In some instances, in the woods, the blooms were so numerous they were not unlike the glades of bluebells we are accustomed to in the UK.

The views north from the Corniche du Causse Noir were magnificent: of the **Tarn** and **Jonte** far below; of **Le Rozier** and Peyreleau shimmering in the heat; and distant vistas of multi-shaded, violently sculptured rock faces and flat-topped plateaux. But, for us, the show at ground level in the woods and pastures behind us had stolen our hearts. All the roads leading east from the Dourbie are an enchantment: the D41 from La Roque to Vessac (F3); the D159 to Revens and Lanuéjols (F4); the D145/D157 past **Cantobre** to Trèves, and the D114 from **St-Jean-du-Bruel** to **Dourbies** (F4), a drive I described in *Favourites.*

I imagine May may be the best month to soak up the visual thrills but, in early June, we missed nothing. Our drive in the Canyon de la Dourbie was a colourful overture: first the weir at St-Jean-du-Bruel (F4); next, the 14th-century covered market at **Nant**; Cantobre, snoozing contentedly on an oversize rock pillow; then past striped rock faces and, towards La Roque-Ste-Marguerite, exceptionally pleasing pictures of a foaming river, medieval bridge, church and tower.

You could spend a month on map sheet 141 and still not do justice to the varied terrain. In the bottom right-hand corner much of Nature's most unusual gouging and carving is below ground; the caves are amazing places and should not be missed. But if you are claustrophobic don't fret, as much of her best handiwork can be admired above ground, in the form of numerous gorges and rugged, brutally-carved giant cliffs – all shaped out of the vast limestone *causses.*

One drive could go like this. Start at **Millau** (E4), sparing time first for the "Fouilles" (excavations) marked on the map, just east of the town. The site is La Graufesenque where, 1,900 years ago, huge amounts of pottery were manufactured by 500 or more potters. On the 24-acre site the remains of both the potters' houses and scores of kilns can be identified. Visit, too, the Musée de Millau which houses seemingly thousands of Gallo-Romain pots and also the exhibits linked to Millau's once renowned manufacture of gloves. (**Roquefort** (D4) cheese – more about that in the map sheet 155 chapter – is made from ewes' milk; the skins of the lambs sacrificed for that purpose have always been used to make high quality kid gloves.)

I would be impatient to leave the town and head for the famed Gorges du Tarn. These begin to arouse one's interest at Le Rozier (E3), literally a rose-festooned village. As you head north you'll see enough white water, albeit gently foaming, to grasp just why so many "Canoe, Kayak, Rafting" signs have sprouted up over the last decade. But perhaps the finest way of enjoying the river and cliff scenery which follows is to use the services of Les Bateliers de **La Malène** (F3): these are the boatmen who steer the *barques* (punts holding four to five people) from La Malène downstream past the famed Les Détroits, multi-shaded limestone cliffs, to the Cirques des Baumes, where the river does a left-hand turn to flow south. The combination of extensive woods covering the steepish sides of the Gorges du Tarn, topped by savage rock sculptures, and the emerald water of the river is an enthralling sight – whether seen from the roads, the cliff tops or a punt. The *bateliers* get you back by vehicle to La Malène and your parked car.

If time is precious do not fail, on any account, to drive up the seven *lacets* (hairpins) from **Les Vignes** (E3) to the viewpoint called Point Sublime: the best vista is to the east (the course the punts take) but you also have an eagle's eye view of the ninety-degree turn the Tarn completes to head southwards. There are many other viewpoints: the lane that takes you to the Roc des Hourtous, south-west of La Malène; the climbs from La Malène and **Ste-Enimie** (F2); the climb east from Les Vignes; and the walks which lead up to Capluc, east of Le Rozier. One spot, worth a detour upstream from Ste-Enimie (whilst there seek out the 14th-century *maison* at the heart of the medieval village which houses the work of numerous Lozère artisans), is tiny Castelbouc, hanging on by its fingernails to a vertical rock face above the Tarn.

Another excursion from any of the hotels I recommend in my various culinary guides (at Millau, **Meyrueis** (F3), St-Jean-du-Bruel or Le Rozier) could incorporate some of the more odd-ball examples of Nature's handiwork. First, the **Chaos de Montpellier-le-Vieux** (E4), north-east of Millau, a collection of weirdly-shaped rocks which litter the *causse* over an extensive area, as if a drunken giant had stumbled this way and left a scene of utter destruction behind him. There's a long, signposted walk through the rocks and, these days, there's also a small mechanised green train which takes the strain if you prefer to give your legs a rest. Most of the rocks have fanciful names: Devil's Chair, Elephant, Arc de Triomphe and even Queen Victoria's Head.

Next, two fabulous underground caves lie to the north-east of the Chaos; one to the north of the Gorges de la Jonte, the other to the south. **Aven Armand**, to the north (F3), is the most renowned: every imaginable shape of stalagmite and stalactite is to be found here, enhanced by some brilliant lighting. There's a funicular, on tyres, to make at least part of the exploration puff-free. The **Grotte de Dargilan** (F3), the pink cavern, is also impressive with vast chambers, a range of natural colourings and a huge bell-shaped sculpture. Modern lighting has done wonders in showing off both these superb marvels.

A tour of the Gorges de la Jonte will please every visitor. The high cliffs, at the western end, near Le Rozier and perched Peyreleau (E3), are orange and pink and they are cut and hacked into all sorts of shapes; you can have some fun working out names for the sculptures. Just west of the Belvédère des Terrasses du Truel (E3) stop at the small viewpoint above the north side of the road – three to four km from Le Rozier. On the cliff tops, high above you, the griffon vulture has been reintroduced to the Cévennes. There's a permanent telescope on site and display boards which explain everything you need to know. Unlike me, knowing nothing of the site and spectacle, I suggest you take your own binoculars. The sight of the giant vultures, with their eight-ft wing spans,

151

gliding in the warm thermals, is excitingly impressive. We counted ten on the morning we saw them. Meyrueis, at the top of the gorge, is a cool spot; there's a touch of character about the place and there are several bars and cafés with shady terraces.

Now head south into the wooded forests of Mont Aigoual (142:B4). The forests, a pleasing mix of broadleaved trees and evergreens, were planted a century ago by Georges Fabre – to stop erosion of the then bare mountainsides. There are many arboretums in the extensive forests. The most notable on map sheet 141 is the Arboretum de la Foux, on the south side of the D986, just west of the **Abîme du Bramabiau** (A4). What's the latter? A gigantic slash in the rock face where a subterranean river gushes out of the mountainside. You get a fine view of the Abîme from the D986 to the north; a visit requires a longish, but highly exciting and entertaining walk, the latter parts of which cling to the rock face and run alongside the rushing water.

I must not devote all five pages of this chapter to the sights on the bottom half of map 141. A quite different "sandwich" of *pays* is on the top half. First a slice of countryside called the Causse de Sévérac and Causse de Sauveterre; then the sandwich filling of the River **Lot**, so different from its southern neighbour, the Tarn; and, finally, a third slice, at the top of the map, the high **Monts d'Aubrac**.

The two *causses* are less barren, more undulating, and greener than their counterparts to the south. Nevertheless, there's nothing special about them to gladden the heart. One man-made site which does please the eye is the Château de Galinières (D2), north of the D45 from **Laissac** to **St-Martin-de-Lenne**: the fortified walls, ramparts and towers are an exceptional treat. Nature tries hard with the massive rock called the Sabot de Malepeyre, south of **La Canourgue** (E2), from which there are lengthy views north, over the Urugne and Lot Valleys to the Monts d'Aubrac. La Canourgue has a fascinating clock tower.

The Lot Valley, on map sheets 140 and 141, is not among my favourite French scenic "top of the pops"; it's attractive enough, wooded, and as far as map 141 is concerned, a pastoral landscape dominates. The best way to approach the Lot is from the D45 at St-Martin-de-Lenne. Descend by the D95. Immediately you leave the village there's a landscape to the east which, for me, is one of the most alluring in France: distant Marnhac, far below, and a surrounding backdrop of rounded, wooded hills, an enveloping womb for the tiny hamlet. Several man-made sites on the Lot's banks capture the imagination. **St-Geniez-d'Olt** (local patois for Lot) is a large, busy place. Much smaller is medieval Ste-Eulalie-d'Olt which has a handsome church, houses and a château wearing a bronze-shaded hat atop its tower. Lower downstream the ancient streets, fortifications and houses of **St-Côme-d'Olt** catch your eye; chuckle, too, at the slightly out-of-sync church tower.

Rising steeply from the Lot Valley are the southern flanks of the basalt and granite Monts d'Aubrac. South of the isolated village of **Aubrac** (D1:

MICHELIN MAP PAGE 141

over 4000 ft) a series of valleys at right angles to the Lot are pretty and pleasantly wooded with extensive views south from the high ridges between the numerous streams. Much the most refreshing surprise is the descent on the D19, from east or west, into the Boralde de St-Chély Valley with **St-Chély-d'Aubrac** (D1) sitting peacefully at the bottom. On the remote, almost treeless, plateau to the north of Aubrac the pastures are covered with sheets of jonquils in late April and May; by June they have gone and, whilst not so numerous, the same ground is spotted with narcissi and dozens of wild flowers.

Make two calls in St-Chély: first to the Hotel Voyageurs-Vayrou; the latter word is the name of the family which, for generations, has owned the hotel. Madame Christiane Vayrou does the cooking, together with her young son-in-law, Patrick Amilhat. Patrick and his wife, Brigitte, have opened a new business, La Conserverie de l'Aubrac, in the basement. During the winter months they do the preparation work to stock up the shelves with *tripoux, cou farci, confit de canard, foie gras d'oie* and *pâté de foie de porc* – just some of the tinned treats, delights which you can try at the hotel during its short summer season. Fifty metres away is the bakery of Jean Denis Auguy: here you must try a slice of *fouace au beurre* – the regional crown-shaped bread made of flour, fresh eggs, butter, salt, sugar, yeast and orange-flower water.

There are other attractions to be found on map sheet 141. Most of which follow are man-made. The first, the most unusual, is north of **Marvejols** (F1): the site is marked on the map by the words Parc des Loups du Gévaudan. Gérard Ménatory has opened a reserve, now around 65 acres, for 100 and more wolves from Siberia, Canada and Mongolia. Financial help from Brigitte Bardot has helped him enormously; the resultant publicity means that large numbers of visitors explore the reserve. There's an exhibit, too, which explains the story of the beast of Gévaudan – supposedly a large wolf which, over two hundred years ago, killed and ate dozens of local people in the very area where the reserve is now situated. To the immediate north-west is a more conventional sight: the Château de la Baume (E1), reached by the D73, to the west of the N9. The fortified château could be in Scotland; the interior is exuberant, with decorations worthy of a mini Versailles.

In the Lot Valley, at Le Villard, west of **Chanac** (F2), is a new enterprise – one which is claimed to be unique, a medieval farm. In a series of buildings all sorts of exhibits tell the story of how an estate would have been managed centuries ago. **Sévérac-le-Château** (E3), soon to be bypassed by the new A75 autoroute, is dominated by the ruins of what once must have been a sizeable and strategically important fortress; today, the old houses in the streets below the castle are much more interesting. Finally, in the woods south of Meyrueis (F3), is the Château de Roquedols; the small 16th-century castle, with towers and staircases, has colourful, handsome walls. The site now serves as an information centre for the vast forests on Mont Aigoual.

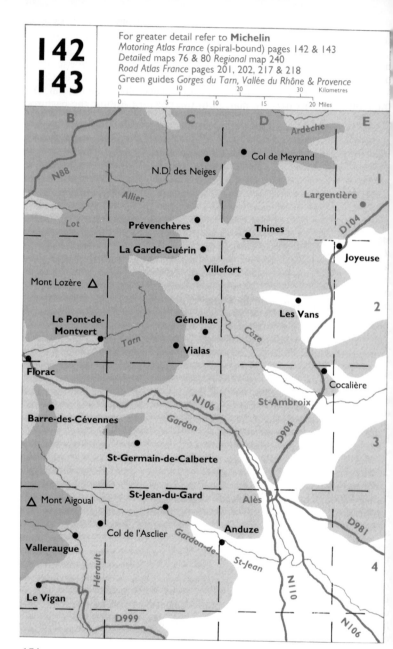

142
143

For greater detail refer to **Michelin**
Motoring Atlas France (spiral-bound) pages 142 & 143
Detailed maps 76 & 80 *Regional* map 240
Road Atlas France pages 201, 202, 217 & 218
Green guides *Gorges du Tarn, Vallée du Rhône & Provence*

0   5   10   15   20   25   30 Kilometres
0   5   10   15   20 Miles

B   **C**   **D**   **E**

Ardèche

N88

Col de Meyrand

N.D. des Neiges

Allier

Largentière

Lot

Prévenchères

Thines

D104

La Garde-Guérin

Joyeuse

Villefort

Mont Lozère △

1

Le Pont-de-Montvert

Génolhac

Tarn

Cèze

Les Vans

Vialas

2

Florac

N106

Cocalière

Barre-des-Cévennes

Gardon

St-Ambroix

D904

St-Germain-de-Calberte

3

△ Mont Aigoual

St-Jean-du-Gard

Alès

D981

Col de l'Asclier

Gardon-de-

Anduze

Valleraugue

Hérault

St-Jean

4

Le Vigan

D999

N110

N106

Before you read on please look again at the opening paragraph for map sheet chapter 141; my words are just as valid here. Most of the terrain on the map to the left is the Cévennes, other than the top right-hand corner which is part of the Ardèche (see map sheet chapter 129).

One word sums up my feelings for map sheets 142/143: stupendous. The varied scenic landscapes are amazing: forests of beech, oak and chestnut; olive trees and vineyards; granite mountains (**Mont Lozère**: B2/C2); limestone gorges and plateaux (west of **Florac**: B2); wooded hills and hidden valleys where the schist is often visible; wild flowers galore; and myriad examples of man's handiwork.

Let's get cracking as I know I shall run out of road by the end of the chapter. I'll start with the Cévennes and finish in the Ardèche.

There are many approach roads to map sheet 142. I suggest you use the least obvious, the D906 (top of grid square C1). The road runs alongside the infant River **Allier**, flowing lazily north in a shallow valley, and the once busy Paris-Nîmes railway line. Make your first stop the Cistercian Abbaye **Notre-Dame des Neiges** (C1), approached along the densely-wooded D4A. Just over a century ago, in 1878, the Presbyterian Scot, Robert Louis Stevenson, came this way with Modestine. The Catholic monks gave him shelter for the night. I doubt whether RLS would recognise the place now: the abbey has the same wooded, oasis-calm site but there's just a touch too much of a tourist trap. No matter, but do attend one of the services (12.30 and 18.30 are ideal) when you can enjoy the soothing chants of the Trappist monks.

Next, a surprise: "La Chocolatière", on the west side of the D906 at **Prévenchères** (C1). Jean-Claude Briet's shop is a mouth-watering teaser: some of his chocolate sculptures are works of art.

At **La Garde-Guérin** (C2) detour 300 metres to the Belvédère du Chassezac. Below you there's a deep gorge with vertical slabs of rock in layer upon layer; there's little water in the river, thanks to the dam upstream. La Garde-Guérin is a tiny, fortified, medieval hamlet. Explore the *hameau* and, from July to mid September, admire the fine designs and crafted work of the area's artisans on display in the stone barn.

Descend to **Villefort**. North of the town head west, beside the man-made lake, to Castanet, where the 16th-century castle, with sausage-like slices off its tower tops, is almost surrounded by water. At Villefort have a cuppa and cake at Georges Riou's super *pâtisserie*.

If time allows make the 30-km drive on the D362 which climbs up the eastern shoulder of the sleeping granite giant, Mont Lozère; the numerous high-altitude views are fabulous. If not, take the low road, the D906, to **Génolhac**. By now you'll be aware of the striking landscape changes: rocky terrain to the north; invigorating woods in the valleys below. The contrasts continue as you head west into the heart of the Parc National des Cévennes. Beyond **Vialas** (C2) the mixed woods are a tonic; as are the tablecloths of narcissi near the top of the Col de la Croix. No wonder "*Miel*" signs are everywhere.

155

Stop at **Le Pont-de-Montvert** (B2). RLS came this way: he slept out overnight, in his fur-lined sleeping sack, on Mont Lozère and he flirted with a waitress over lunch at the Hôtel des Cévennes in the village (the *auberge* is still there). Enjoy the bouncing baby Tarn but then turn your attention to the Ecomusée du Mont Lozère, an unusally-shaped building tucked away behind the village. The museum explains the mountain's human and natural history (May to Sept). Equally interesting are outlying sites, all part of the museum: the splendidly restored, isolated farm at Troubat (to the south-east) where the buildings are constructed from blocks of granite and oak beams; the hamlets of L'Hôpital (north-east) with a thatched *moulin*, and La Fage (north-west) with a small stone bell-tower and a communal *four* (oven).

The park's information centre is at Florac (B2), a modest small resort. Tourists are likely to head south-east on the Corniche des Cévennes (B3), a road running along the crest of high wooded hills. I recommend something better – the D13, D984 and D983: through, literally, **Barre-des-Cévennes** (B3), where houses almost touch above the road; past **St-Germain-de-Calberte** (C3), a *village fleuri par excellence* – awash with roses (the cracking *charcuterie* Therond is a must: on the D13 eastern exit); finishing at **St-Jean-du-Gard** (C4), the town where RLS completed his travels (market on Tues a.m.). The drive is a scenic extravaganza: vast views north and south; and an honour guard of rock roses along much of the winding route.

What other scenic thrills await you? Hundreds. I've seen almost every road in the Cévennes – prime rallying *pays* and classic mapaholics' terrain. Here are a few ideas – from dozens. Drive to the summit of **Mont Aigoual** (B4), the highest point in the national park (1567 m); from the observatory the 360-degree panorama is staggering. You'll see the map identifies an arboretum, l'Hort-de-Dieu, created by the botanist Charles Flahault with the help of his *copain*, Georges Fabre, the mastermind behind the Aigoual *massif* forests a century ago. You can descend, on foot, to the Garden of God from the D269 below the summit (20 mins down; how long up?). Or, like us, use the rather roughish three-ply track from the Col de Prat Peyrol. The arboretum, of exotic trees and plants, is a touch disappointing; the views are heart-stopping.

Drive the hairpins on the D986 west from **Valleraugue** (B4), an almost 3000 ft-high climb. Motor up the narrow road to the Col du Pas, north of the town, where a huge Cross of Lorraine is the monument to the Aigoual *maqui*s. Revel in the D48 or, if you are a rally nut, the D329, both of which snake north from **Le Vigan** (B4), wooded almost all the way (on the town bypass there's a road island with a waterfall; honestly). And share the excitement of rally drivers, and their white-haired navigators, on the thrilling **Col de l'Asclier** (B4).

Some of you will know that the Cévennes was a Protestant stronghold centuries ago. There's no space here for me to recount the persecution they suffered during the Wars of Religion. But under no circumstances bypass the Musée du Désert (the word for a hiding place), north of **Anduze**, the Geneva of the Cévennes (D4). A farmhouse museum tells the story of their persecution and resistance, and the Camisards' revolt at the start of the 18th century (every day March to Nov).

There are many fascinating sites around Anduze. La Bambouseraie de Prafrance, on the way to the *musée*, is a mixture of South-east Asia exotic (acres of high bamboo) and cool, restful water gardens (every day March to Dec). North of the museum is the mysterious underground world of the Grotte de Trabuc with its 100,000 "soldiers" of unknown origin. The Train à Vapeur des Cévennes chugs up the valley from Anduze to St-Jean-du-Gard – ideal for kids and dad (Apl & Oct: Sun. May & Sept: Sun, Tues, Thurs. June: every day but Mon. July & Aug: every day). At St-Jean visit both the Atlantide Parc, a tropical aquarium, and the Musée des Vallées Cévenoles. Before you leave Anduze chuckle at the brightly-tiled pagoda fountain (1649); and marvel at the Poterie de la Madeleine (at La Madeleine, to the south-east), full of *vases d'Anduze* and magnificent pots for the home and garden.

What remains in the top right-hand Ardèche corner? I adore the terrain around **Les Vans** (D2): often, in the space of a mile or so, you'll see olive, cherry and sweet chestnut trees and, *santé*, there's many a vineyard. The local geology is amazing: the weird woods and limestone rocks of the Bois de Païolive and the sculptured *calcaire* at Mazet-Plage (to the east); the tiny Romanesque church at **Thines** (D1), a gem created from granite and sandstone and on a high remote perch at the top of a long dead-end road; the sandstone (*grès*) and granite homes at Chambonas and Champmajour (north of Le Vans); and the houses built from schist at St-Jean-de-Pourcharesse (east of Thines) and remote Malbosc (D2: south-west). Why not hire a bike from Claude Raymond (Le Quay, 07140 Les Vans: 75 37 23 47) and see the lot at leisure?

In the past Anne and I have headed north from Les Vans on the Corniche du Vivarais Cévenol (D10/D4). On the Tanargue massif (D1) we've welcomed the cool woods and, from the **Col de Meyrand**, we've admired the vast views – with the snow-topped Alps sparkling to the east. South of Les Vans, beside the D104, we've been astounded by the endless subterranean *grottes* at **Cocalière**, where water and lighting combine to such good effect (April to Oct: you can take your bike too!).

A couple of museums appeal: the Musée de la Châtaigneraie (scores of objects made from chestnut wood) at **Joyeuse** (E2: 15.00 to 17.00 Mon); and the Les Vans Musée d'Archeologie (July & Aug: Tues to Fri. Rest of year: p.m. Thurs). Off the right edge of my map, but still on 143, are the mighty Gorges de l'Ardèche (E2/F2): drive the spectacular *corniche* road; marvel at the Pont-d'Arc, a natural stone arch over the river; and see at least one of the fabulous underground caves – the Aven d'Orgnac (E2) is a three-star wonder. The river is at its most exciting after heavy rain when the water level can rise metres in a few hours (these sudden rises are called *crues*). Stupendous is the word.

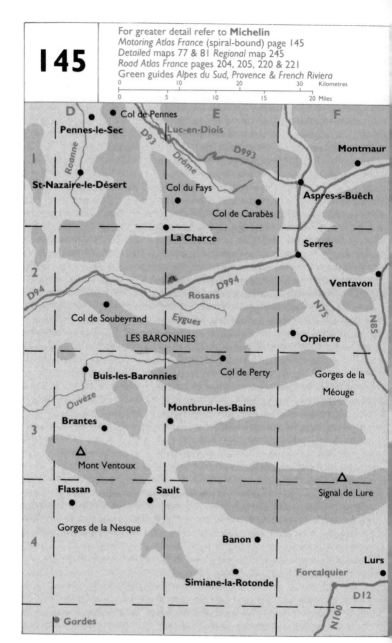

145

For greater detail refer to **Michelin**
Motoring Atlas France (spiral-bound) page 145
Detailed maps 77 & 81 *Regional* map 245
Road Atlas France pages 204, 205, 220 & 221
Green guides *Alpes du Sud, Provence & French Riviera*

Kilometres

0   5   10   15   20 Miles

D   • Col de Pennes   E   F

Pennes-le-Sec   Luc-en-Diois

D93   Drôme   D993   **Montmaur**

Roanne

1   **St-Nazaire-le-Désert**   Col du Fays   **Aspres-s-Buêch**

Col de Carabès

La Charce   **Serres**

D94   Rosans   D994   **Ventavon**

2   Col de Soubeyrand   Eygues   N75   N85

LES BARONNIES   **Orpierre**

Buis-les-Baronnies   Col de Perty   Gorges de la

Ouvèze   Méouge

Brantes   **Montbrun-les-Bains**

3   △   Mont Ventoux   Signal de Lure   △

Flassan   **Sault**

Gorges de la Nesque

4   **Banon** ●   **Lurs**

Forcalquier

Simiane-la-Rotonde   D12

N100

● Gordes

158

f you take a quick glance at the contents map of *Mapaholics' France* ou will soon grasp that I have turned my back on a handful of the ountry's most famous honeypot tourist areas. One is Provence's Roman riangle to the west and south-west of map sheet 145; another is Mayle errain to the immediate south. What follows will prove conclusively that he best of France is only discovered by those willing to make the effort o get off-the-beaten-track, armed with appropriate large-scale maps.

As you travel from south to north across map sheet 145, the landscape hanges, imperceptibly, mile by mile. South of the **D94** and **D994** D2/E2/F1), the light and shades of Provence are unmistakable: olive rees, regimented rows of lavender (at their best in July), soil the colour f rust, and the seductive hues of terracotta roof tiles are a few of the lues. Your sense of smell, awoken by the perfume of herb-scented fields, vill also tell you that this is Provence. By the time you reach the top dge of the map the landscape is almost exclusively Alpine.

I shall start in the north – in an area where, for reasons I have never een able to determine, Michelin's green guide contribution is an empty vhite hole. I'll try to correct that unfair omission.

Leave the **Drôme** Valley on the D135 (130:C4) and follow the River **Roanne** south. I've done this drive at all times of the year but the run is t its best at the end of October, when the extravaganza laid on by Mother Nature is a visual knockout. Trees are myriad torches of every ue imaginable – dark coppers, stunning russets, glowing golds and urning reds; and poplars are giant beacons of yellow light – their long andle-shaped forms burn with a searing, dazzling intensity.

Pennes-le-Sec (D1) is a revelation – restored years ago by Charles Piot 1904-80), a tyre retailer. Beyond the hamlet the road climbs through dry Mediterranean scrub to the summit of the **Col de Pennes** (3412 ft). Then, 100 m over the top, you are in cooler woods where broadleaved rees, in late October, wear their autumn cloaks. The view below you is top-you-in-your-tracks stunning – rated by Bernard Levin in his plendid *Hannibal's Footsteps* as one of the the finest he has ever seen. He omitted one visual fact in his brilliant description of the vista: the vineyards in the valley below contribute their annual share to the efreshing Clairette de Die sparklers (they travel well).

Anne and I have also seen this "white hole" of mountain terrain in une when we set off, one hot day, on the D27 north from **Serres** (F2). At the latter see the town hall, near the Fifi Moulin hotel; the 14th-century Romanesque/Provençale *église*; the rue Peuzin; and the unusual *méridienne* sundial on the primary school façade.) At both Sigottier and La Piarre the stream and road force their way through rock walls. The narrow road climbs through woods and past wild roses to the **Col de Carabès** (E1); on your way up your car will crush hundreds of pine ones strewn across the tarmac. On the northern, cooler side, you'll be velcomed by numerous orchids, lilies and wild flowers.

The Col de la Rossas (E1) is an easy climb; the **Col du Fays** (E1) is

159

quite different with the cooler, northern descent literally tunnelling, for several km, through a heavily-wooded hillside of deciduous trees. At **La Charce** (D1) you'll catch your first sight of lime trees. The flowers are collected in the second half of June (later we saw many folk, up ladders, harvesting the crop), dried, and later sold in local markets to make a delicious tea. Note the distillation plant at the northern entrance to La Charce; relish, too, the view of the village as you climb south through a gorge of multi-coloured rock faces. Near Pommerol (E2) metronome-shaped rock slabs are piled high, on top of each other. Further on, stop - and look back at the village, cradled in the col behind the weird rock formations. On the Col de la Fromagère you'll get your first view of the sulking hulk of **Mont Ventoux** (D3).

Before we enter the *pays* called **Les Baronnies** (D2) I'll list some of the other sights to the north and east. The cols (D1) which lead north to the Roanne Valley and **St-Nazaire-le-Désert** (D1) – a land of lavender pines and oaks, river bathing and chances to buy *chèvre* cheese and *miel*. The ruins of the once vast 12th-century priory at St-André-de-Rosans (E2); only the *église* now remains. The colourful face of the sundial on the *mairie* wall in **Aspres-sur-Buëch** (F1). The 14th-century fortress at **Montmaur** (F1: p.m. July/Aug). The old villages of Savournon and perched **Ventavon** (F2), east of Serres. The **Gorges de la Méouge** (F3) where scenic views, rock sculptures and river bathing all appeal. And, another entry into Les Baronnies, the climb from **Orpierre** (F2) to the **Col de Perty** (E3); at the summit climb 150 m to the *table d'orientation* (4275 ft) for views of Ventoux and, to the east, snow-capped peaks. Detour, too, just after Orpierre, to Ste-Colombe (E3) and its church with a dove (*colombe*) sundial.

I suggest you enter Les Baronnies over the **Col de Soubeyrand** (D2). Lime trees, roses, lavender, apricot and olive trees (the former planted in the most inhospitable spots), vines, herbs and terracotta tiles dominate the landscape in the Ennuye Valley. The same, too, is true of the **Ouvèze** Valley (D3), west of the earlier Baronnies access, the Col de Perty. Hundreds of plane trees make **Buis-les-Baronnies** (D3) one of the shadiest villages in Provence. Every Wednesday there's a renowned market (the famous lime blossom festival is held on the first Wed in July). In June the Ouvèze is a clear, harmless trickle; don't be deceived because, after heavy rain, the same river caused death and destruction in Vaison-la-Romaine (144:C3) in 1992.

Now south towards the ever-closer Mont Ventoux. Most tourists never see Ventoux (in Provençal the name is Ventour, Windy Mountain) from the north. Don't make that mistake. Detour to **Brantes** and its ruined castle (D3), both stuck like wallpaper to the mountainside; across the valley the massive corrugated wall of Ventoux towers above the village. (Seek out, too, the artisans who make such colourful pottery.) Further east, both Reilhanette (D3) and **Montbrun-les-Bains** (E3) have ruined castles above their village houses. From the D542 Montbrun is especially striking: the château sits above a long line of high-walled houses. Walk the narrow lanes and you'll quickly grasp why the houses on the south side have as many floors below street level as they do above. The modern thermal baths are to the south, alongside the D189.

Ventoux fascinates me as much as the mountain has every visitor to its lunar-landscape summit over the centuries. The 6263 ft-high peak is frightening – especially when the maniacal *mistral*, roaring and raving, rages across the barren summit. The climb has long been a cycling hell: could there be a more hateful place to die as the spot where Tom Simpson passed away on 13 July 1967 during a Tour de France stage? Do stop at his memorial just below the summit, on the south side, three miles exactly from the D974/D164 junction (D3). The views from the peak are staggering: Mont Blanc, 130 miles away, is clearly visible.

At lower altitudes on Ventoux forests of pine, beech and holm oaks predominate – with plenty of wild roses and weaver birds' nests looking for all the world like lights on Christmas trees. On the D974 to the south (seemingly with a gradient of 1 in 10 all the way), there are hundreds of shady picnic spots. South of **Flassan** (D4) you're in Côtes du Ventoux wine country; there are plenty of chances to buy direct.

The **Gorges de la Nesque** (D4) are a miniature Verdon (162:C2). The steep sides are scrub and tree-covered almost all the way. What are not covered are the rock faces – of all shapes, sizes and shades. By far the best rock colouring is at the top of the *gorges*, the Rocher du Cire – a high, rounded face hundreds of feet high. There's no sign of water anywhere until the sight of the *plan d'eau* near Monieux (D4).

As you head east you'll be well aware of the many opportunities to buy *miel de lavande*; lavender fields and hives are all too obvious. One man-made surprise is the Aérospatiale rocket-base alongside the D30, south-east of **Sault** (D4). **Simiane-la-Rotonde** (E4) is worth any detour: seen from the D151 to the east – where you are surrounded by acres of perfumed lavender – the perched semi-circular village, topped by a massive round keep, is visual perfection. Walk the lanes in the village to see the stone houses and buildings at their best. **Banon** (E4) has a church tower high above old houses (the famed *chèvre* cheese, wrapped in a chestnut leaf, takes its name from the village). **Lurs** (F4), another must, has light-coloured stone houses and buildings and is perched high above the Durance. In July the views south-west are a mixture of green, old-gold and sand-coloured fields (arable crops), rows of lavender, and orchards of olive and fruit trees.

Finally, to the **Signal de Lure** (5991 ft) atop the Montagne de Lure (F3) – almost a carbon copy of Ventoux; on the south side the D113 climbs through woods of cedars, pines and holm oaks. From the barren, harsh summit the views north-east are superb; both the Ecrins *massif* and Mont Viso are clearly visible. The D53 descent is an exciting series of hairpin bends down a steep high wall of forested mountainside (plenty of beech trees). A fitting end to another face of Provence.

161

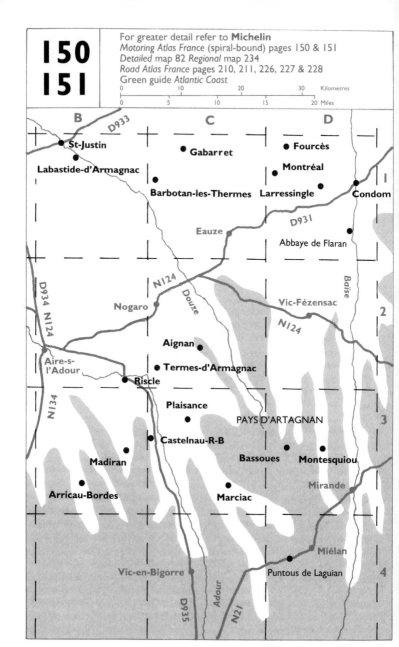

150
151

For greater detail refer to **Michelin**
Motoring Atlas France (spiral-bound) pages 150 & 151
Detailed map 82 *Regional* map 234
Road Atlas France pages 210, 211, 226, 227 & 228
Green guide *Atlantic Coast*

| 0 | 10 | 20 | 30 | Kilometres |
| 0 | 5 | 10 | 15 | 20 Miles |

B   C   D

D933

● St-Justin

Labastide-d'Armagnac

● Gabarret

● Fourcès

● Montréal

Barbotan-les-Thermes   Larressingle ●

● Condom

1

Eauze

D931

Abbaye de Flaran

N124

Douze

Baïse

D934

N124

Nogaro ●

Vic-Fézensac

N124

2

● Aignan

Aire-s-
l'Adour

● Termes-d'Armagnac

N134

● Riscle

Plaisance

●

PAYS D'ARTAGNAN

3

● Castelnau-R-B

● Madiran

● Bassoues

● Montesquiou

Mirande

● Arricau-Bordes

● Marciac

● Miélan

Vic-en-Bigorre ●

● Puntous de Laguian

4

D935   Adour   N21

This is the land of Armagnac – the *pays* where the most heart-warming of brandies is distilled from wine made from white grapes. This is also the heart of Gascony, where locals joke that the crows fly over the region upside down so they can't see how poor the area is below.

What is arguably true is that Gascons are friendly, helpful, proud, and fiercely independent. Much of map sheets 150/151 is the western half of the *département* of Gers, a deeply rural landscape of gentle, curving hills; sleepy river valleys; vineyards and fields of maize; *bastides* and *castelnauds* (*castelnaux*); and few tourists.

I'll try to get under the skin of self-effacing Gers. Let's have a taste of Armagnac first – a name synonymous with Gers. (The "G" is spoken like a soft "J" and the "s" is not silent; so, "Gers" rhymes with "chairs".) Armagnac ("blazing water" or "fire water") was made long before Cognac. Ageing is the key: distilled once, the velvety-smooth brandy, with a long-tasting aroma, develops its unique character in barrels, made from the local black oak, for up to 20 years or longer.

Where can you buy Armagnac and learn more about the brandy? Where better than the Ecomusée de l'Armagnac at the Château Garreau, south of **Labastide-d'Armagnac** (B1). (Use the D626 south-east; in half a mile or so turn right and head south for two miles.) The museum, housed in two 17th-century farms, tells the story of Armagnac over the centuries (open every day except Sun a.m. – Apl to Oct; closed all Sun – Nov to Mar). You can buy Armagnac and *floc* (an *apéritif* of Armagnac and grape juice). Alternatively, seek out the Château de Cassaigne, south-west of **Condom** (D1) – a serene, handsome stone structure where Bernard Faget produces a superb range of brandies; ask him to show you his 16th-century kitchen with an open fire and "thumb-print" brick roof.

This is also a land of fortified *bastides*, mainly built by the English and French during the Hundred Years War (1337-1453). Most have a regular layout of grid patterns with streets laid down at right angles to each other. Any modern-day planner would feel at home in the *bastides* conceived 700 years ago. *Castelnauds* (*castelnaux*) were also fortified but these villages grew fungus-like, clustered around a château or church and often perched on a small hill (*puech*).

Seek out some *bastides* on the top of map sheets 150/151. **St-Justin** (B1), a 13th-century *bastide*, is easily missed. Find the north-east corner of the village; a typical small *place*, arcaded on three sides, and with an eye-catching six-sided, tiled, cone-shaped tower. Walk the lane off the square and past the church, a *rue fleurie* with an intriguing balcony/museum and ramparts to the east. Labastide-d'Armagnac (B1) is a 13th-century *cité médiévale*: an arcaded square, some arcaded side streets, fortified church, and red brick, stone and half-timbered (*colombages*) houses. See also Le Temple des Bastides, a 17th-century Protestant church, which evokes the theme of *bastides*.

Don't miss the perched *bastide* of **Montréal** (built in 1289) with a square, arcaded on three sides, and fortified Gothic church (D1). An even older site (to the south-west) is the remains of the 4th-century Villa Gallo-Romaine de Séviac where colourful mosaics are protected by open-sided, tile-roofed barns (open Easter to Nov). The varied finds on the site are housed in a museum at the tourist office in Montréal (open July/Aug). Detour north to the most magical of *bastides*, the circular 14th-century version at **Fourcès** – built by the English (D1): the mix of arcades, towers, tiny lanes, medieval houses and ancient bridge over the Auzoue is a sumptuous thrill. **Larressingle** (D1) is another fascinating spot. Tagged the "Petite Carcassonne du Gers", the football pitch-sized, 13th-century polygonal fortress, with a minute 13th-century *église* at its heart, is another show-stopper.

Your detour east leads you to Condom (D1) – the capital of Armagnac. There's a Musée d'Armagnac (closed Tues and also Sun from Oct to May); no less than seven *églises*; a 16th-century cathedral and flamboyant Gothic cloisters; and old streets. The 12th-century Cistercian **Abbaye de Flaran**, south of Condom, is an inspiring mix of Romanesque *église*, 14th-century cloisters and handsome stone carvings, columns, capitals, arches and roofs. There's also a Musée des Chemins de St-Jacques-de-Compostelle (the abbey was on one of the pilgrim routes to Spain) and a garden of medicinal plants. (Closed Tues Oct to May.)

Something different is the small, chic spa at **Barbotan-les-Thermes** (C1): walk the smart central street and rest awhile in the cool gardens to the north of the resort, across the road from the modern thermal baths. Just south of the spa the Lac d'Uby has a beach, facilities like tennis and mini-golf, and a children's playground. **Gabarret**, to the north-east, is renowned for its 15th-century half-timbered and small red brick Maison du Gabardan, which houses paintings and sculptures and evokes many aspects of local life.

South now to the heart of map sheets 150/151, to countryside called **Pays d'Artagnan**. Why? Alexandre Dumas, in his legendary and heroic work, *Les Trois Mousquetaires* (a tale of Artagnan, the archetypal, swash-buckling, quick-tempered, hard-drinking Gascon), based his epic on the earlier works of an unknown writer, Gatien de Courtilz de Sandras (*Mémoires de Monsieur d'Artagnan*). The names of Béarn hamlets were used for three famous characters: Aramits (167:E2) for Aramis; Athos (167:D1) for Athos; and Lanne, just west of Aramits, was the home of Monsieur de Porthau, who gave his name to Porthos. Both works, both extravagantly exaggerated, were based on the life story of Charles de Batz, born in 1615 at the Château de Castelmore, north-east of **Aignan** (C2: Castelmore, privately-owned, is on the map, beside the D102).

Pays d'Artagnan stretches from Aignan and **Riscle** (B2) to **Marciac** (C3) and **Montesquiou** (D3). This is hilly country with river valleys running south to north between the high ridges. Start your touring at **Bassoues** (D3), a *bastide* with a fearsome 14th-century *donjon* (keep); but beware, there are over 200 steps to the top. To the west are two further *bastides*: the sizeable version at Marciac (C3), famed too for its

164

August jazz festival; and Beaumarchés (C3), built in 1298 and the site also of a 14th-century Gothic *église*. A trio of *castelnauds* deserve your attention: Montesquiou; L'Isle de Noé, east of Montesquiou; and Tillac (D3), to the south of Bassoues.

Other sites merit a mention. **Termes-d'Armagnac** (C2) is the site of a fearful and impregnable 13th-century tower, on a crest above the right bank of the **Adour** and with fine views of the Pyrénées. There's also a Musée du Panache Gascon with exhibits based on various Gascony themes. **Plaisance** (C3), a deadbeat place, is the home of a glorious, cathedral-sized organ, built by Daniel Birouste. I've told his story before and how the town has benefited from the stupendous efforts of both Daniel and Betrand Lazerme, the organist. Each year many concerts are held. For details write to Ars Organorum, 32160 Plaisance. To the south-west, at Mazères, across the Adour, is a fortified Romanesque *église*, noted for the interior's fine capitals.

Leave the Pays d'Artagnan and detour south to **Puntous de Laguian** on the N21 (D4). By now you will be well aware of the Pyrénées wall lining the entire length of the southern horizon. The Puntous is the best site to study the range: an observation table, created in 1928, details all the peaks; what a pity about the odd oversized tree.

West now to the hills on the Adour's left bank. Start at **Castelnau-Rivière-Basse** (C3). Relish the views and enjoy the attractive fortified church on its cliff-top site. **Madiran** (B3) also has a handsome fortified *église*. In the undulating hills are the vineyards from which grapes are used to make the super deep-coloured Madiran reds and the quality whites called Pacherenc du Vic-Bilh. The finest examples can be bought from Alain Brumont (in the "o" of Maumusson-Laguian: B3); Jean-Marc Laffitte, just north-west of Brumont's *domaine*; and at the Château d'**Arricau-Bordes** (B3). In an elevated position the stately, golden structure, surrounded by vines, is a majestic sight.

I'll end with two unusual sites. South-east of Labastide-d'Armagnac (B1) you'll spot the Chapelle Notre Dame des Cyclistes, an isolated tiny chapel dedicated to cyclists; there's also a nearby Maison des Cyclistes, crammed full of cycling odds and ends (p.m. mid Apl to mid Oct; also a.m. July/Aug). Even more intriguing is the Notre Dame du Rugby at Grenade-sur-l'Adour (A2). Cross the Adour on the D11 and, just before the D52, take the steep lane to the left, by the statue of the Virgin Mary. The perched chapel is dedicated to players and has four stained-glass windows on rugby themes (one a scrum).

The inspiration for the chapel came from the stained glass window in St-Francis' church at Dudley, dedicated to the memory of Duncan Edwards who, in 1958, when only 21, was one of the Manchester United players killed in the crash at Munich. Anne and I were quietly thrilled to discover the chapel: both of us were educated at Dudley and Duncan, born in 1937, like me, was both a schoolboy contemporary of mine and one of my footballing heroes. Life is full of surprises: agreed?

165

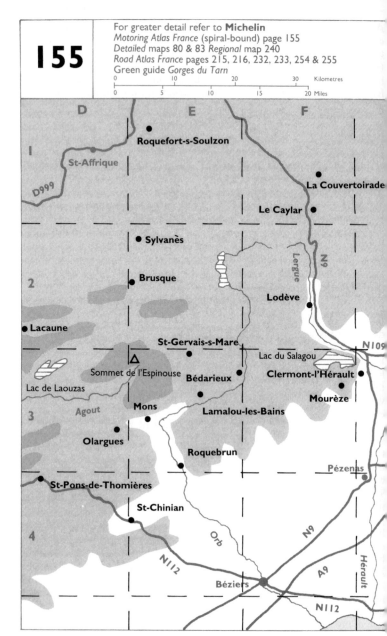

For greater detail refer to **Michelin**
Motoring Atlas France (spiral-bound) page 155
Detailed maps 80 & 83 *Regional* map 240
Road Atlas France pages 215, 216, 232, 233, 254 & 255
Green guide *Gorges du Tarn*

| 0 | 10 | 20 | 30 | Kilometres |

| 0 | 5 | 10 | 15 | 20 Miles |

155

D   **E**   **F**

I

Roquefort-s-Soulzon

St-Affrique

D999

La Couvertoirade

Le Caylar

Sylvanès

Lergue

N9

2

Brusque

Lodève

Lacaune

St-Gervais-s-Mare

Lac du Salagou

N109

△

Sommet de l'Espinouse

Bédarieux

Clermont-l'Hérault

Lac de Laouzas

Mourèze

3

Agout

Mons

Lamalou-les-Bains

Olargues

Roquebrun

Pézenas

St-Pons-de-Thomières

St-Chinian

4

Orb

N9

Hérault

N112

A9

Béziers

N112

166

As hard as I try, I cannot find anything kind to say about the Languedoc coastline (to the east and south of map sheet 155). A year ago Anne and I revisited the stretch of coast between La Grande-Motte (157:D3) and Narbonne-Plage (173:E2) – to check, once again, if my previous criticism had been too harsh. Not at all: we hated every moment and were mightily relieved at the end of two hot days to head inland, to the cool green hills of the Parc Régional du Haut Languedoc (D3).

On our most recent visit, in June, we chose a new way of approaching the regional park. We started at **St-Chinian** (D4/E4) early one Sunday morning; a busy open-air market was much to our liking, as was the large shaded *place.* As you travel the roads across the extensive "white" area on the bottom of map sheet 155 you'll soon realise that almost every nook and cranny is stuffed full of vines: St-Chinian gives its name to one of the best Languedoc red wines; but there are dozens of different classifications, varying from *appellation d'origine contrôlée* to the humble *vin ordinaire.* At least the D20, east of St-Chinian, still very much in wine terrain, was more eye-pleasing than the flatter *pays* to the south-east, a sea of vines I've nick-named "Vinsee".

Roquebrun (E3), above the River **Orb**, was a delight – seemingly stuck to the hillside with house upon house and, above them, a ruined tower brooded silently in the increasingly hot southern sun. A 200-metre long curved weir added both visual and sound effects. Even better was the Jardin Méditerranéen above the village, a terraced site of over 200 different exotic plants (open every day: tel 67 89 55 29).

We followed the Orb upstream; the river was full and cherry trees were laden down with fruit. The landscape changed quickly: to the south we left behind a land of vines, olive trees and orchards of cherries and oranges; most of the vegetation covering the low hills straddling the Orb was small evergreen *chênes verts* (holm oaks); further north we encountered masses of sweet chestnuts and beech trees.

At the junction of the D14 and D908, just east of **Mons** (E3), there are several attractions to the south-west. Ensure you don't miss the first of them – especially after heavy rain or when the rivers are full. The Gorges d'Heric are immediately ahead of you, north of Mons. From the car park the walk north is both long and steepish, though the path is concreted. The waters of the short-lived stream weave a tortuous course between many a rock face being put to good use by climbers. In spring the jumping-jack water spits and sizzles; in summer the gentle trickle is a lifeless squib. If you want to make the trip, without any exertion, then use the small motorised train which runs from the station at Mons to the heart of the *gorges* (June to mid September; every day except Monday. April/May/mid September to October; weekends).

Four more attractions are to the south-west of Mons. First, the medieval perched village of **Olargues** (D3), best seen from the D908 to the west of the huddle of houses. Don't pass the place by. Cross the River Jaur, park, and walk the narrow alleyways; see, too, the museum

167

devoted to the history of the area. **St-Pons-de-Thomières** (D4) has old streets; a richly-decorated cathedral (the organ is especially renowned); and the Musée Municipal de Préhistoire which explains just that and also has fine displays of the megaliths in the mountains to the north (more about them later). Beyond St-Pons is the Grotte de la Devèze, one of many Languedoc underground caves; there's also a Musée de la Spéléologie which explains the world of potholing to the uninitiated. Finally, one great detour from St-Pons is the D907 north to the Col du Cabaretou: the views are sensational.

An easy way of enjoying the valley scenery from Mons to **Bédarieux** (E3) is to use the Train Touristique which chugs between the two locations. Usually a diesel pulls the train but, on Sundays in July and August, a steamer does the job (runs same days as the earlier service).

Another way of approaching Haut Languedoc would be from **Clermont-l'Hérault** (156:A3); here, every Wednesday morning, there's a top-notch market; also see the Gothic church with its three naves. Then seek out Villeneuvette, just east of **Mourèze** (F3) – a tiny 17th-century planned "new town", originally built to house workers weaving woollen cloth for the army. The place is in a time warp, memorable for the buildings, cool streets and massive plane trees. The nearby Cirque de Mourèze is a battlefield of gigantic, dolomitic-shaped rocks; in prehistoric times one needle even had a small fort perched on the summit. The man-made **Lac du Salagou**, to the north, isn't much to write home about; various watersport activities are available.

Head west, through Bédarieux (E3), to Boussagues, a hidden fortified village a few km to the north-west; a ruined castle and Romanesque *église* are extra pluses. Leave to the north – enjoy the great view of Boussagues – and loop south to Hérépian (E3), east of **Lamalou-les-Bains**. Here the Fonderie Bruneau-Garnier, founded in 1600, is an eye-opener: bells are cast and moulded into all sorts of sizes. Lamalou (E3) is a small spa with modern baths and a casino (open every day). Explore the cool, shady main street and then drive north, not from the spa itself, but on the D180 to the south-west of Lamalou.

The climb to the Monts de l'Espinouse is a pleasure at any time: I've seen the hills in spring when wild flowers abound; in June when broom dominates; in August when vast stretches of purple heather flood the high moorland; and in the autumn when thousands of sweet chestnut trees cover the hillsides, their uonopened nuts glistening like a million yellowy-green tennis balls. This a *pays* where you must stop, walk, look and listen— just as we did in June when, north of the **Sommet de l'Espinouse** (D3/E3), we watched skylarks and birds of prey above us and, at our feet, orchids galore competed for our attention.

Back to the D180 climb. Shortly after the Col des Princes turn left on to a small crescent-shaped lane which leads to the Forêt des Ecrivains Combattants. In March 1930 the woods here were washed away by rain. The new forest of pines, chestnuts, oaks and cedars was planted to commemorate the lives of 560 writers who were killed during the 1914-18 war. Detour to minuscule Douch (E3), where the stone houses are "protected" and where, in October, drifts of lilac-tinted autumn crocuses shine brightly in the pastures. If you're a walking nut then make the one-hour climb to Mont Caroux (south of the hamlet). We've yet to make the effort; the views are said to be sensational.

We have driven most of the roads in the park so let me give you some ideas for drives. **St-Gervais-sur-Mare** (E3) is an unprepossessing place with a church above the houses; the Maison Cévenole d'Art et Tradition Populaire explains old local customs and the importance of both sheep and chestnuts to the hill people. Two large lakes, to east and west of La Salvetat-sur-Agout (154:C3), are pleasant sheets of water with woods and roads encircling them; watersports are available at both. The **Lac de Laouzas** (D3) has the Musée de Rieumontagne (open July and August) on its northern banks: the museum evokes prehistoric times in the area and has models of many of the intriguing standing and other stones, many with intricate carvings, in the hills to the north.

Contemplate the scenic contrasts you have encountered in fifty km: from a Med landscape to one more akin to the Welsh borders (note the slate roofs at **Lacaune** – 154:C2); from vineyards to fields of cereal crops; and where farmers earn their income from cows and pigs (Lacaune is famed for *charcuterie*). Visit Lacaune: gamble at the casino if you must but do nose out the rib-tickling Fontaine des Pisseurs in the place de Griffoul (I'll leave you to discover the fine details!).

The D12 which snakes down to **Brusque** (E2) is an eye-pleaser; in the autumn the lofty crag above the village, topped with castle ruins, is aflame with trees changing colour. The Cistercian abbey at **Sylvanès** (E2) is an austere yet graceful building. The abbey is renowned for the successful musical events held each year in the acoustically perfect, high-vaulted interior. For details write to the Abbaye de Sylvanès, 12360 Camarès (65 99 51 83). By the time this book is printed the new cathedral-sized organ should be in place, built by Daniel Birouste at Plaisance (see map sheet chapter 150/151).

What else is there? Don't bypass **Roquefort-sur-Soulzon** (E1), the town which gave its name to the king of cheeses. Visit, free of charge, the caves which are the best natural refrigerators in the world. The blue-veined ewes' milk cheese matures in the caves, eventually emerging into that sharp exquisite taste which makes *Roquefort* unique.

See the medieval walled hamlet of **La Couvertoirade** (F1), once a Templar staging post, on the barren Causse (plateau) du Larzac. Seek out **Le Caylar** (F1). Here, a dead elm tree, over 100 years old, has been shaped into a work of art by Michel Chevray: a variety of images – a shepherd, his dog, an eagle and others – evoke the harsh life of the *causses*. Finish at **Lodève** (F2) with its *ancienne cathédrale* St-Fulcran and, in the hills to the east, the 12th-century Prieuré St-Michel-de-Grandmont with nearby *dolmens* (burial stones).

169

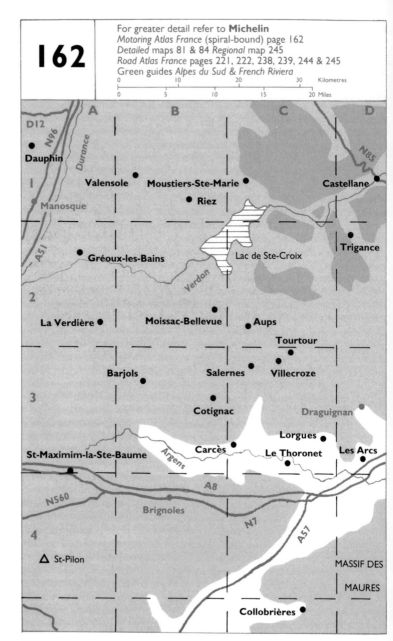

162

For greater detail refer to **Michelin**
Motoring Atlas France (spiral-bound) page 162
Detailed maps 81 & 84 *Regional map* 245
Road Atlas France pages 221, 222, 238, 239, 244 & 245
Green guides *Alpes du Sud & French Riviera*

| 0 | 10 | 20 | 30 | Kilometres |
| 0 | 5 | 10 | 15 | 20 Miles |

A   **B**   **C**   **D**

D12
N96

● **Dauphin**

Durance

1

● **Valensole**   **Moustiers-Ste-Marie** ●

Manosque

● **Riez**

Castellane ●

N85

A51

● **Gréoux-les-Bains**

Lac de Ste-Croix

Trigance ●

Verdon

2

La Verdière ●   **Moissac-Bellevue**

● **Aups**

Tourtour
●

Barjols ●   **Salernes** ●   **Villecroze**

3

● **Cotignac**

Draguignan ●

Argens

Carcès ●

Lorgues ●

Le Thoronet ●   **Les Arcs** ●

St-Maximim-la-Ste-Baume ●

A8

N560

Brignoles ●

N7

A57

4

△ St-Pilon

MASSIF DES

MAURES

● **Collobrières** ●

170

Man and Mother Nature combine majestically in the Provençal terrain contained within map sheet 162. In turn your five senses will be tickled and teased: by the herb-scented air and lavender perfume; by wild flowers, forests of oak, beech and chestnut, savage canyons and perched villages with ancient houses; by refreshing wines and copious fruit and vegetables; by church bells, crickets, nightingales and rushing torrents; by the texture of bark on proud trees, the varying styles of pottery and the cooling pleasure of woods and running water.

I have divided the map into three segments: the countryside south of the **A8** *autoroute* (A4/B4/C4); the terrain between the motorway and the Grand Canyon du **Verdon** (C1/C2); and the *pays* north of the Verdon river. I shall begin with the middle segment – in the Var hills where man's legacy is a series of atmospheric, evocative villages.

Start in the isolated setting of the Cistercian abbey at **Le Thoronet** (C3), a 12th-century creation of simple, exquisite beauty; the cloisters are especially pleasing. Continue west, over the rich red bauxite soil, past the Lac de Carcès and the falls below the dam, to **Carcès** (C3), renowned for its wines and medieval houses. Approach Entrecasteaux (C3) from the south. The part 11th/part 17th-century château, which dominates the village, is a revelation. Restored from a derelict state the interior has all sorts of exhibits (open every day).

On to **Salernes** (C3), famous for the manufacture of colourful glazed tiles (*carrelages*) and pottery. See the shaded *place*, the fountains and alleys, and the ancient *église*, but then seek out some of the workshops which produce such attractive pots and tiles. The clay, with a high iron-oxide content, comes from local deposits. Two establishments caught our fancy: La Poterie du Soleil (made in the traditional style) and the Carrelages Pierre Boutal with a range of tiles and other pottery creations (our "frost-proof" gardenware has proved to be otherwise). Both are on the D560 to the east: the former on the edge of the town, the latter on the outskirts. (Salernes market is on Wed and Sun a.m.)

Now head west. At the D560/D22 junction walk for 15 minutes to the waterfall at Sillans-la-Cascade, where the Bresque cascades over a high, wooded cliff. **Cotignac** (B3) has two pluses: the first is no through traffic; the second is the ideal site – nestling in a hollow, protected from the harsh northern winds by a large wall of rock and wooded hills. Old houses, a handsome fountain and a large shaded *place* all please. But do drive to the sanctuary of Notre Dame de Grâces, one km to the south. Shaded by perfumed pines and ringed by a small, terraced garden, the chapel provides a super view of the town and hills.

Where next? To tiny Fox-Amphoux (B3), north-west of Cotignac. Atop a wooded hill, the hamlet is a gem. The site has always been strategically important: the church dates from the 11th century, built by the Templars who settled there. Between the wars the hamlet fell into disrepair when roofs were removed to escape taxes and rates. Slowly the houses are being rebuilt. **Barjols** (B3), built in the form of an amphitheatre, is renowned for 25 fountains and *lavoirs* (wash-houses), several shaded *places* and a plane tree reputed to be Provence's largest.

A line of four unprepossessing hamlets lie to the north. **La Verdière** (A2) is dominated by an 18th-century château; the first castle on the site was built 1,000 years ago (open every day). Montmeyan (B2) – also founded by the Templars – is a mix of old and new on a small rise. Régusse (B2) sits on a narrow ridge; outside the village is a sports complex of heated pool and tennis courts. **Moissac-Bellevue** (B2) is well named: a perched *village fleuri* with fountain, narrow streets and 12th-century chapel; sadly there are few trees and little shade. **Aups** (C2) is famed for truffles and ham and has a huge shaded *place*, fountains, narrow streets and Provençale Gothic *église*. (A truffle market is held on Thurs a.m. from Nov to Feb.)

Before I finish the Var villages tour let me lead you to a remarkable forest, the like of which is perhaps unique in France. Leave Aups to the north, on the D957; after six km, turn east on the D6 towards Vérignon (C2). In the next four km you'll pass through a medieval oak forest, reckoned to be the oldest in France: how do these stately specimens survive in such difficult cold terrain (over 2000 ft)?

All the southern forests are at risk every year. The *mistral* causes damage of course – but the combination of the maniacal wind plus fire is the most deadly enemy. For example, a decade ago, 2,000 acres of forest were destroyed between Aups and **Tourtour** (C3). All wild life was wiped out; two years passed before birds returned. And, within weeks of the first rain after the fire, myriad wild flowers appeared – many of which had not been seen by local residents for decades.

Ampus (C2) is a tiny spot, ignored by tourists; enjoy the fountain and the views 50 yards to the east. Tourtour, the "village in the sky", came close to being destroyed by fire a decade ago. There are two fountains, a small shaded *place* almost filled with café terrace furniture, and fabulous views from the church above the village (there's also an observation table). At one spot in Tourtour the road is so narrow that traffic lights have been installed to prevent vehicles coming to blows. **Villecroze** (C3) sits sleepily in a protected site, far below Tourtour. North of the village, in the lee of a wooded hill, is a municipal park with gorgeous cypresses, small rose garden, high cascade, stream and caves. Old streets and a Thursday market in the large square are bonuses. Even better is the annual music festival held in the Chapelle St-Victor (an ambitious new custom-built hall is on the drawing board); details from the Syndicat d'Initiative, 83690 Villecroze. See, too, the second branch of La Poterie du Soleil (to the south-east of the village) where more contemporary pottery is displayed and sold.

Finish your tour with this trio. Flaysoc (C3/D3) has a small, cool square, fountains and a Monday market. **Lorgues** (C3) has a lovely shaded *place*, plane trees, fountain, old gates and a large *église*. Medieval Les Arcs-sur-Argens (163:D3; **Les Arcs** on the map) sits atop a rocky spur overlooking the new town; its most noted architectural site is the Provençale-style Romanesque Chapelle Ste-Roseline (to the east) with fine interior treasures (p.m. Wed and Sun; closed Jan/Feb).

Turn now to the map's top segment – where Nature makes a fabulous contribution: the 13 mile-long Grand Canyon du Verdon (C1/C2), one of the most stunning sights in Europe. Every visitor to France should detour to the savagely sculptured slash, up to 2000 ft deep, which the Verdon has carved through the limestone rock. One vital tip: make the trip from **Moustiers-Ste-Marie** (C1) to **Castellane** (163:D1), and back, in a clockwise direction – because then the gorge is always on your right-hand side; you'll park your car more easily at the cliff-side viewpoints and your passengers will get better views.

Surprisingly the canyon is heavily wooded with deciduous trees; in the late autumn the gorge is a luminous, spellbinding sight. One caveat: be careful if you go walking and be sure to set off as well equipped as you can be. Give time to Moustiers-Ste-Marie, clinging to a high cliff, and famed for an overhead star, its individualistic-styled glazed pottery and the Romanesque bell tower of the *église*, built in the Lombard style. Another tip: at La Palud-sur-Verdon (C1) make the D23 23 km-long circuit which is tagged the Route des Crêtes. Rougon (C1) is an eagle's nest high above the Verdon. Stop awhile in Castellane: Napoléon came this way in 1815 on his return from Elba; alleys, fountains, a square, and a giant rock "cube" overlooking the town, all appeal. **Trigance** (163:D2) is a delight, a huddle of ancient houses and medieval castle perched high on a mountainside. Aiguines (C2), with squat château and square-towered church, offers extensive views of the man-made **Lac de Ste-Croix** to the south-west. On the tour stop as often as you can.

All types of watersport facilities are available on the lake. Bauduen (B2), with its toes in the water, and Ste-Croix-du-Verdon (B2), perched above the blue lake, are two alternatives. Further west seek out **Riez** (B1), once an important Roman city, and the vast lavender fields north and south of **Valensole** (B1). **Gréoux-les-Bains** (A2), a cool, shady oasis of a spa, is both ancient and modern and both smart and decrepit at the same time. Tiny, perched **Dauphin** (A1) has covered passageways and old houses built with the local limestone.

What else? In segment three, below the A8, head for **St-Maximin-la-Ste-Baume** (A3) and its Gothic-style basilica. Then south to the Ste-Baume *massif* (A4). Local legend claims that Mary Magdalene spent the last 30 years of her life in a cave on the *massif*. Park at either the D95/D80 junction, or at the Hôtellerie, and allow two hours to climb through the beech forest to the Ste-Baume cave and, later, to the fantastic viewpoint of **St-Pilon** with views of both mountains and the Med. Dense forests are the major attraction of the **Massif des Maures** (C4 and 163:D4); cork oaks dominate but, south of **Collobrières** (161:E3), chestnuts are the scenic highlight in the Forêt du Dom. Fires, alas, have left many a blackened scar in the *massif*.

173

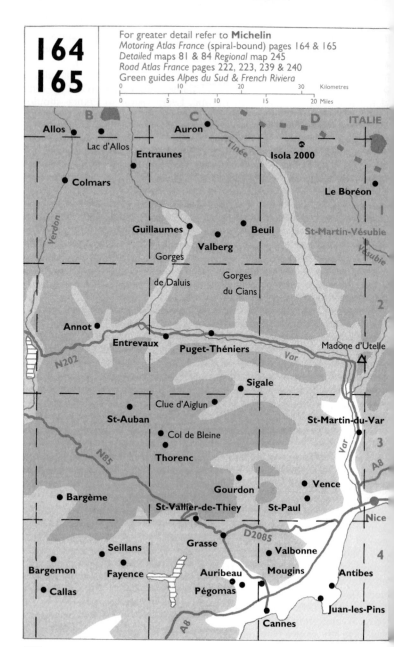

164
165

For greater detail refer to **Michelin**
Motoring Atlas France (spiral-bound) pages 164 & 165
Detailed maps 81 & 84 *Regional* map 245
Road Atlas France pages 222, 223, 239 & 240
Green guides *Alpes du Sud & French Riviera*

Kilometres

0   10   20   30

0   5   10   15   20 Miles

B   C   D   ITALIE

Allos

Lac d'Allos   Auron   Tinée   Isola 2000

Entraunes

Colmars   Le Boréon

St-Martin-Vésubie

Guillaumes   Beuil   Vésubie

Valberg

Gorges

de Daluis   Gorges

du Cians

Annot

Entrevaux   Madone d'Utelle

Puget-Théniers   Var

N202

Sigale

Clue d'Aiglun

St-Auban   St-Martin-du-Var

Col de Bleine

Thorenc   Var

N85   A8

Gourdon   Vence

Bargème   St-Vallier-de-Thiey   St-Paul

Nice

D2085

Seillans   Grasse

Valbonne

Bargemon   Fayence   Auribeau   Mougins   Antibes

Callas   Pégomas

A8   Juan-les-Pins

Cannes

n the introduction to the Côte d'Azur chapter in *French Leave Encore*, was savagely critical about the changes Anne and I have witnessed on he coast during the last 40 years. On our last visit we were horrified, yet igain, to see the apparently never-ending development – on both the coastal strip and, alarmingly, in the ever creeping tentacles spreading 1orth of the **A8** *autoroute*. There seems to be not a single nook or :ranny without some sort of building or "development".

Other than a few references to the coastal strip on the bottom of the nap, I shall concentrate entirely on *l'arrière-pays*; for the purposes of his chapter that means all the countryside north of the busy A8.

We have seen the terrain in each of the seasons. In February we have idmired the "protected" Massif du Tanneron, south-west of **Pégomas** C4), when the hillsides are dressed in yellow – stunning drapes of parkling mimosa which, in midwinter, do wonders for morale. In May ind June we have been bewitched by gardens, terraces and villa walls, ›lanketed with roses, oleander, bougainvillea, veronica, hibiscus and :ountless other cultivated plants. Further inland we have been stunned ›y wild flowers; more about those later. In early summer we have noted he new blooms of the aptly-named "smoke trees" (*cotinus*); but, in)ctober, they become a much more extrovert show, resembling fires of ed-hot coals. In the autumn every mountainside is a massive canvas of nulti-covered confetti – of gold, copper, red, brown and yellow hues.

Without any shadow of doubt I can safely say that I've driven every ›oad on the two map sheets 164/165 during the last 40 years, other than ı dozen or so of the more remote dead-end lanes. One 22-mile stretch of nountain road is, in my opinion, as exhilarating and exciting as any ›ther in the French Alps. I never grow tired of seeking out the lost valley ›f the Gironde and the two mountain walls which guard its scenic hrills; on each visit I enthuse more than ever.

Start your motoring thriller from the D2, just east of **Thorenc** (C3). In Лay we have walked in the pastures south of the Swiss look-alike resort, reading gingerly on white eiderdowns of wild narcissi. In July we have ›een thumped in the eyes by the spectacle of hundreds of exotic orange `urk's-cap lilies, growing wild on the southern slopes of the **Col de 3leine** (Bleyne). At the summit we always turn right and take the dead-›nd climb to the radio masts: in early spring there are snow-capped ›eaks to the north; Thorenc nestles in the woods below you; beyond the ›esort, to the left, are the perched ruins of a 12th-century village Oppidum de Castellaras on the map; a lung-testing hike from the D5 ›elow the site); and, if you're lucky, you will spot birds of prey cruising n the thermals around you (humans, too, use this site for hang-gliding). 3ack at the col note the small memorial to 10 U.S. airmen who ›arachuted to safety from a B24 bomber on 27 May 1944.

Next comes some heart-in-the-mouth stuff. Descend the hairpins to he north and be absolutely certain to stop on the bend where the red igure 5 is on the map. The view east is sensational. A deep, deep valley

175

of cones, slices, humps and lumps stretches into the eastern distance; every slope seems to be covered with trees. In the early morning you look into the sun; the view then is more mysterious. In late afternoon the sun, now behind you, illuminates the entire valley. The over-riding sensation which makes this one of France's finest natural panoramas is the great depth of the valley. On your descent east do not use the easier D110; rather the D10, a classic Monte-Carlo Rally stage when, invariably, the road is a sheet of slippery ice.

Gasp at Le Mas (C3) on a dizzy perch; and even more so at the **Clue d'Aiglun** (C2), an orange and grey gash through slabs of rock hundreds of feet high; later, spot **Sigale** (C2), high above you, clinging on by its fingernails to the mountainside; and don't forget to look right, just after the *clue* (cleft), for the 100 m-high Cascade de Vegay.

Before we head off into the mountains further north let me tell you of the many attractions, most of which are man-made, in the belt of hills to the immediate north of the A8. This is the land of perched villages. **Gourdon** (C3) is the most spectacular: you feel you are in an aeroplane high in the sky as you look down to the vertigo-inducing Gorges du Loup far, far below you. The Château de Gourdon is renowned for its small but dramatic garden; the terraces pack a real visual punch (open all the year, except Tuesday from October to May).

What of the other perched villages? **Auribeau** (C4) is tiny and has a narrow, circular lane within the ancient village. **Mougins** (C4/D4) has the coast's most expensive real estate; at its heart the village resembles a film set. Cabris (C4), west of Grasse, rewards you with extensive views south and is unusual, like St-Vallier-de-Thiey (C3) on the Route Napoléon (RN85), in having a large village green.

Montauroux (C4) and **Fayence** (B4) are biggish places but, as with all the others, both have umbrellas of chestnuts and plane trees and cool fountains. Callian, between the two, also has an unusual waterfall to add to its charms; the site, below a château, is another plus. **Seillans** (B4) has one particularly picturesque fountain (see my drawing on page 77 in *French Leave Favourites*) and some notable *chapelles*. Mons (B4) further inland, is among the oldest of the perched villages; the *table d'orientation* and view are worth the trip alone. Medieval **Bargemon** (B4) is tiny, with a minute shaded *place*; a bonus here, in May/June, is the Col du Bel-Homme, the road a ribbon of wild flowers as you climb to the summit. **Bargème** (B3), further north, is an isolated medieval hamlet, really no more than a church and ruined castle.

Opio (C4), east of Grasse, is a pocket-sized delight. **St-Paul** (D3) is probably the most famous of the perched villages; today the handsome site is a touch too precious and, arguably, is the most crowded.

If time permits, visit them all and also, of course, some of the world renowned resorts on the coast. **Cannes** (D4) has its sophisticated Croisette, alongside the Med, but the narrow rue Meynadier is more of a temptation for us, especially the many food shops. Old **Antibes** (D4) and

176

the glamorous, wooded resort of **Juan-les-Pins** (D4) are totally different in character. **Vence** (D3) is a honeypot tourist trap; and you'll either love or hate Matisse's Chapelle du Rosaire on the northern outskirts. Vallauris (D4), made famous by Picasso, will appeal to any of you interested in pottery; a nearby new motoring museum, financed by Adrien Maeght, is a must for motoring nuts (north of A8).

The names Matisse and Maeght remind me of other museums worth seeking out. Remember the coast was a landscape where the light and vistas inspired many master artists: Matisse, Renoir, Picasso and Chagall among them. Visit the Picasso Museum in the Château Grimaldi at Antibes; Renoir's old home at Les Colettes in Cagnes-sur-Mer (D4); and the Maeght Foundation at St-Paul, a home of fine contemporary art.

Do not leave the southern borders of the map without paying a call on the cool hill station of **Grasse** (despite the ghastly traffic) and its small market: the *parfumeries* Molinard and Fragonard should be seen at least once (guided tours are free; you don't have to buy perfumes though resistance levels are inevitably low by the end). Don't miss either the Confiserie des Gorges du Loup at Pont-du-Loup (D3), west of Vence; here guided tours are also free – but Anne and I have yet to leave empty-handed as the crystallised fruits are just too tempting.

Three quite different shops. First, Roger Casoni's L'Etable cheese shop in the rue Sade, Antibes, where his *chèvre* selection is both an eye-opener and a kick-in-the-mouth experience. Next, the evocative La Bolognaise (Chez César) in Pégomas, a treasure trove of Italian goodies. Finally, the Moulin de **Callas** (B4), north-east of Draguignan, where, since 1928, the finest quality olive oil has been pressed.

Olive oil reminds me to tell you about one of the most impressive characters I know, Marc Streitz. Over a decade ago, when his mother died, Marc returned to the 2,000 olive trees she had so lovingly nursed for over 30 years. "To put my fingers back into the earth, a much better way of life than being a bad architect," he laughingly explains.

Marc's olives and olive oil are second to none. So is his other business, supplying quality vegetables, grown 100 per cent naturally, to a handful of chefs within a brief drive of the estate. One new piece of excellent news: Marc now provides bed and breakfast at his home among the olive trees. Contact him at the Colline de Peirabelle, 06560 **Valbonne** (D4) (tel 93 12 00 29). How do you find him? Head south from Valbonne for one km on the D3; 100 m past the Auberge Fleurie turn right and continue for 500 metres; the estate is on the right.

If Nature's handiwork interests you then visit a trio of underground caves near **St-Vallier-de-Thiey** (C3): the 40 m-long Grottes de St-Cézaire (C4), noted for a rich variety of stalagmites and stalactites and remarkable colourings; the Grotte de la Baume Obscure, where water plays the most important part; and the Domaine des Grottes des Audides, known for impressive formations and river springs.

Now let's head north again, into glorious mountains and valleys. If I have missed out anything among the sights on the southern borders then I apologise: the older I get the more I itch to escape the rush and crush of *la côte* and head for the heavenly peace of the mountains.

There are numerous scenic roads for you to nose out. The Col de Vence (D3) has a panoramic reward at its summit. The D27 (D2), which runs high above the **Var**, is a thrill-a-minute drive from **St-Martin-du-Var** (D3) to **Puget-Théniers** (C2). The run from Sigale (C2), past the Clue du Riolan and down to the Var or, better still, west to **St-Auban** (B3), is not too demanding. Enjoy St-Auban and its *clue*, where the road and stream share the slit in the rocks. Retrace your steps to Briançonnet and climb north on the steep Col du Buis. On to **Entrevaux** and, as you descend, you have a remarkable aspect of the medieval village, on the far bank of the Var, and its citadel, high above the houses, linked together by the nine zigzags of an umbilical wall.

Puget-Théniers (C2) is the home of two fascinating attractions. First, have a look at the map and the gaggle of roads to the north: visit Puget-Rostang; the eagle's nest of Auvare; La Croix, perched above the Gorges de la Roudoule; the high bridge at Pont de St-Léger, a vital link for the village of St-Léger; and remote Léouvé. A highly commendable and inventive enterprise called the Ecomusée du Pays de la Roudoule has been set up in this remote mountain pocket (Easter to end September; closed Monday). Several sites tell the story of man's life in the harsh terrain, describe the surrounding environment, and explain the unusual geology of its red rocks. The main *maison* is at Puget-Rostang (call there first); other villages also make their own contributions. Especially noteworthy are three churches (at Puget-Rostang, La Croix and St-Léger) which, each year, show the rich, colourful 15th-century work (*splendeurs du retable* – altar piece) of Louis Bréa.

The other attraction is the metre-gauge railway which links Digne to Nice (diesel car service). In 1980 an old steam engine was revived to do the short hop between Puget-Théniers and **Annot** (B2); on most Sundays (June to September) this Train des Pignes does the run. Alas, I hear the steamer is under threat of closure; enthusiasts are running up a real head of steam and locals believe the enterprise will be saved. The company which owns the Digne-Nice line is the Chemins de Fer de Provence. They run all sorts of special services; for details write to 40 rue Clément Roassal, 06007 Nice Cedex 1 (93 88 34 72).

For something totally different, leave the N202 a few miles east of Annot and climb to Braux (B2). Then, north of the hamlet, nose out the yard-wide irrigation canal which brings water from the River Coulomp, a few kilometres to the north. You can follow the canal on foot; but take care. If you really want to get off-the-beaten-track, turn off the D908 north of Annot and drive and walk to the remote hamlets of Argenton and La Beauge, above the Coulomp and where the canal starts.

Two fabulous gorges straddle the map squares C1/C2 to the north of Puget-Théniers: the **Gorges du Cians** and the **Gorges de Daluis**. The

178

most fascinating geological feature is the dark iron-ore red band of slate, a few miles deep, which cuts, east to west, across the central sections of both gorges. Today, numerous new tunnels and extensive road widening, in both gorges, have taken away the best parts of what were once memorable driving adventures. The Cians is the more astonishing; park your car at many of the new tunnels and walk the old, narrow roads to appreciate the steep cliffs, almost touching in places, and the turbulent, tumbling river as it rushes down to the Var. Don't rush past the site called Grande Clue (C1) and look out, too, just to the north, for numerous saxifrages growing out of the rust-shaded rock faces. The Daluis is less extrovert but, once again, leave your car at the entrances to the new tunnels and set off on foot to admire the deep gorge below you. In both cases the red rocks provide the special splendour.

At the top of the Cians you enter a refreshingly different world from the dusty Var Valley. By **Beuil** (C1) you're in an Alpine environment of stone and timber houses and chalets, massive pines and emerald pastures. **Valberg** (C1), at 1700 m, is an ever-growing winter sports resort. To the west are several villages worth a detour. Step back in time at: Péone (C1), built of stone and with rock needles dominating the isolated huddle of houses; **Guillaumes** (C1), much bigger, and in the Var Valley, is in the shadow of castle ruins atop a yellow and grey outcrop of rock (market day is Thursday); Sauze, at the end of an eight km climb with endless hairpins, has a richly decorated church; likewise Châteauneuf-d'Entraunes (C1), a perched village facing south; and Villeneuves-d'Entraunes, St-Martin-d'Entraunes and **Entraunes** (B1) – all in the Var Valley and all three with churches and fountains.

Of the three mighty passes that snake north – the Col de la Bonette, 9193 ft (147:E2), the Col de la Cayolle, 7634 ft (147:E2), and the Col d'Allos, 7349 ft (147:D2) – I prefer the last because, at **Allos** village, you can head east up a fantastic dead-end to the **Lac d'Allos**, 7313 ft (147:E3). Allow 45 minutes each way for the pulsating (literally) walk from the car park to the azure lake. Another reason I prefer the Allos is the fortified town of **Colmars** (B1); especially noteworthy are the two Vauban forts straddling the strategic site.

I am running out of space and there's so much more for me to implore you to see. The climb to the **Madone d'Utelle** (D2), a 15 km-run from 285 m to an observation platform, under a strange umbrella-like roof, at 1174 m. The dead-end road to **Le Boréon** (E1), a wonderland of flora and fauna in the Mercantour National Park. The many exhilarating hillclimbs from the left bank of the Var; the most notable is the ascent to La Roquette (D3), a famed rally stage. The winter resorts of **Auron** (147:F3), 5276 ft; and **Isola 2000** (D1), 6562 ft, and the finish of a tortuously cruel stage on the 1993 Tour de France when, after tackling the Izoard (7742 ft), Vars (6912 ft) and Bonette (9193 ft) cols, the cyclists had to face the D97's 31 hairpins as the road snakes 10 miles, and 3675 ft, up into the mountains from Isola.

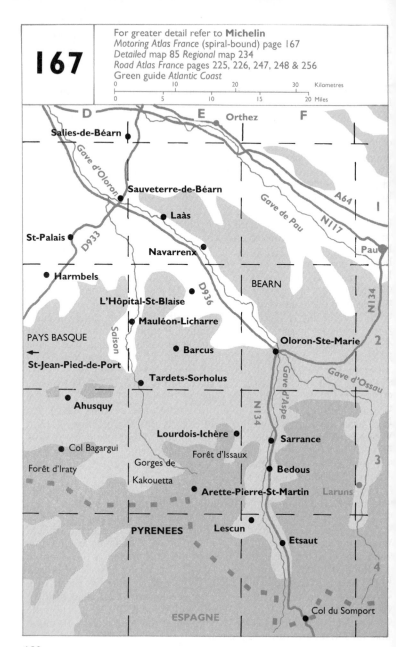

167

For greater detail refer to **Michelin**
Motoring Atlas France (spiral-bound) page 167
Detailed map 85 *Regional* map 234
Road Atlas France pages 225, 226, 247, 248 & 256
Green guide *Atlantic Coast*

| 0 | | 10 | | 20 | | 30 | Kilometres |
| 0 | 5 | | 10 | | 15 | 20 Miles | |

D   E   Orthez   F

Salies-de-Béarn

Gave d'Oloron

Sauveterre-de-Béarn

Laàs

Gave de Pau

A64

N117

I

St-Palais

D933

Navarrenx

Pau

Harmbels

D936

BEARN

N134

L'Hôpital-St-Blaise

Saison

Mauléon-Licharre

PAYS BASQUE

Barcus

Oloron-Ste-Marie

2

St-Jean-Pied-de-Port

Tardets-Sorholus

Gave d'Aspe

Gave d'Ossau

Ahusquy

N134

Col Bagargui

Lourdois-Ichère

Sarrance

Forêt d'Issaux

Forêt d'Iraty

Gorges de

Bedous

Kakouetta

Arette-Pierre-St-Martin

Laruns

3

PYRENEES

Lescun

Etsaut

4

ESPAGNE

Col du Somport

As the years creep by I find myself turning my back on the major *vaut le voyage* and *mérite un détour* French towns and cities. The more I get off-the-beaten-track the more I appreciate the surprises which lie around every corner. In the past I've swarmed, with other tourist bees, to the Biarritz, Bayonne and St-Jean-de-Luz honeypots. Now I look elsewhere for scenic refreshment. Leave the coast and head for the eastern corners of the **Pays Basque** and the western edges of **Béarn**.

Where can we start? Of the many approach roads I think I would choose the **D933** (D1). I would dive down into **Salies-de-Béarn** (149:D3) from the bypass: the thermal spa, protected by low hills, has a Swiss feel. Famed for its brine, there's a Musée du Sel and a salt festival is held on the second Sunday in September. Continue south across the foothills to **Sauveterre-de-Béarn** (D1): walk the narrow streets of the 12th-century *cité médiévale*; enjoy the views of the **Gave d'Oloron** (*gave* is river) and the Pyrénées panorama to the south.

North of **St-Palais** (D1) you will have the first of many typical Basque **Pyrénées** views: mountains and hills shaped in the form of ridges, humps, cones and moulds. (A similar but even better vista is from the D347 midway between **Tardets-Sorholus** and **Barcus** (E2). But, please, don't drive to the viewpoint at La Madeleine: the map shows a "goer" – no way, you'll wreck your suspension.) At St-Palais you're in Basque terrain: the clues are whitewashed houses with red shutters, signs for *gâteau Basque, pelota* courts and men wearing their traditional berets. Amazingly, maize seems to grow in every field; chuckle, too, at the odd palm tree – courtesy of the Gulf Stream.

As you head south-west on the D933 you will see one of the many signs in the area with the shell of St-Jacques; in centuries past pilgrims came this way on their way to Santiago de Compestela in Spain. Accept the invitation at one such sign to visit the 12th-century church of St-Nicolas at Harambeltz (D2: **Harambels** on the map). Drive up the wooded valley, past gorse and heather, to the minute chapel maintained by the local community. The decrepit exterior hides an extravagantly decorated interior (ask at the farm for the key).

St-Jean-Pied-de-Port (166:C2) is a busy place. This is where the numerous pilgrimage routes converged; today, most visitors seem to come from the opposite direction, as the majority are Spanish. The cobbled lanes of the old town, the *maisons médiévales*, the houses with their balconies overlooking the River Nive, the citadel designed by the wily Vauban: all combine to please. If you want to see St-Jean sitting down take the motorised train. (Mon is market day.)

In the past I've driven both the D18 east from St-Jean to the **Col Bagargui** (D3) and the D417 to **Ahusquy** (D3). But last year, for the first time, I drove the D301 south from St-Jean, alongside the Nive, crossing on to map sheet 167 just north of the **Forêt d'Iraty** (D3). What an electrifying drive the mountain road proved to be.

Initially, the D301 runs through the wooded Nive Valley with verdant

181

fields and caramel-hued cattle. You pass signs inviting you to buy *brebi* cheese and *foie gras*. Soon the road becomes steep and there's many a sharp hairpin. I found the D301 reminiscent of the Lake District's Hard Knott Pass and the scenic aspects are similar to many a vista in Cumbria. The road climbs to over 1100 metres and there's a never-ending panorama to the north – one which seems to unfold, scene by scene, as you climb higher. The contrasts are startling: woods, barren peaks, gorse and heather, emerald pastures, bracken and ferns, and flocks of sheep (some with bells). You'll see rock faces, birds of prey, horses grazing freely and *Ardi Gasna* (*brebis*) cheese for sale at remote farms. One gilt edged bonus: you'll have the road to yourself.

That's not all though. The D301 forms a junction with the D18/D19 near the Chalet Pedro (D3); study the board which details six walks in the area. (One walk, using the GR10, takes you to the top of the Sommet d'Occabe at 1456 m.) Now drive south into the heart of one of France's most noble beech forests, the Forêt d'Iraty, at an altitude of between 1000 and 1300 m. In October the trees are a heart-stopping sight; the autumn shades are gargantuan sheets of smouldering colour. Walks abound; there's a café at the Chalet Pedro (you can also buy *brebis* cheese, mountain ham, *confits* and *gâteau Basque*); and a couple of idyllic picnic spots at two lakes – one at the junction, the second as you climb the 1327 metre-high Col Bagargui. As you ascend the western slopes, through beech woods, look out for ponies, roaming freely.

If you use the easier D18 from St-Jean, don't bypass the huge Chapelle St-Sauveur (D3). There are numerous chalets on the climb of the Col Bagargui; many can be rented (details from the local tourist offices). If you want a further dose of a road to yourself then follow the small brown signpost at the col announcing "10 km Ahusquy". The track is stone based and is adequate enough. The views north are more akin to looking down on a relief map. Ahusquy (D3), another pretty spot, is at a lower altitude but is peaceful, pastoral and, scenically, richly eye pleasing. Here you are at the centre of a large circle of country called the Pays de Soule – from **Mauléon-Licharre** (E2), the capital, south to the Spanish border. The eastern descent of the Col Bagargui is long and steep; the best views are from a point just east of the summit.

The map highlights two natural landmarks: the Crevasses d'Holcarté (D3) and the **Gorges de Kakouetta** (E3). Both are 200 metre-deep narrow slashes in the limestone cliffs, carved out by water over millions of years. Both involve long hikes. Kakouetta is more accessible (in places the *crevasse* is just a few metres wide) and there's a car park on the D113. Note, too, the tiny emerald pool just below the start of the walk and, to the east, the Romanesque chapel at Senta.

Two further high cols are beyond Senta: the Col de Suscousse (1216 m), at the head of a wooded valley; and the Col de Soudet at the junction of the D113 and D132 (E3). The latter is 1540 metres high. Continue up the dead-end road to the ski resort of **Arette-Pierre-St-**

Martin (1640 m), out of season a ghostly white lunar landscape under the cone peak of Pic d'Anie. The views north are sensational.

Similar views can be seen from the road between the Pas de Guilhers and the Col de Labays (E3) – the terrain which provides such a memorable vista from the D347 (south-west of Barcus: E2). At the Col de Labays strike out east again, through the dense **Forêt d'Issaux** (E3) – another vast, mainly beech and fir forest. The road is narrow and, at Osse-en-Aspe(F3), the church acts as a road island.

Now we are in the Vallée d'Aspe. Make your first port of call the tourist office on the west side of the **N134**, south of **Bedous** (F3). Some of the best Béarn *pays* is in the high mountains straddling the **Gave d'Aspe**. For the sporting enthusiast there's rock climbing, hang-gliding, white-water rafting and mountain biking. For the more relaxed among us there are endless opportunities for solitary walking. From April to June the high altitude meadows are a wonderland of wild flowers. For example, drive up to **Lescun** (F4), ringed to the west and south by a *cirque* of peaks. Drive the roads as far as they go, park, and then set off on foot: for example the Labadie Valley.

Alternatively, drive to the historic **Col du Somport** (1632 m) with its invigorating mountain and valley views (F4). Try two walks: the easier one, from a point 300 m below the summit, heads west alongside the frontier. The longer hike starts three km below the col; park at the Chalet Cadier and head north on the marked walk; at the point just north of the 2034 m peak the mountainside is known as the Plateau de la Gentiane – renowned in late Spring for just that!

Simpler pleasures are the two Pyrénées bears, Antoine and Segolene, which can be seen at Borce (F4: open every day summer; weekend only mid Sept to mid June). At nearby **Etsaut** there's a *maison du parc* for the Parc National des Pyrénées; call for information about the park's famed flora and fauna. Further north detour west to the *ecomusée*, the Maison de Lourdios, at **Lourdios-Ichère** (E3) – an exhibition which evokes the life of a village in a remote Pyrénées valley.

What else is there to see on map sheet 167? I'll detail some of the man-made sites. As you travel north up the Vallée d'Aspe stop awhile at **Sarrance** (F3); a medieval *église*, cloisters and *musée* are the magnets here. **Oloron-Ste-Marie** (F2) has a rich treasure in the shape of the Eglise Ste-Marie, built in the 13th century; the west door is a stunning sight with its intricate stone carvings. See, too, the nearby Musée du Haut Béarn. Remote **L'Hôpital-St-Blaise** (E2), in the Pays Basque, is the home of a tiny 12th-century Romanesque/Byzantine *église*. **Navarrenx** (E1), in a great site above the Gave d'Oloron, is a medieval *bastide* with solid and formidable ramparts. **Laàs** has an ivy-covered, 17th-century château, more like a small manor house with a lived-in feel (open a.m. and p.m. Apl to Oct – but not Tues).

Anything else? Yes, there are no end of attractions both to the east and west of map sheet 167 – but that's another story.

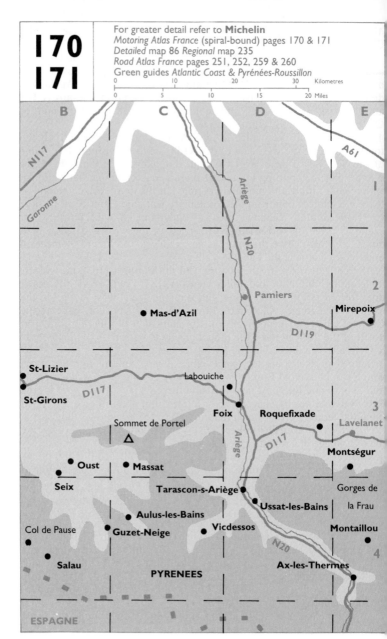

170
171

For greater detail refer to **Michelin**
Motoring Atlas France (spiral-bound) pages 170 & 171
Detailed map 86 *Regional* map 235
Road Atlas France pages 251, 252, 259 & 260
Green guides *Atlantic Coast & Pyrénées-Roussillon*

0   10   20   30   Kilometres
0   5   10   15   20 Miles

B   C   D   E

N117

A61

Garonne

Ariège

N20

1

Pamiers

2

● Mas-d'Azil

Mirepoix

D119

St-Lizier

Labouiche

D117

St-Girons

Foix

Roquefixade

3

Lavelanet

Sommet de Portel
△

Ariège

D117

Montségur

● Oust
Seix

● Massat

Tarascon-s-Ariège

Gorges de
la Frau

Aulus-les-Bains

Ussat-les-Bains

Col de Pause

Guzet-Neige

Vicdessos

Montaillou

4

Salau

N20

PYRENEES

Ax-les-Thermes

ESPAGNE

Forgive me if I devote most of this chapter to the bottom halves of map sheets 170 and 171. Here you'll enjoy exhilarating mountain terrain which, for the most part, tourists seem to ignore.

The small map to the left covers most of the Ariège *département*, literally a cross-section of the **Pyrénées** at their best. As you approach from the north the initial landscape is one of gentle, rounded hills, rising to higher peaks, mainly wooded, and cut by valleys famed for caves and castles. Further south, on the Spanish border, there are many stark, higher peaks, some rising to near or over 10,000 feet.

I'll start right at the heart of the high mountains, in the Pays du Haut Couserans – near **Oust** (170:B3). New roads from **St-Girons** (B2) make access to the Salat Valley easy. At **Seix** (south of Oust), on our last autumn visit, and after weeks of heavy rain, the river was fuming and foaming; the village has a château, large *place* and a church with an ornate four-bell bell-tower. As we headed upstream the river laid on a stupendous show – with white water catching the eye and, here and there, turquoise pools providing restful contrasts. Wild buddleia, with their mauve spikes, seemed to be everywhere (butterflies must love them) and broadleaved trees made a refreshing backdrop.

Continue south to **Salau** (B4). In the summer the river is a hospitable friend; in late October and early November the Salut can be a murderous, bludgeoning enemy. Many times over the centuries torrential rain, falling over several days, has siphoned into the three mighty *cirques* to the south and come roaring down the valley, flattening parts of the village and killing inhabitants. The last inundation was on 7/8 November 1982 when parts of the church were washed away. The nave and apse of the small 12th-century Templars' *église* were still being rebuilt a year ago. In the village (from the first house beyond the church but on the east bank) buy a fascinating booklet, *Huit siècles d'histoire à Salau*, which tells the story of the indefatigable village.

At the far end of Salau park at English-speaking Roland Simenel's Hôtel Les Myrtilles. Tell him you're doing so. Now follow the signposted path from the side of the hotel to the Cirque d'Anglade (1115 m). In spring a one-hour walk will take you to a marvellous display of wild flowers; a two-hour hike will reward you with a breathtaking show. On your return I'm sure you'll want to rest awhile in Roland's café.

There's much more to come. Now head west to one of France's greatest dead-end roads, the **Col de Pause** (B4). I'll be frank and say now that the last few km to the col (you're forbidden to drive beyond the pass) are very rough and require slow, careful driving. At the 1527 metre-high col summit you've entered the lofty and remote Réserve du Massif du Valier – truly a rich kingdom for flora and fauna, one that is renowned for birds of prey and *izards* (cousins of the *chamois*). Needless to say, in June, the wild flowers are stunning.

If you prefer not to drive the last steep few km then at least climb as far as the Bergerie de Capvert (1100 m) where the tarmac is still smooth.

Danièle and Gilbert Gilles will give you a friendly welcome. Buy cheese, *charcuterie*, jams, honey, milk and other *produits fermier*. Better still, ring 24 hours ahead (61 96 55 02) and order a picnic: then walk to your heart's content in any part of the regal Salat Valley.

Another mouthwatering "shop" is the easy-to-find Confiture Artisanale des Pyrénées of Daniel and Anne-Marie Boudet. The modern building is near the Elf garage, on the D3, just north of Oust. The range of home-made *confitures* and *gelées* is saliva-stirring; we're still tucking into the various bottles we bought. (Other produce also available.)

The high peaks surrounding **Aulus-les-Bains** (C4) are another strong magnet. The small spa (780 m) is in a wooded, *cirque*-like valley. Old-world hotels sit side by side with modern thermal baths, behind which is a newly-created park. There are numerous walks and several excellent notice boards in the valley give details of just where they go and how long they take. The spectacular Cascade d'Ars (Arse on map), the Etang du Garbet and, higher still, the Etang Bleu are recommended. In late spring, at altitude, wild flowers are profuse.

Aulus can be approached from four directions. The Vallée du Garbet, to the north-west, is the easiest: wooded, extensively cultivated and with numerous dwellings. The Vallée d'Ustou, to the west, is more rewarding scenically. The ascent from Ustou (B4) provides attractive views of the wooded valleys climbing south towards Spain. Use the new D68 road, built for skiers, which climbs to **Guzet-Neige** (B4) and continue south, ascending on the not-too-rough road towards the Col d'Escots. At the gate two km from Guzet stop and take in the vista of the Garbet Valley far below you. Vast views abound in all directions.

A third approach is from **Massat** (C3), south along the D18 and climbing a wooded valley. Just below the Col d'Agnes, 1630 m on the sign, there's the small Etang de Lers which looks for all the world like a Lakeland tarn; the rocky cradle of mountains has a touch of Cumbria too. From the col there's a panorama to the south of a long line of bare-topped high peaks with several "bowls" gouged out below the summits. The tree-line starts at about 5000 ft and, in summer, there are no signs of snow. The fourth access is from **Vicdessos** (C4); this steep, wooded ascent climbs the Port de Lers pass, east of the *étang*.

The valleys south of Vicdessos and Auzat (C4) lead you to another high-altitude world of flora and fauna among the mountains and mostly man-made *étangs*. There's also plenty to keep outdoor enthusiasts busy: riding, canoeing and hang-gliding as examples. Contact the Maison du Tourisme at 09220 Auzat for details (tel 61 64 87 53).

Before heading east to map sheet 171 let me detail some of the country in the middle of 170. I'll begin at Massat (C3) where the valley is especially nice with wooded domes and high ridges. The village *église* is an austere 15th-century building. One scenic aspect is all too obvious in the terrain to the north: the hills are almost exclusively wooded. One road, the D17, east and west of Burret (C3), is tagged the Route Verte.

The route is just that, wooded every inch of the way.

Spend some time north-east of Massat. Use the D618 east and then the steep lane that connects the Col des Caougnous and Col de Péguère. Don't make the short, sharp climb to the Tour Laffont (Laffon on map): trees have outgrown the tower ruins and obliterate the views. At the Col de Péguère the acoustics are unusually entertaining: still air allows distant sounds of cockerels, birds and cow and sheep bells to be heard distinctly. Enjoy the 360-degree views from the high roads and from the 1485 m **Sommet de Portel** (C3), a short hike from the D72.

Be certain not to miss two sites on 170: the 12th-century cathedral at **St-Lizier** (B2), north-of St-Girons, with octagonal bell-tower, frescoes, fine woodwork and impressive two-tier cloisters; and the Grotte du **Mas-d'Azil** (C2) where a river has carved out a vast tunnel – and also formed prehistoric galleries where man lived tens of thousands of years ago (there's also an excellent *musée* at the site).

Now to 171. **Foix** (D3) sits below a medieval fortress with three different-shaped towers. North and south of the town are more underground attractions. To the north-west is the subterranean river at **Labouiche**: 60 m below ground the river is navigable by boat for 1500 m of its six km length. To the south of **Tarascon-sur-Ariège** (D4) is the massive Grotte de Niaux, famous for cave drawings of bison, horses, deer and goats. Around the corner, in the **Ariège** Valley and near the thermal spa of **Ussat-les-Bains** (with handsome old-fashioned *thermes*), is the Grotte de Lombrives, Europe's largest; access is by a small train which takes you through a succession of galleries and halls with stalactite formations.

There's plenty to see east of Foix. Use the D9 which provides pretty views south-west and leads to **Roquefixade** (D3); there's an arduous hike to the ruins of the Cathar castle high above the village. Climb the Col de **Montségur** (E3) and park below the east side of the pass. You're faced with a lung-testing 30-minute walk to the ruins of the Cathars' last stronghold. I shall write about the Cathars and **Montaillou** (E4) in map sheet chapter 175. (Both the ruins and archaeological *musée* in Montségur are closed from Dec to Feb.)

East of Montségur Nature offers two super contributions: the Fontaine de Fontestorbes – a resurgent source, intermittent in nature, where 1,800 litres of water a second can flow from the cave. The **Gorges de la Frau** (E4), an ever-narrowing valley, is a mix of dense broadleaved woods and a striking mix of rock shapes.

What else? The bustling spa of **Ax-les-Thermes** (E4), where hot water bubbles out of the ground into baths once used by Romans. To the southeast, in the Vallée d'Orlu (two km past the Forge), is the start of the Réserve Nationale d'Orlu, a wildlife paradise particularly reputed for *izards*. **Mirepoix** (E2) is a *cité médiévale* with a 15th-century cathedral (and largest nave in France) and exceptional 12th-century timbered arcades under half-timbered (*colombages*) houses.

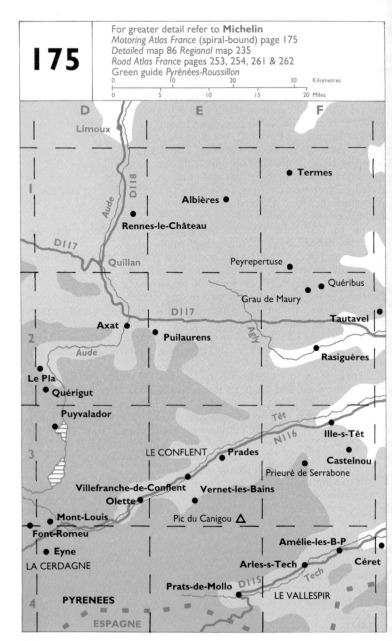

175

For greater detail refer to **Michelin**
Motoring Atlas France (spiral-bound) page 175
Detailed map 86 *Regional* map 235
Road Atlas France pages 253, 254, 261 & 262
Green guide *Pyrénées-Roussillon*

| 0 | 10 | 20 | 30 | Kilometres |

| 0 | 5 | 10 | 15 | 20 Miles |

D   E   F

Limoux

Termes

D118

Aude

Albières

Rennes-le-Château

D117

Quillan

Peyrepertuse

Quéribus

Grau de Maury

D117

Axat

Puilaurens

Agly

Tautavel

Aude

Rasiguères

Le Pla

Quérigut

Puyvalador

Têt

N116

Ille-s-Têt

LE CONFLENT

Prades

Castelnou

Prieuré de Serrabone

Villefranche-de-Conflent

Vernet-les-Bains

Olette

Mont-Louis

Pic du Canigou △

Font-Romeu

Amélie-les-B-P

Eyne

Céret

LA CERDAGNE

Arles-s-Tech

Tech

D115

Prats-de-Mollo

LE VALLESPIR

PYRENEES

ESPAGNE

188

MICHELIN MAP PAGE 175

I started the first chapter in *Mapaholics' France* with a plea for you to "look beyond the obvious". That advice is just as valid in this final chapter – about terrain which is part of Roussillon or, to be more specific, *la terre Catalane*. There's a varied mix of great treats.

Access the area by the following spectacular route. Leave bustling Ax-les-Thermes (174:C2) on the D25 to the east. There's nothing exciting on the ascent of the Port (pass) de Pailhères; the fireworks start at the 2001 m col. To the south and west are jagged lines of high peaks; and to the east the sleeping hulk of Madrès (D3) fills the horizon. As you start the descent take the short new northern loop of road which, I imagine, has been especially built to allow you to gasp at the never-ending northern panorama.

At the pass you enter the Pays de Donézan, a small, circular and secret enclave ringed by a high bowl of mountains, with the River **Aude** as the eastern border and **Quérigut** (D2) at the centre. Head first for the tourist office at **Le Pla**. Ask for leaflets and details of the numerous walks in Donézan – from easy to difficult – which lead you to high pastures, dense woods, lakes and streams, flora and fauna, old Catalane forges, ruined castles and humble villages.

In the past I've always entered the Haute Vallée de l'Aude from **Axat** (D2). I recall one glorious April day when the combination of the river in full flood, fed by melting snow from the high peaks to the south, splendid gorges, the numerous new tints on the trees and a clear blue sky left an indelible memory. I remember, too, the forest south of Carcanières-les-Bains (D2) when, on one hot October day, the beech trees were mammoth drapes of burning autumn shades.

At **Puyvalador** (D3) you enter Le Capcir, a land of lakes, the largest are man-made, and pine forests. Bordered to the west by the twin peaks of Pic Peric and Pic Carlit (174:C3), this high-altitude terrain, most villages are around the 5000 ft mark, is perfect for both the walker and botanist. Head west from the D118 (up the dead-end D60 road from Mont-Louis: D3) to the Lac des Bouillouses (174:C3): numerous *étangs*, wild flowers in the spring, and woods to the east provide bags of interest (both the Aude and **Têt** rivers rise nearby).

As you cross the Col de la Quillane (D3) you catch your first sight of **La Cerdagne**, a high-altitude, broad valley cum plateau renowned for its dry and bracing air and, allegedly, 3,000 hours of sunshine every year. I can believe the latter: ringed by high protective peaks, the Cerdagne is too much of a burnt landscape for me – even when the rest of France has had weeks of rain. But seek out these sites.

First, the remarkable *four solaire* (solar furnace) at Odeillo, just below **Font-Romeu** (174:C4); the space-age marvel is a giant concave wall made up of 10,000 small mirrors which concentrate the sun's energy into useable power. There's also a permanent exhibition at the foot of this Temple du Soleil (every day except mid Nov to mid Dec). Font-Romeu is both a winter ski-resort and, during the summer, a mecca for athletes

189

who use the high-altitude facilities for training. The massive fort at **Mont-Louis** (D4) is yet another Vauban creation (aren't they all?). More to my liking are **Eyne** (D4) and nearby Llo. The latter is renowned for a Romanesque *église* with grotesque capitals; the former for sand-coloured stone houses, famed flora in the Eyne Valley to the south-east, and for many local prehistoric sites (a four-hour walk, every day in July/Aug, starts in the village at 2.30 p.m.: tel 68 04 72 48).

East to differing terrain, the Têt Valley. Where the river starts its long fall from La Cerdagne, to the man-made lake east of Prades (E3), the valley and nearby mountains are known as **Le Conflent**. At the high western end the landscape is dry scrub; so, too, are the south-facing northern hillsides all the way down to **Olette** (D4); the north-facing, cooler slopes seem to be entirely covered with woods. Beyond Olette the countryside has a typical Mediterranean face.

As you descend the Têt Valley from La Cerdagne, along the improved N116, you'll notice the impressive viaducts and bridges of a metre-gauge railway line – a remarkable piece of engineering which allows *Le Petit Train Jaune* to travel from **Villefranche-de-Conflent** (F3: 427 m) to the highest station in the Cerdagne (and for SNCF in all France) at Bolquère/Eyne (D4: 1592 m), a climb of getting on for 4,000 ft. The red and yellow train, nicknamed *le canari*, provides an exciting scenic ride, especially if you sit in one of the open flat-cars.

Three differing small towns are among Conflent's main attractions. Medieval Villefranche-de-Conflent's two long main streets are within high ramparts, redesigned by "guess who?"; the claustrophobic *cité* is notable for the ramparts (climb them), *portes*, 13th-century bridge, 12th-century church and two towers. **Vernet-les-Bains** (E3) is a colourful flower-filled spa with, high above the small resort, a 12th-century *église* and restored castle sitting above the old town's streets. **Prades** (E3) is famed for both its 17th-century church (built on the site of a Romanesque *église* – hence the golden-stone tower) and the interior's ornate Baroque wood carvings; and an annual music festival founded by the celebrated cellist, Pablo Casals (Syndicat d'Initiative, 4 rue Victor Hugo, 66500 Prades: tel 68 96 27 58).

You'll enjoy driving the many roads, some quite taxing, which link Vernet and Prades and snake up the **Pic du Canigou** slopes (2784 m). The most impressive views of this giant slumbering dinosaur of a mountain, with several humps across the top of its back, are from further afield than the Têt Valley; especially good are those from the east and north. But walking on the high wooded Canigou slopes rewards you much, much more (this is true of the ring of country surrounding the *massif*). Woods, wild flowers, birds of prey, *mouflons*, *izards* (cousins of the *chamois*), a *maquis*-like undergrowth scented with thyme and herbs: all combine to tickle the senses. One underground site worth a call is the Grottes des Canalettes, north of Vernet: discovered only 40 years ago, the caves have a collection of illuminated stalagmites,

190

talactites and pillars of varying colours, shapes and textures.

Visit other man-made sites: **Castelnou** (F3), in the eastern Canigou foothills, a restored medieval fortified village with endearing cobbled lanes and houses – the site dominated by a castle; and **Ille-sur-Têt** (F3), enclosed within ramparts, where the old town and its rare geological *orgues* are picturesque attractions.

But much the most alluring man-made pleasures in Le Conflent are the Romanesque treasures. First the *église* at Corneilla-de-Conflent, north of Vernet: see the doorway, choir, apse, wood carvings and marble Virgin with child. South of Vernet is the most spectacularly-sited abbey in France, St-Martin-du-Canigou – perched on a rocky outcrop high above wooded valleys. You have to make a steep 30-35 minute hike to savour the cloisters, square bell-tower, two-level *église*, the capitals and, above all, the remote mountain setting. Next, the Abbaye de St-Michel-de-Cuxa, south of Prades, in a desolate, dry site, with a handsome, multi-arched tower; this is the home of the Pablo Casals festival.

An even more evocative Romanesque site is the **Prieuré de Serrabone** (F3), in an isolated setting off the D618. You wind up eight hairpins, and pass both heather and holm oaks, on the four km D84 drive. Relish the dividends: cloisters, tribune, carvings, pillars, arches, capitals and a Mediterranean garden with hundreds of plants.

The D618 run from the Têt to the **Tech** Valley (F4), only 45 km long, is a real scenic thriller. I doubt if there's a straight longer than 100 metres. The views, as you head south, include distant glimpses of the Med, vistas of Canigou, a mountain much revered by Catalans, and a panorama of the peaks on the Spanish border; and woods, all the way, starting with small holm oaks in the north, then changing, south of the Col Xatard, to a mixture of chestnuts, oaks and beech.

The Tech Valley is part of an area called **Le Vallespir** – a market garden where cherries, oranges, vines and olives grow side by side. In February, mimosa is a fragrant, colourful show; at the end of April and in early May, cherry blossom provides a bright, eye-catching spectacle. **Amélie-les-Bains-Palalda** (F4) is a smart busy thermal spa. **Prats-de-Mollo** (E4) is an old fortified town with a Romanesque *église*. **Céret** (177:D4), with an atmospheric, bustling heart, is famed for its links with Picasso, Matisse, Braque and Dali. The Musée d'Art Moderne has recently been altered and enlarged.

Nature offers many tempting alternatives. Note the source of the Tech in the Roc Colom (E4: 2507 m). By Céret the river has fallen to 120 m, in a distance of just 30 km as the crow flies. As a consequence the valley is subject to severe changes in water levels after heavy rain; you'll see plenty of evidence of the damage caused by the river. Higher up the valley sides woods dominate; walks and views to both north and south are magnificent, as are the many dead-end roads.

If time allows walk the Gorges de la Fou (F4: access from the D115): the gap can be as narrow as three metres in places, yet the cliff walls reach as high as 100 m. If not, do the following drive through cool forests and with great views – but, I implore you, in a clockwise direction: **Arles-sur-Tech**; D54 to Montferrer – past high ochre and grey cave-pocked rock faces; D44 to Corsavy; and Arles.

Now north. **Rasiguères** (F2) used to be called *un village perdu*. No any more. Moura Lympany, the pianist, bought a house there 20 years ago; at the time she was in a trough of depression but both the village and Roussillon did much to rejuvenate her spirits. Her appreciation comes each year in the form of a music festival at the end of June when musicians from all over the globe play (details: Festival Moura Lympany 66720 Rasiguères). **Tautavel** (177:D2) is to the north-east. In 1971, in a cave near the village, the skull of a 20-year-old man was discovered, an individual who had lived 450,000 years earlier. A skilfully-designed museum, above the village, explains the story of Europe's first *Homo erectus* (open every day; cave in July/Aug only).

The northern half of 175 is Cathar country. Cathars wanted to free man from the materialism of the Catholic church and they also repudiated the divinity of Christ; inevitably they clashed with papal authority. From 1209 to 1244 a series of crusades against the Cathars forced them to take refuge in remote castles. The ruins of several can be seen on map sheet 175. **Peyrepertuse** (F1) is the most spectacular – a long line of battlements and towers, astride a high granite ridge (allow 30 minutes to reach the top-most tower). **Quéribus** (F2), to the east, looks for all the world like a fingernail stuck to the top of a rocky finger (approached by a two km-long, first-gear climb; then a 15-min hike). Others are at **Puilaurens** (E2), east of Axat; **Termes** (F1); Quérigut (D2) and Puivert (174:C1). (One must: be sure to read the classic *Montaillou* (Penguin), the story of the Cathars in the remote hamlet (174:C2) during the period 1294-1324.)

Scenically the north-east corner of 175, part of Corbières, has little to offer – other than millions of holm oaks. However, the views from the **Grau de Maury** (F2) are superb – of saw-tooth ridges, Canigou, peaks and the Med. Termes (F1) is a cool delight, care of a couple of dozen plane trees and running water. The D212 north of **Albières** (E1), and the D613 to the west, run through a completely different landscape: forest of beech, chestnut and oak, fine views and little traffic.

Finally, to the unnerving, hill-top village of **Rennes-le-Château** (D1), steeped in a turbulent history. Before you go read the controversial *The Holy Blood and The Holy Grail*. Immediately you arrive seek out the shop adjacent to the *église* and *musée*. At the shop buy the English language *Visitor's Guide* and have a natter with Celia Brooke, an English lady. What was the secret of the Abbé Bérenger Saunière (1852-1917) and his servant, Marie Denarnaud (1868-1953), one which went to the grave with her? (For information about Rennes and its history join Le Reflet de la Fabuleuse Rhédae. Write to Celia, c/o the association, a 11190 Rennes-le-Château for details of regular newsletters.)

FAVOURITES

Anne and I first visited France forty years ago. Then we were teenagers, both innocents abroad. I had just passed my driving test and many of the trips we made in those early days were in our first clapped-out motor cars. By the late Fifties I had acquired the bug for rally navigating and, as a consequence, I soon became an addicted "mapaholic". The end result – a love affair with *la douce France* – was inevitable.

Little did we realise then that forty years on we would have written, published and sold over four hundred thousand books on that adorable country – and penned scores of articles for some of the world's most prestigious newspapers and magazines. Not to mention, too, the twelve thousand and more letters we would receive from readers around the globe; the quiet pleasure we would enjoy from seeing every "Chiltern House" title make the bestseller lists; and last, but not least, the contented satisfaction we would get from taking on, and beating, the publishing "establishment" (we know that many authors and journalists have relished this part of our adventure more than any other).

In 1980, as out-and-out amateurs, we made the decision to turn our hobby into a business when we published the first of our many books, *French Leave*. The trips for pleasure, during the previous 25 years, were replaced by numerous hectic, strictly "professional", research visits – of topography and both hotels and restaurants. Our financial survival depended on the success we made of our do-it-yourselves publishing enterprise. Today, we are most certainly not innocents abroad!

For much of the Eighties I visited France on my own; Anne stayed at home to look after the business and the children. Now, the children are adults so, once again, Anne accompanies me on every visit. I have no idea how many hundreds of thousands of miles I have driven on French roads and I calculate I must have visited a four-figure number of French hotels and restaurants – some of them several times over.

What follows in this middle section of *Allez France!* is a record of the sixty hotels and restaurants we admire and appreciate the most. In *French Leave Favourites* I wrote about the places that readers considered were the best. The pages which make up the filling of the *Allez France!* sandwich are an account of our personal favourites; the list is not influenced in any way by readers. One way of summing them up is to say that these are the places we would visit first – before any others.

What makes one place a favourite – from humble to great – and another an also-ran? There's no mystery about the answer: the common thread running through all our favourites lies in the personalities behind each establishment. An individual, couple, or family, can instil character, talent and life into the dullest of homes. Equally, however grand and glitzy the bricks and mortar, and furnishings and fittings, of a

luxury palace may be, there is often a moribund vacuum *in situ*.

Some readers will be surprised at the omission of many celebrated *cuisiniers*. These chefs have been among our favourites in the past; but our attitudes and tastes have changed – and they've changed too. I said a lot about the shortcomings of the superstars' restaurants in *French Leave Encore*. I repeat: we have grown weary of the "three-star spiral chase". Most three-star, and too many two-star restaurants, have become too precious, pretentious and pompous: you see the 3Ps on the plates, in the trappings and service, and in the owners, who change gradually as they ascend the spiral. The "Enjoyment Factor" at the 3P shrines is often zero out of 10; you can't say that about any of our "Favourites". Progress is not necessarily always in a forward gear!

Everything which follows is self-explanatory. The map on this page shows the location of each favourite (individual entries are listed alphabetically in the text which follows). For details of abbreviations, price bands, cooking ratings, culinary styles, a glossary of menu terms and regional culinary notes – see *Franc-wise France*.

Dear Reader

You asked what did we think of French hotel and restaurant standards during our many 1993/94 visits. "Many" is the right word: Anne and I spent the equivalent of several months in France during the last two years, driving the length and breadth of the country.

Two separate sets of three words sum up our answer to your question. The first set is "a mixed bag". Inconsistency has become an ingrained feature of French hotel and restaurant performance; during the last two years we must have received at least one grumble about every French entry in *French Leave Encore* (*FLE*) – from the greatest to the simplest.

However, a second set of three words, "*Franc-fort France*", sums up our findings even better and, in addition, explains why "a mixed bag" has become such a common occurrence. What does "*Franc-fort France*" mean?

Britain's forced exit from the Exchange Rate Mechanism, in September 1992, brought a significant change of economic policy: inch by inch, we've hauled ourselves out of the recession. France, on the other hand, remains stuck in the recessionary mire. Despite concerted attacks on the currency, the French Government has persisted in clinging to a *franc-fort* policy. The strong franc, high interest rates (now lower), increased taxes, intense competition and a rise in unemployment have all combined to cause mayhem in the hotel and restaurant industry.

Bankruptcies and closures have become commonplace. We've talked to numerous chefs, hoteliers and restaurateurs: their morale has sunk to an all-time low. With few exceptions most have their chins on their chests; the in-word is "*crise*". How heartening it is to meet the exceptions – owners with a smile, a positive attitude, making plans to improve facilities and providing top-notch *rapport qualité-prix* (*RQP*).

In addition, French hoteliers and restaurateurs have to bear crippling extra costs: minimum wage laws (about £700 per month) and sky-high social security taxes are fearful burdens. The inevitable consequence is that staff numbers are pared to the bone in hotels and restaurants.

Are standards affected by all the above? Yes, they are: we found standards at their lowest level in the 40 years we've been visiting France. The tell-tale signs are everywhere: lack of cleaning – with dust, fag ends and animal smells some of the clues; threadbare towels and worn out furnishings all too common; and broken fittings in bedrooms and bathrooms. Meals, too, regularly provide the evidence that corners are being cut through lack of time, shortage of kitchen staff and a need to cut costs. Service, too, has sunk to an all-time low – though, in their defence, French hoteliers and restaurateurs complain bitterly of the difficulty of employing dedicated, professional young staff.

A sure sign of low morale is the stunning apathy we've encountered in one area of our dealings with French hoteliers and restaurateurs. As you well know, they pay nothing to be included in our guides. With both *FLE* and *Allez France!* we sent out hundreds of letters asking owners to provide us with the summary details which we include at the end of each entry. The cost of a reply is at most five francs. Yet to get owners to answer is stunningly difficult; some need three reminders and a few never respond. One can understand owners who don't know of us or our books (we give them scores of French chef references); what is an insult is to hear nothing from establishments which have been in one or more of our guides – with all the business that brings.

In *FLE* we wrote a heartfelt paragraph (p9) in which we implored chefs to provide clients with *RQP* meals. The devaluation of sterling means we all now look twice at every pound we part with in France; the French, too, also think hard about each franc they spend. *RQP* are the buzz words in France these days; even a handful of the culinary gods have opened bistros near their three-star shrines (four are in this book).

How we wish French hoteliers would apply *RQP* to wines, drinks, coffee and breakfasts. The quality, too, of some breakfasts is horrendous.

(Though top-notch *RQP* is harder to nose out on this side of the Channel we maintain that eating-out in provincial Britain is in many ways more enjoyable than the French equivalent: eclectic repertoires and a far greater variety of choice are the big pluses here. Despite our much improved culinary standards, the blinkered French, misinformed as they are in so many ways, still consider us the dustbin of Europe.)

We hear you ask: "What's the state of French cooking?" Fine – most of the time. At the lower levels, the use of freezers and microwaves is now commonplace; that doesn't worry us because if specialities are home-made why shouldn't chefs use the very aids we do at home. Buying-in finished produce is another matter: acceptable perhaps for *charcuterie* and confectionery but another thing when chefs cheat with sauces and "specialities" from bought-in, boil-in-the-bag creations.

At all levels of ability French chefs are now making extensive use of cheaper cuts of meat, offal, oxtail, cod and other less-expensive white fish. That's no bad thing. What is a sin is the gross misuse of French classical cooking terms. A time will come when the correct meanings of some terms will have been lost for ever. (One "adopted" term, seemingly now on every menu in France and used for all sorts of produce, is *carpaccio* – originally a Cipriani creation, a "reddish" raw filet of beef, named after the Venetian artist Vittore Carpaccio.)

Please delete these *FLE* entries (for varying reasons): Epinal p37; Gérardmer (Réserve) p42; Mittelwihr p43; St-Malo p70; Gimel p133; Claix p142; Varces (Matitis) p147; Huisseau p210; Montreuil p211; Onzain p212; Tours (Groison) p213; Artemare p226; Donzère p249; Bourcefranc p304; Montmorillon p307; Bidarray p363; Grenade p364.

Finally, may we commend to you once again (*FLE* p479) Carolyn Hall's peaceful Aux Deux Soeurs (Mich 158/B2) – in 25 wooded acres west of St-Rémy-de-Provence (13150 St-Etienne-du-Grès). In addition to The Lodge and The Cottage, a large apartment, The Granary, can also be rented (as will four *chambres d'hôtes* in 1996). For details ring 0483 303782 (UK).

Keep well and keep enjoying France. **Richard and Anne Binns**

AUXERRE   **Barnabet**

Very comfortable restaurant/Cooking 3
Terrace

Jean-Luc and Marie Barnabet are now well-established at their swish
new Auxerre home (once a garage); what a change from the Petite
Auberge, their previous base, upstream on the Yonne at Vaux. Jean-Luc,
always enthusiastic and looking younger than ever, is proud of his
gleaming kitchen, seen easily by all clients behind its glass wall, and his
spacious dining room and *salons*. He's a supreme example of a *faites
simple cuisinier*: tastes count most in his repertoire; there's no over-
elaboration and there's no problem finishing a meal. Two highlights on
our last visit included a *pot-au-feu de boeuf en gelée* (a three cm-deep
blockbuster burger) and a thumpingly-good, five-part dessert, all based
on a *thème sur le caramel*. Handsome English-speaking Jean Claude
Mourguiart (he worked for Raymond Blanc at Summertown) is still *in
situ*. Debits? Wines are dearish and not enough half-bottles.
Menus DE. Cards Access, AE, Visa. (Rooms: Le Maxime, 200 metres to N.)
Closed Sun evg. Mon. (Park opposite on quayside overlooking Yonne.)
Post 14 quai République, 89000 Auxerre, Yonne. Region Burgundy.
Tel 86 51 68 88. Fax 86 52 96 85. Mich 72/A2.

BADEN   **Le Gavrinis**

Comfortable hotel/Cooking 2
Terrace/Gardens/Parking

As remarkable a family enterprise as any we know in France. Alain
Justum is the chef, assisted in the kitchen by sons Olivier (*le pâtissier*)
and Frédéric (also a keen gardener). Alain's wife, Michèle, and their
daughter, Sybille, run the front of house. Sybille is a delight: fluent
English, dark good looks and an easy way of putting you at ease are just
three of her many talents. Modern and neo-classical quality *plats* are
executed with flair – and what RQP: cracking appetisers; spiky *soupe de
poissons de Roche, gratinée*; *salade de harengs*; an exemplary *saumon
rôti sur peau*; and a beautifully presented *dobostorte* dessert are typical
of the Justum skills. Other pluses: the modern hotel is kept spick and
span (the family do all the decorating); a flower-bedecked, south-facing
terrace, shaded by pines; and, a nice touch, Royal Doulton china.
Menus CDE. Rooms (19) DEF. Cards All.
Closed Dec. Jan. Mon (not evg from June to Sept).
Post Toulbroch, 56870 Baden, Morbihan. Region Brittany.
Tel 97 57 00 82. Fax 97 57 09 47. Mich 62/C2.

A 100frs & under. B 100–135. C 135–165. D 165–250. E 250–350. F 350–500. G 500+

BELCASTEL

Vieux Pont

Comfortable restaurant with rooms/Cooking 3
Quiet/Gardens

I cannot improve on the initial sentence I used in *FLE*. "A sumptuously scenic spot: a huddle of 15th-century houses, dominated by a castle high above the roof tops; a bend in the Aveyron; and a medieval *pont* spanning the 20 yard-wide river." One new man-made plus is the seven-bedroom annexe, across the arched bridge on the river's left bank. *Les patronnes* are the Fagegaltier sisters: Nicole, a self-taught *cuisinière*, was born in the village and has just turned 30; and Michèle, an attentive hostess and *sommelière*. The duo opened their beguiling restaurant in 1983 and, a decade later, they deserve their considerable success. Nicole has fashioned an assured natural and original style of modern cooking – inspired by her local hero, Michel Bras. Extensive use of oil (hazelnut, walnut and olive), light cooking reductions and champion *RQP*.
Menus BDE. Rooms (7) EF. Cards Access, Visa.
Closed Jan. Feb. Sun evg (not July/Aug). Mon (but not midday July/Aug).
Post 12390 Belcastel, Aveyron. Region Massif Central (Cévennes).
Tel 65 64 52 29. Fax 65 64 44 32. Mich 140/B1-B2.

BEUVRON-EN-AUGE

Pavé d'Auge

Very comfortable restaurant/Cooking 3

The restaurant, once the oak-beamed covered market, is at the heart of the unbelievably evocative Beuvron-en-Auge. One new man-made restaurant addition is the high and handsome stone, small red brick and oak fireplace, a typical Pays d'Auge *cheminée*. Chef/*patron* Jérôme Bansard, trained by Michel Roux, is a great supporter of quality produce, mainly local, which he prepares in eminently sensible neo-classical and modern ways. One example is an eclectic *dos de cabillaud poêlé écrasée de pomme à l'andouille de Vire* – an immensely happy and clever marriage of regional products. Susan, a gentle, self-effacing English lass, and now the mother of two boys, is a *pâtissière* second to none; she supervises the opulent desserts. (Rooms? Good news. Use the newly-opened, secluded Manoir de Sens, *sans rest*, 1 km to the east. The house and estate is a lilliputian version of the Pays d'Auge. Tel 31 79 23 05. Rooms (7) FG. Use postcode below.)
Menus cDE. Cards Access, Visa.
Closed 21 Nov to 9 Dec. Feb school hols. Mon (not Midday Apl-Nov). Tues.
Post 14430 Beuvron-en-Auge, Calvados. Region Normandy.
Tel 31 79 26 71. Fax 31 39 04 45. Mich 32/C1.

A100frs & under. B100–135. C135–165. D165–250. E250–350. F350–500. G500+

BLOIS

Rendez-vous des Pêcheurs

Comfortable restaurant/Cooking 3

There's absolutely nothing prissy or pretentious about the tiny home of good-looking, English-speaking Eric Reithler. He's a brilliant young *cuisine moderne* chef. Eric seems to do everything from soup to nuts: he takes the orders, cooks the dishes and still finds time to chat with you at the end of your meal. He's a sympathetic, engaging soul – and those traits reflect in his intimate, personal culinary style. Two dishes illustrate his culinary spectrum: whiter-than-white, fresh-as-daisies *cabillaud*, topped with a tiny teaspoon of caviar and a frothy, herby *beurre d'herbes*; and a step back in time with *pain perdu de Madelaine et sa crème glacée* – French toast with a light *crème*, vanilla ice cream and mated wih orange rind, pineapple and raisins in a refreshing way. Distinctive appetisers and "different" *petits fours*. Informal service – but slow. Welcome air-conditioning. (Rooms: swish new Mercure – 10 min walk upriver; Anne de Bretagne – 5 min walk NW.)
Menus C(menu)DE(à la carte). Cards Access, AE, Visa. (Parking OK.)
Closed Feb school hols. 1st 3 wks Aug. Sun. Mon midday. Public hols.
Post 27 r. Foix, 41000 Blois, Loir-et-Cher, Region Loire.
Tel 54 74 67 48. Fax 54 74 47 67. Mich 68/C3. (S of château, near river.)

BRINON-SUR-SAULDRE

La Solognote

Comfortable hotel/Cooking 3
Quiet/Gardens/Parking

The façade of this well-named hotel is typical of the red-brick cottages throughout La Sologne. The beamed dining rooms, part of an original series of cottages, are the traditional face of the hotel; quiet, more modern bedrooms are at the rear. But the place appeals for different "people" reasons – true of all our greatly admired favourites: Andrée Girard is a warm-hearted, smiling *patronne*; Dominique, her husband, is a gentle, unassuming classical chef. He capitalises on his *pays*, its wines, traditions and rich larder: come the autumn and you'll not find finer game dishes anywhere; the same applies to Dominique's clever use of the region's fungi – *cèpes, girolles* and *champignons sauvages*. An earthy out-of-season *plat* is a *joues de porc braisées au Menetou rouge* – a crafty way of making pork taste like wild boar.
Menus CDE. Rooms (13) EF. Cards Access, Visa.
Closed 15 Feb-15 Mar. Last wk May. 12-22 Sept. Tues evg (Oct-June). Wed.
Post 18410 Brinon-sur-Sauldre, Cher. Region Loire.
Tel 48 58 50 29. Fax 48 58 56 00. Mich 69/F3.

A100frs & under. B100–135. C135–165. D165–250. E250–350. F350–500. G500+

CHAMONIX

Albert 1er

Very comfortable hotel/Cooking 4 (see text)
Gardens/Swimming pool/Lift/Garage/Parking

Together with Le Bosquet at Pégomas this is the French hotel Anne and I love most – for a host of reasons. In the past we've told you about Marcel and Andrée Carrier, a couple we've known for almost 30 years. Today, their son Pierre and his wife, Martine, are the English-speaking hosts – a talented duo with bags of good taste. Pierre is a brilliant young *cuisinier* with a sharp eye for detail. Order menus E or F and put his highly-honed skills to the test. Last year his memorable modern creations included a *consommé de tomate glacé*; a *risotto Piémontais aux champignons des bois et farçon Savoyard au lard fumé* – an inspired marriage; and a Picasso dessert – *larme fondante de chocolate noir à la crème légère de gentiane*, so good you almost shed a tear when breaking into the "picture" and when finishing the heavenly concoction. (The cooking rating does not apply to the *pension* menu d.)
Menus dEF. Rooms (17) G. Cards All.
Closed 1-9 May. 23 Oct to 2 Dec. Rest: Wed.
Post 74400 Chamonix-Mont-Blanc, Haute-Savoie. Region Savoie.
Tel 50 53 05 09. Fax 50 55 95 48. Mich 105/F4.

CHAMONIX

Auberge du Bois Prin

Very comfortable hotel/Cooking 2-3
Secluded/Terrace/Gardens/Lift/Garage/Parking

The pluses are piled Mont Blanc high at the second of the Carrier family hotels. First, the view – surely the most pulsating from any European hotel (shared by all 11 bedrooms). Second, the seclusion of a cosseting Relais & Châteaux flower-bedecked chalet. Third, the caring, English-speaking hosts, Denis and Monique. Last, but not least, the rapidly improving neo-classical and regional cooking skills of Denis. Menu c is a *RQP* bargain. Menu E (low end), a *Savoyarde* showcase, is five *plats* based on regional produce. One, *filets de fera à la crème d'estragon*, lightly pan-fried with a tarragon *jus*, is an explosion of taste and is worthy of a star. Another enjoyable dazzler is *La S'pa* (soup) *de fraises à la rhubarbe sabayon aux bourgeons de sapin* – a clever mix of warm and cold and sweet and tart. Great dessert and cheese chariots.
Menus cEF. Rooms (11) G-G2. Cards All.
Closed 17 Apl to 4 May. 24 Oct to 1 Dec. Rest: Wed (midday).
Post aux Moussoux, 74400 Chamonix-Mt-Blanc, Haute-Savoie.
Tel 50 53 33 51. Fax 50 53 48 75. Mich 105/F4. Region Savoie.

A100frs & under. B100–135. C135–165. D165–250. E250–350. F350–500. G500+

CHATEAU-ARNOUX
L'Oustaou de la Foun

Comfortable restaurant/Cooking 2-3
Terrace/Parking

Young Gérald and Nathalie Jourdan will enjoy great success at their new home, north of the town and south of an A51 exit. (They moved here from their previous Digne base, the nondescript Le Tampinet.) What a gorgeous restaurant: an old farm with cool, spacious and light dining rooms and an evocative central courtyard cum terrace. Bricks and mortar seduce and so does Gérald's *RQP cuisine terroir* – a marvellous mix of modern cooking using the best of Provençal produce. Provençal flavours and perfumes dominate. We recall, with relish, *tête de veau au gelée à l'ancienne petite ratatouille et chèvre frais*; a succulent *gigot d'agneau en cassonade d'ail jus court "piperade"*; and an opulent *nougat glacée aux amandes fruits confits et coulis.* (Rooms: easy 13 km, 5fr toll drive up A51 to an Ibis, just past *péage*; see *FLE* pl42.)
Menus BCD. Cards Access, AE, Visa. (2 km north, west side of N85.)
Closed Wed (out of season). Regions Hautes-Alpes/Provence.
Post Rte Napoléon, 04160 Château-Arnoux, Alpes-de-Haute-Provence.
Tel 92 62 65 30 (and 31). Fax 92 62 65 32. Mich 146/B4.

CHATEAUFORT
La Belle Epoque

Comfortable restaurant/Cooking 3
Terrace

Readers of the 1980-86 *FL* guides will recall that Alain Rayé shared, with Frédy Girardet, a singular honour: the two chefs were by far the most appreciated readers' favourites. He moved from Albertville to Paris in 1986 and two years ago headed south to a new base – one I already knew (*FLE* p157); here he has yet to regain his sparkling Savoie form. Brigitte, his delightful, English-speaking wife watches over the aptly-named dining rooms and tree-shaded terrace. Alain, an innovative modern *maître*, is a small details addict: witness his desserts, the three-star *petits fours maison* and his pre-meal appetisers. Our May lunch was on the terrace with perhaps the best view from any in the Ile de France – below us the wooded Mérantaise Valley, above us an azure blue sky. (Rooms: Port Royal, at Voisins-le-Bretonneux (*FLE* p156); or the Novotel St-Quentin Golf National; both a short drive away.)
Menus DEF. Cards All.
Closed Sun evg. Mon. (Note golf addicts: many courses locally.)
Post 78117 Châteaufort, Yvelines. Region Ile de France.
Tel (1) 39 56 21 66. Fax (1) 39 56 87 96. Mich 35/E4.

A100frs & under. B100–135. C135–165. D165–250. E250–350. F350–500. G500+

CHATEAUNEUF
La Fontaine

Simple restaurant/Cooking 3
Parking

Anne and I first met Yves and Anne Jury 20 years ago at his family's hotel in nearby Chauffailles. For varying reasons, familiar to all family businesses, the couple eventually decided to find fame and fortune elsewhere. They didn't find either. Now they are back in their old familiar *pays*, happy again and content to be their own bosses. The tiny restaurant is an eccentric oddity. But there's nowt oddball about Yves cooking, a mix of neo-classical and modern. Anne, too, wears no airs or graces. Relish precisely cooked creations such as a *terrine de mousserons et chutney de fruits rouges*; a *filet de barbue* with an intense *sauce cèpes*; an earthy *mitonnée de queue de boeuf à la moelle* and *délices de la Fontaine* – a superb dessert of five harmonious concoctions. (Rooms: Relais de l'Abbaye, Charlieu, a 10 km drive SW.)
Menus bCDE. Cards Access, Visa.
Closed 22 Jan to 16 Feb. 2-12 Oct. Tues evg. Wed.
Post 71740 Châteauneuf, Saône-et-Loire. Region Lyonnais.
Tel 85 26 26 87. Mich 101/E3.

CHINON
Au Plaisir Gourmand

Very comfortable restaurant/Cooking 3-4

What a contented, unassuming, happy individual Jean-Claude Rigollet is these days: now his own master and, with his elegant wife, Danielle, the owners of an immaculate 17th-century tufa stone house, asleep beneath the high ramparts of the inspiring, infused-with-history castle. Jean-Claude is a supreme classical master (the equal of most three-star gods but serving meals we can all afford). Superlative standards and consummate saucing – especially those based on Chinon red wine. A pungent *dodine de caneton au marc de Chinon*; a spiky (coriander) *fouée au lard fumé* (a batter hat impregnated with bacon) *au champignons de Ligné* (nearby village); a sensational *géline fermière en matignon de légumes* (with truffles from nearby Richelieu); the list of joys is endless. Note the Wedgwood crockery. *Tour de force* Chinon wines including Jean-Claude's own vineyard, L'Echo. (Rooms: Diderot *sans rest* base hotel – 800 metres to the east; see *FLE* p204.)
Menus DE. Cards Access, AE, Visa. (Park on quayside.)
Closed 6-27 Feb. 13-27 Nov. Sun evg. Mon.
Post Quai Charles VII, 37500 Chinon. Indre-et-Loire. Region Loire.
Tel 47 93 20 48. Fax 47 93 05 66. Mich 81/F1.

A100frs & under. B100–135. C135–165. D165–250. E250–350. F350–500. G500+

COURLANS   Auberge de Chavannes

Very comfortable restaurant/Cooking 3-4
Terrace/Gardens/Parking

For Pierre Carpentier, who hails from Argentan in faraway Normandy, one culinary philosophy matters more than any other: taste is everything. Flavours predominate and so do his ever-improving technical skills – in both preparation and presentation work. Pierre's repertoire includes modern, classical and neo-classical *plats*: luscious *goujonnettes de sole en vinaigrette tiède aux truffes d'été*; *foie gras de canard poêlées* with the counterpoint of an intense *betteraves caramélisées*; and a *suprême de poularde de Bresse en rouelles, galette de riz au gras et morille farcie* – a complex construction of contrasting flavours. Monique Carpentier is an elegant, charming hostess, the daughter of a local *vigneron*; quiz her on Jura wines and capitalise on her magnificent *cave*. (Rooms: Parenthèse at Chille, NE of Lons-le-Saunier; secluded and easy 9 km drive.)
Menus CE. Cards Access, Visa. (Beside N78, 6 km W of Lons-le-Saunier.)
Closed Feb. 26 June to 3 July. Sun evg. Mon.
Post 39570 Courlans, Jura. Region Jura.
Tel 84 47 05 52. Mich 89/D4.

CRISSIER   Girardet

Very comfortable restaurant/Cooking 5

Frédy Girardet, as both a *cuisinier* and restaurateur, sets the standards by which all others must be judged. Every aspect of the culinary arts is demonstrated to perfection; from innovative technique and exemplary good taste to, as just one of scores of examples, the dying skills of carving at the table (a feature of both his menus). Service is professional and friendly with none of the pompous preciousness of some three-star shrines. Usually 80% of clients are Swiss, from families to young couples (spending their all) and celebrating business folk; they all get the same attention from the staff, led by one of the world's most able *maîtres d'hôtel*, English-speaking Louis Villeneuve. Expensive? Yes – the Swiss franc sees to that, in a land where everything costs 65% more. (Consider "Big Mac currency": £1.70 here; £2.80 in Switzerland.) Anne and I would happily forgo any four or five *Franc-wise France RQP* meals for one at Girardet's. (Rooms: Novotel or new Ibis, both minutes away to W.)
Menus SF165(7 courses)-185(8 courses). A la carte SF120-190. Cards None.
Closed 1st 3 wks Aug. 20 Dec to 3 Jan. Sun. Mon. Region Jura.
Post CH 1023 Crissier, Vaud, Switzerland. (NW of Lausanne; E of N1.)
Tel 21 634 05 05 or 21 634 05 06. Mich 105/D1.

A100frs & under. B100–135. C135–165. D165–250. E250–350. F350–500. G500+

DURBAN-CORBIERES

Le Moulin

Very comfortable restaurant/Cooking 3-4
Swimming pool/Parking

What a stunning show. On an elevated site, surrounded by vineyards, the restored windmill looks more like a Foreign Legion fort. The light dining room is semi-circular with eight huge oak beams and panoramic windows; four stained-glass windows are a colourful plus. All the front of house team speak English: Corinne Moreno, her assistant Tania, waitress Carole, and *sommelier* Hervé. The *cave* is exceptional, especially the reasonably priced dozens of Corbières and Minervois vintages. David Moreno, a quietly-spoken, but ball-of-fire Spaniard, is a cook with an overdose of common sense and good taste: how these traits show in his uncomplicated modern repertoire. Witness a clear-cut and simple *tarte fine de tomate et anchois* or a *ravioles de chèvre dans leur jus au safran* where several flavours tease the taste buds. (Rooms: easy drive to hotels S of Narbonne (A9 exit): Novotel, Ibis, Climat etc.)
Menus CDE. Cards Access, Visa.
Closed Mid Oct to mid Mar. Sun evg and Mon (not July/Aug).
Post 11360 Durban-Corbières, Aude. Region Languedoc-Roussillon.
Tel 68 45 81 03. Fax 68 45 83 31. Mich 172/C3.

ESPALION

Le Méjane

Comfortable restaurant/Cooking 3-4

The cooking rating gives the clue to how impressed we were at this most modest of *RQP* restaurants; we can't wait to return. The dining room is small – but the enjoyment factor is gargantuan. The pleasures start with the smiling Régine Caralp – a vivacious hostess and a member of the long-established hotel family in nearby St-Chély-d'Aubrac (see *FWF*). They continue with the myriad talents of her husband Philippe. Every dish is faultless – in technique, presentation and, better still, in the eating: modern panache in dishes like *terrine de poulet fermier au curry et jeunes poireaux* and a bravura *jambonette de pintade rôtie, jus réduit au vin rouge*. This is a young man, in his mid-30s, going places. (Rooms: the Moderne – just that and a 5 minute-walk away, on the other side of the River Lot; or the simpler Central – clean, correct, decrepit in a genteel way, a 15 second-walk away and run by two super sisters.)
Menus BCD. Cards All. (On Lot's left bank; east side of D920.)
Closed Feb school hols. 26 June to 1 July. Sun evg (not Aug). Wed.
Post r. Méjane, 12500 Espalion, Aveyron. Region MC (Auvergne/Cévennes).
Tel 65 48 22 37. Mich 140/C1.

A100frs & under. B100–135. C135–165. D165–250. E250–350. F350–500. G500+

Les EYZIES-DE-TAYAC   Cro-Magnon

Very comfortable hotel/Cooking 3
Terrace/Gardens/Swimming pool/Parking

Anne and I have loved the vine-covered "special" hotel for almost 35 years. Our first visit to Cro-Magnon was a year or two before our son, Andrew, was born. Later, we took him and his sister, Sally, when both were toddlers. The shady terrace and the gardens, over the road, always remind us of happy family days in the sun. Best of all though are the English-speaking owners, Jacques and Christiane Leyssales – genuine, caring hoteliers. Cooking is a mix of modern and easy-to-digest regional dishes. Menus C can include a *morue fraîche à l'anchoïade*, bubbling with subtle tastes of aubergine, anchovy and herbs. A more expensive menu highlight could be a *feuilleté d'oeuf poché au foie gras et aux cèpes* – an impeccable concoction. We consider ourselves very fortunate to have known for so long the evocative Cro-Magnon and its lovable owners.
Menus CDEF. Rooms (18) FG. Cards All.
Closed 10 Oct to end April. Rest: Wed midday.
Post 24620 Les Eyzies-de-Tayac, Dordogne. Region Dordogne.
Tel 53 06 97 06. Fax 53 06 95 45. Mich 123/F3.

FLEURIE   Auberge du Cep

Very comfortable restaurant/Cooking 4

For long one of our most liked favourites. Four years ago, *chef/patron* Gérard Cortembert died, still in his 40s. His widow, Chantal, aided by her daughter Hélène (both English speakers) and young chef Michel Guérin, trained by Gérard, battled on. The first setback was the loss of one of their two Michelin stars. Imagine their ecstatic excitement and intense satisfaction when they won back star two last year. The Cep is an ideal example of just where restaurateurs should draw a line in acquiring flashy fittings and buying-in soulless service to win star three. Here excellence is a way of life. Michel's repertoire is an estimable mix of classical and regional cooking (a roll-call of Bresse, Burgundy and Beaujolais brilliance). Simply reading his mouthwatering menus sets off Pavlovian bells. Ask delectable Hélène to explain the "other" arm of her family tree: a "border" surprise. But which border? (Rooms: nearby Grands Vins – *sans rest* and secluded.)
Menus DEF. Cards Access, AE, Visa.
Closed Dec. Sun evg. Mon.
Post pl. Eglise, 69820 Fleurie, Rhône. Region Lyonnais.
Tel 74 04 10 77. Fax 74 04 10 28. Mich 102/B3.

A100frs & under. B100–135. C135–165. D165–250. E250–350. F350–500. G500+

FORGES-LES-EAUX

Auberge du Beau Lieu

Comfortable restaurant with basic rooms/Cooking 3
Terrace/Parking

Marie-France Ramelet is a *petite*, attentive *patronne* and *sommelière*, proud of her splendid cellar (three cheers for the 40 half-bottles) and her well-lit, beamed dining room – brightened up no end by the numerous paintings of a talented local artist, William Gantier (Wiga). Her chef husband Patrick matches the artist's skills with his own inventive modern culinary canvasses. A succession of tastebud teasing specialities come from Patrick's kitchen, among them a *carpaccio de canard au basilic* (the chef's a *maître-canardier*), a sensuous *foie gras de canard poêlé aux pommes* (apples *confits* and sesame seeds), a drooling *sorbet fromage blanc*, *pigeon rôti sauce Rouennaise* (slices of breast and a tiny leg, stuffed with breadcrumbs and mustard, in an intense black sauce) and a tantalising choice of top-notch desserts. Debits? The bedrooms can be a touch dampish and readers complain about cold floors.
Menus CDE. Rooms (3) E. Cards All. (2 km SE, alongside D915.)
Closed 23 Jan to 8 Feb. Tues (not school hols).
Post Le Fossé, 76440 Forges-les-Eaux, Seine-Maritime.
Tel 35 90 50 36. Fax 35 90 35 98. Mich 16/C2-C3. Region Normandy.

GEVREY-CHAMBERTIN

La Rôtisserie du Chambertin

Very comfortable restaurant/Cooking 3
Parking

There are four good reasons for seeking out La Rôtisserie: the owner, cooking, dining room and *cave* – in that order. Be sure to find time to natter with Anglophile Pierre Menneveau, who has well and truly recovered a real zest for life after Céline, his talented chef wife, died in May 1985. His present-day business partner and *cuisinier* is Jean-Pierre Nicolas; the latter's repertoire includes modern, regional, classical and neo-classical creations. A gutsy *tranche de saumon frais rôti* is not overwhelmed by a Gevrey Chambertin sauce; more artful is a *filet de sandre au vin jaune*. The dining room – in old wine cellars – is a cool mix of stone, wood panelling and discreet lighting. Pierre's collection of Gevrey-Chambertin wines is a treasure-chest of liquid rubies. (Rooms: Les Grands Crus; *sans rest* and a 5 minute walk.)
Menus d(lunch)EF. Cards Access, Visa.
Closed Feb. 1st wk Aug. Sun evg. Mon (not public hols).
Post 21220 Gevrey-Chambertin, Côte-d'Or. Region Burgundy.
Tel 80 34 33 20. Fax 80 34 12 30. Mich 88/B1.

A100frs & under. B100–135. C135–165. D165–250. E250–350. F350–500. G500+

GRASSE
Maître Boscq

Very simple restaurant/Cooking 1-2

No dining room comes smaller or simpler at the tiny home of Patrick and Odile Boscq – both big-hearted *patrons*. You can hardly swing a kitten in the minuscule 300-year-old restaurant, let alone a cat. At the very most only 20 clients or so can be shoe-horned in – all of them looked after with great good humour and charm by Odile. Both she and her chef husband Patrick – now proud grandparents – have an engaging sense of humour. He is the Stormin' Norman of French cuisine and has the girth that all chefs should have. Patrick speaks good English and has a fierce loyalty for *Grassoise* recipes. Where else can you savour the likes of *lou fassum, tourteau Grassois aux herbes*, or *fricot de cacho-fuou*? Herbs, vegetables, game; everything is authentically Provençal. The restaurant is just off the Place aux Aires (Grasse's small open-air market). Park at the nearby bus station or in the underground carpark, at the Place du Cours. (Rooms: du Bosquet, Pégomas; 9 km to the S – see p216.)
Menu B. Cards Access, Visa.
Closed 1–15 Nov. Sunday. Evenings (out of season – except sch. hols).
Post 13 r. Fontette, 06130 Grasse, Alpes-Maritimes.
Tel 93 36 45 76. Mich 164/C4. Region Côte d'Azur.

Les ISSAMBRES
Chante-Mer

Simple restaurant/Cooking 2
Terrace

Mario is the oldest of the three Battaglia brothers – all of whom have have at last had their cooking talents recognised by Michelin. (Why so long Bibendum?) Some of you may remember his delightful wife, Nanette, when she was working for Jean-Pierre at Valbonne in the early 80s. The couple opened their tiny new home ten years ago: the terrace seats two dozen or so; the air-conditioned interior an equal number. Menu B offers a classical/Provençal choice for each of three courses: for example a *soupe de poissons* or a mouthwatering *petit pâté chaud* (in a pastry turnover); a *panaché de poissons* or *contrefilet sauce marchand de vin*; a freshly-made tart or a *parfait glacé*. Order *chapon farci (poisson)* and *bouillabaisse* in advance. In the evening you're likely to be served by Céline and Elise, the couple's teenage daughters.
Menus BCD. Cards Access, Visa. (Rooms: Plage at La Nartelle – 4 km SW.)
Closed 15 Dec-31 Jan. Sun evg (Sept-June). Mon (not evgs July/Aug).
Post 83380 Les Issambres, Var. Region Côte d'Azur.
Tel 94 96 93 23. Mich 163/E4. (N of N98 at Hôtel Les Calanques.)

A100frs & under. B100–135. C135–165. D165–250. E250–350. F350–500. G500+

JAVRON
La Terrasse

Very comfortable restaurant/Cooking 3

What a refreshing breath of culinary virtuosity blows through this unknown village straddling the N12. A talented young English couple are making a great impression: Alison Greenaway, *la patronne*, is as vivacious and charming as any hostess – anywhere; husband Michael, a student of the magnificent Bournemouth Catering College, is the chef. Shame on you Michelin: Michael is worthy of both a star and a *"Repas"* accolade – as awarded elsewhere. Why are you so wretchedly xenophobic? Our last meal was faultless (deserving perhaps a Cooking 3-4 rating): superb home-made *foie gras* served with a *compote de figues* – the perfect foil; an equally delicate *terrine de cèpes maison*; a *filet de barbue persillé aux fumet d'herbes fraîches* – seasoned to perfection; and a well-judged *gratin de fruits frais*. Handsome dining room and great cellar; 106 wines under 150 francs and over 40 half-bottles. One word suffices: GO! (Rooms: Ermitage at Bagnoles-de-l'Orne – an easy 19 km drive to the NW; the new owner, Mme Planche, is an energetic soul.)
Menus ACDE. Cards Access, Visa.
Closed 2-15 Jan. Sun evg. Mon.
Post 53250 Javron-les-Chapelles, Mayenne. Region Normandy.
Tel 43 03 41 91. Mich 50/B2.

KAYSERSBERG
Remparts

Comfortable hotel (no restaurant)
Quiet/Garage/Parking

The Remparts, extensively refurbished during the last few years, has modern amenities and a quiet location. So have hundreds of other hotels. But what the others don't have is one of the most talented hoteliers we've ever met – Christiane Keller, an effervescent, intelligent angel who speaks excellent English and makes both her hotel and Kaysersberg buzz. She's the energetic, tireless driving force behind both the famed Christmas market (see *Mapaholics' France* – map sheets 60/61) and the "Horizons d'Alsace" venture – a group of 11 hoteliers where clients can permutate overnight stops between any of the hotels, walking from one to another in the knowledge that their luggage is taken to the next base. The 11 are in a small semi-circle to the west of Kaysersberg (details from Christiane).
Rooms (31) EF. Cards Access, AE, Visa.
Post 68240 Kaysersberg, Haut-Rhin. Region Alsace.
Tel 89 47 12 12. Fax 89 47 37 24. Mich 61/D3.

A100frs & under. B100–135. C135–165. D165–250. E250–350. F350–500. G500+

LAPOUTROIE
du Faudé

Comfortable hotel/Cooking 2-3
Terrace/Gardens/Swimming pool (indoor)/Parking

What a happy family atmosphere envelopes this always improving Vosges hotel. Jean Marie and Mariette Baldinger still play an important part but these days the most involved family members are Thierry, the couple's capable chef son, and his bubbling, English-speaking young wife, Chantal. The dining room has been spruced up no end and whether you order one of the cheapest three menus (all a last year), or the four more expensive alternatives, you'll not be disappointed by either the quantities served or the quality. On one hand, at the inexpensive end, a silky *terrine de foie de volailles au poivre vert* – served with a dozen *hors d'oeuvre* and *crudités* (they're left at the table – a nice touch); or, on the more expensive menus, the formidable *foie gras* made by Thierry or his *la tour du Faudé* dessert – a towering, toothsome confection of chocolat, *parfait pralin*, *crème* and caramel sauce.
Menus aCD. Rooms (25) EF. Cards All.
Closed 8-23 Mar. 13 Nov to 7 Dec.
Post 68650 Lapoutroie, Haut-Rhin. Region Alsace.
Tel 89 47 50 35. Fax 89 47 24 82. Mich 60/C3.

MARLENHEIM
Le Cerf

Very comfortable restaurant with rooms/Cooking 4
Terrace/Gardens/Parking

All the major French guides shower stars, *toques* and *palmarès* on the Cerf. Deservedly so: the cooking is excellent – a mix of modern, neo-classical and reworked regional; the dining room is small and intimate – with some Spindler marquetry gems; the service is unfussy; and there's a strong family influence at every turn. Robert Husser, nearing 60 now, and his son, Michel, are the innovative chefs; their wives, Marcelle and Cathy, are caring, informed *patronnes*; and Robert's mother, Irmgard, over 80, still lends a hand. Add to this quintet the so capable *maître d'hôtel*, English-speaking Daniel Krier. The "Menu clin d'oeil au terroir d'Alsace" is a revealing study: six "with a wink" *plats* making clever use of regional produce and traditions – among them a sensual *pinot noir* sauce accompanying a *dos de sandre rôti*.
Menus EFG. Rooms (15) FG. Cards Access, AE, Visa.
Closed Tues. Wed.
Post 67520 Marlenheim, Bas-Rhin. Region Alsace.
Tel 88 87 73 73. Fax 88 87 68 08. Mich 43/D4.

A100frs & under. B100–135. C135–165. D165–250. E250–350. F350–500. G500+

MARQUISE Grand Cerf

Very simple restaurant/Cooking 3

This is our "maverick" favourite – chosen mischievously as the "joker in the pack". Marquise is a down-at-heel town; and the Grand Cerf, an historic *relais*, is in need of a face-lift – neither the exterior nor the dining room would win any prizes for looks. But don't be fooled: what counts is the fare prepared by 34-year-old, English-speaking chef Stéphane Pruvot. On our last visit he thumped us for six. Normally Anne and I hate crab: a *croustillant de crabe à la fondue de poireaux* was an unbeatable creation – worthy of any 3-star chef; a simple pan-fried *rascasse*, with a purée of courgettes and a thin potato *crêpe*, was laced with subtle hints of basil and pepper; and who would have thought a *compote de Granny Smith au coulis d'abricot* could taste so tantalisingly good.(Rooms: several *sans rest* hotels in Boulogne and Calais.)
Menus A(two *plats*)BDE. Cards Access, Visa.
Closed Sun evg. Mon.
Post 62250 Marquise, Pas-de-Calais. Region North.
Tel 21 87 55 05. Fax 21 33 61 09. Mich 2/A2.

MILLAU La Marmite du Pêcheur

Simple restaurant/Cooking 2
Terrace

I have sad news to pass on: Albert Négron died last year, aged 79 and after working 65 years in various kitchens. The good news is that his widow, the ever-smiling, always helpful Janine is carrying on at their most recent Millau restaurant – aided by 31-year-old Christian Aveline, for so long at his late master's side. The Négron repertoire continues: numerous regional and classical dishes sit side by side – among them *trénels*, *tête de veau sauce ravigote* and *confit de canard à l'ancienne*. The *pièce de résistance* is *la marmite du pêcheur* – a fish soup worthy of a fishing port. The 16 desserts are extrovert showpieces, showing off Christian's delicate touch: both the *charlotte aux trois chocolats avec crème anglaise vanille* and the *bolet du chef Albert* are worthy of a star. Ask Janine to explain the names and reasons for various *coupes* – including one tagged "Marie-Astérie". (Rooms: use Jane Rouquet's *FLE sans rest* hotel, La Capelle, a two minute-walk to the north.)
Menus ABCD. Cards Access, AE, Visa. (Park in large *place* opp. hotel.)
Closed Wed evg (not high season).
Post 14 bd Capelle, 12100 Millau, Aveyron. Region MC (Cévennes).
Tel 65 61 20 44. Mich 141/E4.

A100frs & under. B100–135. C135–165. D165–250. E250–350. F350–500. G500+

MIMIZAN   Au Bon Coin du Lac

Very comfortable restaurant with rooms/Cooking 3-4
Quiet/Terrace/Gardens/Garage/Parking

Before your meal walk the 250 metre-long *promenade fleurie* which
starts at the restaurant and runs alongside the still Etang d'Aureilhan. At
the end of the rainbow walk note, in the distance, Woolsack, the Tudor-
style house built by the Duke of Westminster in 1910 (Churchill and
Lloyd George were regular guests). Later, enjoy the idyllic, well-named
restaurant home of Jean-Pierre and Jacqueline Caule. She's a vivacious,
larger-than-life extrovert; he's a beguiling chef who capitalises on the
rich harvests of the nearby ocean. A *petite crabe farci*, *chartreuse de
homard breton* and a *sole soufflée aux langoustines* were an exuberant
trio – fresh and tantalisingly tasty. Desserts are both light and numerous.
Breakfast is one of the best in France – especially the small serving of
scrambled eggs and bacon, a sunny start to the day.
Menus cEF. Rooms (4) G. Cards Access, AE, Visa.
Closed Feb. Sun evg and Mon (not July/Aug).
Post 40200 Mimizan, Landes. (North of Mimizan-Bourg.) Region Southwest.
Tel 58 09 01 55. Fax 58 09 40 84. Mich 134/A3.

MOIDREY   Au Vent des Grèves

Comfortable restaurant/Cooking 2
Terrace/Parking

This *RQP* outpost is an oasis of culinary pleasure. The "boss" is English-
speaking Jean-Claude Pierpaoli – an effervescent professional and one of
the most likable of front-of-house hosts. Aided by a capable chef duo –
Patrice Soisnard and Christian Bourrée – Jean-Claude offers a quartet of
classical and regional menus, backed up by a craftily constructed *carte*
(the *grand plateau de fruits de mer* is a stunner). Menu C, as one *RQP*
example, could include a cracking mini version of the *grand plateau*
(tagged *grande assiette*); a juicy, perfectly-cooked *gigot d'agneau de
pré-salé* (lamb pastured on the nearby salt marshes; Jean-Claude was
taught how to cook lamb in Wales – by a wizard Welsh chef, Colin
Pressdee); three pungent *fromages Normands*; and a virtuoso apple
sorbet, laced with *calvados*. (Rooms: Le Pratel at Avranches and Moulin
de Ducey at Ducey – both *FLE sans rest* hotels.)
Menus ACDE. Cards Access, Visa.
Closed Mid Jan to mid Feb. Tues evg and Wed (not Aug).
Post 50170 Moidrey, Manche. Regions Brittany/Normandy.
Tel 33 60 01 63. Mich 30/C4. (On D976 6 km south of Le Mont-St-Michel.)

A100frs & under. B100–135. C135–165. D165–250. E250–350. F350–500. G500+

MONESTIER-DE-CLERMONT   Au Sans Souci

Simple hotel/Cooking 2
Quiet/Terrace/Gardens/Swimming pool/Tennis/Garage/Parking

Au Sans Souci does indeed have a "carefree" setting, north of Monestier and, importantly, a couple of minutes drive west from the hectic N75. *Au milieu des sapins* claims the hotel letterhead: that's spot on. But the pleasant site would go to waste without Frédéric and Michelle Maurice, the fourth generation of a family which, in 1994, celebrated 60 years at the hotel they founded in 1934. Classical and *Bourgeois* menus: B provides plenty of choice and the chance to try regional treats – among them *gigotin de lapin au vin de noix* (the renowned Dauphiny walnut version) *et ravioles du Royans* (the latter on the western flanks of the Vercors – the mountain fortress to the west of the hotel), *omble chevalier aux amandes* and a *carré du Trièves* (a cow's milk cheese from the *pays* below the hypnotic table-top Mont Aiguille to the south).
Menus ABCD. Rooms (15) DE. Cards Access, Visa.
Closed 20 Dec to end Jan. Sun evg. Mon.
Post St-Paul-lès-Monestier, 38650 Monestier-de-Clermont, Isère.
Tel 76 34 03 60. Mich 131/E3. Regions Hautes-Alpes/Savoie.

MOUGINS   Feu Follet

Comfortable restaurant/Cooking 2-3
Terrace

To make a restaurant pay in film-set Mougins is hideously difficult (the most expensive real estate on the *côte*). In this case, where overheads are high, quality is above average, and prices are not wallet-emptying, one essential requirement must be met: you have to have every table in the restaurant full – all the time. Jean-Paul and Micheline Battaglia (both speak English) have made a resounding success of their restaurant venture: they've bought the house next door; added a high-tech, million-franc kitchen; put in new loos; and have a genuine non-smoking dining room. They also remain unspoilt, likable people. One notable plus: there's no stinting with portions. Some fine wines too. Cooking is neo-classical and Provençale: *saumon au basilic*, *boeuf sauce Béarnaise* and *soupe de poissons* are typical dishes. Desserts are the highlights.
(Rooms: our favourite, du Bosquet, at Pégomas; see p216.)
Menus CD. Cards Access, Visa.
Closed Sun evg (out of season). Mon. Tues midday (mid June to mid Sept).
Post pl. Mairie, 06250 Mougins, Alpes-Maritimes. Region Côte d'Azur.
Tel 93 90 15 78. Fax 92 92 92 62. Mich 163/F2. Note: book ahead.

A100frs & under. B100–135. C135–165. D165–250. E250–350. F350–500. G500+

MOUGINS
Relais à Mougins

Very comfortable restaurant/Cooking 3
Terrace

André Surmain is the most wily and knowledgeable *cuisinier* I know.
Trained by Dumaine and once owner of the Big Apple's Lutèce, André is
a born survivor. After all sorts of personal setbacks and professional
difficulties (true of all class restaurants with high overheads in recession-
hit France), André is as bouncy and canny as ever. His new pricing
formula provides a menu/à la carte selection where *RPQ* is manifest. We
recall, with relish, a champion starter – *gelée d'ailerons de raie aux
câpres à la crème de citron*; an impeccable *selle d'agneau rôtie à la
crème d'estragon* and tingling-with-flavour Marc Streitz young
vegetables; and an ethereal *tiramisu*. Dominique Louis is an
accomplished chef; Gigi, André's daughter, is a fluent English-speaking
hostess with more than a fair share of her father's sense of humour and
gritty personality. (Rooms: du Bosquet, Pégomas; see p216.)
Menus CG. (Also bar Le Zinc: menu A.) Cards Access, AE, Visa.
Closed Mon (not evgs July/Aug). Tues midday.
Post pl. Mairie, 06250 Mougins, Alpes-Maritimes. Region Côte d'Azur.
Tel 93 90 03 47. Fax 93 75 72 83. Mich 163/F2.

MOUSTIERS-STE-MARIE
Les Santons

Comfortable restaurant/Cooking 3-4
Terrace

I concluded my *FLE* entry with these words: "Anne and I cannot return
to Les Santons soon enough." We returned earlier this year, to
encounter, once again, the magical spell spun by two culinary magicians
– English-speaking André Abert and his partner Claude Fichot. Make
the short, steep climb from the bridge to their tiny cottagey dining room,
fizzing with vitality and illuminated by some exhilarating paintings.
Classical and regional specialities sparkle with the sunny tastes of
Provence: olive bread and oil; *caviare ou flan d'aubergines* – a masterly
duo; *ratatouille*, artichokes, herbs, *truffes* and *asperges*; Sisteron lamb
or *poulet fermier au miel de lavande aux aromates et épices doux*; a 3-
star *nougat glacé aux noisettes et amandes de Valensole*; the list is
endless. (Rooms: two-minutes-by-car, *sans rest* and quiet Le Colombier.)
Menus CDF. Cards Access, DC, Visa. Note: book ahead.
Closed Dec. Jan. Mon evg (mid Sept to mid July). Tues.
Post pl. Eglise, 04360 Moustiers-Ste-Marie, Alpes-de-Haute-Provence.
Tel 92 74 66 48. Mich 162/C1. Regions Côte d'Azur/Hautes-Alpes.

A100frs & under. B100–135. C135–165. D165–250. E250–350. F350–500. G500+

MUR-DE-BRETAGNE
Auberge Grand'Maison

Very comfortable restaurant with rooms/Cooking 3-4

The "Argoat" (inland Brittany; "land of the woods") is blessed with a human treasure. No, two: Jacques and Brigitte Guillo. Both are helpful, self-effacing and courteous – and are such talented restaurateurs. Jacques, a chef who has both good taste and confidence flowing through his veins, has honed his talents to a razor-sharp edge of perfection. A *gratin de queues de langoustines aux légumes croquants* is a taste of old France; *carré d'agneau pané au pain d'épices, garnitures Bretonnes* (breaded with spices and served with Brittany's *haricots blancs*) is lip-smacking good; *pigeonneau cuisiné comme au retour de chasse* is melt-in-the mouth magic; and sweets rate a "formidable" tag. Other pluses: first-class breakfasts; and effective insulation for the bedroom windows. The *auberge* is rated by readers as one of their top favourites: we agree 100%. We pray, too, that Jacques' health improves.
Menus DEF. Rooms (12) EFG. Cards All.
Closed Feb school hols. Oct. Sun evg. Mon.
Post 22530 Mur-de-Bretagne, Côtes d'Armor. Region Brittany.
Tel 96 28 51 10. Fax 96 28 52 30. Mich 28/B4.

NARBONNE
L'Olibo

Comfortable restaurant/Cooking 3-4

Many of you will know the high regard I have for the culinary skills of Claude Giraud who, for ten years or more, never failed to impress me immensely at his Réverbère restaurant in Narbonne. Shortly after winning his second Michelin star a few years ago the restaurant went under – an early victim of the French recession. The good news is that Claude and Sabine Giraud have resurfaced again – this time following a far more sensible *rapport qualité-prix* path. The welcome dividend from their decision is that you now get the same tremendous cooking skills coupled to remarkable value-for-money prices. Two menus provide many a chance to savour original masterpieces – modern, neo-classical and reworked regional *plats*: among them a *jambonneau de poulette farci à la girolle*, simple *jus d'églacé à l'ail doux*; a sumptuous *salmigondis de pigeonneau fermier*; and an aromatic *bourride de morue fraîche*. (Rooms: La Résidence to the NE, 3 min walk, *sans rest* and quiet; see *FLE* p185.)
Menus BD. Cards Access, AE, Visa. (Parking across the road.)
Closed 1-15 Mar. 1-21 Aug. Sun. Wed evg.
Post 51 r. Parerie, 11100 Narbonne, Aude. Region Languedoc-Roussillon.
Tel 68 41 74 47. Fax 68 42 84 90. Mich 173/D2.

A100frs & under. B100–135. C135–165. D165–250. E250–350. F350–500. G500+

Le NOIRMONT

La Gare

Very comfortable restaurant with rooms/Cooking 4

If we were asked to name the four favourites we appreciate most then the Wengers' La Gare would most certainly be one of the quartet. The ever-appreciating Swiss franc ensures La Gare is a touch expensive but Anne and I would be happy to compensate for this by spending one night less in France and not begrudging the decision one iota: that's how good the Wengers are. Georges' eye for detail is prodigious and he's a culinary neuro-surgeon. He's also a consummate modern master, able to create a succession of dishes, invariably based on his amazingly rich regional larder. Every creation incorporates many differing subtle tastes – with no discordant notes. Andrea, who like her husband speaks fluent English, is an attractive, sparkling hostess; she, too, has an eye for detail – witness the dining room tables and her bedrooms, the latter the best we encountered on our 1993/94 researches. One final bonus: in the words of Paul Henderson (of Gidleigh Park), whose opinion I respect immensely, the wine list is one of the 25 best "anywhere".

Menus SF48(weekday lunch)-56-68-113-130. Rooms (3) SF130-250 (inc' super Swiss bkft). Cards Acc, AE, Visa. Closed 2nd half Jan. Rest: Sun evg. Mon.
Post CH 2725 Le Noirmont, Jura, Switzerland. Region Jura.
Tel 39 53 11 10. Fax 39 53 10 59. Mich 91/D1. (Parking outside rest.)

NOUAN-LE-FUZELIER

Le Dahu

Comfortable restaurant/Cooking 2-3
Terrace/Gardens/Parking

In the winter a log fire crackles in the oak-beamed dining room of the old *Solognote* farm. In the summer there's a pretty, English-style garden to admire, either from the terrace or through the clever glass panels between the roof's oak supports. The indoor flowers are worthy of a gold medal award. Marie-Thérèse Germain looks after the front of house with cool, friendly efficiency; her chef husband, Jean-Luc, paddles a light, modern-style culinary canoe. His succulent home-made *foie gras* is also a gold medal winner. Other enjoyable *plats* include tender veal with excellently cooked vegetables, including perfect *haricots verts*; and a colourful, flamboyant *turbot aux moules et à l'orange*. Super local cheeses. (Rooms: Charmilles, a short walk away, quiet and *sans rest*.)

Menus bCD. Cards Access, AE, Visa.
Closed 19 Feb to 19 Mar. Tues evg and Wed (not July/Aug).
Post 14 r. H. Chapron, 41600 Nouan-le-Fuzelier, Loir-et-Cher.
Tel 54 88 72 88. Mich 69/E3. Region Loire.

A100frs & under. B100–135. C135–165. D165–250. E250–350. F350–500. G500+

PAILHEROLS
Auberge des Montagnes

Simple hotel/Cooking 2
Quiet/Swimming pools (indoor and outdoor)/Parking

I first nosed out this appealing mountain hotel, 3400 ft high, in 1982 when I was researching *Hidden France.* A warm-hearted, friendly and willing family, led by André and Denise Combourieu, fusses over you at the l00-year-old farm. André's cooking, a mix of classical, *Bourgeoise* and appetite-quenching *Auvergnate*, is another rewarding benefit. Menu B, tagged Gastronomique, offers a wide choice and gives you the chance to tuck into some knockout local specialities: homely *pounti aux pruneaux, salade Cantalouse* – a sterling marriage of a *jeune* Cantal cheese and *saucisse sèché* (dried), *pavé de Salers* (renowned beef), *chou farci* and *truffade.* As a contrast some light-as-air, lip-smacking *pâtisseries* are a welcome counterpoint. Great walking, cross-country skiing, mountain bikes, gym and games room are all additional pluses.
Menus AB. Rooms (19) D. Cards Access, Visa.
Closed Mid Oct to 20 Dec.
Post 15800 Pailherols, Cantal. Region Massif Central (Auvergne).
Tel 71 47 57 01. Fax 71 49 63 83. Mich 126/C3.

PEGOMAS
du Bosquet

Simple hotel (no restaurant)
Secluded/Gardens/Swimming pool/Tennis/Parking

For 30 years Anne and I have been enchanted by the utterly adorable Bernardi family and their superlative yet simple, value-for-money hotel, which they opened in 1965. Together with the Albert 1er in Chamonix, this is our most loved French favourite. The locomotive of the family, Simone, is supposedly not so involved these days (impossible for anyone who knows this irrepressible lady); her daughter, Chantal, a look-alike of her mother, now runs the show. Her father, Jean-Pierre, after a bout of ill-health, wisely does take things a bit easier. The pluses are endless here: see the long list in the line above this paragraph. Add to that the handful of studios with kitchens; breakfasts on the patio beneath the trees – with Simone's jams made from the fruit harvested from the garden's trees; a perfect site, ideal for both the coast and the hills; nightingales; and the Bernardi family – *bien sûr.*
Rooms (18) CDE. Studios with kitchen (7) EF. Cards None.
Closed 10 Jan to 10 Feb. Region Côte d'Azur.
Post 74 ch. des Périssols, 06580 Pégomas, Alpes-Maritimes.
Tel 93 42 22 87. Mich 163/F2. (On Mouans-Sartoux road.)

A 100frs & under. B 100–135. C 135–165. D 165–250. E 250–350. F 350–500. G 500+

PEILLON
Auberge de la Madone

Comfortable hotel/Cooking 2-3
Secluded/Terrace/Gardens/Tennis/Parking

Escape Nice's ghastly suburbs, the nearby (out of sight) grotesque quarries, and hairpin up seven *lacets* to a quiet haven of contentment (marred only by the twice-striking church clock). The heavenly perched oasis is tended by a friendly family: Aimée Millo, *la mère*, and still helping in the kitchen; her son, Christian – a master chef with the flavours of Provence flowing through his veins; and his sister, Marie-Josée, a charismatic and adorable smasher (her English is an infectious tonic). (Please note you famed cookery book writers: she's Christian's sister – not his wife.) And let's not forget Roger, the perpetual-motion waiter. Savour the tastes of *la vrai Provençale* cooking: among them delights like *asperges* with herbs, an olive-oil dressing and a purée of olives; and *loup*, simply steamed, with its skin crisp and accompanied by superb vegetables. (The E band bedrooms are in Lou Pourtail, a newly-acquired annexe across the dead-end road.)
Menus b(lunch)CDE. Rooms (26) EFG. Cards Access, Visa.
Closed 19 Oct to 19 Dec. Wed.
Post 06440 Peillon, Alpes-Maritimes. Region Côte d'Azur.
Tel 93 79 91 17. Fax 93 79 99 36. Mich 164/E3.

PLAISANCE
Les Magnolias

Comfortable restaurant with rooms/Cooking 2-3
Quiet/Terrace/Gardens

I regret I took so long to check out this bewitching spot, one I first referred to eight years ago in *FLFavourites* (p112). The nearby terrain is a refreshing wooded *apéritif*; the village, topped by an *église Romane*, is a super appetiser; the old vine-covered *logis* with sturdy beams and stones, shady terrace and an exquisite jewel of a garden (you go upstairs to admire the emerald gem) is a beguiling *entrée*; and to top all that you have the welcoming charms of English-speaking Marie-France Roussel and the culinary wizardry of her husband Francis. A satisfying mix of regional and light neo-classical: how welcome the easily digested *quenelle de haddock en habit vert à l'huile d'olive* and *dos de truite et son court bouillon à l'ail rose de Lautrec* were on a hot summer's day.
Menus ABDE. Rooms (6) DE. Cards Access, AE. Visa.
Closed Mid Nov to end Mar.
Post 12550 Plaisance, Aveyron. Region Languedoc-Roussillon.
Tel 65 99 77 34. Fax 65 99 70 57. Mich 154/C1.

A100frs & under. B100–135. C135–165. D165–250. E250–350. F350–500. G500+

ROYE
La Flamiche

Very comfortable restaurant/Cooking 3

Gérard Borck and Marie-Christine Klopp (her father's name and the chef who founded the restaurant) do a sterling job at their dull-looking home opposite the Hôtel de Ville. There's nothing dull about the stylish dining room where the glorious flowers would rate as good as any in France. Service is masterminded by Gérard (Marie-Christine has bravely taken over responsibility for *la cuisine*); his young team of girls and boys are utterly professional. A fabulous *cave*: menu G gives you the chance to try a different glass of wine with each of five courses (cost of wine included); and the Alsace choice is superb. Cooking is primarily modern: a simple *barbue aux haricots cocos* are perfect mates; and a *terrine de melon et fraises au Monbazillac* is a heavenly marriage. (Rooms: Motel des Lions – at A1 junction 12; tel 22 87 20 61.)

Menus dEFG. Cards All. (Park in large *place* opposite restaurant.)
Closed 20 Dec to 9 Jan. Sun evg. Mon.
Post pl. H. de Ville, 80700 Roye, Somme. Region North.
Tel 22 87 00 56. Mich 18/B2.

ST-GUIRAUD
Mimosa

Comfortable restaurant/Cooking 3-4
Terrace

Why no Michelin star Monsieur Naegellen? This is another example of your wretched xenophobia. No couple deserve the accolade more than this lovable, talented duo. Bridget and David Pugh had already made a huge success of their previous careers – she as a Royal Ballet prima ballerina, he as a violinist with the same company's orchestra – when, on 29 February 1984, they started anew at Le Mimosa, a restaurant awash with colour and character. Bridget's culinary repertoire is the epitome of common sense and good taste and her eclectic specialities are full of natural, harmonious flavours. One example – perfection on a plate – is *rouget*, not overcooked, served with slices of courgette, lime and a coriander *pesto*. David, now a formidable wine buff, has a superb cellar. Bravo, too, for "wines by the glass" – including the Daumas Gassac and Mas Jullien classics; and don't miss the Folle Blanche *apéritif*. (Rooms: the Hauts de Mourèze, Mourèze: *sans rest* and secluded; *FLE* p185.)

Menus c(lunch)E(low-end *menu dégustation*). Cards Access, Visa.
Closed Nov-Feb. Sun evg (not July/Aug). Mon (not midday on public hols).
Post 34725 St-Guiraud, Hérault. Region Languedoc-Roussillon.
Tel 67 96 67 96. Mich 156/A2. (North of junction of N9 & N109.)

A100frs & under. B100–135. C135–165. D165–250. E250–350. F350–500. G500+

FAVOURITES

ST-HILAIRE-LE-CHATEAU

du Thaurion

Very comfortable restaurant with rooms/Cooking 3
Terrace/Gardens/Parking

Five menus welcome you at the completely refurbished home of Gérard (he was born in the building) and English-speaking Marie-Christine Fanton. (The dining room is much improved and the modernised bedrooms are a world away from the previous versions.) The two cheapest offer *RQP* treats as good as any, for the francs handed over, in France. The three top-priced menus provide Gérard with the chance to show you just why he's such a brilliant chef. A soup of local *cèpes* is delicate silk; *turbotin beurre blanc* has elegant depth of flavour; and *ravioles de homard avec girolles* is a blue-chip marvel. Snags? Only one: when the restaurant is busy service can be slow. But nothing would ever stop us from returning to this Limousin outpost of culinary excellence and how good it is to see that Michelin have at long last woken up to Gérard's talents; let's hope a star is soon added to the *"Repas"* accolade.
Menus aCDEF. Rooms (10) DEFG. Cards All.
Closed Jan to end Feb. 21-27 Dec. Wed. Thurs midday.
Post 23250 St-Hilaire-le-Château, Creuse. Region Poitou-Charentes.
Tel 55 64 50 12. Fax 55 64 90 92. Mich 111/D1.

ST-JEAN-DU-BRUEL

Midi-Papillon

Simple hotel/Cooking 2
Quiet/Gardens/Swimming pool/Parking

Fourth-generation hosts Maryse and Jean-Michel Papillon are involved, able *patrons*. The *logis* has been spruced up no end over the years; the latest plus is the small swimming pool built in the garden of the newly-acquired *maison Bourgeoise* across the road. The Cévennes is a wild flower and orchid sea; I write about this wonderland elsewhere – see *Mapaholics' France* map sheet chapter 141. Admire the Papillon orchid on the front of the menu (ask, too, to see Maryse's two albums of orchids found locally); then tuck into Jean-Michel's wide range of unfussy specialities: home-grown vegetables; home-reared poultry; home-made *charcuterie, confits, foies gras* and *tripoux*; the *faites simple* flavours of a *carré d'agneau persillé* – served with a cracking "crackling"; *champignons* and *cèpes* from the *causses*; the list is a long one.
Menus aBD. Rooms (19) ACD. Cards Access, Visa.
Closed 11 Nov to 24 Mar.
Post 12230 St-Jean-du-Bruel, Aveyron. Region Massif Central (Cévennes).
Tel 65 62 26 04. Fax 65 62 12 97. Mich 141/F4.

A100frs & under. B100–135. C135–165. D165–250. E250–350. F350–500. G500+

ST-MARTIN-DU-VAR
Jean-François Issautier

Very comfortable restaurant/Cooking 4-5
Parking

Jean-François and Nicole Issautier deserted their remote mountain hotel 20 years ago (at St-Etienne-de-Tinée) and headed south to the Auberge de la Belle Route (the previous name). Since we first tested their talents at St-Etienne we've gown to admire the couple immensely; now we would perhaps rate their flower-filled home our favourite Michelin two-star restaurant. The recession has hit them hard: we pray they survive. Enjoy J-F's classical skills and admire the way he puts local disparate produce to such triumphant effect. Relish "real" French cooking: *terrine de canard comme à la ferme* is authentic brilliance; *agnolotti* (*ravioles*) *aux herbes dans un bouillon de sauge* is sunny Provence on a plate; superb sweets; the roll-call of classics is never-ending. Menu D (lunch) is a *RQP tour de force*. Try the super Villars wines (to the north, round the River Var bend). (Rooms: Servotel, one km to the south.)
Menus D(lunch)EF. Cards All. (On E side of N202, 19 km N of A8.)
Closed Mid Feb to mid Mar. 1st wk Nov. Sun evg. Mon.
Post 06670 St-Martin-du-Var, Alpes-Maritimes. Region Côte d'Azur.
Tel 93 08 10 65. Fax 93 29 19 73. Mich 165/D3.

ST-MEDARD
Le Gindreau

Very comfortable restaurant/Cooking 3-4
Terrace

The contemplative views south over the well-named Vert Valley remain the same – as does the evocative, tree-shaded terrace. But how the old school house has changed over the years. Alexis and Martine Pélissou have done a remarkable job with the décor; at the prices they charge clients get astounding *RQP*. Alexis' cooking, based mainly on local produce, oozes quality. Punchy appetisers; a *crème de fèves, sans peau*; succulent *foie gras de canard poêlée*, served with a counterpoint of earthy lentils; and a fresh and crisp *tronçon de turbot grillée, beurre blanc* remain vivid memories from our last visit. The fine wine list has over 50 half bottles; the *sommelier* is first class; the flowers are gorgeous; and, best of all, *les patrons* are a sheer delight. (Rooms: France & Campanile, Cahors – to the SE; La Source Bleu, Touzac – to the west.)
Menus CDE. Cards Access, AE, Visa.
Closed 13 Nov to 7 Dec. Sun evg (out of season). Mon (not public hols).
Post 46150 St-Médard, Lot. Region Dordogne.
Tel 65 36 22 27. Fax 65 36 24 54. Mich 138/B1.

A100frs & under. B100–135. C135–165. D165–250. E250–350. F350–500. G500+

STES-MARIES-DE-LA-MER

Pont de Gau

Comfortable restaurant with rooms/Cooking 2-3
Terrace/Parking

I'll give you five reasons why this *Logis de France* is a favourite. For a start it is well away from tourist-infested Stes-Maries. A second is that the Pont de Gau is next door to the Information Centre for the Parc Ornithologique – a birdwatchers' paradise. A third is the warm welcome from Monique Audry and a fourth is the all-too-evident eye she has for good taste in furnishings and flowers (bearing in mind the *RQP* charges). The fifth and best reason is the vivid *Camarguaise* and classical cooking from chef Jean Audry: enjoy a variety of tastes and textures – like a beefy *marinade de toros à la provençale avec riz de Camargue*, a spiky *petite bouillabaisse* or an intense *râble de lièvre en civet*.
Menus ABD. Rooms (9) D. Cards Access, AE, Visa. (D570 – 5 km to north.)
Closed 3 Jan to 19 Feb. Wed (mid Oct to Easter – but not school hols).
Post 13460 Stes-Maries-de-la-Mer, Bouches-du-Rhône. Region Provence.
Tel 90 97 81 53. Fax 90 97 98 54. Mich 157/E3-E4.

SARPOIL

La Bergerie

Comfortable restaurant/Cooking 3
Parking

Chef Laurent Jury, like Englishman John Burton-Race, has evolved a highly-individualistic personal style where lots of work goes into the preparation, assembly and presentation of almost all his creations. Dishes combine contrasting tastes in anything but bland marriages: a colourful rainbow of lentils, trout and smoked salmon; *rouelles de lapereau désossé, pâtes fraîches et morilles farcies*; a gutsy *pansettes* (faggots) of lamb stuffed with wild thyme and herbs; and 12 glorious Auvergne cheeses (served with all menus) are typical delights. Isabelle Jury is a *petite*, friendly soul who becomes more and more talkative as the evening matures. (Rooms: the exquisite small Château de Pasredon, 63500 St-Rémy-de-Chargnat – 2 km NW, beside D999. Henriette Marchand is a charming, informed hostess. The secluded château nestles contentedly in a large park; views; super bedrooms and *salons*; two friendly dogs – an Airedale and terrier; and prices at the bottom end of F (including breakfasts). Tel 73 71 00 67. *Chambres d'hôtes par excellence.*)
Menus BCDE. Cards All. (La Bergerie is 10 km south-east of Issoire.)
Closed Jan. Sun evg. Mon.
Post Sarpoil, 63490 St-Jean-en-Val, Puy-de-Dôme. Region MC (Auvergne).
Tel 73 71 02 54. Mich 113/E3.

A100frs & under. B100–135. C135–165. D165–250. E250–350. F350–500. G500+

SERRIERES

Schaeffer

Comfortable restaurant with rooms/Cooking 3
Terrace/Garage

I have included the Schaeffer as a personal favourite because the modern present-day *logis* is a classic example of what a dedicated, hard-working young couple can achieve, bit by bit, year by year. The long-established family hotel, on a busy site, has been improved hugely since my first visit nearly 10 years ago. But chef Bernard Mathe more than matches the site's shortcomings. Colour plays a striking part in his repertoire; he gives this element of his *métier* much thought – witness his appetisers and sumptuous desserts. One memorable dish is a *suprème de volaille fermière, jus au vinaigre, palaisson de pomme Ardèchois*; and, under no account, miss the *St-Marcellin* cheese come *fromages* time. In the autumn his *carte de chasseur* (a variety of game dishes) is a bravura collection of vivid, emphatic tastes. Quiz Bernard and his wife, Joëlle, about the site's past history; and don't miss the old photographs.
Menus bDE. Rooms (12) DE. Cards Access, Visa.
Closed 1-15 Jan. Mon evg and Tues (not July/Aug).
Post 07340 Serrières, Ardèche. Region Massif Central (Ardèche).
Tel 75 34 00 07. Fax 75 34 08 79. Mich 130/A1.

TALLOIRES

Les Prés du Lac

Very comfortable hotel (no restaurant)
Secluded/Gardens/Lake swimming/Parking

What a magical marriage of seductive charms. First, the setting is as captivating as any in France: the hotel is 100 metres from Lac d'Annecy – with nothing but a *prés* (meadow) separating you from the picturesque waters of the lake; and the views, in all directions, are rejuvenating tonics. Second, the light, airy rooms are furnished and decorated with style and flair – attractive tributes to *la patronne* (her breakfasts, too, don't come better). Third, and best of all, is the fluent English-speaking owner, Marie-Paule Conan (a clue to a distant relation is in her name!) – a lovely, bubbly lady, not unlike the late Joyce Grenfell (whom we adored). Some rooms have terraces leading onto the *prés*; others have balconies. "People come as clients – and return as friends." That sums up Marie-Paule and her jewel of a hotel to a tee.
Rooms (16) G-G2. Cards All.
Closed Nov to mid Feb.
Post 74290 Talloires, Haute-Savoie. Region Savoie.
Tel 50 60 76 11. Fax 50 60 73 42. Mich 118/B1.

A100frs & under. B100–135. C135–165. D165–250. E250–350. F350–500. G500+

TETEGHEM   La Meunerie

Very comfortable restaurant with rooms/Cooking 3-4
Quiet/Gardens/Garage/Parking

Some readers will know that Jean-Pierre Delbé, approaching the summit
of his culinary powers, died in August 1992, aged 42. Marie-France, his
widow, has battled on through the recession – as courteous and
welcoming as ever. At her side is the couple's English-speaking, pretty
young daughter, Laurence: she's a friendly girl and has a sharp eye for
detail. The dining room, divided cleverly into four segments, is as
invigorating as ever – as are the glorious flowers. The bedrooms,
designed by Jean-Pierre, are magnificent and represent fantastic value for
money. Chef Alain Gellé, who worked with Jean-Pierre for 12 years,
does a terrific job. Neo-classical specialities with a wide spectrum of
choice: from *raie* in a mustard sauce with a mound of small-grained rice
laced with herbs; to *noisettes de chevreuil* – tender as the night; and 18
desserts where Alain's execution and conviction is exemplary.
Menus EF. Rooms (8) FG. Cards Access, DC, Visa.
Closed 23 Dec to 12 Jan. Rest: Sun evg and Mon. Region North.
Post 59229 Tétéghem, Nord. (S of village, at junction of D2 and D4.)
Tel 28 26 14 30. Fax 28 26 17 32. Mich 3/D1.

TORNAC   Demeures du Ranquet

Very comfortable hotel/Cooking 2-3
Quiet/Terrace/Gardens/Swimming pool/Parking

Georges Renault (who publishes a Languedoc-Roussillon restaurant
guide) led me to this heavenly *Cévenole* farmhouse, beside the D982 and
south of Tornac – itself south of Anduze. Some farmhouse! *Ranquet*
means "rocky hill": maybe, but the holm oaks enveloping the site hide
the large bedrooms which are on the hillside overlooking the pool. The
dining room and reception area are light and airy with modern paintings
and classical music playing in the background. The welcome is delicious.
Anne Majourel, a self-taught *cuisinière*, leads an all-lady kitchen team.
Their offerings are not faultless but you leave with vivid memories of rich
southern flavours – among them an exotic *filet de canette de Barbarie,
peau croustillante laquée au miel et Banyuls* and a spiky *dos de
daurade aux citrons confits, pommes boulangères*.
Menus CDE. Rooms (10) G. Disabled. Cards Access, Visa.
Closed Jan to Mar. Tues evg and Wed (mid Sept to mid June).
Post Tornac, 30140 Anduze, Gard. Regions Languedoc-Roussillon/Provence.
Tel 66 77 51 63. Fax 66 77 55 62. Mich 143/D4.

A100frs & under. B100–135. C135–165. D165–250. E250–350. F350–500. G500+

TOURTOUR
Les Chênes Verts

Comfortable restaurant with rooms/Cooking 4
Quiet/Gardens/Parking

What a joy to witness such consistent improvements over the last decade; in both the isolated restaurant, surrounded by woods, and in the cooking skills of Paul Bajade. He's a superb modern *cuisinier*: confidence, experience and good taste influence every aspect of his repertoire. You see and meet Paul; he takes the orders and follows up later. He's a quiet, thoughtful personality with an infectious sense of humour. Our last meal at Tourtour was truly memorable and one dish we rated among the finest creations we have ever eaten: a *risotto aux petites cèpes "bouchons" et rapée du truffes de pays* – a supreme masterpiece. Another dish, a *pieds d'agneau en surprise et mikado de légumes au jus de truffes*, was also a bravura knockout. (Cheaper rooms: the nearby Mas de Collines or the Petite Auberge – both secluded and with pools.)

Menus d(lunch)FG. Rooms (apartments) G-G2. Cards None.
Closed Jan to mid Feb. Tues evg. Wed.
Post rte Villecroze, 83690 Tourtour, Var. Region Côte d'Azur.
Tel 94 70 55 06. Fax 94 70 59 35. Mich 162/C3. (D51, 2 km west.)

TREBEURDEN
Ti al-Lannec

Very comfortable hotel/Cooking 3
Secluded/Gardens/Lift/Parking

Why should I try to re-invent the wheel? The words I used in *FLE* sum up exactly what Anne and I feel about Ti al-Lannec: "a little piece of heaven on earth." Nature has been kind: a secluded, wooded site; extensive sea views; and a beach 50 metres below you and a five minute-walk away. But the gilt-edged dividend which you'll appreciate most is the couple who are the heart and soul of the hotel: English-speaking Danielle and Gérard Jouanny – both masterful hoteliers. Dominique Lanos, their chef for eight years, brings a modern, light and appetising touch to the kitchen: Anne rated her meal as one of the best she had in France during 1993/94. Certainly the cooking is up to Michelin one-star standard. Helpful English-speaking staff and a fabulous health centre where the sauna, solarium, jacuzzi and gym facilities are provided free of charge for clients. To all that add lounges and a billiards room.

Menus b(lunch)DF. Rooms (29) FG. Disabled. Cards All.
Closed Mid Nov to mid Mar.
Post 22560 Trébeurden, Côtes d'Armor. Region Brittany.
Tel 96 23 57 26. Fax 96 23 62 14. Mich 27/F1.

A100frs & under. B100–135. C135–165. D165–250. E250–350. F350–500. G500+

VALBONNE
Auberge Fleurie

Comfortable restaurant/Cooking 2-3
Terrace/Parking

This is the restaurant, more than any other, which Anne and I wish we had on our doorstep back home. Why? Here is the *RQP* gold medal winner – a blazing beacon of just what the term means. Quality is often up to Michelin one-star standard; but low prices provide the *raison d'être* for seeking out this *RQP* shrine. For us the special thrill is to have watched Jean-Pierre Battaglia succeed over the 18 years we've known him (Bibendum took far too long to recognise his talents). His classical cooking is faultless: whether the dishes are *escalope de saumon en salade*, a *feuilleté chaud de lapin* or a *filet de rascasse au vin rouge*. Occasionally something new surfaces: a world-beating terrine of fresh goat's milk cheese with slices of artichoke heart in the interior, served with tomatoes and artichoke hearts in olive oil. Top marks, too, to Colette who runs the busy show so efficiently. Finally, what a joy it was to see Stéphanie, Jean-Pierre's eldest daughter and now 17, working with Dad in his kitchen. (Rooms: du Bosquet, Pégomas; see p216.)
Menus BCD. Cards Access, Visa. (On D3, south of village.)
Closed Mid Dec to end Jan. Wed.
Post 06560 Valbonne, Alpes-Maritimes. Region Côte d'Azur.
Tel 93 12 02 80. Fax 93 12 22 27. Mich 163/F2.

VALS-LES-BAINS
Europe

Comfortable hotel (no restaurant)
Lift

The opening lines for the Europe in *FLE* capture succinctly the reasons why the hotel is a favourite: "Guide book shorthand is all very well but abbreviations and symbols can't sum up the soul of a place; they tell you nowt 'bout folk who make the very air hum." The sad news here is that Albert Mazet (50 years a chef) has *quitté ses fourneaux*. His retirement should not deter you from continuing to share the happy tonic of the sainted duo – Albert and Renée; delightful, amiable folk, full of character and, like their hotel, the very essence of *la vrai France* as she used to be. Buffet breakfast with a chance to tuck into Albert's home-made jams. (See *FWF* for nearby Vals-les-Bains *RQP* restaurants.)
Rooms (32) DEF. Cards All. (Parking across the road.)
Closed Oct to Apl.
Post 86 r. J. Jaurès, 07600 Vals-les-Bains, Ardèche.
Tel 75 37 43 94. Fax 75 94 66 62. Mich 129/E4. Region MC (Ardèche).

A100frs & under. B100–135. C135–165. D165–250. E250–350. F350–500. G500+

VIALAS

Chantoiseau

Very comfortable restaurant with rooms/Cooking 3-4
Quiet/Swimming pool

For years we've been told to seek out this out-of-the-way corner of Lozère. We eventually did – and we fell in love instantly with the wooded terrain, the south-facing setting of the 17th-century *relais* and, above all, the remarkable Patrick and Christiane Pagès. Patrick is invigoratingly intelligent, a poet, consummate wine expert (over 1,000 different wines in his cellar – perhaps France's best; ask him to show you his Aladdin's *cave*) and, most importantly, a creative *cuisinier par excellence*. His style is modern "involved": time-consuming preparation and *plats* with many contrasting tastes. He uses little cream and butter; but be sure to savour one superlative dairy product – a *fromage fermier de brebis*, treated with *vin jaune* and made in the Lozère by Gilbert Négron. Chuckle over the chef's *lexique*. Admire, too, Christiane's supremely well thought-out bedrooms; everything you need is at hand.
Menus bEFG. Rooms (15) F. Cards All.
Closed 11 Nov to 6 Apl. Tues evg. Wed.
Post 48220 Vialas, Lozère. Regions Massif Central (Cévennes)/Provence.
Tel 66 41 00 02. Fax 66 41 04 34. Mich 142/C2.

VIVONNE

La Treille

Very simple restaurant with very basic rooms/Cooking 2

La Treille is the last of our favourites and has by far the simplest facilities of the 60 entries – but arguably there are no happier *patrons* anywhere else in this guide. Geneviève Monteil is the most helpful, cheerful hostess in all France; and her husband Jacquelin does as much as anybody I know to protect and promote the specialities of his *pays* – Poitou-Charentes. Here you'll have to refer often to the regional lists at the back of the guide: *farci Poitevin, mouclade Vendéenne, embeurrée de choux, mojettes* and *bouilliture d'anguilles* are just some of the treats. Of its type there's no better *RQP* in France – Jacquelin is a classical and *cuisine terroir* champ. La Treille is away from the N10 and faces the wooded Parc du Vounant (seek out the River Vonne weir; *FLF* p169). (If you want better rooms with *en suite* facilities head 14 km north on the N10 to the Mondial at Croutelle – *sans rest* and quiet.)
Menus ACD. Rooms (4) ABC. Cards Access, AE, Visa. (Parking easy.)
Closed Feb school hols. Wed (not midday in high season).
Post av. Bordeaux, 86370 Vivonne, Vienne. Region Poitou-Charentes.
Tel 49 43 41 13. Mich 95/D2.

A100frs & under. B100–135. C135–165. D165–250. E250–350. F350–500. G500+

FRANC-WISE FRANCE

Abbreviations

Few abbreviations are used in *Franc-wise France* (*FWF*). Each entry has an introductory summary of the main facilities provided and a concluding section where essential information is shown as follows:

Menus   range of cost of fixed-price menus (*prix-fixe*) or, if not available, the minimum cost of three courses from the à la carte menu; see price bands listed below

Rooms   number of bedrooms (in brackets) and price band range (for the bedroom). The word "Disabled" indicates that some bedrooms are accessible to guests in wheelchairs

Cards   accepted: Access (also MasterCard and Eurocard); AE American Express; DC Diners Club; Visa. Always check ahead

Closed   annual holidays (if any) and days of the week closed. Always check ahead, as changes are often made. If no details provided then the establishment is open all the year

Post   post code, village or town name, *département*

Region   for details of both regional cuisine and regional specialities see the region(s) indicated at the back of *Franc-wise France*

Tel   telephone number

Fax   fax number, where available

Mich   page number and grid square on which the entry is located in the spiral-bound *Michelin Motoring Atlas France*

Map   map number (1 to 6 – these follow the four introductory pages) on which the entry is located

Prices

(Bands D to G: see notes below)

A	under 100 Francs	D	165 to 250 Francs
B	100 to 135 Francs	E	250 to 350 Francs
C	135 to 165 Francs	F	350 to 500 Francs
		G	over 500 Francs

(a) (b) etc: menus not available at weekends or on public holidays.
G2: multiply G by figure indicated. Price bands include service and taxes but not wines and breakfasts. Agree *pension* terms in advance.

All recommendations in *FWF* offer one or more menus in price bands A, B or C. At least one qualifying menu should also be available at weekends and on public holidays. More expensive menus (price bands D to G) may also be available. Bedroom prices will probably be outside the price bands A, B and C.

227

Introduction

Franc-wise France has one objective: to identify quality cooking for the fewest francs possible. ("Fine fare for few francs" would make an apt alternative title.) The French have the ideal label to summarise exactly what I mean: *rapport qualité-prix (RQP)*. *Rapport*, a precise word, emphasises the all-important balance between quality and price.

"Good-value", "value-for-money" and "bargain-price" cooking are inadequate English labels. Not one of them stresses the importance of "quality". There has never been any difficulty nosing out low-cost menus in France. The only snag is you eat many a disappointing meal along the way; cheap menus save francs but often quality is non-existent.

To qualify for inclusion in *Franc-wise France (FWF)* all recommended hotels and restaurants must offer clients quality cooking in **one or more menus** within three price bands: **A** (under 100 francs); **B** (between 100 and 135 francs); and **C** (between 135 and 165 francs). At current exchange rates that means a range covering from about £10 ($15) to a ceiling of £20 ($30). One onerous additional condition of entry is that at least one qualifying menu must be available at all times – including weekends and public holidays. Many prospective candidates fail on this count. (All French menu prices include both service and taxes.)

Michelin multi-starred chefs fail to meet my price criteria. However, many one-star chefs do offer a *RQP* menu – and several are included. Starred restaurants have had a tough time in recent years but those lower down the ambition scale, guided by the lifesaving *RQP* culinary lighthouse, have had fewer problems and continue to flourish.

Your hard-earned cash is better spent when you seek out the hotels and restaurants in this guide. Any rough edges here and there matter not one iota. You are not paying for a theatrical extravaganza; what counts is the food on the plate. Owners are *in situ* and the enjoyment factor is high. As a bonus, value-for-money prices stretch your francs further.

Three caveats. First, like all my guides, *FWF* is for the independent motorist. **I deliberately do not direct you into the centres of cities and the largest towns** – where noise, traffic, thefts from cars, parking and navigation are all nightmares. Visit them during the day to admire their architectural glories but, come the evening, look elsewhere for a meal and a place to lay your head. (I've provided an overnight hotel recommendation for every restaurant *sans chambres*.) Second, when I use the word **basic** to describe bedrooms, that's exactly what I mean. Third, standards at Michelin *"Repas"* (*"R"*) restaurants vary wildly; many have been excluded from *FWF*.

Of the 351 recommendations in *Franc-wise France* approximately one-third have been "inspected" by 22 of my readers – all of whom have long understood what I mean by *rapport qualité-prix*. My very special thanks go to Mike Millbourn who checked out 30 of the entries.

For campers and caravanners I recommend *The Alan Rogers' Good Camps Guide France*. Another indispensable travelling companion is Alastair Sawday's *Guide to French Bed & Breakfast*.

Let me tell you how I categorise cooking standards – a system which has taken years to evolve and which I first used in *French Leave Encore* (*FLE*). I use five ratings – but with four important variations which allow me to solve the problem where, from day to day or even from course to course, standards can vary up or down. I know of no better system.

Cooking 1 Simple, straightforward cooking which, more often than not, will consist of *cuisine Bourgeoise* specialities. Many readers could do as well, or better, at home. This rating is not considered adequate enough to gain an entry in *Franc-wise France* (*FWF*).

Cooking 2 Good, competent cooking – Gault-Millau one *toque* and most Michelin *"Repas"* (*"R"*) restaurants. When standards vary, up or down, I use **Cooking 2-3** or **Cooking 1-2** as a rating.

Cooking 3 Very good level of cooking. Some faults but close or equal to a Michelin one-star restaurant standard. If standards are sometimes higher I use **Cooking 3-4** as a rating (awarded to several *FWF* chefs).

Cooking 4 Excellent cooking, often innovative and ambitious and rarely flawed. (No chef in *FWF* wins either this or a **Cooking 4-5** rating.)

Cooking 5 Superb, flawless cooking. (No *FWF* chef wins this rating.)

Most entries in *FWF* have a **Cooking 2** or **2-3** rating. The place names of 39 recommendations with a **Cooking 3** or **3-4** rating are highlighted on the maps which follow in this way: **Belcastel***)

Finally, some comments on culinary terms. I have included the Glossary of Menu Terms and all the Regional Cuisine/Specialities notes and lists from *FLE* (see the last section of *FWF*). I would also like to provide you with thumbnail-sized descriptions of the different French cooking styles - key terms which I refer to constantly in the guide.

La cuisine Bourgeoise. Simple, family, home cooking using good produce and invariably done well. The repertoire often seems to revolve around 20 to 30 dishes – wherever you are in France: *terrine, escalope, jambon, côte de veau, côte d'agneau, entrecôte, gigot, poulet* and so on.
La cuisine Régionale. Self-explanatory. Alas, authentic regional cooking continues to wither away at an alarming rate. (*Cuisine terroir*: cooking of the local area, including both produce and ancient recipes.)
La haute cuisine (classical cooking). A repertoire of hundreds of rich sauces and garnishes combined with carved-in-stone recipes, techniques and preparation, developed over the last 200 years, make this style of cooking France's greatest contribution to the culinary arts. Many chefs have worked hard to bring a lighter touch to classical cuisine – described in this guide as neo-classical cooking.
La cuisine moderne. Dishes prepared to preserve natural flavours and with the simplest of sauces. Simplicity, and the quality and purity of produce, are essential keys. Improvisation, too, plays a vital part.

229

Specimen Letters of Reservation

To reserve bedrooms; options on right (in brackets)

1 Would you please reserve a room	(2 rooms, etc.,)
2 with a double bed	(with 2 single beds)
	(one room with) (each room with)
3 and bathroom/WC	(and shower/WC)
4 for one night	(2 nights, etc.,)
5 *(indicate day, date, month)*	
6	(We would like *pension* (half-*pension*) terms for our stay)
7 Please confirm the reservation as soon as possible and please indicate the cost of the rooms	(your *pension* terms for each person)
8 An International Reply Coupon is enclosed	
9 Yours faithfully	
1 Pouvez-vous, s'il vous plaît, me réserver une chambre	**(2 chambres, etc.,)**
2 avec un grand lit	**(avec les lits jumeaux)**
	(une chambre avec)
	(chaque chambre avec)
3 avec salle de bains/WC	**(et douche/WC)**
4 pour une nuit	**(2 nuits, etc.,)**
5 le *(indicate day, date, month)*	
6	**(Nous voudrions pension complète (demi-pension) pour notre séjour)**
7 Veuillez confirmer la réservation dès que possible, et indiquer le tarif des chambres	**(le tarif de pension par personne)**
8 Ci-joint un coupon-réponse international	
9 Je vous prie, Monsieur, d'accepter l'expression de mes salutations distinguées	

If appropriate: Can I have a room/table overlooking the water
Puis-je avoir une chambre/une table qui donne sur l'eau

To reserve tables; options (in brackets)

Would you please reserve a table for ＿＿ persons for lunch (dinner) on *(indicate day, date, month)*. We will arrive at the restaurant at ＿＿ hours *(use 24-hour clock)*. (We would like a table on the terrace.) Please confirm the reservation. An International Reply Coupon is enclosed. Yours faithfully

Pouvez-vous me réserver une table pour ＿＿ personnes pour déjeuner (dîner) le *(indicate day, date, month)*. Nous arriverons au restaurant à ＿＿ heures *(use 24-hour clock)*. (Nous aimerons une table sur la terrasse.) Veuillez confirmer la réservation. Ci-joint etc., (see 8 above). Je vous prie, etc., (see 9 above)

I

Cooking 3 or 3-4: **Roscoff***

0   40   80 Kilometres
0   25   50 Miles

I

1 | 2 | 3
Rennes | PARIS • Tours | Strasbourg
4 | 5 | 6
Bordeaux | Clermont-Fd • Toulouse | Lyon • Marseille

CHERBOURG

Barfleur
St-Vaast-le-Hougue

N13

• **Marigny**
Villers-Bocage •

Ploumanac'h
Roscoff* •
• **Cléder**
Perros-Guirec

St-Pierre-Langers

Flers •

Le Conquet
St-Thégonnec
Guingamp
St-Cast-le-Guildo
St-Malo
St-Méloir-des-Ondes*
Ducey
Moidrey
BREST
Le Faou
Dinan •
Dol-de-Bretagne

N165
N12
N175

Mayenne

• **Carhaix-Plouguer**

• **Roudouallec**
La Prénessaye
Noyal-s-Vilaine
Ty Sanquer
• **Vitré**
Chateaubourg
A81

Concarneau
Bignan
RENNES
N24
Raguenès-Plage

N137

Arradon
Baden
Vannes
Carnac
La Trinité-s-Mer
Sarzeau

N165

A11

Loire

NANTES

• **Les Moutiers-en-Retz**

N137

231

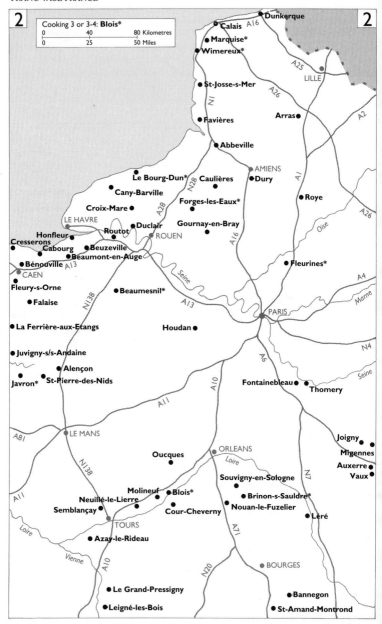

2

Cooking 3 or 3-4: **Blois***

| 0 | 40 | 80 Kilometres |
| 0 | 25 | 50 Miles |

2

Dunkerque
Calais • A16
• Marquise*
• Wimereux*

LILLE

• St-Josse-s-Mer

A26

Arras•

A2

• Favières

• Abbeville

AMIENS

Le Bourg-Dun* • • Caulières
• Dury
Cany-Barville •

• Roye

A26

Croix-Mare • • Forges-les-Eaux*

Gournay-en-Bray

Oise

LE HAVRE

Routot • • Duclair
Honfleur • ROUEN
Cresserons • Beuzeville
Cabourg • • Beaumont-en-Auge
• Bénouville A13

• Fleurines*

A4

CAEN

Fleury-s-Orne

Seine

Marne

• Beaumesnil*

A13

PARIS

• Falaise

• La Ferrière-aux-Étangs

Houdan •

N4

• Juvigny-s/s-Andaine

A6

Seine

• Alençon
Javron* • St-Pierre-des-Nids

Fontainebleau • • Thomery

A10

A11

A81

LE MANS

N138

Joigny • •
Migennes

ORLEANS

Auxerre
Vaux •

• Oucques

Loire

N7

Souvigny-en-Sologne •

A11

Molineuf • • Blois*
Neuillé-le-Lierre • • Brinon-s-Sauldre*
Semblançay • Cour-Cheverny Nouan-le-Fuzelier

Loire

TOURS

• Léré

• Azay-le-Rideau

Vienne

A10

N20

BOURGES

• Le Grand-Pressigny

• Bannegon

• Leigné-les-Bois

• St-Amand-Montrond

3 3

Cooking 3 or 3-4: **Stainville***

0	40	80 Kilometres
0	25	50 Miles

Oise

A26

•Bièvres

•Neufchâtel-s-Aisne

A4

○REIMS

A4

•Ste-Menehould

○METZ St-Avold

•Niedersteinbach

Marne

•Pont-à-Mousson

A31

A4

•Stainville* N4 ○NANCY

•Wangenbourg

STRASBOURG

🏭 •St-Dizier

A31

N57

•Ottrott-le-Haut

A26

•Chaumousey

•Baldenheim*

•Thannenkirch
•Lapoutroie
Les Trois-Epis

A35

🏭 •Bar-s-Aube

○TROYES

A5

•Colombey-les-2-Eglises

•Gérardmer •Artzenheim
•Rouffach*

Seine

•Langres

N19

•Froideterre

N66

A35

•Beine

•Combeaufontaine

BALE

Saône

A31

•Avallon

A6

A36

•St-Père-s/s-Vézelay •Velars-s-Ouche •Goumois

A38

•Gevrey-Chambertin DIJON

A31

•Echigey

•Flagey-Echezeaux

•Mouchard

•Autun •Beaune •Chaussin •Mouthier-Hte-Pierre

•Etang-s-Arroux •Meursault

A6

•Poligny

•Torcy •St-Martin-en-Bresse N5

Loire •Courlans* •Passenans
•Lons-le-Saunier

233

4 4

Fontenay-le-Comte
Luçon
Coulonges-s-l'Autize
N148
Marans
Coulon
La Flotte
N11
La Rochelle
Bouhet
A10
Rochefort
●Cognac
N10
Margaux ●
N89
BORDEAUX
Dordogne
Garonne
A62
N10
Villeneuve-de-Marsan
Eugénie-les-Bains*
St-Martin-d'Armagnac
Peyrehorade*
Amou
Plaisance*
A64
BIARRITZ
Madiran
Hendaye
A63
PAU ●
●St-Pée-s-Nivelle
Gan
N21
Barcus ●
Oloron-Ste-Marie
Lurbe-St-Christau
Argelès-Gazost

Cooking 3 or 3-4: **Eugénie-les-Bains***

0	40	80 Kilometres
0	25	50 Miles

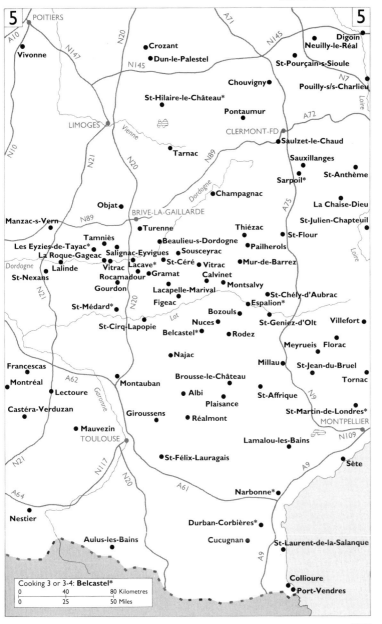

5

POITIERS

A10

Vivonne

N147

N20

N145

Crozant

Dun-le-Palestel

A71

N145

Digoin

Neuilly-le-Réal

St-Pourçain-s-Sioule

N7

Pouilly-s/s-Charlieu

Chouvigny

St-Hilaire-le-Château*

Pontaumur

A72

LIMOGES

Vienne

CLERMONT-FD

Saulzet-le-Chaud

N10

N21

N20

Tarnac

N89

Sauxillanges

Sarpoil*

St-Anthème

Champagnac

Dordogne

A75

La Chaise-Dieu

St-Julien-Chapteuil

Objat

N89

BRIVE-LA-GAILLARDE

Turenne

Thiézac

St-Flour

Loire

Manzac-s-Vern

Tamniès

Les Eyzies-de-Tayac*

La Roque-Gageac*

Salignac-Eyvigues

Beaulieu-s-Dordogne

Sousceyrac

Pailherols

Dordogne

Lalinde

Vitrac

Lacave*

St-Céré

Vitrac

Mur-de-Barrez

St-Nexans

Rocamadour

Gramat

Calvinet

N21

Gourdon

Lacapelle-Marival

Montsalvy

St-Médard*

N20

Figeac

Lot

St-Chély-d'Aubrac

Espalion*

Bozouls

St-Cirq-Lapopie

Nuces

St-Geniez-d'Olt

Villefort

Belcastel*

Rodez

Najac

Meyrueis

Florac

Millau

St-Jean-du-Bruel

Francescas

A62

Montréal

Lectoure

Garonne

Montauban

Brousse-le-Château

Tornac

Albi

St-Affrique

N9

Castéra-Verduzan

Giroussens

Plaisance

St-Martin-de-Londres*

Réalmont

MONTPELLIER

N109

Mauvezin

TOULOUSE

Lamalou-les-Bains

N21

N117

St-Félix-Lauragais

A9

Sète

N20

A61

A64

Narbonne*

Nestier

Aulus-les-Bains

Durban-Corbières*

Cucugnan

A9

St-Laurent-de-la-Salanque

Cooking 3 or 3-4: **Belcastel***

| 0 | 40 | 80 Kilometres |
| 0 | 25 | 50 Miles |

Collioure

Port-Vendres

6

6

Tournus
Louhans
Bonlieu*
Pont-de-Vaux*
Cuiseaux
Les Rousses
La Clayette
MACON
Attignat
Bons-en-Chablais
Fuissé
Vonnas
Mézériat
GENEVE
Verchaix
Châteauneuf*
Juliénas
Bourg-en-Bresse
Anse
Rumilly
Cordon
Chamonix
Alix
Duingt
Thônes
Les Houches
Chasselay*
Chaparon
Megève*
Pusignan
Faverges
Les Halles
LYON
Bourgoin-Jallieu
Montmélian
Montbrison
Chambéry*
Bonneval-s-Arc
ST-ETIENNE
Le Bessat
Chonas l'Amballan*
St-Vallier
St-Marcellin
Allemont
Valloire
Tence*
GRENOBLE
L'Alpe d'Huez
Les Deux-Alpes
Briançon
Monestier-de-Clermont
Corps
Die
Crest
Vals-les-Bains
Gap
Embrun
Nyons
Gigondas
Château-Arnoux
Méjannes-lès-Alès
Lurs
Annot
Joucas
Dabisse
Plan-du-Var
Levens
Forcalquier*
Tourrettes-s-Loup
St-Paul
St-Rémy-de-Provence
Aups
Opio
NICE
Maussane-les-Alpilles
Valbonne
La Colle-s-Loup
Aigues-Mortes
Montferrat
Mougins*
Stes-Maries-de-la-Mer
Flayosc
Fréjus
St-Raphaël
Les Issambres
MARSEILLE
Hyères

Cooking 3 or 3-4: **Megève***

| 0 | 40 | 80 Kilometres |
| 0 | 25 | 50 Miles |

ABBEVILLE   Auberge de la Corne

Comfortable restaurant/Cooking 2

Two dining rooms: one described as *anglo-normande*; the other a warm, panelled *salle*. There's an equally warm welcome from English-speaking *patronne*, Maryse Lematelot. Her husband, Yves, walks a classical path and is competently adept with alternative specialities ranging from *morue fraîche, fondue et poireaux* to a hearty *faux filet de sauce échalote*. One regional must is a filling *ficelle picarde*.
Menus ACDE. Cards All. (Rooms: nearby Relais Vauban – 100 m walk E.)
Closed 19 Feb to 9 Mar. Sun evg. Mon. (W of station, parking and N1.)
Post 32 chaussée du Bois, 80100 Abbeville, Somme. Region North.
Tel 22 24 06 34. Fax 22 24 03 65. Mich 6/C3. Map 2.

AIGUES-MORTES   Arcades

Comfortable restaurant with rooms/Cooking 2
Terrace

A 16th-century house with a stone, beamed and flower-filled dining room; an arcade; tiny patio garden; and stylish bedrooms. Classical fare: savour home-made *soupe de poissons*, flavoursome *rable de lapin farci sauce à la sauge*, and simple *fraises au sucre*. Enter the fortified town by the gate halfway along the north wall (bd Gambetta).
Menus BCD. Rooms (6) FG. Cards All. (Cheaper rooms: Croisades.)
Closed Feb. Rest: Mon (not July/Aug). Region Languedoc-Roussillon.
Post 23 bd Gambetta, 30220 Aigues-Mortes, Gard.
Tel 66 53 81 13. Fax 66 53 75 46. Mich 157/D3. Map 6.

ALBI   Jardin des Quatre Saisons

Comfortable restaurant/Cooking 2-3

Georges Bermond, after an absence of 20 years, has returned to his *pays*. The inventive, modern *cuisinier*, together with his blond wife Martine, weave a *RQP* cloth of gold. No less than seven starters, a dozen main courses (divided equally between fish and meat offerings) and nine scrumptious desserts. In addition, a limited choice menu C includes a half-bottle of Gaillac. Right bank, near river and town bridge.
Menus BC. Cards Access, AE, Visa. (Rooms: Cantepau, 150 m E; parking.)
Closed Mon (not public hols).
Post 19 bd Strasbourg, 81000 Albi, Tarn. Region Languedoc-Roussillon.
Tel 63 60 77 76. Fax 63 60 77 77. Mich 154/A1. Map 5.

A 100frs & under. B 100–135. C 135–165. D 165–250. E 250–350. F 350–500. G 500+

ALENCON
Au Petit Vatel

Very comfortable restaurant/Cooking 2-3

The town's most famous restaurant – rightly so, as the window-boxed exterior provides an attractive *entrée* to the culinary patterns so delicately woven by classicist, Michel Lerat. (The restaurant is almost next door to the Musée des Beaux-Arts with its fine lace collection.) Precision *plats* like *délice de cèpes, duo de sole et saumon sauce cardinal, coq au vin à la Solognotte* and super *sorbets et glaces*.
Menus BCD. Cards All. (Rooms: Ibis, 300 metre-walk away to E.)
Closed Feb school hols. 1-23 Aug. Sun evg. Wed.
Post 72 pl. Cdt Desmeulles, 61000 Alençon, Orne. Region Normandy.
Tel 33 26 23 78. Mich 51/D2. Map 2. (Plenty of parking nearby.)

ALIX
Le Vieux Moulin

Simple restaurant/Cooking 1-2
Terrace/Parking

Annie and Gérard Umhauer's mill shines with pride – literally, as the *moulin* is constructed from the local golden stone (*pierres dorées*). Gérard's cooking is Lyonnais fare at its most Pavlovian: temptations tagged *terrine maison, grenouilles, poulet à la crème, andouillette de "Chez Besson" sauce moutarde, fromage blanc* and *sorbet vigneron*.
Menus BCD. Cards Access, Visa. (Rooms: A6 *autoroute* hotels Limonest.)
Closed 7 Aug to 5 Sept. Mon and Tues (not pub hols). (See *FLE* p222.)
Post 69380 Alix, Rhône. Region Lyonnais. (Limonest is SE of Alix.)
Tel 78 43 91 66. Fax 78 47 98 46. Mich 115/F1. Map 6.

ALLEMONT
Giniès

Simple hotel/Cooking 1-2
Quiet/Terrace/Gardens/Parking

A colourful, shady garden is one big bonus; a second is the enterprising Giniès family – Robert and Gilberte, their chef son, Philippe, and his wife, Isabelle. Run-of-the-mill *Bourgeoise* and classical cuisine – of the *terrine maison, truite meunière, escalope de veau* variety. Order *râclette* and *fondue* (regional winners) at least two hours in advance.
Menus aBCD. Rooms (28) DE. Cards Access, Visa.
Closed Rest: 10 Apl to 2 May; mid Sept to Jan.
Post 38114 Allemont, Isère. Regions Hautes-Alpes/Savoie.
Tel 76 80 70 03. Fax 76 80 73 13. Mich 132/B2. Map 6.

A100frs & under. B100–135. C135–165. D165–250. E250–350. F350–500. G500+

L'ALPE D'HUEZ   Le Lyonnais

Comfortable restaurant/Cooking 2-3

As you drive the 3000-ft climb with two dozen *lacets* think of the Tour de France cyclists using only pedal power to reach the top. Your car-aided efforts are well rewarded by Gérard Astic's classical and Lyonnais *plats: carpaccio de thon frais à la coriandre, quenelle de brochet soufflé au coulis crustacés* (what memories) and *cervelle de Canut (fromage frais aux herbes)* are typical. Closed at lunchtime.
Menus bCD. Cards Access, Visa. (Rooms: Alp'Azur, 500m-walk away to NE.)
Closed Lunch. May-June. Sept-Nov. Regions Htes-Alpes/Savoie/Lyonnais.
Post rte du Coulet, 38750 L'Alpe d'Huez, Isère.
Tel 76 80 68 92. Mich 132/B2. Map 6.

AMOU   Commerce

Simple hotel/Cooking 2
Terrace/Garage/Parking

As colourful an exterior as you'll find in France: window boxes, blinds, awnings and creeping vines. The Darracq family enterprise is geared up for entertaining individuals and large gatherings. Classical, *Bourgeois* and regional repasts: *terrine maison, quenelles d'oie, confit de porc* and *gâteau Basque* (from wide-choice menu B) will quench any appetite.
Menus aBCD. Rooms (20) DE. Cards All.
Closed 14-28 Feb. 11-30 Nov. Mon (not high season).
Post 40330 Amou, Landes. Region Southwest.
Tel 58 89 02 28. Fax 58 89 24 45. Mich 149/E3. Map 4.

ANNOT   Avenue

Simple hotel/Cooking 2

A warm welcome at this much-liked *FLE* favourite (now "discovered" by Michelin) – ideally placed to explore the mountains to the north. Enterprising *Bourgeoise* and classical cooking with Italian touches from *chef/patron* Jean-Louis Genovesi: starters such as *cannellonis de homard au coulis de crustacés* and *millefeuille de truites rosées*; and welcome main courses like *daube légère de pigeon en couronne de fettucine.*
Menus AB. Rooms (12) DE. Cards Access, Visa.
Closed Nov to March. Regions Côte d'Azur/Hautes-Alpes.
Post 04240 Annot, Alpes-de-Haute-Provcence.
Tel 92 83 22 07. Fax 92 83 34 07. Mich 147/E4. Map 6.

A100frs & under. B100–135. C135–165. D165–250. E250–350. F350–500. G500+

ANSE

St-Romain

Comfortable hotel/Cooking 2
Quiet/Terrace/Gardens/Parking

Easily found if you have my *En Route* (p58). A quiet site, sunny terrace, beamed and flower-filled *salle* and smiling *patronne* are all pluses. So, too, is the classical cuisine of Bruno Levet: try perhaps a *melon glacé aux 4 fruits rouges* or a well-executed *truite de mer en crépinette, crème ciboulette*. Alas, only "so-so" sweets from the trolley.
Menus aBCDE. Rooms (24) DE. Cards All.
Closed 27 Nov to 4 Dec. Sun evg (Nov to Apl).
Post rte Graves, 69480 Anse, Rhône. Region Lyonnais.
Tel 74 60 24 46. Fax 74 67 12 85. Mich 116/A1. Map 6.

ARGELES-GAZOST

Hostellerie Le Relais

Comfortable hotel/Cooking 2
Terrace/Lift (being installed)/Parking

Jeannette Hourtal's flowers on the shady terrace and in the main rooms are colourful eye-catchers. Husband Jean's copious classical, regional, and *Bourgeoise* fare is not prissy stuff. Highly satisfying grub of the *flan de cèpes, pâté de lièvre confiture d'oignons, tranche de gigot de mouton poêlée* and *coupe aux myrtilles flambées* variety.
Menus abCD. Rooms (23) DE. Cards Access, Visa.
Closed 10 Oct to 8 Feb. Region Southwest.
Post 25 r. Mar. Foch, 65400 Argelès-Gazost, Hautes-Pyrénées.
Tel 62 97 01 27. Mich 168/B3. Map 4.

ARRADON

L'Arlequin

Comfortable restaurant/Cooking 2
Terrace/Gardens/Parking

On the D101, at the spot marked Boloré on the map. Prices have remained the same for four years – a remarkable record. Fine *cave* (many halves). Lunch under umbrellas on the terrace. Modern, classical and regional touches: witness *millefeuille de saumon, crème d'agrumes; tournedos de rumsteack*; and *petit far minute aux pommes et calvados*.
Menus aBCD, Cards All. (Rooms: Le Logis de Parc er Gréo; off D101 to W.)
Closed Sun evg. (Above is *sans rest*, secluded and has swimming pool.)
Post Parc Botquelen, 56610 Arradon, Morbihan. Region Brittany.
Tel 97 40 41 41. Fax 97 40 52 93. Mich 62/C2. Map 1.

A100frs & under. B100–135. C135–165. D165–250. E250–350. F350–500. G500+

ARRAS
Ambassadeur

Very comfortable restaurant/Cooking 2-3

A posh name for a swish show. But, for all railway nuts, this is the
ultimate *buffet de gare* – a real "stop" *par excellence. Haute cuisine*
TGV classics share the line with regional, anything but punk, puffers: the
latter could include *tarte aux maroilles, ficelles à la Picarde and
andouillette d'Arras*; the former may number *escalope de saumon à la
crème d'aneth* and *rable lapin à la crème de moutarde de Meaux.*
Menus BCD. Cards All. (Rooms: Les 3 Luppars – a brisk 5 m walk to N.)
Closed Sun evg. (Parking for restaurant adjacent to station.)
Post gare, pl. Foch, 62000 Arras, Pas-de-Calais. Region North.
Tel 21 23 29 80. Fax 21 71 17 07. Mich 8/A2. Map 2.

ARTZENHEIM
Auberge d'Artzenheim

Comfortable restaurant with rooms/Cooking 2
Quiet/Terrace/Gardens/Parking

A colourful mix of old and new – with, in true Alsace fashion, flowers
everywhere. Some bedrooms smallish. Chef Edgar Husser, who trained
at the nearby three-star Aub. de l'Ill, mixes regional and both old and
new: a filling *assiette des terrines et crudités*, tasty *mignons de porc aux
choux rouges* and a heady finale, a smooth *mousse au kirsch.*
Menus b(lunch)CDE. Rooms (10) E. Cards Access, Visa.
Closed Mid Feb to mid Mar. Mon evg. Tues.
Post 68320 Artzenheim, Haut-Rhin. Region Alsace.
Tel 89 71 60 51. Fax 89 71 68 21. Mich 61/E3. Map 3.

ATTIGNAT
Dominique Marcepoil

Very comfortable restaurant with rooms/Cooking 2-3
Terrace/Gardens/Parking

A perfect lunch: a covered terrace with a retina-piercing tapestry and
vast colourful mural; and, better still, eye-catching cooking from
chef/patron, the bubbly DM. A well-balanced *repas* of *saumon*
marinaded in olive oil and dill, a *quiche de ris de veau au Côtes de
Jura*, a fresh goat's cheese *quenelle* and strawberry tart. Perfection?
Menus bCDE. Rooms (9) EF. Cards Access, AE, Visa. (On D975.)
Closed 11-17 Sept. 13-19 Nov. Sun evg. Mon.
Post 01340 Attignat, Ain. Region Lyonnais.
Tel 74 30 92 24. Fax 74 25 93 48. Mich 103/D3. Map 6.

A100frs & under. B100–135. C135–165. D165–250. E250–350. F350–500. G500+

AULUS-LES-BAINS   Terrasse

Simple hotel/Cooking 2
Terrace

Step over the bridge and travel back in time 30 years – furnishings, service and cooking as they used to be; so, too, is Madame, Rose Amiel, a headmistress martinet. No modern frills here. Chef Jean-François Maurette is a true-blue classics/regional fan: savour rich dishes like *tourte de foie gras de canard* and *cuisse de canard confite du Gers*.
Menus b(lunch)CDE. Rooms (19) DE. Cards Access, Visa (cash preferred!).
Closed Oct to Apl (but not school hols). (Essential to book ahead.)
Post 09140 Aulus-les-Bains, Ariège. Region Southwest.
Tel 61 96 00 98. Mich 170/C4. Map 5.

AUPS   Le Chalet

Very simple restaurant/Cooking 2
Terrace & Gardens (newly-created)

Philippe La Montagne, in his mid-30s, is a classical chef, a self-confessed disciple of Escoffier. Wife Béatrice is a welcoming *patronne*. A flurry of rich, tasty specialities: *pièce de boeuf grillée à l'essence de truffe et au foie gras* is just one memorable example. Mouthwatering sweets, especially an irresistible hot *soufflé au Grand Marnier*.
Menus ABC. Cards None. (Rooms: hotels at Tourtour & Moustiers-Ste-M.)
Closed Mon evg & Wed evg (out of seas). (Best: Le Colombier, Moustiers.)
Post 3 r. Maréchal Foch, 83630 Aups, Var. Region Côte d'Azur.
Tel 94 70 04 22. Mich 162/C2. Map 6.

AUTUN   Chalet Bleu

Comfortable restaurant/Cooking 2

Papa Bouché, Georges, was once the chef at the French Embassy in London. Here he runs the front of house and his son, Philippe, is the chef. Regional, classical and neo-classical alternatives: *saupiquet de jambon vieux Morvan, jambon persillé à la Bourguignonne, pièce de boeuf rôtie au fumet de Bourgogne* and *fondant de crabe océan* are a representative quartet. Terrific old-time desserts. (Near *mairie* – town hall.)
Menus aBCD. Cards Access, AE, Visa. (Rooms: Arcades – 5 min walk to NW.)
Closed 5-20 Feb. Mon evg. Tues.
Post 3 r. Jeannin, 71400 Autun, Saône-et-Loire. Region Burgundy.
Tel 85 86 27 30. Mich 87/E3. Map 3.

A100frs & under. B100–135. C135–165. D165–250. E250–350. F350–500. G500+

AUXERRE Le Moulin

Comfortable restaurant/Cooking 2
Terrace/Parking

Just north of the Auxerre-Sud A6 exit (follow signs). Jean-Pierre Vaury is highly thought of by his regional peers. A mainly classical repertoire confirms their opinions: a rarely seen *pied de veau, sauce ravigote*; a smooth and full-of-flavour *saumon grillée beurre blanc*; a cheese chariot (regional varieties); and drooling *tarte aux pommes*.
Menus bCDEF. Cards Access, Visa. (Rooms: Ibis near A6 exit.)
Closed 15-31 Jan. 19-30 Aug. Sun evg. Mon.
Post La Coudre, 89290 Venoy, Yonne. Region Burgundy.
Tel 86 40 23 79. Fax 86 40 23 55. Mich 72/A2. Map 2.

AVALLON Le Morvan

Very comfortable restaurant/Cooking 2
Terrace/Gardens/Parking

Step back to France as she used to be; not for those influenced by lightness and brightness cooking and served on black octagonal plates. Jean, the chef, and Marinette Breton are loyal regional and classical troopers: dig into a meaty *duo de terrine, jambon sec de pays, saucisson chaud au canard fumé* and *filets de lapin farcis Bourguignonne*.
Menus BD. Cards All. (Rooms: Avallon-Vauban – a 5 min walk to SE.)
Closed Jan. Feb. Sun evg. Mon (not public hols).
Post 7 rte de Paris (N6), 89200 Avallon, Yonne. Region Burgundy.
Tel 86 34 18 20. Mich 72/B3. Map 3.

AZAY-LE-RIDEAU Aigle d'Or

Comfortable restaurant/Cooking 2-3
Terrace

A pleasure in every sense: a pastel-shaded dining room with flowers on each table; a garden terrace for eating out; an attractive hostess, Ghislaine Fèvre; and traditional cooking from her husband, Jean-Luc. *Crème d'oseille et quenelles de brochet, jambonnette de volaille à la crème de morilles* and *craquant aux fraises* are lip-smacking memories.
Menus a(lunch)CDE. Cards Access, Visa. (Rooms: De Biencourt.) Closed 6 Feb-2 Mar. 4-10 Sept. 15-25 Dec. Sun evg. Tues evg (Oct-mid May). Wed.
Post 37190 Azay-le-Rideau, Indre-et-Loire. Region Loire.
Tel 47 45 24 58. Fax 47 45 90 18. Mich 82/A1. Map 2.

A100frs & under. B100–135. C135–165. D165–250. E250–350. F350–500. G500+

BADEN   Le Gavrinis

Comfortable hotel/Cooking 2
Terrace/Gardens/Parking

A sparkling, multi-faceted family affair. Alain Justum and sons, Olivier and Frédéric, man the stoves; mum, Michèle, and daughter Sybille run the front of house. English-speaking Sybille is a knowledgeable delight. Modern and neo-classical *plats* excecuted with flair, harmony and good taste. Modern, spick and span hotel with flower-bedecked terrace.
Menus CDE. Rooms (19) DEF. Cards All.
Closed Dec. Jan. Mon (not evg from June to Sept).
Post Toulbroch, 56870 Baden, Morbihan. Region Brittany.
Tel 97 57 00 82. Fax 97 57 09 47. Mich 62/C2. Map 1.

BALDENHEIM   La Couronne

Very comfortable restaurant/Cooking 3

Chefs Argèle Trébis and her son-in-law, Daniel Rubiné, marry regional and classical in their culinary offerings. Marcel Trébis and his pretty daughter, Chantal, watch over their flower-filled, panelled dining rooms with courtesy and flair. Typical qualifying menu: *amuse bouche*, *filet de hareng mariné*, gutsy *civet de chevreuil* and sumptuous *sorbets*. Champion *matelote de Ried* (the name for the marshy Rhine plain).
Menus CDE. Cards Access, AE, Visa. (Rooms: several hotels N of Colmar.)
Closed 3-10 Jan. 25 July to 5 Aug. Sun evg. Mon (not public hols).
Post 67600 Baldenheim, Bas-Rhin. Region Alsace.
Tel 88 85 32 22. Fax 88 85 36 27. Mich 61/E2. Map 3.

BANNEGON   Auberge Moulin de Chaméron

Comfortable restaurant with rooms/Cooking 2-3
Secluded/Terrace/Gardens/Swimming pool/Parking

English-speaking Jacques and Annie Candoré are the informed *patrons* at the 18thC mill (with milling museum). Son-in-law, chef Jean Mérilleau, conjures up neo-classical and modern tricks: a *flan de langoustines au vin blanc de Sancerre* and a *feuillantine de framboises* are examples of his skills. Drink Menetou, Quincy, Reuilly and St-Pourçain wines.
Menus CD. Rooms (12) EF. Disabled. Cards Access, AE, Visa.
Closed Mid Nov to end Feb. Tues (out of season).
Post 18210 Bannegon, Cher. Region Berry-Bourbonnais. Map 2.
Tel (R) 48 61 84 48. (H) 48 61 83 80. Fax 48 61 84 92. Mich 85/D4.

A 100frs & under. B 100–135. C 135–165. D 165–250. E 250–350. F 350–500. G 500+

BARCUS Chez Chilo

Very comfortable restaurant with rooms/Cooking 2
Terrace/Gardens/Parking

Pierre and Martine Chilo are the third generation *patrons* (a family renowned locally for their rugby links). Scrum down for Pierre's classical and regional culinary balls – among them bright *piments "piquillos" farcis à la morue*, hearty *civet de marcassin* and yummy *gâteau Basque au coulis de cerises noires*. Eight super new bedrooms.
Menus aC. Rooms (14) BDEF. Cards Access, AE, Visa.
Closed 15-31 March. Sun evg and Mon (not high season).
Post 64130 Barcus, Pyrénées-Atlantiques. Region Southwest.
Tel 59 28 90 79. Fax 59 28 93 10. Mich 167/E2. Map 4.

BARFLEUR Moderne

Comfortable restaurant with rooms/Cooking 2

A small pepperpot tower is an unusual man-made exterior feature. Mme Le Roulier is a friendly, helpful *patronne*. Her husband, chef Evrard, steams a classical course and capitalises on the nearby ocean's piscatorial harvests: *soupe de poisson*, oysters and a *choucroute de poisson au beurre blanc* are typical treats. Patterned plates reflect the rather busy cooking style. Home-made breads/pasta. Many half-bottles.
Menus aBD. Rooms (8) BD. Cards Access, Visa.
Closed Mid Jan to 20 Mar. Tues and Wed (mid Sept to mid Jan).
Post 50760 Barfleur, Manche. Region Normandy.
Tel 33 23 12 44. Fax 33 23 91 58. Mich 12/C1. Map 1.

BAR-SUR-AUBE Relais des Gouverneurs

Comfortable restaurant with rooms/Cooking 2
Garage/Parking

A dour-looking *relais* at the heart of Bar-s-Aube. A small flower-filled courtyard provides limited off-the-road parking. Modern creations from the 23-year-old chef son of Mme Guilleminot. Examples include a colourful *levée de rougets aux haricots* and a *sorbet à la framboise avec fruits* (served, intelligently, with a glass of Coteaux Champenois).
Menus aBC. Rooms (15) E. Cards All.
Closed Sat midday. Sun evg. Mon midday (not public hols).
Post 38 r. Nationale, 10200 Bar-s-Aube, Aube. Region Champagne-Ardenne.
Tel 25 27 08 76. Fax 25 27 20 80. Mich 57/E3. Map 3.

A100frs & under. B100–135. C135–165. D165–250. E250–350. F350–500. G500+

BEAULIEU-SUR-DORDOGNE   Central Hôtel Fournié

Simple hotel/Cooking 1-2
Terrace/Parking

A fairly modern, brown-shuttered *logis* with easy parking in the large *place* opposite. An all-fish menu (how welcome) is only just outside the C price range ceiling. Menu B includes a *pillau de calmar d'encre, foie gras de canard frais en terrine* and a middling only *navarin d'agneau et ses pâtes fraîches*. Overall, enjoyable grub from Bernard Bessière.
Menus aBCDE. Rooms (27) CDE. Cards Access, Visa.
Closed Nov to Mar. Region Dordogne.
Post 4 pl. Champ-de-Mars, 19120 Beaulieu-sur-Dordogne, Corrèze.
Tel 55 91 01 34. Fax 55 91 23 57. Mich 125/D3. Map 5.

BEAUMESNIL   L'Etape Louis XIII

Comfortable restaurant/Cooking 3
Terrace/Gardens/Parking

A line of evocative 17th-century half-timbered Normandy cottages is the initial eye-tickler. Next the welcome from Françoise Sureau. Only one qualifying menu (top-end A) – but what palette-tickling classical largesse from chef Philippe Sureau: *fricassée de légumes aux herbes, choux farci de sa pintade au romarin*, cheese and *mousse au chocolat*.
Menus ADE. Cards Access, AE, Visa. (Rooms: Acropole to SW of Bernay.)
Closed 18 Jan to 9 Feb. 21 June to 12 July. Sun evg. Mon. Tues.
Post 27410 Beaumesnil, Eure. Region Normandy.
Tel 32 44 44 72. Mich 33/F2. Map 2.

BEAUMONT-EN-AUGE   La Haie Tondue

Comfortable restaurant/Cooking 1-2
Parking

Chef Dominique Tolmais is a champion menu changer; every three weeks a new version appears. Menus B&C provide a choice of five starters, five main courses, followed by many cheeses and even more puds. Appetite-quenching classical and *Bourgeoise* grub: like *terrine campagnarde, terrine de poisson verte* and *faux-filet grillé maître d'hôtel*.
Menus BCD. Cards Access, Visa. (Rooms: Climat de France, Pont-l'Evêque.)
Closed 1-15 Mar. 19 June-4 July. 2-17 Oct. Mon evg (not Aug). Tues.
Post 14130 La Haie Tondue, Beaumont-en-Auge, Calvados. Region Normandy.
Tel 31 64 85 00. Fax 31 64 69 34. Mich 32/C1. Map 2. (2 km to S.)

BEAUNE Central

Comfortable hotel/Cooking 2

At the heart of the flower-covered town, a tennis court length from the multi-hued Hôtel-Dieu patterned roof. Bright, pretty patterns also grace the Central plates: menu B includes *petites salades mélangées au blanc de volaille fumé maison* and *saumon cuit sur peau à l'encre de seiche, gnocchi de moelle.* Regional classics – *jambon persillé fait maison* and *véritable coq au vin à l'ancienne mode* – are on menu C.
Menus a(lunch)BCD. Rooms (20) EFG. Cards Access, Visa.
Closed 21 Nov to 22 Dec. Sun evg (Nov to Mar). Wed (Nov to June).
Post 2 r. V. Millot, 21200 Beaune, Côte-d'Or. Region Burgundy.
Tel 80 24 77 24. Fax 80 22 30 40. Mich 88/A2. Map 3.

BEINE Le Vaulignot

Comfortable restaurant/Cooking 1-2

Alongside the D965, six km west of Chablis, six km from an A6 exit and in the thick of vineyard terrain. Jean-Claude Dubois believes in choice and seems to have a low opinion of all slimmers. *Bourgeoise*, classical and regional grub. Forget your diet, loosen your belts and tuck into a nostalgic *saucisson chaud du Beaujolais pommes à l'huile*; *sole meunière; fromage blanc*; and *baba au rhum et sa crème anglaise.*
Menus aCD. Cards Access, Visa. (Rooms: Les Lys, Chablis; Ibis, A6 exit.)
Closed Feb. 2nd half Oct. Sun evg. Mon.
Post Beine, 89800 Chablis, Yonne. Region Burgundy.
Tel 86 42 48 48. Mich 72/B2. Map 3.

BELCASTEL Vieux Pont

Comfortable restaurant with rooms/Cooking 3
Quiet/Gardens

A sumptuously scenic spot and a seductive modern, natural style of cooking from self-taught *cuisinière*, Nicole Fagegaltier-Rouquier; sister Michèle runs the front of house. Extensive use of oil (olive, walnut and hazelnut) and light cooking reductions: examples are *essence de morilles* and *lait d'amandes.* New bedroom annexe on opposite bank of the river.
Menus BDE. Rooms (7) EF. Cards Access, Visa.
Closed Jan. Feb. Sun evg (not July/Aug). Mon (but not midday July/Aug).
Post 12390 Belcastel, Aveyron. Region Massif Central (Cevénnes).
Tel 65 64 52 29. Fax 65 64 44 32. Mich 140/B1-B2. Map 5.

A100frs & under. B100–135. C135–165. D165–250. E250–350. F350–500. G500+

BENOUVILLE

Manoir d'Hastings et la Pommeraie

Very comfortable restaurant with rooms/Cooking 2-3
Quiet/Gardens/Parking

New owners, Carole and José Aparicio, praised by readers, have injected a new lease of life into the 17thC priory. Classical/regional cooking and a wide choice for each course is a plus. Faultless technique with specialities such as *terrine de foie gras au vieux porto*, *ris de veau aux morilles*, *goujonnettes de soles poêlées* and *tarte chaude Normande*.
Menus b(lunch)CDEF. Rooms (11) G. Cards All.
Closed Feb school hols. 15-30 Nov. Rest: Sun evg and Mon (not July/Aug).
Post 14970 Bénouville, Calvados. Region Normandy.
Tel 31 44 62 43. Fax 31 44 76 18. Mich 32/B1. Map 2.

Le BESSAT

La Fondue

Comfortable restaurant with rooms/Cooking 1-2
Garage

The over 3800 ft-high village is at the heart of the Pilat Regional Park, a green lung for industrial St-Etienne, 18 km to the NW. La Fondue comes in a wedge-shaped stone building. Enjoy *Bourgeois* and classical basics like mussels and leeks in a cream sauce, *venison à l'ancienne*, stuffed *lapereau*, goat's cheese and desserts from a trolley.
Menus aBCDE. Rooms (9) CDE. Cards All.
Closed Dec to Feb.
Post 42660 Le Bessat, Loire. Region Massif Central (Ardèche).
Tel 77 20 40 09. Fax 77 20 45 20. Mich 115/E4. Map 6.

BEUZEVILLE

Petit Castel/Aub. Cochon d'Or

Comfortable hotel (annexe) & restaurant with rooms/Cooking 2
Gardens (hotel)

A much-liked family show: Charles and Monique Folleau, aided by their English-speaking daughter, Catherine, and her husband, Olivier Martin. Classical and regional delights: spiky *safranée de truite aux champignons*, stylish *gâteau de pleurotes au beurre échalotes* and saucy *faux-filet grillé Béarnaise*. Annexe (Petit Castel) across the road.
Menus aCD. Rooms (21 of which 16 in annexe) CDE. Cards Access, Visa.
Closed Mid Dec to mid Jan. Mon. (Park in large *place*.)
Post 27210 Beuzeville, Eure. Region Normandy. Map 2.
Tel (R) 32 57 70 46. (H) 32 57 76 08. Fax 32 42 25 70. Mich 15/D4.

A100frs & under. B100–135. C135–165. D165–250. E250–350. F350–500. G500+

BIEVRES
Relais de St-Walfroy

Comfortable restaurant/Cooking 1-2
Parking

A hidden hamlet, north-west of Montmédy and south of the N43. Michel Vignol is the mayor and *directeur* of the small, rustic *relais*. Chef Jean-Noël Vignol treads *Bourgeois* and regional paths: *truite belle meunière, quiche Ardennaise, jambon d'Ardenne, faux-filet maître d'hôtel, sorbets* and similar. Franc-wise is the Vignol motto.
Menus ABC. Cards Access, Visa. (Rooms: Le Mady at Montmédy to SE.)
Closed Tuesday.
Post Bièvres, 08370 Margut, Ardennes. Region Champagne-Ardenne.
Tel 24 22 61 62. Mich 22/B3. Map 3.

BIGNAN
Auberge La Chouannière

Comfortable restaurant/Cooking 2

Jean Luc and Anne-Marie Simon opened their restaurant, with a Louis XVI-style dining room, almost 25 years ago. A typical menu C could include a silky *mousse de foie gras de volaille au porto*, a crunchy and moist *croustillant de saumon à l'oseille* (or, loosen the belts, a *pièce de boeuf grillée, sauce verte* with a robust *galette de pomme de terre*), Brie *de Meaux* and *nougat maison glacé*. Champion classical fare.
Menus aCD. Cards Access, AE, Visa. (Rooms: L'Argoat at Locminé, 5 km.)
Closed Feb school hols. 2-13 Oct. Sun evg. Mon. (Rest. SE of Locminé.)
Post 56500 Bignan, Morbihan. Region Brittany.
Tel 97 60 00 96. Fax 97 44 24 58. Mich 62/C1. Map 1.

BLOIS
Rendez-vous des Pêcheurs

Comfortable restaurant/Cooking 3

Menu C (low-end) at the tiny home of young master chef Eric Reithler does not appear in written form. Ask the waitress to get Eric to explain the daily-changing menu – in French or English. The three courses which follow are modern gems, bursting with flavours: examples are *rouelles de cabillaud aux pommes de terre en anchoïade* and a consummate *nougat glacé sur beurre d'oranges*. (Rooms: many hotels within walking distance.)
Menus C(menu)DE(à la carte). Cards Access, AE, Visa. (S of château.)
Closed Feb school hols. 1st 3 wks Aug. Sun. Mon midday. Public hols.
Post 27 r. Foix, 41000 Blois, Loir-et-Cher. Region Loire.
Tel 54 74 67 48. Fax 54 74 47 67. Mich 68/C3. Map 2.

A100frs & under. B100–135. C135–165. D165–250. E250–350. F350–500. G500+

BONLIEU   La Poutre

Comfortable restaurant with rooms/Cooking 3
Parking

Don't judge a restaurant by a dismal exterior – as at least one reader has done here (he drove on). Inside the well-named "beamed" home of Denis Moureaux lurks an able chef and his delicious regional/classical dishes. Menu B could include *tête de veau, crêpes Jurassiennes; filet de poisson aux petits légumes*; *pintade aux champignons*; and *sorbets*.
Menus BDEF. Rooms (10) DE. Cards Access, Visa.
Closed Mid Oct to mid Feb.
Post 39130 Bonlieu, Jura. Region Jura.
Tel 84 25 57 77. Mich 89/F4. Map 6.

BONNEVAL-SUR-ARC   Auberge Le Pré Catin

Simple restaurant/Cooking 1-2
Terrace

Alpine from boots to helmet: a stone-built chalet; mountain flowers and decorations; and filling *Bourgeoise* and regional fare. Daniel Delaplace, a Parisian, and his wife, Josiane, from Normandy, serve up gutsy grub: mainly grills (*feu de bois*) – like *entrecôte* and *agneau*; tasty cheeses, *jambon de Savoie*, locally-dried meats and *ravioles de Royans*.
Menus ABC. Cards Access, Visa. (Rooms: A la Pastourelle.)
Closed 3 May to 16 June. 18 Sept to 15 Dec. Mon. (Above *sans rest*.)
Post 73480 Bonneval-sur-Arc, Savoie. Region Savoie.
Tel 79 05 95 07. Mich 119/F4. Map 6.

BONS-EN-CHABLAIS   Progrès

Comfortable hotel/Cooking 2
Lift/Parking

The dining room is alongside the main road; the modern bedrooms in an annexe behind the restaurant (note the lift). Brigitte Colly is an obliging *patronne*. Her husband, Charles, is a champion classicist: reference an excellently executed *filet de féra au Crépy* (a local white wine) and an intense *suprême de pintade à la crème d'échalottes*.
Menus a(Tues-Thurs)BCE. Rooms (10) E. Disabled. Cards Access, Visa.
Closed 2-22 Jan. Last wk June. Sun evg & Mon (not 15 July-15 Aug).
Post 74890 Bons-en-Chablais, Haute-Savoie. Region Savoie.
Tel 50 36 11 09. Fax 50 39 44 16. Mich 104/C2. Map 6.

A100frs & under. B100–135. C135–165. D165–250. E250–350. F350–500. G500+
250

BOUHET   Auberge du Vieux Moulin

Comfortable restaurant with rooms/Cooking 2
Terrace/Parking

Nelly and Stéphane Jacob have won the hearts of many readers at their
working mill (the wheel and grinding mechanism still turn). Both worked
in the UK and speak good English. Neo-classical *plats* with idiosyncratic
touches – *terrine de poisson sauce Tyrolienne* – and a flavoursome
fricassée de volaille au thym et à la sarriette. Good breakfasts.
Menus BD. Rooms (6) DE. Cards Access, Visa.
Closed Rest: Sun evg and Mon (not public hols). Rooms: out of season.
Post 17540 Bouhet, Charente-Maritime. Region Poitou-Charentes.
Tel 46 68 20 86. Mich 93/E3. Map 4.

Le BOURG-DUN   Auberge du Dun

Comfortable restaurant/Cooking 3
Parking

What a classy restaurant: Pierre Chrétien is as smart a chef as his dining
rooms are stylish. Menu B (perhaps low-end C by publication)
epitomised *RQP* at its most exhilarating: *aumônière de coquillages*,
paupiettes de saumon aux épinards, a selection of creamy regional
cheeses and *sable au citron meringué* was a masterly neo-classical feast.
Menus BDE. Cards Acc, Visa. (Rooms: Altea, St-Valery-en-Caux to W.)
Closed 9-27 Feb. 24 Aug to 9 Sept. Sun evg and Mon (not public hols).
Post 76740 Le Bourg-Dun, Seine-Maritime. Region Normandy.
Tel 35 83 05 84. Mich 15/F1. Map 2.

BOURG-EN-BRESSE   La Galerie

Comfortable restaurant/Cooking 2

A modest, shop-fronted look about La Galerie but, when added to the
Mail and Jacques Guy (both in *FLE*), you have a redoubtable Bourg *RQP*
trio to choose from. Here Michel, the chef, and Dominique Chanteloup
beguile with regional, neo-classical and classical treats – reference *persillé
de tête de veau*, *crépinette de sanglier aux châtaignes*, *noisettes de
lièvre au genièvre* and *fromage frais de Bresse à la crème*.
Menus BCD. Cards Access, Visa. (Rooms: Logis de Brou, 800 m walk to SE.)
Closed Sat midday. Sun. (La Galerie is SW of Notre-Dame church.)
Post 4 r. Th. Riboud, 01000 Bourg-en-Bresse, Ain. Region Lyonnais.
Tel 74 45 16 43. Mich 103/D3. Map 6. (Logis is *sans rest*, parking.)

A100frs & under. B100–135. C135–165. D165–250. E250–350. F350–500. G500+

BOURGOIN-JALLIEU   Chavancy

Very comfortable restaurant/Cooking 2

An air-conditioned, orange-hued oasis in bustling Bourgoin-Jallieu (400 metres north of the N6, near the hospital and close to parking). Bruno Chavancy drives all carriageways. Menu C (low-end) offers a chance to try a Bresse culinary landmark – *petit pâté chaud*, followed by a light *saumon beurre aux herbes*. Another regional treat comes in the chance to savour a Bresse *suprême de volaille* (mated to *curry*, *riz sauvage*).
Menus CDE. Cards All. (Rooms: Ibis & Climat de France to W of town.)
Closed 24 July to 22 Aug. Sun evg. Mon.
Post av. Tixier, 38300 Bourgoin-Jallieu, Isère. Region Lyonnais.
Tel 74 93 63 88. Fax 74 28 42 44. Mich 116/C3. Map 6.

BOZOULS   Le Belvédère

Comfortable restaurant with rooms/Cooking 1-2
Quiet/Terrace

Overlooking the Trou de Bozouls (a small, wooded, meandering *cirque* – and the plus of a handsome *église*), Marcel Girbelle keeps matters plain and simple in his rustic dining room. The chimney's roaring fire provides grills for the main courses (*boeuf* or *magret de canard*); *Roquefort* cheese features in tasty first and second courses.
Menus aBC. Rooms (11) DE. Cards Access, Visa.
Closed Dec. Sat and Sun evg (out of season).
Post 12340 Bozouls, Aveyron. Regions MC (Auvergne/Cévennes).
Tel 65 44 92 66. Fax 65 48 87 33. Mich 140/C2. Map 5.

BRIANCON   Le Péché Gourmand

Very comfortable restaurant/Cooking 2
Parking

A modern dining room and stylish neo-classical cooking from 22-year-old Sandrine Bellet. Emphatic full-of-flavour dishes: witness the *confit de lapin aux endives* or the *velouté de lentilles et canard fumé*; the enlightened *papillote de pintade de citron*; and silky-smooth *marquise aux deux chocolats*. Some wines sold by the glass: just ask.
Menus BCDE. Cards Access, AE, Visa. (Rooms: Mont-Brison; 2 min walk E.)
Closed 4-24 Jan. Sun evg and Mon (mid Sept to June). (Above *sans rest*.)
Post 2 rte Gap, 05100 Briançon, Hautes-Alpes. Regions Htes-Alpes/Savoie.
Tel 92 20 11 02. Mich 133/D3. Map 6.

A100frs & under. B100–135. C135–165. D165–250. E250–350. F350–500. G500+

BRIANCON   Vauban

Comfortable hotel/Cooking 2
Gardens/Lift/Parking

A striking apricot and cream façade ensures you can't miss the Semiond family hotel in the lower town. Utterly straightforward classical and *Bourgeoises* specialities: *quenelles aux fruits de mer, canard à l'orange, tarte Tatin* and *soufflé au Grand Marnier* – all well executed and precisely cooked. André Semiond speaks fluent English.
Menus BD. Rooms (44) EF. Cards Access, Visa.
Closed 5 Nov to 18 Dec. Regions Hautes-Alpes/Savoie.
Post 13 av. Gén. de Gaulle, 05100 Briançon, Hautes-Alpes.
Tel 92 21 12 11. Fax 92 20 58 20. Mich 133/D3. Map 6.

BRINON-SUR-SAULDRE   La Solognote

Comfortable hotel/Cooking 3
Quiet/Gardens/Parking

Andrée Girard is a warm-hearted, smiling *patronne*; husband Dominique is a classical specialist, capitalising on his *pays* and its rich larder. Beamed dining rooms in old red-brick Sologne cottages; bedrooms in modern extension at rear. Menu C *plats* such as *feuilleté de lotte au fenouil* and earthy *joues de porc braisées au Menetou rouge*.
Menus CDE. Rooms (13) EF. Cards Access, Visa.
Closed 15 Feb-15 Mar. Last wk May. 12-22 Sept. Tues evg (Oct-June). Wed.
Post 18410 Brinon-sur-Sauldre, Cher. Region Loire.
Tel 48 58 50 29. Fax 48 58 56 00. Mich 69/F3. Map 2.

BROUSSE-LE-CHATEAU   Relays du Chasteau

Simple hotel/Cooking 1-2
Quiet/Parking

An endearing riverside village pleases the eye; and the efforts of young English-speaking Sybile and Philippe Senegas please both the spirits and taste buds at their unfussy home. Copious regional, *Bourgeois* and classical offerings: *canard aux olives* and *filet de truite à la mer à la crème de Roquefort* most certainly pleased us. Modernised bedrooms.
Menus ACD. Rooms (12) D. Cards Access, Visa.
Closed 19 Dec to 19 Jan. Fri evg and Sat midday (Oct to Apl).
Post 12480 Brousse-le-Château, Aveyron. Region MC (Cévennes).
Tel 65 99 40 15. Mich 140/C4. Map 5.

A100frs & under. B100–135. C135–165. D165–250. E250–350. F350–500. G500+

CABOURG
Pied de Cochon

Comfortable restaurant/Cooking 1-2

You'll nose out the pig's trotter on the D514, just inland from the beach at Le Hôme, 2 km W of Cabourg. Jacqueline and Claude Renard are crafty *patrons*, living up to their surname. Choose from his fish dishes – *moules à la créme crue, soupe de poisson* or fresh-as-daisies filets of fish; or from spit-roasted grills (turned in the dining room fireplace). One highlight: *pied de cochon* with *frites et cresson – bien sûr*.

Menus BDE. Cards Access, Visa. (Rooms: Le Cottage, 2 km to E on D514.)
Closed 16 Jan to 1 Feb. 28 Nov to 14 Dec. Mon evg. Tues.
Post Le Hôme, 14390 Cabourg, Calvados. Region Normandy.
Tel 31 91 27 55. Mich 32/B1. Map 2.

CALAIS
Au Côte d'Argent

Comfortable restaurant/Cooking 2

For many readers Bertrand Lefebvre is the best chef in the busy Channel port. His modern restaurant, overlooking both the Channel and the bustling port entrance – plus the bonus of a huge public car park at the door – is a classical haven. The Menu Douceur (A) keeps wallets full: a filling *caudière*, a fresh-from-the-sea filet of cod in a tangy, perfectly executed *beurre blanc* sauce and a knockout sweet to finish.

Menus ACDE. Cards All. (Rooms: Richelieu & Windsor; both 5 min walk.)
Closed Sun evg. Mon. (Both above *sans rest*; Windsor has garage.)
Post 1 digue G. Berthe, 62100 Calais, Pas-de-Calais. Region North.
Tel 21 34 68 07. Fax 21 96 42 10. Mich 2/B1. Map 2.

CALAIS
Le Channel

Comfortable restaurant/Cooking 2

José (Jo) and Monique Crespo do a great job but don't call with excessive expectations as they can't match the over-the-top sycophancy of some British food writers. Monique speaks English and Jo digs a classical tunnel with, not surprisingly, a significant reliance on fish delights: from *langoustines* to *turbotin*. A channel-wide choice for all courses on menu C (low-end). Cellar? 600 wines and 60,000 bottles.

Menus aCDE. Cards All. (Rooms: Richelieu & Windsor; both 3 min walk.)
Closed 19 Dec to 16 Jan. 5-14 June. Sun evg. Tues. (See previous entry.)
Post 3 bd Résistance, 62100 Calais, Pas-de-Calais. Region North.
Tel 21 34 42 30. Fax 21 97 42 43. Mich 2/B1. Map 2.

A100frs & under. B100–135. C135–165. D165–250. E250–350. F350–500. G500+

CALVINET
Beauséjour

Comfortable restaurant with rooms/Cooking 2
Terrace/Parking

Louis-Bernard Puech is an unsmiling host – which matches the style of the renovated, whitewashed interior. His cooking has a brighter face (*la cuisine d'hier et d'aujourd-hui*) using both local produce and fish and shellfish from distant oceans; examples are a punchy *filet de boeuf rôti sauce Béarnaise* and *chartreuse de tourteaux au jus de crustacés*.
Menus ACE. Rooms (12) DE. Cards Access, Visa.
Closed Mid Jan-mid Feb. 2-9 Oct. Sun evg & Mon (mid Sept-mid June).
Post 15340 Calvinet, Cantal. Region Massif Central (Auvergne).
Tel 71 49 91 68. Fax 71 49 98 63. Mich 126/A4. Map 5.

CANY-BARVILLE
Manoir de Barville

Very comfortable restaurant with rooms/Cooking 2
Secluded/Gardens/Parking

A gorgeous spot, south of the town at the marked *gué* (ford); to avoid the latter approach from the D131. Magnificent trees, the River Durdent, colourful gardens and a handsome house – plus Lionel Morin's classical cooking: a menu of *brouillade d'oeuf aux champignons des bois et avocat, filet de truite de la Durdent* (the delectable river which forms the ford mentioned earlier), cheese and strawberry tart was most enjoyable.
Menus CDE. Rooms (4) DF. Cards Access, Visa.
Post 76450 Cany-Barville, Seine-Maritime. Region Normandy.
Tel 35 97 79 30. Fax 35 57 03 55. Mich 15/E1-E2. Map 2.

CARHAIX-PLOUGUER
Auberge du Poher

Comfortable restaurant/Cooking 1-2
Gardens/Parking

Robert Le Roux's modern *auberge* is at Port de Carhaix, south of the Nantes-Brest Canal. An austere dining room, attractive gardens, stream and views. Classical and *Bourgeoise* grub with a wide choice for each course. Loosen your belts for homely *soupe de poisson, terrine de chef, faux filet grillée, boeuf en daube, truite au Roquefort* and similar.
Menus ABCD. Cards Acc, Visa. (Rooms: D'Ahès, Carhaix-Plouguer.)
Closed 1-21 Feb. 5-18 Sept. Mon.
Post 29270 Carhaix-Plouguer, Finistère. Region Brittany. (SW of town.)
Tel 98 99 51 18. Mich 46/A1. Map 1.

A100frs & under. B100–135. C135–165. D165–250. E250–350. F350–500. G500+

CARNAC
Alignements

Comfortable hotel/Cooking 2
Lift

An all-modern, three-storey hotel with every room having its own minuscule terrace. (On D781 Lorient road.) Menu C offers choice, quality and quantity: a wholesome *assiette de fruits de mer*, an entire *canette de Challans aux épices* (for two) and a calorie-boosting *gâteau aux deux chocolats* will test readers with even the most whopping appetites.
Menus ACD. Rooms (27) EF. Cards Access, Visa.
Closed Hotel: Oct to Easter. Rest: Oct to Apl. Fri midday. Mon. Tues.
Post 45 r. St-Cornély, 56340 Carnac, Morbihan. Region Brittany.
Tel 97 52 06 30. Fax 97 52 76 56. Mich 62/B2. Map 1.

CASTERA-VERDUZAN
Hôtel Ténarèze/Rest. Florida

Simple restaurant with rooms/Cooking 2
Terrace

The stone-built Florida is in a tiny thermal spa. Bernard Ramounéda, a third-generation chef (his grandmother kicked off in 1935), mixes classical, regional and *Bourgeoise*: a typical filling menu C could be *potage, poule farci Henri IV, épaule d'agneau rôtie aux herbes* and *trois chocolates* (*marquise, mousse, glace*). Hotel run as separate business.
Menus a(lunch)CD. Rooms (24) CD. Cards All.
Closed Feb. Sun evg & Mon (Oct to Mar). Rest: Wed (Apl to Sept).
Post 32410 Castéra-Verduzan, Gers. Region Southwest. Map 5.
Tel (R) 62 68 13 22. (H) 62 68 10 22. Fax 62 68 14 69. Mich 151/E2.

CAULIERES
Auberge de la Forge

Very comfortable restaurant/Cooking 2

Once the village *café/tabac/épicerie* and facing the forge which, in times past, must have been kept busy shoeing horses whilst their riders fed *en face*. Alan, the *cuisinier*, and Michele Mauconduit make you welcome at their rustic dining room. Regional and classical fare: from *cuisse de lapin au cidre* (a Normandy tempter) and *ficelle Picarde* (a northern teaser) to *saumon à l'oseille*. (Bedroom annexe planned.)
Menus aBCDE. Cards Access, Visa. (Rooms: Le Cardinal, Poix-de-Picardie.)
Closed Feb school hols. 7-20 Aug. (7 km W of Poix-de-Picardie.)
Post 80590 Caulières, Somme. Regions Normandy/North.
Tel 22 38 00 91. Fax 22 38 08 48. Mich 17/E2. Map 2.

A100frs & under. B100–135. C135–165. D165–250. E250–350. F350–500. G500+

La CHAISE-DIEU   Au Tremblant

Simple hotel/Cooking 1-2
Gardens/Garage/Parking

Jean and Josette Boyer are the third generation at this family *logis*, first opened in 1902. Josette has a beaming smile. Jean's menus are beaming classical and *Bourgeois* with a sofa-wide range of choice: *soufflé de foies de volailles forestières, truite belle meunière, pâté de brochet, loup farci au safran* and *coquelet au vin* are typical.
Menus ABD. Rooms (27) CDE. Cards Access, Visa.
Closed Nov to Apl. (On D906.)
Post 43160 La Chaise-Dieu, Haute-Loire. Region MC (Auvergne).
Tel 71 00 01 85. Mich 128/B1. Map 5.

CHAMBERY   L'Essentiel

Very comfortable restaurant/Cooking 3

As good as any *RQP* cooking in the French Alps. Young Jean-Michel Bouvier, trained by Guérard and Senderens, is a modern cooking addict: a *filet de rouget poêlé à la tapenade dans son jus acidulé aux herbes fraîches* is the Med on a plate; and a *moëlleux au chocolat chaud, glace pistache aux zestes d'orange confits* is an intense, yummy sweet.
(On the ground floor of the Hôtel Mercure – which has its own garage.)
Menus a(lunch)CD. Cards Access, AE, Visa. (Rooms: see Mercure above.)
Closed Sat midday. (Opposite station.)
Post 183 pl. Gare, 73000 Chambéry, Savoie. Region Savoie.
Tel 79 96 97 27. Fax 79 96 17 78. Mich 117/F3. Map 6.

CHAMONIX   Eden

Comfortable restaurant with rooms/Cooking 2
Parking

A blue and white exterior and a stylish, light interior. Odette Lesage is the elegant *patronne*; husband Gérard skis the classical cooking *piste*. Relish the majestic views and also the restrained mastery of accomplished specialities like *terrine de poisson à la croûte d'algues* (in the Alps!) and a tasty *contre filet de boeuf marchand de vin*.
Menus bCDE. Rooms (10) EF. Cards All. (Les Praz is NE of Chamonix.)
Closed 1-15 June. Nov. 1st wk Dec. Tues (not high season).
Post Les Praz, 74400 Chamonix, Haute-Savoie. Region Savoie.
Tel 50 53 06 40. Fax 50 53 51 50. Mich 105/F4. Map 6.

A100frs & under. B100–135. C135–165. D165–250. E250–350. F350–500. G500+

CHAMPAGNAC

Le Lavendès

Comfortable hotel/Cooking 2
Secluded/Gardens/Swimming pool/Parking

The hotel, a handsome old manor house, is gorgeously situated – between the high Auvergne and green Périgord. Louisette Gimmig is the hostess; husband Gérard, a prize-winning desserts champ, paddles classical and regional courses: a *chartreuse de canard confit vinaigrette de pied de porc* and *fondant et sa glace au miel de pays* confirm the latter.
Menus b(lunch)CDE. Rooms (8) FG. Cards Access, Visa.
Closed 15 Nov-Feb. Rest: Sun evg (Oct-15 May). Mon (not evg 15 May-Oct).
Post 15350 Champagnac, Cantal. Regions Dordogne/MC (Auvergne).
Tel 71 69 62 79. Fax 71 69 65 33. Mich 112/A4. Map 5.

CHAPARON

La Châtaigneraie

Comfortable hotel/Cooking 1-2
Secluded/Terrace/Gardens/Tennis/Parking

An alluring setting for a family hotel, led by English-speaking Martine Millet and her husband Robert – a friendly, helpful duo. Competent classical and *Bourgeoise* cooking with a repertoire ranging from *terrine maison* and *filet de haddock fumé sur lit de salade* to a more ambitious, thumpingly good *jambonette de volaille farcie sauce poivre vert.*
Menus a(lunch)BCDE. Rooms (25) F. Cards All. (S of Brédannaz.)
Closed 20 Oct to end Jan. Sun evg and Mon (Oct to Apl).
Post Chaparon, 74210 Faverges, Haute-Savoie. Region Savoie.
Tel 50 44 30 67. Fax 50 44 83 71. Map 118/B1. Map 6.

CHASSELAY

Guy Lassausaie

Comfortable restaurant/Cooking 3
Parking

Brilliant is the word which sums up the efforts of Guy Lassausaie – an imaginative modern master chef. Menu C is culinary largesse: four exuberant courses with two *petites surprises* at start and finish (melon balls in a cream sauce; and a small *crème brûlée*). Of the four courses a *cuisse de lapin braisée à la coriandre et basilic* was scented heaven.
Menus CDEF. Cards All. (Rooms: A6 *autoroute* hotels; Limonest 9 km SW.)
Closed Aug. Tues evg. Wed. (See *FLE* p222 for details of above hotels.)
Post r. Belle-Cize, 69380 Chasselay, Rhône. Region Lyonnais.
Tel 78 47 62 59. Fax 78 47 06 19. Mich 116/A1. Map 6.

A100frs & under. B100–135. C135–165. D165–250. E250–350. F350–500. G500+
258

CHATEAU-ARNOUX

L'Oustaou de la Foun

Comfortable restaurant/Cooking 2-3
Terrace/Parking

Young Natalie and Gérald Jourdan (the chef) have moved from Digne to a gorgeous old farm with cool, stylish, spacious rooms and a pleasing central courtyard. Great emphasis on regional produce and specialities. Gérald's claims that the tastes and perfumes of Haute-Provence dominate his cooking are vividly demonstrated. (2 km N, on N85; near A51 exit.)
Menus BCD. Cards Access, AE, Visa. (Rooms: Ibis, Sisteron; end of A51.)
Closed Wed (out of season). Regions Hautes-Alpes/Provence.
Post Rte Napoléon, 04160 Château-Arnoux, Alpes-de-Haute-Provence.
Tel 92 62 65 30 (and 31). Fax 92 62 65 32. Mich 146/B4. Map 6.

CHATEAUBOURG

Pen'Roc

Comfortable hotel/Cooking 2
Terrace/Gardens/Swimming pool/Lift/Parking

Top marks on all counts for this modern hotel, next door to the Eglise Notre Dame at La Peinière, 6 km east of the town. Colour and brightness dominate both Mireille Froc's rooms and husbands Joseph's cuisine. Clever choice formula. Highlights: an assertive *gelée de lapereau et sa confiture d'oignons* and filling *choucroute du pêcheur.*
Menus bCDE. Rooms (33) EF. Cards All. Regions Brittany/Normandy.
Closed School hols Feb and Nov. Rest: Sun evg (mid Sept to Apl).
Post La Peinière, 35220 Châteaubourg, Ille-et-Vilaine.
Tel 99 00 33 02. Fax 99 62 30 89. Mich 49/D3. Map 1.

CHATEAUNEUF

La Fontaine

Simple restaurant/Cooking 3
Parking

Yves and Anne Jury's tiny home is a touch odd-ball. But there's nowt odd-ball about his modern and neo-classical cooking. Menu C is a superlative *RQP* bargain: perhaps a *salade de saumon fumé au vinaigre balsamique*; some *noix d'agneau au coulis d'olive*; a *fromage du charolais chaud en salade*; and brilliant sweets tagged *délices de la Fontaine.*
Menus bCDE. Cards Access, Visa. (Rooms: Relais de l'Abbaye, Charlieu.)
Closed 22 Jan to 16 Feb. 2-12 Oct. Tues evg. Wed. (Above 10 km to SW.)
Post 71740 Châteauneuf, Saône-et-Loire. Region Lyonnais.
Tel 85 26 26 87. Mich 101/E3. Map 6.

A100frs & under. B100–135. C135–165. D165–250. E250–350. F350–500. G500+
259

CHAUMOUSEY   Le Calmosien

Comfortable restaurant/Cooking 2
Terrace

On the D460, west of Epinal. A whitewashed, window-boxed exterior
hides a *belle époque* interior. Chef Jean-Marc Béati paddles all streams:
huîtres de Cancale aux épinards, julienne de citrons au sel; a
thumpingly tasty *saucisson de canard au foie gras* with *chutney de
pommes vertes*; and *gratin de poires aux amandes* are the proof.
Menus BCDE. Cards All. (Rooms: Epinal; Mercure, Ibis, Ariane & Europe.)
Closed Sun evg. (10 km SW of Epinal.)
Post 37 r. d'Epinal, 88390 Chaumousey, Vosges. Region Alsace.
Tel 29 66 80 77. Fax 29 66 89 41. Mich 59/F3. Map 3.

CHAUSSIN   Voyageurs Chez Bach

Comfortable hotel/Cooking 2
Quiet/Parking

Near *la gare*: don't take ear plugs – there's no line now. Modern *logis*
with forests of greenery in the cool dining room. A cascade of menus
from young Christophe Vernay who plays Bach's Jura tunes adroitly: a
robust *assiette Jurassienne* (mountain ham, *brési, terrine*, etc.); and
feuilleté de quenelles de volaille au vin jaune – a polished melody.
Menus BCDE. Rooms (22) DE. Cards Access, Visa.
Closed 1st 3 wks Jan. Fri evg and Sun evg (not July to Sept).
Post pl. Ancienne Gare, 39120 Chaussin, Jura. Region Jura.
Tel 84 81 80 38. Fax 84 81 83 80. Mich 89/D2. Map 3.

CHONAS L'AMBALLAN   Domaine de Clairefontaine

Comfortable hotel/Cooking 3
Quiet/Terrace/Gardens/Tennis/Parking

Mme Girardon and her chef sons, Philippe (ex-Michel Roux student)
and Hervé, have injected new life into this ideally-situated hotel. Menu
B (top-end) is a good excuse for a visit: *velouté de moules aux fins
légumes, cuissot de volaille farci Grande-mère, fromage blanc* and
caramelised *gratin de poires William* is impressive neo-classical fare.
Menus BDEF. Rooms (14) DEF. Cards All. Regions Lyonnais/MC
(Ardèche). Closed Dec. Jan. Rest: Sat midday (July/Aug). Sun evg. Mon (not
evg July/Aug). Post 38121 Chonas l'Amballan, Isere. (9 km S of Vienne.)
Tel 74 58 81 52. Fax 74 58 80 93. Mich 116/A4. Map 6.

CHOUVIGNY
Gorges de Chouvigny

Simple restaurant with rooms/Cooking 1-2
Secluded/Terrace/Parking

West of Ebreuil and the A71 junction 12 – in a riverside setting on the Sioule's north bank. Bedrooms are in an ivy-covered house across the road. Young Eric and Sylvie Fleury do a sound job. *Cuisine Bourgeoise*: *terrine de saumon*, *truite menunière*, *filet de boeuf Fleury*, *petite friture* and *jambon sec d'Auvergne* – all plain, homely cooking.
Menus ABCD. Rooms (8) DE. Cards Access, Visa.
Closed 19 Dec to end Feb. Tues evg and Wed (mid Sept to May).
Post 03450 Chouvigny, Allier. Regions Berry-Bourbonnais/MC (Auvergne).
Tel 70 90 42 11. Mich 99/F4. Map 5.

La CLAYETTE
Gare

Comfortable restaurant with rooms/Cooking 2
Terrace/Gardens/Swimming pool/Garage/Parking

The well-kitted out *logis* is in the capable hands of Simone Thoral and her classicist *cuisinier* husband Michel. Even menu A is a humdinger: perhaps a *dodine de colvert aux noisettes*, *confiture d'oignons* to start; then *cuisse de pain farcie à l'ail et aux olives noires*, *sauce au romorain*; finishing with *fromage blanc à la crème*. Beat that for RQP.
Menus ABCDE. Rooms (8) DEF. Cards Access, Visa. (S entrance to town.)
Closed 25 Dec to 15 Jan. Sun evg (not July/Aug). Mon.
Post av. Gare, 71800 La Clayette, Saône-et-Loire. Region Lyonnais.
Tel 85 28 01 65. Fax 85 28 03 13. Mich 101/E3. Map 6.

CLEDER
Le Baladin

Comfortable restaurant/Cooking 2

In a quiet side street, east of the church. One welcome innovation is that you can try different wines by the glass: just ask. Monsieur Queffelec's dining room is spartan but his cooking is most certainly not. Modern and classical: an aromatic *fricassée de rable de lapin et tabac forestière* with the counterpoint of a spicy *jambonette de canard aux poivres vertes*. (For rooms use Roscoff's *sans rest* hotels.)
Menus ACD. Cards Access, Visa. (Rooms: several hotels at Roscoff to NE.)
Closed Mon and Tues evg (not July and Aug).
Post 9 r. Armorique, 29233 Cléder, Finistère. Region Brittany.
Tel 98 69 42 48. Mich 27D1. Map 1.

A100frs & under. B100–135. C135–165. D165–250. E250–350. F350–500. G500+

COGNAC
Pigeons Blancs

Very comfortable restaurant with rooms/Cooking 2-3
Terrace/Gardens/Parking

A young family trio: Jacques Tachet is *le cuisinier*; brother Jean-Michel is *le sommelier*; and sister Catherine is *la patronne*. Elegance radiates in all areas: in the 17thC *relais de poste*; in the furnishings; and in the neo-classical dishes. Menu C, Le Nez du Marché, is a spontaneous affair: *⅓ produits extra frais, ⅓ savoir, ⅓ d'amitié*.
Menus BCD. Rooms (7) EF. Cards All. (On D731 Poitiers road.)
Closed Rest: 6-19 Jan. Sun evg.
Post 110 r. J.-Brisson, 16100 Cognac, Charente. Region Poitou-Charentes.
Tel 45 82 16 36. Fax 45 82 29 29. Mich 107/E2. Map 4.

La COLLE-SUR-LOUP
La Belle Epoque

Comfortable restaurant/Cooking 2
Terrace/Gardens/Parking

The clue to the décor is in the restaurant name: old-world charm, a seductive terrace and clever lighting come darkness. Michelle Frédéric is a seductive hostess; husband Jean-Pierre is happy with both classical and Provençal plats. Home-made *assiette de ravioli, daube d'agneau à l'Avignonnaise* and all the chef's desserts have won readers' praise.
Menus BCD. Cards All. (Rooms: nearby Marc Hély.). Closed 5 Jan-5 Feb. Tues *midi* & Wed *midi* (July/Aug). Mon evg & Tues (Sept-June).
Post 06480 La Colle-sur-Loup, Alpes-Maritimes. Region Côte d'Azur.
Tel 93 20 10 92. Fax 93 20 29 66. Mich 165/D4. Map 6. (On D6 to SE.)

La COLLE-SUR-LOUP
La Stréga

Comfortable restaurant/Cooking 2
Terrace/Parking

An unprepossessing exterior (easily missed) but a pretty Provençal interior. A light, neo-classical and modern approach from chef Gilbert Stella. *Fleurs de courgette farcies à la mousseline de rascasse* can be so fresh you may even see the flowers being delivered. Wine and coffee included on cheapest menu; and *Brie* cheese on more expensive version.
Menus CD. Cards Access, Visa. (Rooms: nearby Marc Hély. Both on D6.)
Closed Jan. Feb. Sun evg (out of season). Mon. Tues *midi* (July/Aug).
Post 06480 La Colle-sur-Loup, Alpes-Maritimes. Region Côte d'Azur.
Tel 93 22 62 37. Mich 165/D4. Map 6. (On D6 to SE of village.)

A100frs & under. B100–135. C135–165. D165–250. E250–350. F350–500. G500+

COLLIOURE La Frégate

Comfortable hotel/Cooking 2
Terrace/Lift

A fiery, English-speaking maverick, Yves Costa has managed to fall out with both the main French guides. Short-fuse Catalan he may be – but he's a cracking chef, capable of creative fireworks. A wide choice of *Catalane*, classical and modern: *anchois de Collioure à l'escalivade*, *moules à la "Sang et Or"*, *riz Frégate* (a *paella* filler), *filet de boeuf sauce Béarnaise* and *crème Catalane* are typical sparklers.
Menus BCD. Rooms (24) EFG. Cards Access, Visa. Region Languedoc-Rouss.
Post 24 bd Camille-Pelletan, 66190 Collioure, Pyrénées-Orientales.
Tel 68 82 06 05. Fax 68 82 55 00. Mich 177/F3. Map 5. (NW of château.)

COLLIOURE Nouvelle Vague

Comfortable restaurant/Cooking 2
Terrace

Claude Nourtier, the young owner, is a passionate champion of both *Catalane* cuisine and Roussillon wines. The Menu Catalan (low-end C) could include *les rillettes de pain à la fleur de thym*, *les figues au vinaigre* (two flavours not quite jelling); *"paupilles" d'agneau aux pignons et à la Soubressade*; and a luscious *crème Catalane*.
Menus ACE. Cards Access, Visa. (Rooms: Casa Païral and Madeloc.)
Closed 1-18 Mar. 1-18 Dec. Sun evg (out of season). Mon (not evgs high season). Post 7 r. Voltaire, 66190 Collioure, Pyrénées-Orientales.
Tel 68 82 23 88. Mich 177/F3. Map 5. Region Lang-Rouss. (S of château.)

COLOMBEY-LES-DEUX-EGLISES Auberge Montagne

Comfortable restaurant with rooms/Cooking 2
Quiet/Gardens/Parking

A hatful of pluses here: away from the busy N19; Arlette Natali is an attentive *patronne*; and her extrovert husband Gérard is a competent chef. Appetite-quenching *plats*: a duo of *hures – sanglier et lapereau* composed of one slice of each in jelly; and several rounds of tasty *noix de veau aux pleurottes*. Debits? Small bedrooms; moody waitress.
Menus bCDE. Rooms (7) DE. Cards Access, Visa.
Closed Mid Jan to mid Feb. Mon evg. Tues. Region Champagne-Ard.
Post 52330 Colombey-les-deux-Eglises, Haute-Marne.
Tel 25 01 51 69. Fax 25 01 53 20. Mich 57/F3. Map 3.

A100frs & under. B100–135. C135–165. D165–250. E250–350. F350–500. G500+

COMBEAUFONTAINE

Balcon

Comfortable hotel/Cooking 2
Garage

Yvette & Christian Parnet (Oye-et-Pallet: Jura *FLE* p175) gave me the nod about their *copains* – Claudine, *la patronne*, and chef Gérard Gauthier. He's a classical/neo-classical fan but also finds room for exemplary Jura gems: *petite salade de brési au vinaigre de Xérès* and *poulet au vin jaune et morilles* are two examples. Super passion fruit *bavarois*.
Menus CDEF. Rooms (18) CDEF. Cards All.
Closed 27 Dec to 12 Jan. 25 June to 3 July. Sun evg. Mon.
Post 70120 Combeaufontaine, Haute-Saône. Regions Jura/Champagne-Ard.
Tel 84 92 11 13. Fax 84 92 15 89. Mich 75/E2. Map 3.

CONCARNEAU

Les Sables Blancs

Comfortable hotel/Cooking 1-2
Terrace

The aptly-labelled Chabrier family *logis*, north-west of the port, has its toes in the beach and sea. Dishes are artistically presented. Aromatic *soupe de poissons maison, moules à la crème* (60 no less), melt-in-the-mouth *magret de canard*, *riz au curry* as a vegetable, and flashy *galette Concarnoise flambée*. Plenty of half-bottles of wine.
Menus ABC. Rooms (48) E. Cards Access, DC, Visa.
Closed November to March. Region Brittany.
Post Plage Sables Blancs, 29182 Concarneau, Finistère. Mich 45/D3.
Tel 98 97 01 39 (98 97 86 93 – out of season). Fax 98 50 65 88. Map 1.

Le CONQUET

Pointe Ste-Barbe

Comfortable hotel/Cooking 1-2
Lift/Parking

An ugly, ultra-modern concrete and glass structure with a spectacular site on rocks above the sea – west of Brest. Great views. Menu C has vast choice with fish specialities predominating. Classical sauces – *Béarnaise, hollandaise, beurre blanc* and *mayonnaise* – served with salmon, white fish and crab as examples. Also various meat dishes.
Menus aCDF. Rooms (49) CEFG. Disabled. Cards All.
Closed 11 Nov to 16 Dec. Mon (mid Sept to June).
Post 29217 Le Conquet, Finistère. Region Brittany.
Tel 98 89 00 26. Fax 98 89 14 81. Mich 26/A3. Map 1.

A100frs & under. B100–135. C135–165. D165–250. E250–350. F350–500. G500+

CORDON   Le Cordonant

Comfortable hotel/Cooking 1-2
Secluded/Terrace/Parking

A flower-bedecked chalet with the most friendly of owners in the shape of Gisèle Pugnat. Stand on the flower-filled terrace, turn your eyes south-east and revel in the superb view of the Mont Blanc *massif*. Alain Pugnat keeps his fare simple: *fera au beurre blanc, gigot d'agneau rôti, osso bucco* and similar temptations. Utterly enjoyable in every sense.
Menus bCD. Rooms (16) E. Cards Access, Visa.
Closed 1st 2 wks May. 24 Sept to 18 Dec.
Post 74700 Cordon, Haute-Savoie. Region Savoie.
Tel 50 58 34 56. Mich 105/E4. Map 6.

CORPS   Poste

Comfortable restaurant with rooms/Cooking 2
Terrace/Garage

Young Gilbert and Christiane Delas are steaming ahead. Their extrovert N85 outpost is a huge success. Now they've also opened the swish Ch. des Herbeys at St-Firmin (to the SE; pool and calm). A classical course at the Poste from Gilbert, once chef on the liner *France*. Even the cheapest menu offers wide-choice, four-course, appetite-scuttling grub.
Menus bCD. Rooms (20) DEF. Cards Access, Visa.
Closed Dec to 20 Jan.
Post 38970 Corps, Isère. Regions Hautes-Alpes/Savoie.
Tel 76 30 00 03. Fax 76 30 02 73. Mich 132/A3. Map 6.

COULON   Central

Comfortable restaurant/Cooking 1-2
Terrace

The name is spot on; central it is. Anny Monnet is the *cuisinière* at this smart *logis*; husband Jean is the attentive front-of-house boss. Be sure to make a reservation if you want to punt with classical treats such as *daube de joue de boeuf à l'ancienne* and *oeufs à la neige*. Lots of local produce: *mogettes* (small pulse beans) for example.
Menus aCD. Cards Access, Visa. (Rooms: Espace; N11, 5 km SW of Niort.)
Closed 8 Jan to 1 Feb. 18 Sept to 12 Oct. Sun evg. Mon.
Post 79510 Coulon, Deux-Sèvres. Region Poitou-Charentes.
Tel 49 35 90 20. Fax 49 35 81 07. Mich 93/F2. Map 4.

A100frs & under. B100–135. C135–165. D165–250. E250–350. F350–500. G500+

COULONGES-SUR-L'AUTIZE   Citronnelle

Simple restaurant/Cooking 1-2
Terrace

An airy dining room with a sun-trap terrace for warm days. *Chef/patron*
Eddy Zefner is mad keen on red cars (note the Ferrari models); his own
runabout is an Alfa. Colourful cooking covering the spectrum of culinary
styles: *salade multicolore à la hure de langue, omble chevalier fourré à
la crème de St-Jacques aux pistaches* and *mouclade au curry*.
Menus ABCD. Cards Access, AE, Visa. (Rooms: St-Nicolas, Maillezais.)
Closed Sun evg. Mon. (Above *sans rest* hotel easy drive to SW.)
Post 79160 Coulonges-sur-l'Autize, Deux-Sèvres.
Tel 49 06 17 67. Mich 93/F1. Map 4. Region Poitou-Charentes.

COUR-CHEVERNY   Trois Marchands

Comfortable hotel/Cooking 1-2
Parking

The Bricault family, from father to son, have owned the hotel since 1865.
Classical cooking from the past, too, with some Sologne flavours: among
them *fricassée de girolles*, *cuisse de grenouilles fraîches*, asparagus and
chicken breast in a cream sauce. Jean-Jacques, the latest Bricault, is an
uncommunicative *patron*. Readers dislike annexe rooms.
Menus bCDE. Rooms (37) CDE. Cards All.
Closed Feb to mid March. Mon (Oct to Easter).
Post 41700 Cour-Cheverny, Loir-et-Cher. Region Loire.
Tel 54 79 96 44. Fax 54 79 25 60. Mich 68/C3. Map 2.

COURLANS   Auberge de Chavannes

Very comfortable restaurant/Cooking 3-4
Terrace/Gardens/Parking

Taste is everything to chef Pierre Carpentier. Flavours dominate his
modern, classical and neo-classical repertoire. Menu C (top-end) is a
steal (choice for each course). How about a luscious *terrine fondante de
pigeon*, a *poupeton de volaille de Bresse rôti* and *chariot de desserts*.
Monique Carpentier is an elegant, knowledgeable *patronne/sommelière*.
Menus CE. Cards Access, Visa. (Rooms: Comfort Inn Primevère, N of Lons.)
Closed Feb. 26 June to 3 July. Sun evg. Mon. Region Jura.
Post 39570 Courlans, Jura. (On N78, 6 km W of Lons-le-Saunier.)
Tel 84 47 05 52. Mich 89/D4. Map 3.

A100frs & under. B100–135. C135–165. D165–250. E250–350. F350–500. G500+

CRESSERONS

La Valise Gourmande

Very comfortable restaurant/Cooking 2-3
Terrace/Gardens/Parking

A wisteria-clad, 18thC *maison Bourgeoise*. Jean-Jacques Hélie's culinary *valise* includes classical and regional tricks. From menu B (low-end) choose from *moules marinières, soupe de poissons* or *terrine de foies de volaille*; next *coq au vin, pavé aux poivres* or *poisson*; then *tartes aux fruits, glaces* or *teurgoule (terrine de riz au lait à la cannelle)*.
Menus BDE. Cards Access, AE, Visa. (Rooms: Novotel, Ibis, etc. at Caen.)
Closed Xmas to New Year. Sun evg. Mon. (All above hotels N side Caen.)
Post rte Lion-sur-Mer, 14440 Cresserons, Calvados. Region Normandy.
Tel 31 37 39 10. Mich 32/B1. Map 2.

CREST

Grand Hôtel

Simple hotel/Cooking 2

Danielle and René Lattiers' *logis* is 200 metres or so from the Tour de Crest, a formidable medieval dungeon reckoned to have the highest walls in France. Chef René's cooking is no less formidable with classical and *Bourgeois plats* in each of the multi-choice menus. Step back in time to *terrine de foies, truite meunière, faux filet marchand de vin, gigot d'agneau au thym, crème caramel* and *pêche Melba* (an ubiquitous dame).
Menus aBD. Rooms (22) CDE. Cards Access, Visa. Closed 22 Dec to 20 Jan. School hols Feb. Sun evg (Sept to mid June). Mon (not evg Apl to Oct).
Post 60 r. Hôtel de Ville, 26400 Crest, Drôme. Regions Hte-Alpes/Savoie.
Tel 75 25 08 17. Fax 75 25 46 42. Mich 130/B4. Map 6.

CROIX-MARE

Auberge de la Forge

Comfortable restaurant/Cooking 2
Parking

Don't be put off by the run-down, decrepit exterior. Three immaculate rustic dining rooms (once separate cottages) will cheer you up no end. A mix of styles from Christian Truttmann: *oeufs cocotte crème de haddock, escalope de saumon frais crème de courgettes au curry* and *pièce de boeuf sauce marinade* are a typical filling, flavoursome trio. (Park at rear.)
Menus ACE. Cards Acc, AE, Visa. (Rooms: Havre at nearby Yvetot to NW.)
Closed Tues evg and Wed (not public hols).
Post N15, Croix-Mare, 76190 Yvetot, Seine-Maritime. Region Normandy.
Tel 35 91 25 94. Mich 15/F3. Map 2.

A 100frs & under. B 100–135. C 135–165. D 165–250. E 250–350. F 350–500. G 500+

CROZANT   Auberge de la Vallée

Comfortable restaurant/Cooking 1-2

I've had mixed reports on the *auberge* (hence the low rating) – with waitresses dressed in Marchois folk costumes. Françoise Guilleminot and daughter Béatrice are *les patronnes*; and husband Jean turns classical, regional and *Bourgeoises* pedals in the kitchen. *Jambon demi sel au porto*; *aloyau* (sirloin) *Limousin rôti* (famed beef); and *magret de canard aux cèpes* (equally acclaimed local mushrooms) are three examples.
Menus aBCE. Cards Access, DC, Visa. (Rooms: nearby Lac – *sans rest.*)
Closed Jan. Mon evg and Tues (not July/Aug).
Post 23160 Crozant, Creuse. Region Poitou-Charentes.
Tel 55 89 80 03. Mich 97/E2. Map 5.

CUCUGNAN   Auberge de Cucugnan

Simple restaurant/Cooking 1-2
Parking

Climb the stepped lanes to reach the *auberge*, once a barn. The village is within sight of two of the famous Cathar castles. Menu A is not for the diet squeamish: start with either a plate of *crudités* or a *charcuterie* assortment; then *coq au vin*, *lapin au saupiquet* or *pintadeau en salmis*; vegetables; cheese; dessert. Surely you are not still peckish?
Menus ACD. Cards Access, Visa. (Rooms: Alta Riba at Rivesaltes to ESE.)
Closed Wed (Jan to March.) (Above has lift, garage and parking.)
Post 11350 Cucugnan, Aude. Region Languedoc-Roussillon.
Tel 68 45 40 84. Fax 68 45 01 52. Mich 175/F2. Map 5.

CUISEAUX   Commerce

Comfortable restaurant with rooms/Cooking 2
Swimming pool/Garage/Parking

A stone-built *logis* in an evocative village, bypassed by the very busy N83. Jean and Viviane Vuillot are regional addicts, *naturellement* – but we chose the oh-so-welcome, light Menu Pêcheur: a *rosace de langoustines au beurre de safran* (choice of 3 courses); *filet de sandre à l'oseille* (choice of 2); *fromage blanc à la crème*; and strawberry ice-cream.
Menus ABCDE. Rooms (16) DE. Cards Access, Visa.
Closed 20 June-4 July. 30 Sept-8 Oct. Mon (not bedrooms in season).
Post 71480 Cuiseaux, Saône-et-Loire. Regions Jura/Lyonnais.
Tel 85 72 71 79. Fax 85 72 54 22. Mich 103/E1. Map 6.

A100frs & under. B100–135. C135–165. D165–250. E250–350. F350–500. G500+

DABISSE
Vieux Colombier

Comfortable restaurant/Cooking 2-3
Terrace/Parking

An old farm and once a *relais de poste*. A rustic dining room with a handsome terrace, shaded by two proud trees. Sylvain Nowak is an inventive modern cook, doing a remarkable job in an out-of-the-way spot. Worth a detour for tomatoes stuffed with *ratatouille* and *chèvre, sauce basilic*; and *pintadeau poêlée aux gousses d'ail en chemise*.
Menus CD. Cards Access, Visa. (Rooms: Villiard at St-Auban to N.)
Closed 2-8 Jan. Sun evg (Oct to May). Wed. Regions Htes-Alpes/Provence.
Post Dabisse, 04190 Les Mées, Alpes-de-Haute-Provence.
Tel 92 34 32 32. Fax 92 34 34 26. Mich 146/A4. Map 6. (S of village.)

Les DEUX-ALPES
Chalet Mounier

Comfortable hotel/Cooking 2
Gardens/Swimming pools (indoor & outdoor)/Tennis/Lift/Parking

Great facilities (see above) and a heart-stopping view from the cliff at the end of the gardens – over Venosc and the Véneon Valley. The chalet is busy; some details need polishing up. Menu C could include a starter, then spicy *meurson en brioche* (a tasty pork sausage), *filet de flétan à la creme de ciboulette* and an absolutely top-notch dessert.
Menus bCD. Rooms (48) EFG. Cards Access, Visa.
Closed May. June. 4 Sept to 17 Dec.
Post 38860 Les Deux-Alpes, Isère. Regions Hautes-Alpes/Savoie.
Tel 76 80 56 90. Fax 76 79 56 51. Mich 132/B2. Map 6.

DIE
La Petite Auberge

Comfortable restaurant with rooms/Cooking 2
Terrace/Parking

No wonder readers have enthused over the years about Maryse Montero and her warm welcome and the classical cooking of her husband Patrick. The chef, now 45, once worked for three-star gods Bocuse and Outhier in his 20s; the couple settled in Die in 1979. Culinary fireworks could include *le meilleur du boeuf poêlé à la moelle* – lip-smackingly good.
Menus aBD. Rooms (11) CDE. Cards Access, Visa. Closed 15 Dec-15 Jan. 17-24 Sept. Sun evg & Wed (not July/Aug). Mon (July/Aug).
Post av. Sadi-Carnot, 26150 Die, Drôme. Regions Hautes-Alpes/Savoie.
Tel 75 22 05 91. Fax 75 22 24 60. Mich 131/D4. Map 6. (Opposite *gare*.)

A 100frs & under. B 100–135. C 135–165. D 165–250. E 250–350. F 350–500. G 500+

DIGOIN

Gare

Comfortable restaurant with rooms/Cooking 2-3
Gardens/Parking

Jean-Pierre and Jacqueline Mathieu have won praise from readers since they bought the Gare – after Billoux moved to Dijon. Jean-Pierre paints a classical canvas. Menu C has a palette of brights colours: *feuilletés chauds de lièvre sur son lit de verdure* and *panaché de poissons de mer aux baies roses* are invigorating *plats.* (Some rooms noisy.)
Menus bCDE. Rooms (13) EF. Cards Access, Visa.
Closed Mid Jan to mid Feb. Wed (not July & Aug). Region Berry-Bourb.
Post 79 av. Gén. de Gaulle, 71160 Digoin, Saône-et-Loire.
Tel 85 53 03 04. Fax 85 53 14 70. Mich 101/D2. Map 5.

DINAN

Caravelle

Comfortable restaurant/Cooking 2-3

Menu B is a wide-choice *RQP* stunner. Consider the evidence: to start perhaps a *lapereau en gelée, crépinette aux herbes, marmalade d'oignons et de primeurs* – intense and colourful; then a *tranche de lieu doré au paprika* – pretty and punchy; next pungent cheeses; and, finally, an unabashedly sweety treat – *crêpes soufflé aux cerises à la verveine de jardin.* Bravo Jean-Claude (the chef) and Christiane Marmion.
Menus BDEF. Cards All. (Rooms: Arvor – 5 min walk SE; parking.)
Closed 14-23 Mar. 11 Nov to 3 Dec. Sun evg. Wed (Oct to mid June).
Post 14 pl. Duclos, 22100 Dinan, Côtes d'Armor. Region Brittany.
Tel 96 39 00 11. Mich 29/F3. Map 1.

DINAN

Les Grands Fossés

Comfortable restaurant/Cooking 2
Parking

The bespectacled duo, Alain and Jacqueline Colas, opened their *maison Bourgeoise*, opposite the ramparts (NW corner), in 1990. Relish Alain's neo-classical offerings in two handsome dining rooms: an ace *terrine de ris de veau à l'hydromel*; melting *ballotin de julienne* (fish), *sauce à l'oseille*; and a pretty-as-a-picture *palette des sorbets.*
Menus ACE. Cards Access, Visa. (Rooms: du Bas Frêne, 2 km to W.)
Closed 25-31 Jan. Thurs.
Post 2 pl. Gén. Leclerc, 22100 Dinan, Côtes d'Armor. Region Brittany.
Tel 96 39 21 50. Mich 29/F3. Map 1.

A100frs & under. B100–135. C135–165. D165–250. E250–350. F350–500. G500+

DOL-DE-BRETAGNE
La Bresche Arthur

Comfortable restaurant with rooms/Cooking 2
Gardens/Parking

Philippe Martel's refurbished *logis* (fire damaged shortly after he bought the property) is liked by readers. Revitalised, pick-me-up, modern fare (he's well named): *carpaccio de saumon à la vinaigrette de concombre, escalopes de barbue en vapeur d'algues et petits oignons nouveaux* and a *crème brûlée à la vanille* remain Cognac-clear memories.
Menus ABD. Rooms (24) DE. Cards Access, Visa.
Closed 2nd half Jan. Rest: Wed (Oct to June). Region Brittany.
Post 36 bd Deminiac, 35120 Dol-de-Bretagne, Ille-et-Vilaine.
Tel 99 48 01 44. Fax 99 48 16 32. Mich 48/B1. Map 1.

DUCEY
Auberge de la Sélune

Comfortable hotel/Cooking 2
Gardens

The small, weed-choked gardens have a view of the Sélune, a famed salmon river. Chef Jean-Pierre Girres and his wife Josette offer classical catches such as *terrine d'aubergine, paupiettes de saumon, pie au crabe* (soup with a pastry topper), *truite soufflée à la ducéene* and, alas, an absolutely comatose *tarte aux pommes* (cooking rating of zero).
Menus aBCD. Rooms (19) E. Cards All.
Closed Mid Jan to mid Feb. Mon (Oct to Feb).
Post 50220 Ducey, Manche. Regions Brittany/Normandy.
Tel 33 48 53 62. Fax 33 48 90 30. Mich 30/C4. Map 1.

DUCLAIR
Poste

Comfortable restaurant with rooms/Cooking 2
Lift

A busy site beside the Seine. The restaurant is on the first floor and the bustling river traffic and ferry ensure there's never a dull visual moment. Eric Montier does the same with his classical dishes: *terrine de canard au porto, filet de lotte sauce Nantua, fromage blanc* and a *tarte Normande* makes a great lunch. (Also separate cheaper "Grill".)
Menus aBCD. Rooms (19) DE. Cards All.
Closed School hols in Feb, Nov and at Xmas. Sun evg. Mon.
Post 76480 Duclair, Seine-Maritime. Region Normandy.
Tel 35 37 50 04. Fax 35 37 39 19. Mich 15/F3. Map 2.

A100frs & under. B100–135. C135–165. D165–250. E250–350. F350–500. G500+

DUINGT

Lac

Comfortable hotel/Cooking 2
Terrace/Gardens/Lake swimming/Lift/Parking

An exquisite setting: gorgeous views and the modernised hotel's toes literally in Lac d'Annecy. Thierry and Anne Borsoi are justifiably proud of their tonic hotel. Chef Marc Catellani treads water in the modern cooking pool: delight in exuberant catches like *bisquit de truite rose au curry* and *carpaccio de volaille en marinière de sauce vierge*.
Menus BCD. Rooms (23) EF. Cards Access, Visa.
Closed Hotel: Nov to 8 Feb. Sun (not May to Sept). Rest: Oct to Apl.
Post 74410 Duingt, Haute-Savoie. Region Savoie. Map 6.
Tel (R) 50 68 95 87. (H) 50 68 90 90. Fax 50 68 50 18. Mich 118/B1.

DUNKERQUE

Le Soubise

Very comfortable restaurant/Cooking 2
Gardens/Parking

Well clear of Dunkerque – at Coudekerque-Branche, south of the A16 and on W side of D916. Don't be put off by the scruffy frontage. Michel Hazebroucq is a creative classicist. His *saumon et canard* menu C has six starters and seven main courses. How about *carpaccio de canard*, *cotelettes de saumon grillées Béarnaise* and a *chocolat/nougat* dessert?
Menus ACD. Cards All. (Rooms: Campanile & Hôtel du Lac, 5 km W, Lac d'Armbouts-Cappel.) Closed Sat midday. Sun evg.
Post 49 rte Bergues, 59210 Coudekerque-Branche, Nord. Region North.
Tel 28 64 66 00. Fax 28 25 12 19. Mich 3/D1. Map 2.

DUN-LE-PALESTEL

Joly

Simple hotel/Cooking 2

The Creuse *département* is ideal walking and cycling *pays*. No wonder then that Claude Monceaux is happy to welcome walkers and cyclists to his *logis*; he's well equipped to give you sound advice on the best terrain. Step back in time at Joly: to Jacqueline's dining room; and to her husband's classical treats. A *faux-filet de Limousin mousseline de cèpes* is a local *terroir* joy. Also a welcome Special Poissons Menu (A).
Menus ACD. Rooms (26) DE. Cards Access, Visa.
Closed 1st 3 wks Mar. 4-24 Oct. Sun evg. Mon midday.
Post 23800 Dun-le-Palestel, Creuse. Region Poitou-Charentes.
Tel 55 89 00 23. Fax 55 89 15 89. Mich 97/E3. Map 5.

A100frs & under. B100–135. C135–165. D165–250. E250–350. F350–500. G500+

DURBAN-CORBIERES   Le Moulin

Very comfortable restaurant/Cooking 3-4
Swimming pool/Parking

What a stunning show. All the staff, led by Corinne Moreno, speak English. The dining room is semi-circular with panoramic windows. Chef David Moreno, a Spaniard, lives and breathes good taste. Menu C could be a *tarte fine de tomate et anchois* – clearcut simplicity; a fish creation; a choice of 40 cheeses; and a sumptuous *crème brûlée*.
Menus CDE. Cards Acc, Visa. (Rooms: *autoroute* hotels S Narbonne.)
Closed 15 Oct-15 Mar. Sun evg & Mon (not July/Aug). (Above easy drive.)
Post 11360 Durban-Corbières, Aude. Region Languedoc-Roussillon.
Tel 68 45 81 03. Fax 68 45 83 31. Mich 172/C3. Map 5.

DURY   La Bonne Auberge

Comfortable restaurant/Cooking 2
Parking

A retina-searing, flower-covered exterior with a touch forced rustic interior. Nowt forced or prissy about Raoul Beaussire's regional and classical juggling. Menu C has a good range of choice: a typical meal could start with *ficelles Picardes*, move on to *pintade crème de champignon* and finish with a copious *fruits de jour Melba*.
Menus CD. Cards Access, AE, Visa. (Rooms: Novotel to E; N of Boves.)
Closed Sun evg and Mon. (Above hotel near junction N29/D934.)
Post 63 rte National (N1), 80480 Dury, Somme. Region North.
Tel 22 95 03 33. Mich 17/F1. Map 2.

ECHIGEY   Place (Rey)

Comfortable restaurant with basic rooms/Cooking 1-2
Gardens/Parking

A quiet village, south-east of Dijon. The *logis* is well-appointed and has basic but adequate bedrooms. Chef Dany Rey offers a good choice for each course. Nothing flashy with *plats* such as a shrimp and avocado cocktail; gutsy *pièce de boeuf* – touch spoiled by veg overpowered with nutmeg; top-notch cheese chariot; and dessert trolley. All on menu a.
Menus aCD. Rooms (13) BCD. Cards Access, DC, Visa.
Closed Jan. 1st wk Aug. Sun evg. Mon (not public hols).
Post Echigey, 21110 Genlis, Côte-d'Or. Region Burgundy.
Tel 80 29 74 00. Fax 80 29 79 55. Mich 88/C1. Map 3.

A100frs & under. B100–135. C135–165. D165–250. E250–350. F350–500. G500+

EMBRUN   Mairie

Simple hotel/Cooking 1-2
Terrace

The *logis* is at the heart of Embrun, opposite the Fontaine St-Pierre (follow signs for Centre Ville/Hôtel de Ville). Jean-Pierre François is from the Southwest, hence his fondness for *foie gras de canard* and *magret de canard fumé*. Menu A represents great *RQP* with a good choice (extra for *foie gras*, *bien sûr*). Classical and *Bourgeoise* grub.
Menus A. Rooms (22) DE. Cards All.
Closed 10-29 May. Oct. Nov. Sun and Mon (Oct to May but not sch. hols).
Post pl. Mairie, 05200 Embrun, Hautes-Alpes. Regions Htes-Alpes/Savoie.
Tel 92 43 20 65. Fax 92 43 47 02. Mich 147/D1. Map 6.

ESPALION   Le Méjane

Comfortable restaurant/Cooking 3-4

The cooking rating gives the clue to how impressed we were at this most beguiling of *Franc-wise France* recommendations; we can't wait to return. A young couple going places: Régine Caralp, a vibrant, vivacious hostess; and husband Philippe, a confident, modern master with an eye for technique, presentation and good taste. One dish, a *jambonette de pintade rôtie, jus reduit au vin rouge* was a superb showpiece.
Menus BCD. Cards All. (Rooms: Moderne or simpler Central—20 m away.)
Closed Feb school hols. 26 June to 1 July. Sun evg (not Aug). Wed.
Post r. Méjane, 12500 Espalion, Aveyron. Regions MC (Auvergne/Cévennes).
Tel 65 48 22 37. Mich 140/C1. Map 5. (South of Lot, E of D920.)

ETANG-SUR-ARROUX   Hostellerie du Gourmet

Comfortable restaurant with basic rooms/Cooking 1-2

The geranium-edged frontage is a bright and welcome sight at the Caboche *hostellerie* on the southern main road (D994) entrance to the village. Copious and anything but dull could describe a lunch of *salade de noix de pétoncles au vinaigre de framboise*; followed by, first, a *filet de julienne sauce crustacé* and, next, a *contrefilet vigneronne*; then *fromage* and, to finish, a large slice of *tarte aux pommes*.
Menus aCD. Rooms (12) CD. Cards Access, Visa.
Closed January.
Post 71190 Etang-sur-Arroux, Saône-et-Loire. Region Burgundy.
Tel 85 82 20 88. Mich 87/D3-E3. Map 3.

A100frs & under. B100–135. C135–165. D165–250. E250–350. F350–500. G500+

EUGENIE-LES-BAINS
La Ferme aux Grives

Simple restaurant/Cooking 3
Terrace

Enterprise 4 in the growing *"Village Minceur"* Eugénie empire of 3-star chef Michel Guérard. Rustic conversion and *la cuisine rustique* – using local produce and old recipes. Vast choice: a suckling pig turning on the spit in the huge fireplace, superb soups, Landes *terrines*, black puddings, *cochon de lait*, roast duck, meringues and *tartes*. First-class service.
Menus C. Cards Access, Visa. (Rooms: Maison Rose or Adour at Aire to E.)
Closed Dec/Jan (not Xmas/New Yr). Mon evg & Tues (10 July-10 Sept).
Public hols. Post 40320 Eugénie-les-Bains, Landes. Region Southwest.
Tel 58 51 19 08. Fax 58 51 13 59. Mich 150/A2. Map 4.

Les EYZIES-DE-TAYAC
Cro-Magnon

Very comfortable hotel/Cooking 3
Terrace/Gardens/Swimming pool/Parking

Anne and I have loved the vine-covered hotel and the genuine, caring owners, Jacques and Christiane Leyssales, for almost 35 years. Menu C (low-end) gives you the chance to understand another one of the reasons why you should visit: a subtle tasting *morue fraîche à l'anchoïade*; *fricassée de pintadeau aux Xérès*; and strawberries and cream.
Menus CDEF. Rooms (18) FG. Cards All.
Closed 10 Oct to end April. Rest: Wed midday.
Post 24620 Les Eyzies-de-Tayac, Dordogne. Region Dordogne.
Tel 53 06 97 06. Fax 53 06 95 45. Mich 123/F3. Map 5.

FALAISE
Poste

Comfortable hotel/Cooking 1-2
Parking

The only debit at the Poste is the main road site. Everything else is a credit: an informative *patronne*, Simone Collias, is one pleasing plus; another is her judo-loving husband Michel's classical repertoire. (He's also a pilot: take an aerial tour.) Limited choice: *tête de veau ravigote* and *entrecôte grillée sauce moelle* are typical dishes.
Menus aBCD. Rooms (21) DEF. Cards Access, AE, Visa.
Closed 17-23 Oct. 20 Dec to 20 Jan. Sun evg. Mon (not hotel).
Post 38 r. G. Clemenceau, 14700 Falaise, Calvados. Region Normandy.
Tel 31 90 13 14. Fax 31 90 01 81. Mich 32/B3. Map 2.

A 100frs & under. B 100–135. C 135–165. D 165–250. E 250–350. F 350–500. G 500+

Le FAOU   Vieille Renommée

Comfortable hotel/Cooking 1-2
Lift

Readers usually give their vote to Mme Philippe's modern hotel, rather than Michelin's favourite, the Relais de la Place. Chef Daniel Bourhis' repertoire is a lengthy roll call of *Bretonne* and *Bourgeoise* fare with highlights like *truite saumonée au coulis de crustacés* and a gutsy *pot-au-feu de la mer*. Park in the football pitch-sized *place*.
Menus aCD. Rooms (38) E. Cards Access, Visa.
Closed Sun evg and Mon (not July/Aug).
Post pl. Mairie, 29580 Le Faou, Finistère. Region Brittany.
Tel 98 81 90 31. Fax 98 81 92 93. Mich 26/C4. Map 1.

FAVERGES   Florimont

Comfortable hotel/Cooking 2
Terrace/Gardens/Lift/Parking

Jacques and Marie-Josèphe Goubot (as unsmiling as ever) let their son, Jean-Christophe, run the kitchen show in their new home, north-east of Faverges. Classical and *Bourgeoise* fare: *cuisse de canard aux olives*, *omble chevalier rôti*, *magret de canard poêlé et sa sauce aux mûres* and similar. Marie-Claire, J-C's wife, provides a happier, warmer welcome.
Menus bCDF. Rooms (27) EF. Disabled. Cards All.
Closed Rest: Sun evg (Oct to June).
Post 74210 Faverges, Haute-Savoie. Region Savoie.
Tel 50 44 50 05. Fax 50 44 43 20. Mich 118/C2. Map 6.

FAVERGES   Gay Séjour

Simple hotel/Cooking 2-3
Secluded/Terrace/Parking

A cascade of pluses have made this a readers' top favourite: a 17thC *Savoyarde* farmhouse; a captivating site – near mountains, Lac d'Annecy and Tamié Abbey; and the caring family Gay – led by Bernard, a likeable dynamo of a chef. Neo-classical and *Savoyards plats* with great emphasis on fish dishes (from the lake and oceans). Superb regional cheeses.
Menus CDE. Rooms (12) F. Cards All. (Take D12 S from Faverges.)
Closed 27 Dec to 27 Jan. Sun evg and Mon (not school hols).
Post Tertenoz, 74210 Faverges, Haute-Savoie. Region Savoie.
Tel 50 44 52 52. Fax 50 44 49 52. Mich 118/C2. Map 6.

A100frs & under. B100–135. C135–165. D165–250. E250–350. F350–500. G500+

FAVIERES
La Clé des Champs

Comfortable restaurant/Cooking 2
Parking

'The key" leads you to blue and white cottages and a rustic interior with plenty of flowers – at the heart of a hamlet in the Somme estuary. Isabelle and Bruno Flasque charm clients in many ways: a warm welcome, competent service, sensible wines and appetising neo-classical dishes: *terrine de poissons aux 3 couleurs* and *filet de turbotin* were champion.
Menus aBC. Cards Access, DC, Visa. (Rooms: Lion d'Or at Rue 3 km to N.)
Closed 2 Jan to 4 Feb. 28 Aug to 16 Sept. Sun evg. Mon.
Post 80120 Favières, Somme. Region North.
Tel 22 27 88 00. Mich 6/C2. Map 2.

La FERRIERE-AUX-ETANGS
Auberge de la Mine

Comfortable restaurant/Cooking 2-3

What an off-putting name; but please don't bypass this colourful oasis. A talented young couple – Catherine and Hubert Nobis – have an eye for detail. A bright-as-a-button dining room is the first eye-catcher; followed by Hubert's inventive, modern repertoire: full-of-verve dishes such as *pavé de brochet rôti au gingembre frais*; *filet de rascasse en nage de coriandre*; and *pudding chocolat, creme de réglisse.*
Menus aBC. Cards Access/AE/Visa. (Rooms: Ermitage, Bagnoles-de-l'Orne.)
Closed 4-25 Jan. 1-15 Sept. Tues evg. Wed. (Above easy drive to SE.)
Post Le Gué-Plat, 61450 La Ferrière-aux-Etangs, Orne. Region Normandy.
Tel 33 66 91 10. Mich 32/A4. Map 2. (2 km S, via D21 and D825.)

FIGEAC
des Carmes

Very comfortable hotel/Cooking 2-3
Terrace/Swimming pool/Tennis/Lift/Parking

A capable *directeur*, Jean-Louis Tillet, and an equally able chef, Daniel Raynaud, ensure that standards are kept high. Classical and regional specialities: from many worthy alternatives choose delights such as an earthy-scented *brouillade d'oeufs aux truffes*; a punchy *noix d'agneau à la crème d'ail* and a voluptuous *trilogie de chocolat.*
Menus BDE. Rooms (40) EF. Cards All.
Closed Xmas to New Year. Sat (Oct to Apl). Sun evg.
Post Enclos des Carmes, 46100 Figeac, Lot. Region Dordogne.
Tel 65 34 20 78. Fax 65 34 22 39. Mich 139/E1. Map 5.

A100frs & under. B100–135. C135–165. D165–250. E250–350. F350–500. G500+

FLAGEY-ECHEZEAUX Robert Losset

Simple restaurant/Cooking 2

What a disarming surprise. You'll see no signs – just "Bar" and "Tabac" in the small *place* north of the church. No airs and graces here – just emphatic, exemplary classics: an intense *terrine de caille*; a light, restrained *mousseline de saumon*; an unabashed *lapin farci façon chasse* or a hit-in-the-mouth *rognon veau à la moutarde*; finishing with a flourish – a *vacherin*. An endearing experience – in every way.
Menus a(lunch)BCD. Cards Access, Visa. (Rooms: St-Georges, Nuits.)
Closed Wed. (St-Georges hotel at A31 exit 1; see *FLE* p80 for details.)
Post Flagey-Echezeaux, 21640 Vougeot, Côte-d'Or. Region Burgundy.
Tel 80 62 88 10. Mich 88/B1. Map 3.

FLAYOSC L'Oustaou

Comfortable restaurant/Cooking 1-2
Terrace

Pleasant village square setting; lovely out of doors on terrace, a touch confined inside. Provençale cuisine with several hunky dory *Bourgeois* tummy fillers: *pâté, boeuf en daube, coq au vin, pieds et paquets, magrets grillés*, goat's milk cheeses and above average sweets. One nice touch: help yourself from copper pans brought to the table.
Menus BCD. Cards Access, AE, Visa. (Rooms: Les Oliviers, 3 km to E.)
Closed 13-20 Mar. 13 Nov to 11 Dec. Sun evg. Mon.
Post 83780 Flayosc, Var. Region Côte d'Azur. (7 km W of Draguignan.)
Tel 94 70 42 69. Mich 162/C3. Map 6.

FLERS Au Bout de la Rue

Comfortable restaurant/Cooking 2

The smile-forcing name is a happy start; the cascade of flowers over the shop-front façade is even better. Marie-Noël Lebouleux is a warm-hearted hostess and husband Jacky a classical/neo-classical chef. Huge choice on menu C (low-end) including *salade terre-mer en vapeur de poissons tiède, saumon d'Ecosse rôti aux graines de sésame, rognons de veau à la moutarde* and 10 cracking desserts. Also cheaper bistro.
Menus A(bistro)C. Cards Acc, Visa. (Rooms: Galion; *sans rest*, parking.)
Closed Sunday. Pub hols. (Above hotel 2 minute-walk to NE, same road.)
Post 60 r. Gare, 61100 Flers, Orne. Region Normandy.
Tel 33 65 31 53. Fax 33 65 46 81. Mich 32/A4. Map 1.

A100frs & under. B100–135. C135–165. D165–250. E250–350. F350–500. G500+

FLEURINES
Vieux Logis

Very comfortable restaurant/Cooking 3
Terrace/Gardens

North of Senlis (and A1 exit 8) and at the heart of the Forêt d'Halatte. Yann and Valérie Nivet have assembled a knockout formula – which pleases both the eyes and taste buds. Faultless classical and regional fare. Some autumn examples: pungent *gibier, champignons, cul de lapin à la bière Picarde* and a Normandy marvel, *douillon aux poires sauce caramel.*
Menus CDF. Cards All. (Rooms: Ibis, just W of A1 exit 8.)
Closed 1st 3 wks Aug. Sun evg. Mon. Regions Normandy/North
Post 105 av. Gén. de Gaulle, 60700 Fleurines, Oise.
Tel 44 54 10 13. Fax 44 54 12 47. Mich 36/B1. Map 2.

FLEURY-SUR-ORNE
L'Ile Enchantée

Comfortable restaurant/Cooking 2

Well-named: a pretty, wooded setting, across the road from the River Orne and adjacent to an easily accessible riverside "green". Luscious classical food with a varied choice of tastes: light *gourmandise de saumon à la crème d'herbettes* and *minute de saumon aux huîtres, sauce lie de vin*; or loosen-your-belts *médaillon de veau a l'anglaise, crème Vallée d'Auge* and *fine tarte aux pommes chaudes, sauce caramel.*
Menus BCDE. Cards Access, Visa. (Rooms: Novotel & Ibis – N of Caen.)
Closed Feb sch hols. 1-8 Aug. Sun evg. Mon. (Use E bypass for above.)
Post 14123 Fleury-sur-Orne, Orne. (4 km S of Caen.) Region Normandy.
Tel 31 52 15 52. Mich 32/A1-B1. Map 2.

FLORAC
Grand Hôtel Parc

Comfortable hotel/Cooking 1-2
Gardens/Swimming pool/Lift/Parking

The large hotel is a mixture of modern and old, overlooking a large, shady garden with an almost hidden, cool swimming pool. Claude Gleize, *chef/patron*, rows in regional and classical boats: put your oars into gutsy, filling grub – including *charcuteries Cévenoles, salade Cévenole, tripoux Lozèriens, civet de caneton* and *côtes d'agneau grillées.*
Menus aCD. Rooms (66) CD. Cards All.
Closed Dec to mid March. Sun evg (not hotel). Mon (not high season).
Post 48400 Florac, Lozère. Region Massif Central (Cévennes).
Tel 66 45 03 05. Fax 66 45 11 81. Mich 142/B2. Map 5.

A100frs & under. B100–135. C135–165. D165–250. E250–350. F350–500. G 500+

La FLOTTE (Ile de Ré) Le Lavardin

Comfortable restaurant/Cooking 2-3

Georges and Patricia Barbet, the owners, look after the front of house while young chef William Donny, not yet 30, mixes neo-classical, *Charentaises* and Danish culinary cocktails. Refreshing, salty and sweet cocktails of flavours they are too: try a shaker mix of *harengs marinés Baltique*, *saumon grillé à la fleur de sel de Ré*, *bavette d'aloyau* (sirloin) *aux échalotes* and what else but *Ile Flottaise*!
Menus b(lunch)CDE. Cards Access, Visa. (Rooms: Hippocampe.)
Closed 10 Jan-10 Feb. 13 Nov-13 Dec. Mon evg & Tues (out of season).
Post r. H.Lainé, 17630 La Flotte, Charente-Maritime. Region Poitou-Char.
Tel 46 09 68 32. Mich 92/C3. Map 4.

FONTAINEBLEAU Napoléon/Rest. La Table des Marcéchaux

Very comfortable hotel/Cooking 2
Terrace/Lift

Opposite the palace. Bedroom prices are as elevated as the emperor's ego. (The Ibis, 200 m away, has a garage and cheaper rooms.) The menu is *RQP* plus in the expensive Ile de France. Enjoy classical *plats* with a view of the interior garden – a real bonus: *agneau grillée*, *sauce Béarnaise*; *brandade de morue fraîche*; and superb *Bries* are typical.
Menus B. Rooms (56) G-G2. Cards All.
Closed 18 Dec to 2 Jan. Regions Ile de France/Champagne-Ardenne.
Post 9 r. Grande, 77300 Fontainebleau, Seine-et-Marne.
Tel (1) 64 22 20 39. Fax (1) 64 22 20 87. Mich 54/C2. Map 2.

FONTENAY-LE-COMTE Chouans Gourmets

Comfortable restaurant/Cooking 2

Alongside the Vendée's right bank and at the heart of handsome Fontenay. Stone features overpoweringly in the main dining room; a smaller *salle* overlooks the dull river view. Madame is an eagle-eyed *patronne*. *Chef/patron* Robert Vrignon weaves a mix of culinary patterns: witness *emincé de porc Cantonnaise*, succulent *canette rôtie au miel et coriandre* and tender, pink *brochette de gigot d'agneau grillée aux herbes*.
Menus ABCD. Cards All. (Rooms: Rabelais or St-Nicolas at Maillezais.)
Closed 2-17 Jan. 4-11 July. Sun evg. Mon. (Maillezais easy 12 km to SE.)
Post 6 r. Halles, 85200 Fontenay-le-Comte, Vendée. Region Poitou-Char.
Tel 51 69 55 92. Mich 93/E2. Map 4.

A100frs & under. B100–135. C135–165. D165–250. E250–350. F350–500. G500+

FORCALQUIER   Host. des Deux Lions

Comfortable hotel/Cooking 3
Garage

Old France in a time warp: gentle, caring hosts, Robert & Claude Audier and Michel Montdor-Florent, a classical/regional chef. No-choice menu B (top-end) confirms his old-fashioned skills: dishes like *oeuf brouillé au crabe et aux crevettes en aumônière croustillante*; *poitrine d'agneau mitonnée puis grillée aux herbes*; and *mousse au chocolat noir*.
Menus BDE. Rooms (17) EF. Cards Access, Visa.
Closed Jan. Feb. Mid Nov to 18 Dec. Region Provence.
Post 11 pl. Bourguet, 04300 Forcalquier, Alpes-de-Hte-Provence.
Tel 92 75 25 30. Fax 92 75 06 41. Mich 145/F4. Map 6.

FORGES-LES-EAUX   Auberge du Beau Lieu

Comfortable restaurant with basic rooms/Cooking 3
Terrace/Parking

Marie-France Ramelet is a *petite*, attentive *patronne* and *sommelière* – proud of her *cave* (with 40 halves) and beamed dining room (with many paintings by local artist, William Gantier). Patrick Ramelet is an inventive modern master: *gâteau d'andouille aux pommes confites* and *millefeuille de haddock mariné et salade* are two *RQP* treats.
Menus CDE. Rooms (3) E. Cards All. (2 km SE, alongside D915.)
Closed 23 Jan to 8 Feb. Tues (not school hols). Region Normandy.
Post Le Fosse, 76440 Forges-les-Eaux, Seine-Maritime.
Tel 35 90 50 36. Fax 35 90 35 98. Mich 16/C2-C3. Map 2.

FORGES-LES-EAUX   Paix

Comfortable restaurant with basic rooms/Cooking 1-2
Gardens/Parking

Régine and Rémy Michel claim that their culinary philosophy is to uphold *tradition et terroir*. They do just that at their modest town-centre *logis* with beamed dining rooms. Examples of regional *plats* using *terroir* produce: *andouillete à la Normande*, *terrine de canard à la Rouennaise*, *filets de sole Dieppoise*, *Bray* cheeses and hot apple tart.
Menus ABC. Rooms (5) BC. Cards All. Region Normandy.
Closed 20 Dec-15 Jan. Sun evg (not high seas). Mon (not evg high seas).
Post 15 r. Neufchâtel, 76440 Forges-les-Eaux, Seine-Maritime.
Tel 35 90 51 22. Fax 35 09 83 62. Mich 16/C2-C3. Map 2.

A100frs & under. B100–135. C135–165. D165–250. E250–350. F350–500. G500+

FRANCESCAS

Relais de la Hire

Very comfortable restaurant/Cooking 2-3
Terrace/Gardens

A high-ceilinged *salle* in an 18thC house with a *parc ombragé* – all at
the door of heart-stirring Gascony. Jean-Noël Prabonne adds his own
brand of musketeer bravura. Tuck into two menus – l'Ecuyer (a) and
Chevalier (C) – and savour classical largesse like *cromesquis de Ste-
Maure* and *petit salé de saumon à la crème de lentilles.*
Menus aCD. Cards All. (Rooms: Trois Lys & Logis des Cordeliers, Condom.)
Closed Sun evg (not July and Aug). Mon. (Both *sans rest*; 15 km to SW.)
Post 47600 Francescas, Lot-et-Garonne. Region Southwest.
Tel 53 65 41 59. Fax 53 65 86 42. Mich 136/C4. Map 5.

FREJUS

La Toque Blanche

Very comfortable restaurant/Cooking 2

At east end of Fréjus-Plage, as you enter St-Raphaël. Stylish, service *sous
cloches* and goldfish-bowl glasses. Jacky Collin is a classicist with a light
hand: *gratin de moules et huîtres, cervelles beurre noir, tournedos
sauté forestière* and *sorbets* are menu B possibilities. (Prices in francs &
écus – a horrible reminder that an EU single currency may be forced
upon us one day. Please – no; let's pull out of the EU now.)
Menus BDE. Cards All. (Rooms: L'Oasis, quiet, parking – 1 km away to W.)
Closed 9 June to 9 July. Mon. (See *FLE* – p111 – for details of above.)
Post 394 av. V.Hugo, 83600 Fréjus-Plage, Var. Region Côte d'Azur.
Tel 94 52 06 14. Mich 163/E3. Map 6.

FROIDETERRE

Hostellerie des Sources

Comfortable restaurant/Cooking 2
Terrace/Parking

Well-named with springs and pools – the latter used to breed *écrevisses.*
Marcel Brocard is a savvy wine buff and son Valéry an able young chef.
In the beamed dining room dig into eclectic French dishes: *soupe de
poisson à la Provençale*; *gras-double à la Lyonnaise*; *gigot des
Pyrénées*; and the ubiquitous *crème brûlée à la vanille* (hot or cold).
Menus ABDE. Cards Access, Visa. (Rooms: Eric Hôtel, Lure – 3 km to SW.)
Closed 1st wk Feb. Last wk July. 1st 2 wks Aug. Sat midday. Mon.
Post 4 r. du Grand Bois, 70200 Froideterre, Haute-Saône. Region Alsace.
Tel 84 30 13 91. Fax 84 30 29 87. Mich 76/B2. Map 3.

A 100frs & under. B 100–135. C 135–165. D 165–250. E 250–350. F 350–500. G 500+

FUISSE
Pouilly Fuissé

Comfortable restaurant/Cooking 2
Terrace

Eric and Dominique Point (she's the fourth generation owner) entice with lick-your-lips *RQP* classical, *Bressane* and *Lyonnaise* cuisine. From an avalanche of five menus dig into the likes of *saladier Lyonnais*, *filet de perche sauce Duglérée* (sic), *grenouilles poëlées à la persillade* and the encore-please *crêpes Parmentier sucrées* (potato pancakes).
Menus aBCD. Cards Access, Visa. (Rooms: Ibis; SE at A6 Mâcon-Sud exit.)
Closed Mid Feb to mid Mar. 1st wk Aug. Sun evg. Tues evg. Wed.
Post 71960 Fuissé, Saône-et-Loire. Region Lyonnais.
Tel 83 35 60 68. Mich 102/B3. Map 6.

GAN
Le Tucq

Simple restaurant/Cooking 1-2
Terrace/Parking

If pennies count and if you would like to lose yourself in the exquisite foothills of the Pyrénées – and if you relish down-to-earth *Béarnaise* and *Bourgeoise* grub – then nose out Michel and Simone Rances. Take an appetite: *garbure Béarnaise, assiette de charcuterie, truite meunière, confit de canard* and six desserts all appear on the low-end menu B.
Menus aB. (Rooms: Bilaa, quiet, 6 km NW of Pau. Pau is 8 km N of Gan.)
Closed Oct. Mon evg, Tues and Wed (but not Aug). Region Southwest.
Post rte de Laruns, 64290 Gan, Pyrénées-Atlantiques. (4 km S – on D934.)
Tel 59 21 61 26. Mich 168/A1. Map 4.

GAP
Carré Long

Comfortable restaurant/Cooking 2-3

There are no gaps in Gap on the *RQP* front. Bernard Fiore-Rappelin is a modern *maître* with a sense of humour (read his menus carefully) and a taste for extrovert marriages: a *craquant de dorade aux petits légumes, sauce à la fleur d'aubépine* (hawthorn) is a tasty pastry-wallet treat. Monique, Bernard's wife, is an interesting, intelligent hostess. (Try, too, a Vin des Hautes-Alpes. A Vin de Théus no less! New to you?)
Menus BDE. Cards All. (Rooms: Ibis with garage – 5 min walk to E.)
Closed 1-15 May. Sun. Mon.
Post 32 r. Pasteur, 05000 Gap, Hautes-Alpes. Regions Htes-Alpes/Savoie.
Tel 92 51 13 10. Mich 146/B1. Map 6.

A100frs & under. B100–135. C135–165. D165–250. E250–350. F350–500. G500+

GAP — La Musardière

Simple restaurant/Cooking 2

Bravo Christophe Fouilloux! A tiny, rustic dining room, seating 20. But big-hearted offerings from a chef who clearly adores the Ecrins *montagnes* to the north (each menu has a name linked to a mountain in the *massif*). Menu C (low-end) is a memorable repast, including *St-Marcellin* (cheese) *rôti* with almonds, *gigot d'agneau son jus au porto*, *fromages de nos montagnes* and *nougat glacé au miel du Queyras*.
Menus ACD. Cards All. (Rooms: Ibis with garage – 3 min walk to SE.)
Closed 1-15 Jan. 1-15 July. Sun evg. Mon.
Post 3 pl. Révelly, 05000 Gap, Hautes-Alpes. Regions Htes-Alpes/Savoie.
Tel 92 51 56 15. Mich 146/B1. Map 6.

GERARDMER — Grand Hôtel Bragard/Rest. Le Grand Cerf

Luxury hotel/Cooking 2-3
Terrace/Gardens/Swimming pool/Lift/Parking

Talented Fabienne and Claude Remy have injected a new lease of life into the old-fashioned hotel (in the second *FL*). Chef Dominique Mervelay tempts with modestly-priced menus, eaten in a deluxe environment. Relish the latter and tuck into the fare: perhaps a *marmite du pêcheur*, then an *emincé de canard aux raisins*, followed by the cheese chariot and a plate of *pâtisseries*. Work the inches off in the gym, sauna and solarium.
Menus bCDEF. Rooms (56) FG. Cards All. (Cheaper rooms: nearby Bains.)
Post pl. du Tilleul, 88400 Gérardmer, Vosges. Region Alsace.
Tel 29 63 06 31. Fax 29 63 46 81. Mich 60/B3. Map 3.

GEVREY-CHAMBERTIN — Le Bonbistrot

Simple restaurant/Cooking 1-2
Terrace/Parking

Pierre Menneveau's *bistrot* is at ground level, above his rightly famed Rôtisserie, and is served by the same kitchen. Admire the l9thC pewter bar and chuckle at the toilets' washbasin. Emphatic regional tunes on the Bonbistrot piano: among them *jambon persillé, fricassée de coq au vin à l'ancienne* and *ami du Chambertin* cheese. Wines by the glass.
Menus ABC(à la carte). Cards Access, Visa. (Rooms: Les Grands Crus.)
Closed Feb. 1st wk Aug. Sun evg. Mon (not pub hols). (Above easy walk.)
Post 21220 Gevrey-Chambertin, Côte-d'Or. Region Burgundy.
Tel 80 34 35 14. Fax 80 34 12 30. Mich 88/B1. Map 3.

A100frs & under. B100–135. C135–165. D165–250. E250–350. F350–500. G500+

GIGONDAS   Les Florets

Comfortable restaurant with rooms/Cooking 2
Secluded/Terrace/Gardens/Parking

A large tree-shaded terrace is a plus: cool at midday and with lights in the evening. Service can be off-hand. Menu C has a choice of classical, regional and *Bourgeois plats*: *tourte de lapereau au romarin et morilles* and *roulade de pintadeau aux ravioles* have been praised. *Patrons* Martine and Pierre Bernard's family also own their own Gigondas vineyard.
Menus a(lunch)CD. Rooms (15) F. Cards All. (To the E; shown on map.)
Closed Jan. Feb. Tues evg (out of season). Wed.
Post 84190 Gigondas, Vaucluse. Region Provence.
Tel 90 65 85 01. Fax 90 65 83 80. Mich 144/C3. Map 6.

GIROUSSENS   L'Echauguette

Comfortable restaurant with rooms/Cooking 2
Terrace

La cuisinière, Pierrette Canonica, puts her fingers in all sorts of French regional cooking pots: take your pick from varied delights such as *salade Aveyronnaise*, *gras-double à la Lyonnaise*, *andouillettes* (Normandy) and an earthy *daube de boeuf au Madiran* (Gascony). Sumptuous home-made *pâtisseries*. Pierrette's husband, Claude, is *le patron*.
Menus ABCDE. Rooms (5) CDE. Cards All.
Closed 1st 3 wks Feb. 15-30 Sept. Sun evg and Mon (Oct to June).
Post pl. de la Mairie, 81500 Giroussens, Tarn. Region Languedoc-Rouss.
Tel 63 41 63 65. Mich 153/E2. Map 5.

GOUMOIS   Taillard

Comfortable hotel/Cooking 2-3
Secluded/Terrace/Gardens/Swimming pool/Parking

A blissful spot with rejuvenating views across the wooded Doubs Valley. A long-established, now modernised family hotel, founded in 1875. Regional and modern creations from Jean-François Taillard: *truites* in various guises (including *au vin jaune*), *feuilleté forestier flanqué de morilles* and super palate-tickler *sandre aux 7 épices, sauce estragon*.
Menus BCDE. Rooms (13) EF. Cards All.
Closed Nov to Feb. Wed (not Apl to Sept).
Post 25470 Goumois, Doubs. Region Jura.
Tel 81 44 20 75. Fax 81 44 26 15. Mich 77/D4. Map 3.

A100frs & under. B100–135. C135–165. D165–250. E250–350. F350–500. G500+

GOURDON
Host. de la Bouriane

Comfortable hotel/Cooking 2
Quiet/Gardens/Lift/Parking

A modern *logis* south of Gourdon's medieval centre. A host of little details make their mark: tasty appetisers and *petits fours* for example. Pretty dining room and caring *patrons*. A spiky *escalope de saumon grillée au beurre d'épices* and a luscious *coq au vin de Cahors* – with a dark pool of sauce – were the high points of an enjoyable *repas*.
Menus aBCDE. Rooms (20) EF. Cards Access, AE, Visa.
Closed Mid Jan to mid Mar. Rest: Mon (not evgs June to Oct).
Post pl. Foirail, 46300 Gourdon, Lot. Region Dordogne.
Tel 65 41 16 37. Fax 65 41 04 92. Mich 124/B4. Map 5.

GOURNAY-EN-BRAY
Aux Trois Maillets

Simple restaurant with rooms/Cooking 2-3
Terrace/Parking

The are two menus B: one *poisson*, the other *viande*. Panache describes both: *bisque de homard* and *filet de daurade* on the former; *chou farci de canard* and *pot au feu* on the latter. Philippe Colignon is a classicist and Maître Canardier: two D duck menus (above the *FWF* ceiling) offer the chance, in half-a-dozen ways, to confirm he's not a quack chef.
Menus BDE. Rooms (30) DE. Disabled. Cards All. Closed Rest only: mid Jan to mid Feb. Tues midday (mid Sept to Mar). Sat midday. Sun evg.
Post 6 r. Barbacane, 76220 Gournay-en-Bray, Seine-Maritime.
Tel 35 90 82 50. Fax 35 09 99 77. Mich 17/D3. Map 2. Region Normandy.

GRAMAT
Le Relais des Gourmands

Comfortable hotel/Cooking 2
Terrace/Gardens/Swimming pool

An enticing mix of ingredients beguile clients: colourful, bright decorations and furnishings in a modern building; a Scots' welcome from multi-lingual Susy Curtet and a confident *palette* of regional and classical specialities from husband Gérard. Memorable *assiette de deux terrines* and a blockbuster *cassoulet Périgourdin au confit d'oie.*
Menus aCD. Rooms (16) EF. Cards Access, Visa.
Closed Rest: Sun evg (winter) and Mon midday (not July/Aug).
Post av. Gare, 46500 Gramat, Lot. Region Dordogne.
Tel 65 38 83 92. Fax 65 38 70 99. Mich 125/D4. Map 5.

A100frs & under. B100–135. C135–165. D165–250. E250–350. F350–500. G500+

GRAMAT   Lion d'Or

Very comfortable hotel/Cooking 2
Terrace/Lift

A handsome stone façade with a vine-shaded terrace and a warm welcome
from Suzanne and René Mommejac. René seduces with treats like *carpaccio
de jambon d'Aoste au melon des côteaux du Quercy* (a tasty French and
Italian marriage) and a mouthwatering *saumon rôti au lard, poireaux et
tatin de champignons aux pommes.* Neo-classical and regional cooking.
Menus bCDE. Rooms (15) EF. Cards All. (Park in huge *place.*)
Closed Mid Dec to mid Jan. Rest: Mon midday (Nov to Feb).
Post pl. République, 46500 Gramat, Lot. Region Dordogne.
Tel 65 38 73 18. Fax 65 38 84 50. Mich 125/D4. Map 5.

Le GRAND-PRESSIGNY   Espérance

Comfortable restaurant with basic rooms/Cooking 2-3
Parking

Times change. Once unfussy; now the tag "grand" can be applied to
whitejacketed waiters, a plague of plate covers, and to some of Bernard
Torset's neo-classical and modern repertoire. Some older gems remain:
terrine de lapereau and *brochet au beurre blanc* are a Menu B duo; and
the lip-licking home-made breakfast jams of *la patronne*, Pauline Torset.
Menus BCD. Rooms (10) CD. Cards Access, DC, Visa.
Closed 5 Jan to 5 Feb. Mon (not public hols). Regions Loire/Poitou-Char.
Post 37350 Le Grand-Pressigny, Indre-et-Loire.
Tel 47 94 90 12. Mich 82/B3. Map 2.

GUINGAMP   Relais du Roy

Very comfortable restaurant with rooms/Cooking 2-3
Quiet

Victoria and Jacques Mallégol's 16th-century *hôtel particulier* (town
house) has swish bedrooms. Neo-classical cooking with a Brittany
flourish. Four fish creations – *petite marmite des Pêcheurs, moules de
la Côte au cidre, filet de mérou bisquine* and *filet de truite de l'Argoat*
– evoke to a tee the chef's well-crafted regional objectives.
Menus BCD. Rooms (7) G. Cards All. (Cheaper rooms at D'Armor.)
Closed Xmas. Sun. (Parking in *place.*)
Post pl. Centre, 22200 Guingamp, Côtes d'Armor. Region Brittany.
Tel 96 43 76 62. Fax 96 44 08 01. Mich 28/B2. Map 1.

A100frs & under. B100–135. C135–165. D165–250. E250–350. F350–500. G500+

Les HALLES   Charreton

Comfortable restaurant with rooms/Cooking 2
Parking

The *auberge*, on the D489 and at the heart of the Monts du Lyonnais, has views from the rear of both hills and woods. Pierre Charreton is both a master baker and *cuisinier*. Regional and neo-classical specialities: an enterprising *Pithiviers au Roquefort*; a sweet toothsome *cuisse de canard au Banyuls et orange*; and, no surprise, a *fromage blanc* with cream.
Menus bCD. Rooms (5) E. Cards Access, Visa.
Closed Sun evg. Wed.
Post 69610 Les Halles, Rhône. Region Lyonnais.
Tel 74 26 63 05. Mich 115/E2. Map 6.

HENDAYE   Chez Antoinette

Simple hotel/Cooking 1-2
Gardens

A mile or so from Hendaye Plage and not that far from the Spanish border. A green-shuttered (for a change) family *logis*, led by Bernard Haramboure, the *chef de cuisine*. Enjoy both *Basque* and classical fare: *merlu salsa verde, lotte au coulis de crabe, confit de cannette maison* and *noisette d'agneau à la Navarraise* are typical copious alternatives.
Menus bC. Rooms (16) DEF. Cards Access, Visa.
Closed Nov to Easter. Mon (not July/Aug). Public hols.
Post pl. Pellot, 64700 Hendaye Ville, Pyrénées-Atlantiques.
Tel 59 20 08 47. Fax 59 48 11 64. Mich 166/A1. Map 4. Region SW.

HONFLEUR   Au P'tit Mareyeur

Simple restaurant/Cooking 2

Christian Chaillou is an assured *cuisinier*. Behind the blue-fronted, ship-shape façade lies a small 18th-century dining room. There's a single-price, neo-classical menu which confirms Christian's culinary nous: a punchy *velouté de petits crabes son croûton à la crème d'ail*, an artful *escalope de saumon mi-cuit a la réglisse douce* and a saliva-stirring *tarte paysanne au miel et pommeau* are cracking creations.
Menus B. Cards Access, Visa. (Rooms: many *sans rest* hotels nearby.)
Closed 4-19 Jan. 2nd Half Nov. Thurs. Fri midday. (Parking nearby.)
Post 4 r. Haute, 14600 Honfleur, Calvados. Region Normandy.
Tel 31 98 84 23. Mich 14/C3. Map 2. (Rest. NW of La Lieutenance.)

A100frs & under. B100–135. C135–165. D165–250. E250–350. F350–500. G500+

Les HOUCHES   Auberge Beau Site/Rest. Le Pèle

Comfortable hotel/Cooking 1-2
Terrace/Gardens/Lift/Parking

Mont Blanc towers over the hotel but it is the extrovert, colourful gardens which almost steal the show. Nicole Perrin is an obliging hostess and husband Christian is a skilled chef. Primarily classical offerings such as *magret de canard au miel de montagne, féra du lac au beurre blanc, travers de porc à la Dijonnaise* and *tarte au citron*.
Menus bCD. Rooms (18) F. Cards All.
Closed 15-30 Apl. Oct to Xmas. Wed (May to 15 June & 15-30 Sept).
Post 74310 Les Houches, Haute-Savoie. Region Savoie.
Tel 50 55 51 16. Fax 50 54 53 11. Mich 119/E1. Map 6.

HOUDAN   Plat d'Etain

Comfortable restaurant with rooms/Cooking 2

Once a 16th-century *relais de poste* with a half-timbered, beamed interior and *grande cheminée*. With man-made skills from the past preserved in stone and timber no wonder, then, that the cooking is authentic classical with varying regional flourishes. Among the specialities are the famed *poule de Houdan, foie gras de canard au vieil Armagnac* and a sunny *millefeuille de boeuf à la ratatouille*.
Menus BD. Rooms (9) E. Cards Access, Visa.
Closed 1st 3 wks Aug. Mon evg. Tues. Regions Ile de France/Normandy.
Post 94 r. Paris, 78550 Houdan, Yvelines.
Tel (1) 30 59 60 28. Mich 34/C4. Map 2. (The busy N12 bypasses Houdan.)

HYERES   Jardins de Bacchus

Comfortable restaurant/Cooking 2-3
Terrace

An elegant spot with the Bacchus theme used at every turn. A top-notch *cave, bien sûr* – presented by *la patronne/sommelière*, the charming Claire Santioni. Her husband, Jean-Claude, paddles in modern Provençale pools: a right *champion marinade de canard en tapendae et huile d'olive* and a tingling-with-flavour *tian de filets de rougets et ratatouille*.
Menus BDE. Cards Acc, AE, Visa. (Rooms: Ibis & Centrotel nearby – to S.)
Closed Sat midday (summer). Sun evg (winter). Mon.
Post 32 av. Gambetta, 83400 Hyères, Var. Regions Côte d'Azur/Provence.
Tel 94 65 77 63. Mich 161/D4. Map 6.

A100frs & under. B100–135. C135–165. D165–250. E250–350. F350–500. G500+

Les ISSAMBRES   Chante-Mer

Simple restaurant/Cooking 2
Terrace

A tiny spot where 20 or so clients eat out on the covered terrace and an equal number share the air-conditioned interior. Chef Mario Battaglia is a classical fan; wife Nanette is a delightful, smiling hostess. Tuck into tempting *soupe de poissons*, drooling *petit pâté chaud*, *contrefilet sauce marchand de vin*, a freshly-made tart or *parfait glacé*.
Menus BCD. Cards Access, Visa. (Rooms: Plage at La Nartelle – 4 km SW.)
Closed 15 Dec-31 Jan. Sun evg (Sept-June). Mon (not evgs July/Aug).
Post 83380 Les Issambres, Var. Region Côte d'Azur.
Tel 94 96 93 23. Mich 163/E4. Map 6. (N of N98 at Hôtel Les Calanques.)

JAVRON   La Terrasse

Very comfortable restaurant/Cooking 3

One of the great highlights of our research for *FWF*. One word suffices: GO! Stylish modern *RQP* cuisine of an impeccable standard from a gifted and talented English duo: Alison Greenaway is the vivacious hostess (she puts most French *patronnes* to shame); husband Michael is a champion chef. Handsome dining room. Great cellar with over 40 halves. Come on Michelin, Michael deserves a star: don't be so wretchedly xenophobic.
Menus ACDE. Cards Access, Visa. (Rooms: Ermitage, Bagnoles-de-l'Orne.)
Closed 2-15 Jan. Sun evg. Mon. (Easy 19 km drive NW to Bagnoles.)
Post 53250 Javron-les-Chapelles, Mayenne. Region Normandy.
Tel 43 03 41 91. Mich 50/B2. Map 2.

JOIGNY   Le Rive Gauche

Comfortable hotel/Cooking 1-2
Quiet/Terrace/Gardens/Lift/Tennis/Parking/Helicopter pad

The "pad" is the sure sign that this has to be a 3-star chef's bistro; this one belongs to Michel Lorain. The riverside green-roofed hotel (zero marks for looks) is across the Yonne from his 3-star palace. Vast choice in the busy dining room. The big attraction is the buffet-style *grande table de hors d'oeuvre* – followed by main courses such as an *entrecôte marchand de vin* and sweets like *profiteroles au chocolat*.
Menus aCD. Rooms (42) EFG. Disabled. Cards All.
Post Port au Bois, 89300 Joigny, Yonne. Region Burgundy.
Tel 86 91 46 66. Fax 86 91 46 93. Mich 71/E1. Map 2.

A100frs & under. B100–135. C135–165. D165–250. E250–350. F350–500. G500+

JOUCAS
Host. le Phébus

Very comfortable hotel/Cooking 2-3
Secluded/Terrace/Gardens/Swimming pool/Tennis/Parking

A super dry-stone complex in 10 acres of *garrigue*. Luxury is the word; bedrooms prices are steep (see below for nearby alternative). Enjoy the setting and chef Xavier Mathieu's classical and Provençale offerings in the two menus C: *fleurs de courgette farcies de morue fraîche* and *charlotte d'agneau de Sisteron au romarin* remain tasty memories.
Menus CDE. Rooms (17) G-G2. Disabled. Cards Access, AE, Visa.
Closed Nov to Feb. (Rooms: cheaper Résidence des Ocres, Roussillon.)
Post route Murs, 84220 Joucas, Vaucluse. Region Provence.
Tel 90 05 78 83. Fax 90 05 73 61. Mich 159/D1. Map 6.

JULIENAS
Le Coq au Vin

Simple restaurant/Cooking 2
Terrace

Multi-coloured *coqs* reign supreme at Claude Clévenot's blue-shuttered bistro – lifted, it would seem, from the pages of *Clochemerle*. The fare is a mix of modern, neo-classical and regional – with Georges Duboeuf wines almost on tap. Among many offerings we voted one cock of the walk: what else but *coq au vin de Juliénas* – the perfect mating.
Menus aCD. Cards All. (Rooms: nearby des Vignes, *sans rest.*)
Closed Tues evg and Wed (Jan/Feb).
Post pl. Marché, 69840 Juliénas, Rhône. Region Lyonnais.
Tel 74 04 41 98. Fax 74 69 68 41. Mich 102/B3. Map 6.

JUVIGNY-SOUS-ANDAINE
Au Bon Accueil

Comfortable restaurant with rooms/Cooking 2
Garage

André Cousin dips his fingers into many a French regional culinary pool at his modern *logis*: *jambon de Bayonne, terrine de canard à la Rouennaise, foie gras d'oie des Landes, escargots de Bourgogne* and *sorbet Granny Smith* are an eclectic jumble. *Bourgeoise* and classical – *ancien régime* cooking which guarantees you leave with tummies contentedly full.
Menus BCE. Rooms (8) E. Cards Access, Visa.
Closed Feb school hols. Tues evg. Wed.
Post 61140 Juvigny-sous-Andaine, Orne. Region Normandy.
Tel 33 38 10 04. Fax 33 37 44 92. Mich 50/B1. Map 2.

A100frs & under. B100–135. C135–165. D165–250. E250–350. F350–500. G500+

LACAPELLE-MARIVAL   Terrasse

Simple hotel/Cooking 2
Gardens

A smart, whitewashed *logis* near the château and church. Young chef
Eric Boussac and his English-speaking wife, Clarisse, are highly thought
of by their Quercy peers and nothing is too much trouble for them. Proof
of Eric's talent shines forth in a herby *terrine de lapereau a là sauge* and
a drooling *filet de truite, beurre d'échalotes et Bergerac blanc*.
Menus ABD. Rooms (15) DE. Cards Access, Visa.
Closed Jan to mid Mar. Sun evg and Mon (Oct to Mar).
Post 46120 Lacapelle-Marival, Lot. Region Dordogne.
Tel 65 40 80 07. Mich 125/D4. Map 5.

LACAVE   Pont de l'Ouysse

Very comfortable restaurant with rooms/Cooking 3
Secluded/Terrace/Gardens/Swimming pool/Parking

A roll-call of man-made and natural pleasures: a site beside the River
Ouysse, downstream from Rocamadour, just before it joins the Dordogne;
Belcastel château; cosseting comforts; and modern and regional dishes
from master chef Daniel Chambon. Especially appetising are poultry and
lamb specialities, simply roasted – made-in-heaven creations.
Menus CDEFG. Rooms (12) FG. Cards All.
Closed Jan. Feb. Mon (not evgs from May to Sept).
Post 46200 Lacave, Lot. Region Dordogne.
Tel 65 37 87 04. Fax 65 32 77 41. Mich 124/C3. Map 5.

LALINDE   Château

Comfortable restaurant with rooms/Cooking 2
Terrace/Swimming pool

A down-at-heel façade for the *logis* (once a prison!) alongside the right
bank of the River Dordogne. Culinary treats generally match the fine site
and views: an *omelette aux queues de langoustines* made a pleasant
change; and both a *blanquette d'agneau aux trompettes de mortes* and
a *tarte aux pommes chaudes* were well executed, accomplished dishes.
Menus a(lunch)CD. Rooms (7) FG. Cards Access, Visa.
Closed Dec to Feb. Fri (not evgs July/Aug).
Post 1 r. Verdun, 24150 Lalinde, Dordogne. Region Dordogne.
Tel 53 61 01 82. Fax 53 24 74 60. Mich 123/D3-E3. Map 5.

A 100frs & under. B 100–135. C 135–165. D 165–250. E 250–350. F 350–500. G 500+

LAMALOU-LES-BAINS   Mas

Comfortable hotel/Cooking 1-2
Terrace/Lift/Parking

A small, shady, cool spa. The *belle époque* hotel is opposite the spa's casino. Ask English-speaking Ernest Bitsch, a friendly host, to show you the fine frescoes in the vast *salon*. Neo-classical/classical dishes: *tournedos Bordelaise à la moelle* and *omelette Norvégienne* are typical of the latter. The large terrace is a shady oasis on hot days. (For nicer bedrooms ask Ernest to put you up at a sister hotel, L'Arbousier.)
Menus ABCD. Rooms (40) BCD. Cards All.
Post 34240 Lamalou-les-Bains, Hérault. Region Languedoc-Roussillon.
Tel 67 95 62 22. Fax 67 95 67 78. Mich 155/E3. Map 5.

LANGRES   Grand Hôtel Europe

Comfortable hotel/Cooking 1-2
Parking

Highly regarded by *En Route* users (p134). A 17th-century town house at the heart of the walled town and south of the cathedral. A taste of nostalgia in the rooms, furnishings and cooking. Nothing flashy – but neither is the grub cheap and cheerful. Readers have praised the *terrine maison*, *bavarois de saumon fumé* and *poulet rôti à la broche*.
Menus ABD. Rooms (28) DE. Cards All.
Closed 7-21 May. 1-23 Oct. Sun evg. Mon (not evgs May to Oct).
Post 23 r. Diderot, 52200 Langres, Hte-Marne. Regions Burg/Champ-Ard.
Tel 25 87 10 88. Fax 25 87 60 65. Mich 74/C1. Map 3.

LAPOUTROIE   Les Alisiers

Comfortable restaurant with rooms/Cooking 2
Secluded/Terrace/Gardens/Parking

A longtime readers' favourite. Jacques and Ella Degouy's *logis* (2300 ft high) has a panoramic vista, a Chartreuse-shaded distillation of Vosges scenery. Raining? Enjoy the view from the dining room with its glass walls. Alsace and *Bourgeois plats*: *choucroute à l'ancienne, faux-filet au pinot noir, tarte à l'oignon* and *gâteau au chocolat sauce anglaise.*
Menus ABC. Rooms (10) DE. Cards Access, Visa.
Closed Jan. 1st wk July. Xmas. Mon evg & Tues (not rooms Mar to Nov).
Post 68650 Lapoutroie, Haut-Rhin. Region Alsace. (SW of village.)
Tel 89 47 52 82. Fax 89 47 22 38. Mich 60/C3. Map 3.

A100frs & under. B100–135. C135–165. D165–250. E250–350. F350–500. G500+

LAPOUTROIE

du Faudé

Comfortable hotel/Cooking 2-3
Terrace/Gardens/Swimming pool (indoor)/Parking

The much loved Baldinger family makes the *logis* zing. Thierry is the able chef; wife Chantal the English-speaking *patronne*. A cascade of menus: with stomach-fillers like *coq au Riesling* and *choucroute garnie* to personal favourites such as a silky *terrine de foie de volaille au poivre* served with *12 hors d'oeuvre et crudités* left at the table.
Menus aCD. Rooms (25) EF. Cards All.
Closed 8-23 Mar. 13 Nov to 7 Dec. (In village, which is bypassed.)
Post 68650 Lapoutroie, Haut-Rhin. Region Alsace.
Tel 89 47 50 35. Fax 89 47 24 82. Mich 60/C3. Map 3.

LAPOUTROIE

Host. A La Bonne Truite

Simple hotel/Cooking 2
Parking

At Hachimette, alongside the N415 to the east. Danièle Zavialoff is an efficient hostess; husband Michel conjures up both regional and more modern creations. Choose from alternative ends of the culinary spectrum: perhaps a thumpingly good *choucroute royale au Riesling* or a smooth *terrine de sandre et du saumon au saumon fumé avec mousse au curry*.
Menus ABCDE. Rooms (10) DE. Cards Access, AE, Visa.
Closed Jan. 20-29 June. 6-22 Nov. Tues. Wed (Oct to June).
Post Hachimette, 68650 Lapoutroie, Haut-Rhin. Region Alsace.
Tel 89 47 50 07. Fax 89 47 25 35. Mich 60/C3. Map 3.

LECTOURE

De Bastard

Comfortable hotel/Cooking 2-3
Quiet/Terrace/Swimming pool/Garage

A handsome 18th-century building with stylish rooms and exhilarating views. English-speaking Anne Arnaud is an informed hostess and her chef husband, Jean-Luc, thankfully offers more than just the usual Gers goose and duck permutations. Savour lighter, modern dishes such as *terrine de poissons aux champignons* and *soupe de moules aux courgettes et safran*.
Menus aCD. Rooms (29) DEF. Cards All.
Closed 23 Dec-15 Feb. Rest: Fri evg, Sat midday & Sun evg (Oct-Apl).
Post r. Lagrange, 32700 Lectoure, Gers. Region Southwest.
Tel 62 68 82 44. Fax 62 68 76 81. Mich 151/E1-F1. Map 5.

A100frs & under. B100–135. C135–165. D165–250. E250–350. F350–500. G500+

LEIGNE-LES-BOIS   Gautier

Comfortable restaurant/Cooking 2

An unpretentious little country restaurant – in a hamlet and across the road from the *église* – with smartly kitted-out, beamed dining rooms and trying hard to get small details right. Classical pleasures arrive on chef Bernard Gautier's plates: a taste of the local fields with *gâteau de lapereau en geleé*; a fresh, unfussy *cabillaud au beurre d'échalotes*; and an out-for-the-count *tournedos B. Gautier* (loosen the belts).
Menus ACD. Cards Access, Visa. (Rooms: Europe at La Roche-Posay.)
Closed Feb. Nov. Sun evg. Mon. (La Roche-Posay, a spa, 10 km to E.)
Post 86450 Leigné-les-Bois, Vienne. Regions Loire/Poitou-Charentes.
Tel 49 86 53 82. Mich 82/B4. Map 2.

LERE   Lion d'Or

Comfortable restaurant with rooms/Cooking 2-3
Terrace/Garage

A quietish site, west of the D751. Patron Jean-Paul Ridon, engineer turned chef (also past Formula 3000 driver and African reserve guide) is an ingenious cook. Elaborate creations include *petit bavarois d'araignée de mer en rémoulade* and *royale de poissons de Loire, beurre blanc, au vinaigre de canne à sucre*. Choice of over 250 wines.
Menus BCD. Rooms (8) D. Cards Access, Visa.
Closed Sun evg. Mon.
Post 18240 Léré, Cher. Regions Berry-Bourbonnais/Loire.
Tel 48 72 60 12. Fax 48 72 58 01. Mich 70/C4. Map 2.

LEVENS   Les Santons

Simple restaurant/Cooking 1-2
Terrace

Tucked away in Levens, high above the Var and Vésubie valleys. The Pellerins ask you to take your time and enjoy their hospitality. Madame is a charmer. Provençale fare and numerous fish specialities. Three-star *amuses-geules*; gutsy *timbale de moules, noisette en beurre*; a *chèvre quintet*; and sweet trolley. Note: closed evenings other than Fri & Sat.
Menus bCD. Cards Access, Visa. (Rooms: nearby La Vigneraie – to SE.)
Closed 2 Jan-8 Feb. 26 June-5 July. 2-11 Oct. Wed. Evgs (not Fri & Sat).
Post 06670 Levens, Alpes-Maritimes. Region Côte d'Azur.
Tel 93 79 72 47. Mich 165/D2. Map 6. (Near village church.)

A100frs & under. B100–135. C135–165. D165–250. E250–350. F350–500. G500+

LONS-LE-SAUNIER
Comédie

Comfortable restaurant/Cooking 2-3

A tiny dining room in a pretty-as-a-picture square where every terraced house seems to be washed in a different pastel shade. Single menu A is down-to-earth largesse. Main courses have a special panache: both *joues de loup grillée au riz noir* and *cuisse de canard de Challans aux mousserons et navets confits* are exotic, virtuoso gems. A *Roquefort terrine* is a perfectly-balanced starter. Bravo Bernard Hémery.

Menus A. Cards Access, Visa. (Rooms: Nouvel, parking, 5 min walk to W.)
Closed 2nd half Apl. 1st 3 wks Aug. Sun. Mon evg.
Post 65 r. Agriculture, 39000 Lons-le-Saunier, Jura. Region Jura.
Tel 84 24 20 66. Mich 89/D4. Map 3. (Park in place Comédie opposite.)

LOUHANS
La Cotriade

Comfortable restaurant/Cooking 2

The clue for Philippe Coulon's home *pays* is in the name: Brittany *bien sûr*. He's no introvert: study the couple of dozen framed diplomas in the hall for proof of his culinary abilities. Being a Breton he's fond of fish: a Menu du Pêcheur has an *assiette de fruits de mer* and a *dos de sandre au beurre blanc*. Otherwise regional and classical numbers: *volaille de Bresse rôti, à la crème et morilles* is one highlight.

Menus ABE. Cards Access, DC, Visa. (Rooms: Host. Cheval Rouge.)
Closed 1st wk July. 15-30 Nov. Tues evg & Thurs evg (not July/Aug).
Post 4 r. Alsace, 71500 Louhans, Saône-et-Loire. Region Lyonnais.
Tel 85 75 19 91. Mich 103/D1. Map 6. (Cheval Rouge is at 5 r. Alsace.)

LUCON
La Mirabelle

Comfortable restaurant/Cooking 2-3

A UK Michelin one-star chef inspected La Mirabelle twice during a 1993 holiday. Benoît and Véronique Hermouet are a friendly and talented duo. Benoît punts both classical and Vendée streams: a *préfou* appetiser (a garlic bread *galette*); a simple and tender *filet de canard aux aromates et sa garniture* was a well-sauced classic; and *terrine froid de jarret de porc, purée légère mojettes et préfou* a mouthwatering Vendée winner.

Menus aCDE. Cards Access, Visa. (Rooms: Central at St-Michel-en-l'Herm.)
Closed Feb & Nov school hols. Tues. Sat midday. (Above 15 km to SW.)
Post 35 r. de Gaulle, 85400 Luçon, Vendée. Region Poitou-Charentes.
Tel 51 56 93 02. Fax 51 56 35 92. Mich 92/C2. Map 4.

A 100frs & under. B 100–135. C 135–165. D 165–250. E 250–350. F 350–500. G 500+

LURBE-ST-CHRISTAU   Au Bon Coin

Comfortable hotel/Cooking 2
Terrace/Swimming pool/Parking

His regional chef peers rate Thierry Lassala and his English-speaking wife highly. A well-named hotel – a modern blue and cream, chalet-styled building east of the village. A thumpingly good *garbure*, melting *saumon braisée au Jurançon* and an assiduously executed *charlotte d'agneau au beurre de tomate* confirmed his regional and classical cooking skills.
Menus ACD. Rooms (18) E. Disabled. Cards Accss, AE, Visa.
Closed Mid Jan to mid Feb. Tues (mid Oct to Mar). Region Southwest.
Post rte des Thermes, 64660 Lurbe-St-Christau, Pyrénées-Atlantiques.
Tel 59 34 40 12. Fax 59 34 46 40. Mich 167/E3. Map 4.

LURS   Bello Visto

Simple restaurant/Cooking 1-2

Extensive views over the Durance Valley and two indoor fans are welcome distractions on a hot summer's day (note closing details). François Grisolle is the chef; wife Dominique *la patronne*. A *mélange* of regional, classical and *Bourgeois* dishes: main courses are especially flavoursome – *lapin rôti avec sa sauce poivrade* or *grillade d'agneau au miel de thym.* Simple sweets: fruit, *pâtisserie* and *glace à la Chantilly.*
Menus aBCD. Cards Access, Visa. (Rooms: Aub. Charembeau to W, off N100.) Closed Oct. Wed. Evgs (not high season). (*Auberge* easy drive.)
Post Lurs, 04700 Oraison, Alpes-de-Hte-Prov. Regions Htes-Alpes/Prov.
Tel 92 79 95 09. Mich 146/A4. Map 6.

MADIRAN   Le Prieuré

Simple hotel/Cooking 2
Quiet/Terrace/Gardens/Parking

Michel (the chef) and Danielle Cuénot's handsome stone hotel was once the abbey at the famous wine village. Cleverly modernised public rooms and bedrooms (once monks' cells!). Clever neo-classical and regional cooking too – like light *filets de rougets aux oignons frits* and tender *agneau de lait des Pyrénées à l'ail confit.* Top-notch sweets.
Menus aCDE. Rooms (10) DE. Cards All.
Closed 22-29 Jan. 13-24 Nov. Sun evg and Mon (Oct to Easter).
Post 65700 Madiran, Hautes-Pyrénées. Region Southwest.
Tel 62 31 92 50. Fax 62 31 90 66. Mich 150/B3. Map 4.

A100frs & under. B100–135. C135–165. D165–250. E250–350. F350–500. G500+

MANZAC-SUR-VERN   Lion d'Or

Comfortable restaurant with basic rooms/Cooking 2
Terrace/Gardens

Jean-Paul and Nelly Beauvais created their oasis of *RQP* charm 14 years
ago. Bright and airy applies to both the dining room and cooking. Menu
B may offer a first-rate *terrine de foie gras* or *salade de St-Jacques et
saumon*; *méli-mélo* (an assortment) *de poissons au beurre de safran* or
magret de canard poêlée sauce au vin de noix; and one of six desserts.
Menus ABCD. Rooms (7) D. Cards All.
Closed Feb school hols. 24 Oct to 9 Nov. Sun evg (not July/Aug). Mon.
Post 24110 Manzac-sur-Vern, Dordogne. Region Dordogne.
Tel 53 54 28 09. Mich 123/D2. Map 5.

MARANS   Porte Verte

Simple restaurant/Cooking 2
Terrace

Colourful: flowers, greenery and gourds. Once a fisherman's quayside
home with a small, cool, handsome interior. Even smaller terrace. Didier
Montéran keeps things classically simple: *assiette de fruits de mer* or
terrine de lapin; *bavette sauce porto* or various fish alternatives (so
fresh, still wriggling); cheese and dessert (like iced *nougat terrine*).
Menus ABC. Cards Access, Visa. (Rooms: St-Nicolas, Maillezais – to NE.)
Closed Feb school hols. Sun evg (mid Sept to mid June). Wed.
Post 20 quai Foch, 17230 Marans, Charente-Maritime. Region Poitou-Char.
Tel 46 01 09 45. Mich 93/D2. Map 4.

MARGAUX   Auberge Le Savoie

Comfortable restaurant/Cooking 2
Terrace

Yves Fougeras' two *RQP* menus boldly state his culinary philosophy: *la
cuisine est un art; tout art est patience.* How right he is: even low-cost
classical and neo-classical menus need sure, skilled hands and Yves
certainly has those. Two memorable menu B (low-end) *plats: terrine
d'aileron de raie aux câpres* and *crème de pommes au cidre doux.*
Menus A(not Sat evg)B. (Rooms: Pont Bernet, Louens – to S.)
Closed 1-22 Feb. Sun. Public hols. (Above is an easy 12 km-drive away.)
Post 33460 Margaux, Gironde. Region Southwest.
Tel 57 88 31 76. Mich 121/D2. Map 4.

A100frs & under. B100–135. C135–165. D165–250. E250–350. F350–500. G500+
298

MARIGNY   Poste

Comfortable restaurant/Cooking 2

The odd-ball blue-and-white façade – with three large panels depicting the varied harvests garnered from land, sea and air (and vines to boot) – leaves you in no doubt about the Manche-wide repertoire of award-winning chef, Joël Meslin. Examples include *filet de carrelet au Camembert* – a happy marriage; and an artful *noisettes de jeune cerf sur petite vinaigrette aux ciboulettes.* Banal sweets. Stylish dining room.
Menus bCDEF. Cards All. (Rooms: Ibis, St-Lô to E. Easy 12 km drive.)
Closed 1-15 Jan. 2 wks end Sept/early Oct. Sun evg. Mon.
Post pl. Wesport, 50570 Marigny, Manche. Region Normandy.
Tel 33 55 11 08. Fax 33 55 25 67. Mich 31/D2. Map 1.

MARQUISE   Grand Cerf

Very simple restaurant/Cooking 3

A down-at-heel village and a drooping Cerf – in need of a face-lift. Don't be put off: English-speaking Stéphane Pruvot is a brilliant chef. Our lunch menu B – *croustillant de crabe à la fondue de poireaux* was worthy of a 3-star God; followed by a pan-fried *rascasse* with a purée of courgettes and a potato *crêpe*; finishing with an *omelette aux pommes sauce pistache* – was the essence of modern simplicity and subtlety.
Menus A(two *plats*)BDE. Cards Access, Visa.
Closed Sun evg. Mon. (Rooms: several hotels in Boulogne and Calais.)
Post 62250 Marquise, Pas-de-Calais. Region North.
Tel 21 87 55 05. Fax 21 33 61 09. Mich 2/A2. Map 2.

MAUSSANE-LES-ALPILLES   La Petite France

Comfortable restaurant/Cooking 2-3
Parking

Regional tunes from the culinary piano of young, neo-classicist chef, Thierry Maffre-Bogé. Order anything which features the famed olive oil from nearby Mouriès and tuck into evocative specialities like *tomates tièdes farcies de brandade de morue au pistou* (Provence on a plate) and *terrine de gigot d'agneau à l'ail confit.* Scrumptious desserts.
Menus CDE. Cards Access, Visa. (Rooms: Touret, short walk away to W.)
Closed Jan. 16-23 Nov. Wed. Thurs midday. Region Provence.
Post av. Vallée-des-Baux, 13520 Maussane-les-Alpilles, Bouches-du-Rhône.
Tel 90 54 41 91. Mich 158/B2. Map 6. (On D17, W of village.)

A100frs & under. B100–135. C135–165. D165–250. E250–350. F350–500. G500+

MAUVEZIN   La Rapière

Comfortable restaurant/Cooking 2
Terrace

Michel Fourreau, soon to be 50, started cooking at the age of 14 in the
Loire's Sologne. Marie-Thérèse, his wife, welcomes you and Michel then
challenges you to a classical and regional duel with menus notable for their
exceedingly generous choice. Signature *plats*: *terrine de faisan, saumon
sauce hollandaise* and luscious *glace aux pruneaux à l'Armagnac.*
Menus ABCDE. Cards All. (Rooms: Coin de Feu, Gimont; 14 km to S.)
Closed 14 June to 4 July. 4-19 Oct. Tues evg. Wed. (Above easy drive.)
Post 32120 Mauvezin, Gers. Region Southwest.
Tel 62 06 80 08. Mich 152/A2. Map 5.

MEGEVE   Michel Gaudin

Comfortable restaurant/Cooking 3

Alongside the N212 through Megève. Attentive English-speaking Monique
Gaudin looks after the minute dining room while husband Michel, a
modern master, does the culinary juggling backstage. Blockbusting Mont
Blanc-sized RQP. Consider the evidence in menu B: three *amuse-bouche,
soupe de poissons, canard cuit en cocotte aux olives et poivres vert,
fromage blanc, coupe de fraises à la crème Chantilly* and *petits fours.*
Menus ABCDE. Cards Access, Visa. (Rooms: L'Auguille, 3 min walk to N.)
Closed Tues (not high season). (Above quiet, *sans rest* and parking.)
Post carrefour d'Arly, 74120 Megève, Haute-Savoie. Region Savoie.
Tel 50 21 02 18. Mich 119/D1. Map 6.

MEJANNES-LES-ALES   Auberge des Voutins

Comfortable restaurant/Cooking 2-3
Terrace/Gardens/Parking

To the south-east of Alès, alongside the D981. A stone-built villa with
shady terrace and neat gardens please the eye. So, too, does the modern,
inventive cooking of René Turonnet: *filet de rascasse demi-sel* with
tomato, garlic and olive oil is just one typical taste explosion. A big plus
feature of his repertoire is the clever use he makes of regional wines.
Menus CDE. Cards All. (Rooms: Ibis, at St-Christol, to SW – easy drive.)
Closed 1st wk Mar. 1st wk Sept. Sun evg. Mon (not public hols).
Post Méjannes-lès-Alès, 30340 Salindres, Gard. Region Provence.
Tel 66 61 38 03. Mich 143/D4. Map 6.

A100frs & under. B100–135. C135–165. D165–250. E250–350. F350–500. G500+

MEURSAULT
Relais de la Diligence

Comfortable restaurant/Cooking 2
Parking

Beside the D23, south-east of the N74 (near *la gare*). A modern building with four dining rooms and fine views west of *la côte*. Several menus, efficient service and pleasing ambience. Typical *plats* include a tasty *mousse d'avocat* with fresh shrimps; a well-chosen *panaché de poisson aux deux sauces*; and a multi-choice *plateau de fromages*.
Menus ABC. Cards All. (Rooms: Les Magnolias or Les Charmes in village.)
Closed 21 Dec to 10 Feb. Tues evg. Wed. (Both above *sans rest* & quiet.)
Post r. de la gare, 21190 Meursault, Côte-d'Or. Region Burgundy.
Tel 80 21 21 32. Fax 80 21 64 69. Mich 88/A2-A3. Map 3.

MEYRUEIS
Mont Aigoual

Comfortable hotel/Cooking 2
Gardens/Swimming pool/Lift

The Robert family – Frédéric, Stella and Jean-Paul (the chef) – own two Meyrueis hotels: Mont Aigoual and the nearby Europe. Both (from father to son since 1902) have been much liked by readers for 12 years now. I've been castigated over the *FLE* Cooking 1 rating. The new rating does justice to the above average classical and *Bourgeoise* cuisine.
Menus ABC. Rooms (30) E. Cards Access, Visa.
Closed Nov to Mar. (Hotel's facilities available to Europe clients.)
Post r. Barrière, 48150 Meyrueis, Lozère. Region MC (Cévennes).
Tel 66 45 65 61. Fax 66 45 64 25. Mich 141/F3. Map 5.

MEZERIAT
Les Bessières

Comfortable restaurant with rooms/Cooking 1-2
Terrace

To the west of the sizeable *village fleuri*, near the railway station. Joël and Raymonde Foraison are gentle, friendly folk – complementing perfectly the unassuming restaurant, shady terrace and classical and regional fare. Enjoy Bresse *plats* – *mousse de brochet sauce Nantua*, *filet de carpe des Dombes aux cerfeuil* and *fromage blanc à la crème*.
Menus BD. Rooms (6) D. Cards Access, Visa.
Closed Mid Dec to end Jan. Mon and Tues (Sept to May).
Post 01660 Mézériat, Ain. Region Lyonnais.
Tel 74 30 24 24. Mich 102/C3. Map 6.

A 100frs & under. B100–135. C135–165. D165–250. E250–350. F350–500. G500+

MIGENNES

Par▮

Comfortable restaurant with rooms/Cooking 2

A vine-covered building alongside a busy main road (D943). Ghast▮ décor – in the style only the French know how to do so brilliantl▮ Attentive service, with a touch of humour, and plenty of flowe▮ compensate – as does the classical cooking of Patrice Chauvin, th▮ *chef/patron*. Notable touches include a deliciously flavoured *assiette d*▮ *poissons* and a lip-smackingly good *île flottante crème anglaise*.
Menus aC. Rooms (9) DEF. Cards Access, Visa.
Closed 1-15 Jan. Aug. Fri evg. Sat midday. Sun evg.
Post 57 av. J.Jaurès, 89400 Migennes, Yonne. Region Burgundy.
Tel 86 80 23 22. Fax 86 80 31 04. Mich 72/A1. Map 2.

MILLAU

Château de Creisse▮

Comfortable hotel/Cooking 1-2
Quiet/Terrace/Gardens/Parking

A pleasing step back in time at the Austruy family hotel 2 km SW ▮ Millau. There's an old tower and medieval church next door (at night th▮ clock is silent). Bedrooms are well-appointed, a counterpoint to the ol▮ world gentility of the main rooms. Classical, *Bourgeois* and region▮ menus (wide choice). *Roquefort* used too excessively in many dishes.
Menus ABCD. Rooms (33) DEF. Disabled. Cards All. (Alongside D992.
Closed 28 Dec to 15 Feb. Rest: Sun evg and Mon midday (not high season
Post rte St-Affrique, 12100 Millau, Aveyron. Region MC (Cévennes).
Tel 65 60 16 59. Fax 65 61 24 63. Mich 141/E4. Map 5.

MILLAU

La Marmite du Pêcheu▮

Simple restaurant/Cooking 2
Terrace

Albert Négron is no longer with us. He died last year, aged 79 and aft▮ working 65 years in various kitchens. His widow, the smiling Janin▮ continues Albert's classical and regional traditions – aided by 31-yea▮ old chef, Christian Aveline. Best treats are *petite marmite du pêche▮* and, among 16 sweets, *bolet du chef Albert* – a 3-star winner.
Menus ABCD. Cards Access, AE, Visa. (Rooms: La Capelle, 200 metres N
Closed Wed evg (not high season). (Above hotel *sans rest* and quiet.)
Post 14 bd Capelle, 12100 Millau, Aveyron. Region MC (Cévennes).
Tel 65 61 20 44. Mich 141/E4. Map 5. (Park in large *place* opp. hotel.)

A100frs & under. B100–135. C135–165. D165–250. E250–350. F350–500. G500

MOIDREY

Comfortable restaurant/Cooking 2
Terrace/Parking

One-time director of the legendary Mère Poulard hotel/restaurant on Le Mont-St-Michel, the talented and friendly, English-speaking Jean-Claude Pierpaoli now entices clients to his own lair. A rich sea-water pool of pleasures – *assiette de fruits de mer* is one example – and, just as commendable, a juicy *gigot d'agneau de pré-salé* from the nearby marshes. Menus ACDE. Cards Access, Visa. (Rooms: Digue, on D976, 3 km to N.) Closed Mid Jan to mid Feb. Tues evg and Wed (not Aug). Post 50170 Moidrey, Manche. Regions Brittany/Normandy. Tel 33 60 01 63. Mich 30/C4. Map 1. (D976 6 km S of Le Mont-St-M.)

MOLINEUF

Comfortable restaurant/Cooking 2
Parking

An attractive village in terrific wooded country. A modern, light dining room with striking wall frescoes. An up-and-coming young chef, Thierry Poidras, certainly means business. Classical and neo-classical dishes: a hunky dory duo of *dos de flétan au coulis et ravioli de homard* and *magret de canard aux langoustines et jus de truffes* were perfection. Menus aCD. Cards All. (Rooms: several hotels at Blois, 9 km to E.) Closed Feb. Sun evg. Wed. (Ibis, Campanile & Cottage near A10 exit.) Post 41190 Molineuf, Loir-et-Cher. Region Loire. Tel 54 70 03 25. Fax 54 70 12 46. Mich 68/B3. Map 2.

MONESTIER-DE-CLERMONT

Simple hotel/Cooking 2
Quiet/Terrace/Gardens/Swimming pool/Tennis/Garage/Parking

The Maurice family celebrated 60 years of ownership in 1994. The fourth generation, Frédéric, the chef, and Michelle, *la patronne*, do a sterling job at their mountain *logis*. Extensive choice on the classical and *Bourgeois* menus: *ravioles du Royans* (W of Vercors), *omble chevalier aux amandes, filet d'agneau aux cèpes* and *fromage blanc* – winners all. Menus ABCD. Rooms (15) DE. Cards Access, Visa. Closed 20 Dec to end Jan. Sun evg. Mon. (N of Monestier; W of N75.) Post St-Paul-lès-Monestier, 38650 Monestier-de-Clermont, Isère. Tel 76 34 03 60. Mich 131/E3. Map 6. Regions Hautes-Alpes/Savoie.

A100frs & under. B100–135. C135–165. D165–250. E250–350. F350–500. G500+

MONTAUBAN   Ambroisie

Comfortable restaurant/Cooking 2

The welcome new eastern N20 bypass means that Montauban is a bit
quieter these days. Sybette Fournales is the hostess at the contemporary-
styled restaurant; husband Jean-Pierre mans the *fours* in the kitchen.
Copious, multi-choice menus with classical, *Bourgeoises* and regional
specialities of the *parfait de foie de volaille, filet de truite poêlée aux
champignons, faux-filet sauce au poivre vert, îles flottantes* variety.
Menus ABCE. Cards Access, Visa. (Rooms: Climat de France, 4 km N, N20.)
Closed Sun. Public hols. (Also in town: Ingres, on Tarn's opp. bank.)
Post 41 r. Comédie, 82000 Montauban, Tarn-et-Garonne. Region Southwest.
Tel 63 66 27 40. Mich 138/B4. Map 5.

MONTAUBAN   Orsay/Rest. La Cuisine d'Alain

Comfortable restaurant with rooms/Cooking 2-3
Terrace/Lift

Opposite the station but soundproofed rooms take the sting out of
moving trains. Alain Blanc regales clients with a neo-classical display,
notable for a mix of fish dishes – *gratin de poissons aux poireaux* is one
example – and filling creations such as a *galinette de veau pâtes
fraîches.* Terrific trolley of light sweets. Nicole is *la patronne.*
Menus BCDE. Rooms (20) E. Cards All.
Closed 1st wk May. 6-22 Aug. 23 Dec-7 Jan. Sun. Mon midday. Public hols.
Post face gare, 82000 Montauban, Tarn-et-Garonne. Region Southwest.
Tel 63 66 06 66. Fax 63 66 19 39. Mich 138/B4. Map 5.

MONTBRISON   Rest. Yves Thollot/Hôtel Marytel

Comfortable restaurant & simple hotel/Cooking 2
Terrace (restaurant)/Parking

At Savigneux, beside D946 to E. Two colourful, ultra-modern buildings
side-by-side. Odd-ball bright umbrellas in dining room. Nothing odd-ball
about Yves' neo-classical repertoire: a spirited *panaché de lotte et
saumon* and an accomplished, full-of-flavour marriage of *magret de
canard aux chanterelles* are sunny memories under the indoor umbrellas.
Menus aCDE. Rooms (33) DE. Disabled. Cards Acc, AE, DC (H only), Visa.
Closed Rest only: Feb school hols. 1-15 Aug. Sun evg. Mon. Map 6.
Post 93/95 rte Lyon, 42600 Montbrison, Loire. Region MC (Auvergne).
Tel (R) 77 96 10 40. (H) 77 58 72 00. Fax (H) 77 58 42 81. Mich 115/D3.

A100frs & under. B100–135. C135–165. D165–250. E250–350. F350–500. G500+

MONTFERRAT   Ferme du Baudron

Simple restaurant/Cooking 1-2
Terrace/Gardens/Swimming pool/Tennis/Parking

Note: lunch only at the Faivre family farm. Rustic is the tag at this
Alpine-like ski-lodge, complete with vast chimney and log fire where
Daniel Faivre does most of the cooking. Readers adore the sauces and a
mushroom sextet *façon de grand-mère. Pâtés*, grilled *faux-filet* and *côte
de porc*, ice creams – and similar (and instant-whip chocolat mousse?).
Menus A (not Sun when à la carte C). Lunch only. (Studios for rent.)
Closed Mid Jan to end Feb. Wed. (1 km S of Montferrat.)
Post 83131 Montferrat, Var. Region Côte d'Azur.
Tel 94 70 91 03. Mich 163/D2. Map 6.

MONTMELIAN   Viboud

Simple restaurant with basic rooms/Cooking 1-2
Parking

On the hill in the old town, well away from the N6. Jacques Viboud is a
great rugger enthusiast – witness the intriguing memorabilia and the
town team's many cups displayed in the bar. Old-fashioned cooking
(little choice) with classics such as *terrine de canard au pistaches et
noisettes* and a mundane but appetising *faux-filet poêlé.*
Menus ABC. Rooms (17) BCD. Cards All.
Closed 1st 3 wks Jan. 25 Sept to 22 Oct. Sun evg. Mon.
Post 73800 Montmélian, Savoie. Region Savoie.
Tel 79 84 07 24. Mich 118/B3. Map 6.

MONTREAL   Chez Simone

Simple restaurant/Cooking 1-2
Terrace

Chez Simone, tucked away near the fortified *église* in the perched
bastide of Montréal, is a cool oasis of culinary Gers charm. Three plane
trees provide a shady terrace; a beamed *salle* is the indoor option.
Blockbusting Landes and Gers tummy fillers: *salmis de palombe* and
confit de canard are typical. Bravo for the toothsome *hors d'oeuvre.*
Menus aBCD. Cards All. (Rooms: Trois Lys & Logis des Cordelirs, Condom.)
Closed Sat. (Above hotels are *sans rest* and easy 15 km drive to E.)
Post pl. Eglise, 32250 Montréal, Gers. Region Southwest.
Tel 62 29 44 40. Mich 151/D1. Map 5.

A100frs & under. B100–135. C135–165. D165–250. E250–350. F350–500. G500+

MONTSALVY

Nord

Comfortable hotel/Cooking 2
Parking

Jean Cayron, a cheerful, energetic *patron*, runs the front of house; his wife, Mauricette, is *la cuisinière* at the much modernised hotel. Readers speak warmly of her artistic skills with regional, classical and *Bourgeoises* offerings such as *terrine de légumes en jardinière, quiche crèmeuse aux girolles* and *filet de St-Pierre, doré, au Noilly.*
Menus ABCD. Rooms (26) DE. Cards All.
Closed Jan to Mar.
Post 15120 Montsalvy, Cantal. Region Massif Central (Auvergne).
Tel 71 49 20 03. Fax 71 49 29 00. Mich 126/B4. Map 5.

MOUCHARD

Chalet Bel'Air/Rôtisserie

Comfortable restaurant with rooms/Cooking 1-2
Terrace (Rôtisserie)/Gardens/Parking

Chalet-style *logis* between the village and N83. Bruno and Monique Gatto do an enterprising job at their "Rôtisserie". From the open fire in the large chimney relish tasty grills with vegetables – cooked in olden-day ways: *jambon grillée, côtes d'agneau, faux-filet grillé maître d'hôtel, caille dorée en broche* and other alternatives. (Note: the *logis* and *rôtisserie* are open every day; the separate restaurant is not.)
Menus ABC (à la carte). (ADEF in rest.) Rooms (9) DEF. Cards All.
Post 39330 Mouchard, Jura. Region Jura.
Tel 84 37 80 34. Fax 84 73 81 18. Mich 89/E2. Map 3.

MOUGINS

Feu Follet

Comfortable restaurant/Cooking 2-3
Terrace

At the heart of film-set Mougins, the most expensive real estate on the coast. English-speaking Jean-Paul and Micheline Battaglia have worked wonders in creating such a success; the place is always busy. Classical cooking, no stinting on portions and quality, wide choice and opulent desserts. Take a peek at the high-tech kitchen (cost 1 million francs).
Menus CD. Cards Acc, Visa. (Rooms: du Bosquet, Pégomas to W.)
Closed Sun evg (out of season). Mon. Tues midday (mid June to mid Sept).
Post pl. Mairie, 06250 Mougins, Alpes-Maritimes. Region Côte d'Azur.
Tel 93 90 15 78. Fax 92 92 92 62. Mich 163/F2. Map 6. Note: book ahead.

A100frs & under. B100–135. C135–165. D165–250. E250–350. F350–500. G500+

MOUGINS

Relais à Mougins

Very comfortable restaurant/Cooking 3
Terrace

André Surmain's wily pricing provides a top-notch bargain in some style. Menu C can include 3 virtuoso *plats*: *gelée d'ailerons de raie aux câpres à la crème de citron* – masterful; *morue fraîche au beurre de tomates* (with superb Streitz young veg); and a dream *tiramisu*. Bravo André, daughter Gigi (both speak fluent English) & chef Dominique Louis.
Menus CG. Cards Acc, AE, Visa. (Rooms: du Bosquet, Pégomas to W.)
Closed Mon (not evg July/Aug). Tues midday. (Also Le Zinc: menu A.)
Post pl. Mairie, 06250 Mougins, Alpes-Maritimes. Region Côte d'Azur.
Tel 93 90 03 47. Fax 93 75 72 83. Mich 163/F2. Map 6.

MOUTHIER-HAUTE-PIERRE

La Cascade

Comfortable hotel/Cooking 1-2
Quiet/Parking

The *logis* has scintillating views of the wooded Loue Valley far below. *Chef/patron* René Savonet juggles regional and *Bourgeoises* balls on menu B (classical, too, in DE): *croûte forestière, pâté aux foies de volaille ou crudités; truite belle meunière, épaule de veau sauce paprika ou côtes d'agneau grillée*; cheeses; dessert. One blot: awful tea.
Menus BDE. Rooms (23) E. Cards Access, Visa.
Closed Mid Nov to mid Feb.
Post 25920 Mouthier-Haute-Pierre, Doubs. Region Jura.
Tel 81 60 95 30. Fax 81 60 94 55. Mich 90/A2-B2. Map 3.

Les MOUTIERS-EN-RETZ

Bonne Auberge

Comfortable restaurant/Cooking 2

Patrice and Catherine Raimbault have bags of nous: neo-classical and classical *plats*; a smart dining room with flowers; and a profusion of professional touches. A clever *nouvelle formule* menu allows you to permutate five different prices (good choice). Chef Patrice's talents shine in numerous fish/shellfish dishes like *palourdes farcies au beurre d'ail, marinade d'anguilles* and *coquillage à la crème de curry*.
Menus bCDE. Cards Access, AE, Visa. (Rooms: Alizes; Pornic, 8 km NW.)
Closed Feb sch. hols. Mid Nov-mid Dec. Sun evg & Mon (not July/Aug).
Post av. Mer, 44580 Les Moutiers-en-Retz, Loire-Atlantique.
Tel 40 82 72 03. Mich 78/B2. Map 1. Regions Loire/Poitou-Charentes.

A100frs & under. B100–135. C135–165. D165–250. E250–350. F350–500. G500+

MUR-DE-BARREZ   Auberge du Barrez

Comfortable hotel/Cooking 1-2
Quiet/Parking

A contemporary-styled, ultra-modern *auberge*, to the south-east of high-on-a-hill Mur-de-Barrez. Christian Gaudel's culinary brush is a lot more traditional and unfussy: few regional colours but this is more than compensated for by well-judged flavoursome dishes such as *terrine de lapin en gelée, canette braisée au vin rouge* and *terrine de fraises*.
Menus aBD. Rooms (10) DEF. Cards Access, AE, Visa.
Closed Jan to mid Feb. Rest: Sun evg (Nov to Easter). Mon.
Post 12600 Mur-de-Barrez, Aveyron. Region Massif Central (Auvergne).
Tel 65 66 00 76. Fax 65 66 07 98. Mich 126/C3. Map 5.

NAJAC   Oustal del Barry

Very comfortable restaurant with rooms/Cooking 2-3
Quiet/Terrace/Gardens/Lift

Sixth generation owners, Catherine Miquel and husband, chef Jean-Marie, weave light, colourful, modern culinary tapestries at picturesque Najac. Typical personalised creations include *filet de poisson à l'infusion d'anis et d'algues, fenouil et céleri aux moules* and *tarte aux poires et crème d'amandes, crème glacée au miel*. Slow, slow service.
Menus b(lunch)CDE. Rooms (21) EF. Cards Access, AE, Visa.
Closed Nov to Mar. Mon midday (not high season and not public hols).
Post 12270 Najac, Aveyron. Regions Dordogne/Massif Central (Cévennes).
Tel 65 29 74 32. Fax 65 29 75 32. Mich 139/E3. Map 5.

NARBONNE   L'Olibo

Comfortable restaurant/Cooking 3-4

A Michelin two-star chef at his previous Réverbère restaurant, Claude Giraud and his delectable wife, Sabine, have resurfaced in Narbonne after the financial failure of the business. At L'Olibo there's no better *RQP* goldmine in France. Examples of the modern nuggets on menu B are two gold medal winners: *bourride de morue fraîche* and j*ambonneau de poulette, farci à la girolle*. Welcome back Claude!
Menus BD. Cards Access, AE, Visa. (Rooms: La Résidence, 3 min walk NE.)
Closed 1-15 Mar. 1-21 Aug. Sun. Wed evg. (Above *sans rest* and quiet.)
Post 51 r. Parerie, 11100 Narbonne, Aude. Region Languedoc-Roussillon.
Tel 68 41 74 47. Fax 68 42 84 90. Mich 173/D2. Map 5. (Park opp. rest.)

A100frs & under. B100–135. C135–165. D165–250. E250–350. F350–500. G500+

NESTIER
Relais du Castéra

Comfortable restaurant with rooms/Cooking 2-3
Terrace/Parking

At the northern door of spectacular terrain (Col d'Aspin to the SW; St-Bertrand-de-Comminges to the SE). Man and Nature tease the eyes; here Serge Latour tempts the taste buds with regional and neo-classical creations: put my claims to the test with *croustillant de truite*, *cassoulet* and *feuilleté tiède aux pruneaux*. Rooms not very comfy.
Menus aCDE. Rooms (8) E. Cards All.
Closed 5-25 Jan. 9-16 June. Sun evg. Mon.
Post 65160 Nestier, Hautes-Pyrénées. Region Southwest.
Tel 62 39 77 37. Fax 62 39 77 37 (same no.). Mich 169/E2. Map 5.

NEUFCHATEL-SUR-AISNE
Le Jardin

Comfortable restaurant/Cooking 2
Gardens

The A26 (junc. 14) is 10 km away (ideal for a last lunch). Well-named; the glassed-in terrace overlooking the garden is a delight. Jean-Claude Chevallier is *le patron* and master pastry cook; son Thierry is the chef. Limited choice on menu a. Knockout regional *plats*: *soufflé d'anguille et filet de carpe*; and *croustillant de Picardie* (dessert).
Menus aCDE. Cards Access, Visa. (Rooms: Novotel & Ibis W of Reims.)
Closed 15-31 Jan. Sun evg. Mon. Tues evg. (Above at junc. of A26 & A4.)
Post 02190 Neufchâtel-sur-Aisne, Aisne. Regions North/Champ-Ard.
Tel 23 23 82 00. Fax 23 23 84 05. Mich 20/C3. Map 3.

NEUILLE-LE-LIERRE
Auberge de la Brenne

Comfortable restaurant/Cooking 2
Parking

François Sallé is the helpful host (ask him to fix up a nearby *chambre d'hôte*) and his wife, Ghislaine, conjures up unfussy classical/regional culinary tricks – among them *salade tourangelle*, *rillettes* of pork, duck and goose cooked slowly and perfectly over a log fire and *joue de boeuf mijotée* with an unctuous black sauce (*vin de Bourgueil*).
Menus aCD. Cards Acc, AE, Visa. (Rooms: Novotel & Belle Vue, Amboise.)
Closed 24 Jan to mid Mar. Tues evg. Wed. (Above easy 12 km drive to SE.)
Post 37380 Neuillé-le-Lierre, Indre-et-Loire. Region Loire.
Tel 47 52 95 05. Mich 68/A3. Map 2.

A100frs & under. B100–135. C135–165. D165–250. E250–350. F350–500. G500+

NEUILLY-LE-REAL

Logis Henri IV

Comfortable restaurant/Cooking 2
Terrace

Valdi and Patricia Persello are justly proud of their authentic 16th-century hunting lodge. They should be just as chuffed by their *RQP* menu B. Consider the evidence: a *cassolette de moules au safran, compotée d'endives*, tender *noisettes d'agneau de pays à la sarriette, fromage* and a mouthwatering *nougat glacé au miel des Cévennes*.
Menus a(lunch)BD. Cards Access, Visa. (Rooms: Ibis (N7) S of Moulins.)
Closed 15 days Feb. 28 Aug-1 Sept. Sun evg. Mon. (Above 12 km to NW.)
Post 03340 Neuilly-le-Réal, Allier. Region Berry-Bourbonnais.
Tel 70 43 87 64. Mich 100/B2. Map 5.

NIEDERSTEINBACH

Cheval Blanc

Comfortable hotel/Cooking 1-2
Quiet/Terrace/Gardens/Swimming pool/Tennis/Parking

Charles and Michel Zinck, father and son, run a successful show at their *logis* – interconnected buildings, both old and new – in the densely wooded northern Vosges. Regional and classical cooking: *presskopf de lapereau* (rabbit terrine), *truite au bleu, entrecôte Béarnaise, civet de gibier, tarte maison* and *vacherin glacé* is all safe-as-houses fare.
Menus aCDE. Rooms (29) E. Cards Access, Visa.
Closed Feb to mid Mar. 15-29 June. 1-15 Dec. Thurs.
Post 67510 Niedersteinbach, Bas-Rhin. Region Alsace.
Tel 88 09 55 31. Fax 88 09 50 24. Mich 43/D2. Map 3.

NOUAN-LE-FUZELIER

Le Dahu

Comfortable restaurant/Cooking 2-3
Terrace/Gardens/Parking

A beamed and cleverly glassed-in dining room in an old Solognote farm with English-style gardens and English-speaking chef, Jean-Luc Germain. Some menu C alternatives: *salade Nordique au saumon fumé* or *soupe de moules au thym*; *sandre aux poireaux* or *magret de canard à la moutarde*. Marie-Thérèse Germain is a friendly hostess.
Menus bCD. Cards Acc, AE, Visa. (Rooms: Charmilles, a short walk away.)
Closed 19 Feb to 19 Mar. Tues evg and Wed (not July/Aug).
Post 14 r. H. Chapron, 41600 Nouan-le-Fuzelier, Loir-et-Cher.
Tel 54 88 72 88. Mich 69/E3. Map 2. Region Loire.

A100frs & under. B100–135. C135–165. D165–250. E250–350. F350–500. G500+

NOYAL-SUR-VILAINE
Hostellerie les Forges

Comfortable restaurant with rooms/Cooking 2-3
Parking

André Pilard, ex-student of the Strasbourg hotel school, is the chef; his wife, Laurette, is *la patronne*. André plays a classical cooking cello, his bow tuned to the sauces strings. Among a rich repertoire of nostalgic culinary tunes the likes of *filet de boeuf sauté Périgourdine* and *gratin d'oranges au Grand Marnier* are hard to resist.
Menus BCDE. Rooms (11) DE. Cards All.
Closed 2nd half Feb. Sun evg. Public hols (evgs only).
Post 35530 Noyal-sur-Vilaine, Ille-et-Vilaine. Region Brittany.
Tel 99 00 51 08. Fax 99 00 62 02. Mich 48/C3. Map 1.

NUCES
La Diligence

Very comfortable restaurant with rooms/Cooking 2-3
Terrace/Garage/Parking

Alongside the busy N140. Don't be put off. What a surprise the stylish, cool dining room is – matched by the terrace, shaded by four large trees. Jean-Claude Lausset is the dining room boss; Joël Delmas is the chef. Neo-classical, inventive *plats* with desserts stealing the show – witness a *biscuit au chocolate noisette, glace à l'amande amère.*
Menus a(lunch)BDE. Rooms (7) E. Cards Access, Visa.
Closed Jan. 4-10 Sept. Tues evg & Wed (Sept to June but not pub. hols).
Post Nuces, 12330 Valady, Aveyron. Region Massif Central (Cévennes).
Tel 65 72 60 20. Mich 140/B2. Map 5.

NYONS
La Charrette Bleue

Comfortable restaurant/Cooking 2
Terrace/Parking

Four menus to choose from – *tradition, découverte, régal* and *saveur* – at this single-storey, stone-built "cart". Extremely popular with locals; join them and dig into regional, classical and *Bourgeoise* cooking. Great olives – no surprise – and two memorable highlights: *terrine de lapin aux senteurs de Provence* and *bavette poêlée à la tapenade.*
Menus aBC. Cards Access, Visa. (Rooms: Caravelle & Les Alizés, Nyons.)
Closed 11 Jan to 7 Feb. 1st wk Dec. Tues evg (not July/Aug). Wed.
Post rte de Gap, 26110 Nyons, Drôme. Region Provence. (7 km to NE.)
Tel 75 27 72 33. Fax 75 26 05 72. Mich 144/C2. Map 6.

A100frs & under. B100–135. C135–165. D165–250. E250–350. F350–500. G500+

NYONS
Le Petit Caveau

Comfortable restaurant/Cooking 2-3

An aptly-named medieval site at the heart of Nyon. Christian Cormont's seven-year stint with Joël Robuchon in Paris gave him a modern cooking itch. This, married to a Provençale style, results in many flavoursome humdingers: *bouillabaisse minute de rouget et rascasse aux pistils de safran* is just one. Muriel Cormont, an expert hostess/*sommelière*, offers an enterprising three different glasses of wine at a sensible price.
Menus ACDE. Cards Access, Visa. (Rooms: Caravelle & Les Alizés, Nyons.)
Closed Dec. Sun evg and Mon (not high season).
Post 9 r. V. Hugo, 26110 Nyons, Drôme. Region Provence.
Tel 75 26 20 21. Mich 144/C2. Map 6. (Park in large *place* to the W.)

OBJAT
Pré Fleuri

Comfortable restaurant with rooms/Cooking 2-3
Terrace/Gardens

On the road to the "horse" town of Arnac-Pompadour. Jacques and Ingrid Chouzenoux have been joined by their son, Stéphane. Father and son ride regional, classical and neo-classical cooking mounts: *saumon fumé maison à la crème d'herbes* and *volaille fermière sauté aux olives et citron* are typical of the culinary hurdles jumped by the duo.
Menus aCE. Rooms (7) D. Cards Access, AE, Visa.
Closed 9-24 Jan. Mon (not in Aug).
Post rte Pompadour, 19130 Objat, Corrèze. Region Dordogne.
Tel 55 25 83 92. Mich 124/B1. Map 5.

OLORON-STE-MARIE
Alysson

Very comfortable hotel/Cooking 2
Terrace/Swimming pool/Lift/Parking

A spanking-new hotel to the west of the town. Mod-cons everywhere plus stirring views of the Pyrénées wall to the south. Plenty of choice between Philippe Maré's stop-the-tummy-rumbling regional *plats* and lighter fish alternatives: take your pick from the likes of *eminé de magret de canard au fumet de cèpes* and *tranche de thon poêlé Basquaise.*
Menus ACD. Rooms (32) EF. Disabled. Cards Access, Visa.
Closed Rest: 1st 3 wks Feb. Sat midday. Sun evg. Region Southwest.
Post bd Pyrénées, 64400 Oloron-Ste-Marie, Pyrénées-Atlantiques.
Tel 59 39 70 70. Fax 59 39 24 47. Mich 167/F2. Map 4.

A 100frs & under. B 100–135. C 135–165. D 165–250. E 250–350. F 350–500. G 500+

OPIO
Mas des Géraniums

Very simple restaurant/Cooking 2
Terrace/Gardens/Parking

The new owners of this jewel of a *mas*, English-speaking Colette and Michel Creusot, worked for Surmain at Mougins. Michel's classical and Provençal repertoire has many appealing facets: menu C could include *mousseline de rascasse à la vinaigrette de tomates, marengo de poulet aux écrevisses, fromage blanc* and dessert (choice for each course).
Menus CD. Cards Access, Visa. (Rooms: Novotel & Ibis SE of Valbonne.)
Closed 8 Nov-8 Dec. Tue evg (out of seas). Wed. Thur *midi* (July/Aug).
Post 06650 Opio, Alpes-Maritimes. Region Côte d'Azur.
Tel 93 77 23 23. Mich 163/F2. Map 6. (Beside D7, S of D2085.)

OTTROTT-LE-HAUT
A l'Ami Fritz

Comfortable restaurant with rooms (annexe)/Cooking 2
Secluded (annexe)/Gardens (annexe)/Terrace/Parking

A 200-year-old restaurant and a spanking-new annexe 300 metres or so away. Sophie and Patrick Fritz are a competent couple. Bravo Patrick for your efforts to re-create old *recettes Alsaciennes*. There's nothing prissy about *strudel de boudin noir, salade Ganzeliesel, gilerle* (cockerel) *au Riesling* and *boeuf au rouge d'Ottrott*.
Menus BCDE. Rooms (17) DE. Cards All.
Closed 3-20 Jan. Rest: Wed.
Post 67530 Ottrott-le-Haut, Bas-Rhin. Region Alsace. Map 3.
Tel (R) 88 95 80 81. (H) 88 95 87 39. Fax 88 95 84 85. Mich 61/D1.

OTTROTT-LE-HAUT
Beau Site

Very comfortable hotel/Cooking 2-3
Terrace/Garage/Parking

Martin and Brigitte Schreiber are *les patrons*: young Pascal Steffan is *le cuisinier*. In the beamed "Spindler" dining room (noted for its marquetry) you can order neo-classical specialities cooked in the modern French style. Superb cellar. For cheaper, stomach-filling Alsace nosh head for the glass-fronted "Les 4 Saisons" bistro (menus AB).
Menus (Spindler) CEF. Rooms (7) EFG. Cards All.
Closed Rest: Sun evg. Mon.
Post 67530 Ottrott-le-Haut, Bas-Rhin. Region Alsace.
Tel 88 95 80 61. Fax 88 95 86 41. Mich 61/D1. Map 3.

A100frs & under. B100–135. C135–165. D165–250. E250–350. F350–500. G500+

OUCQUES   Commerce

Comfortable restaurant with rooms/Cooking 2

The dark-shuttered *logis* is beside the D917, to the east of the D924. The
very much contemporary-styled, colourfully-upholstered dining room
and bedrooms come as quite a surprise. *La patronne*, Jo Lanchais, is a
delight; her husband, Jean-Pierre, drives classical and *Bourgeoises*
routes: enjoy *filet de daurade et sa brunoise de légumes* and a robust
crépinette de poularde aux champignons des bois – just the ticket.
Menus aCD. Rooms (12) DEF. Cards Access, Visa.
Closed 20 Dec-31 Jan. Sun evg (Sept-June). Mon (not evgs July/Aug).
Post 41290 Oucques, Loir-et-Cher. Region Loire.
Tel 54 23 20 41. Fax 54 23 02 88. Mich 68/B2. Map 2.

PAILHEROLS   Auberge des Montagnes

Simple hotel/Cooking 2
Quiet/Swimming pools (indoor and outdoor)/Parking

A warm-hearted family, led by André and Denise Combourieu, fusses over
you at the high-altitude *auberge*. *Bourgeois*, classical and *Auvergnats*
appetite-quenching meals: *pounti*, *truffade*, *tripoux* and *cornet de Murat*
on one of the A menus; *terrine d'aiglefin*, *pavé de Salers* (beef) and a
light, tempting plate of three high-quality *pâtisseries* on menu B.
Menus AB. Rooms (19) D. Cards Access, Visa.
Closed Mid Oct to 20 Dec.
Post 15800 Pailherols, Cantal. Region Massif Central (Auvergne).
Tel 71 47 57 01. Fax 71 49 63 83. Mich 126/C3. Map 5.

PASSENANS   Le Revermont

Comfortable hotel/Cooking 2
Secluded/Terr./Gardens/Swim. pool/Tennis/Lift/Garage/Parking

Michel and Marie-Claude Schmit, the owners, are an uncommunicative
duo at this odd-looking, modern *logis*, run as a "business", in a lovely
setting north of the village. Principally classical offerings: *mitonnée de
magret de canard à la creme de lentilles* (an in-vogue dish) is a stomach
filler; *petite assiette de pâtisseries* a sumptuous sweet.
Menus BCDE. Rooms (28) DEF. Cards Access, AE, Visa.
Closed Jan. Feb. Sun evg and Mon (Oct to Mar).
Post 39230 Passenans, Jura. Region Jura.
Tel 84 44 61 02. Fax 84 44 64 83. Mich 89/E3. Map 3.

A 100frs & under. B 100–135. C 135–165. D 165–250. E 250–350. F 350–500. G 500+

PERROS-GUIREC   Les Feux des Iles

Comfortable hotel/Cooking 2
Quiet/Gardens/Parking

Gardens, sea views and a modern stone building impress as much as *chef/patron* Antoine Le Roux's cooking. Menu B could include a rainbow-hued *terrine de poissons et saumon tiède au velouté vert*; a tasty and tarty *fricassée de volaille au cidre et pommes acidulées*; a *rouelle de chèvre (avec salade)*; and a lip-smacking strawberry *pâtisserie*.
Menus BDE. Rooms (15) EFG. Disabled. Cards All. Region Brittany.
Closed Feb school hols. 2-8 Oct. Sun evg and Mon (Oct to Apl).
Post 53 bd Clemenceau, 22700 Perros-Guirec, Côtes d'Armor.
Tel 96 23 22 94. Fax 96 91 07 30. Mich 28/A1. Map 1.

PEYREHORADE   Central

Comfortable hotel/Cooking 3
Lift

A fizzing *RQP* crackler. What a transformation at the hotel I've known for 20 years. Sylvie de Lalagade has worked wonders; the building is now a contemporary-styled sparkler; and her brother, Eric Galby, is a young *cuisine moderne* dazzler. Past tastebud teasers have included *sandre soufflé aux pleurottes* and *sablé aux fraises, crème vanillée*.
Menus ACD. Rooms (16) E. Cards All.
Closed 1st 3 wks Mar. 11-27 Dec. Sun evg and Mon (not July/Aug).
Post pl. A. Briand, 40300 Peyrehorade, Landes. Region Southwest.
Tel 58 73 03 22. Fax 58 73 17 15. Mich 149/D3. Map 4.

PLAISANCE   Les Magnolias

Comfortable restaurant with rooms/Cooking 2-3
Quiet/Terrace/Gardens

A bewitching spot: an old vine-covered *logis* with stones and beams and an emerald of a garden. Marie-France and Francis Roussel are charmers too. She's the English-speaking *patronne*; he's a capable *cuisinier* with a light, neo-classical touch. Hereabouts dishes like *dos de truite et son court bouillon à l'ail rose de Lautrec* are a welcome surprise.
Menus ABDE. Rooms (6) DE. Cards Access, AE, Visa.
Closed Mid Nov to end Mar.
Post 12550 Plaisance, Aveyron. Region Languedoc-Roussillon.
Tel 65 99 77 34. Fax 65 99 70 57. Mich 154/C1. Map 5.

A100frs & under. B100–135. C135–165. D165–250. E250–350. F350–500. G500+

PLAISANCE

La Ripa Alta

Comfortable restaurant with rooms/Cooking 3 (see text)

Generous-hearted, English-speaking Maurice Coscuella, cooking for almost 35 years, has had his fair share of problems over the decades I've known him and his gentle wife, Irène. Maurice is one of a rare breed – a truly innovative chef capable of pulling modern, regional and neo-classical tricks from his culinary *valise. Quod sapit nutrit* he claims: spot-on with delights like a *soupe de châtaigne aux grattons de foie gras.*
Menus ACD (menu A – rating 2). Rooms (12) DE. Cards All.
Closed Jan. Mon midday (not mid May to mid Sept).
Post 32160 Plaisance, Gers. Region Southwest.
Tel 62 69 30 43. Fax 62 69 36 99. Mich 150/C3. Map 4.

PLAN-DU-VAR

Cassini

Comfortable restaurant with rooms/Cooking 2
Terrace

Beside the N202. A rural-style dining room and a warm welcome from the Cassini-Martin foursome – all talented restaurateurs. Philippe Martin is a clever classicist with many light-fingered touches. Two main courses epitomise those skills: a super *truite saumonée à la crème de persil* and a gutsy *pavé de boeuf aux morilles.* Delicious desserts.
Menus BCD. Rooms (22) CDE. Cards Access, AE, Visa. Region Côte d'Azur.
Closed 8-21 Jan. 12-25 June. Sun evg & Mon (not July/Aug).
Post rte Nationale, Plan-du-Var, 06670 Levens, Alpes-Maritimes.
Tel 93 08 91 03. Fax 93 08 45 48. Mich 165/D2-D3. Map 6.

PLOUMANAC'H

Rochers

Very comfortable restaurant with rooms/Cooking 2-3

Bracing views of a landlocked bay from Renée Justin's acclaimed restaurant will leave laser-etched memories. Whether the classical *plats* will impress as much is open to doubt. Menu C offers no choice: to start, a well-executed *terrine de lapereau aux fruits sec, chutney de légumes* followed by a fresh-as-daisies *filet de carrelet au coulis de langoustines* finishing with a *parfait glacé St-James, crème vanille.*
Menus CDF. Rooms (15) E. Cards Access, Visa.
Closed Oct to Easter. Rest: Wed (out of season).
Post Ploumanac'h, 22700 Perros-Guirec, Côtes d'Armor. Region Brittany.
Tel 96 91 44 49. Fax 96 91 43 64. Mich 28/A1. Map 1.

A100frs & under. B100–135. C135–165. D165–250. E250–350. F350–500. G500+

POLIGNY   Paris

Simple hotel/Cooking 1-2
Swimming pool (indoor)/Garage

André Biétry's ugly *logis* is in the centre of Poligny. A choice for each
course is a big plus – as is the indoor pool. Choose from alternatives
such as *terrine* or *soupe de poissons*; *truite meunière, civet de lièvre* –
the latter both rich and filling – or *lapereau aux herbes garni*; Jura
cheeses and a vast selection of desserts, including *vacherin glacé*.
Menus ACD. Rooms (25) CDE. Cards Access, Visa.
Closed Nov to Jan. Rest: Mon and Tues midday (not July/Aug).
Post 7 r. Travot, 39800 Poligny, Jura. Region Jura.
Tel 84 37 13 87. Mich 89/E3. Map 3.

PONT-A-MOUSSON   Auberge des Thomas

Simple restaurant/Cooking 2
Terrace

Flowers caress the eyes both inside and in the gardens at Michel and
Solange Thomas' *auberge* – at Blénod, two km south of the town in the
unattractive Moselle Valley. Thierry Pernot is the neo-classical chef: he
makes good use of the local wine in a tasty *sandre à la lie de pinot noir
de Toul*. Brilliant desserts – like *charlotte à la poire*.
Menus BCD. Cards All. (Rooms: Bagatelle, *sans rest*, in Pont-à-Mousson.)
Closed Feb school hols. 1st 3 wks Aug. Sun evg. Mon. Wed evg.
Post 100 av. V. Claude, 54700 Blénod-lès-Pont-à-Mousson, Meurthe-et-M.
Tel 83 81 07 72. Mich 41/D3. Map 3. Regions Alsace/Champagne-Ard.

PONTAUMUR   Poste

Simple hotel/Cooking 1-2
Garage

Pierrette Quinty is a welcoming hostess; and her husband, Jean-Paul, is
both an enthusiastic rugger fan and lover of *Auvergnats*, classical and
Bourgeois specialities: *tête de veau gribiche, jambon d'Auvergne* and
râble de lièvre aux figues are among the many Quinty pleasures. A top-
notch sweet is a lip-licking *nougat glacé au miel et aux noix*.
Menus aCD. Rooms (15) DE. Cards Access, Visa.
Closed Mid Dec to end Jan. Sun evg and Mon (not July/Aug).
Post 63380 Pontaumur, Puy-de-Dôme. Region Massif Central (Auvergne).
Tel 73 79 90 15. Fax 73 79 73 17. Mich 112/C1. Map 5.

A100frs & under. B100–135. C135–165. D165–250. E250–350. F350–500. G500+

PONT-DE-VAUX   Commerce

Comfortable restaurant with rooms/Cooking 2-3
Garage

Monique Patrone is an attractive, attentive *patronne*. Competition is murderous in the small town, its houses looking quite colourful these days. What about this for a colourful menu B? Silky *gâteau de foies de volaille*; *escalope de saumon sauce curry et fruits* – a stormy marriage; and a *tarte aux pommes chaude, caramel et glace canelle*.
Menus a(lunch)BCD. Rooms (10) DE. Cards All.
Closed 19 Nov to 21 Dec. Tues and Wed (not July/Aug and public hols).
Post 01190 Pont-de-Vaux, Ain. Region Lyonnais.
Tel 85 30 30 56. Mich 102/C2. Map 6.

PONT-DE-VAUX   Le Raisin

Comfortable restaurant with rooms/Cooking 3
Garage

A coffee-shaded façade in a street of houses with many-hued exteriors. The menus, too, have many shades of taste and choice. Consider the cheapest: from 4 starters a *terrine de chef* and *assiette de crudités*; from a main-course trio, a robust *paillard de boeuf grillée*; *crêpes Parmentier*; and, from four sweets, *fromage blanc à la crème*.
Menus bCDE. Rooms (8) DE. Cards All.
Closed Jan. Sun evg and Mon (not public hols).
Post 01190 Pont-de-Vaux, Ain. Region Lyonnais.
Tel 85 30 30 97. Fax 85 30 67 89. Mich 102/C2. Map 6.

PORT-VENDRES   Côte Vermeille

Comfortable restaurant/Cooking 2

The brothers Bessière – Philippe, younger by two years, is the chef; Guilhem runs the front of house – are fish addicts; there's no use coming here if you're a carnivore. The trawler alternatives are a knockout: like *soupe de poissons, anchois de Collioure marinés, fantasie de poissons et crustacés marinés, merlan de palangre et pétoncles* and *filets de rougets de roche en salmis*. (You'll be hard pressed to find such a roll-call of super fish dishes anywhere.) Forget the chips!
Menus a(lunch)CD. Cards Access, Visa. (Rooms: St-Elme, *sans rest*.)
Post quai du Fanal, 66660 Port-Vendres, Pyrénées-Orientales.
Tel 68 82 05 71. Mich 177/F3. Map 5. Region Languedoc-Roussillon.

A100frs & under. B100–135. C135–165. D165–250. E250–350. F350–500. G500+

POUILLY-SOUS-CHARLIEU

de la Loire

Very comfortable restaurant/Cooking 2
Terrace/Gardens/Parking

Brigitte and Alain Rousseau (he trained at Troisgros in Roanne) have a handsome dining room and lime-shaded terrace – 100 m from the Loire. Alain rings all the culinary-style bells: *rillette aux deux saumons*; a blockbuster pan-fried *pièce Charolaise au beurre vigneron* or a lighter *filet de cabillaud à la Basquaise*; and a dessert duo – all on menu C.
Menus aCDE. Cards All. (Rooms: Relais de l'Abbaye, Charlieu.) Closed 2-7 Jan. Feb sch. hols. 1-10 Sept. Sun evg. Mon. Wed evg (not high seas).
Post 42720 Pouilly-sous-Charlieu, Loire. Region Lyonnais.
Tel 77 60 81 36. Mich 101/E3. Map 5. (Hotel is easy 5 min-drive to E.)

La PRENESSAYE

Motel d'Armor/Rest. Le Boléro

Comfortable hotel/Cooking 2
Gardens/Parking

Beside the N164, 8 km east of Loudéac. Wooded grounds, a warm welcome from Madeleine Fraboulet and modern cooking from her husband Daniel. Clever menu choice. First-class fish dishes served on huge plates: *le délice Nordique* (*galette de blé noir, poisson fumé*) and *le superbe filet de lieu côtier à l'estragon* are among the memorable highlights.
Menus aBCD. Rooms (10) E. Cards Access, Visa.
Closed Feb school hols. Rest: Sun evg. Mon midday.
Post La Prénessaye, 22210 Plémet, Côtes d'Armor. Region Brittany.
Tel 96 25 90 87. Fax 96 25 76 72. Mich 47/D1. Map 1.

PUSIGNAN

La Closerie

Very comfortable restaurant/Cooking 2-3
Terrace/Gardens/Parking

Gilles Troump's Louis XV-styled restaurant is more easily found if Pusignan is approached from the A432 Satolas road. Classical is the best tag for the cooking, service and fittings. An original *carpaccio de canard* – which didn't quite work – and impressive *blanquette de veau* (no relation to the basic mundane version) were enjoyable. Pretty gardens.
Menus BCDE. Cards All. (Rooms: Sofitel & Climat de France, – 7 km to S.)
Closed 7-21 Aug. Sun evg. Mon. (Both above at Lyon-Satolas airport.)
Post 4 pl. Gaîté, 69330 Pusignan, Rhône. Region Lyonnais.
Tel 78 04 40 50. Mich 116/B2. Map 6. (Pusignan is 23 km E of Lyon.)

A100frs & under. B100–135. C135–165. D165–250. E250–350. F350–500. G500+

RAGUENES-PLAGE

Chez Pierre

Comfortable hotel/Cooking 1-2
Quiet/Terrace/Gardens/Parking

Chez Pierre has had many a face-lift over the decades – including a new modern annexe. Gentle, English-speaking *patronne*, Dany Guillou, and her chef husband, Xavier, work hard to please their largely *pension* clients. Copious classical and *Bourgeoises plats*: *colin au champagne* and *gigot d'agneau* as examples. *Vacherin* a mini Mt-Blanc concoction.
Menus bCD. Rooms (35) DEF. Disabled. Cards Access, Visa.
Closed Oct to Mar. Rest: Wed (June to mid Sept).
Post Raguenès-Plage, 29139 Névez, Finistère. Region Brittany.
Tel 98 06 81 06. Mich 45/E3. Map 1.

REALMONT

Noël

Very comfortable restaurant with rooms/Cooking 2
Terrace

Young chef Jean-Paul Granier hangs classical and regional *plats* on the Noël tree; and his wife Michèle takes your requests. The green-shuttered house and shady terrace remain the same from times past – as does the cooking. Menu B could be a *salade de foie de dinde au vinaigre de Xérès*; *noix de boeuf au poivre*; cheeses; and *croustillant aux pommes*.
Menus BDE. Rooms (9) DE. Cards All.
Closed Feb school hols. Sun evg and Mon (not July/Aug).
Post r. H. de Ville, 81120 Réalmont, Tarn. Region Languedoc-Roussillon.
Tel 63 55 52 80. Mich 154/A2. Map 5.

ROCAMADOUR   Beau Site et Notre Dame/Rest. Jehan de Valon

Very comfortable hotel/Cooking 2-3
Terrace/Lift/Parking

A well-named site, halfway up the cliff-hanger medieval *cité*. Modern and old apply to the two buildings (straddling the pedestrian-crowded road) and to Christophe Besse's cooking. On one hand a melting *millefeuille de truite rose à la crème de ciboulette*; on the other a belt-stretching *cuisse de canard confite à l'ancienne*. Wide choice on menus.
Menus ACD. Rooms (44) EF. Cards All.
Closed Mid Nov to Mar.
Post 46500 Rocamadour, Lot. Region Dordogne.
Tel 65 33 63 08. Fax 65 33 65 23. Mich 124/C4. Map 5.

A100frs & under. B100–135. C135–165. D165–250. E250–350. F350–500. G500+

ROCHEFORT Tourne-Broche

Comfortable restaurant/Cooking 1-2

Dina Klein and her husband, chef Jean, contrive to pull off a series of culinary rope tricks with no less than four qualifying menus. The two C menus are largesse: *nos propositions du marché* offers a wide choice for each course; a *dégustation* has eight courses. Fish, shellfish, *grillades au feu de bois*, classical and regional alternatives provide the most varied of options. Simpler grills on the two cheapest menus.

Menus BCD. Cards Access, AE, Visa. (Rooms: Ibis to N – with parking.)
Closed 20-28 Feb. 24 June to 7 July. Last wk Oct. Sat midday.
Post 56 av. Ch. de Gaulle, 17300 Rochefort, Char.-Mar. Region Poit-Char.
Tel 46 99 20 19. Fax 46 99 72 06. Mich 106/B1-Cl. Map 4.

La ROCHELLE L'Entracte

Comfortable restaurant/Cooking 2-3

Easy to get to from the western side; park near the famous Tour de la Lanterne. L'Entracte is Michelin 2-star chef Richard Coutanceau's bistro (about 300 metres from his restaurant). A "theatre-programme" menu: four acts (starters, fish, *viandes*, desserts) and you choose from three. Wide choice of modern, classical and regional *plats* like *mouclade*, *norue fraîche*, *faux-filet grillée sauce Bordelaise* and *jonchée*.

Menus C Cards Access, Visa. (Rooms: Les Brises & Majestic – both to W.)
Closed Sun. (Les Brises has super site/parking; Majestic much cheaper.)
Post 22 r. St-Jean du Pérot, 17000 La Rochelle, Charente-Maritime.
Tel 46 50 62 60. Fax 41 41 99 45. Mich 92/C3. Map 4.

RODEZ St-Amans

Comfortable restaurant/Cooking 2

Jack Amat is fast approaching his 50th birthday. Thirty years ago he won the coveted best apprentice chef in France award; he also had a long seven-year stint at Taillevent in Paris. That honed and buffed polish in Paris shows in his classical and neo-classical repertoire: menu B could be *oeuf poché aux asperges*, *saumon poêlé aux algues*, a *granité*, *filet de porc au citron vert*, *fromage* and a cracking sweet.

Menus BE. Cards Access, Visa, (Rooms: Tour Maje – adjacent to parking.)
Closed Mid Feb to mid Mar. (Above 200 metres-walk to NW.)
Post 12 r. Madeleine, 12000 Rodez, Aveyron. Region MC (Cévennes).
Tel 65 68 03 18. Mich 140/B2-C2. Map 5.

A100frs & under. B100–135. C135–165. D165–250. E250–350. F350–500. G500+

La ROQUE-GAGEAC   Belle Etoile

Comfortable hotel/Cooking 1-2
Terrace/Garage

Guy and chef Régis Ongaro's *logis* has a fabulous Dordogne-side site.
The first-floor terrace is a cool haven for summer lunches. Plenty of
choice but no little extras. A typical menu could be a drooling *ballotine
de canard au foie gras et sa salade*, a *magret de canard sauce citron*,
cabécou de Rocamadour and a "so-so" *crème brûlée à la cassonade*.
Menus BCDE. Rooms (17) DEF. Cards Access, Visa.
Closed Mid Oct to Easter.
Post 24250 La Roque-Gageac, Dordogne. Region Dordogne.
Tel 53 29 51 44. Fax 53 29 45 63. Mich 124/A3. Map 5.

ROSCOFF   Le Temps de Vivre

Very comfortable restaurant/Cooking 3

If you are using Roscoff to cross the Channel then find an excuse to nose
out Jean-Yves Crenn, one of Brittany's best chefs. A modern master
creating gilt-edged *plats* and capitalising cleverly on Finistère's rich and
varied larder. Simple, complex and robust sit cheek by jowl: *choux farcis
d'araignée aux oignons roses de Roscoff* and a *museau de cochon farci*
are both star-winning stunners – and ample evidence of what I mean.
Menus bCDE. Cards Access, Visa. (Rooms: adjacent Ibis.)
Closed Feb and Nov school hols. Sun evg. Mon.
Post pl. Eglise, 29680 Roscoff, Finistère. Region Brittany.
Tel 98 61 27 28. Mich 27/D1. Map 1.

ROUDOUALLEC   Bienvenue

Comfortable restaurant/Cooking 2-3
Parking

A run-of-the-mill exterior but don't be fooled: the airy, cool dining room
is a refreshing tonic (the turquoise wall covering is English). Refined and
intense neo-classical cuisine from Jean-Claude Spégagne. Two cracking
specialities have links with Scotland: Scottish salmon in a sorrel sauce
and giant *langoustines grillées flambées au whisky*.
Menus aCDE. Cards Access, AE, Visa. (Rooms: Relais de Cornouaille – at)
Closed 1-15 Feb. Tues evg & Wed (out of season). (Châteauneuf-du-Faou.)
Post 56110 Roudouallec, Morbihan. Region Brittany.
Tel 97 34 50 01. Mich 45/E1. Map 1. (Easy drive NW to Chat.-du-Faou.)

A100frs & under. B100–135. C135–165. D165–250. E250–350. F350–500. G500+

ROUFFACH A la Ville de Lyon/Rest. Philippe Bohrer

Simple hotel and very comfortable restaurant/Cooking 3
Lift/Parking

Two adjacent buildings (the hotel exterior needs a face-lift). Attentive waitress service. Neo-classical fare from chef Philippe Bohrer: a wholesome *hure de queue de boeuf en gelée*, flavoursome *blanc de volaille aux senteurs des Mascareignes* and a saliva-stirring *terrine de quetsches et sa glace cannelle*. Also cheaper Chez Julien *winstub* (wine bar).
Menus BDEF (winstub AB). Rooms (43) EF. Cards All.
Closed 1st 3 wks Mar. Rest: Mon. (On town's northern exit.)
Post r. Poincaré, 68250 Rouffach, Haut-Rhin. Region Alsace. Map 3.
Tel (R) 89 49 62 49. (H) 89 49 65 51. Fax 89 49 76 67. Mich 61/D4.

Les ROUSSES France

Very comfortable hotel/Cooking 3
Terrace/Parking

For many decades Roger Petit has been charming both French and Swiss clients (the border is just minutes away) at his mountain chalet-hotel 1100 metres above sea-level. Step back many decades, to the days of the legendary Fernand Point, for painstakingly-created classical offerings. One more endearing dividend: plenty of half-bottles of wine.
Menus CDF. Rooms (33) F. Cards All.
Closed 20 Nov to 14 Dec. 5-30 June.
Post 39220 Les Rousses, Jura. Region Jura.
Tel 84 60 01 45. Fax 84 60 04 63. Mich 104/B1. Map 6.

ROUTOT L'Ecurie

Comfortable restaurant/Cooking 2-3

Danièlle and Jacques Thierry are a delightful, ambitious duo. Great dining room (not the *écurie* – stable – which is used for large parties) and equally stylish menus, a roll-call of sumptuous classical dishes. Try these for size: *les rouelles de lapereau tièdes, vinaigrette au jus de truffe*; *trois terrines maison*; *canard de Duclair façon Ecurie*; Normandy cheeses; and *charlotte au chocolat crème au café*.
Menus aCD. Cards Acc, Visa. (Rooms: Normotel-La Marine, Caudebec.)
Closed Feb school hols. 1st wk Aug. Sun evg. Mon. Wed evg (Oct-June).
Post 27350 Routot, Eure. Region Normandy. (Caudebec 20 km to N.)
Tel 32 57 30 30. Mich 15/E4. Map 2. (Park in huge *place*.)

A100frs & under. B100–135. C135–165. D165–250. E250–350. F350–500. G500+

ROYE Central/Rest. Florentin

Comfortable restaurant with rooms/Cooking 2

A modern, smart-looking spot in the centre of the town (near the huge place H. de Ville). The dining room, with garish neo-classical pillars and murals, is much too crowded for comfort. Chef Denis Devaux does a competent classical/regional job: enjoy, from a wide choice for each course on menu C (low-end), *tourteau froid mayonnaise*; gutsy *coq au vin*; cheese; and a filling, intense *gâteau au chocolat*.
Menus aCD. Rooms (8) DE. Cards All.
Closed 23 Dec to 4 Jan. 6-13 Mar. 19-27 Aug. Sun evg. Mon.
Post 36 r. Amiens, 80700 Roye, Somme. Region North.
Tel 22 87 11 05. Fax 22 87 42 74. Mich 18/B2. Map 2.

RUMILLY L'Améthyste

Comfortable restaurant/Cooking 2-3

Easily found if you enter the town from the north; the restaurant is on the right, before the river bridge. Chef Julien Valéro, a modern *cuisinier*, was once a student of glamour-puss Marc Veyrat (near Annecy). Julien's invention shows – though not that well in a *noisettes de thon au curry*. More resounding successes are *cuisse de lapereau au jus de thyme* and a clever *duo chaud-froid* strawberry dessert.
Menus BDEF. Cards Access, Visa. (Rooms: Relais du Clergeon at Moye.)
Closed 23 July to 11 Aug. (Moye is 4 km to NW – quiet village and site.)
Post 27 r. Pont-Neuf, 74150 Rumilly, Haute-Savoie. Region Savoie.
Tel 50 01 02 52. Mich 118/A1. Map 6.

ST-AFFRIQUE Moderne

Comfortable hotel/Cooking 2

A considerable favourite with readers over the years. Built in 1970, the *logis* lives up to its modern-day name as the place has been extensively refurbished and painted up a treat; the interior is a permanent art exhibition. Jean-François Decuq does the brush work front of house; brother Yves mixes the colours in the kitchen. Classical and regional canvases with *Roquefort* (down the road) popping up all over the show.
Menus ACDE. Rooms (28) EF. Cards Access, AE. Visa.
Closed 18 Dec to 15 Jan. 9-15 Oct (not hotel).
Post 54 av. A.-Pezet, 12400 St-Affrique, Aveyron. Region MC (Cévennes).
Tel 65 49 20 44. Fax 65 49 36 55. Mich 155/D1. Map 5.

A 100frs & under. B 100–135. C 135–165. D 165–250. E 250–350. F 350–500. G 500+

ST-AMAND-MONTROND Boeuf Couronné

Simple restaurant/Cooking 2
Parking

Three dining rooms in this small restaurant at a busy junction NW of the town. A Grand Canyon wide choice of dishes is an impressive feature. Menu B has 6 starters, 4 main course dishes and 11 desserts. Typical bounty could include *saumon fumé* (home-made and delicious), gutsy *confit de canard maison aux cèpes* and a simple *crème caramel*.
Menus aBCD. Cards Access, Visa. (Rooms: Le Noirlac, 2 km to NW.)
Closed 3-17 Jan. 28 June to 12 July. Tues evg. Wed. (Above on N144.)
Post 86 r. Juranville, 18200 St-Amand-Montrond, Cher.
Tel 48 96 42 72. Mich 84/C4. Map 2. Region Berry-Bourbonnais.

ST-ANTHEME Pont de Raffiny

Simple hotel/Cooking 2
Parking

Alain Beaudoux has to try so much harder at this remote *logis* 5½ km south of St-Anthème. Modernised bedrooms and an unusual dining room with fountain and small pool; ask, too, to see the *salon*. Classical fare: *civet de sanglier sauce Grand Marnier*, *pavé de boeuf au poivre* and *rable de lièvre aux pâtes fraîches* will stop tummies rumbling for days.
Menus aBC. Rooms (12) D. Cards Access, Visa.
Closed Jan to mid Feb. Sun evg and Mon (mid Sept to June).
Post Raffiny, 63660 St-Anthème, Puy-de-Dôme. Region MC (Auvergne).
Tel 73 95 49 10. Fax 73 95 80 21. Mich 114/C3. Map 5.

ST-AVOLD Europe

Comfortable hotel/Cooking 2
Lift/Garage/Parking

I first visited Eugène and Charlotte Zirn's modern hotel when I was researching my *En Route* guide (p41). Eugène drives both traditional and modern cooking *autoroutes*: *jarret de porc sur choucroute nouvelle*, *moules marinières*, *escalope de saumon à la crème de ciboulette* are typical *plats*. (S from A4; left after Novotel; right at T.)
Menus BCDE. Rooms (34) EF. Cards All.
Closed Rest: 1-15 Aug. Sat midday. Sun.
Post 7 r. Altmayer, 57500 St-Avold, Moselle. Region Alsace.
Tel 87 92 00 33. Fax 87 92 01 23. Mich 41/F1. Map 3.

A100frs & under. B100–135. C135–165. D165–250. E250–350. F350–500. G500+

ST-CAST-LE-GUILDO

Le Biniou

Comfortable restaurant/Cooking 2
Parking

Panoramic views of the sea from the smart modern Breton "bagpipe". Yvette and Jean-Claude Menard are the pipers at "Le Biniou". The Armor's piscatorial harvests – treasures all – dominate the menus: oysters, mussels, *soupe de poissons aux étrilles, filet de lieu, terrine de poissons, maquereaux, saumon*. Who needs to eat meat here?
Menus aBDE. Cards Access, Visa. (Rooms: Dunes & Bon Abri.)
Closed Mid Nov to mid Mar. Tues (mid Sept to mid June).
Post Plage de Pen-Guen, 22380 St-Cast-le-Guildo, Côtes d'Armor.
Tel 96 41 94 53. Mich 29/E2. Map 1. Region Brittany.

ST-CERE

France

Comfortable hotel/Cooking 2
Terrace/Gardens/Swimming pool/Parking

A modern *logis*, away from St-Céré's busy centre, with spacious lounges, dining room and shady terrace/garden. English-speaking Isabelle Lherm is an attractive young hostess; husband Patrick an assured, able chef. Classical and regional offerings: invigorating *soupe paysanne en croûte, saumon fumé Parmentier* and a diet-killing *pièce de boeuf grillée*.
Menus bCDE. Rooms (22) EF. Cards Access, Visa.
Closed Mid Nov to Feb. Tues midday. Sat midday.
Post av. F. de Maynard, 46400 St-Céré, Lot. Region Dordogne.
Tel 65 38 02 16. Fax 65 38 02 98. Mich 125/D3. Map 5.

ST-CHELY-D'AUBRAC

Voyageurs-Vayrou

Simple hotel/Cooking 1-2

Christiane Vayrou and her son-in-law, Patrick Amilhat (his wife, Brigitte, is the sister of Régine Caralp at Le Méjane, Espalion), are the cooks at the long-established family hotel. Classical and regional *cuisine soignée* (see the dining room photographs): *tripoux, terrine de canard, assiette de charcuterie, cou farci et magret fumé* and *aligot du chef* – all dishes which are the very essence of Aubrac.
Menus ABC. Rooms (14) E. Cards Access, Visa.
Closed Oct to Mar. Sat (not July/Aug).
Post 12470 St-Chély-d'Aubrac, Aveyron. Region Massif Central (Auvergne).
Tel 65 44 27 05. Mich 141/D1. Map 5.

A100frs & under. B100–135. C135–165. D165–250. E250–350. F350–500. G500+

ST-CIRQ-LAPOPIE   Auberge du Sombral "Aux Bonnes Choses"

Comfortable restaurant with rooms/Cooking 1-2
Quiet/Terrace

The medieval village, high above the Lot, is a photographer's dream; so, too, is Gilles Hardeveld's *auberge* and the evocative place de la Mairie. Unabashed regional nosh: *salade de cabécous rôtis, cuisse de canarde confite, poulet aux champignons, truite au vieux Cahors* and *gigot d'agneau* are typical. Tricky parking.
Menus ACD. Rooms (8) EF. Cards Access, Visa.
Closed 11 Nov to end Mar. Tues evg. Wed.
Post 46330 St-Cirq-Lapopie, Lot. Region Dordogne.
Tel 65 31 26 08. Fax 65 30 26 37. Mich 138/C2. Map 5.

ST-DIZIER   La Gentilhommière

Comfortable restaurant/Cooking 1-2

New owners, Florémond, the chef, and Corinne Descharmes, have worked in numerous swish French and Swiss hotels since they won their hotel school diplomas a decade ago. Flowers and shutters dominate the façade (are the two figures still there?). Elegant interior. Neo-classical treats from the chef: *rouelles de dos de lapin à la sauge et ses graines de moutarde* is a typical assured creation. (Rooms: simple Picardy or Ibis.)
Menus ABC. Cards Access, Visa. (Ibis N of town; Picardy 600 m walk.)
Closed Sat midday. Sun evg. Mon evg. Region Champagne-Ardenne.
Post 29 r. J. Jaurès, 52100 St-Dizier, Haute-Marne.
Tel 25 56 32 97. Mich 57/F1. Map 3. (Alongside D384 Troyes road.)

ST-FELIX-LAURAGAIS   Auberge du Poids Public

Comfortable hotel/Cooking 2-3
Terrace/Gardens/Garage/Parking

Panoramic views from the large beamed dining room appeal – perhaps as much as the cooking of acclaimed chef, Claude Taffarello. Both modern and regional dishes. Menu B could be a block of *rillettes de canard, confiture d'oignons; thon poêlé, beurre de tomate; noisettes* (rissoles) *de pied de porc au jus*; and *pain perdu à l'ancienne* (French toast).
Menus BCDE. Rooms (13) E. Cards Access, AE, Visa.
Closed Jan. Sun evg (Oct to Apl). Region Languedoc-Roussillon.
Post 31540 St-Félix-Lauragais, Haute-Garonne.
Tel 61 83 00 20. Fax 61 83 86 21. Mich 153/E4. Map 5.

A100frs & under. B100–135. C135–165. D165–250. E250–350. F350–500. G500+

ST-FLOUR   Grand Hôtel Voyageurs

Comfortable hotel/Cooking 2-3
Lift/Garage

In the *haute ville* with the most delectable of secret sun-trap terraces (alas, not used for meals). Diego Quinonero mixes creative neo-classical with regional. The latter, in menu B, included a *cochonnaille des Monts d'Auvergne* (*charcuterie*), a pungent *volaille fermière Brayaude aux morilles, lentilles, fromages* and yummy *milliard aux griottes*.
Menus aBCD. Rooms (33) CDE. Cards Access, DC, Visa.
Closed Nov to Mar.
Post 25 r. College, 15100 St-Flour, Cantal. Region MC (Auvergne).
Tel 71 60 34 44. Fax 71 60 00 21. Mich 127/D2. Map 5.

ST-FLOUR   Les Messageries/Rest. Nautilus

Comfortable hotel/Cooking 2
Terrace/Swimming pool/Garage/Parking

North of the busy N9, in the low town and near the station. Chef Bruno Giral (son of the high town Europe's owners) and his wife, Catherine, do a sound job. Mix of regional, neo-classical and modern creations: on one hand a light *sandre grillé aux mousserons* and at a more basic, gutsy level both *tripoux* and *noisette de porc au curry*.
Menus ABCDE. Rooms (16) DEF. Cards Access, Visa.
Closed Mid Jan to mid Feb. Fri and Sat midday (Nov to Mar).
Post 23 av. Ch. de Gaulle, 15100 St-Flour, Cantal. Region MC (Auvergne).
Tel 71 60 11 36. Fax 71 60 46 79. Mich 127/D2. Map 5.

ST-GENIEZ-D'OLT   France

Comfortable hotel/Cooking 1-2
Lift/Swimming pool & Tennis (see text)

St-Geniez, beside the River Lot (Olt is local *patois*), is a busy place. Clients of Madeleine and Michel Crouzet can use the facilities (see above) at their Club Marmotel, one km away. France's cooking? Regional and classical. Especially noteworthy is the Menu Aveyronnais (A): *charcuterie, terrine de tripoux, aligot* and *cabécou grillé*.
Menus ACD. Rooms (48) E. Cards Access, Visa.
Closed Mid Nov to mid Mar.
Post 12130 St-Geniez-d'Olt, Aveyron. Regions MC (Auvergne/Cévennes).
Tel 65 70 42 20. Fax 65 47 41 38. Mich 141/D2. Map 5.

A100frs & under. B100–135. C135–165. D165–250. E250–350. F350–500. G500+

ST-HILAIRE-LE-CHATEAU   du Thaurion

Very comfortable restaurant with rooms/Cooking 3
Terrace/Gardens/Parking

Either qualifying menu (a or C) is *RQP* at its best: the first offers a choice
at each of three courses; the second, with no choice, provides the chance
for you to try five regional *plats*. Regional, neo-classical and modern
fare: whatever your choice, I cannot recommend chef Gérard Fanton
and his English-speaking wife, Marie-Christine, enough.
Menus aCDEF. Rooms (10) DEFG. Cards All.
Closed Jan to end Feb. 21 to 27 Dec. Wed. Thurs midday.
Post 23250 St-Hilaire-le-Château, Creuse. Region Poitou-Charentes.
Tel 55 64 50 12. Fax 55 64 90 92. Mich 111/D1. Map 5.

ST-JEAN-DU-BRUEL   Midi-Papillon

Simple hotel/Cooking 2
Quiet/Gardens/Swimming pool/Parking

At the heart of one of Nature's most beguiling corners this spruced-up
logis appeals to all: a riverside setting; involved fourth-generation
owners, Maryse and Jean-Michel Papillon; and the latter's cooking, of all
styles, makes clever use of his own home-grown vegetables, home-reared
poultry and home-made *charcuterie, foies gras et confits.*
Menus aBD. Rooms (19) ACD. Cards Access, Visa.
Closed 11 Nov to 24 Mar.
Post 12230 St-Jean-du-Bruel, Aveyron. Region Massif Central (Cévennes).
Tel 65 62 26 04. Fax 65 62 12 97. Mich 141/F4. Map 5.

ST-JOSSE-SUR-MER   Le Relais de St-Josse

Simple restaurant/Cooking 2

A four-star *village fleuri* where a young couple are working wonders.
Fabienne Delmer is a quiet, English-speaking *patronne*; husband Etienne
a classical cavalier chef. Stylish, assured specialities (three choices for
each course). Examples in C: *marbre de queue de boeuf, pot-au-feu de
lotte, plâteau de fromages* and *tarte Tatin servi tiède*. Only debit: barn-
like dining room. (Rooms: many hotels at Le Touquet.)
Menus ACDE. Cards Access, Visa. (Ibis, on beach, recommended.)
Closed Mid Jan to early Feb. Sun evg. Mon. (Le Touquet 9 km to NW.)
Post 62170 St-Josse-sur-Mer, Pas-de-Calais. Region North.
Tel 21 94 61 75. Mich 2/A4. Map 2.

A 100frs & under. B 100–135. C 135–165. D 165–250. E 250–350. F 350–500. G 500+

ST-JULIEN-CHAPTEUIL   Vidal

Very comfortable restaurant/Cooking 2-3

I can vouch for chef Jean-Pierre Vidal's references (he was trained by Forges at Riorges, Troisgros at Roanne and Rostang at Antibes – all in my earlier guides). Neo-classical virtuosity – exemplified by an accomplished aromatic *cannette rôtie aux épices et pommes gaufrettes*. Chantal Vidal is a bespectacled, smiling *patronne/sommèliere*. (Rooms: Moulin de Barette, Pont de Sumène – N88, 13 km to WNW: also see below.)
Menus bCDEF. Cards Access, AE, Visa. (Rooms: also Barriol in village.)
Closed 19 Jan to end Feb. Mon evg. Tues (out of season).
Post 43260 St-Julien-Chapteuil, Haute-Loire. Region MC (Ardèche).
Tel 71 08 70 50. Fax 71 08 40 14. Mich 129/D2. Map 5.

ST-LAURENT-DE-LA-SALANQUE   Auberge du Pin

Simple hotel/Cooking 2
Terrace/Gardens/Parking

Philippe Got, after stints elsewhere in France, California and other overseas outposts, took over from his parents a few years ago. Readers enjoy his *Catalane* and neo-classical cooking. Menu C is typical: *filets de rougets au coulis d'olives*; *magret de canard au Banyuls*; *chèvre frais aux figues*; and the ubiquitous *crème Catalane*.
Menus BCD. Rooms (19) DE. Cards Access, Visa.
Closed Jan. Feb. Sun evg and Mon (out of season). Region Lang-Rouss.
Post rte Perpignan, 66250 St-Laurent-de-la-Salanque, Pyr.-Or.
Tel 68 28 01 62. Fax 68 28 39 14. Mich 173/D4. Map 5.

ST-LAURENT-DE-LA-SALANQUE   Commerce

Comfortable restaurant with rooms/Cooking 2
Garage

Raymonde Siré is the hostess; husband Jean-Louis is the chef. Enjoy classical cuisine, with the odd dip in the *Catalane* pool, in a light, yellow-washed dining room. Noteworthy specialities on menu C include an exemplary *bouillabaisse de lotte à la Catalane*, a sea-scented *méli-mélo* (mixture) *de palourdes et moules bouchots* and *crème Catalane* .
Menus aCD. Rooms (14) DE. Cards Access, Visa. Region Lang-Rouss.
Closed School hols in Feb and Nov. Sun evg and Mon (not July/Aug).
Post 2 bd Révolution, 66250 St-Laurent-de-la-Salanque, Pyr.-Or.
Tel 68 28 02 21. Mich 173/D4. Map 5.

A100frs & under. B100–135. C135–165. D165–250. E250–350. F350–500. G500+

ST-MALO   Le Chalut

Comfortable restaurant/Cooking 2

At last! Michelin have woken up to the talents of chef Jean-Philippe Foucat (true, too, of at least a dozen old *FL* favourites); he wins an entry and an accolade. My *FLE* words still apply: go once and you'll return often. What better compliment can I pay this congenial fish restaurant? Fresh fish is laid out on an open-air counter; shellfish are in a dining room tank. Classical fare. Not for carnivores.

Menus aCD. Cards Access, AE, Visa. (Rooms: several nearby hotels.)
Closed 15-31 Oct. Sun evg (out of season). Mon. Region Brittany.
Post 8 r. Corne de Cerf, 35400 St-Malo, Ille-et-Vilaine.
Tel 99 56 71 58. Mich 30/A4. Map 1. (In NE corner of walled town.)

ST-MARCELLIN   Savoyet-Serve

Simple hotel (comfortable annexe)/Cooking 1-2
Lift/Parking

The multi-floored annexe is soulless modern – but with all mod-cons. St-Marcellin is famed for its cow's milk cheese; Jean-Pierre Serve's restaurant is acclaimed locally for his classical and regional *RQP* menus: *ravioles de Royans* (down the road) – don't miss 'em; *poulet sauté aux écrevisses*; and *chevreuil Grand Veneur* are typical *plats*.

Menus aBCD. Rooms (60) BCDEF. Cards Access, Visa.
Closed Sun evg. Regions Hautes-Alpes/Savoie.
Post 16 bd Gambetta, 38160 St-Marcellein, Isère.
Tel 76 38 04 17. Fax 76 64 02 99. Mich 130/C2. Map 6.

ST-MARTIN-D'ARMAGNAC   Auberge du Bergerayre

Comfortable restaurant with rooms/Cooking 2-3
Secluded/Terrace/Gardens/Swimming pool/Parking

Pierrette Sarran is *la cuisinière* at this delectable old farm – west of the village and surrounded by vineyards and fields – seemingly infused with the spirit of Armagnac. Rustic dining rooms. Madame's classical and regional repertoire epitomises Gers: witness *salade paysanne aux gésiers confits* and *pintadeau rôti, jus court à l'ail* as evidence.

Menus aBD. Rooms (14) EF. Disabled. Cards Access, Visa.
Closed Mid Jan to mid Feb. Rest: Wed.
Post 32110 St-Martin-d'Armagnac, Gers. Region Southwest.
Tel 62 09 08 72. Fax 62 09 09 74. Mich 150/B2. Map 4.

A100frs & under. B100–135. C135–165. D165–250. E250–350. F350–500. G500+

ST-MARTIN-DE-LONDRES

Les Muscardins

Very comfortable restaurant/Cooking 3

Multi-prize-winning *cuisinier* Georges Rousset, a longtime *FL* favourite leaves much of the modern and neo-classical cooking these days to his talented 30-year-old son, Thierry. The contents of menu b vary each day – depending what's at the market. Menu C can include a lipsmackingly good *cabillaud demi-sel en croûte légère* and a brilliantly conceived *agneau en trilogie (noisettes, poitrine farci et navarin).*
Menus b(lunch)CDEF. Cards All. (Rooms: Juvena – 18 km SE, D986.)
Closed Feb. Mon (not public hols). Tues (not evgs in summer).
Post 19 rte Cévennes, 34380 St-Martin-de-Londres, Hérault.
Tel 67 55 75 90. Fax 67 55 70 28. Mich 156/B2. Map 5. Region Lang-Rouss.

ST-MARTIN-EN-BRESSE

Au Puits Enchanté

Simple hotel/Cooking 2
Parking

Well-named and a worthwhile detour from the A6. Chef Jacky Chateau and his wife, Nadine, are *RQP* winners. Elegant but simple applies to both furnishings and cooking: start with a sumptuous *terrine de pintade aux foies de canards en gelée blonde*; then a lighter *rosettes de saumon à la fondue les jeunes poireaux*, cheese and sweet (typical menu B).
Menus aBCD. Rooms (14) CDE. Cards Access, Visa. Closed 16-31 Jan. Feb sch. hols. 1-7 Sept. Sun evg (not July/Aug). Mon (out of season). Tues.
Post 71620 St-Martin-en-Bresse, Saône-et-Loire. Regions Burg/Lyonnais.
Tel 85 47 71 96. Fax 85 47 74 58. Mich 88/B3. Map 3.

ST-MEDARD

Le Gindreau

Very comfortable restaurant/Cooking 3-4
Terrace

An old school house with green views over the Vert Valley and a cool chestnut-shaded terrace. Some school house – these days very chic. Elegant Martine and Alexis Pélissou, the chef, beguile with a flavour-personified RQP menu: wide choice including *magret de canard macéré façon carpaccio*, local lamb and drooling *gateau aux trois chocolats*.
Menus CDE. Cards Acc, AE, Visa. (Rooms: Campanile & France, Cahors.)
Closed 13 Nov to 7 Dec. Sun evg (out of season). Mon (not public hols).
Post 46150 St-Médard, Lot. Region Dordogne.
Tel 65 36 22 27. Fax 65 36 24 54. Mich 138/B1. Map 5.

A100frs & under. B100–135. C135–165. D165–250. E250–350. F350–500. G500+

ST-MELIOR-DES-ONDES   Le Coquillage

Comfortable restaurant/Cooking 2-3
Secluded/Gardens/Parking

I'm no fan of the latest French chef comet, two-star Olivier Roellinger –
Gault Millau's 1994 Chef of the Year. He, too, has opened a bistro –
housed in the Hôtel de Bricourt-Richeux, a deluxe Relais & Châteaux
annexe for his famed Cancale restaurant. "Sea" and "spices" are the
words which flood the aromatic *RQP* repertoire. Superb views.
Menus BC. Cards All. (Rooms: Nuit & Jour, Cancale; Terminus, Rotheneuf.)
Closed Mid Nov to mid Dec. Mon. Tues midday (not July/Aug).
Post le Point-du-Jour, 35350 St-Méloir-des-Ondes, Ille-et-Vilaine.
Tel 99 89 64 76. Fax 99 89 88 47. Mich 30/A4. Map 1. Region Brittany.

ST-MELOIR-DES-ONDES   Hôtel Tirel-Guérin

Very comfortable hotel/Cooking 3
Gardens/Swimming pool (indoor)/Tennis/Parking

A family closed shop: Roger Tirel (son of the owners) married Annie
Guérin; her brother, Jean-Luc, hitched-up with Roger's sister, Marie-
Christiane. Great favourite with readers. Modern and classical *plats*.
Fresh-as-daisies fish and shellfish: oysters, mussels, scallops, *colin*,
saumon, *lieu et al*. Fine sauces. *RQP* grub with cosseting comforts.
Menus BDE. Rooms (60) EF. Disabled. Cards All. (S of St-Méloir.)
Closed Mid Dec to mid Jan. Rest: Sun evg (Oct to Easter).
Post la gare, La Gouesnière, 35350 St-Méloir-des-Ondes, Ille-et-Vilaine.
Tel 99 89 10 46. Fax 99 89 12 62. Mich 30/A4. Map 1. Region Brittany.

ST-NEXANS   La Vieille Grange

Comfortable restaurant/Cooking 1-2
Terrace/Gardens/Parking

An old barn, 6 km SE of Bergerac. A mixture of rustic and Louis XIII –
and Italian and Périgourdine cuisine from Catherine Cassaresi, born
locally and married to an Italian. There's nothing bland about her varied
specialities – among them *mignon de veau au gorgonzola*, *tortellini aux
quatre fromages*, *caneton rôti au miel au citron* and *tiramisu*.
Menus BCD. Cards All. (Rooms: Climat de France & Campanile, Bergerac.)
Closed Tues evg and Wed (not July/Aug). (Above SW of Bergerac – D936.)
Post La Petite Forêt, 24520 St-Nexans, Dordogne. Region Dordogne.
Tel 53 24 32 21. Mich 123/D4. Map 5.

A100frs & under. B100–135. C135–165. D165–250. E250–350. F350–500. G500+

ST-PAUL-DE-VENCE   La Brouette

Simple restaurant/Cooking 1-2
Terrace/Parking

The English-speaking Danish family Bornemann – Olé, Birgitte and son
Michel – mix Scandinavian and French at their extrovert base. Menu C is
"salty and smoky" goodies galore – with a *terrine de foie* (Viking recipe),
filet mignon, *flétan fumé* (*ou saumon mariné*), *harengs marinées ou
saumon fumé* (both *Danois*), *truite fumé* and dessert. *Olé*!
Menus ACD. Cards Acc, Visa. (D36 Cagnes-Vence road, E of St-Paul.)
Closed Feb. Mon (out of season). (Rooms: Le Hameau, D7 W of St-Paul.)
Post 830 rte de Cagnes, 06570 St-Paul, Alpes-Mar. Region Côte d'Azur.
Tel 93 58 67 16. Mich 165/D3. Map 6.

ST-PEE-SUR-NIVELLE   Fronton

Comfortable restaurant with rooms/Cooking 2-3
Terrace

Jean-Baptiste and Maritxu (Maritchu) Daguerre are passionate about their
métier. It shows in their unpretentious, flower-dominated Basque home.
Menu B is primarily neo-classical: dishes like *filet de truite saumonée au
beurre blanc*, *civet de canard aux petits oignons* and *île flottante*. A
super menu of reworked old Basque recipes is, alas, in price range D.
Menus BD. Rooms (7) E. Cards All. (At Ibarron – 2 km to W.)
Closed Mid Feb to mid Mar. Tues evg and Wed evg (not high season).
Post 64310 St-Pée-sur-Nivelle, Pyrénées-Atlantiques. Region Southwest.
Tel 59 54 10 12. Mich 148/B4. Map 4.

ST-PERE-SOUS-VEZELAY   Le Pré des Marguerites

Comfortable restaurant/Cooking 2-3
Terrace/Gardens/Parking

Another three-star chef's bistro (Marc Meneau). How's this for a low-end
menu C with a choice for each course: a bravura *galantine de canard* or
unfussy *saucisson chaud pommes*; a feisty, ear-to-the-ground *oreilles de
porc aux lentilles*; and a discreetly flavoured *sable aux pommes crème
anglaise* or a robust *tarte aux raisins de vendange*. Fine service.
Menus aCD. Cards All. (Rooms: La Renommée, *sans rest*, at St-Père.)
Closed Mon (not public holidays).
Post Gde-Rue, 89450 St-Père-sous-Vézelay, Yonne, Region Burgundy.
Tel 86 33 33 33. Fax 86 33 34 73. Mich 72/B4. Map 3.

A100frs & under. B100–135. C135–165. D165–250. E250–350. F350–500. G500+

ST-PIERRE-DES-NIDS

Dauphin

Comfortable restaurant with rooms/Cooking 2
Parking

Don't be put off by the exterior. Hidden behind the dull façade is the remarkable Jean Etienne, an English-speaking *patron/chef* (once with the *French Line*) and dynamic promoter of his *pays*. *French Line* classical cooking: *escalope de saumon d'Ecosse sur lit vert* and a local *cuisse de canard confite à la Pôôtéenne* (the local *pays*) are show stoppers.
Menus ACDE. Rooms (9) CDE. Cards Access, Visa.
Closed Feb school hols. 2nd half Aug. Wed.
Post rte Alençon, 53370 St-Pierre-des-Nids, Mayenne. Region Normandy.
Tel 43 03 52 12. Fax 43 03 55 49. Mich 50/C2. Map 2.

ST-PIERRE-LANGERS

Le Jardin de l'Abbaye

Very comfortable restaurant/Cooking 2
Parking

Two rustic dining rooms, both with chimneys, at the happy home of Alain and Catherine Duval. The couple love their *métier*; she's a friendly hostess; he walks the classical cloisters. Relish the Menu Abbaye (three choices for each of three courses; top-end B): *nage de daurade au basilic* and *faux-filet au poivre de Guinéc* are top of the pops treats.
Menus ABE. Cards Access, Visa. (Rooms: Michelet, Granville, 11 km NW.)
Closed 3 wks Feb. 23 Sept to 9 Oct. Sun evg (not July/Aug). Mon.
Post Croix Barrée, 50530 St-Pierre-Langers, Manche. Region Normandy.
Tel 33 48 49 08. Fax 33 48 18 50. Mich 30/C3. Map 1.

ST-POURCAIN-SUR-SIOULE

Chêne Vert

Comfortable hotel/Cooking 2-3
Terrace/Garage

A welcome gale of fresh air, in the shape of new owners Jean-Guy and Martine Siret, has blown away the old cobwebs. The tag spick and span describes the beefed up hotel fabric and J-G's neo-classical dishes. Get stuck into *saumon cru mariné au gros sel*, *terrine de faisan en gelée*, *omble chevalier poêlé*, *civet de chevreuil* and a selection of *sorbets*.
Menus aBCD. Rooms (32) EF. Cards All.
Closed Last 3 wks Jan. Sun evg (Oct to Apl). Rest: Mon.
Post bd Ledru-Rollin, 03500 St-Pourçain-sur-Sioule, Allier.
Tel 70 45 40 65. Fax 70 45 68 50. Mich 100/A3. Map 5. Region Berry-B.

A100frs & under. B100–135. C135–165. D165–250. E250–350. F350–500. G500+

ST-RAPHAEL   Pastorel

Comfortable restaurant/Cooking 2-3
Terrace

At the heart of old St-Raphaël, north of the railway line. There's nowt
flippant about the restaurant or the cooking; chef Charles Floccia has
both Provençal and classical nous. An almost faultless meal of a tasty
amuse-bouche, nine oysters with rye bread, an as-it-should-be *blanquette
d'agneau à l'ancienne, salade de Roquefort aux noix* and a sweet.
Menus CD. Cards All. (Rooms: Epulias, next door; L'Oasis, Fréjus-Plage.)
Closed Midday in Aug. Sun evg & Mon (not Aug). (L'Oasis: quiet/parking.)
Post 54 r. Liberté, 83700 St-Raphaël, Var. Region Côte d'Azur.
Tel 94 95 02 36. Fax 94 95 64 07. Mich 163/E3. Map 6.

ST-REMY-DE-PROVENCE   La Maison Jaune

Comfortable restaurant/Cooking 2-3
Terrace

A three-storey town house in the centre of St-Rémy. Chef François
Pérraud (previously at La Regalido in Fontvieille – *FLE* p325) and his
English-speaking wife, Catherine, opened their new home at the end of
1993. Stylish and clever taste combinations like *minestrone, toasts aux
olives noires* and *blanc de volaille à l'aïoli et au safran.*
Menus b(lunch)CDE. Cards Access, Visa. (Rooms: Soleil – 3 min-walk S.)
Closed Mid Feb to mid Mar. Sun evg. Mon. (Above quiet/parking/pool.)
Post 15 r. Carnot, 13210 St-Rémy-de-Provence, Bouches-du-Rhône.
Tel 90 92 56 14. Mich 158/B2. Map 6. Region Provence.

ST-THEGONNEC   Auberge St-Thégonnec

Comfortable hotel/Cooking 2
Terrace/Gardens/Parking

A modern, stone-built *logis* across the road from one of the famed
enclos paroissiaux. English-speaking Alain Le Coz (he gives a lot of
help to Leicester Catering College students) favours flavour in his
cuisine: witness a *salade de magret tièdes à l'huile de noix* and a *poêlée
de rougets barbets aux pleurottes.* Finish with local Plougastel *fraises.*
Menus aBCD. Rooms (19) EFG. Disabled. Cards All.
Closed Mid Dec to end Jan. Sun evg & Mon (mid Sept to mid June).
Post 29410 St-Thégonnec, Finistère. Region Brittany.
Tel 98 79 61 18. Fax 98 62 71 10. Mich 27/D2. Map 1.

ST-VAAST-LA-HOUGUE

France et Fuchsias

Comfortable hotel/Cooking 1-2
Terrace/Gardens

Famed for exceptional gardens. The owners, the Brix family, make good use of produce grown on their farm. Plenty of fish courses, too: *crabe mayonnaise* and *filet de cabillaud* are champion; so, too, are *tarte framboise* and *nougat glace.* Cooking rating scuppered by kindergarten standard *amuse-guèle* (offal), vegetable soup and chicken-liver terrine.
Menus aBCD. Rooms (32) CDEF. Cards All.
Closed 9 Jan to 19 Feb. Mon (mid Sept to Apl). Tues midday (Nov to Apl).
Post 50550 St-Vaast-la-Hougue, Manche. Region Normandy.
Tel 33 54 42 26. Fax 33 43 46 79. Mich 12/C3. Map 1.

ST-VALLIER

Terminus/Rest. Albert Lecomte

Very comfortable restaurant with rooms/Cooking 2-3
Garage

Don't be put off by the exterior and the site – by *la gare* and beside the N7. Double-glazed bedrooms, a modern dining room and a first-class classical chef more than compensate. Albert hails from St-Jean-en-Royans (Vercors) – the area's famed *ravioles* appear in a salade with *magret fumé* and with a *filet de sandre.*
Menus CDEF. Rooms (10) EF. Cards All.
Closed Feb school hols. 14-25 Aug. Sun evg. Mon.
Post 116 av. J. Jaurès, 26240 St-Vallier, Drôme. Region MC (Ardèche).
Tel 75 23 01 12. Fax 75 23 38 82. Mich 130/A1. Map 6.

STE-MENEHOULD

Cheval Rouge

Simple hotel/Cooking 1-2

Catherine and François Fourreau are the hosts at the vine-covered *logis*; Jean-Robert Lafois is the busy chef. He juggles classical, *Bourgeois* and varying regional culinary trotters. Relish *choucroute d'empereur* or an *onglet de veau à la Niçoise*; or tuck into local treats like the famed *pied de cochon à la Ste-Menehould* and *délice d'Argonne.* Some rooms noisy: Le Jabloire (*sans rest*) at Florent-en-Argonne much quieter.
Menus aCD. (Brasserie A.) Rooms (18) DE. Cards All. (Above 8 km to NE.)
Closed Sun evg (not hotel). Mon (Sept to Apl).
Post 1 r. Chanzy, 51800 Ste-Menehould, Marne. Region Champagne-Ard.
Tel 26 60 81 04. Fax 26 60 93 11. Mich 39/E2. Map 3.

A100frs & under. B100–135. C135–165. D165–250. E250–350. F350–500. G500+

STES-MARIES-DE-LA-MER Pont de Gau

Comfortable restaurant with rooms/Cooking 2-3
Terrace/Parking

Jean and Monique Audry's *logis*, at the heart of the Camargue, is next door to the renowned Parc Ornithologique. Vivid regional and classical *plats* from chef Jean – including a gutsy Menu Camarguais. Tuck into the likes of *bouille de congre à la rouille*, a beefy *marinade de toros à la provençale* or *faux-filet grillé sauce forestière au poivre*.
Menus ABD. Rooms (9) D. Cards Access, AE, Visa. (5 km N – D570.)
Closed 3 Jan to 19 Feb. Wed (mid Oct to Easter – but not school hols).
Post 13460 Stes-Maries-de-la-Mer, Bouches-du-Rhône. Region Provence.
Tel 90 97 81 53. Fax 90 97 98 54. Mich 157/E3-E4. Map 6.

SALIGNAC-EYVIGUES La Meynardie

Comfortable restaurant/Cooking 2-3
Terrace/Gardens/Parking

A dead-end road (follow signs N) leads you to an exquisite setting (woods and pastures) and an old farm with stone walls and deep casement windows. Little touches abound. Hearty regional – *assiette gourmand du Périgord (foie, magret, gésiers, d'oie, crudités)* – and lighter dishes like a spirited *saumon à la feuille de chou, sauce gingembre.*
Menus ACDE. Cards Access, Visa. (Rooms: La Terrasse in village.)
Closed Mid Nov to mid Dec. Mon midday (July to Sept). Wed (Oct to June).
Post 24590 Salignac-Eyvigues, Dordogne. Region Dordogne.
Tel 53 28 85 98. Fax 53 28 82 79. Mich 124/B3. Map 5.

SARPOIL La Bergerie

Comfortable restaurant/Cooking 3
Parking

Menu B at Laurent and Isabelle Jury's remote *bergerie* is superb *RQP*. Clever use of regional produce in Laurent's creative culinary rainbow: terrine of lentils, trout and smoked salmon; *pansettes* (faggots) of lamb stuffed with wild thyme & herbs; 12 Auvergne cheeses; and *oeufs à la neige*. (Rooms: use the exquisite Château de Pasredon, 2 km to the NW.)
Menus BCDE. Cards All. (Above *chambres d'hôtes*; low-end F inc' bkft; at)
Closed Jan. Sun evg. Mon. (63500 St-Rémy-de-Chargnat; tel 73 71 00 67.)
Post Sarpoil, 63490 St-Jean-en-Val, Puy-de-Dôme. Region MC (Auvergne).
Tel 73 71 02 54. Mich 113/E3. Map 5. (La Bergerie 10 km SE of Issoire.)

A 100frs & under. B 100–135. C 135–165. D 165–250. E 250–350. F 350–500. G 500+

SARZEAU   Espadon

Comfortable restaurant/Cooking 2-3
Parking

A modern façade gives no inkling of the art museum interior with stone,
beams and panelling; almost every square inch of wall is covered with
pictures. Bravura classical cooking: *soupe de poisson, blanc de poulet*
bourguignonne and *île flottante* on a give-away menu A which will
please anyone keen to keep wallets full. Excellent fish *plats* & sweets.
Menus ACDE. Cards All. (Rooms: Mur du Roy – Penvins.)
Closed Sun evg & Mon (Oct to May). (Penvins 1 km N.)
Post La Grée-Penvins, 56370 Sarzeau, Morbihan. Region Brittany.
Tel 97 67 34 26. Fax 97 67 38 43. Mich 62/C3. Map 1. (SE of Sarzeau.)

SARZEAU   Le Tournepierre

Simple restaurant/Cooking 2

A tiny, beamed dining room in a small stone cottage opposite the village
church of St-Colombier (NE of Sarzeau). Rich, gutsy classical offerings:
fricassée de ris d'agneau et ses copeaux de foie gras de canard (a bit
too high-octane opulent for me), *noisettes d'agneau poêlés aux cocos*
blancs et son beurre de noix, chèvre chaud and a dessert of *pommes*
rôti au miel is a typical appetite-satisfying menu C.
Menus a(lunch)CDE. Cards Access, AE, Visa. (Rooms: see previous entry.)
Closed 15-31 Jan. 15-30 Nov. Sun evg & Mon (not July/Aug).
Post St-Colombier, 56370 Sarzeau, Morbihan. Region Brittany.
Tel 97 26 42 19. Mich 62/C2-C3. Map 1.

SAULZET-LE-CHAUD   Auberge de Montrognon

Comfortable restaurant/Cooking 2
Parking

By the end of 1994 Gilles and Florence Bettiol should have moved into
their spanking new restaurant. Spanking good menus too – changed every
three days. Dig into Gilles' varied kaleidoscope of specialities: among
them *meunière de saumon au coulis de crustacés, vinaigrette de*
volaille aux myrtilles and *rable de lapereau aux champignons des bois*.
Menus bCDE. Cards Acc, Visa. (Rooms: La Châtaigneraie, Ceyrat; 2 km N.)
Closed Tues evg. Wed. Region Massif Central (Auvergne).
Post Saulzet-le-Chaud, 63540 Romagnat, Puy-de-Dôme.
Tel 73 61 30 51. Fax 73 61 34 09. Mich 113/D2. Map 5.

A 100frs & under. B 100–135. C 135–165. D 165–250. E 250–350. F 350–500. G 500+

SAUXILLANGES   Chalut

Very simple restaurant with basic rooms/Cooking 2
Garage

Have you a sweet tooth? Then head here for a 5-pudding dessert menu
(C). Most of us will be content with François Chalut's neo-classical and
regional concoctions: a *salade de lapereau tiède et sa ballotine*, *filet de
canard aux poires épicées*, Auvergne cheeses and *crème brulée aux
mûres* all appear on an aptly-named, multi-choice Menu Plaisir (C).
Menus aBCE. Rooms (6) CD. Cards Access, Visa.
Closed 1-25 Feb. 4-24 Sept. Sun evg & Mon (not July/Aug).
Post 63490 Sauxillanges, Puy-de-Dôme. Region Massif Central (Auvergne).
Tel 73 96 80 71. Fax 73 96 87 25. Mich 113/E3. Map 5.

SEMBLANCAY   Mère Hamard

Simple hotel/Cooking 2
Gardens/Parking

An elegant dining room and friendly owners – English-speaking Patrick
and Monique Pégué. The gardens and rear aspect are more eye-pleasing
than the modest façade. Nothing modest about the grub: a satisfying menu
B of *terrine de canard au foie gras*, rich *rognons de veau au Bourgueil et
à l'échalote, salade au Ste-Maure chaude* and a chocolate sweet.
Menus aBD. Rooms (9) D Cards Access, Visa.
Closed Sch. hols Feb/Nov. Sun evg & Mon (not hotel mid Apl-mid Oct).
Post pl. Eglise, 37360 Semblançay, Indre-et-Loir. Region Loire.
Tel 47 56 62 04. Fax 47 56 53 61. Mich 67/E3. Map 2.

SETE   Les Terrasses du Lido

Comfortable hotel/Cooking 2
Terrace/Swimming pool/Lift/Garage/Parking

West of Sète, on La Corniche (on D2 – not the N112), and with views of
the distant Med and famed Bassin de Thau. Cool elegance prevails: in
the dining room and on the flower-bedecked terrace beside the first-floor
pool. Colette Guironnet is *la cuisinière*. A welcome emphasis on fish
dishes (mainly classical) and *coquillages* from the nearby *bassin*.
Menus BDE. Rooms (8) EF. Disabled. Cards All.
Closed Feb. Rest: Sun evg & Mon (not July/Aug).
Post rond-point Europe, 34200 Sète, Hérault. Region Languedoc-Rouss.
Tel 67 51 39 60. Fax 67 53 26 96. Mich 156/B4. Map 5.

A100frs & under. B100–135. C135–165. D165–250. E250–350. F350–500. G500+

SOUSCEYRAC
Au Déjeuner de Sousceyrac

Comfortable restaurant with basic rooms/Cooking 2-3

Fluent English-speaking Laurence Piganiol and her brilliant young chef husband, Richard, do a great job in an unprepossessing village. A panelled dining room is a handsome backdrop. Starters – *terrine de boeuf froide en gelée* and a *brandade de morue et crispie de poitrine fumée* – were star quality; alas, meat dishes were undercooked to the point of being almost inedible; and desserts were flamboyantly top notch.
Menus bCD. Rooms (10) CD. Cards Access, Visa.
Closed Jan (rooms only). Feb. Sun evg and Mon (not July/Aug).
Post 46190 Sousceyrac, Lot. Region Dordogne.
Tel 65 33 00 56. Fax 65 33 04 37. Mich 125/E3. Map 5.

SOUVIGNY-EN-SOLOGNE
Perdrix Rouge

Comfortable restaurant/Cooking 2
Gardens

A super village with pretty "green" and unusual church with *caquetoir*. The English-speaking *patronne*, Dominique Beurienne, and the small, beamed dining room are also eye-pleasers. Husband, Jean-Noël, treads all cooking paths – witness *filet de sandre au beurre blanc, émincé de boeuf au poivre vert* and *tarte tiède aux pommes façon Sologne*.
Menus aCDE. Cards Acc, Visa. (Rooms: Charmilles, Nouan-le-Fuzelier, SW.)
Closed 2-11 Jan. 24 Fe-15 Mar. 28 Au-5 Sep. Mon (not *midi* Ap-Oct). Tues.
Post 41600 Souvigny-en-Sologne, Loir-et-Cher. Region Loire.
Tel 54 88 41 05. Fax 54 88 05 56. Mich 69/F3. Map 2.

STAINVILLE
La Petite Auberge

Comfortable restaurant/Cooking 3

Why is it that guides like Gault Millau turn their backs on outposts of old-fashioned excellence like La Petite Auberge? Owner Mme Abalti first won a Michelin star in the 70s. Today, chef Philippe Perée conjures up the same classical culinary tricks. Refined *ancien régime* cooking with *filet de boeuf (avec pleurotes ou morilles), filet de poisson poché au champagne* and an unbeatable old-timer – *gâteau au chocolat*.
Menus CDE. Cards All. (Rooms: Ibis, N of St-Dizier; 18 km W on N4.)
Closed 21 July to 12 Aug. Fri evg. Sat. Sun evg.
Post 55500 Stainville, Meuse. Region Champagne-Ardenne.
Tel 29 78 60 10. Mich 39/F4. Map 3.

A100frs & under. B100–135. C135–165. D165–250. E250–350. F350–500. G500+

TAMNIES

Laborderie

Comfortable hotel/Cooking 2
Secluded/Terrace/Gardens/Swimming pool/Parking

A much modernised and extended *logis* "business" on a hilltop site with fine views over the Beune Valley. A *Périgourdin* menu C includes feisty, filling dishes such as *foie gras d'oie mi-cuit, cuisse de canarde confite avec cèpes et pommes forestière, cabécou chaud* with an aromatic walnut-oil salad and an inevitable *soufflé glace aux noix.*
Menus BCDE. Rooms (36) EF. Cards Access, Visa.
Closed Nov to Mar.
Post 24620 Tamniès, Dordogne. Region Dordogne.
Tel 53 29 68 59. Fax 53 29 65 31. Mich 124/A3. Map 5.

TARNAC

Voyageurs

Simple hotel/Cooking 2
Quiet

Readers have consistently praised this modest *logis*, tucked away in adorable Corrèze. The same adjective could be tied to both Ghislaine and Jean Deschamps – and to his classical and *Bourgeoise* cuisine. Sauces with all beef dishes are considered "wonderful" and *escargots* "the best ever". Autumn bonuses of *cèpes, pleurottes* and *girolles.*
Menus aBC. Rooms (17) CD. Cards Access, Visa.
Closed Mid Dec to mid Mar. Sun evg & Mon (Oct to May; not public hols).
Post 19170 Tarnac, Corrèze. Region Poitou-Charentes.
Tel 55 95 53 12. Fax 55 95 40 07. Mich 111/E2. Map 5.

TENCE

Grand Hôtel Placide

Comfortable hotel/Cooking 3
Gardens/Parking

A string of compliments from readers for the young, 4th-generation *chef/patron*, Pierre-Marie Placide (trained by Chabran at Pont-de-l'Isère) and his bubbling, English-speaking wife, Véronique. Modern and regional masterpieces: dither over choices like lightly-smoked *cochon aux lentilles de Puy* and *terrine chaude de cèpes, sauce au brebis frais.*
Menus bCDEF. Rooms (17) EF. Cards Access, AE, Visa.
Closed Mid Nov to mid Feb. Sun evg and Mon (not high season).
Post av. Gare, 43190 Tence, Haute-Loire. Region MC (Ardèche).
Tel 71 59 82 76. Fax 71 65 44 46. Mich 129/E2. Map 6.

A 100frs & under. B 100–135. C 135–165. D 165–250. E 250–350. F 350–500. G 500+

THANNENKIRCH
Auberge la Meunière

Simple hotel/Cooking 2
Terrace/Parking

Timber predominates in this bright *logis* – both inside and out – and in the extensive Vosges forest views. Other pluses: a jacuzzi, sauna and billiards. Francesca Dumoulin is the hostess; husband, Jean-Luc, mans the stoves. Particularly tasty starters and sweets; among them *canapés de Munster chaud au cumin* and *parfait aux griottes de Thannenkirch*.
Menus aBCD. Rooms (15) EF. Cards Access, AE, Visa.
Closed Mid Nov to end Mar.
Post 68590 Thannenkirch, Haut-Rhin. Region Alsace.
Tel 89 73 10 47. Fax 89 73 12 31. Mich 61/D2. Map 3.

THIEZAC
Casteltinet

Comfortable hotel/Cooking 2
Terrace/Lift/Parking

Built a decade ago with extensive views and now less noise from the main road (new bypass to E). Nelly Macua is a helpful hostess; husband Faust is a creative chef. One dish alone – a bursting with flavour *escalopes de sandre, fondue de poireaux et fricassée de trompettes aux lardons* – made the trip worthwhile. Another bonus: great Auvergne cheeses.
Menus aBCD. Rooms (23) DE. Cards Access, Visa.
Closed Mid Oct to Xmas. Easter to mid May.
Post 15450 Thiézac, Cantal. Region Massif Central (Auvergne).
Tel 71 47 00 60. Mich 126/C2. Map 5.

THOMERY
Le Vieux Logis

Very comfortable restaurant with rooms/Cooking 2-3
Terrace/Swimming pool/Parking

Punt upstream on the Seine and Loing and you are in Impressionist *pays*. Monique-Antonia Plouvier's *hostellerie* is equally eye-pleasing. Jean-Luc Daligault continues the theme with vibrant modern cooking canvases: menu C could include *saumon croustillé en peau, polenta et jus de viande* and a luscious *crème brûlée à la cassonade et vanille Bourbon*. Another plus: a dozen sensibly-priced, first-class half-bottles of wine.
Menus CD. Rooms (14) F. Cards Access, AE, Visa. Region Ile de France.
Post 5 r. Sadi-Carnot, 77810 Thomery, Seine-et-Marne.
Tel (1) 60 96 44 77. Fax (1) 60 96 42 71. Mich 54/C2. Map 2.

A100frs & under. B100–135. C135–165. D165–250. E250–350. F350–500. G500+

THONES   Nouvel Hôtel du Commerce

Comfortable hotel/Cooking 2
Lift/Garage

Don't be put off by either the name or the façade. The 3rd-generation owners of the 80-year-old *logis* are a cracking duo. Attractive Christiane Bastard-Rosset is the welcoming hostess; husband Robert is an assertive chef. Classical & *Savoyards* menus: the former could include a *mousse de brochet soufflé*; the latter, a filling *farcement*.
Menus aBCDE. Rooms (25) DEF. Cards Access, Visa.
Closed Nov. Rest: Sun evg and Mon (not high season).
Post r. Clefs, 74230 Thônes, Haute-Savoie. Region Savoie.
Tel 50 02 13 66. Fax 50 32 16 24. Mich 118/Cl. Map 6.

TORCY   Vieux Saule

Very comfortable restaurant/Cooking 2-3
Terrace/Parking

South of Le Creusot. Marie-Madeleine Hervé is a helpful *patronne*; and her husband Christian is a down-to-earth *cuisinier*. His Menu du Terroir (C) is a four-course, appetite-quenching blockbuster with two especially hearty *plats* – a *chausson d'escargots au beurre d'orties* and *estouffade de joues de boeuf à la charolaise*. Excellent desserts.
Menus b(lunch)CDE. Cards Access, Visa. (Rooms: Novotel, Montchanin.)
Closed Sun evg. Mon. (Above easy 4 km drive to SE; use N80.)
Post 71210 Torcy, Saône-et-Loire. Region Burgundy.
Tel 85 55 09 53. Mich 87/F4. Map 3.

TORNAC   Demeures du Ranquet

Very comfortable hotel/Cooking 2-3
Quiet/Terrace/Gardens/Swimming pool/Parking

A heavenly wooded site south of Tornac. Anne Majourel is a self-taught *cuisinière* and her Menu du Terroir (C) is the sole *FWF* qualifier: relish a *tarte fine chaude à la brandade de morue; cuisse de canard confite aux lentilles; salade au pélardon frit*; and a sweet. Lunch is perfect: afterwards relax by the pool. Cheaper rooms? See two lines below.
Menus CDE. Rooms (10) G. D'bled. Cards Acc, Visa. (Porte des Cévennes.)
Closed Jan to Mar. Tues evg & Wed (mid Sept-mid June). (NW of Anduze.)
Post Tornac, 30140 Anduze, Gard. Regions Languedoc-Roussillon/Provence.
Tel 66 77 51 63. Fax 66 77 55 62. Mich 143/D4. Map 5.

A100frs & under. B100–135. C135–165. D165–250. E250–350. F350–500. G500+

TOURNUS

Terminus

Comfortable restaurant with rooms/Cooking 2
Terrace/Parking

Alongside both the N6 and station. A bright exterior, lined with boxes of geraniums; the interior hides the exciting surprise of a 1900 Gasparini mechanical organ – in the dining room! Michel Rigaud pulls out all the stops in his classical/regional tunes. How about a prize-winning *gâteau de foie blond* and an evocative *quenelle de brochet soufflé*?
Menus aBCDE. Rooms (13) DE. Cards Access, Visa.
Closed 3-25 Jan. 21-29 Nov. Tues evg and Wed (not July/Aug).
Post 21 av. Gambetta, 71700 Tournus, Saône-et-Loire. Region Lyonnais.
Tel 85 51 05 54. Fax 85 32 55 15. Mich 102/C1. Map 6.

TOURNUS

Terrasses

Comfortable restaurant with rooms/Cooking 2
Garage/Parking

Competition is fierce in this "intriguing" town (see *Mapaholics' France*; map sheet 102). Like the entry above, the vine-covered, busy-lizzied *logis* is also alongside the N6. Michel Carrette is a friendly host and competent chef. Menu B (low-end) is bravura classical: we recall, with relish, a pungent *cuisse de lapin en civet au Mâcon rouge*.
Menus aBCD. Rooms (18) E. Cards Access, Visa.
Closed 2-31 Jan. 19-25 June. Sun evg. Mon.
Post 18 av. 23-Janvier, 71700 Tournus, Saône-et-Loire. Region Lyonnais.
Tel 85 51 01 74. Fax 85 51 09 99. Mich 102/C1. Map 6.

TOURRETTES-SUR-LOUP

Petit Manoir

Comfortable restaurant/Cooking 2

A perched *cité*. The manoir is *petit*, accessible only on foot (for the sure-footed only), 150 metres from the D2210. Françoise and Dominique Taburet make you welcome at their old stone house. Chef Dominique is a classical master: savour carefully sauced and prepared *croustade d'escargots, beurre Provençal*; filling *aiguillettes de boeuf braisée aux carottes*, cheese and a choice of desserts. English spoken.
Menus a(lunch)CD. Cards Access, AE, Visa. (Rooms: Floréal or Miramar.)
Closed 2nd half Feb. 15-30 Nov. Sun evg. Wed. (Above at Vence to E.)
Post 21 Gde Rue, 06140 Tourrettes-s-Loup, Alpes-Mar.
Tel 93 24 19 19. Mich 163/F2. Map 6. Region Côte d'Azur.

A100frs & under. B100–135. C135–165. D165–250. E250–350. F350–500. G500+

La TRINITE-SUR-MER   L'Azimut

Very comfortable restaurant/Cooking 2-3
Terrace

Blue and white umbrellas and awnings brighten up the stone-built house overlooking the port. Marie-Hélène & Hervé Le Calvez have an impressive culinary c.v. (in France & Switzerland). Menu du Terroir (B), Menu Marin (C) and grills from the open fire. *Saumon, bar et haddock fumés*, sardines stuffed with an artichoke cream, *saumon sauvage laqué en peau au miel* and a lime charlotte is a typical menu C.
Menus ABCD. Cards Access, Visa. (Rooms: La Licorne, *sans rest*, Carnac.)
Post 56470 La Trinité-s-Mer, Morbihan. Region Brittany. (Above 5 km W.)
Tel 97 55 71 88. Fax 97 55 80 15. Mich 62/B2. Map 1.

Les TROIS-EPIS   Croix d'Or

Simple hotel/Cooking 1-2
Terrace/Parking

Views are the highlight at this small hotel, 2000 ft above sea-level and only 14 km from Colmar. Catherine Bruley and Marianne Gebel stick with a regional, classical and *Bourgeoise* repertoire – a formula which includes *canard de Barbarie à l'orange*, *choucroute garnie* and the buffet-style *hors d'oeuvre*, tagged *la table Hans im Schnokeloch*.
Menus aBCD. Rooms (12) DE. Cards Access, Visa.
Closed Mid Nov to mid Dec. Tues.
Post 68410 Les Trois-Epis, Haut-Rhin. Region Alsace.
Tel 89 49 83 55. Fax 89 49 87 14. Mich 61/D3. Map 3.

TURENNE   Maison des Chanoines

Simple restaurant with comfortable rooms/Cooking 2
Quiet/Terrace

A tiny, 16th-century stone-built house at the heart of the *bourg* – with a shady terrace across the alley. Plenty of choice. A typical regional meal could incorporate an inventive *terrine chaude aux noix, Roquefort et poires*; a filling *médaillon de veau du Limousin sauce Quercynoise*; and a refreshing *glace aux noix maison*. All appetising grub.
Menus b(lunch)CD. Rooms (3) EF. Cards Access, Visa.
Closed 11 Nov to end Feb. Tues evg and Wed (not July/Aug).
Post 19500 Turenne, Corrèze. Region Dordogne.
Tel 55 85 93 43. Mich 124/C2. Map 5.

TY SANQUER Auberge Ty Coz

Comfortable restaurant/Cooking 1-2
Parking

Beside the D770 – 7 km N of Quimper and E of the N165 *voie express* – the sombre, dark granite exterior is brightened-up no end by a splash of flowers. Jean-Pierre Marrec's classical and *Bourgeois* wide-choice menus brighten-up spirits and fill empty stomachs: oysters, mussels, smoked salmon, *gigot, faux-filet, confit de canard* and similar.
Menus aCD. Cards Access, Visa. (Rooms: Ibis, NE corner of Quimper.)
Closed 25 Apl to 14 May. 5-24 Sept. Sun evg. Mon. (Above easy drive.)
Post Ty Sanquer, 29000 Quimper, Finistère. Region Brittany.
Tel 98 94 50 02. Mich 45/D2. Map 1.

VALBONNE Auberge Fleurie

Comfortable restaurant/Cooking 2-3
Terrace/Parking

A top *RQP* favourite. Jean-Pierre Battaglia's *métier* is polished classical. Good choice for each course on all menus. Even menu B has gems like *pâté de canard et ses aubergines confites, filet de rascasse au vin rouge* and *pavé de chocolat crème anglaise*. How rewarding it has been to see Jean-Pierre succeed so well during the 18 years we've known him.
Menus BCD. Cards Access, Visa. (Rooms: Novotel/Ibis 6 km to SE.)
Closed Mid Dec to end Jan. Wed. (Both above at Sophia-Antipolis.)
Post 06560 Valbonne, Alpes-Maritimes. Region Côte d'Azur.
Tel 93 12 02 80. Fax 93 12 22 27. Mich 163/F2. Map 6. (On D3, to S.)

VALLOIRE La Sétaz/Rest. Le Gastilleur

Comfortable hotel/Cooking 2
Gardens/Swimming pool/Parking

The large modern *logis* has two attractive amenities (see above). But, for me, the first-floor dining room and the chef, whom I was fortunate enough to meet, are better bonuses. Jacques Villard is a clever classicist: a superlative *suprême de poulet avec morilles et champignons des bois* and a lip-smacking dessert trolley remain vivid memories.
Menus bCD. Rooms (22) EF. Cards Access, AE, Visa.
Closed 25 Apl to 2 June. 25 Sept to 15 Dec.
Post 73450 Valloire, Savoie. Regions Hautes-Alpes/Savoie.
Tel 79 59 01 03. Fax 79 59 00 63. Mich 132/C1. Map 6.

A100frs & under. B100–135. C135–165. D165–250. E250–350. F350–500. G500+

VALS-LES-BAINS   Chez Mireille

Simple restaurant/Cooking 1-2

The sainted duo, Albert and Renée Mazet, now run their Hôtel Europe *sans rest* (an ideal base – a short walk away). This alternative, in the same *rue*, does very nicely thank you. A warm welcome from Colette Martin and classical temptations from husband Daniel. How about this permutation? A salad of fresh and smoked salmon; *petits rôtis de pintade à la crème de laurier*; cheese; and a *parfait aux marrons*. Or, *escargots au St-Péray* to start; then *filet de sole à la crème de homard*? Menus ABCD. Cards Access, Visa. (Rooms: see text above.)
Post 3 r. J. Jaurès. 07600 Vals-les-Bains, Ardèche. Region MC (Ardèche). Tel 75 37 49 06. Mich 129/E4. Map 6.

VALS-LES-BAINS   Vivarais

Comfortable hotel/Cooking 2-3
Terrace/Swimming pool/Lift/Parking

A fifth-generation chef, Christiane Guiliani-Brioude, is making a name for herself at the multi-floored, 30s-style spa hotel. Neo-classical delights mixed with reworked, old regional recipes: a typical meal could be a mysterious *salade picodonne*; *parmentier d'agneau en crépinettes* with a wild mushroom sauce; and a seductive sweet (choose from 14).
Menus CDE. Rooms (47) EFG. Cards All.
Closed Rest: Feb.
Post av. C. Expilly, 07600 Vals-les-Bains, Ardèche. Region MC (Ardèche). Tel 75 94 65 85. Fax 75 37 65 47. Mich 129/E4. Map 6.

VANNES   La Morgate

Simple restaurant/Cooking 2

Vannes is a busy town and came close to not being included. This small beamed restaurant, between the cathedral and *gare*, is well worth the detour. Exceptionally helpful *patrons*, Vincenza and Daniel Le Blay. Chef Daniel stirs classical pots: tuck into the likes of 10 oysters, an invigorating *dos de bar rôti en peau, fleur de sel de Guérande*, cheese and a mouthwatering *fondant au chocolat amer, compote d'oranges*. Menus ABCD. Cards Access, Visa. (Rooms: Anne de Bretagne, near *gare*.)
Closed Mar. Sun evg (out of seas). Mon. (Above 5 min walk N; garage.)
Post 21 r. La Fontaine, 56000 Vannes, Morbihan. Region Brittany. Tel 97 42 42 39. Mich 62/C2. Map 1.

A100frs & under. B100–135. C135–165. D165–250. E250–350. F350–500. G500+

VAUX

La Petite Auberge

Comfortable restaurant/Cooking 2
Terrace/Parking

The duo Mansour took over the tiller here, a Yonne-side *auberge*, a few years back when the Barnabets paddled downstream to their new restaurant in Auxerre. Classical cuisine with safe, assured specialities such as *compote de lapereau en gelée, pièce de boeuf à la moutarde* and *île flottante, creme anglaise à la vanille*.
Menus CD. Cards Access, Visa. (Rooms: Ibis, A6 Auxerre-Sud exit.)
Closed Sun evg. Mon (not public hols). (Also several hotels in Auxerre.)
Post Vaux, 89290 Auxerre, Yonne. Region Burgundy. (6 km SE of Auxerre.)
Tel 86 53 80 08. Fax 86 53 65 62. Mich 72/A2. Map 2.

VELARS-SUR-OUCHE

Auberge Gourmande

Very comfortable restaurant/Cooking 2
Terrace/Parking

The stone-built, flower-bedecked restaurant – rustic, yet refined – is west of Dijon and south of the A38 exit. Chef André Barbier and his wife, Louise, play a Burgundy fiddle: *escargots, oeufs pochés en meurette, coq au vin* and *jambon persillé dijonnais* are all on the menus. You'll not complain about lack of choice here – that's for sure.
Menus aCD. Cards Access, Visa. (Rooms: La Bonbonnière, Talant, 6 km E.)
Closed 15-31 Jan. Sun evg. Mon. (Above *sans rest* & quiet, W of Dijon.)
Post 21370 Velars-sur-Ouche, Côte-d'Or. Region Burgundy.
Tel 80 33 62 51. Fax 80 33 65 83. Mich 74/A4. Map 3.

VERCHAIX

Rouge Gorge

Very simple restaurant/Cooking 1-2

Simplicity personified in a fabulous valley (be sure to head east to the dead-end *cirque* before or after your meal). *"Derrière la poste"* and between the village and D907. Françoise Thirvaudey tends the tiny *salle*; Roland, her chef husband, paints a classical *palette*: a *feuilleté de Chavignol sur salade verte, darne de saumon sauce tartare, plateau de fromages* and a *tarte* is a typical tempting menu C.
Menus ACD. Cards Access, Visa. (Rooms: simple Chalet Fleuri nearby.)
Closed 15-30 June. 15 Nov-6 Dec. Sun evg. Mon. (More hotels at Samoëns.)
Post 74440 Verchaix, Haute-Savoie. Region Savoie.
Tel 50 90 16 77. Mich 105/E3. Map 6.

A100frs & under. B100–135. C135–165. D165–250. E250–350. F350–500. G500+

VILLEFORT
Balme

Simple hotel/Cooking 2-3
Terrace/Garage

A small, handsome corner of old-world France. Michel Gomy, an English-speaking Parisian (and tennis nut), and his wife, Micheline, work hard to promote their adopted *pays* (Lozère) in the Far East every year. Touches of the Orient surface in Michel's work – together with modern creations and *Cévenols* treats. Mont Lozère-sized choice in menu C.
Menus BCD. Rooms (20) CDE. Cards All.
Closed 4-9 Oct. Mid Nov to mid Feb. Sun evg and Mon (out of season).
Post 48800 Villefort, Lozère. Region Massif Central (Cévennes).
Tel 66 46 80 14. Fax 66 46 85 26. Mich 142/C2. Map 5.

VILLENEUVE-DE-MARSAN
Europe

Comfortable hotel/Cooking 2-3
Terrace/Gardens/Swimming pool/Parking

I'm giving another chance to Robert and Maïté Garrapit (dropped from *FLE* because of Madame's wayward *addition* arithmetic). Robert has had health problems and now leaves the cooking to young Franck Augé, a *cuisine moderne* chef. Among typical menu B treats are *gelée de tête de veau, croustillant de filet de saumon, lapin farci au basilic et son jus réduit* and a masterly *gratin de fruits frais à la crème d'amandes*.
Menus BDE. Rooms (13) CDE. Cards All.
Post 40190 Villeneuve-de-Marsan, Landes. Region Southwest.
Tel 58 45 20 08. Fax 58 45 34 14. Mich 150/A1. Map 4.

VILLERS-BOCAGE
Trois Rois

Very comfortable restaurant with rooms/Cooking 2
Gardens/Parking

The modern *logis*, alongside the N175, will, one of these days, have a welcome bypass (has any ever taken so long to complete?). Chef Henri Martinotti is a classical champ: he's renowned for his *tripes à la mode de Caen*; he boxes clever with numerous fish dishes; an appetite-busting *tournedos sauté*; and an artful, heady *nougat glace au Cointreau*.
Menus BDE. Rooms (14) DEF. Cards All.
Closed Jan. Last wk June. Sun evg and Mon (not public hols).
Post 14310 Villers-Bocage, Calvados. Region Normandy.
Tel 31 77 00 32. Fax 31 77 93 25. Mich 31/F2. Map 1.

A100frs & under. B100–135. C135–165. D165–250. E250–350. F350–500. G500+
350

VITRAC
Auberge de la Tomette

Simple hotel/Cooking 1-2
Quiet/Terrace/Gardens/Swimming pool

A warm welcome from kindly Odette Chausi at her stone-built *logis* in chestnut-tree terrain. There's nothing prissy about husband Daniel's regional fare. From a trio of choices for each course on the regional menu B dig into *plats* such as *jambon de pays, bouriol à la crème fraîche, poulet farci aux pruneaux*, Auvergne cheeses and *tarte*.
Menus ABC. Rooms (20) E. Cards Access, AE, Visa.
Closed Jan to Mar.
Post 15220 Vitrac, Cantal. Region Massif Central (Auvergne).
Tel 71 64 70 94. Fax 71 64 77 11. Mich 126/A4. Map 5.

VITRAC
La Ferme

Simple restaurant/Cooking 1-2
Parking

An isolated site, 200 metres from the River Dordogne – at Caudon, east of Vitrac. *Périgourdine* fare at Dominique and Arlette Lacour-Escalier's long-established business. Gutsy grub: *soupe de campagne au pain de seigle*; *rillettes Sarladaises*; *faux-filet grillé* and *côtes d'agneau* are some of the non-cissy stomach fillers. Air-conditioned *salle*.
Menus ABC. Cards Access, Visa. (Rooms: Mas de Castel, 3 km S of Sarlat.)
Closed Oct. Xmas to end Jan. Sun evg (not high season). Mon.
Post Caudon-de-Vitrac, 24200 Sarlat-la-Canéda, Dordogne.
Tel 53 28 33 35. Mich 124/A3-B3. Map 5. Region Dordogne.

VITRAC
La Sanglière

Comfortable restaurant/Cooking 2
Gardens/Swimming pool/Parking

A pleasant drive west and north from Vitrac leads you to an isolated and elevated modern restaurant "home" in extensive gardens. Unrelenting regional dishes dominate the menus: *salade de magret ou gésier, cuisse de canard garnie* and a heavyweight *civet de gésier* are typical. A lightweight option is *flétan à l'oseille*. Top-notch desserts.
Menus ACDE. Cards Access, Visa. ((Rooms: see previous entry.)
Closed Jan. Feb. Sun evg and Mon (not July/Aug).
Post 24200 Vitrac, Dordogne. Region Dordogne.
Tel 53 28 33 51. Fax 53 28 52 31. Mich 124/A3-B3. Map 5.

A100frs & under. B100–135. C135–165. D165–250. E250–350. F350–500. G500+

VITRE   Hôtel Petit Billot/Rest. Petit Billot

Simple hotel and restaurant/Cooking 1-2

I first visited the simple, beamed restaurant when researching *En Route*, my *autoroute* guide (p109). Marie-Thérèse Lancelot welcomes you; husband Bernard works both *Bourgeoises* and classical chopping blocks (*billot* – block): *fromage de tête, rillettes de pays, terrine de maison et son chutney, escalope de veau Viennoise, crème caramel* and *île flottante* are typical. The hotel is run as a separate business by M. Fournel.
Menus AB. Rooms (22) CDE. Cards Access, Visa. Map 1.
Closed Mid Dec to mid Jan. Fri evg (not high season). Sat. Hotel: Sun.
Post 5 pl. Mar. Leclerc, 35500 Vitré, Ille-et-Vilaine. Region Normandy.
Tel (R) 99 74 68 88. (H) 99 75 02 10. Fax 99 74 72 96. Mich 49/D3.

VIVONNE   La Treille

Very simple restaurant with very basic rooms/Cooking 2

A couple I love dearly will please all readers – especially those with few francs to spare. Geneviève Monteil is a bubbly angel; husband, chef Jacquelin, is an ardent supporter of both regional and classical *plats*. Refer to the regional lists for notes on *mouclade, farci Poitevin, bouilliture d'anguilles*, etc. (Better rooms: Mondial, quiet, *sans rest*, at Croutelle, N10, 14 km to N; and Ibis-Sud, near A10 exit 20.)
Menus ACD. Rooms (4) ABC. Cards Access, AE, Visa.
Closed Feb school hols. Wed (not midday in high season).
Post av. Bordeaux, 86370 Vivonne, Vienne. Region Poitou-Charentes.
Tel 49 43 41 13. Mich 95/D2. Map 5.

VONNAS   La Résidence des Saules/Rest. L'Ancienne Auberge

Comfortable hotel & simple restaurant/Cooking 2-3
Quiet (hotel)/Terrace

3-star chef George Blanc's bistro. Watch supplements on menu C (with 8 dessert options). Two finger-licking hits: a *pâté chaud feuilleté sauce porto* and *crème de champignons aux petites quenelles de volaille*. One disaster: overcooked, mushy *filet de lieu jaune à l'échalote*. Great service. Vonnas? No – "Blancville" ("*le business*" at every turn).
Menus a(lunch)CD. Rooms (6) G. Cards All. (Cheaper rooms: Beaujolais.)
Closed 2 Jan-9 Feb. Sun evg & Mon (not pub hols). (Mâcon, E bank Saône.)
Post pl. Marché, 01540 Vonnas, Ain. Region Lyonnais.
Tel 74 50 11 13. Fax 74 50 08 80. Mich 102/C3. Map 6.

A100frs & under. B100–135. C135–165. D165–250. E250–350. F350–500. G500+

WANGENBOURG

Parc

Comfortable hotel/Cooking 2
Quiet/Gardens/Swimming pool (indoor)/Tennis/Lift/Parking

A super site in wooded, hilly terrain nicknamed the Swiss Vosges. Owned by the same family for 150 years; the 6th generation, Elisabeth and Daniel Gihr, are spirited owners. A gym and sauna – and walks galore – to sweat off the inches after tucking into the likes of *truite au Riesling* and *civet de chevreuil* (infused with *essence de genièvre*).
Menus BCDE. Rooms (34) DEF. Cards Access, Visa.
Closed 2 Jan to 20 Mar. 2 Nov to 21 Dec.
Post 67710 Wangenbourg, Bas-Rhin. Region Alsace.
Tel 88 87 31 72. Fax 88 87 38 00. Mich 42/C4. Map 3.

WIMEREUX

Atlantic Hôtel

Very comfortable restaurant with rooms/Cooking 2-3
Lift/Parking

New owners, Aron and Marie-France Misan (he worked in London for many years), and young chef, Alain Morville, have blown bracing air through the first-floor restaurant. Classical offerings with emphasis on fish creations: *terrine de turbotin à la mousse de crabe* and *feuilleté de fruits de mer sauce corail* are typical. (Also cheaper *brasserie*.)
Menus bCD. Rooms (11) F. Cards Access, Visa.
Closed Dec to Feb. Sun evg and Mon (not July/Aug).
Post digue de mer, 62930 Wimereux, Pas-de-Calais. Region North.
Tel 21 32 41 01. Fax 21 87 46 17. Mich 2/A2. Map 2.

WIMEREUX

Epicure

Comfortable restaurant/Cooking 3

A small, whitewashed restaurant on the corner of the D940 and rue de la Gare. Claudette Carrée is *la patronne*; husband Philippe is the *cuisine moderne* magician. How welcome a mixture of eclectic flavours are: *cabillaud au cerfeuil et poivre de Sichuan* (a Chinese-cracker trick); *navarin de langoustines aux lentilles* (contemporary sleight of hand); and *tarte croustillant de banane et noix de coco* (Indies deception).
Menus CD. Cards Access, Visa. (Rooms: Ibis-Plage, Boulogne, 6 km D940.)
Closed 9-29 Oct. Sun evg. Wed. (Above easy drive to S.)
Post 1 r. Gare, 62930 Wimereux, Pas-de-Calais. Region North.
Tel 21 83 21 83. Mich 2/A2. Map 2.

A 100frs & under. B 100–135. C 135–165. D 165–250. E 250–350. F 350–500. G 500+

A point medium rare
Abatis (Abattis) poultry giblets
Abats offal
Ablette freshwater fish
Abricot apricot
Acajou cashew nut
Acarne sea-bream
Achatine snail (from Far East)
Ache celery
Acidulé(e) acid
Affiné(e) improve; ripen, mature (common term with cheeses)
Africaine (à l') African style: with aubergines, tomatoes, *cèpes*
Agneau lamb
Agneau de pré-salé lamb fed on salt marshes
Agnelet young lamb
Agnès Sorel thin strips of mushroom, chicken and tongue
Agrumes citrus fruits
Aïado lamb with herbs and garlic
Aiglefin haddock
Aigre-doux sweet-sour
Aigrelette sharp sauce
Aiguillette thin slice
Ail garlic
Aile (Aileron) wing (winglet)
Aillade garlic sauce
Aïoli mayonnaise, garlic, olive oil
Airelles cranberries
Albert white cream sauce, mustard, vinegar
Albuféra *béchamel* sauce, sweet peppers
Alénois watercress-flavoured
Algues seaweed
Aligot purée of potatoes, cream, garlic, butter and fresh Tomme de Cantal (or Laguiole) cheese
Allemande a *velouté* sauce with egg yolks
Allemande (à l') German style: with sauerkraut and sausages
Allumette puff pastry strip
Alose shad (river fish)

Alouette lark
Alouette de mer sandpiper
Aloyau sirloin of beef
Alsacienne (à l') Alsace style: with sauerkraut, sausage and sometimes *foie gras*
Amande almond
Amande de mer small clam-like shellfish with nutty flavour
Amandine almond-flavoured
Amer bitter
Américaine (à l') Armoricaine (à l') sauce with dry white wine, cognac, tomatoes, shallots
Amourettes ox or calf marrow
Amuse-bouche appetiser
Amuse-geule appetiser
Amusette appetiser
Ananas pineapple
Anchoïade anchovy crust
Anchois anchovy
Ancienne (à l') in the old style
Andalouse (à l') Andalusian style: tomatoes, sweet red peppers, rice
Andouille smoked tripe sausage
Andouillette small chitterling (tripe) sausage
Aneth dill
Ange angel
Ange à cheval oyster, wrapped in bacon and grilled
Angevine (à l') Anjou style: with dry white wine, cream, mushrooms, onions
Anglaise (à l') plain boiled
Anguille eel
Anis aniseed
Anis étoile star anise (a star-shaped fruit)
Ansé basted with liquid
Arachide peanut
Araignée de mer spider crab
Arc en ciel rainbow trout
Ardennaise (à l') Ardenne style: with juniper berries
Arête fish bone

Argenteuil asparagus flavoured (usually soup)
Arlésienne stuffed tomatoes *à la provençale*, eggplant, rice
Armoricaine see *Américaine*
Aromates aromatic; either spicy or fragrant
Arômes à la gêne Lyonnais cow's or goat's cheese soaked in *marc*
Artichaut artichoke
Asperges asparagus
Assaisonné flavoured or seasoned with; to dress a salad
Assiette (de) plate (of)
Aubergine aubergine, eggplant
Aulx (plural of *ail*) garlic
Aumônière pancake drawn up into shape of beggar's purse
Aurore (à l') pink sauce, tomato flavoured
Auvergnate (à l') Auvergne style: with cabbage, sausage and bacon
Aveline hazelnut
Avocat avocado pear
Avoine oat(s)
Azyme unleavened (bread)
Baba au rhum sponge dessert with rum syrup
Baguette long bread loaf
Baie berry
Baigné bathed or lying in
Ballotine boned and stuffed poultry or meat in a roll
Banane banana
Bar sea-bass
Barbarie Barbary duck
Barbeau barbel
Barbeau de mer red mullet
Barbue brill
Barigoule (à la) brown sauce with artichokes and mushrooms
Baron de lapereau baron of young rabbit
Barquette boat-shaped pastry
Basilic basil
Basquaise (à la) Basque style:

Bayonne ham, rice and peppers
Bâtarde butter sauce, egg yolks
Bâtarde pain crusty white loaf
Batavia salad lettuce
Bâton stick-shaped bread loaf
Baudroie monkfish, anglerfish
Bavaroise bavarois mould, usually of custard, flavoured with fruit or chocolate. Can describe other dishes, particularly shellfish
Bavette skirt of beef
Baveuse runny
Béarnaise thick sauce with egg yolks, shallots, butter, white wine and tarragon vinegar
Béatilles (Malin de) sweetbreads, livers, kidneys, cockscombs
Beaugency *Béarnaise* sauce with artichokes, tomatoes, marrow
Bécasse woodcock
Bécassine snipe
Béchamel creamy white sauce
Beignet fritter
Beignet de fleur de courgette courgette flower in batter
Belle Hélène poached pear with ice cream and chocolate sauce
Belon oyster (see *Huîtres*)
Berawecka Christmas fruit bread stuffed with dried fruit, spices and laced with *kirsch*
Bercy sauce with white wine and shallots
Bergamot variety of pear or orange
Bergamote orange-flavoured sweet
Berlingot mint-flavoured sweet
Berrichone *Bordelaise* sauce
Bêtisse hard mint
Betterave beetroot
Beuchelle à la Tourangelle kidneys, sweetbreads, morels, cream and truffles
Beurre (Echiré) butter. (Finest butter from Poitou-Charentes)
Beurre blanc sauce with butter, shallots, wine vinegar and

sometimes dry white wine

Beurre noir sauce with browned butter, vinegar, parsley

Biche female deer

Bière à la pression beer on tap

Bière en bouteille bottled beer

Bifteck steak

Bigarade (à la) orange sauce

Bigarreau type of cherry

Bigorneau winkle

Billy By mussel soup

Biscuit à la cuiller sponge finger

Bisque shellfish soup

Blanc (de volaille) white breast (of chicken): can describe white fish fillet or white vegetables

Blanchaille whitebait

Blanquette white stew

Blé corn or wheat

Blé noir buckwheat

Blettes Swiss chard

Blinis small, thick pancakes

Boeuf à la mode beef braised in red wine

Boeuf Stroganoff beef, sour cream, onions, mushrooms

Boletus type of edible fungi

Bombe ice cream

Bon-chrétien variety of pear

Bonne femme (à la) white wine sauce, shallots, mushrooms

Bonne femme (à la) potato, leek and carrot soup

Bordelais(e) (à la) Bordeaux style: brown sauce with shallots, red wine, beef bone marrow

Bouchée mouthful size (either a tart or *vol-au-vent*)

Boudin sausage-shaped mixture

Boudin blanc white coloured; pork and sometimes chicken

Boudin noir black pudding

Bouillabaisse Mediterranean fish stew and soup

Bouilliture eel stew (see *matelote d'anguilles*)

Bouillon broth, light consommé

Boulangère sauce of onions and potatoes

Boulette small ball of fish or meat

Bouquet prawn

Bouquet garni bunch of herbs used for flavouring

Bourdaloue hot poached fruit

Bourdelot whole apple pastry

Bourgeoise (à la) sauce of carrots, onions and diced bacon

Bourguignonne (à la) Burgundy style: red wine, onions, bacon and mushrooms

Bouribot duck stewed in red wine

Bourrache borage, a herb used in drinks and salads

Bourride creamy fish soup with *aïoli*

Bourriole sweet or savoury pancake

Boutargue grey mullet roe paste

Braisé braised

Brandade de morue salt cod

Brassado (Brassadeau) doughnut

Bréjaude cabbage and bacon soup

Brème bream

Brési thin slices dried beef

Bretonne sauce with celery, leeks, beans and mushrooms

Brioche sweet yeast bread

Broche (à la) spit roasted

Brochet pike

Brochette (de) meat or fish on a skewer

Brouet broth

Brouillade stewed in oil

Brouillés scrambled

Broutard young goat

Brugnon nectarine

Brûlé(e) toasted

Brunoise diced vegetables

Bruxelloise sauce with asparagus, butter and eggs

Bucarde cockle

Buccin whelk

Bugne sweet pastry fritter
Cabillaud cod
Cabri kid (young goat)
Cacahouète roasted peanut
Cacao cocoa
Caen (à la mode de) cooked in Calvados and white wine
Café coffee
Cagouille snail
Caille quail
Caillé milk curds
Caillette pork and vegetable faggot
Cajasse sweet pastry (sometimes made with black cherries)
Cajou cashew nut
Calissons almond and crystallised fruit sweetmeats
Calmar (Calamar) inkfish, squid
Campagne country style
Canapé a base, usually bread
Canard duck
Canard à la presse (Rouennaise) duck breast cooked in blood of carcass, red wine and brandy
Canard au sang see above
Canard sauvage wild duck
Caneton (canette) duckling
Cannelle cinnamon
Capilotade small bits or pieces
Capoum scorpion fish
Caprice whim (a dessert)
Capucine nasturtium
Carbonnade braised beef in beer, onions and bacon
Cardinal *béchamel* sauce, lobster, cream, red peppers
Cardon cardoon, a large celery-like vegetable
Cari curry powder
Caroline chicken consommé
Carpe carp
Carré d'agneau lamb chops from best end of neck
Carré de porc pork cutlets from best end of neck
Carré de veau veal chops from best end of neck
Carrelet flounder, plaice
Carvi caraway seed
Casse-croûte snack
Cassis blackcurrant
Cassolette small pan
Cassonade soft brown sugar
Cassoulet casserole of beans, sausage and/or pork, goose, duck
Caviar d'aubergine aubergine (eggplant) purée
Cebiche raw fish marinated in lime or lemon juice
Cedrat confit a crystallised citrus fruit
Céleri celery
Céleri-rave celeriac
Cendres (sous les) cooked (buried) in hot ashes
Cèpe fine, delicate mushroom
Cerfeuil chervil
Cerise (noire) cherry (black)
Cerneau walnut
Cervelas pork garlic sausage
Cervelle brains
Cévenole (à la) garnished with mushrooms or chestnuts
Champignons (des bois) mushrooms (from the woods)
Chanterelle apricot-coloured mushroom
Chantilly whipped cream, sugar
Chapon capon
Chapon de mer *rascasse* or scorpion fish
Charbon de bois (au) grilled on charcoal
Charcuterie cold meat cuts
Charcutière sauce with onions, white wine, gherkins
Charlotte sponge fingers, cream, etc.
Charolais (Charollais) beef
Chartreuse a mould shape
Chasse hunting (season)

Chasseur sauce with white wine, mushrooms, shallots
Châtaigne sweet chestnut
Chateaubriand thick fillet steak
Châtelaine garnish with artichoke hearts, tomatoes, potatoes
Chaud(e) hot
Chaudrée fish stew
Chausson pastry turnover
Chemise (en) pastry covering
Cheveux d'ange vermicelli
Chevreau kid (young goat)
Chevreuil roe-deer
Chevrier green haricot bean
Chichi doughnut-like fritter
Chicon chicory
Chicorée curly endive
Chiffonnade thinly-cut
Chinoise (à la) Chinese style: with bean sprouts and soy sauce
Chipirones see *calmars*
Choisy braised lettuce, sautéed potatoes
Choix (au) a choice of
Choron *Béarnaise* sauce with the addition of tomatoes
Chou (vert) cabbage
Choucroute (souring of vegetables) usually white cabbage (sauerkraut), peppercorns, boiled ham, potatoes and Strasbourg sausages
Chou-fleur cauliflower
Chou-frisé kale
Chou-pommé white-heart cabbage
Chou-rave kohlrabi
Chou-rouge red cabbage
Choux (au fromage) puffs (made of cheese)
Choux de Bruxelles Brussels sprouts
Choux (pâte à) pastry
Ciboule spring onion
Ciboulette chive
Cidre cider
Citron (vert) lemon (lime)

Citronelle lemon grass
Citrouille pumpkin
Civet stew
Civet de lièvre jugged hare
Clafoutis cherries in pancake batter
Claires oysters (see *Huîtres*)
Clamart with petits pois
Clou de girofle clove (spice)
Clouté (de) studded with
Clovisse small clam
Cocherelle type of mushroom
Cochon pig
Cochonailles pork products
Coco coconut; also small white bean
Cocotte (en) cooking pot
Coeur (de) heart (of)
Coeur de palmier palm heart
Coffret (en) in a small box
Coing quince
Colbert (à la) fish, dipped in milk, egg and breadcrumbs
Colin hake
Colvert wild duck
Compote stewed fruit
Concassé(e) coarsely chopped
Concombre cucumber
Condé creamed rice and fruit
Confiserie confectionery
Confit(e) preserved or candied
Confiture jam
Confiture d'oranges marmalade
Congre conger eel
Consommé clear soup
Contrefilet sirloin, usually tied for roasting
Copeaux literally shavings
Coq (au vin) chicken in red wine sauce (or name of wine)
Coque cockle
Coque (à la) soft-boiled or served in shell
Coquelet young cockerel
Coquillages shellfish
Coquille St-Jacques scallop

Corail (de) coral (of)
Coriandre coriander
Cornichon gherkin
Côte d'agneau lamb chop
Côte de boeuf side of beef
Côte de veau veal chop
Côtelette chop
Cotriade Brittany fish soup
Cou (d'oie) neck (of goose)
Coulemelle mushroom
Coulibiac hot salmon *tourte*
Coulis (de) thick sauce (of)
Coupe ice cream dessert
Courge pumpkin
Courgette baby marrow
Couronne circle or ring
Court-bouillon aromatic
poaching liquid
Couscous crushed semolina
Crabe crab
Crambe sea kale
Cramique raisin or currant loaf
Crapaudine (à la) grilled game
bird with backbone removed
Crapinaude bacon pancake
Craquelot herring
Crécy with carrots and rice
Crème cream
Crème (à la) served with cream or
cooked in cream sauce
Crème à l'anglaise light custard
sauce
Crème brûlée same, less sugar and
cream, with praline (see *brûlée*)
Crème pâtissière custard filling
Crème plombières custard filling:
egg whites, fresh fruit flavouring
Crémets fresh cream cheese,
eaten with sugar and cream
Crêpe thin pancake
Crêpe dentelle thin pancake
Crêpe Parmentier potato pancake
Crêpe Suzette sweet pancake
with orange liqueur sauce
Crépinette (de) wrapping (of)
Cresson watercress

Cressonière purée of potatoes and
watercress
Crête cockscomb
Creuse long, thick-shelled oyster
Crevette grise shrimp
Crevette rose prawn
Cromesquis croquette
Croque Monsieur toasted cheese
or ham sandwich
Croquette see *boulette*
Crosne Chinese/Japanese
artichoke
Croustade small pastry mould
with various fillings
Croûte (en) pastry crust (in a)
Croûtons bread (toast or fried)
Cru raw
Crudité raw vegetable
Crustacés shellfish
Cuillère soft (cut with spoon)
Cuisse (de) leg (of)
Cuissot (de) haunch (of)
Cuit cooked
Cul haunch or rear
Culotte rump (usually steak)
Cultivateur soup or chopped
vegetables
Dariole basket-shaped pastry
Darne slice or steak
Dartois savoury or sweet filled
puff-pastry rectangles
Datte date
Daube stew (various types)
Daurade sea-bream
Décaféiné decaffeinated coffee
Dégustation tasting
Délice delight
Demi-glace basic brown sauce
Demi-sel lightly salted
Diable seasoned with mustard
Diane (à la) peppered cream
sauce
Dieppoise (à la) Dieppe style:
white wine, cream, mussels,
shrimps
Dijonnaise (à la) with mustard

sauce

Dijonnaise (à la belle) sauce made from blackcurrants

Dinde young hen turkey

Dindon turkey

Dindonneau young turkey

Diot pork and vegetable sausage

Dodine (de canard) cold stuffed duck

Dorade sea-bream

Doré cooked until golden

Doria with cucumbers

Douceurs desserts

Douillon pear wrapped in pastry

Doux (douce) sweet

Dragée sugared almond

Du Barry cauliflower soup

Duxelles chopped mushrooms, shallots and cream

Echalote shallot

Echine loin (of pork)

Echiquier in checkered fashion

Eclade (de moules) (mussels) cooked over pine needles

Ecrasé crushed (as with fruit)

Ecrevisses freshwater crayfish

Ecuelle bowl or basin

Effiloché(e) frayed, thinly sliced

Emincé thinly sliced

Encornet cuttlefish, squid

Encre squid ink, used in sauces

Endive chicory

Entrecôte entrecôte, rib steak

Entremets sweets

Epaule shoulder

Eperlan smelt (small fish)

Epice spice

Epinard spinach

Epis de maïs sweetcorn

Escabèche fish (or poultry) marinated in *court-bouillon*; served cold

Escalope thinly cut (meat or fish)

Escargot snail

Espadon swordfish

Estouffade stew with onions, herbs, mushrooms, red or white wine (perhaps garlic)

Estragon tarragon flavoured

Esturgeon sturgeon

Etrille crab

Etuvé(e) cooked in little water or in ingredient's own juices

Exocet flying fish

Façon cooked in a described way

Faisan(e) pheasant

Fane green top of root vegetable

Far Brittany prune flan

Farci(e) stuffed

Farine flour

Faux-filet sirloin steak

Favorite a garnish of *foie gras* and truffles

Favouille spider crab

Fécule starch

Fenouil fennel

Fenouil marin samphire

Féra lake fish, like salmon.

Ferme (fermier) farm (farmer)

Fermière mixture of onions, carrots, turnips, celery, etc.

Feuille de vigne vine leaf

Feuilleté light flaky pastry

Fève broad bean

Ficelle (à la) tied in a string

Ficelles thin loaves of bread

Figue fig

Filet fillet

Financière (à la) Madeira sauce with truffles

Fine de claire oyster (see *Huîtres*)

Fines herbes mixture of parsley, chives, tarragon, etc.

Flageolet kidney bean

Flamande (à la) Flemish style: bacon, carrots, cabbage, potatoes and turnips

Flambé flamed

Flamiche puff pastry tart

Flan tart

Flétan halibut

Fleur (de courgette) flower

(courgette flower, usually stuffed)
Fleurons puff pastry crescents
Flie small clam
Florentine with spinach
Flûte long thin loaf of bread
Foie liver
Foie de veau calves liver
Foie gras goose liver
Foies blonds de volaille chicken liver mousse
Foin (dans le) cooked in hay
Fond (base) basic stock
Fondant see *boulette*: a bon-bon
Fond d'artichaut artichoke heart
Fondu(e) (de fromage) melted (cheese with wine)
Forestière bacon and mushrooms
Fouace dough cakes
Four (au) baked in oven
Fourré stuffed
Frais (Fraîche) fresh or cool
Fraise strawberry
Fraise des bois wild strawberry
Framboise raspberry
Française (à la) mashed potato filled with mixed vegetables
Frangipane almond custard filling
Frappé frozen or ice cold
Friandises sweets (*petits fours*)
Fricadelle minced meat ball
Fricandeau slice topside veal
Fricassée braised in sauce of butter, egg yolks and cream
Frisé(e) curly
Frit fried
Frite chip
Fritot fritter
Frittons see *grattons*
Friture small fried fish
Frivolle fritter
Froid cold
Fromage cheese
Fromage de tête brawn
Fruit de la passion passion fruit
Fruits confits crystallised fruit
Fruits de mer seafood

Fumé smoked
Fumet fish stock
Galantine cooked meat, fish or vegetables in jelly, served cold
Galette pastry, pancake or cake
Galimafrée (de) stew (of)
Gamba large prawn
Ganache chocolate and *crème fraîche* mixture used to fill cakes
Garbure (Garbue) vegetable soup
Gardiane beef stew with red wine, black olives, onions and garlic
Gardon small roach
Gargouillau pear tart or cake
Garni(e) with vegetables
Garniture garnish
Gasconnade leg of lamb roasted with anchovies and garlic
Gâteau cake
Gâtinaise (à la) with honey
Gaufre waffle
Gayette faggot
Gelée aspic jelly
Géline chicken
Gendarme smoked or salted herring: flat, dry sausage
Genièvre juniper
Génoise rich sponge cake
Gentiane liqueur made from gentian flowers
Germiny sorrel and cream soup
Germon long-fin tuna
Gésier gizzard
Gibelotte see *fricassée*
Gibier game
Gigot (de) leg of lamb. Can describe other meat and fish
Gigot brayaude leg of lamb in white wine with red beans and cabbage
Gigue (de) shank (of)
Gingembre ginger
Girofle clove
Girolle apricot-coloured fungus
Givré frosted

Glacé iced. Crystallised. Glazed

Glace ice cream

Gnocchi dumplings of semolina, potato or *choux* paste

Godard see *financière (à la)*

Gougère round-shaped, egg and cheese *choux* pastry

Goujon gudgeon

Goujonnettes (de) small fried pieces (of)

Gourmandises sweetmeats; can describe *fruits de mer*

Gousse (de) pod or husk (of)

Graine (de capucine) seed (nasturtium)

Graisse fat

Graisserons duck or goose fat scratchings

Grand Veneur sauce with vegetables, wine vinegar, redcurrant jelly and cream

Granité water ice

Gratin browned

Gratin Dauphinois potato dish with cream, cheese and garlic

Gratin Savoyard potato dish with cheese and butter

Gratiné(e) sauced dish browned with butter, cheese, breadcrumbs, etc.

Gratinée Lyonnaise clear soup with port, beaten egg and cheese (grilled brown)

Grattons pork fat scratchings

Gravette oyster (see *Huîtres*)

Grecque (à la) cooked vegetables served cold

Grelette cold sauce, based on whipped cream, for fish

Grenade pomegranate

Grenadin thick veal escalope

Grenouille (cuisses de grenouilles) frog (frogs' legs)

Gribiche mayonnaise sauce with gherkins, capers, hardboiled egg yolks and herbs

Grillade grilled meat

Grillé(e) grilled

Grilot small bulb onion

Griotte (Griottine) bitter red cherry

Griset mushroom

Grisotte parasol mushroom

Grive thrush

Grondin gurnard, red gurnet

Gros sel coarse rock or sea salt

Groseille à maquereau gooseberry

Groseille noire blackcurrant

Groseille rouge redcurrant

Gruyère hard, mild cheese

Gyromitre fungus

Habit vert dressed in green

Hachis minced or chopped-up

Hareng herring

  à l'huile cured in oil

  fumé kippered

  salé bloater

  saur smoked

Haricot bean

Haricot blanc dried white bean

Haricot rouge red kidney bean

Haricot vert green/French bean

Hochepot thick stew

Hollandaise sauce with butter, egg yolk and lemon juice

Homard lobster

Hongroise (à la) Hungarian style: sauce with tomato and paprika

Hors d'oeuvre appetisers

Huile oil

Huîtres oysters

  Les claires: the oyster-fattening beds in Marennes terrain (part of the Charente Estuary, between Royan and Rochefort, in Poitou-Charentes).

  Flat-shelled oysters:

  Belons (from the River Belon in Brittany);

  Gravettes (from Arcachon in the Southwest);

  both the above are cultivated in

their home oyster beds.
Marennes are those transferred
from Brittany and Arcachon to
les claires, where they finish
their growth.

Dished oysters (sometimes
called *portugaises*):
these breed mainly in the
Gironde and Charente
estuaries; they mature at
Marennes.
Fines de claires and *spéciales*
are the largest; *huîtres de parc*
are standard sized.
All this lavish care covers a time
span of two to four years.

Hure (de) head (of). Brawn. Jellied
Ile flottante unmoulded soufflé of
beaten egg white and sugar
Imam bayeldi aubergine with rice,
onions and sautéed tomatoes
Impératrice (à la) desserts with
candied fruits soaked in kirsch
Indienne (à l') Indian style: with
curry powder
Infusion herb tea
Italienne (à l') Italian style:
artichokes, mushrooms, pasta
Jalousie latticed fruit or jam tart
Jambon ham
Jambonneau knuckle of pork
Jambonnette (de) boned and
stuffed (knuckle of ham or
poultry)
Jardinière diced fresh vegetables
Jarret de veau stew of shin of veal
Jarreton cooked pork knuckle
Jerez sherry
Jésus de Morteau smoked Jura
pork sausage
Joinville *velouté* sauce with
cream, crayfish tails and truffles
Joue (de) cheek (of)
Judru cured pork sausage
Julienne thinly-cut vegetables:
also ling (cod family, see *lingue*)

Jus juice
Kaki persimmon fruit
Lait milk
Laitance soft roe
Laitue lettuce
Lamproie eel-like fish
Langouste spiny lobster or craw-
fish
Langoustine Dublin Bay prawn
Langue tongue
Languedocienne (à la) mush-
rooms, tomatoes, parsley garnish
Lapereau young rabbit
Lapin rabbit
Lapin de garenne wild rabbit
Lard bacon
Lard de poitrine fat belly of pork
Lardons strips of bacon
Laurier bay-laurel, sweet bay leaf
Lavaret lake fish, like salmon trout
Lèche thin slice
Léger (Légère) light
Légume vegetable
Lieu cod-like fish
Lièvre hare
Limaçon snail
Limande lemon sole
Limon lime
Lingue ling (cod family)
Lit bed
Livèche lovage (like celery)
Longe loin
Lotte de mer monkfish, anglerfish
Lotte de rivière (de lac) burbot, a
river (or lake) fish, like eel; liver
a great delicacy
Lou magret see *magret*
Loup de mer sea-bass
Louvine (loubine) grey mullet,
like a sea-bass (Basque name)
Lyonnaise (à la) Lyonnais style:
sauce with wine, onions, vinegar
Macédoine diced fruit or veg
Mâche lamb's lettuce; small, dark,
green leaf
Macis mace (spice)

Madeleine tiny sponge cake

Madère sauce *demi-glace* and Madeira wine

Madrilène Madrid style: with chopped tomatoes

Magret (de canard) breast (of duck); now used for other poultry

Maigre fish, like sea-bass

Maigre non-fatty, lean

Maillot carrots, turnips, onions, peas and beans

Maïs maize flour

Maison (de) of the restaurant

Maître d'hôtel sauce with butter, parsley and lemon

Maltaise an orange flavoured *hollandaise* sauce

Manchons see *goujonnettes*

Mandarine tangerine

Mangetout edible peas and pods

Mangue mango

Manière (de) style (of)

Maquereau mackerel

Maraîchère (à la) market-gardener style: *velouté* sauce with vegetables

Marais marsh or market-garden

Marbré(e) marbled

Marc pure spirit

Marcassin young wild boar

Marché market

Marchand de vin sauce with red wine, chopped shallots

Marée fresh seafood

Marengo tomatoes, mushrooms, olive oil, white wine, garlic, herbs

Marennes (blanche) flat-shelled oyster (see *Huîtres*)

Marennes (verte) green shell

Mareyeur fishmonger

Marinade, Mariné(e) pickled

Marinière see *moules*

Marjolaine marjoram

Marjolaine almond and hazelnut

sponge cake with chocolate cream and praline

Marmite stewpot

Marquise (de) water ice (of)

Marrons chestnuts

Marrons glacés crystallised sweet chestnuts

Massepains marzipan cakes

Matelote (d'anguilles) freshwater red wine fish stew (of eels)

Matignon mixed vegetables, cooked in butter

Mauviette lark

Médaillion (de) round piece (of)

Mélange mixture or blend

Melba (à la) poached peach, with vanilla ice cream, raspberry sauce

Mélisse lemon-balm (herb)

Ménagère (à la) housewife style: onions, potatoes, peas, turnips and carrots

Mendiant (fruits de) mixture of figs, almonds and raisins

Menthe mint

Mer sea

Merguez spicy grilled sausage

Merlan whiting (in Provence the word is used for hake)

Merle blackbird

Merlu hake

Merluche dried cod

Mérou grouper (sea fish)

Merveilles hot, sugared fritters

Mesclum mixture of salad leaves

Meunière (à la) sauce with butter, parsley, lemon (sometimes oil)

Meurette red wine sauce

Miel honey

Mignardises *petits fours*

Mignon (de) small round piece

Mignonette coarsley ground white pepper

Mijoté(e) cooked slowly in water

Milanaise (à la) Milan style: dipped in breadcrumbs, egg,

cheese
Millassou sweet maize flour flan
Mille-feuille puff pastry with numerous thin layers
Mimosa chopped hardboiled egg
Mique stew of dumplings
Mirabeau anchovies, olives
Mirabelles golden plums
Mirepoix cubes carrot, onion, ham
Miroir smooth
Miroton (de) slices (of)
Mitonée (de) soup (of)
Mode (à la) in the manner of
Moelle beef marrow
Mojettes pulse beans in butter
Moka coffee
Montagne (de) from mountains
Montmorency with cherries
Morilles edible, dark brown, honeycombed fungi
Mornay cheese sauce
Morue cod
Morvandelle (jambon à la) ham with a piquant cream sauce, wine and wine vinegar (from Burgundy)
Morvandelle rapée baked eggs, cream and cheese, mixed with grated potato (from Burgundy's Morvan)
Mostèle (Gâteau de) cod mousse
Mouclade mussel stew
Moule mussel
Moules marinière mussels cooked in white wine and shallots
Mourone Basque red bell pepper
Mourtayrol stew with beef, chicken, ham, vegetables and bread (from the Auvergne)
Mousse cold, light, finely-minced ingredients with cream and egg whites
Mousseline *hollandaise* sauce with whipped cream
Mousseron edible fungus
Moutarde mustard

Mouton mutton
Mulet grey mullet
Mûre mulberry
Mûre sauvage (de ronce) blackberry
Muscade nutmeg
Museau de porc (de boeuf) sliced muzzle of pork (beef) with shallots and parsley in *vinaigrette*
Myrtille bilberry (blueberry)
Mystère a meringue desert with ice cream and chocolate; also cone-shaped ice cream
Nage (à la) *court-bouillon*: aromatic poaching liquid
Nantua sauce for fish with crayfish, white wine, tomatoes
Nappé sauce covered
Nature plain
Navarin stew, usually lamb
Navets turnips
Nègre dark (e.g. chocolate)
Newburg sauce with lobster, brandy, cream and Madeira
Nid nest
Nivernaise (à la) Nevers style: carrots and onions
Noilly sauce based on vermouth
Noisette hazelnut
Noisette sauce of lightly browned butter
Noisette (de) round piece (of)
Noix nuts
Noix (de veau) topside of leg (veal)
Normande (à la) Normandy style: fish sauce with mussels, shrimps, mushrooms, eggs and cream
Nouille noodle
Nouveau (nouvelle) new or young
Noyau sweet liqueur from crushed stones (usually cherries)
Oeufs à la coque soft-boiled eggs
Oeufs à la neige see *île flottante*
Oeufs à la poêlé fried eggs
Oeufs brouillés scrambled eggs

Oeufs durs hard-boiled eggs
Oeufs moulés poached eggs
Oie goose
Oignon onion
Oison rôti roast gosling
Omble chevalier freshwater char; looks like large salmon trout
Ombre grayling
Ombrine fish, like sea-bass
Omelette brayaude omelette with bacon, cream, potatoes and cheese
Onglet flank of beef
Oreille (de porc) ear (pig's)
Oreillette sweet fritter, flavoured with orange flower water
Orge (perlé) barley (pearl)
Origan oregano (herb)
Orléannaise (à l') Orléans style: chicory and potatoes
Orly dipped in butter, fried and served with tomato sauce
Ortie nettle
Ortolan wheatear (thrush family)
Os bone
Oseille sorrel
Osso bucco à la Niçoise veal braised with orange zest, tomatoes, onions and garlic
Ouillat Pyrénées soup; onions, tomatoes, goose fat, garlic
Oursins sea-urchins
Pageot sea-bream
Paillarde (de veau) grilled veal escalope
Paille fried potato stick
Pailletté (de) spangled (with)
Paillettes pastry straws
Pain bread
  bis brown bread
  de campagne round white loaf
  d'épice spiced honey cake
  de mie square white loaf
  de seigle rye bread
  doré bread soaked in milk and eggs and fried

  entier/complet wholemeal
  grillé toast
Paleron shoulder
Palmier palm-shaped sweet puff pastry
Palmier (coeur de) palm (heart)
Palombe wood pigeon
Palomête fish, like sea-bass
Palourde clam
Pamplemousse grapefruit
Pan bagna long split bread roll, brushed with olive oil and filled with olives, peppers, anchovies, onions, lettuce
Panaché mixed
Panade flour or bread paste
Panais parsnip
Pané(e) breadcrumbed
Panier basket
Panisse fried chickpea or maize fritter
Pannequets like *crêpes*, smaller and thicker
Pantin pork filled small pastry
Paon peacock
Papeton fried or puréed aubergines, arranged in ring mould
Papillon small oyster (butterfly) from the Atlantic coast
Papillote (en) cooked in oiled paper (or foil)
Paquets (en) parcels
Parfait (de) a mousse (of)
Paris-Brest cake of *choux* pastry, filled with butter cream, almonds
Parisienne (à la) leeks, potatoes
Parmentier potatoes
Pascade sweet or savoury pancake
Pascaline (de) see *quenelle* (of)
Passe Crassane variety of pear
Passe-pierres seaweed
Pastèque watermelon
Pastis (sauce au) aniseed based
Pâté minced meats (of various types) baked. Usually served

cold

Pâte pastry, dough or batter

Pâte à choux cream puff pastry

Pâte brisée short crust pastry

Pâte d'amande almond paste

Pâté en croûte baked in pastry crust

Pâtes (fraîches) fresh pasta

Pâtés (petits) à la Provençale anchovy and ham turnovers

Pâtisserie pastry

Pâtisson custard marrow

Patte claw, foot, leg

Pauchouse see *pochouse*

Paupiettes thin slices of meat of fish, used to wrap fillings

Pavé (de) thick slice (of)

Pavot (graines de) poppy seeds

Paysan(ne) (à la) country style

Peau (de) skin (of)

Pêche peach

Pêcheur fisherman

Pèlerine scallop

Perce-pierre samphire (edible sea fennel)

Perche perch

Perdreau young partridge

Perdrix partridge

Périgourdine (à la) goose liver and sauce *Périgueux*

Périgueux sauce with truffles and Madeira

Persil parsley

Persillade mixture of chopped parsley and garlic

Petit-beurre biscuit made with butter

Petit gris small snail

Petite marmite strong consommé with toast and cheese

Petits fours miniature cakes, biscuits, sweets

Petits pois tiny peas

Pétoncle small scallop

Pets de nonne small soufflé fritters

Picanchâgne (piquenchânge) a

pear tart with walnut topping

Picholine large green table olives

Pied de cheval large oyster

Pied de mouton blanc creamcoloured mushroom

Pied de porc pig's trotter

Pigeonneau young pigeon

Pignon pine nut

Pilau rice dish

Pilon drumstick

Piment (doux) pepper (sweet)

Pimpernelle burnet (salad green)

Pintade (pintadeau) guinea-fowl (young guinea-fowl)

Piperade omelette or scrambled eggs with tomatoes, peppers, onions and, sometimes, ham

Piquante (sauce) sharp-tasting sauce with shallots, capers, wine

Piqué larded

Pissenlit dandelion leaf

Pistache green pistachio nut

Pistil de safran saffron (*pistil* from autumn-flowering crocus)

Pistou vegetable soup bound with *pommade*

Plateau (de) plate (of)

Pleurote mushroom

Plie franche plaice

Plombières sweet with vanilla ice cream, *kirsch,* candied fruit and *crème chantilly*

Pluche sprig

Pluvier plover

Poché(e) Pochade poached

Pochouse freshwater fish stew with white wine

Poêlé fried

Pogne sweet brioche flavoured with orange flower water

Poire pear

Poireau leek

Pois peas

Poisson fish

Poitrine breast

Poitrine fumée smoked bacon

Poitrine salée unsmoked bacon

Poivrade a peppery sauce with wine vinegar, cooked vegetables

Poivre noir black pepper

Poivre rose red pepper

Poivre vert green pepper

Poivron (doux) pepper (sweet)

Pojarsky minced meat or fish, cutlet shaped and fried

Polenta boiled maize flour

Polonaise Polish style: with buttered breadcrumbs, parsley, hard-boiled eggs

Pommade thick, smooth paste

Pomme apple

Pommes de terre potatoes
  à l'anglaise boiled
  allumettes thin and fried
  boulangère sliced with onions
  brayaude baked
  château roast
  dauphine croquettes
  duchesse mashed with egg yolk
  en l'air hollow potato puffs
  frites fried chips
  gratinées browned with cheese
  Lyonnaise sautéed with onions
  vapeur boiled

Pomponette savoury pastry

Porc (carré de) loin of pork

Porc (côte de) pork chop

Porcelet suckling pig

Porchetta whole roasted young pig, stuffed with offal, herbs, garlic

Porto (au) port

Portugaise (à la) Portuguese style: fried onions and tomatoes

Portugaises oysters with long, deep shells (see *Huîtres*)

Potage thick soup

Pot-au-crème dessert, usually chocolate or coffee

Pot-au-feu clear meat broth served with the meat

Potée heavy soup of cabbage, beans, etc.

Potimarron pumpkin

Potjevleisch northern terrine of mixed meats (rabbit, pork, veal)

Pouchouse see *pochouse*

Poularde large hen

Poulet chicken

Poulet à la broche spit-roasted chicken

Poulet Basquaise chicken with tomatoes and peppers

Poulet de Bresse corn-fed, white flesh chicken

Poulet de grain grain-fed chicken

Poulette young chicken

Poulpe octopus

Pounti small, egg-based, savoury soufflé with bacon or prunes

Pourpier purslane (salad green, also flavours dishes); a weed

Pousse-pierre edible seaweed

Poussin small baby chicken

Poutargue grey mullet roe paste

Praire small clam

Praline caramelised almonds

Praslin caramelised

Pré-salé (agneau de) lamb raised on salt marshes

Primeur young vegetable

Princesse *velouté* sauce, asparagus tips and truffles

Printanièr(e) (à la) garnish of diced vegetables

Produit (de) product (of)

Profiterole *choux* pastry, custard filled puff

Provençale (à la) Provençal style: tomatoes, garlic, olive oil, etc.

Prune plum

Pruneau prune

Purée mashed

Quasi (de veau) thick part of loin of veal (chump)

Quatre-épices four blended ground spices (ginger, cloves, nutmeg and white pepper)

Quatre-quarts cake made with equal weights of eggs, butter, sugar and flour (four-quarters)
Quenelle light dumpling of fish or poultry
Quetsche small, purple plum
Queue tail
Queue de boeuf oxtail
Quiche (Lorraine) open flan of cheese, ham or bacon
Râble de lièvre (lapin) saddle of hare (rabbit)
Raclette scrapings from specially made and heated cheese
Radis radish
Ragoût stew, usually meat, but can describe other ingredients
Raie (bouclée) skate (type of)
Raifort horseradish
Raisin grape
Raïto sauce served over grilled fish (red wine, onions, tomatoes, herbs, olives, capers and garlic)
Ramequin see *cocotte (en)*
Ramier wood pigeon
Rapé(e) grated or shredded
Rascasse scorpion fish
Ratafia brandy and unfermented Champagne. Almond biscuit
Ratatouille aubergines, onions, courgettes, garlic, red peppers and tomatoes in olive oil
Ratte de Grenoble white potato
Raves (root) turnips, radishes,etc.
Ravigote sauce with onions, herbs, mushrooms, wine vinegar
Ravioles ravioli
Ravioles à la Niçoise pasta filled with meat or Swiss chard and baked with cheese
Ravioles du Royans small ravioli pasta with goat cheese filling (from the terrain under the western edges of the Vercors)
Régence sauce with wine, truffles, mushrooms

Réglisse liquorice
Reine chicken and cream
Reine-Claude greengage
Reinette type of apple
Réjane garnish of potatoes, bone-marrow, spinach and artichokes
Rémoulade sauce of mayonnaise, mustard, capers, herbs, anchovy
Rillettes (d'oie) potted pork (goose)
Rillons small cubes of fat pork
Ris d'agneau lamb sweetbreads
Ris de veau veal sweetbreads
Rissettes small sweetbreads
Rivière river
Riz rice
Riz à l'impératrice cold rice pudding
Riz complet brown rice
Riz sauvage wild rice
Robe de chambre jacket potato
Robert sauce *demi-glace*, white wine, onions, vinegar, mustard
Rocambole wild garlic
Rognon kidney
Rognonnade veal and kidneys
Romanoff fruit marinated in liqueur; mostly strawberries
Romarin rosemary
Roquette salad green
Rosé meat cooked to pink stage
Rosette large pork sausage
Rossini see *tournedos*
Rôti roast
Rouelle (de) round piece or slice
Rouget red mullet
Rouget barbet red mullet
Rouget grondin red gurnard (larger than red mullet)
Rouille orange-coloured sauce with peppers, garlic and saffron
Roulade (de) roll (of)
Roulé(e) rolled (usually *crêpe*)
Rousette rock salmon; dog fish
Roux flour, butter base for sauces
Royan fresh sardine

Rutabaga swede
Sabayon sauce of egg yolks, wine
Sablé shortbread
Sabodet Lyonnais sausage of pig's head, pork, beef; served hot
Safran saffron (see *pistil de*)
Sagou sago
Saignant(e) underdone, rare
Saindoux lard
St-Germain with peas
St-Hubert sauce *poivrade*, bacon and cooked chestnuts
St-Jacques (coquille) scallop
St-Pierre John Dory
Saisons (suivant) depending on the season of the year
Salade Niçoise tomatoes, beans, potatoes, black olives, anchovy, lettuce, olive oil, perhaps tuna
Salade panachée mixed salad
Salade verte green salad
Salé salted
Salicornes marsh samphire (edible sea-fennel)
Salmigondis meat stew
Salmis red wine sauce
Salpicon meat or fish and diced vegetables in a sauce
Salsifis salsify (vegetable)
Sanciau thick sweet or savoury pancake
Sandre freshwater fish, like perch
Sang blood
Sanglier wild boar
Sanguine blood orange
Sanguines mountain mushrooms
Santé potato and sorrel soup
Sarcelle teal
Sarrasin buckwheat
Sarriette savory, bitter herb
Saucisse freshly-made sausage
Saucisson large, dry sausage
Saucisson cervelas saveloy
Sauge sage
Saumon salmon
Saumon blanc hake

Saumon fumé smoked salmon
Sauté browned in butter, oil or fat
Sauvage wild
Savarin see *baba au rhum*
Savoyarde with Gruyère cheese
Scarole *endive* (chicory)
Scipion cuttlefish
Seiche squid or cuttlefish
Sel salt
Selle saddle
Selon grosseur (S.G.) according to size
Serpolet wild thyme
Sévigné garnished with mushrooms, roast potatoes, lettuce
Smitane sauce with sour cream, onions, white wine
Socca chickpea flour fritter
Soissons with white beans
Soja (pousse de) soy bean (soy bean sprout)
Soja (sauce de) soy sauce
Sole à la Dieppoise sole fillets, mussels, shrimps, wine, cream
Sole Cardinale poached fillets of sole in lobster sauce
Sole Dugléré sole with tomatoes, onions, shallots, butter
Sole Marguéry sole with mussels and prawns in rich egg sauce
Sole Walewska *mornay* sauce, truffles and prawns
Sorbet water ice
Soubise onion sauce
Soufflé(e) beaten egg whites, baked (with sweet or savoury ingredients)
Soupière soup tureen
Sourdon cockle
Souvaroff a game bird with *foie gras* and truffles
Spaghettis (de) thin strips (of)
Spoom frothy water ice
Strasbourgeoise (à la) Strasbourg style: *foie gras*, *choucroute*, bacon

Sucre sugar
Suppion small cuttlefish
Suprême sweet white sauce
Suprême boneless breast of
poultry; also describes a fish
fillet
Sureau (fleurs de) elder tree
(flowers of); delicious liqueur
Tacaud type of cod
Talleyrand truffles, cheese, *foie
gras*
Talmousse triangular cheese pastry
Tanche tench
Tapé(e) dried
Tartare raw minced beef
Tartare (sauce) sauce with
mayonnaise, onions, capers,
herbs
Tarte open flan
Tarte Tatin upside down tart of
caramelised apples and pastry
Telline small clam
Tergoule Normandy rice pudding
with cinnamon
Terrine container in which mixed
meats/fish are baked; served
cold
Tête de veau vinaigrette calf's
head *vinaigrette*
Thé tea
Thermidor grilled lobster with
browned *béchamel* sauce
Thon tunny fish
Thym thyme
Tiède mild or lukewarm
Tilleul lime tree
Timbale mould in which contents
are steamed
Tomate tomate
Topinambour Jerusalem artichoke
Torte sweet-filled flan
Tortue turtle
Tortue sauce with various herbs,
tomatoes, Madeira
Toulousaine (à la) Toulouse style:
truffles, *foie gras*, sweetbreads,

kidneys
Tournedos fillet steak (small end)
Tournedos chasseur with shallots,
mushrooms, tomatoes
Tournedos Dauphinoise with
creamed mushrooms, *croûtons*
Tournedos Rossini with goose
liver, truffles, port, *croûtons*
Touron a cake, pastry or loaf
made from almond paste and
filled with candied fruits and
nuts; also see *ouillat*, a
Pyrénées soup
Tourte (Tourtière) covered
savoury tart
Tourteau large crab
Tourteau fromager goat's cheese
gâteau
Tranche slice
Tranche de boeuf steak
Traver de porc spare rib of pork
Tripes à la mode de Caen beef
tripe stew
Tripettes small sheep tripe
Tripoux stuffed mutton tripe
Trompettes de la mort fungi
Tronçon a cut of fish or meat
Trou water ice
Truffade a huge sautéed pancake,
or *galette*, with bacon, garlic
and Cantal cheese
Truffe truffle; black, exotic, tuber
Truffée with truffles
Truite trout
Truite (au bleu) trout poached in
water and vinegar; turns blue
Truite saumonée salmon trout
Tuiles tiles (thin almond slices)
Turbot (turbotin) turbot
Vacherin ice cream, meringue,
cream
Valenciennes (à la) rice, onions,
red peppers, tomatoes, white
wine
Vallée d'Auge veal or chicken;
sautéed, flamed in Calvados and

371

served with cream and apples

Vapeur (à la) steamed

Varech seaweed

Veau veal

Veau à la Viennoise (escalope de) slice of veal coated with egg and breadcrumbs, fried

Veau Milanaise (escalope de) with macaroni, tomatoes, ham, mushrooms

Veau pané (escalope de) thin slice in flour, eggs and breadcrumbs

Velouté white sauce with *bouillon* and white *roux*

Velouté de volaille thick chicken soup

Venaison venison

Ventre belly or breast

Verdurette *vinaigrette* dressing with herbs

Vernis clam

Véronique grapes, wine, cream

Verte green mayonnaise with chervil, spinach, tarragon

Vert-pré thinly-sliced chips, *maître d'hôtel* butter, watercress

Verveine verbena

Vessie (en) cooked in a pig's bladder; usually chicken

Viande meat

Vichy glazed carrots

Vichyssoise creamy potato and leek soup, served cold

Viennoise coated with egg and breadcrumbs, fried (usually veal)

Vierge (sauce) olive oil sauce

Vierge literally virgin (best olive oil, the first pressing)

Vigneron vine-grower (wine-maker)

Vinaigre (de) wine vinegar or vinegar of named fruit

Vinaigre de Jerez sherry vinegar

Vinaigrette (à la) French dressing with wine vinegar, oil, etc.

Viroflay spinach as a garnish

Volaille poultry

Vol au vent puff pastry case

Xérès (vinaigre de) sherry (vinegar)

Yaourt yogurt

Zeste (d'orange) rubbing from (orange skin)

Regional Cuisine

In the notes which follow I examine first the French regions with Atlantic seaboards, starting in the north and finishing at the Spanish frontier; then the regions bordering Belgium, Germany, Switzerland, Italy and the Mediterranean; and, finally, the regions of inland France.

North Fish takes pride of place, freshly landed at the ports of Boulogne, Calais, and smaller ones like Le Crotoy. *Sole, turbot, maqueraux, barbue, lotte de mer, flétan, harengs, merlan, moules, crévettes*; all appear on menus. So do soups and stews, many with root vegetables: *waterzooï* – fish or chicken stew; *hochepot* – meat and vegetable *pot-au-feu*; *carbonnade* – beef stew with beer. Leeks are super; enjoy *flamiche aux poireaux* (*quiche*-like pastry). Seek out the *hortillonages* (water-gardens) of Amiens and their fine vegetables. Try *gaufres* (yeast waffles) and *ficelles* (variously stuffed pancakes). Beer, too, is good.

Normandy Land of cream, apples and the pig. Vallée d'Auge gives its name to many dishes, including chicken, veal and fish; the term means cream, apples or cider, or apple brandy (Calvados) have been added. Cider is first class. Pork products are everywhere: *andouilles* – smoked tripe sausages, eaten cold; *andouillettes* – small grilled tripe sausages. Fish are superb: *sole à la Normande, à la Dieppoise, à la Fécampoise, à la Havraise* (the last three are ports); *plats de fruits de mer*; shrimps; oysters; *bulots* (whelks); mussels. Enjoy tripe; *ficelles* – pancakes; cow's milk cheeses; rich cream; butters, both salty and sweet; salad produce and potatoes from Caux; exquisite apple tarts; *canard à la Rouennaise*; and fish stews.

Brittany Fish and shellfish are commonplace: lobsters, *huîtres, langoustes*, crabs, of varying sorts, *moules*, prawns, shrimps, *coquilles St-Jacques*; to name just a few. Enjoy *cotriade* – a Breton fish stew with potatoes and onions; *galettes* – buckwheat flour pancakes with savoury fillings; *crêpes de froment* – wheat flour pancakes with sweet fillings; *far Breton* – a batter mixture with raisins; *gâteau Breton* – a mouthwatering concoction; *agneau de pré-salé* – from the salt marshes near Mont-St-Michel (fine omelettes are also made there); and *poulet blanc Breton*. Brittany is one of France's market-gardens: enjoy artichokes, cauliflowers, cabbages, onions and strawberries.

Charentes/Vendée western half of Poitou-Charentes. La Rochelle is a famed fishing port; consequently fish predominates. Oysters are glorious (see *Huîtres* in Glossary). The port of La Cotinière, on the island of Oléron, is renowned for its shrimps. Challans, in the Vendée, is reputed for its quality ducks. Charentes is second to none for butter, goat's milk cheeses, Charentais melons, Cognac, cabbages, mussels, *mojette* (white beans) and salt-marsh lamb from the Marais Poitevin.

Southwest One of the great larders of France; can be divided into several distinct areas. From the countryside that lies in a semicircle to the north-west, west, south and south-east of Bordeaux comes: lamb from Pauillac; oysters (*gravettes*) from Arcachon; eels (*pibales*); beef (*entrecôte Bordelaise* is the bestknown); onions and shallots; *cèpes*; *alose* (shad); and *lamproie* – lamprey (eel-like fish). The Garonne Valley is one vast orchard: try prunes from Agen; peaches; pears and dessert grapes.

South of the Garonne is **Gascony**: famed for *foie gras* (duck and goose); *confit* (preserved meat from both birds); jams and fruits; and Armagnac. Try a *floc* (Armagnac and grape juice).

To the south and west of Gascony are **Béarn** and the **Landes**. From the latter came *palombes* and *ortolans*, ducks and chickens. Among traditional Béarn specialities are *garbue* – the most famous of vegetable soups; *poule au pot* – the chicken dish given its name by Henri IV; *tourin, ouliat* and *cousinette (cousinat)*. See the Southwest for further details.

West of Béarn is **Basque** country: tuna, anchovies, sardines and salmon (from Béarn also) are great; Bayonne ham, *piments* (peppers), *piperade, ttoro* (fish stew) and *gâteau Basque*.

Champagne-Ardenne & Ile de France Many of the specialities listed earlier in the North appear in the former, renowned for its potatoes and turkeys. In the Ardenne you'll enjoy smoked hams, sold in nets; *sanglier; marcassin;* and red and white cabbages. West of Verdun, at Ste-Menehould, try *pieds de cochon* (pig's trotters); *petits gris* (snails); and the many differing sweets and sugared almonds (Verdun is famous for them). Troyes is renowned for pork and *andouillettes*.

Regional specialities and produce are all but non-existent in the Ile de France. Look out for cherries from Poissy, beans from Arpajon and tomatoes from Montlhéry. Enjoy *pâtés* and *terrines* and tempting *pâtisseries* and *galettes*.

Alsace There is a strong German influence in much of the cooking; pork, game, goose and beer are common. *Foie gras* (fattened goose liver) is superb. So, too, is a range of tarts; *flammekuchen* – flamed open tart; and some with fruit (*linzertorte* – raspberry or bilberry open tart); jams, fruit liqueurs and *eaux-de-vie* (see Alsace wines). Stomach-filling *choucroute* and local sausages are on most menus; as are *kougelhopf, beckenoffe* and *lewerknepfle* (see Alsace specialities). Enjoy *tourte Alsacienne* – pork pie. Use *winstubs* (wine bars).

Lorraine on the north-west borders is known for its *madeleines* (tiny sponge cakes), *macarons*, mouthwatering *quiche Lorraine*, fruit tarts, omelettes and *potée*.

Jura This is dairy country; witness the numerous excellent cheeses encountered in the region. Try *Jésus de Morteau* – a fat pork sausage smoked over pine and juniper; *brési* – wafer-thin slices of dried beef; and many local hams. *Morilles* and other fungi are common; so are freshly-caught trout and other freshwater fish.

Savoie & Hautes-Alpes *Plat gratiné* applies to a wide variety of dishes; in the Alps this means cooked in breadcrumbs; *gratins* of all sorts show how well milk, cream and cheese can be combined together. Relish *fondue* and *gougère*. Freshwater lake fish are magnificent (see the regional specialities for Savoie). Walnuts, chestnuts, all sorts of fruits and marvellous wild mushrooms are other delights.

Côte d'Azur & Provence A head-spinning kaleidoscope of colours and textures fills the eyes: aubergines, peppers, beans, tomatoes, cauliflowers, asparagus, olives, garlic, artichokes, courgettes; the list is endless. Fruit, too, is just as appealing: melons from Cavaillon; strawberries from Monteux; cherries from Remoulins; glacé fruit from Apt; truffles from

Valréas and Aups. Fish from the Med are an extra bonus: *bar* and *loup de mer, daurade, St-Pierre*, monkfish and mullet; these are the best. Lamb from the foothills of the Alps near Sisteron; herbs of every type from the *département* of Var; nuts from Valensole; honey and olive oil; *ratatouille*; sardines; *saucisson d'Arles*; *bouillabaisse* and *bourride*; *soupe de poissons* and *soupe au pistou*; what memories are stirred as I write.

Corsica Savour game and charcuterie: *prisuttu* – raw ham, like Italian *prosciutto*; *figatelli* – grilled pig's liver sausage; *lonzu (lonza)* – slice of pork pickled in salt and herbs; *coopa (copa)* – pork sausage or shoulder of pork. Chestnut flour is used in many ways, particularly in desserts. Fine citrus fruits and, befitting the island of the *maquis*, superb herbs.

Languedoc-Roussillon & Cévennes The same products and dishes listed under Provence are available here. Also oysters and mussels (*les coquillages*) from the lagoons (particularly the Bassin de Thau; visit Mèze and Bouzigues). Excellent shellfish; cherries from Céret; anchovies; apricots and pumpkins. Enjoy *brandade de morue* (salt cod), *confit d'oie* (and *canard*), *cassoulet* and *saucisses de Toulouse*.

Loire The river and its many tributaries provide *alose, sandre, anguille*, carp, perch, pike, salmon and *friture*. A tasty *beurre blanc* is the usual sauce with fish. *Charcuterie* is marvellous: *rillettes, rillons, andouillettes, saucissons, jarretons* and other delights. Cultivated mushrooms come from the limestone caves near Saumur.

The **Sologne** is famous for asparagus, frogs, game, fungi, lake and river fish and wildfowl. You'll be offered, too, many a *pâté*, fruit tarts (it's the home of *tarte Tatin*) and pies.

Burgundy Refer to the often seen regional specialities. Many dishes are wine based: *coq au Chambertin* and *poulet au Meursault* are examples. Enjoy hams, freshwater fish, vegetables, *escargots*, mustard and gingerbread from Dijon and blackcurrants (used for *cassis*, the term for both the fruit and the liqueur made from them).

Lyonnais The culinary heart and stomach of France. There is a variety of top-class produce on hand: Bresse poultry (*chapons* – capons – are unforgettable treats); *grenouilles* and game from Les Dombes; Charolais cattle from the hills west of Beaujolais; fish from the rivers and pools (pike *quenelles* appear everywhere); *charcuterie* from Lyon, particularly sausages called *sabodet, rosette, saucisson en brioche* and *cervelas*; and chocolates and *pâtisseries* from Lyon.

Auvergne & Ardèche Both areas which keep alive old specialities. Refer to the regional lists but here are some of the best: *potée Auvergnate* – a stew of cabbage, vegetables, pork and sausage; *friand Sanflorin* – pork meat and herbs in pastry; *aligot* – a purée of potatoes, cheese, garlic and butter; *pounti* – a small egg-based savoury souffle with bacon or prunes; and delectable *charcuterie*, hams, *saucisson, saucisses sèches* (dried sausages), *pâtés* and so on. The quality and variety of cheeses are second to none. Cabbages, potatoes, bacon and cheese feature on menus. The area around Le Puy is famed for its lentils and Verveine du Velay – yellow and green liqueurs made from over 30 mountain plants. The Ardèche is renowned for its sweet chestnuts (relish *marrons glacés*).

Berry-Bourbonnais & Poitou – eastern half of Poitou-Charentes. The flat terrain of Berry-Bourbonnais is dull country, the granary of France. The area is renowned for beef, deer, wild boar, rabbits, hares, pheasants and partridge.

Much of Poitou lies in the deserted, wooded hills of Limousin (as do the western edges of Auvergne). Apart from the specialities listed look out for *mique* – a stew of dumplings; *farcidure* – a dumpling, either poached or sauteed; and *clafoutis* – pancake batter, poured over fruit (usually black cherries) and baked. Limousin is reputed for its *cèpes* – fine, delicate, flap mushrooms; and also for its reddish-coloured cattle.

Dordogne A land of truffles, geese, ducks, walnuts, *cèpes*, chestnuts, sunflowers and fruit. *Foie gras* (goose and duck) is obligatory on menus; as are *confits* of both birds (preserved in their own fat) and *magrets* (boned duck breasts which have become so popular in the last decade throughout France). *Pâtés* incorporating either poultry or game, and truffles, are common place. If you see *miques* (yeast dumplings) or *merveilles* (hot, sugar-covered pastry fritters) on menus, order them. In the south, in the Lot Valley and towards the Garonne, it's a land of orchards: plums, prunes, figs, peaches, pears and cherries.

Regional Specialities

ALSACE

Beckenoffe (Baeckeoffe) (Baeckaoffa) "baker's oven"; a stew, or hotpot, of potatoes, lamb, beef, pork and onions, cooked in a local wine
Choucroute garnie sauerkraut with peppercorns, boiled ham, pork, Strasbourg sausages and boiled potatoes. Try it with a beer (*bière*)
Chou farci stuffed cabbage
Flammekueche (Tarte flambée) bacon, onion and cream tart
Foie gras goose liver
Kougelhopf a round brioche with raisins and almonds
Krapfen fritters stuffed with jam
Lewerknepfle (Leber Knödel) liver dumpling (pork liver dumpling)

Matelote Alsacienne in Alsace made with stewed eels (in the past from the River Ill) – sometimes with freshwater fish
Pflutters Alsacienne potato puffs
Potage Lorraine potato, leek and onion soup
Schifela shoulder of pork with turnips
Tarte (aux mirabelles) golden plum tart. Also with other fruits
Tarte à l'oignon Alsacienne onion and cream tart

BERRY-BOURBONNAIS

Bignons small fritters
Bouquettes aux pommes de terre grated potato, mixed with flour, egg white and fried in small, thick pieces
Brayaude (gigot) lamb cooked in white wine, onions and herbs
Chargouère (Chergouère) pastry turnover of plums or prunes
Cousinat (Cousina) chestnut soup (*salée* – salted) with cream, butter and prunes; served with bread
Gargouillau a *clafoutis* of pears
Gouèron a cake of goat cheese and eggs
Gouerre (Gouère) a cake of potato purée, flour, eggs and *fromage blanc* (fresh cream cheese), cooked in an oven as a *tourtière*
Lièvre à la Duchambais hare cooked slowly in a sauce of cream, chopped-up shallots, vinegar and pepper
Milliard (Millat) (Milla) a *clafoutis* of cherries (see Poitou-Charentes)
Pâté de pommes de terre a tart of sliced potatoes, butter, bacon and chopped-up onions, baked in an oven. Cream added to hot centre
Poirat pear tart
Pompe aux grattons a cake, in the shape of a crown, made up of a mixture of small pieces of pork, flour, eggs and butter
Sanciau thick sweet or savoury pancake; made from buckwheat flour
Truffiat grated potato, mixed with flour, eggs and butter and baked

BRITTANY

Agneau de pré-salé leg of lamb, from animals pastured in the salt marshes and meadows of Brittany
Bardatte cabbage stuffed with hare, cooked in white wine and served with chestnuts and roast quail
Beurre blanc sauce for fish dishes; made from the reduction of shallots, wine vinegar and the finest butter (sometimes with dry white wine)
Cotriade fish soup with potatoes, onions, garlic and butter
Crêpes Bretonnes the thinnest of pancakes with a variety of sweet fillings; often called **Crêpes de froment** (wheat flour)
Far Breton batter mixture; vanilla-flavoured sugar, rum, dried prunes
Galette takes various forms: can be a biscuit, a cake or a pancake; the

latter is usually stuffed with fillings like mushrooms, ham, cheese or seafood and is called a **Galette de blé noir** (buckwheat flour)
Gâteau Breton rich cake with butter, flour, egg yolks and sugar
Gigot de pré-salé same as *agneau de pré-salé*
Kouign-amann crisp, flaky pastries of butter, sugar and yeast
Palourdes farcies clams in the shell, with a *gratiné* filling
Poulet blanc Breton free-range, fine quality white Breton chicken

BURGUNDY

Boeuf Bourguignon braised beef simmered in red wine-based sauce
Charolais (Pièce de) steak from the excellent Charolais cattle
Garbure heavy soup; mixture of pork, cabbage, beans and sausages
Gougère cheese pastry, based on Gruyère cheese
Jambon persillé parsley-flavoured ham, served cold in its jelly
Jambon en saupiquet, **Jambon à la crème**, **Jambon à la Morvandelle** ham with a piquant cream sauce, wine and wine vinegar
Matelote freshwater fish soup, usually based on a red wine sauce
Meurette red wine-based sauce with small onions. Accompanies fish or poached egg dishes
Pain d'épice spiced honeycake from Dijon
Pochouse (Pouchouse) stew of freshwater fish and garlic, usually white wine based. Rarely seen on restaurant menus
Potée see *Garbure*

CHAMPAGNE-ARDENNE

Flamiche aux Maroilles see *Tarte aux Maroilles*
Flamiche aux poireaux puff-pastry tart with cream and leeks
Goyère see *Tarte aux Maroilles*
Rabotte (Rabote) whole apple wrapped in pastry and baked
Tarte aux Maroilles a hot creamy tart based on the local cheese

COTE D'AZUR

Aïgo Bouido garlic and sage soup – with bread (or eggs and cheese)
Aïgo saou fish soup (no *rascasse* – scorpion fish) with *rouille*
Aïoli (ailloli) a mayonnaise sauce with garlic and olive oil
Anchoïade anchovy crust
Berlingueto chopped spinach and hard-boiled eggs
Bouillabaisse a dish of Mediterranean fish (including *rascasse, St-Pierre, baudroie, congre, chapon de mer, langoustes, langoustines, tourteaux, favouilles, merlan* and, believe it or not, many others) and a soup, served separately with *rouille, safran* and *aïoli*
Bourride a creamy fish soup (usually made with big white fish), thickened with *aïoli* and flavoured with crawfish

Brandade (de morue) à l'huile d'olive a mousse of salt cod with cream, olive oil and garlic

Capoum a large pink *rascasse* (scorpion fish)

Pain Bagna bread roll with olive oil, anchovies, olives, onions, etc.

Pieds et paquets small parcels of mutton tripe, cooked with sheep trotters and white wine

Pissaladière Provençal bread dough with onions, anchovies, olives, etc.

Pistou (Soupe au) vegetable soup bound with *pommade*

Pollo pépitora Provençal chicken *fricassée* thickened with lemon-flavoured mayonnaise

Pommade a thick paste of garlic, basil, cheese and olive oil

Ratatouille aubergines, courgettes, onion, garlic, red peppers and tomatoes in olive oil

Rouille orange-coloured sauce with hot peppers, garlic and saffron

Salade Niçoise tomatoes, beans, potatoes, black olives, anchovy, lettuce and olive oil. Sometimes tuna fish

Tapénade a purée of stoned black olives, anchovy fillets, capers, tuna fish and olive oil

Tarte (Tourte) aux blettes open-crust pastry with filling of Swiss chard (not unlike Chinese cabbage) and pine nuts

Tian Provençal earthenware dish

DORDOGNE

Bourrioles d'Aurillac sweet pancakes, made from buckwheat flour

Cèpes fine, delicate mushrooms. Sometimes dried

Chou farci stuffed cabbage. Sometimes *aux marrons* – with chestnuts

Confit de canard (d'oie) preserved duck (goose)

Cou d'oie neck of goose

Foie de canard (gras) duck liver (goose)

Friands de Bergerac small potato cakes

Merveilles hot, sugar-covered pastry fritters

Mique stew or soup with dumplings

Pommes à la Sarladaise potatoes, truffles, ham or *foie gras*

Rilletes d'oie soft, potted goose

Sobronade soup with pork, ham, beans and vegetables

Tourin Bordelais (Ouillat) onion soup

Tourin Périgourdine vegetable soup

Truffes truffles; black and exotic tubers or fungi, as large as walnuts, which grow on the roots of certain oak and hazelnut trees

Truffes sous les cendres truffles, wrapped in paper (or bacon) and cooked in ashes

HAUTES-ALPES

See those listed in the Savoie region

ILE DE FRANCE

Refer to these five regions: Normandy to the west; the North; Champagne-Ardenne to the east; and Burgundy and the Loire on the southern borders of the Ile de France.

JURA

Brési wafer-thin slices of dried beef
Gougère hot cheese pastry – based on Comté cheese
Jésus de Morteau fat pork sausage smoked over pine and juniper
Poulet au vin jaune chicken, cream and *morilles*, cooked in *vin jaune*

LANGUEDOC-ROUSSILLON

Aïgo Bouido garlic soup. A marvellous, aromatic dish; the garlic is boiled, so its impact is lessened. Served with bread
Boles de picoulat small balls of chopped-up beef and pork, garlic and eggs – served with tomatoes and parsley
Bouillinade a type of *bouillabaisse*; with potatoes, oil, garlic and onions
Boutifare a sausage-shaped pudding of bacon and herbs
Cargolade snails, stewed in wine
Millas cornmeal porridge
Ouillade heavy soup of bacon, *boutifare*, leeks, carrots and potatoes
Touron a pastry of almonds, pistachio nuts and fruit

LOIRE

Alose à l'oseille grilled shad with a sorrel sauce
Bardette stuffed cabbage
Beuchelle à la Tourangelle kidneys, sweetbreads, morels, truffles, cream
Bourdaines apples stuffed with jam and baked
Rillauds chauds strips of hot bacon
Rillettes potted pork
Sandre freshwater fish, like perch
Tarte à la citrouille pumpkin tart
Tarte Tatin *upside-down* tart of caramelised apples and pastry
Truffiat potato cake

LYONNAIS

Bresse (Poulet, Poularde, Volaille de) the best French poultry. Fed on corn and, when killed, bathed in milk. Flesh is white and delicate
Gras-double ox tripe, served with onions
Poulet demi-deuil *half-mourning*; called this because of the thin slices of truffle placed under the chicken breast; cooked in a *court-bouillon*

Poulet au vinaigre chicken, shallots, tomatoes, white wine, wine vinegar and a cream sauce
Rosette a large pork sausage;
Sabodet see *Glossary of Menu Terms*
Tablier de Sapeur *gras-double* coated with flour, egg-yolk, breadcrumbs

MASSIF CENTRAL (Auvergne, Ardèche and Cévennes)

Aligot purée of potatoes with Tomme de Cantal cheese, cream, garlic and butter
Bougnette a stuffing of pork, bread and eggs – wrapped in *crépine* (caul)
Bourriols d'Aurillac sweet pancakes, made from buckwheat flour
Brayaude (gigot) lamb cooked in white wine, onions and herbs
Cadet Mathieu pastry turnover filled with slices of apple
Clafoutis baked pancake batter, poured over fruit, usually cherries
Confidou Rouergat ragout of beef, red wine, tomatoes, garlic and onions
Cousinat (Cousina) chestnut soup (*salée* – salted) with cream, butter and prunes and served with bread
Criques grated potato, mixed with eggs and fried – in the form of pancakes. Related to the *truffiat* of Berry
Farçon large *galette* of sausage, sorrel, onions, eggs and white wine
Farinette buckwheat flour pancakes – meat and vegetable filling
Friand Sanflorin pork meat and herbs in pastry
Jambon d'Auvergne a tasty mountain ham
Manouls see *Trénels*
Milliard (Millat) (Milla) a *clafoutis* of cherries (see Poitou-Charentes)
Mourtayol a stew with beef, chicken, ham, vegetables and bread
Omelette Brayaude eggs, pork, cheese and potatoes
Perdrix à l'Auvergnate partridge stewed in white wine
Potée Auvergnate stew of vegetables, cabbage, pork and sausage
Pountari a mince of pork fat in cabbage leaves
Pounti small, egg-based savoury soufflé with bacon or prunes
Rouergat(e) Rouergue; the name of the area to the west of Millau
Salmis de colvert Cévenole wild duck, sautéed in red wine, onions, ham and mushrooms
Soupe aux choux soup with cabbage, ham, pork, bacon and turnips
Trénels mutton tripe, white wine and tomatoes
Tripoux stuffed sheep's feet
Truffade a huge *galette* of sautéed potatoes

NORMANDY

Andouillette de Vire small chitterling (tripe) sausage
Barbue au cidre brill cooked in cider and Calvados
Cauchoise (à la) with cream, Calvados and apple
Douillons de pommes à la Normande baked apples in pastry

Escalope (Vallée d'Auge) veal sautéed, flamed in Calvados and served with cream and apples

Ficelle Normande pancake with ham, mushrooms and cheese

Marmite Dieppoise a fish soup with some, or all of the following: sole, turbot, *rouget*, *moules*, *crevettes*, onions, white wine, butter and cream

Poulet (Vallée d'Auge) chicken cooked in the same way as *Escalope Vallee d'Auge*

Tripes à la mode de Caen stewed beef tripe with onions, carrots, leeks, garlic, cider and Calvados

Trou Normand Calvados – a "dram", drunk in one gulp, between courses; claimed to restore the appetite

NORTH

Carbonnade de Boeuf à la Flamande braised beef with beer, onions and bacon; if only more chefs would prepare this great dish

Caudière (Chaudière, Caudrée) versions of fish and potato soup

Ficelles Picardes ham pancakes with mushroom sauce

Flamiche aux Maroilles see *Tarte aux Maroilles*

Flamiche aux poireaux puff-pastry tart with cream and leeks

Gaufres yeast waffles

Goyère see *Tarte aux Maroilles*

Hochepot a *pot-au-feu* of the North (see *Pepperpot*)

Pepperpot stew of mutton, pork, beer and vegetables

Sanguette black pudding, made with rabbit's blood

Soupe courquignoise soup with white wine, fish, *moules*, leeks and Gruyère cheese

Tarte aux Maroilles a hot creamy tart based on Maroilles cheese

Waterzooï a cross between soup and stew, usually of fish or chicken (Don't bypass Serge Pérard's exhilarating fish restaurant at 67 rue de Metz in Le Touquet; his *soupe de poissons* is fabulous. Robin Yapp at Mere (my favourite wine supplier) stocks the soup (0747) 860423)

POITOU-CHARENTES

Bouilliture (Bouilleture) a freshwater eel stew with shallots and prunes in Sauvignon white wine

Boulaigou thick sweet or savoury pancake

Bréjaude cabbage, leek and bacon soup

Cagouilles (also called **Lumas**) snails from the Charentes

Casserons en matelote squid in red wine sauce with garlic and shallots

Cèpes fine, delicate, flap mushrooms; please do try them

Chaudrée a ragout of fish cooked in white wine, shallots and butter

Chevrettes local name for *crevettes* (shrimps)

Clafoutis pancake batter, poured over fruit (usually black cherries), and then baked; another treat you must not miss

Embeurrée de chou white-heart cabbage, cooked in salted water, crushed and served with butter
Farcidure a dumpling – either poached or sautéed
Farci Poitevin a *pâté* of cabbage, spinach and sorrel, encased by cabbage leaves and cooked in a *bouillon*
Migourée a sort of *chaudrée*
Mique a stew of dumplings
Mogette (Mojette) small pulse beans in butter and cream
Mouclade mussels cooked in wine, egg yolks and cream; can be served with some Pineau des Charentes
Oysters for an explanation of *les claires*, *belons*, *gravettes*, *marennes* and other terms see the *Glossary of Menu Terms* (under *Huîtres*)
Soupe aux fèves des Marais soup of crushed broad beans with bread, sorrel, chervil and butter
Soupe de moules à la Rochelaise soup of various fish, mussels, saffron, garlic, tomatoes, onions and red wine
Sourdons cockles from the Charentes
Tartisseaux fritters
Tourtou thick buckwheat flour pancake

PROVENCE

Please see the specialities listed in the Côte d'Azur

SAVOIE

Farcement (Farçon Savoyard) potatoes baked with cream, eggs, bacon, dried pears and prunes; a hearty stomach filler
Féra a freshwater lake fish
Fondue hot melted cheese and white wine
Gratin Dauphinois a classic potato dish with cream, cheese and garlic
Gratin Savoyard another classic potato dish with cheese and butter
Lavaret a freshwater lake fish, like salmon
Longeole a country sausage
Lotte a burbot, not unlike an eel
Omble chevalier a char, it looks like a large salmon trout

SOUTHWEST

Besugo *daurade* – sea-bream
Chorizos spicy sausages
Confit de canard (d'oie) preserved duck meat (goose)
Cousinette (Cousinat) vegetable soup
Echassier a wading bird of the Landes
Garbure (Garbue) vegetable soup with cabbage and ham bone
Gâteau Basque a shallow, custard pastry – often with fruit fillings

Grattons (Graisserons) a *mélange* of small pieces of rendered down duck, goose and pork fat; served as an appetiser – very filling

Hachua beef stew

Jambon de Bayonne raw ham, cured in salt. Served as paper-thin slices

Lamproie eel-like fish; with leeks, onions and red Bordeaux wine sauce

Lou-kenkas small, spicy sausages

Loubine (Louvine) grey mullet (like a sea-bass)

Ortolan a small bird (wheatear) from the Landes

Ouillat (Ouliat) Pyrénées soup; onions, tomatoes, goose fat, garlic

Palombes (Salmis de) wild doves and wood pigeons from the Landes and Béarn, sautéed in red wine, ham and mushrooms

Pastiza see *Gâteau Basque*

Ramereaux ring doves

Salda a thick cabbage and bean soup

Tourin (Tourain) see *Ouillat*. (*Touron*: see Languedoc-Roussillon)

Tourtière Landaise a sweet of Agen prunes, apples and Armagnac

Ttoro (Ttorro) a Basque fish stew

CORSICA

Aziminu the Corsican *bouillabaisse*. Large *rascasse* (called *capone* or *capoum*), red peppers and pimentos are among the local ingredients

Canistrelli an almond cake flavoured with *anis*

Cédrat a sour lemon-like fruit used in sweets and liqueurs

Falculelle (Falculella) a cheesecake using Broccio cheese

Fiadone an orange-flavoured flan made with Broccio cheese

Fritelle chestnut flour fritter

Panizze a fried cake made from chestnut flour (or cornmeal)

Piverunata (Pebronata) a stew of kid (young goat), or beef, or chicken – in a sauce of red peppers, garlic and tomatoes

Pulenta (Polenta) in Corsica this is usually made from chestnut flour – similar in appearance to the Italian boiled commercial version

Stufatu the Italian influence is strong in Corsican cooking – especially pasta. This dish is macaroni with mushrooms and onions

Torta castagina a tart covered with crushed almonds, *pignons*, *raisins secs* and a dash, or two, of rum

Ziminu a pimento and red pepper sauce for fish

FRENCH WINES & CHEESES

For details of one thousand or so French wines and cheeses I refer you to the regional introductions of my guide, *French Leave Encore*. Apart from providing details of the wines and cheeses the accompanying regional maps also show their respective birthplaces and, in addition, two invaluable indexes make tracking them all down child's play. Use the indexes both in France and at home.